mdeltree

`mdeltree msdosdirectory [msdosdirectory ...]`
The mdeltree command deletes one or more MS-DOS directories. It is similar to the DOS DELTREE command.

mkdir

`mkdir [-p] [-m mode] [-parents] [-mode=mode] [-help]`
`➥ [-version] directory ...`
The mkdir command creates one or more directories.

more

`more [-dlfs] [-number] [+number] [file ...]`
The more command displays one or more files, screen-by-screen, and allows for searching and jumping to an arbitrary location in the file.

mount

`mount -a [-rvw] [-t vfstype]`
`mount [-rvw] [-o options [,...]] device | dir`
`mount [-rvw] [-t vfstype] [-o options] device dir`
The mount command mounts a file system to a specified directory.

nslookup

`nslookup [host | - [server]]`
The nslookup command queries a DNS name server. It can be run in interactive mode. If no host name is provided, then the program enters interactive mode. By default, the DNS server, as specified in /etc/resolv.conf, is used unless otherwise specified. If you want to specify a server but not look up a specified host, you must provide a - in place of the host.

passwd

`paste [-s] [-d delim-list] [-serial]`
`➥ [-delimiters list] [file...]`
The passwd command changes a user's password. When run by the root user, it can be used to change a specific user's password by providing the username as an argument.

ping

`ping [-fR] [-c number] [-i seconds]`
`➥ [-s packetsize] host`
The ping command sends echo request packets to a network host to see if it is accessible on the network.

ps

`ps [lumaxwr] [txx] [pid ...]`
The ps command displays status reports for currently running processes. Given a specific process ID as an argument, ps displays information about that particular process. Without options or arguments, ps displays the current user's processes.

pwd

`pwd`
The pwd command displays the name of the current directory.

rm

`rm [-firR] [-force] [-inter active] [-recursive]`
`➥ file | directory ...`
The rm command deletes one or more files or directories.

rmdir

`rmdir [-p] [-parents] directory ...`
The rmdir command deletes empty directories.

rsh

`rsh [-Knx] [-l username] host [command]`
The rsh command opens a shell on a remote system. If a command is provided, the command is executed on the remote host, the results are returned, and the connection is terminated.

su

`su [-flmp] [-c command] [-s shell] [-login] [-fast]`
`➥ [-preserve-environment] [-command=command]`
`➥ [-shell=shell] [-] [user]`
The su command runs a new shell under different user and group IDs. If no user is specified, the new shell will run as the root user.

tar

`tar [-crtuxz] [-f file] [-file file] [-create] [-delete]`
`➥ [-preserve] [-append] [-same-owner] [-list]`
`➥ [-update] [-extract] [-get] [-gzip] [-gunzip]`
`➥ [file | directory ...]`
The tar command creates an archive file of one or more files or directories.

top

`top [d delay] [q] [c] [S] [s]`
The top command displays a regularly updated report of processes running on the system.

unzip

`unzip [-cflptuz] file[.zip]`
The unzip command manipulates and extracts ZIP archives.

zcat

`zcat [-f] [file ...]`
The zcat command uncompresses one or more compressed files and displays the results to the standard output. If no files are specified, then the standard input is uncompressed and displayed.

zip

`zip [-efFgmrSu@] [ zipfile [ file1 file2 ...]]`
The zip command creates a ZIP archive from one or more files and directories.

zmore

`zmore [file ...]`
The zmore command displays the contents of compressed text files, one screen at a time, allowing searching in much the same way as the more command. If no files are specified, the standard input will be used.

D1463843

Mastering Red Hat Linux 6

Mastering™ Red Hat® Linux 6

Arman Danesh

SYBEX®

San Francisco • Paris • Düsseldorf • Soest • London

Associate Publisher: Gary Masters
Contracts and Licensing Manager: Kristine O'Callaghan
Acquisitions & Developmental Editor: Ellen Dendy
Editor: Sarah Lemaire
Project Editors: Kelly Winquist and Julie Sakaue
Technical Editor: Brian Horakh
Book Designer: Kris Warrenburg
Graphic Illustrator: Tony Jonick
Electronic Publishing Specialist: Nila Nichols
Project Team Leader: Jennifer Durning
Proofreaders: Catherine Morris
Indexer: Ted Laux
Companion CD: Ginger Warner
Cover Designer: Design Site
Cover Photographer: Jack D. Myers, Design Site

Screen reproductions produced with either The GIMP (a graphics package included with Red Hat Linux 6), xv (a graphics package for Linux), or Collage Plus.

Collage Plus is a trademark of Inner Media Inc.

SYBEX is a registered trademark of SYBEX Inc.
Mastering is a trademark of SYBEX Inc.

Netscape Communications, the Netscape Communications logo, Netscape, and Netscape Navigator are trademarks of Netscape Communications Corporation.

Netscape Communications Corporation has not authorized, sponsored, endorsed, or approved this publication and is not responsible for its content. Netscape and the Netscape Communications Corporate Logos are trademarks and trade names of Netscape Communications Corporation. All other product names and/or logos are trademarks of their respective owners.

TRADEMARKS: SYBEX has attempted throughout this book to distinguish proprietary trademarks from descriptive terms by following the capitalization style used by the manufacturer.

The author and publisher have made their best efforts to prepare this book, and the content is based upon final release software whenever possible. Portions of the manuscript may be based upon pre-release versions supplied by software manufacturer(s). The author and the publisher make no representation or warranties of any kind with regard to the completeness or accuracy of the contents herein and accept no liability of any kind including but not limited to performance, merchantability, fitness for any particular purpose, or any losses or damages of any kind caused or alleged to be caused directly or indirectly from this book.

Photographs and illustrations used in this book have been downloaded from publicly accessible file archives and are used in this book for news reportage purposes only to demonstrate the variety of graphics resources available via electronic access. Text and

images available over the Internet may be subject to copyright and other rights owned by third parties. Online availability of text and images does not imply that they may be reused without the permission of rights holders, although the Copyright Act does permit certain unauthorized reuse as fair use under 17 U.S.C. Section 107.

Library of Congress Card Number: 99-66176
ISBN: 0-7821-2613-8

Manufactured in the United States of America

10 9 8 7 6 5 4 3 2 1

To my parents-in-law who, through their steadfastness in their Faith in the face of persecution and suffering, offer a shining example to all those who strive to stand by their beliefs.

ACKNOWLEDGMENTS

In producing a book of this scope, there are countless people who contribute to its development, and all are deserving of recognition and acknowledgment.

Most notably, the numerous staff and contributors brought together by Sybex—including Gary Masters, Ellen Dendy, Kelly Winquist, Julie Sakaue, Sarah Lemaire, Brian Horakh, and Jim Pire—as well as all staff involved in the production and design of this book—including Nila Nichols and Jennifer Durning—deserve recognition for their hard work and commitment to this project. Nick Wells also helped ensure that this book is the best it can be by contributing to the book.

At the same time, my colleagues and coworkers at Landegg Academy, especially Tom Garraway and Shoba Sukumaran, deserve to be commended for their patience in the face of my sudden and mysterious periods of absence from the office while I raced to meet deadlines.

Finally, my wife, Tahirih, is owed my greatest gratitude. She tolerated the long hours and the resulting exhaustion that writing a book entails and managed to make it all bearable.

CONTENTS AT A GLANCE

TABLE OF CONTENTS

Appendices

INTRODUCTION

Thank you for buying this book, and welcome to the world of Linux. As one of the few alternatives to Microsoft operating systems on affordable desktop-class personal computers, Linux has gained notoriety and, more recently, acclaim as an example of what can be done by a group of motivated people without any fiscal incentive.

Linux is a freely distributable, efficient, fast operating system that offers the power of Unix—once the domain of expensive servers and workstations—on hardware affordable to the budget-conscious home computer user. This has sparked a mini-revolution in the computer world leading to acceptance of free software for a wide range of tasks—from mission-critical Web sites to corporate information systems infrastructure to education applications.

This book is designed as an introduction to the installation and use of Red Hat Linux 6. Red Hat Linux 6 is a widely used version of Linux that is well-suited to use on server systems, as well as Linux workstations and desktop computers. Any operating system with the breadth of features and capabilities offered by Linux cannot be covered completely in a single book. Still, this book provides the sound knowledge of Linux, and Red Hat in particular, needed for users to move on and learn more on their own as they use Linux in their everyday work.

Who Should Read This Book?

This book is really designed for anyone who uses a PC. Although Linux may not yet have all the ease-of-use refinements found in commercial desktop operating systems such as Windows 95/98 and the Mac OS, Linux can be used by almost anyone and mastered by anyone who can master Windows.

Having said that, learning to use any operating system is always easier if you already possess some basic computer knowledge, including an understanding of the difference between a hard disk and RAM, an understanding of the basic configuration (in Windows) of peripherals such as video cards and sound cards, and a sense of how data is organized and stored by computers (for instance, the difference between directories, subdirectories, and files).

This book aims to open the world of Linux to the average computer user. In doing so, a passing familiarity with Windows (or the Mac OS) and basic PC hardware is assumed. Without this assumption, this book would be a primer on basic computing concepts rather than a robust introduction to the Linux operating system.

If you are already comfortable using a Windows or Macintosh system and you haven't experimented with the DOS prompt, it would be helpful to do so before diving into the world of Linux, where the command line is more powerful, and therefore more heavily used, than in the Windows arena.

If you are already a power user of Windows, then you are more than ready to become a power user of Linux. Just as this book will make the everyday computer user proficient at getting their work done using Linux, it will help you become an advanced Linux user.

This book also has something to offer for the SOHO (Small Office/Home Office) user or manager of a small network. You will learn how to use Linux in many situations in your office environment, in roles that include file server, intranet Web server, and router.

What You Need to Use This Book

To use this book, you will need access to a personal computer with the following minimum specifications:

- A 486 CPU or higher (In theory, you can run Linux on a 386 system, but the performance will likely be poor enough that it isn't worthwhile for most users.)

- 16MB of RAM or more (You will notice a significant performance gain if Linux has 32MB or more of memory.)

- A hard disk with at least 500MB of free disk space (If you can afford 1GB or more, this will greatly enhance your freedom to experiment with Linux and Linux applications.)

- A CD-ROM drive (preferably an ATAPI/IDE CD-ROM or a SCSI CD-ROM drive)

- A backup of your current system in case you need to recover existing data or applications

- A video card and VGA or better monitor

- A keyboard and mouse

You may also want to have the following options:

- A printer (opt for a PCL or PostScript printer if you have a choice)

- A sound card and speakers

- A modem or ISDN modem

How This Book Is Organized

This book is divided into seven sections:

Welcome to Linux   This section introduces you to Linux as an operating system and as the foundation of the GNU General Public License software model. It looks at the most popular distributions (versions) of Linux and helps you make preparations to install Linux on your system.

Installing Red Hat Linux 6   This section covers the installation of a stand-alone Linux system. It includes discussion of how to prepare to install Red Hat Linux 6 and special installations (such as on systems with no CD-ROM drive).

Using Desktop Environments in Red Hat Linux 6   This section looks at the use of X Windows with the GNOME desktop manager (the standard Red Hat Linux GUI). This discussion includes an overview of some common X Windows applications.

Mastering the Essentials   This section describes a range of essential skills needed to truly master Linux. Topics covered include file management, system configuration, and printers and peripherals.

Basic Connectivity   This section explains how to connect a Linux system to the Internet using a dial-up connection. Topics covered include accessing the World Wide Web and working with e-mail.

Using Linux in the SOHO   As an inexpensive but powerful computing environment, Linux is well-suited to many small or home office tasks. This section looks at the installation of Red Hat Linux 6 in a networked office environment and the use of Linux as a file or print server for Unix and Windows networks and will give you an awareness of basic security issues when using Linux in a networked environment. Finally, this section examines DOS and Windows compatibility and integration in Linux, which allows many organizations to migrate from their current Windows environments to Linux without sacrificing their current investment in software and applications.

Using Red Hat Linux 6 as a Web and E-mail Server   In addition to being an ideal file and print server for the SOHO, Linux can be used to create robust enterprise Web and mail servers. This section describes how to set up Linux-based Web and mail servers.

If you already have some experience with Linux, you probably can skip straight to the second section of the book, "Installing Red Hat Linux 6," and begin installing a Linux system. If you have never used Linux before, start at the beginning with "Welcome to Linux," to get your feet wet and become comfortable with the world of Linux and its dynamic nature. Whatever your background, though, always remember that computers are tools that bring added power to your work, and Linux is a great way to enhance that role.

PART I

Welcome to Linux

CHAPTER
ONE

1

What Is Linux?

- Linux History

- Linux as an Operating System

- Linux as Free Software

- Commercial Applications for Linux

If you have made it this far—buying this book, wading through the front matter, and looking at the table of contents—then you probably have some idea of what Linux and the Linux phenomenon are all about. If you don't, read on.

Linux is a truly amazing development in the computer industry. It shows that quality software isn't necessarily dependent on the financial blessing of the commercial software industry. The history of Linux illustrates how free software can evolve, grow, and become an attractive alternative to the commercial software packages with which most of you are familiar.

In addition, the technical excellence of Linux shows why it is a serious contender against rival operating systems from Microsoft, Novell, and IBM.

This chapter will paint a quick picture of the history of Linux and then look at the key features that make Linux a powerful alternative operating system for a variety of technical applications. Finally, this chapter will look at the free software model used in Linux and examine its implications for the whole software industry.

Linux History

The emergence of Linux onto the computing scene grew out of the Unix culture. As an operating system (really a variety of different operating systems with similar features), Unix long predates the era of desktop computers; Unix was developed in the mid-1970s when minicomputers and mainframe computers were the norm in the corporate world. Unix continues to be widely used in this corporate environment, as well as in the educational world, although it is also often found running on today's client-server intranet networks.

The problem with Unix, historically, has been its inaccessibility to programmers and developers who want to work with it outside the context of corporate or university computing centers. While versions of Unix have long been available for PCs, they never had the grace or power of the operating systems available for minicomputers, mainframes, and today's servers. In addition, the early commercial versions of Unix were costly, sometimes costing more than the PC hardware they were destined to run on.

This lack of accessibility ultimately gave birth to Linux as a means to make a Unix-like operating system available on a widespread basis.

Linux's life began in the hands of Linus Torvalds at the University of Helsinki in Finland. While the Linux you know today was developed with the assistance of programmers worldwide, Linus Torvalds still retains control of the evolving core of the Linux operating system: the *kernel*.

Torvalds originally intended to develop Linux as a hobby. Early versions of Linux didn't have the end user in mind; instead, they provided the barest bones of functionality to allow Unix programmers the apparent joy of programming the kernel. As the core of the operating system, the kernel keeps everything running smoothly—without a stable, powerful kernel, you don't *have* an operating system.

But as the team of programmers grew and the base software for a complete operating system emerged, it became clear to those involved that Linux was evolving to the state where it could respectably be called an operating system. In March 1992, version 1.0 of the kernel came into being, marking the first official release of Linux. At this point, Linux ran most of the common Unix tools from compilers to networking software to X Windows.

Linux continues to evolve as the preeminent Unix-clone operating system for PCs. Hardware support is now broad, including the most popular and common peripherals; performance is strong, giving many PCs power comparable to that of mid-range workstations such as Sun Microsystems' SPARC systems. Although technically today's Linux is not Unix because it fails to qualify for the brand name, efforts are under way to add to Linux the features needed to receive full certification as a Unix operating system.

Linux as an Operating System

The term "Linux" is actually somewhat vague. "Linux" is used in two ways: specifically to refer to the kernel itself—the heart of any version of Linux—and more generally to refer to any collection of applications that run on the kernel, usually referred to as a *distribution*. The kernel's job is to provide the basic environment in which applications can run, including the basic interfaces with hardware and the systems for managing tasks and currently running programs.

In the specific sense, there is only one current version of Linux at any one time: the current revision of the kernel. Torvalds keeps the kernel as his domain in the world of Linux development, leaving all the applications and services that sit on top of the kernel to any of the thousands of other Linux developers in the world.

In the general meaning of the term "Linux," referring to cohesive collections of applications that run on top of the Linux kernel, there are numerous versions of Linux. Each distribution has its own unique characteristics, including different installation methods, different collections of features, and different upgrade paths. But since all distributions are fundamentally Linux, in almost every case an application that works with a current version of one distribution will work with a current version of another distribution.

> **NOTE**   Chapter 2, "Choosing a Distribution," contains a complete discussion of Linux distributions.

The interesting thing about this dichotomous use of the term "Linux" is that it exactly parallels the same confused usage of the term "operating system." In the commercial sense, an operating system has come to mean a large collection of applications centered around a kernel. This is what Windows 95 and 98, Windows NT, and Windows 2000 are. This is what the Macintosh OS is.

In a purist, technical sense, an operating system is a much smaller core kernel that provides those basic system functions needed to develop any application.

Taken in both senses, Linux is an operating system. One of the features of the Linux kernel that sets it apart from other operating systems designed to run on desktop PCs is that it is both multitasking and multiuser.

A Multitasking Operating System

You are probably familiar with the term "multitasking" even if you are not really sure what it means.

When desktop computing graduated from Windows 3.1 to Windows 95, the multitasking capabilities of the then-new Windows 95 were among its biggest claims to fame.

To say that a system can multitask is to say that it can appear to be running more than one application, or process, at a time. For example, the system can print a document, copy a file, and dial into the Internet while the user is comfortably typing in a word processing program. Even with these background tasks happening, the foreground word processor should not freeze up or be unusable.

This is the wonder of multitasking: it allows a computer with a single processor to appear to be performing multiple tasks simultaneously. Of course, a single CPU can only execute a single instruction at a time—that is, only one action can be taking place at any one time. Multitasking creates the appearance of simultaneous activity by switching rapidly between tasks as the demands of those processes dictate.

When multitasking works well, a user running a word processor while several other things happen will not be aware of the extra work the computer is doing. All processes will seem to be running smoothly and the computer will be responsive.

Historically, Unix systems have been much better than Windows at multitasking; Unix is able to run large numbers of simultaneous applications in a way that made it ideal for large corporate servers and high-powered workstations. Today, only Windows 2000, and its predecessor Windows NT, can really claim to offer a similarly robust multitasking implementation. Even Windows 95, despite all of its fanfare, has trouble effectively handling large numbers of simultaneous processes.

To take things further, Linux, like Windows NT and Windows 2000, offers support for computers with multiple processors such as dual-Pentium II systems. These systems can in fact perform two actions at exactly the same time. Combining multitasking with multiple processors greatly increases the number of simultaneous applications a computer can run smoothly.

A Multiuser Operating System

Even more important than being a multitasking operating system, Linux—like all versions of Unix and Unix clones—is a multiuser operating system.

All versions of Windows and the Mac OS are single-user systems. While some Windows NT services provide a semblance of multiuser capabilities, only one user can be logged in and running applications at any one time in these operating systems. It is only recently that efforts have been made to extend Windows NT into a multiuser platform under the guise of the Windows NT Terminal Server Edition.

By comparison, Linux allows multiple simultaneous users, fully leveraging the multitasking capabilities of the operating system. The great advantage of this is that Linux can be deployed as an applications server. From their desktop computers or terminals, users can log into a Linux server across a LAN and actually run applications on the server instead of on their desktop PCs.

Linux Applications

As an operating system, Linux can be used to develop almost any type of application. Among the applications available for Linux are:

Text and word processing applications   In addition to commercial word processing software such as WordPerfect, StarOffice, and Applixware, Linux offers powerful tools for editing text files and processing text in an automated fashion.

Programming languages   There is a wide variety of programming and scripting languages and tools available for Linux and all Unix operating systems. This abundance of programming tools makes it easy to develop new applications that can run not only on Linux but also on most Unix and Unix-like operating systems.

X Windows   X Windows is Unix's answer to the graphical user interface (GUI). X Windows is a highly flexible and configurable GUI environment that runs on Linux as well as on most Unix systems. Numerous applications that run in X Windows help to make Linux an easy-to-use operating system.

NOTE   Chapters 6 through 12 provide complete coverage of X Windows.

Internet tools   In addition to supporting well-known software such as Netscape Communicator and Mosaic, Linux provides a wide range of Internet software, including character-based and graphical mail-reading applications, the full range of software needed to create Internet servers (Web servers, mail servers, and news servers), plus complete network support to connect to the Internet via local network or modem.

Databases   Like all Unix platforms, Linux provides a robust platform for running client-server database applications. From its earliest days, powerful, free databases such as mSQL and Postgre have been available for Linux. As Linux has grown in popularity, especially in corporate information systems, the number of commercial relational database servers for Linux has grown. Today, Oracle, Sybase, and Informix all offer relational database products for Linux.

DOS and Windows compatibility software   As you will see in Chapter 30, "Red Hat Linux 6 and DOS/Windows," Linux can be made to run DOS software with a high degree of stability and compatibility and offers several approaches to running Windows software. In fact, the entire text of this book was written using Microsoft Word for Windows on a computer running Linux. This provides strong evidence of Linux's ability to work well in a Windows environment. In addition, emulators are available for other popular computer systems, including the Macintosh and Atari ST computer lines.

This list only touches the tip of the iceberg. Many more applications exist for Linux. A good source for finding Linux software is the Linux Software Map, which can be found on the World Wide Web at `http://www.linux.org/apps/lsm.html`.

Linux as Free Software

Given all the capabilities promised by Linux, you might think that the operating system is expensive. On the contrary, the Linux kernel and most of the applications written for Linux are available for free on the Internet, often with no restriction on the copying and redistribution of the software.

To begin with, the Linux kernel is distributed under the GNU General Public License (GPL). This special software license, developed by the Free Software Foundation, promotes the open distribution and, more importantly, open development of software. Unlike the software licenses common with most commercial software, the GNU license allows anyone to redistribute software, even for a fee, so long as in the redistribution, the terms of the GNU license are still in force. In other words, anyone can take GNU software, alter it if they wish, and redistribute it, but they can't stop someone who buys GNU-licensed software from them from turning around and redistributing it again.

Most of Linux is available under the GNU General Public License. This makes it possible for many different vendors to produce both free and commercially available Linux distributions.

This approach to free software is not the same as public domain software. With GNU products, the software developers retain the rights to the software and may choose in the future to stop distributing that software under the GNU license. What is special about the GNU license is that it encourages iterative development of applications by many people, each making changes that they consider important or necessary and then redistributing the software.

This process is enabled by the fact that all GNU-licensed software must be distributed with its complete source code. Unlike commercial software, where the original code is unavailable and hence unalterable, GNU software not only makes it possible to alter and customize software but actually encourages interested and capable users to do so.

In fact, this model has been so successful in the development of Linux and applications for Linux that it has been adopted by Netscape for its Communicator product line. Using basic GNU principles, Netscape makes Communicator freely available and allows anyone to license the source code for Communicator or to redistribute Communicator.

Commercial Applications for Linux

As you will see later in this book, there are commercial applications for Linux as well as commercial distributions of Linux. In these cases, most products are licensed under terms more restrictive than the GNU standards of the Linux world.

But even if a distribution of Linux includes commercial components that cannot be redistributed freely, this doesn't change the underlying GNU license that applies to the Linux kernel and those core applications found in all Linux distributions. If the original license of an application is the GNU General Public License, then the license of the redistributed copy of the software is likewise the GNU General Public License.

Looking Ahead

In this chapter, you have taken the first step into the world of Linux. You now know what the basic components and philosophy of Linux are, and have become acquainted with the features that make it an excellent choice for many applications.

Chapter 2 examines the Linux distribution philosophy and the many distributions, or flavors, of Linux that are available.

Chapter 3 describes the practical steps of preparing to install Red Hat Linux 6 on a PC. Chapters 4 and 5 walk you through various different installations and associated issues and potential pitfalls. Then you will be ready to look at Linux desktop environments described in Chapters 6 through 12.

Chapters 4 and 5 describe how to install Linux on a stand-alone PC; they also address any special installation issues, such as PCs with no CD-ROM drive. From that point, the book is divided into five sections dealing with using Linux; these sections cover X Windows and GNOME, essential Linux skills, connecting Linux to the Internet, and using Linux in a small or home office (the so-called SOHO environment).

CHAPTER
TWO

Choosing a Distribution

- What Is a Distribution?

- An Overview of Major Distributions

- Red Hat Linux

As you saw in Chapter 1, the entire approach to the development of Linux breaks with traditional commercial software development. Most of the components that go into making a complete Linux system—including the kernel (the heart of the operating system), modules for devices, and all the applications and utilities that make the system do useful things—are developed by small or large loosely knit groups of developers scattered around the globe.

To top it all off, most of these components are distributed under licenses allowing free redistribution, such as the GNU Public License. (Appendix D contains a copy of this license.)

This all leaves the potential user of Linux at a bit of a loss as to how to put together a working Linux system and what components to include in that system.

The answer to this quandary has emerged in the form of Linux *distributions*. Distributions are prepackaged Linux systems that are ready to install. They come in numerous flavors from the freely available to the fully commercial, and they all offer different core sets of applications, utilities, and management tools to ease the use of Linux.

This chapter will take a broad look at some of the major and more well-known distributions and then take a somewhat closer look at the latest release of Red Hat Linux, the distribution included on the CD-ROM with this book.

What Is a Distribution?

The concept of a distribution can be a little hard to understand in a world of commercial operating systems such as Windows 98 and NT, Mac OS, and even commercial Unix systems such as Solaris and HP-UX.

After all, in all these cases, the name of the operating system denotes a very specific product. For instance, Windows 98 defines the complete set of Windows utilities, applications, and drivers that Microsoft ships. There is no room for variation. Any application, driver, or utility that users adds to their systems is not considered part of Windows 98, and Windows 98 doesn't technically exist as a product with less than its complete set of software and tools.

In the Linux world, however, this definition becomes blurred. The term "Linux" can refer to everything from the kernel (the heart of the operating system) to any collection of Linux-based applications put together with a kernel to produce a functioning system running Linux.

This lack of a clear set of applications, utilities, drivers, and a kernel that together can clearly be identified exists because Linux has opened the door to different flavors of Linux that meet different needs. These are the distributions.

Distributions can be built on different versions of the kernel, can include different sets of applications, utilities, tools, and driver modules, and can offer different installation and upgrade programs to ease management of the system.

It might seem that with this type of flexibility would come chaos. This is a logical deduction. After all, how is it possible to have potentially infinite varieties of Linux and yet have some level of reasonable assurance that Linux applications can be installed and run on any of these systems?

Luckily, this tends to work: in all the diversity that is Linux is an underlying thread of similarity that provides the compatibility needed to develop applications that can be used on most Linux systems.

At the heart of most Linux distributions is a common set of basic programs, utilities, and libraries that application developers can reasonably expect to find in a Linux system. In addition, most Linux distributions now adhere to such standards as the Linux File System Hierarchy Standard (FHS).

Therefore, large-scale commercial applications such as Netscape Communicator or Corel WordPerfect can be developed for Linux and be expected to work on the majority of Linux systems. Even if a component, such as a program or library, upon which an application depends is missing, it can be downloaded from one of the large Linux software repositories on the Internet to enable the application to work.

An Overview of Major Distributions

The majority of Linux distributions are freely available. They can be downloaded from the Internet from Linux software archives such as the Metalab FTP site or the TSX-11 Linux Repository at MIT.

TIP   See Appendix B, *Sources of Linux Information*, for a complete list of Linux sites offering distributions and for a list of CD-ROM vendors.

Of course, the average Linux distribution can be quite large, ranging from a few dozen to a few hundred megabytes in size, and most users will not want to spend valuable online time and bandwidth downloading a complete Linux distribution. To handle this, there are numerous sources of Linux distributions available on CD-ROM, including the organizations that produce the distributions or third-party sources that bundle one or more distributions into CD-ROM sets that also include additional Linux software and documentation.

For instance, the Linux Developer's Resource is a set of six CD-ROMs from InfoMagic (`www.infomagic.com`). This is released quarterly and contains the latest Red Hat, Slackware, S.u.S.E., and Debian distributions.

Generally, CD-ROM copies of free Linux distributions range in price from $10 to $50, with more popular sets such as the Linux Developer's Resource costing less than $30.

The Major Distributions

There are numerous Linux distributions. In recent years, though, five distributions have emerged as the most common: Red Hat, Slackware, Caldera, S.u.S.E., and Debian. These distributions have some of the longest histories in the Linux community, and together they control the lion's share of the market. In addition, all five distributions are freely available, which has made them the bases for other distributions and for commercial packages that include a Linux distribution.

After these five, there is a second tier of Linux distributions that includes some long-standing distributions such as Yggdrasil, and newer distributions such as Turbo Linux.

Red Hat

By most counts, the Red Hat Linux distribution from Red Hat Software (`www.redhat.com`) has emerged as the favorite Linux distribution for most users. This distribution is the target, or base, distribution for many commercial Linux software developers and is the benchmark against which many Linux distributions are measured.

Red Hat has gained fame particularly for its tools for installing and upgrading the operating system and for its well-designed system for installing, uninstalling, and tracking software application packages.

Red Hat Linux has also won awards, including *InfoWorld*'s Reader's Choice and Browser's Choice Awards in March 1998. Red Hat Linux came first in a survey of *InfoWorld*'s Web site visitors that asked readers to indicate their choice for product of the year (receiving 27 percent of the vote, well ahead of the number two package, OS/2 Warp 4, which had just over 8 percent). Red Hat Linux has also been used in projects that have proven the commercial viability of Linux, including animation work for the movie *Titanic*.

Red Hat Linux is available in a free version that can be downloaded from popular Linux archives on the Internet and in a reasonably priced $50 commercial version that includes a manual, a CD-ROM, and several commercial applications to supplement its collection of free software.

Red Hat Linux 6 is the current version of the distribution and is the distribution included with this book. This chapter will take a deeper look at Red Hat.

NOTE   In addition to the Red Hat Linux 6 distribution included on the CD-ROM, you can always download the latest version from the Red Hat FTP server at `mirrors.red-hat.com` or from the Metalab Linux Archive at `metalab.unc.edu/pub/Linux/distributions/slackware`.

Slackware

Before Red Hat Linux came to fame, Slackware was the distribution to beat. Slackware is still a popular distribution and is found on CD-ROMs from many vendors, including InfoMagic and Walnut Creek (`www.slackware.com`), the official home of Slackware, which offers a CD-ROM set of Slackware that includes support.

The version of Slackware available from Walnut Creek at the time of this writing was Slackware 3.6. The distribution offers the full range of expected utilities, tools, and applications, including X Windows, development tools such as the GNU C Compiler, PPP support, full Java support, and the Java SDK (Developer's Kit) for Linux. Like most Linux distributions, Slackware offers the Apache Web server for using Linux to set up an intranet or Internet Web site, as well as several freely available Web browsers.

Slackware can be downloaded from Walnut Creek's FTP site at `ftp.cdrom.com` or from the SunSite Linux archive at `metalab.unc.edu/pub/Linux`.

Caldera OpenLinux

Caldera caused a stir in both the Linux and the broader computer markets by trumpeting the call of supportable commercial Linux. Now the call has been roundly taken up by other Linux vendors, most notably Red Hat. The idea is to offer tested, stable, and supported versions of Linux that appeal to the corporate market and to application developers who want a secure target distribution of Linux to develop for.

To some extent, this strategy has worked. WordPerfect 6 for Linux was targeted for (and only distributed with) Caldera's Network Desktop distribution. Previous versions of StarOffice for Linux were aimed at Caldera distributions, and the Linux version of Netscape's FastTrack Web server package has been ported by Caldera and is available as part of the OpenLinux package.

OpenLinux 1.3, the current Caldera distribution, can be purchased or downloaded from the Web. The complete distribution includes:

- The K desktop Environment (which you will learn about in Chapter 11, "KDE: An Alternative to GNOME")

- A non-commercial license of StarOffice for Linux

- NetWare support

- A license of DR-DOS for DOS compatibility

Caldera currently is working on several initiatives that promise to broaden the reach of Linux, including a powerful, customizable Linux administration system that it plans to make available to the Linux community.

Caldera's OpenLinux won the *Byte* Magazine Editor's Choice Award of Distinction in December 1997. In awarding OpenLinux this honor, *Byte*'s editors noted the combination of value for price, compared with other commercial server operating systems, as a strong point in favor of Caldera OpenLinux.

OpenLinux can be downloaded at no cost from Caldera's Web site at `www.calderasystems.com`.

S.u.S.E. Linux

S.u.S.E. Linux is a popular Linux distribution available primarily in Europe and is offered in both English and German versions.

The version of S.u.S.E. available at the time of this writing is unique in several ways when compared against the major distributions. S.u.S.E. offers:

- KDE, the latest version of the XFree86 X Windows server where some distributions are one version behind

- A system administration tool called YaST, which is useful for configuring everything from dial-up Internet connections to scanners and network cards

- A custom utility for configuring X Windows

- A copy of the latest version of StarOffice

S.u.S.E.'s menu-driven installation program has been lauded by some magazines as the simplest around, although the competition for easy-to-install distributions is heating up considerably. The boxed version of the distribution also includes a 400-page manual. The distribution can be downloaded at no cost from www.suse.com.

Debian/GNU

As one of the three major Linux players, Debian/GNU (www.debian.org) is the odd man out, because it has no commercial organization backing it. Where Red Hat is developed by Red Hat Software and Slackware has a home at Walnut Creek, Debian/GNU Linux is produced by a team of volunteers in much the same way as Linux development itself takes place.

Debian offers more than 1,000 software packages using its own package management system, which is designed to offer similar functionality to that offered by the Red Hat distribution.

The Debian distribution is unique in some ways. Their Web site highlights a commitment to giving back any code they generate to the free software world: They publicize their bugs, making bug reports easy to find, and they won't include applications in their distribution that don't match Debian's definition of free software (which includes free redistribution rights, available source code, and allowances for modifications and derived work).

Other Distributions

Other English-language distributions of Linux that are worth noting include LinuxPro, LinuxWare, Turbo Linux, and Yggdrasil, among others. In addition, there are several non-English distributions, particularly in French and German, which are covered in Appendix A, "Linux Around the World."

You can learn more about other distributions and find links to the relevant Web sites from Linux Online's English-language distributions page at `www.linux.org/dist/english.html`.

Red Hat Linux

The distribution of Linux used in this book is Red Hat Linux. As mentioned earlier, Red Hat Linux is currently one of the most well-known and widely used Linux distributions.

The feature that launched Red Hat Linux into popularity was its package management system. This system allows software applications to be tested, configured, and provided in a ready-to-run state for Red Hat Linux. Using simple package management tools, new packages can be downloaded, installed, and run without the sometimes tortuous configuration required with other packages—such as software that is distributed with its own special installation program or that doesn't use the Red Hat (or the similar Debian) package management system.

Of course, package management alone is not enough to explain the success of Red Hat Linux. After all, the key software needed to implement the Red Hat package management system is made freely available by Red Hat, and other distributions also use the system.

One benefit provided by package management is upgradability. It is possible to upgrade versions of Red Hat without having to reinstall Linux from scratch. This problem plagued earlier distributions by Slackware, when it was the leading distribution, and still plagues some distributions today.

Another major feature of the Red Hat distribution is that it is available not only on the Intel PC platform but also on two other platforms: Digital Alpha–based computers and Sun SPARC–based computers. These two platforms offer higher performance hardware than the typical Intel PC but generally require expensive commercial versions of Unix. Red Hat makes it possible to use Linux on all three systems and, because the distributions are fundamentally the same, management and configuration of systems running Red Hat Linux for any of the three platforms is simplified, as is the porting of software.

What's New About Red Hat Linux 6

Version 6 of Red Hat Linux offers a lot of new features not found in earlier versions and still not found in all distributions of Linux. These features include

- Improved installation
- New and improved system administration tools
- The introduction of GNOME

Improved Installation

The Red Hat installation software continually improves; it now does many things that earlier versions of Red Hat failed to do. This includes

- Improved ability to recognize PCI devices
- Adoption of new disk-partitioning software (which eases initial configuration and offers features such as growable disk partitions that can increase in size as disk space is available)
- The ability to choose which services load automatically at boot time once the system is installed

New and Improved Administration Tools

Linux has always had a strong set of both command-line and graphical tools for configuring and administering a Red Hat Linux–based system. With Version 5, these were expanded to include a user information tool to set user information such as name and phone number, a user password tool that makes it easy to change users' passwords, and a file system tool that allows the mounting and dismounting of file systems from a graphical interface.

Now, in Red Hat Linux 6, LinuxConf, a powerful graphical Linux configuration tool, has been added to the tools available for administering Red Hat Linux systems.

Red Hat Linux also offers a tool for configuring the free version of X Windows, XFree86, called Xconfigurator. Xconfigurator has always been superior to the configuration program included with XFree86, and in Red Hat Linux, Xconfigurator offers additional improvements such as automatic detection of video cards and their features.

All together, these improvements make Red Hat Linux easy to manage for most users and help bring to the Linux world the types of graphical management tools found in rival systems such as Windows NT.

Introduction of GNOME

Red Hat has begun including current snapshots of the GNOME desktop environment in recent versions of Red Hat Linux on its CD-ROMs with plans to integrate it into the Red Hat distribution in an upcoming distribution.

GNOME is a desktop environment for X Windows designed to make application development easier and to provide a more consistent, professional-quality desktop environment for Linux users. GNOME is discussed in detail in Chapter 8, "Using GNOME."

Improved Performance Features

Red Hat Linux 6 offers several new or improved features, which can be used to leverage high-end hardware to improve performance and stability of Red Hat Linux systems. These features include better implementation of symmetric multiprocessing (SMP), which allows Red Hat Linux to leverage the performance gain offered by multiprocessor systems.

In addition, Red Hat Linux 6 has introduced software-based RAID (Redundant Array of Inexpensive Disks). RAID provides a mechanism for combining multiple disks to improve both reliability and performance.

Looking Ahead

Now that you have a firm sense of what Linux is all about and what the options are in terms of the various distributions, you are ready to focus on actually working with Red Hat Linux (which is on the enclosed CD-ROM).

The next chapter will cover the preparation that is needed to ensure that installing Red Hat Linux will go smoothly. This includes understanding some of the hardware issues involved in getting a Linux system up and running with minimum fuss and also making sure you have all the necessary information on hand to provide the installation program the data it needs to do its job.

Following that, in Chapter 4, you will walk through the actual steps involved in installing a Red Hat Linux system.

PART II

Installing Red Hat Linux 6

Getting Ready to Install Red Hat Linux 6

- What You Need

- Checking Your Hardware for Compatibility

- Recording Your Hardware Information

- Choosing an Installation Method

- Arranging Your Hard Disk

In this chapter, you finally get down to the business of installing Linux. Most of this chapter will be concerned with decisions that affect the installation process, rather than with the actual installation process itself, but this decision-making is an essential step to ensure that your Linux installation goes smoothly and that you end up with a well-configured system.

This chapter starts with a brief discussion of the minimum Linux system. What hardware is necessary to run a useful Linux system? It is possible to boot Linux from a single floppy disk, but the resulting system will be so limited that it will be useless for most purposes. This chapter describes what equipment you need in order to make Linux a useful tool in your computing arsenal.

From there, this chapter discusses a crucial issue: hardware compatibility. Even in the Windows world where vendors provide drivers quickly for almost every conceivable piece of hardware, things go wrong and hardware incompatibility can be the cause of long, sleepless nights trying to get the Windows operating system to work. In Linux, there is equal potential for problems, especially if you try to use hardware for which there is currently limited or no support.

What You Need

Before you can install Linux, it is important to step back and consider exactly what type of computer you need.

Linux can be installed on a wide range of hardware, including the following:

- ARM processors
- Motorola 68000 series processors
- 8086 CPUs
- Alpha processors
- MIPS systems
- PowerPC-based systems
- Acorn computers
- Power Macintoshes
- Intel-based PCs

By far, though, Intel-based PC hardware is the most common Linux platform. It generally provides the lowest cost-performance ratio for Linux and is the primary development platform for most Linux tools. Intel Linux offers the best selection of device drivers for peripheral hardware, the largest body of available applications (both commercial and free), and the strongest user community on the Internet that can be turned to for support and assistance.

For these reasons, this book focuses on Linux for Intel *x*86-based computers; the companion CD-ROM for this book contains Red Hat Linux 6 for the Intel platform.

The Minimum PC for Linux

As an operating system, Linux has amazingly modest requirements for computer resources. It is possible to get Linux up and running on a 386-based computer with only 4MB of RAM. Such a machine will, of course, be limited:

- It can't run X Windows (so, no GUI interface).

- The number of simultaneous programs it can run is limited by the amount of physical RAM.

- Its performance will be slow enough to prevent its use in most mission-critical applications (for instance, as a mail server or Web server).

Given these limitations, a system like this can still play a role in an organization, as

- A terminal to another Linux or Unix server where applications are running

- A low-end server for services such as DNS (Domain Name Server, which helps computers translate host names such as www.yahoo.com into actual numeric [IP] addresses) or an authentication server for a small network

In fact, Linux can provide a better way to leverage this type of old hardware than DOS can. DOS has limited networking capabilities and cannot handle the server duties described above.

If you want to try to run this type of minimalist Linux system, turn to the Small Memory Mini HowTo at http://metalab.unc.edu/mdw/HOWTO/mini/Small-Memory.html for some basic tips to help you get Linux up and running in a system with limited memory.

A Good PC for Linux

This book's main focus is on running Linux on a personal workstation or as a small intranet server. Needless to say, just as you wouldn't want to run Windows on the type of machine described in the previous section, you need a more robust PC to fully enjoy the features and benefits of Linux.

Linux actually requires far fewer resources to perform far more functions than the average Windows 98 or Windows NT system. For instance, a functional workstation can be put together with a 486-100MHz processor and 16MB of RAM. This system will be able to run X Windows (for a graphical interface), access the Internet, run Netscape Communicator, and, all the while, perform as a low-end server on a network.

Still, the average user will want a somewhat more powerful Linux system. A respectable Linux workstation needs the following specifications:

- A Pentium-class CPU. Even a Pentium 133 will do just fine for most users. It is wise to avoid certain clone chips, such as the Cyrix 686 line, because of some reported difficulties people have had running these chips. Generally, though, most Pentium-class systems work just fine. Of course, if you are buying a new PC today, you won't be able to find a Pentium, so choose a Pentium II–class system.

- 32MB of RAM. Linux is exceptionally good at taking advantage of any extra memory you throw at it. 32MB is enough for the average workstation, but you will notice the difference if you can afford 64MB of RAM.

- A 2GB hard disk. You can get away with a 1GB (or even smaller) hard disk, but a roomier disk is preferable. Larger disks tend to perform better than the older, smaller ones.

- A supported video card. (See the section on hardware compatibility later in this chapter.)

With a system like this, you will have more than sufficient resources to run Linux as a desktop operating system. You don't need to go out and buy the latest 400MHz Pentium II system with all the bells and whistles to get Linux up and running at a respectable speed.

Added Bonuses

Of course, in today's computing environment, you will probably want to extend your PC's capabilities into areas such as multimedia and the Internet. There are a few add-ons that greatly enhance any Linux system, and you should consider them as a way to round out your workstation:

- A CD-ROM drive. If you are going to install one, consider an IDE/ATAPI CD-ROM drive or, if you can afford it, a SCSI CD-ROM drive. Generally, it is best to avoid proprietary CD-ROM drives that work with their own interface cards or connect directly to special interfaces on sound cards. These CD-ROM drives are usually poor performers and difficult to configure in Linux.

- A sound card. Most Sound Blaster®–compatible cards are supported in Linux; check the hardware compatibility section of this chapter.

- A modem. In terms of speed, the same rules apply here as with Windows: it is generally best to get the fastest modem you can that will be able to connect at its top speed to your Internet service provider (ISP). If your ISP can't offer 56Kbps connections, then you may not want a 56Kbps modem at this time. One caveat, though. It is generally wise to opt for external modems in Linux. This is especially true for ISDN modems, because there is limited support in Linux for internal ISDN modems. The advantage of external modems (ISDN or analog) is that they are easier to configure and they offer external indicators so you can more easily debug configuration problems.

If you plan to use Linux as a small server on your intranet, you should consider the following add-ons:

- A SCSI card. SCSI offers much better performance for hard drives than the IDE interface and has better support for multiple devices. If you plan to run any type of multiuser system (for instance, file server, Web server, or applications server) you really need to use a SCSI card. Make sure to consult the hardware compatibility section before selecting a SCSI card and, if possible, choose a card with Ultra-Wide SCSI support.

- SCSI hard drive(s). The function of the SCSI card is to be able to use SCSI hard drives. If possible, use Ultra-Wide SCSI drives for the best performance. You may want to consider multiple disk drives. For instance, if you estimate you need 8GB of space for your users' data as well as the operating system and all installed applications, you may want to consider two 4GB drives (one for the user data and the other for the system and software). By splitting software and data, you will probably find that performance improves because the same disk is not being accessed for both.

- A tape drive. If you plan to run a server, you will want to do backups to ensure that your data is safe from system failure and other disasters. While it is possible to use some tape drives that connect through the floppy disk bus, you will find that life is a lot easier if you opt for a SCSI tape drive, if you can afford one. They are faster and better supported by Linux.

Checking Your Hardware for Compatibility

As with a Windows (especially Windows NT) system, it is important to check that your hardware will work with your Linux operating system and with the rest of the hardware in your computer before committing the dollars to purchase. Hardware incompatibility with the operating system and other hardware can be the source of endless difficulty and time spent trying to debug and reconfigure a computer.

This issue is especially important in the Linux community. Because Linux does not yet enjoy widespread support among hardware vendors, vendors generally do not provide Linux drivers for their hardware, and their support staff is unable or unwilling to work with users to debug hardware conflicts and problems in a Linux environment. This means that the hardware needs to be supported by drivers included in the user's Linux distribution or by add-on software that provides drivers for the hardware in question. In addition, users must rely on the Linux community for help when problems arise.

Because of the current Linux support situation, it is wise to do some research before installing Linux, or before purchasing new hardware for a Linux-based system. Here's what you can do:

- Consult the *Linux Hardware Compatibility HowTo.* This document, authored by Patrick Reijnen, contains extensive lists of hardware known to work with Linux, hardware known not to work with Linux, and issues related to both types of hardware. If you purchase hardware that has the stamp of approval from this HowTo guide, your life will be easier.

- Consult the `comp.os.linux.hardware` newsgroup. This is a good source of information about hardware issues as they relate to Linux. If you are unsure if your intended hardware purchase is wise, post a question to the group asking if anyone has had any experience with the hardware in question. You will usually find that others have tried what you are considering, and their collective wisdom is an invaluable resource in making informed purchase decisions.

- If you are running the Red Hat Linux version that ships with this book, try consulting the archives of the Red Hat mailing list. The mailing list can be found in the support section of the Red Hat home page at `http://www.redhat.com/`.

- Try to evaluate the hardware before purchasing it. If you are considering making a corporate purchase of hardware from a vendor you use regularly, it may be possible to borrow hardware to test it with Linux before actually purchasing it. This, of course, is the only way to be certain that the hardware will work the way you want it to.

Recording Your Hardware Information

Once you have put together your target Linux PC, you need to collect the hardware-related information necessary to get your hardware working. This section will quickly look at the information you should be aware of in order to get your hardware working quickly with Linux.

Video Cards

If you install Linux without X Windows (the graphical user interface for Unix systems), you will probably have no difficulties with any video card. However, with X Windows you need care and attention to detail to get your card working. Record the following information about your video card before installing Linux:

- Vendor and model of the card

- Video chipset used on the card (Sometimes X Windows may not provide explicit support for a particular card but will offer general support for the chipset used in the card.)

- Amount of video memory on the card

- Type of clock chip on the card (If there is one; many common cards do not have clock chips.)

- Type of RAMDAC on the card (If there is one; many common cards do not have RAMDACs.)

All of this information should be available in the documentation that came with your card.

Sound Cards

Sound cards require that you supply very specific information in order to get them working. The following information is critical to configuring most sound cards:

- Vendor and model of the card

- IRQ(s) of the card

- I/O address(es) of the card

- DMA address(es) of the card

You may have to set the IRQ, I/O address, and DMA address manually, using jumpers or DIP switches. Refer to the card's documentation for instructions.

Monitors

As with your video card, it is important to record the technical specifications of your monitor in order to get it working optimally with X Windows. If you don't have this information, or use the wrong information, there is a risk that your monitor could be damaged. Record the following specifications after consulting your monitor's documentation:

- Vendor and model of the monitor

- Top resolution of the monitor

- Top refresh rate of the monitor when running at its top resolution

- Horizontal sync range of your monitor

- Vertical sync range of your monitor

Consult Chapter 7, "Installing and Configuring X Windows," for a discussion of horizontal and vertical sync ranges as they apply to the configuration of X Windows.

Mice

In order to get your mouse working, both in Linux's character-based console mode and in X Windows, you need to note the following information:

- Vendor and model of the mouse

- Number of mouse buttons

- Protocol of the mouse (Consult the mouse's documentation for this; common protocols include the Microsoft protocol, the Mouse Systems protocol, and the PS/2 protocol.)

- Port where your mouse is connected to your computer (In DOS terms, this is generally COM1:, COM2:, or the PS/2 mouse port.)

Hard Drives

If you plan to use Linux to repartition your hard drive during installation (see the section later in this chapter about arranging your hard disk's partitions), you may need the following information:

- Total storage capacity of the hard disk

- Number of cylinders

- Number of heads

- Number of sectors per track

Generally, you will not need to provide this information because Linux will successfully auto-detect it when the system is booted.

Modems

If you have a modem, you should record the following information:

- Vendor and model of the modem

- Speed of the modem
- Port that your external modem is connected to or that you have configured your internal modem to use (In DOS terms, this is generally COM1: or COM2:.)

Other Peripherals

Many other peripherals have specific requirements for configuration. The number and type of possible peripherals are too varied to list here; the details needed to configure these peripherals are left to those sections of this book where the hardware types are discussed. Generally, additional hardware such as specialized serial cards, specialized network hardware, and tape drives are not configured and installed at the time Linux is installed but rather after you have a running Linux system.

If you are planning to install your Linux system on a local area network, consult Chapter 27, "Installing Red Hat Linux 6 for the SOHO," for information pertaining to network cards and Linux installation.

Choosing an Installation Method

Generally, Linux is distributed on CD-ROMs because of its sheer size. While Linux can be downloaded from the Internet, it is too large for most people to download unless they have access to a high-speed, dedicated Internet connection.

A CD-ROM, then, is usually at the core of installing Linux, as it is in the case of the Red Hat Linux 6 distribution included with this book. While it is theoretically possible to install Linux directly off the Internet, this is too time-consuming or too expensive to be practical for most Linux users.

This section will consider different approaches to installing Linux from the CD-ROM included with this book. The procedures will be similar to most other Linux distributions that are available on CD-ROM; consult the documentation for those distributions to determine the differences.

From CD-ROM

If you have an IDE/ATAPI CD-ROM drive and a computer with a recent enough BIOS, it is possible to boot your computer from the Linux CD-ROM to start the installation process.

To check this, consult your computer's or main board's manual, or enter the BIOS setup of your computer while it is booting and see if you can switch the default boot device to your CD-ROM drive. If you can boot from the CD-ROM drive, insert the Red Hat Linux 6 CD-ROM and attempt to boot your system. You should see a Red Hat Linux 6 boot message and a boot prompt that says Lilo:.

NOTE   Even though a CD-ROM may be designed to be bootable, it still may not boot in all PCs that support bootable CD-ROMs. If you experience difficulty booting the copy of Linux that comes with this book or your own copy of Linux, then try installing from a floppy disk and CD-ROM as described in the "From Floppy Disk and CD-ROM" section in this chapter.

From Floppy Disk and CD-ROM

If you have a CD-ROM drive but can't boot from it, the next best thing is to install Linux from a combination of floppy disk and CD-ROM. In this scenario, you boot from one or more floppy disks to start the installation process and then proceed to install the actual Linux software from the CD-ROM.

Some preparation is necessary to do this. For most distributions of Linux, you need to prepare a boot floppy disk and, possibly, one or more supplementary disks. Everything you need to do this should be included on the CD-ROM containing your Linux distribution.

In the case of Red Hat Linux 6, you need a boot disk and a supplementary disk. From DOS or the Windows DOS prompt, you can build these two disks off the Red Hat 6 CD-ROM.

On the Red Hat 6 CD-ROM, the Images subdirectory contains two files, boot.img and supp.img, that are disk images of the floppy disks used for installing Red Hat Linux 6. To produce the necessary floppy disks, you will need two blank, formatted, high-density 1.44MB floppies and will use the rawrite.exe utility.

For instance, assuming that your CD-ROM drive is drive D, you use rawrite.exe as follows to create the Red Hat boot install disk:

```
C:\>d:\dosutils\rawrite.exe
Enter disk image source file name: d:\images\boot.img
Enter target diskette drive: a
Please insert a formatted diskette into drive A: and press -ENTER- :
```

Similarly, you enter **d:\images\supp.img** as the source filename to create the supplementary installation disk.

Once this is done, you can boot from the boot install disk to start the installation process.

From Hard Disk

If you have plenty of disk space, you may want to copy the entire contents of the CD-ROM to your hard disk and install from the hard disk. In order to do this, use Windows Explorer (or the Windows 3.1 File Manager) to copy the contents of the CD-ROM to a location on your hard disk with sufficient free space to hold about 650MB of data. In addition, you need to create the Red Hat Linux boot installation floppy disks as explained previously.

Of course, if you have access to a CD-ROM drive to copy the necessary data to your hard drive, then you don't need to install from a hard disk. The only time this should really become necessary is if the Red Hat Linux installation software won't recognize your CD-ROM drive.

Arranging Your Hard Disk

When it comes time to install Linux, you are going to have to make some fundamental decisions regarding where to place the operating system on your hard disk(s). If you are extremely lucky, then one of the following two situations applies to you:

- You have a blank hard disk, or one you can reformat, available in which to install Linux.

- You have a blank partition, or one you can reformat, available in which to install Linux.

Unfortunately, most users who are looking at installing Linux for the first time want Linux to coexist with their current Windows and DOS installations and do not want to reformat an existing partition or hard disk to do this.

Partitioning Concepts

In order to install Linux into an existing system with no free partitions or hard disks, you need to find sufficient disk space and then carefully adjust your system's partitioning to free up a partition to work with during the Linux installation. Generally, if you want to install a fairly complete Linux system, you should free up at least 500MB of disk space. The space you free up should be on a single partition. (In Windows, each partition appears as a separate drive letter such as C, D, or E, so you need to find a drive with 500MB or more of free space.)

A Sample Partition Scheme for a Windows 98 System

Let's look at a simple example. You have a computer with a single 4GB hard disk divided into two 2GB partitions as drives C and D under DOS. You are able to free up 1GB of disk space on drive D and want to use this to install Linux.

There are two steps to be done before you are ready to install Linux:

1. Defragment the drive to ensure you have a large, continuous area of free space at the end of the partition.

2. Repartition the drive to make the space available for Linux installation.

Defragmenting a Drive

Defragmenting a drive under Windows 98 is fairly simple:

*   In My Computer or the Windows Explorer, right-click the Drives icon.

*   Select Properties from the drop-down menu.

*   Click the Tools tab at the top of the Properties window.

*   Click the Defragment Now button. Wait until defragmentation is complete and then proceed to the next section.

Partitioning Your Disk with Windows 98

Once you have defragmented a drive with sufficient space to install Linux, you need to create a new partition out of the free space. Most Linux distributions, including Red Hat Linux 6, come with a free DOS tool called fips.exe, which is in the dosutils subdirectory or in a subdirectory of this directory. In the Red Hat version included with this book, you can find the program in the \dosutils\ fips20 subdirectory.

This tool allows you to adjust the size of an existing partition, making it smaller by removing empty space at the end of the partition. This empty space is then converted into another partition.

To use fips.exe, you first need to be in MS-DOS mode. To do this, select Shut Down from the Start menu and choose Restart in MS-DOS Mode. Windows 98 should shut down and switch to a full-screen DOS environment.

WARNING This is a critical step. You shouldn't use a program like fips.exe inside a DOS window or full-screen DOS environment while Windows 98 is running. Unlike DOS, Windows 98 allows multiple programs to run simultaneously, so it is possible for other programs to try to access the partition being worked with by fips.exe. If this happens, your data may be corrupted and irretrievable.

Once in DOS mode, run fips.exe from your CD-ROM. If your CD-ROM drive is drive E, use the command:

c:\>e:\dosutils\fips20\fips.exe

The program first presents your partition table. In the previous example of a two-partition drive, this will look something like:

```
Partition table:

      |        |    Start    |      |      End     | Start  |Number of|
Part.|bootable|Head Cyl. Sector|System|Head Cyl. Sector| Sector |Sectors  |  MB
---+-----+---------+----+---------+-----+------+---
1    |  yes |  1    0     1|  06h| 254  222     63|      63|  3582432|1749
2    |  no  |  0   223    1|  05h| 254  286     63| 3582495|  1028160| 502
```

On most systems, identifying your partitions is easy since drive C is partition 1, drive D is partition 2, and so on. If you have trouble, use the size of the partition in megabytes in the last column to help.

You are prompted to choose a partition. In this case, choose 2, since you want drive D to be adjusted. Once you choose, the partition will be scanned and summary information about the partition, similar to the following, is presented:

```
Bytes per sector: 512
Sectors per cluster: 8
Reserved sectors: 1
Number of FATs: 2
Number of rootdirectory entries: 512
Number of sectors (short): 0
Media descriptor byte: f8h
Sectors per FAT: 145
Sectors per track: 63
Drive heads: 16
Hidden sectors: 63
Number of sectors (long): 141057
Physical drive number: 80h
Signature: 29h
```

Assuming you have free space at the end of the partition you have chosen, you are asked which disk cylinder to use as the line where the partition is cut and split. You can use the left and right arrow keys to change the selected cylinder. As you do this, the size of the partitions in megabytes are shown so you can make sure the new partition is large enough. The fips.exe program handles the job of making sure that you can't choose a cylinder to split that would leave some of the data of your current partition on the new partition.

Finally, a revised partition table appears and you are asked to confirm that everything looks OK. In this example, you should now have three partitions, with the third being your new partition and the second being smaller in size than it was originally.

TIP

To protect against mistakes, copy fips.exe, restorrb.exe, and errors.txt from the **dosutils** subdirectory of the Red Hat CD-ROM to a bootable floppy disk. When asked if you want to write backup copies of your boot and root sectors to a floppy disk, answer **Yes**. Then, if you need to recover from a mistake, you can boot from the floppy and run restorrb.exe to restore your original boot and root sectors.

Looking Ahead

In this chapter, you conducted the basic preparation needed to install Linux. Now you are ready for the actual installation.

In Chapter 4, you will run through a basic installation of Linux, discussing each screen of the installation program and how to decide what choices to make.

In Chapter 5, you will look at special cases, such as how to install Linux on multiple hard drives and how to install Linux onto an existing DOS partition.

CHAPTER
FOUR

Installing Red Hat Linux 6

- ■ Starting the Installation

- ■ The Installation Process

You're finally here: you are going to install Linux. By now you should be able to boot the Red Hat Linux 6 installation CD-ROM or should have produced a set of Linux boot floppy disks. You should also have determined where you will be installing Linux and made the space available.

Now you can begin. While the installation program may ask questions unfamiliar to you if you have not used a Linux-like operating system before, in reality the whole process is quite simple and many of the tough decisions are made for you by the installation software.

In fact, for the average user who is installing Linux as a second operating system in a Windows 95 or Windows 98 system, the process is generally straightforward, with a few odd turns required.

Starting the Installation

This chapter will look at a straightforward installation: installing Linux from the CD-ROM onto a non-networked, stand-alone PC.

In order to do this, you need to have selected which media to boot from to start the installation. As outlined in the last chapter, your two options are:

- Booting directly from the Red Hat CD-ROM. This requires that your computer's BIOS supports booting from your CD-ROM drive.

- Booting from a set of boot floppy disks and then installing from the CD-ROM.

In either case, insert your boot disk (floppy or CD-ROM) and boot your computer. When the computer starts booting from the floppy disk or CD-ROM, you will be presented with an initial welcome screen as shown in Figure 4.1.

```
                    Welcome to Red Hat Linux!

  o  To install or upgrade a system running Red Hat Linux 2.0
     or later, press the <ENTER> key.

  o  To enable expert mode, type: expert <ENTER>.  Press <F3> for
     more information about expert mode.

  o  This disk can no longer be used as a rescue disk.  Press <F4> for
     information on the new rescue disks.

  o  Use the function keys listed below for more information.




[F1-Main] [F2-General] [F3-Expert] [F4-Rescue] [F5-Kickstart] [F6-Kernel]
boot:
```

Here you have three main options:

- Press Enter to start the normal installation process.

- Provide boot parameters that allow the installation software to detect some types of obscure hardware, and then Press Enter to start the normal installation process. (Most hardware is detected automatically during installation.)

- Type **expert** and press Enter to boot in expert mode. (In expert mode, hardware detection is not performed and you will need to provide configuration parameters for all your hardware during the installation. You should only revert to this option if your hardware is not being detected properly and you are fairly confident of the parameters to enter.)

Generally, most users will find that all of their hardware will be successfully detected if they choose the first option, so simply press Enter to start the boot process.

NOTE
If you fail to press any key within 60 seconds, the installation automatically starts as if you had pressed Enter without providing any options. To disable this timer, press one of the help keys (F1–F6). Then you will have all the time you need to decide how to start the installation program.

The Installation Process

The installation process has several steps, which will be considered in turn. However, before doing that, you should learn how to use the keyboard to work in the installation program.

Keyboard Controls

As shown in Figure 4.2, there are several elements to the average installation screen. These elements include text input fields, check boxes, and buttons.

FIGURE 4.2:

A typical installation screen

This screen contains the following elements:

- Text input fields (FTP site name and Red Hat directory)

- A check box (Use non-anonymous ftp or a proxy server.)

- Buttons (OK and Cancel)

You can move between these elements using the Tab key (or the Alt+Tab combination to move backward). The arrow keys can also be used to move between fields.

To toggle the state of a check box, move to the check box and press the space bar. To press a button, move the cursor to the button using the Tab or arrow keys and then press the space bar or the Enter key. With an OK button, the F12 key generally works the same as pressing Enter or the space bar.

Choosing a Language

After starting the installation program at the boot screen as described earlier in this chapter, a welcome screen appears. Pressing the OK button brings you to the first screen of the installation process: language selection.

As you can see in Figure 4.3, the language selection screen has a selection list field and an OK button. When the cursor is in the selection list field, you can use the arrow keys or the Page Up and Page Down keys to move through the available languages until the desired one is selected. This selection determines the language that will be used during the installation process. (This is distinct from the language of the actual operating system, which is English, and the keyboard layout, which is chosen later.)

FIGURE 4.3:

Choosing a language

Choosing a Keyboard Type

The next screen presents a selection list field for choosing a keyboard type. In the United States and Canada, the correct choice will almost always be "us." Other common codes include those listed in Table 4.1.

TABLE 4.1: Codes for Keyboard Types

Code	Description
uk	British English keyboard
sg	Swiss German keyboard
sf	Swiss French keyboard
fr	French keyboard (France)
de	German keyboard

PCMCIA Support

Once you have chosen a keyboard type, you are prompted about your need for PCMCIA support during the installation process.

Generally, this is necessary only if you are installing Red Hat Linux 6 on a notebook computer and need to access a PCMCIA device during the installation. For example, you may have an external CD-ROM drive connected to your PC through a PCMCIA SCSI card.

If you need to use PCMCIA support, select this. You are instructed to insert your supplementary boot disk at this time.

Once Red Hat Linux 6 is installed, PCMCIA support is available. Only choose PCMCIA support here if you need it for the installation process.

Choosing an Installation Method

Once you have made your decision about PCMCIA support and, if necessary, provided the supplementary boot disk, another selection list appears asking you to choose the media you want to install from. Possible options are:

- CD-ROM

- Hard drive (from a hard drive partition; discussed in the next chapter)

In your case, you are installing from the enclosed Red Hat Linux 6 CD-ROM, so select CD-ROM and press the OK button.

When you choose to install from a CD-ROM, the installation program attempts to find an IDE/ATAPI CD-ROM drive, since this is the type available on most PCs today. If it fails to find your CD-ROM drive, you are prompted to tell the installation program what type of CD-ROM drive you have. The options are SCSI or Other.

You should select SCSI if you have a SCSI CD-ROM drive. You are prompted to select a driver for your SCSI card. Choose the driver that most closely matches your card and, if necessary, specify any options for your card.

If you have neither a SCSI nor an IDE CD-ROM drive, then you need to select Other. This allows you to choose from a list of proprietary CD-ROM drives such as those directly connected to certain sound cards or proprietary interfaces. You may be prompted to provide configuration information such as I/O addresses and IRQs once you select your drive.

Installing or Upgrading

Once you have selected your installation media (a CD-ROM drive in your case), you are asked if you are upgrading an existing installation or installing a new copy of Red Hat Linux. One of the benefits of Red Hat Linux, as opposed to some other distributions, is that it can be upgraded over old versions of Red Hat Linux. This is a great benefit; some other distributions still require a complete reinstallation to upgrade to a new version of the distribution.

Because you are installing from scratch, press the Install button.

Choosing an Installation Class

After you choose to install Linux (as opposed to upgrading a current installation), you will asked to select an installation class. There are three possible choices:

- Workstation: Performs a default installation for a Linux workstation. This option automatically erases all existing Linux partitions on your system.

- Server: Performs a default installation for a Linux server. This option automatically erases all existing Linux partitions on your system.

- Custom: Provides complete control over all aspects of the installation process.

In order to learn the details of Red Hat Linux installation, you will work with the third option, Custom, throughout this chapter and in Chapter 5, "Special Installations," and in Chapter 27, "Installing Red Hat Linux 6 for the SOHO."

Checking for SCSI Adapters

If you are installing a fresh copy of Red Hat Linux, you may be asked if you have any SCSI adapters. If you do, you should indicate this so that all attached devices can be detected by the installation software.

If you indicate that you have SCSI adapters, you are presented with a list of available drivers for SCSI cards from which you should choose the card that most closely matches your card. You may be prompted to give configuration information for the card once you choose the driver.

If you have no SCSI adapters in your system, it is important to choose No.

Setting Up Your Disk Partitions

After you provide the necessary information about your SCSI adapters, if any, you face a decision about how to allocate disk space for your Linux installation. This is a crucial step in the process because a mistake can erase existing data on your system that you want to keep. Care needs to be taken.

Let's assume that you have a single hard drive in your system; that, as directed in Chapter 3, "Getting Ready to Install Red Hat Linux 6," you created an area of free space (preferably larger than 500MB) using the techniques described there; and that the space is now ready to be used.

The first question you are asked is which tool you want to use to set up your partitions. The two choices are Disk Druid or fdisk.

Fdisk is the standard Linux tool for configuring disk partitions and is available for every Linux distribution. However, it is difficult to use and can be especially daunting for first-time Linux or Unix users.

To help ease this process, Red Hat Linux 6 provides its own tool for disk partition management called Disk Druid. This section will focus on using Disk Druid because it eases the initial installation process for users new to the Linux environment.

If you select the Disk Druid button, the main Disk Druid screen appears, as shown in Figure 4.4.

FIGURE 4.4:

The main Disk Druid screen

This screen has three main sections: the Current Disk Partitions section, the Drive Summaries section, and the button row.

In the Current Disk Partitions section, a single row is displayed for each existing disk partition on your system. The following information is presented about each partition:

- Mount Point: This indicates where the partition appears in your Linux directory structure. Linux directories all appear as subdirectories of the root directory. The root directory is / and all subdirectories start with a /, such as /home, /opt, and /usr/X11R6. At a minimum, you need to have a partition mounted as /. If you choose to mount additional partitions as subdirectories, this will spread your Linux distribution across two directories. For instance, if you mount a partition as /usr, then any content stored under this subdirectory is stored on the /usr partition while all other data is on the root-mounted (/) partition. The primary roles of the standard top-level Red Hat Linux directories are as follows:

  - /bin: Standard system utilities are stored here.

  - /dev: Device files are stored here.

  - /home: Users' home directories are stored here.

  - /opt: Optionally installed software is stored here.

  - /sbin: Standard system administration files are stored here.

  - /usr: Additional system software and administration tools are stored here.

- Device: This indicates the Linux device name for each partition. For IDE disks, the drives are labeled hdx, where *x* is a letter designating a drive (a for the primary master drive, b for the primary slave, c for the secondary master, and d for the secondary slave). Thus, if you have a single IDE hard disk, it is disk hda. SCSI disks are labeled sdx with *x* again designating a drive. Partitions on the disk are then numbered consecutively starting with hda1 and moving up. Generally, partitions 1 through 4 are primary partitions and 5 and above represent the extended and logical partitions common on many DOS systems. In Figure 4.4, you see a single pre-existing DOS partition, hda1.

- Requested: This indicates the minimum size of the partition in megabytes.

- Actual: This indicates the actual space allocated for a partition. Disk Druid allows the creation of growable Linux partitions, which increase in size as free space is available on the hard disk and space runs out in the partition. DOS partitions should have matching actual and requested values.

- Type: This field indicates the type of partition. Possible values include Linux native, Linux swap, and DOS 16-bit.

The next main section of the screen is the Drive Summaries section. This presents one line for each hard disk on your system and includes the following information about the drives:

- Drive: This is the device name for the hard drive, discussed previously.

- Geometry: This indicates the number of cylinders, heads, and sectors (in that order) for the drive.

- Total: This indicates the total available space on the drive, in megabytes.

- Used: This indicates the total used space on the drive, in megabytes. This number actually reflects how much is used in the sense of how much has been allocated to partitions. These partitions may not be full, but the space is no longer available to be allocated to other partitions.

- Free: This indicates how much free, allocated space is available on the drive, both numerically and as a bar graph. This number must be more than zero and should be more than 500MB before proceeding, because you need to use this space to create partitions to install Linux in. If you don't have any free space, consult the discussion in Chapter 3, "Getting Ready to Install Red Hat Linux 6," which describes how to allocate space for your Linux installation.

Finally, the button bar across the bottom of the screen has three task buttons, an OK button, and the typical Back button that you have already seen on some screens. You use the Add task button to create the necessary Linux partitions for your installation and the Edit button to make sure your existing DOS and Windows data is accessible in Linux. Then you will learn how to use the Delete button.

Adding New Partitions

To add a new partition, you simply press the Add button on the main Disk Druid screen. A screen appears asking for the following main information:

- Mount point.

- Size in megabytes.

- Partition type (from a selection list field).

- Whether the drive can grow to use unallocated disk space as needed (through the Growable check box).

- Which drives the partition can be created on. If more than one drive is indicated as allowed and all allowed drives have sufficient space to create the partition, then Disk Druid will decide which disk to use. If you want to create the partition on a specific disk, make sure only that disk is checked.

You need to use the Add button twice to create the following partitions:

- A swap partition: Linux needs a separate partition to use for swapping. This is necessary when you use up all your physical RAM and the operating system must draw on virtual memory (disk space masquerading as RAM) to keep functioning. At a minimum, you want to match the amount of physical RAM you have on your system; if you have plenty of free disk space, make the size of the swap partition as much as double your physical RAM. So, on a 32MB system, create a swap partition of between 32 and 64MB. The partition type should be set to Linux Swap, no mount point should be indicated, and the Growable check box should be unselected.

- A root partition: In this chapter, you are going to install Linux in a single partition. (The next chapter discusses the use of multiple partitions or drives for the installation of Linux.) To do this, you need to add another partition. You will probably want the partition to be at least 500MB to give you room to work once Linux is installed. This partition should be type Linux Native, should have a mount point of /, and can be marked as growable if there is unallocated free space on your drive that you want to use if the partition grows larger than its initial size.

NOTE   When determining your swap partition size, keep in mind that Linux currently limits the size of a swap partition to 128MB, so you don't want to create partitions larger than that.

Editing a Partition

You can edit existing partitions by selecting them on the list of current partitions and then clicking the Edit button. This brings up a window like the one you used when adding a new partition, except that here all the fields are filled in to match the settings of the partition you are editing.

If you have pre-existing DOS partitions, you can make them available by specifying a mount point for them. To do this, select the partition you wish to make accessible in Linux, press the Edit button, and then fill in a mount point for the partition.

If you have a single DOS partition, you could mount it as /dos, for instance. If you have two DOS partitions, which are drives C and D in DOS and Windows, you could choose /dosc and /dosd (or /c and /d) respectively, as the mount points.

TIP   If, you have Windows 95 or 98 FAT32 partitions, you are out of luck at the moment, since Linux currently doesn't support reading to or writing from this type of partition. In this case, don't indicate a mount point for the partition.

Deleting a Partition

If, in the process of creating your Linux swap and root partitions you make a mistake (maybe the swap partition is too large or your root partition too small), you can delete the partitions and then re-add them. To do this, select the partition in the list of current partitions and then press the Delete button.

WARNING   Take care when doing this. Don't accidentally delete any partitions that already existed before you started installing Linux and that contain important data or software you want to keep.

Moving On

Once you have finished creating and configuring your partitions, you are ready to move on. You can do this by pressing the OK button.

Preparing Your Swap Space

The next step in the installation process is to prepare your swap space. A screen appears like the one in Figure 4.5.

FIGURE 4.5:

Preparing your swap space

This screen lists all available partitions of type swap with a check box next to them. Any partitions that you actually want to use as swap space should be checked.

An additional check box is used to indicate that the partitions should be checked for bad blocks while being formatted for use as swap space. If the drive you are using is new, you definitely should check this option. Formatting will take longer but any problems with your hard disk will be caught early. If you are using a disk that has been in use on your computer for some time, you can consider not checking for bad blocks. Note, however, that bad blocks on your swap partition can cause your Linux system to crash. You could lose your current work when this happens, and it is even possible for data saved on your root partition to become corrupted if there are bad blocks in your swap partition.

Formatting Your Linux Partitions

The next step is to format your Linux partitions in preparation for installing Linux. A list of partitions of type Linux Native appears with indications of the mount points they have. Any newly created partitions should be marked for formatting by selecting the check box next to the drive.

If you have additional partitions of type Linux Native, they should be formatted if they are new partitions. If they already existed (this is unlikely for new Red Hat users) and you want to retain the data they hold, don't mark them for formatting.

As with the swap partition, you can indicate that a bad block check should be performed during formatting. This is a good idea, especially for new hard drives.

Selecting Packages

Now that your hard disks are configured and your Linux partitions are formatted, you are ready to begin installing the actual software. The default installation includes all the necessary core software, but several optional components are also available, including those shown in Figure 4.6.

FIGURE 4.6:

Selecting additional components

Each component is a collection of related packages for specific tasks such as dial-up connections, Web surfing, and others. You can choose the packages individually by marking their respective check boxes or you can choose the Everything option, which is the last entry in the list.

The Select Individual Packages option that appears below the list field indicates that you want to select individual packages within each component. However, if you are a first-time Linux user, it will be hard to choose the packages. Leaving this option unselected means that each component is installed in its entirety.

If you have plenty of disk space (more than 700MB; 1GB is preferable), then select everything so that you have a complete Red Hat Linux 6 installation. If your space is in more limited supply, consider installing the following components at a minimum:

- Printer support (If you don't have a printer, then this is unnecessary.)
- X Windows system
- Mail/WWW/News tools
- DOS/Windows Connectivity
- X multimedia support
- Console multimedia
- Dial-up workstation
- Extra documentation

Once you select the components you want to install, you are informed that a log of your installation process will be saved on your new Linux system as the file /tmp/install.log, and then installation will begin.

During the installation of the software, a screen displays the current status of the installation, indicating which package is currently being installed, how many packages and how many megabytes remain, and the overall progress of the installation.

Configuring Your Mouse

Once the Linux software has been successfully installed, the installation proceeds to the configuration process.

The first item to be configured is your mouse. First, the installation software attempts to detect your mouse and informs you of the success of this process. Then, you are presented with a list of possible mouse types from which to select (if automatic detection was successful, then the appropriate mouse type is pre-selected). The two most common types are Microsoft-compatible serial mice and

PS/2 mice. Consult your mouse's documentation to determine the type of mouse you have.

If your mouse is a two-button mouse, make sure that you check the box for three-button mouse emulation. Linux expects a three-button mouse, as do all Unix operating systems. This emulation allows you to click the left and right mouse buttons together to simulate clicking on the middle mouse button.

Network Configuration

The next item to be configured is your network. Because you are installing a stand-alone system in this chapter, choose not to configure your network. Chapter 27, "Installing Red Hat Linux 6 for the SOHO," discusses networked configuration in more detail.

Time Zone Configuration

The next step is to configure your computer's clock and time zone. You need to make two decisions.

First, you need to indicate whether you want your system's clock set to your local time or to Greenwich Mean Time (GMT). If you run only Linux on your computer, choose to set the clock to GMT. Red Hat Linux then converts GMT to the current time for your time zone. But if you also run other operating systems on your PC, don't select this option—leave the system's clock set to your local time.

Second, you need to choose the actual time zone from the list of available time zones.

Selecting Services

In Linux, you can easily control which services start when you boot your system. Services do everything from controlling the movement of e-mail to scheduling automated batch tasks.

Because you can change the scheduling of tasks at any point, leave the default settings on this screen for now. Later, once you have learned about many of these services, you can make changes to the start-up configuration.

Configuring a Printer

The next step is configuring a printer. Printer configuration is covered in some depth in Chapter 18, "Using Peripherals," but it will be reviewed briefly here. If you have no printer, you can skip this step.

This section only discusses configuring a local printer—that is, a printer physically connected to your computer (as opposed to a network printer). To start this procedure, choose Local from the options presented on the first printer configuration screen.

The next screen asks for standard printer options: the name of the queue and the directory where the data should be stored while being printed. It is best to accept the defaults until later discussions of Linux printing.

After you choose these standard options, the installation program detects and displays available parallel ports that a printer could be attached to. Linux parallel ports are named /dev/lp0, /dev/lp1, and so on, with lp0 mapping to LPT1: in DOS and lp1 mapping to LPT2:. Make sure the correct device is indicated in the Printer Device field.

Next, the Configure Printer screen appears. Here you can choose the type of printer that most closely matches your printer. If the exact model is not on the list, choose the closest available type of printer. This leads to a screen where you can specify settings for the printer that include paper size and default resolution.

The Fix Stair-Stepping of Text option is needed if your printer doesn't automatically put a carriage return at the end of each line of text. If you aren't sure, leave this option unselected for now.

Finally, you are presented with the configuration information for your printer and you are asked to confirm that everything is correct.

Setting a Root Password

As a multiuser operating system, Linux needs at least one user to exist in order for it to be used. On all systems, you have to have a root user, so you are prompted to provide a root password (twice, for confirmation). The root user is the all-powerful system administrator. When logged in as the root user, you can view all users' files, perform all system administration tasks, and, if you want to, delete all files on your system. This is a powerful account, and you need to keep this password secure if other people are going to have access to your system.

After setting the root password, you are prompted to make authentication configuration selections. There are three options on this screen and each can be selected individually. They are not mutually exclusive. The options are:

- Enable NIS: This is a type of network authentication common in many Unix networks, especially those with Sun Solaris–based servers. By default, this option is not selected.

- Use Shadow Passwords: Using shadow passwords is a technique designed to make it harder for an attacker or a regular system user to steal the user database and then attempt to crack the system administration password at their own leisure. By default, this option is selected.

- Enable MD5 Passwords: Typically, Unix systems have used a relatively weak encryption scheme for storing passwords. This option makes Linux use a more rigorous encryption scheme for storage of user passwords. By default, this option is selected.

Unless you are familiar with these options and have compelling reasons to alter them, leave the default selections the way they are and move on.

Creating a Boot Disk

This step gives you the chance to create a boot disk for your system. This is a wise decision, because it allows you to boot your system in case of emergencies and then attempt to resurrect a sick system.

By choosing to create a boot disk, you need to provide a blank floppy disk to be used for the boot disk.

Setting Up LILO

LILO is the Linux boot loader. In order for your system to boot properly, you need to configure and install LILO. LILO also provides the dual-boot features that can allow you to choose what operating system to launch at boot time, providing you with access to your existing Windows or DOS system as well as Linux.

The screen asks you to indicate where to install LILO. You can do this in the Master Boot Record (which is recommended) or on the first sector of your root partition. If you are running an operating system such as OS/2 or Windows NT that has its own boot loader, you may want to choose the latter option, but then you will need to know how to make that boot loader launch your Linux system in order to get Linux working.

WARNING   If you choose to skip installing LILO at this point, you need the boot disk from the last step in order to boot your Linux system. It is highly recommended that you install LILO during this initial installation.

The next screen prompts you to provide default options to be given to Linux at boot time. You probably don't need to use these options, but if your hard drive is configured to use logical block addressing (LBA) mode (check your BIOS), then choose the Use Linear Mode option.

Finally, a screen appears in which all partitions are displayed and a boot label is assigned to all bootable partitions—in this case, one for your Linux system and one for your DOS/Windows system. The boot label is the name you use to select which operating system will boot when you start your computer.

The Default column indicates which operating system will boot by default if the user makes no selection at boot time. To change this, select the operating system you wish to be your default and press F2.

Configuring X Windows

X Windows is Linux's graphical user interface (GUI). Chapter 7, "Installing and Configuring X Windows," discusses configuring X Windows in detail. For now, let's quickly run through the configuration process. Configuration can be quite complex and a whole chapter is devoted to it, so any problems will be left to that chapter for resolution.

First, an attempt is made to determine what type of video card you have. If this fails, a list of available video cards appears. Select the one that most closely matches your card (if none match, leave the configuration of X Windows until Chapter 7).

Next, a list of monitor types appears. If you find an exact match for your monitor, choose it; otherwise, hold off until Chapter 7. An incorrectly configured monitor can cause damage to the monitor. The match should be exact.

Next, you are asked for the amount of video memory available on your video card. Consult your video card's documentation for this information.

Once you specify the video memory, a list of clock chips appears. If your card doesn't have a clock chip or you don't know whether it does, choose No Clockchip. Do not guess on this question. If you indicate No Clockchip, you are given a chance to probe your card for clock settings. Give this a try. If it fails, leave things until Chapter 7.

Finally, a list of video modes appears. Select the one you want to use for X Windows.

Rebooting Your System

Finally, you are prompted to remove any floppy disks from the computer and reboot. If you left Linux as the default operating system, the system boots into Linux, giving you five seconds at the boot: prompt during start-up to select an alternate operating system.

If you chose another operating system as your default, then at the boot: prompt you need to type the boot label of your Linux partition in order to boot into Linux.

If all goes well, a Red Hat Linux login appears. You can log in here as the root user using the username root and the password you provided earlier. A command prompt appears similar to the following:

```
[armand@localhost armand]$
```

You will learn about commands later, but the premise is simple: type the command and press the Enter key to execute it. Type **exit** and press Enter to log out.

Linux allows you to log in more than once, even in the initial character-based mode. Using the combinations of Alt+F1 through Alt+F6, you can switch between up to six virtual consoles. You need to log in separately in each virtual console. You can log in as different users and perform different tasks, or log in to different virtual consoles as the same user—this is one of the features of Unix and Linux that make them such flexible environments to work in.

Looking Ahead

By now you should have a working Linux system. If you are one of the few readers who have special circumstances that made it impossible to get your Linux system running by following the steps in this chapter, then take a look at the Chapter 5, "Special Installations," which discusses some special-case installations:

- Installing from a hard drive partition. (This is important if, for some reason, you cannot get Linux to install from your CD-ROM drive.)

- Installing to multiple partitions or hard disks. (This is useful if you have lots of disk space spread over multiple disks or need the performance gain from splitting Linux in this way.)

- Using fdisk instead of Disk Druid to configure your partitions. (Disk Druid is useful but not standard for Linux; using fdisk allows you to learn the workings of this standard tool and provides access to the more powerful tools desired by the expert user.)

If any of these special installations are useful, turn to the Chapter 5. If your system booted correctly, though, you are ready to move on and learn about X Windows. Skip to Chapter 6, "An Overview of X Windows," and continue from there.

CHAPTER

FIVE

Special Installations

- ■ Installing from a Hard Disk Partition

- ■ Installing Linux on Multiple Partitions

- ■ Using Fdisk instead of Disk Druid

In Chapter 4, you learned how to take the straightforward approach to installing Linux: from a local CD-ROM to a single hard disk partition.

This chapter will look at a few installation variations that are not uncommon. First among these is installing from a hard disk partition. There are cases where installing from the local CD-ROM drive is not practical. For instance, you may have one of the few CD-ROM drives that the Red Hat installation software can't recognize, or you may have only temporary access to a CD-ROM drive. In these cases, one option is to copy the contents of the Red Hat CD-ROM to blank space on a hard drive and then install from the hard drive.

In addition, with the low cost of hard drives today, you may have available multiple partitions or hard drives that you can use for your Linux installation. In these cases, you can maximize the performance of your system by spreading your Linux system across multiple partitions and disks.

Finally, this chapter will look at how to use the fdisk program instead of Disk Druid for configuring your hard disk partitions. Fdisk is standard with all distributions of Linux; Disk Druid is available only with Red Hat Linux.

Installing from a Hard Disk Partition

For some users, there are compelling reasons to install Linux from a different hard disk partition than the one they plan to run Linux from. Possible reasons include:

- A CD-ROM drive that the Red Hat Linux installation program fails to recognize

- Lack of a permanent CD-ROM drive, but access to a CD-ROM drive to copy the CD-ROM to a hard disk

- A notebook with a switchable floppy drive and a CD-ROM drive that cannot be booted from the CD-ROM drive

In all these cases, the process of installing from a hard disk partition is basically the same:

1. Copy the contents of the Red Hat CD-ROM to a dedicated hard disk partition.

2. Make sure you have the correct installation floppy disks ready.

3. Start the installation process by booting from the boot installation floppy disk.

Copying the CD-ROM to a Hard Disk Partition

In order to install from a hard disk partition, you need a dedicated partition available to store the contents of the Red Hat CD-ROM. This partition should contain at least 650MB of free space in order to accommodate the complete contents of the Red Hat CD-ROM.

You can copy the contents of the CD-ROM to a partition from your current Windows environment using the xcopy command from a DOS prompt window. If you have your CD-ROM drive at drive F: and the free disk partition where you want to copy the contents of the CD-ROM drive is drive E:, then you can use the command:

```
# xcopy /e f: e:
```

The /e flag indicates that all directories on the CD-ROM should be created in the copy, even if the directory is empty.

Preparing the Installation Floppies

Chapter 3, "Getting Ready to Install Red Hat Linux 6," discusses how to create the necessary installation floppy disks. Refer to the section "From Floppy Disk and CD-ROM" in that chapter for all the details.

In order to install from a hard disk partition, you may need both the primary boot installation floppy disk and the supplementary floppy disk, so it is best to have them both prepared before starting the installation process.

The Actual Installation Process

To begin the installation, boot from the boot floppy. Follow the steps used for a normal installation from CD-ROM (set out in Chapter 4, "Installing Red Hat Linux 6") with the following exceptions:

1. When selecting an installation method, select Hard Drive instead of Local CD-ROM.

2. After selecting Hard Drive, you are prompted to indicate which partition contains your Red Hat source image. Refer back to Chapter 4 for a discussion of Linux device names for disk partitions. If you aren't sure which partition contains the Red Hat software, refer to the list of available partitions provided on the screen to try to determine which one contains your copy of

the Red Hat CD-ROM. If that is not sufficient, then choose Cancel to return to the Disk Druid list of partitions, which provides more detailed information about your partitions.

Other than these two differences, the rest of your installation should proceed in much the same way as outlined in Chapter 4.

Installing Linux on Multiple Partitions

The title of this section is something of a misnomer. After all, for any Linux installation, you are using at least two partitions: one for storing Linux and one for your swap space. However, there can be compelling reasons to use more than one partition for storing Linux.

One obvious reason for this would be if you have a disk that has two available partitions that are not physically contiguous. There is no way to delete these partitions and create one larger partition on which to store Linux. In this case, you can divide your Linux installation across the two partitions.

Even more compelling, though, is to install Linux on more than one disk. There are several ways to take advantage of having more than one disk for your Linux installation.

Putting Swap on a Separate Disk

If you have a large partition on one disk and a smaller partition (of anywhere from 32 to 200MB) on a second disk, you may want to consider putting your swap partition on a second disk. This can noticeably improve performance if you find yourself swapping a lot.

Consider this scenario: Your Linux installation and your swap partition are on the same physical disk. You are running many applications and your system has already been swapping a lot. You attempt to launch a new application, but in order for it to be launched, it needs to be loaded from disk into memory—and at the same time, existing data in memory needs to be swapped out to disk. Since the disk can perform only one operation at once, your disk suddenly becomes a bottleneck as the operating system tries to perform both actions nearly at the same time.

But if your swap partition is on a separate disk, there is less of a bottleneck: one disk can be reading data from the disk into memory while the other is still finishing the process of moving data from memory onto the disk. Even though the computer can't perform two instructions at the same time, the fact that the slow disk operations are spread over two disks helps minimize the time the CPU is left waiting for the disks to finish their work.

Splitting Linux Across Multiple Partitions

Another way to use two or more partitions for your Linux software is to split the storage of your Linux software across the partitions in a logical manner. This can provide two benefits:

- Expanding the disk space available in critical Linux directory trees such as the /home directory tree

- Improving performance by splitting disk accesses across multiple hard disks if the available partitions are on more than one disk

Let's consider how you might want to split your Linux distribution across two partitions. As mentioned in Chapter 4, "Installing Red Hat Linux 6," when discussing how to specify the mount point for an existing DOS partition, you use your additional disks by specifying their mount points.

For example, if you want to store all users' home directories on a separate partition, then make the mount point for that partition /home while leaving the mount point for your main Linux partition as /. Then, when you write to or read from any subdirectory under /home, you are actually accessing a different partition than when you access other directory trees outside /home.

There are several popular ways to split your Linux installation across two partitions:

- If you plan to install a lot of your own software (including commercial software such as word processors, Web browsers, and Windows emulation software), you will find that much of it is installed in the /opt directory tree. If your main Linux partition has plenty of room for the operating system plus user data, then consider mounting your additional partition as /opt. This will give you a separate area for all of your applications, and when you launch applications, the main system disk is still free for accessing data or running the system utilities and background tasks that Linux is always performing.

- If you expect to have a lot of users or plan to store a lot of data in users' home directories, then consider mounting your additional partition as /home. This way, you can separately monitor user disk usage, and you will get a performance gain when many users are accessing their data while other users are trying to launch applications, because these two actions will require access to separate disk partitions.

- If you find that neither partition on its own can contain your complete Linux installation, you may want to choose a fairly large directory tree such as /usr/X11R6 (the X Windows directory tree) and install that to a separate partition so that you can install your complete Linux system.

- While many new packages are installed in /opt, if you do lots of software installation you will find that /usr may also fill up quickly, making it a good candidate for a separate partition.

- If you are using Linux as a busy mail server or a heavily used, multiuser server, consider giving /var its own partition, since mail spool queues and system logs sit in this directory and can grow quickly in these types of servers.

Using *Fdisk* instead of Disk Druid

In Chapter 4, "Installing Red Hat Linux 6," you used Disk Druid to configure your disk partitions when installing Red Hat Linux 6. Disk Druid, however, is a program that is only available in the Red Hat installation process. Normally, Linux users use fdisk to configure their disk partitions, both during the installation process and later when they need to adjust their disk geographies.

In fact, fdisk is so familiar to power Linux users that Red Hat acknowledges its predominance as a tool for configuring disk partitions by offering it as an alternative to Disk Druid.

While fdisk is an extremely complex and powerful tool (and a potentially dangerous and destructive one if misused), the job of performing basic tasks such as displaying a partition table, creating a new partition from free space, and assigning types to partitions is fairly simple.

When you select fdisk instead of Disk Druid during the installation process, first a screen appears and asks you which disk to work with. Unlike Disk Druid, fdisk works with only one physical disk at a time. Once you select a disk to work with, you temporarily leave the now-familiar Red Hat installation program and are presented with the initial fdisk screen shown in Figure 5.1.

FIGURE 5.1:

The fdisk welcome screen

Fdisk operates using simple commands, each a single character long. To issue a command, simply type the command and press the Enter key. If the command needs additional information to perform its task, it prompts you for the missing information.

The simplest command is m or ?. Either of these characters causes fdisk to display the help screen shown in Figure 5.2. This screen lists all the common fdisk commands, including all the commands described in this section.

FIGURE 5.2:

The fdisk help screen

```
Using /dev/hda as default device!

Command (m for help): m
Command action
   a   toggle a bootable flag
   b   edit bsd disklabel
   c   toggle the dos compatibility flag
   d   delete a partition
   l   list known partition types
   m   print this menu
   n   add a new partition
   p   print the partition table
   q   quit without saving changes
   t   change a partition's system id
   u   change display/entry units
   v   verify the partition table
   w   write table to disk and exit
   x   extra functionality (experts only)

Command (m for help):
```

Displaying the Partition Table

One of the most useful tasks performed by fdisk is to display the current partition table for the active disk being worked with. This looks like the table in Figure 5.3.

```
Command (m for help): p

Disk /dev/hda: 255 heads, 63 sectors, 525 cylinders
Units = cylinders of 16065 * 512 bytes

   Device Boot   Begin    Start     End    Blocks   Id  System
/dev/hda1    *       1        1     223   1791216    6  DOS 16-bit >=32M
/dev/hda2          224      224     287    514080    5  Extended
/dev/hda3          288      288     515   1831410   83  Linux native
/dev/hda4          516      516     525     80325   82  Linux swap
/dev/hda5          224      224     287    514048+   6  DOS 16-bit >=32M

Command (m for help):
```

For each partition on the current disk, the device name, start and end blocks, partition size in blocks, and system type are displayed.

Adding a Partition Using Free Space

To add a new partition using existing free space on your hard disk, use the n command. As shown in Figure 5.4, you are prompted for a partition type. Generally, you should choose Primary as the type. With Linux fdisk, you can create four primary partitions as compared to DOS's single primary partition.

Once the partition type is selected, you assign the partition number and finally the start and end blocks. To use all remaining space (assuming all available space is at the end of the drive), take the default first and last block for your partition.

```
Command (m for help): n
Command action
   e   extended
   p   primary partition (1-4)
p
Partition number (1-4): 2
First cylinder (224-525):
```

Changing the Partition Type

By default, all new partitions created with fdisk are assigned the type Linux Native (type number 83). To change the type of a partition, use the t command.

You are prompted for a partition to work with, which you can select numerically, as shown in Figure 5.5, and then you are prompted for the type ID. To view a list of type IDs, use the L command at this point to see the list shown in Figure 5.5.

FIGURE 5.5:

Changing partition type ID
in fdisk

```
Command (m for help): t
Partition number (1-4): 1
Hex code (type L to list codes): 82
Changed system type of partition 1 to 82 (Linux swap)
```

The most commonly used partition types are shown in Table 5.1.

TABLE 5.1 Commonly Used Partition Types

ID	Type
5	Extended
6	DOS 16-bit (larger than 32MB)
7	OS/2 HPFS
b	Windows 95 FAT32
82	Linux Swap
83	Linux Native

Deleting a Partition

Sometimes you want to delete an existing partition to create one or more new partitions for your Linux installation. To do this, simply use the d command and, when prompted, enter the partition number you wish to delete.

Committing Your Changes

While you are working with fdisk, none of the changes you make are actually made to the physical disk. This is a safety precaution so that if you accidentally delete a partition with important data, you will be able to revert to your previous configuration before permanently deleting the partition containing the data.

For that reason, the changes you make are not actually processed until you explicitly ask fdisk to do so at the time of quitting. Therefore, before you quit from fdisk, take care to view the partition table to be sure you have done exactly what you want. If you exit and commit the changes, they are permanent, and going back is not really an option. (In theory, you can save the partition table of your disk to a floppy disk before working with fdisk and then recover from a serious mistake by replacing the new partition table with the saved one; however, this is a complicated procedure and not foolproof. You are better off taking care and making sure that the changes you make to your partition table are exactly the way you want them before committing the changes.)

The two alternative commands for quitting from fdisk are:

Command	Effect
q	Quits from fdisk without processing or saving any of your changes.
w	Processes and saves all your changes and then exits from fdisk. This is a permanent action, so take care.

Looking Ahead

Finally, you are ready to get into the business of actually using Linux. As your first step on that path, you will look at the X Windows environment. X Windows gives all Unix operating systems, including Linux, a highly flexible, mouse-driven graphical user interface (GUI).

Many Linux books start with the command line because this is really the heart of Linux. But X Windows enables new users to quickly start using Linux before they have a thorough grasp of the Linux command line.

The next chapter gives you an overview of X Windows; you will learn what it offers and how it compares with the Microsoft Windows environment. Then you will move on to configuration and use of X Windows and take a look at some common X Windows applications.

PART III

Using Desktop Environments in Red Hat Linux 6

CHAPTER

SIX

6

An Overview of X Windows

- What Is X Windows?

- Microsoft Windows versus X Windows

- X Servers, Window Managers, and Desktop Environments

- What Is Motif?

Now that you have succeeded in installing Linux, you will start your learning process by diving straight into the X Windows environment. Many Linux diehards will shudder at our considering X Windows before mastering the intricate details of the Linux command line and the Linux configuration. But it is X Windows that makes Linux an acceptable alternative to Windows and to the Mac OS as a productive operating system for everyday tasks such as word processing, desktop publishing, and browsing the World Wide Web.

This chapter starts by describing exactly what X Windows is. X Windows offers a graphical user interface (GUI) to the Unix world. X Windows provides a way to deliver all the now commonplace user interface paradigms such as windows, dialog boxes, buttons, and menus. It is X Windows that enables the creation of the sophisticated graphics that make Unix-based workstations the systems of choice for many engineering and design applications, and it is X Windows that has made it possible for Linux to emerge as a strong contender in the PC operating-system market.

To fully understand what X Windows is all about, this chapter will provide a detailed comparison of Microsoft Windows and X Windows. Having done that, the chapter wraps up by looking at some key components of X Windows such as X servers, window managers, desktop environments, and Motif.

What Is X Windows?

Put in its simplest terms, X Windows is a complete graphics interface for Unix, and by extension, for Linux. But this doesn't say it all. X Windows is a highly configurable environment that provides a broad range of flexible options for both the user and the application developers producing software to run under X Windows.

The core X Windows concept is the client-server framework. What this means in practical terms is that X Windows provides an environment that is not bound to a single processor. Applications can run on different servers and machines on a network, and applications can display to X Windows terminals and workstations elsewhere on the network.

This separation between where an application runs and where it is displayed is a concept missing in the Windows and Macintosh environments, which tie the application to the display. The benefit of this separation is that in a networking environment, it is possible to have sophisticated graphics desktops displaying applications that are running on well-maintained, powerful, and easy-to-manage central application servers. In fact, this very capability is what gives Unix and X Windows such a good reputation among professional system administrators of large networks.

Another concept introduced in the X Windows environment is the separation of windowing from the interface. On an X Windows system, two applications must run to provide a complete GUI. The first is the X server, which sets up the graphics display (i.e., resolution, refresh rate, and color depth), displays the windows, and tracks mouse movements, keystrokes, and multiple windows. But an X server does not provide menus, window borders, or mechanisms for moving, switching, minimizing, or maximizing windows. If you look at Figure 6.1, you can see how an X server screen looks without a window manager.

FIGURE 6.1:

An X server display with no window manager

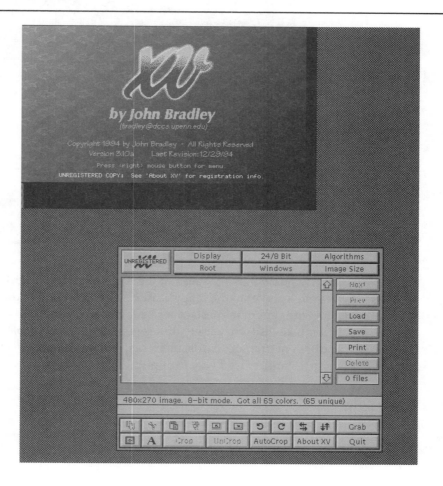

Notice the bare simplicity in Figure 6.1. There is no fancy color background, no sophisticated window borders or menu controls, and no other features that make a complete GUI. All these features are provided by a second application called a *window manager*. Figure 6.2 shows a complete X Windows desktop running the fvwm95 Window Manager. Notice the features of the window frames, the control buttons, and the control menus, as well as a taskbar and a virtual desktop system. All of these are provided by the window manager.

FIGURE 6.2:

An X Windows display running a window manager

The window manager talks to the X server in a standard, predefined way, as does the X server to the X applications. This means that different window managers with different interface features can all talk in this standard way to the X server. Likewise, the variety of X servers that are available, which offer support for different graphics cards, monitors, and other performance features, can also talk in a standardized way to applications.

Microsoft Windows versus X Windows

Given some of the descriptions of X Windows you've seen, it would be natural to assume that Microsoft Windows and X Windows are pretty much the same thing. The reality, though, is that they are fundamentally different beasts.

For example, Microsoft Windows is a complete operating system, with everything from a kernel to a shell to a windowing environment and more. X Windows is just one piece of that operating system puzzle: the windowing environment. Another contrast is in the interface: the Microsoft Windows interface is fairly rigid while the X Windows interface has an amazingly flexible and customizable design.

Similarities

So, what is similar about X Windows and Microsoft's de facto standard operating system? The main similarities are that they both provide graphical interfaces and make it possible to work with multiple windows. On top of this, they allow the user to interact with information using more than a keyboard and plain characters. Users can utilize a mouse as well as a keyboard and can create interfaces that combine menus, forms, windows, and dialog boxes.

Differences

There are numerous differences between the two windowing systems. The main differences are in the following areas:

- Flexibility of the interface
- Fine-tuned control over the interface configuration
- Client-server technology

Flexible Interface

The flexibility of the X Windows interface is one of the joys of this environment for many users. As discussed already, the separation of the user interface layer from the basic windowing layer makes it possible to create multiple interfaces for X Windows through the creation of different window managers.

Multiple interfaces don't simply provide subtle differences in appearance, as some customization tools for the Microsoft Windows interface offer; rather, they allow complete redesigns of the user interface from window manager to window manager.

By way of example, Figure 6.3 shows a sample window interface running a window manager that resembles the user interface of the NeXT operating system. Compare that to Figure 6.4, running on the same system and displaying the same applications, which shows a user interface resembling none of the popular PC or Macintosh operating systems.

FIGURE 6.3:

The Afterstep window manager

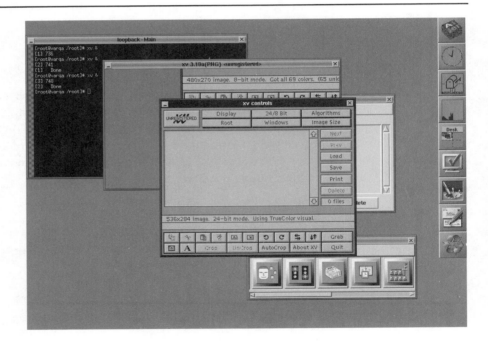

FIGURE 6.4:

The Lesstif window
manager

These examples represent just two of the many look-and-feel designs offered
by X Windows window managers. The better known window managers are discussed briefly later in this chapter.

Fine-Tuned Control

Another advantage of the X Windows environment is that it offers fine-tuned
control over all aspects of the windowing environment and the interface. By setting any of dozens of settings, it is possible to control all aspects of the environment, from the background and foreground window colors to cursor color,
default font, and default window size. Users can also define modes of interaction.
For instance, it is possible to use the mouse pointer to make a window automatically jump to the foreground or to change cursor focus to a background window.

In addition, these and other features can be defined on a per-application basis,
creating different settings for each application so that each application launches
in the most convenient way possible.

It is also possible to define which windows and applications open each time the X environment starts, as well as to have the system make logical choices about which window manager to use when starting X Windows.

Chapter 7, "Installing and Configuring X Windows," discusses the basic X Windows configuration options.

Client-Server Environment

As mentioned previously, the X Windows world works on a client-server model in which applications are clients to an X server that drives the physical display. This has made X Windows well adapted to network environments, allowing applications to run on one machine on the network while displaying their output on another.

Microsoft Windows lacked this ability until very recently, and now has it only in a limited fashion on high-end multiuser Windows NT systems. In the Linux, Unix, and X worlds, even the lowliest system is capable of playing either the client or the server role in this X Windows client-server model.

X Servers, Window Managers, and Desktop Environments

Now that you have a sense of where X Windows fits into things, you need to understand the fundamental components of X Windows: X servers, window managers, and desktop environments. It is these components and the modularity that they represent that provide the power and flexibility of X Windows.

X Servers

As you have already seen, the core of the X Windows system is the X server. The X server handles several tasks:

- Support for a variety of video cards and monitor types
- Resolution, refresh rate, and color depth of the X Windows display
- Basic window management: displaying and closing windows, tracking mouse movements and keystrokes

Multiple X servers with these basic capabilities have sprung up. In the Linux world, there are three main choices: XFree86, Metro-X, and Accelerated-X.

XFree86

XFree86 is the default X server with almost every noncommercial Linux distribution because it is available for free under the same sort of terms as Linux. Full source code is available, users are free to change the code to meet their own needs, and anyone can redistribute it. Red Hat Linux 6 ships with XFree86 3.3.3, the current version at the time of this writing.

The XFree86 Web server is designed to provide broad support for common hardware in the Intel $x86$ PC environment and, in more recent versions, for other platforms. While its performance is not always stellar, XFree86 is the norm for X servers in Linux and other Intel-based Unix variants and therefore is the X server that most people are familiar with.

Among the popular graphics card chipsets supported by XFree86 are Tseng's ET3000, 4000, and 6000, the full range of Trident chips, most of the Cirrus Logic line, Chips & Technologies graphics chips, and many others. You can find a full list in the XFree86 HOWTO, which was installed if you opted to install the complete documentation when you installed Linux. Use the command

```
$ zless /usr/doc/HOWTO/XFree86-HOWTO.gz
```

to read this documentation.

While the XFree86 X server goes a long way toward making Linux a complete, free, Unix-like operating system, it does suffer from some drawbacks that make it less than attractive for corporate or mission-critical environments. XFree86 sometimes requires painstakingly difficult configuration and installation, has less than stable or perfect support for some graphics cards and monitors, and often will not take advantage of the accelerated features of a graphics card.

Luckily, Red Hat Linux 6 ships with an excellent utility called Xconfigurator, which greatly eases the job of configuring XFree86, even to the point of auto-detecting some hardware and suggesting the best options for that hardware. This works great unless you present the tool with problematic hardware combinations, in which case you will be right back to configuring XFree86 manually.

Commercial X Servers

In addition to the XFree86 project, which is a vital part of making Linux a complete and free solution, there are two leading commercial X servers for the Linux world: Metro-X and Accelerated-X.

These products offer the advantage of broader support for different graphics chips and cards, and generally take full advantage of the accelerated features of those chips and cards. In addition, Metro-X and Accelerated-X offer more intelligent configuration and can usually be installed and working in a matter of minutes.

Metro-X Metro-X from MetroLink ships along with XFree86 in the commercial version of Red Hat Linux as one of the added-value features of the commercial package. This gives you the option to choose the server that meets your needs.

Among the many benefits of Metro-X are a well-designed graphical configuration interface like the one in Figure 6.5, support for multi-headed displays (more than one graphics card with attached monitor on a system), support for some brands of touch screens, and more.

FIGURE 6.5:

Metro-X's configuration window

Complete information about the Metro-X server is available on the MetroLink home page at `http://www.metrolink.com/`. Metro-X costs U.S. $39 for Linux.

Accelerated-X   X-Inside actually offers a range of X servers for Linux. These include the Accelerated-X server for Linux, a 3D Accelerated-X server, Multi-head Accelerated-X server, and a specialized Laptop Accelerated-X server. The Laptop Accelerated-X server is significant because the chipsets found on laptops are different than those in desktop graphics cards and because LCD screens have their own set of requirements ignored by desktop drivers.

In fact, support for laptop displays is quite limited in XFree86, and a small mistake can mean that your LCD will be damaged. If you plan to use a notebook full-time as a Linux system, look at the list of systems supported by the Laptop Accelerated-X server to see if yours is there.

Accelerated-X offers support for more than 500 graphics cards using more than 130 chipsets and promises the best performance by 20 percent of any X server for Linux.

The Multi-head Accelerated-X server supports up to eight screens (Metro-X supports four screens) and offers all the features of Accelerated-X on each screen.

Overall, X-Inside's servers are competitively priced. Accelerated-X costs U.S. $99.95, the Laptop server is $199.95, and the Multi-head server is $299.95. Complete information is available on the X-Inside Web site at `http://www .xinside.com/`.

Window Managers

Window managers fill out the niceties of the GUI not provided by X servers. Among other features, window managers include window decorations (which provide the means to resize, move, close, and minimize windows) and mechanisms for launching applications (such as desktop menus, control panels, and button bars).

The remainder of this section will take a brief look at some of the main window managers that are available for Linux, including FVWM, fvwm95, twm, olvwm, and others. The default window manager with Red Hat Linux 6 is Enlightenment, but any reasonably complete installation will include FVWM and other alternative window managers.

An overview of window managers for X Windows is available online at `http://www.plig.org/xwinman/`.

FVWM and fvwm95

By far the most common window manager for Linux until recently has been FVWM or some variation on this package. The name FVWM is a strange one because no one is sure what the "F" stands for in the name. Some say it stands for "Feeble" Virtual Window Manager; others argue that it is "Fine" Virtual Window Manager; still others argue that the meaning of the "F" has long been forgotten and isn't important anyway. (I tend to agree with the latter.)

FVWM is a lightweight window manager that provides a flexible, customizable windowing environment designed to look a bit like the Motif Window Manager (a commercial product). FVWM provides multiple virtual desktops and a module system for extending the window manager, and, in the more recent version 2, allows on-the-fly configuration changes and window-specific feature customization. The FVWM home page is at `http://fvwm.math.uh.edu/`. Figure 6.6 contains a sample FVWM desktop.

FIGURE 6.6:

A sample FVWM desktop

FVWM ships with almost every Linux distribution and is known for its useful-ness as the basis for newer window managers with their own look and feel, including the following:

- fvwm95: designed to look like Windows 95

- Afterstep: designed to look like the NeXT environment

- SCWM (Scheme Configurable Window Manager): configurable using the Scheme language

Figure 6.7 contains a screen of fvwm95 in action.

FIGURE 6.7:

Fvwm95 provides a Win-dows 95–like environment.

Fvwm95 is based on version 2 of FVWM and retains the flexible, easy configu-ration of that release. It continues to support FVWM modules but adds the mod-ules needed to implement Windows 95 features such as the Taskbar. Fvwm95 information is available on the Web at `http://www.plig.org/xwinman/ fvwm95.html`.

twm

The Tab Window Manager (twm), often called Tom's Window Manager after the name of its primary developer, is a basic, functional environment that is included with Red Hat Linux 6 as an alternate window manager. Figure 6.8 shows a typical twm desktop.

FIGURE 6.8:

The twm desktop

The twm window manager offers many key features that users expect in an X Windows window manager, including click-to-type or pointer-driven keyboard focus and user-defined key and button bindings. However, the interface is visually simple and some would see it as limited. Vtwm, a version of twm that includes a virtual desktop, is also available and can be downloaded from `ftp://ftp.x.org/R5contrib/vtwm-5.3.tar.gz`.

olvwm

Olvwm, the OpenLook Virtual Window Manager, is an extension of the Open-Look Window Manager (olwm), which was the standard window manager on Sun systems for many years. While Sun systems now sport Motif and the

Common Desktop Environment (discussed later in this chapter), the unique OpenLook interface is still popular among many users. Olvwm adds support for virtual desktops to the OpenLook package. Figure 6.9 shows a sample olvwm desktop.

The interface used in olvwm will feel awkward to many users, especially in terms of the way in which menus and windows respond to mouse buttons. This is one reason why OpenLook didn't gain huge popularity outside the Sun world. Olvwm can be downloaded from `ftp://ftp.x.org/R5contrib/olvwm4.tar.Z`.

FIGURE 6.9:

The olvwm interface

Afterstep

Afterstep, another variant on the original FVWM code, also ships as an alternative window manager in Red Hat Linux 6. This product is based on an earlier window manager called Bowman and is designed to provide the look and feel of the NeXTSTEP window manager from the NeXT platform. Figure 6.10 shows a sample Afterstep desktop.

Major features drawn from NeXTSTEP are the look of title bars, buttons, and borders, the look of the style menu, and the NeXTSTEP-like icons and button bar. Since it is based on FVWM version 1 code, any modules from that version of FVWM should continue to work with Afterstep.

The Afterstep home page is at http://www.afterstep.org/.

FIGURE 6.10:

The Afterstep desktop

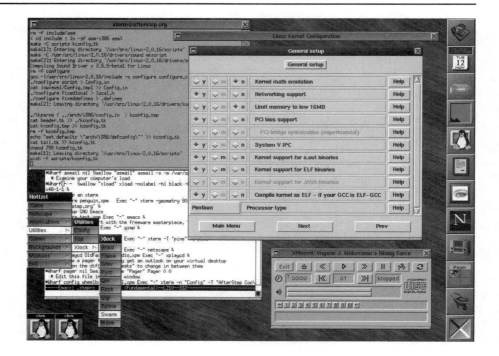

AmiWm

If you are a former user of the Amiga computer and fell in love with its interface, then AmiWm may be the window manager for you. AmiWm emulates the Amiga workbench, as shown in Figure 6.11. With support for multiple screens such as that found on the Amiga, AmiWm can ease the move to X Windows for former Amiga users.

You can learn about AmiWm and download the software from the AmiWm home page at http://www.lysator.liu.se/~marcus/amiwm.html.

FIGURE 6.11:

The AmiWm window manager

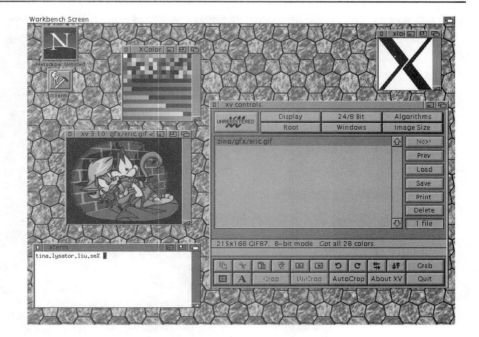

Enlightenment

Enlightenment is a grand project, attempting to develop a window manager that goes beyond the conventional. It provides a useful but also visually attractive environment, and allows the user to define everything from functionality to the appearance of the window manager. Figures 6.12 and 6.13 show just two possible configurations of the Enlightenment environment. Among the many features that help Enlightenment stand out are the abilities it gives users to hand-craft the look and feel and to embed new features easily.

FIGURE 6.12:

The Enlightenment window manager

FIGURE 6.12:

The Enlightenment window manager

While Enlightenment is an ambitious project and offers visually stunning interfaces, installation can be a bit of a challenge for the novice user, often requiring the user to compile and install new libraries. The Enlightenment home page is at `http://www.enlightenment.org/`. Note also that the authors consider Enlightenment in an early pre-release stage and therefore warn of bugs and the potential for crashes. Still, this is an interesting project and a unique concept among window managers.

FIGURE 6.13:

Users can fully customize the Enlightenment environment

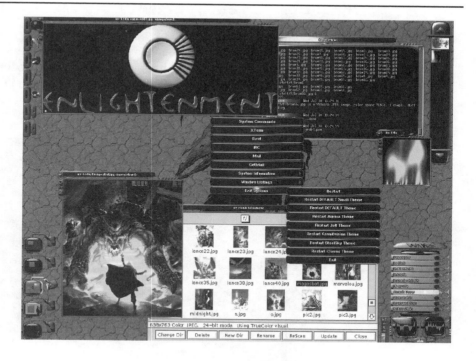

Desktop Environments

Desktop environments are more than just window managers. Desktop environments aim to provide a complete, cohesive GUI. With simple window managers, there is no guarantee of consistency of look and feel between applications and features found in other operating systems, such as drag-and-drop between applications and cross-application data embedding.

There are different desktop environments for Linux that provide robust, integrated GUIs and provide a target platform for application developers to build software with a common look and feel and include integration features such as drag-and-drop.

Two of these desktop environments, the K Desktop Environment and GNOME, are freely available and have emerged as competitors for the de facto standard Linux desktop environment.

The K Desktop Environment

The K Desktop Environment (KDE) is an attempt to provide a free alternative to the Common Desktop Environment (discussed later in this section). In this effort, KDE combines a set of applications such as a file manager, terminal emulator, and display configuration system, together with a window manager to create a consistent look and feel for X applications. Figure 6.14 shows a typical KDE desktop.

FIGURE 6.14:

A KDE desktop

Part of the planning behind KDE is that standards be specified and the development environment be such that developers can create applications that are consistent in features as well as appearance. KDE provides an attractive, professional-looking environment in which to work, and if the necessary applications are developed for KDE, it will become a likely proposition for the business desktop. The KDE Web site is at `http://www.kde.org/`. Chapter 11, "KDE: An Alternative to GNOME," covers KDE in detail.

GNOME: The GNU Network Object Model Environment

GNOME is the result of an alternative effort to develop a comprehensive, free desktop environment for Linux. Unlike KDE, which includes a built-in window manager, GNOME is window manager independent. It provides a programming interface which allows window manager developers to integrate full support for GNOME in their window manager.

Red Hat Linux 6 ships with GNOME as the default desktop environment using the Enlightenment window manager. Other window managers and KDE are included with this distribution, but since the default installation uses GNOME and Enlightenment, this book will use GNOME and Enlightenment as the target desktop. For an introduction to using GNOME, refer to Chapter 8, "Using GNOME and X Windows."

MWM

MWM, the Motif Window Manager, is a commercial window manager that is part of the Motif distribution. Motif as a complete environment is discussed in more detail in the next section of this chapter.

The Common Desktop Environment

The Common Desktop Environment (CDE), is an ambitious project to standardize the graphical environment and development arena on various Unix platforms including AIX, Digital Unix, HP/UX, and Solaris. Now CDE is also available for Linux from Red Hat (`http://www.redhat.com/`) and from X-Inside (`http://www.xinside.com/`).

In addition to a consistent graphical environment based on Motif, CDE offers a set of cohesive tools and applications to standardize administrative procedures and ease the configuration and management of a user's graphical work environment. Among the enhancements brought to the X environment by CDE are drag-and-drop capabilities and the types of folders and icons found in other GUI operating systems. Figure 6.15 shows a sample CDE desktop running Red Hat's TriTeal CDE for Linux.

FIGURE 6.15:

A CDE desktop

What Is Motif?

If you begin to look around the Web for X Windows applications to install on your Linux system, you will inevitably come across applications that refer to the fact that they use the Motif library or the Motif toolkit.

Motif is a development environment for X Windows that was introduced by the Open Software Foundation (OSF) in the late 1980s to provide a consistent policy for X Windows applications. Motif provides a toolkit of widgets that developers can use in developing their applications. By using these widget libraries, Motif developers produce applications that adhere to Motif policies for a consistent look and feel.

Motif, however, is commercial. Developers who want to build and distribute applications based on the Motif libraries must pay for the privilege, and users who want to have copies of the Motif libraries on their systems to improve the performance of Motif-based applications must pay for a client set of libraries.

In addition to the toolkit and libraries, the Motif distribution includes its own window manager, MWM, after which the original FVWM look and feel was patterned. Figure 6.16 shows a sample MWM desktop.

FIGURE 6.16:

An MWM desktop

Do I Need Motif?

For most Linux users, there is probably no need to buy Motif. Users who should consider purchasing Motif include:

- Developers who want to develop applications using the Motif toolkit

- Users who want to run applications that require the presence of the Motif libraries. Most commercial applications that use the Motif libraries either embed the necessary Motif code in the application (so it is not necessary for the user to own the license) or include a complete version of the runtime Motif libraries.

Vendors selling Motif for Linux include Red Hat (`http://www.redhat.com/`), InfoMagic (`http://www.infomagic.com/`), and X-Inside (`http://www.xinside.com/`).

An Alternative to Motif

Like so many things in the Linux world, efforts are under way to produce a freely available alternative to Motif so that developers and users don't have to pay to purchase Motif. The Lesstif Project has developed a product that is compatible with Motif version 1.2 and available under the GNU Public License. Simply put, this means the product is completely free.

Lesstif hasn't reached full maturity yet (the version at the time of this writing is 0.88), but Lesstif can already be used to develop some applications and run some software. The Lesstif FAQ on the Lesstif home page (`http://www.lesstif.org/`) is quick to point out that Lesstif is still not complete. Even so, some of the applications that use Motif can work with Lesstif 0.88, including Mosaic 2.7 and the acclaimed GIMP graphics package for Linux.

Looking Ahead

This discussion of X Windows is your first step toward hands-on use of the Linux operating system.

In the next two chapters, you will master the basics of the X Windows interface using the default desktop environment for Red Hat Linux 6: GNOME. You will learn to install X Windows and begin to experiment with using some of the most common X Windows and GNOME applications.

Chapter 7 serves as a step-by-step guide to installing and configuring X Windows.

CHAPTER
SEVEN

7

Installing and Configuring X Windows

- ■ Obtaining X Windows

- ■ Preparing to Configure X Windows

- ■ Configuring XFree86 with Xconfigurator

- ■ Configuring XFree86 with Xf86config

- ■ Testing Your Configuration

Now that you have a sense of what X Windows is all about, it is time to install and configure the software so that you have a system up and running X Windows as quickly as possible.

This chapter will discuss where to obtain X Windows for your system if you don't or can't install the version of X Windows that shipped with your distribution of Linux. Following that, this chapter will describe how to configure XFree86 so that it works optimally on your computer.

Obtaining X Windows

If you are using the copy of Red Hat Linux 6 that came with this book and you chose to install all the key X Windows components suggested in Chapter 4, "Installing Red Hat Linux 6," then you don't need to read this section because you already have obtained and installed the X Windows files. You can skip ahead to the section entitled "Preparing to Configure X Windows."

Installing from the Red Hat Linux 6 CD-ROM

If you are using Red Hat Linux 6 but didn't install X Windows when you installed Linux, then installing X Windows is a fairly easy process. The procedure outlined here relies on techniques described in Chapter 14, "Working with Files," for accessing your CD-ROM drive.

Using rpm

In this section, you will be using **rpm**, a tool that is shipped with Red Hat Linux for managing Red Hat packages.

Rpm allows you to install new packages, uninstall installed packages, and look at information about packages such as what files they include.

To install a package, use the following command:

```
$ rpm -i package-file-name
```

Continued on next page

To view a list of all installed packages, use this command:

```
$ rpm -qa | more
```

This command presents the list of installed packages one screen at a time; you can scroll down to the next screen by pressing the space bar. The package names shown on the list are not the filenames originally used when installing the packages. They are used, however, in uninstalling a package with the following command:

```
$ rpm -e package-file-name
```

In order to install X Windows from your Red Hat 6 CD-ROM, the first step is to mount your CD so that Linux can access it. This process is not as straightforward as it seems, because it will vary depending on the type of CD-ROM drive you have (IDE/ATAPI, SCSI, or proprietary) and on how the drive is installed. An extensive discussion of CD-ROM options is found in Chapter 19, "Linux Multimedia."

The directions that follow assume that you have an IDE CD-ROM drive, since these are extremely common in today's multimedia PCs. These directions also assume that the CD-ROM drive is installed as the secondary IDE slave device, since most off-the-shelf computers sold today contain only one hard drive.

Given these assumptions, your CD-ROM drive will be device /dev/hdb. For other drive types and configurations, refer to the discussion in Chapter 19 to determine what device your drive is.

Insert the Red Hat Linux 6 CD-ROM into your drive and type the following command:

```
$ mount /dev/hdb /mnt/cdrom
```

to mount the disk and make it accessible to Linux. You can use the following command to look at the contents of the CD-ROM and make sure it is accessible:

```
$ ls /mnt/cdrom
```

The results should look like those shown here:

```
COPYING    README       Red Hat    boot.cat    dosutils    misc
CVS        RPM-PGP-KEY  TRANS.TBL  doc         images      rr_moved
```

The next step is to change into the directory on the CD-ROM that contains all the packages that make up Red Hat Linux 6. This directory is the RedHat/RPMS subdirectory. Use the following command:

```
$ cd /mnt/cdrom/RedHat/RPMS
```

If you type the command

```
$ ls
```

you should see a long list of files scroll by, and all of them should end in the extension .rpm, indicating that they are Red Hat package files.

Now you are ready to install the X Windows packages. In order to do this, you need to determine which packages to install. To start with, you need the general XFree86 files that are in the file XFree86-3.3.3.1-22.i386.rpm. Next, you need all the X Windows fonts, which are in the following files:

```
XFree86-100dpi-fonts-3.3.3.1-49.i386.rpm
XFree86-75dpi-fonts-3.3.3.1-49.i386.rpm
```

In addition, you need the shared XFree86 libraries and the X Windows font server:

```
XFree86-libs-3.3.3.1-49.i386.rpm
XFree86-xfs-3.3.3.1-49.i386.rpm
```

You also need the XFree86 configuration utility provided by Red Hat, which is in the file Xconfigurator-4.1-4.i386.rpm, and you want the collection of X Windows programs that can be found in X11R6-contrib-3.3.2-6.i386.rpm.

The final piece of the puzzle is to choose which XFree86 server package to install. This depends on your monitor and your video card. Check your video card documentation to find out what type of card you have and what chipset it uses. Compare this information to the following descriptions of the different servers designed for specific cards and video chips (the descriptions are those provided in the package files):

- XFree86-3DLabs-3.3.3.1-49.i386.rpm: X server for cards built around 3D Labs GLINT and Permedia chipsets, including GLINT 500TX with IBM RGB526 RAMDAC, GLINT MX with IBM RGB526 and IBM RGB640 RAMDAC, Permedia with IBM RGB526 RAMDAC and the Permedia 2 (classic, 2a, 2v).

- `XFree86-8514-3.3.3.1-49.i386.rpm`: If you are installing the X Window System and the video card in your system is an older IBM 8514 or a compatible from a company such as ATI, you should install XFree86-8514.

- `XFree86-AGX-3.3.3.1-49.i386.rpm`: This is the X server for AGX-based cards, such as Boca Vortex, Orchid Celsius, Spider Black Widow, and Hercules Graphite.

- `XFree86-I128-3.3.3.1-49.i386.rpm`: This is the X server for the #9 Imagine 128 and similar video boards.

- `XFree86-Mach32-3.3.3.1-49.i386.rpm`: XFree86-Mach32 is the X server package for video cards built around ATI's Mach32 chip, including the ATI Graphics Ultra Pro and the Ultra Plus.

- `XFree86-Mach64-3.3.3.1-49.i386.rpm`: XFree86-Mach64 is the server package for cards based on ATI's Mach64 chip, such as the Graphics Xpression, GUP Turbo, and WinTurbo cards. Note that this server is known to have problems with some Mach64 cards.

- `XFree86-Mach8-3.3.3.1-49.i386.rpm`: XFree86-Mach 8 is the X server for video cards built around ATI's Mach8 chip, including the ATI 8514 Ultra and Graphics Ultra.

- `XFree86-P9000-3.3.3.1-49.i386.rpm`: XFree86-P9000 is the X server for video cards built around the Weitek P9000 chip, such as most Diamond Viper cards and the Orchid P9000 card.

- `XFree86-S3-3.3.3.1-49.i386.rpm`: XFree86-S3 is the X server for video cards based on S3 chips, including most #9 cards, many Diamond Stealth cards, Orchid Farenheits, Mirco Crystal 8S, most STB cards, and some motherboards with built-in graphics accelerators (such as the IBM ValuePoint line). Note that if you have an S3 ViRGE-based video card, you'll need XFree86-S3V instead of XFree86-S3.

- `XFree86-S3V-3.3.3.1-49.i386.rpm`: XFree86-S3V is the X server for video cards based on the S3 ViRGE chipset.

- `XFree86-W32-3.3.3.1-49.i386.rpm`: XFree86-W32 is the X server for cards built around ET4000/W32 chips, including the Genoa 8900 Phantom 32i, the Hercules Dynamite, the LeadTek WinFast S200, the Sigma Concorde, the STB LightSpeed, the TechWorks Thunderbolt, and the ViewTop PCI.

In addition to these servers that are specific to certain cards or video chips, there are three generic servers that should work with most cards and video chipsets (although they won't take advantage of any accelerated features of your video card):

- `XFree86-VGA16-3.3.3.1-49.i386.rpm`: XFree86-VGA16 is a generic 16-color server for VGA boards. XFree86-VGA16 works on nearly all VGA style graphics boards, but only supports a low-resolution, 16-color display.

- `XFree86-SVGA-3.3.3.1-49.i386.rpm`: The XFree86-SVGA is an X server for most simple framebuffer SVGA devices, including cards built from ET4000 chips, Cirrus Logic chips, Chips and Technologies laptop chips, Trident 8900 and 9000 chips, and Matrox chips. It works for Diamond Speedstar, Orchid Kelvins, STB Nitros and Horizons, Genoa 8500VL, most Actix boards, the Spider VLB Plus, etc. It also works for many other chips and cards, so try this server if you are having problems.

- `XFree86-Mono-3.3.3.1-49.i386.rpm`: XFree86-Mono is a generic monochrome (two-color) server for VGA cards. XFree86-Mono works for nearly all VGA compatible cards, but only supports a monochrome display.

If you can match your video card precisely to one of the accelerated servers, you only need to install that server. If you think you have a close match but can't be 100 percent certain, install that accelerated server along with one of the three generic servers. If you definitely can't match one of the accelerated servers, you should only install a generic server.

Choosing which generic server to install is fairly straightforward:

- If you have a monochrome monitor and not a color monitor, you should choose the `XFree86-Mono-3.3.3.1-49.i386.rpm` server.

- If you have an older monitor that only supports 640×480 resolution (and nothing higher) and your video card has fewer than 512KB of video RAM, you probably want to choose the `XFree86-VGA16-3.3.3.1-49.i386.rpm` server.

- If you have a newer multisync monitor that supports resolutions higher than 40×480 and your video card has more than 512KB of RAM, choose the `XFree86-SVGA-3.3.3.1-49.i386.rpm` server.

Now that you have built a list of the files that you need to install, you can use the command `rpm -i` to install those files. Everyone needs to install the following files:

```
$ rpm -i XFree86-3.3.3.1-49.i386.rpm
$ rpm -i XFree86-100dpi-fonts-3.3.3.1-49i386.rpm
$ rpm -i XFree86-75dpi-fonts-3.3.3.1-49.i386.rpm
$ rpm -i XFree86-libs-3.3.3.1-49.i386.rpm
$ rpm -i XFree86-xfs-3.3.3.1-49.i386.rpm
$ rpm -i Xconfigurator-4.2.3-1.i386.rpm
$ rpm -i X11R6-contrib-3.3.2-5.i386.rpm
```

Next, you need to install your selected servers. For instance, to install the generic SVGA server, use the command

```
$ rpm -i XFree86-SVGA-3.3.3.1-49.i386.rpm
```

or to install the server for S3 ViRGE chips, use the command

```
$ rpm -i XFree86-S3V-3.3.3.1-49.i386.rpm
```

Once all of this is done, all the necessary X Windows files should be installed on your system.

Installing from the Internet

If you want to install a newer version of XFree86 than is available with Red Hat Linux 6, you can download the necessary files from the Internet and then install them.

NOTE   Chapter 22, "Connecting Linux to the Internet," discusses connecting to the Internet, and Chapter 23, "Using the World Wide Web," discusses using Netscape Communicator. If you aren't ready to take on these tasks in Linux and you kept your old Windows or DOS installation on your system, you can use the Windows or DOS Internet connection to download the files and then access your Windows or DOS partition from Linux to install the files.

XFree86 is developed by the XFree86 Project, which is on the Web at `http://www.xfree86.org`. Figure 7.1 shows the XFree86 Web page.

FIGURE 7.1:

The XFree86 Web page

From this Web site, you can access the directory containing the files for the latest version of XFree86 at `ftp://ftp.xfree86.org/pub/XFree86/3.3.3.1/binaries/`. Here you will find libraries available for many versions of Linux, including:

- `Linux-axp`: Linux for Digital's Alpha processors

- `Linux-m68k`: Linux for Macintosh computers running the 68000 series processor

- `Linux-pppc-glibc-1.99`: Linux for PowerPC processors

- `Linux-ix86-libc5`: Linux for Intel *x*86 processors, including the Pentium and Pentium II

- `Linux-ix86-glibc`: Linux versions for Intel *x*86 processors that use the newer `Glibc` libraries. As of this writing, very few Linux distributions use `Glibc`—with the notable exception of Red Hat Linux 6, which is widely publicized for its adoption of `Glibc`.

Once you have chosen the library for your version of Linux, download the following files:

preinst.sh	postinst.sh
Extract	
Xbin.tgz	Xdoc.tgz
Xfnts.tgz	
Xlib.tgz	Xman.tgz
Xset.tgz	
Xfsrv.tgz	Xcfg.tgz
Xf100.tgz	

In addition, you need to download the file X332VG16.tgz from the Servers directory, as well as any other relevant servers based on the following descriptions provided in the release notes for XFree86 3.3.2:

- X3DL.tgz: 3D Labs server

- X8514.tgz: 8514/A server

- XAGX.tgz: AGX server

- XI128.tgz: I128 server

- XMa32.tgz: Mach 32 server

- XMa64.tgz: Mach 64 server

- XMa8.tgz: Mach 8 server

- XMono.tgz: Mono server

- XP9K.tgz: P9000 server

- XS3.tgz: S3 server

- XS3V.tgz: old S3 ViRGE server (please use SVGA server)

- XSVGA.tgz: SVGA server

- XVG16.tgz: VGA server

- XW32.tgz: ET4000/W32, ET6000 server

Refer to the discussion of selecting a server in the previous section, "Installing from the Red Hat Linux 6 CD-ROM."

The next step is to create the necessary directory for the installation. You do this with the mkdir command, which is discussed in detail in Chapter 14, "Working with Files:"

```
$ mkdir /usr/X11R6
```

Next, you need to run the installation programs provided in the files you have downloaded. Let's assume that you downloaded them to the temp directory of your Windows partition and that in the installation process in Chapter 4, "Installing Red Hat Linux 6," you chose to mount this partition as /dos. If this is the case, you can issue the following commands to run the preinstallation script (some of these commands are discussed later in the book; just use them for now to get X Windows running and you will learn what they all mean later):

```
$ cd /usr/X11R6
$ sh /dos/temp/preinst.sh
```

The next step is to prepare and extract the files from the archives you downloaded. You do this with the following commands:

```
$ chmod 755 /dos/temp/extract
$ /dos/temp/extract /dos/temp/X332[8-z]*.tgz
$ /dos/temp/extract /dos/temp/X3322upd.tgz
```

The final step is to run the postinstallation script:

```
$ sh /dos/temp/postinst.sh
```

As cryptic as it all may seem at this point, the end result of all this typing is that the necessary files for X Windows will be installed on your Linux system.

Preparing to Configure X Windows

Before you can actually configure X Windows, you need to gather some critical information about your hardware to ensure that you do not damage your monitor in the process of trying to optimize X Windows. The information you need is:

- The make and model of your video card
- The make and model of your monitor
- The video memory on your video card
- The type of mouse you are using

- The horizontal sync range for your monitor
- The vertical sync range for your monitor

Without this information, it is possible to make mistakes in configuring XFree86 that could potentially damage your monitor. Let's take this information one piece at a time.

Make and Model of Your Video Card

These specifications shouldn't be too difficult to obtain. Generally, if you check your card's manual you can glean this information.

If you have purchased a non–name brand video card, then the make isn't relevant. In this case, check the documentation for the video card to see what chipset is being used on the card. Common chipsets include those from Cirrus Logic, S3, and Chips and Technologies, among others. In all cases, be sure to record the model number of the chipset as well as the maker of the chips.

If you have a computer with video support built into the motherboard, check the documentation for your computer or motherboard to determine the chipset maker and model number.

Make and Model of Your Monitor

Check the manual of your monitor for the make and model of the monitor. This information may be useful in configuring XFree86 if your monitor is the type of monitor that the configuration software knows about.

Video Memory on Your Video Card

Check the manual for your video card for the amount of memory on the card. In modern computers this is generally no less than 2MB, and on some PCs it may be 4MB or as much as 8MB. On older computers or video cards, you may find as little as 256KB of video memory.

If you can't determine the amount of memory on your card from the manual, try powering on your PC and restarting it. The first screen to appear, usually very quickly, after you power on your computer is often generated by your video card and will display the make, model number, and possibly the amount of video memory on the card.

Type of Mouse You Are Using

This information is necessary in order to get your mouse working under X Windows. If you configured your mouse when installing Linux in Chapter 4, "Installing Red Hat Linux 6," then you need the same information on hand to configure X Windows.

If you didn't configure your mouse then, you need to check the type of mouse you have. Possible types include:

- Microsoft-compatible serial mouse (usually with two buttons)
- Mouse Systems–compatible serial mouse (usually with three buttons)
- Bus Mouse
- PS/2 Mouse
- Logitech serial mouse
- Logitech MouseMan (Microsoft-compatible)
- Microsoft IntelliMouse

Most mice should be compatible with one of these types.

Horizontal Sync Range for Your Monitor

This information is crucial, especially should it turn out that your monitor is not explicitly supported by the configuration software. Without this number (and the vertical sync range discussed in the next section), you risk damaging your monitor by asking your video card to provide a signal to your monitor that is outside its display capability.

You will find the information for horizontal sync range (sometimes referred to as *horizontal scanning range*) in your manual, either under the monitor specifications or in the section discussing video modes. This information will be presented as a range of values in kilohertz, such as 30–70kHz. Generally, this range starts somewhere around 30kHz. You should also make note of the maximum possible value and choose a setting that is slightly less than the maximum.

Vertical Sync Range for Your Monitor

Like the horizontal sync range, the vertical sync range (sometimes called the *vertical scanning range*) is essential to preventing damage to your monitor. You should find the information in the same location as the horizontal sync range. It should appear as a range of values in hertz (not kilohertz like the horizontal value), such as 50–160Hz. (Generally, the larger number should exceed 75Hz unless you have an extremely low-end or old monitor. Monitors that cannot produce vertical scanning speeds higher than 72Hz suffer from flicker problems that can lead to eyestrain and headaches during even short-duration use.) Be sure also to note the maximum possible value for the vertical sync range.

Configuring XFree86 with Xconfigurator

Red Hat Linux comes with Xconfigurator, a configuration program for XFree86 that is much easier to use than the one that comes with XFree86. Let's look first at using Xconfigurator to configure X Windows and then at configuring XFree86 on systems that do not have Xconfigurator available.

Xconfigurator is a simple, menu-driven tool that greatly simplifies the process of configuring XFree86. To run the program, use the command

```
$ Xconfigurator
```

which should run the program and display a welcome screen like the one in Figure 7.2.

FIGURE 7.2:

The Xconfigurator welcome screen

TIP You need to be the root user to successfully complete all the steps involved in configuring X Windows.

To start using the program, press Enter to move past the welcome screen to the first menu, shown in Figure 7.3.

FIGURE 7.3:

The video card menu

Here you choose the type of video card or chipset your system is running. Use the up and down arrows (or the PgDn and PgUp keys) to scroll through the long list of video cards and chipsets, which are presented alphabetically.

It is important to make sure that you have an exact match for your card or chipset. If you don't, it is unwise to guess and choose something that seems similar—a "similar" card can in fact be distinctly different from yours. In this case, select Unlisted Card at the bottom of the list. Once you have made your selection, press Enter to move to the next screen.

If you select Unlisted Card, a second menu appears where you can choose the appropriate server for your card, as shown in Figure 7.4. If you are uncertain about which server to choose, use the generic server you selected earlier in the section on installing X Windows. For most modern multimedia computers, this will be the SVGA server.

FIGURE 7.4:

The X server menu

Once you have selected your card and possibly specified a server, the next step is to indicate your monitor on the monitor selection menu, shown in Figure 7.5.

FIGURE 7.5:

The monitor selection menu

If you can't find your specific monitor on the list, then you have three choices:

- Select Custom and then specify the horizontal and vertical sync ranges for your system (as explained previously).

- If you don't have the sync ranges available for your monitor and you know your monitor is a multisync monitor, select Generic Multisync.

- If you don't have the sync ranges available for your monitor and you don't know whether your monitor is a multisync monitor, then select Generic Monitor (this is the lowest common denominator and should be your selection of last resort).

After making your selection, you may be offered a chance to probe your hardware for the correct resolution and color depth of your video card. Many modern PCI cards support this, and if you have one, it is worth trying to probe. If you have an older card or probing fails, you can still configure the relevant settings manually.

If you select Custom in the monitor selection menu and you choose not to probe or the probing fails, a warning screen appears reminding you that entering the correct ranges is critical to avoiding damage to your monitor. Press Enter to proceed to the horizontal sync range menu shown in Figure 7.6.

FIGURE 7.6:

The horizontal sync range menu

Scan through the list and see if you find an entry that matches your monitor precisely. If you do, press Enter with that entry selected. In Xconfigurator, the choices are not by range, but by maximum possible value. This information is provided in the same place as the sync ranges in your monitor manual. Try to match the entry with the highest resolution and sync rate possible. Never choose an entry that offers a value beyond that listed in your monitor's manual.

Xconfigurator doesn't allow you to manually specify the horizontal and vertical sync ranges of your monitor. If you want to do this to take advantage of a high-end monitor, try using the alternate configuration method described below in the section on xf86config.

Once you make that selection, a menu of vertical sync ranges appears, as shown in Figure 7.7.

FIGURE 7.7:

The vertical sync range menu

Choose a value from this menu where the larger number doesn't exceed the larger number in the vertical sync range for your monitor and the smaller number is not smaller than the smaller number in the vertical sync range for your monitor.

The next screen offered by Xconfigurator is the choice of whether or not to probe your video card for possible video modes. Generally, most new cards can be probed successfully, although attempting this with old cards and certain recent cards can cause problems.

The best bet here is to try probing. If there is an error, you are notified and you have to proceed with manual configuration as outlined here. If probing succeeds, then you save yourself several steps.

If you choose not to probe or if probing fails, the next screen you will see will be the video memory menu shown in Figure 7.8. Choose the value that matches your video card, as discussed earlier in the section on preparing for configuration.

FIGURE 7.8:

The video memory menu

The next screen offers a selection of clock chip settings. Unless you are certain that your card has a clock chip and know the exact type of clock chip, you are better off selecting the default No Clockchip setting, as shown in Figure 7.9.

FIGURE 7.9:

The clock chip menu

At this point you are asked if Xconfigurator should try running X -probeonly. This command attempts to detect the clock information that is needed when a clock chip is unavailable. Not all cards can be probed successfully, however. If you have selected a card that does not support probing, probing will fail. If you attempt to probe your hardware and get a failure notice or Xconfigurator crashes, then you know your card can't be probed.

After choosing a clock chip, a screen appears like the one in Figure 7.10 where you can choose your preferred video modes.

FIGURE 7.10:

The video modes screen

The higher bit depth you choose, the more colors will be displayed, but the slower your video performance will be. Similarly, the higher your resolution, the more desktop real estate you will have, but at the price of the size of letters and icons on the screen. You will probably want to experiment with these settings to find the best one for your system, but generally the best resolutions are 640×480 for a 14-inch monitor, 800×600 for a 15-inch monitor, and 1024×768 for a 17-inch monitor. If you have the resources for it, 16-bit or 24-bit color is worthwhile, especially for color-intensive applications such as Netscape Communicator.

To make your selection, use the Tab key to move between bit depths and the arrow keys to move between resolutions. Use the space bar to select a mode. When you have selected a mode (you can select multiple modes—there is a way to switch between modes when you are running X Windows), use the Tab key to select the OK button and press Enter.

This completes the configuration process. You are informed that a configuration file has been created, and then you can press Enter to exit Xconfigurator. In Red Hat Linux 6, the file that is created is called XF86Config and is placed in the directory /etc/X11.

Configuring XFree86 with Xf86config

Xconfigurator provides only one way to configure XFree86, and this method is only available with Red Hat Linux. XFree86 itself comes with a configuration program that is available in any distribution of Linux that includes XFree86: xf86config.

Xf86config is also menu-driven, but it does less of the work for you and is somewhat more cumbersome to use than Xconfigurator. However, xf86config is more flexible, allowing you to manually specify some settings where Xconfigurator does the job for you and prevents you from controlling those values precisely.

To run xf86config, use the following command:

```
$ xf86config
```

A welcome screen appears like the one in Figure 7.11.

FIGURE 7.11:

The xf86config welcome screen

```
This program will create a basic XF86Config file, based on menu selections you
make.

The XF86Config file usually resides in /usr/X11R6/lib/X11 or /etc. A sample
XF86Config file is supplied with XFree86; it is configured for a standard
VGA card and monitor with 640x480 resolution. This program will ask for a
pathname when it is ready to write the file.

You can either take the sample XF86Config as a base and edit it for your
configuration, or let this program produce a base XF86Config file for your
configuration and fine-tune it. Refer to /usr/X11R6/lib/X11/doc/README.Config
for a detailed overview of the configuration process.

For accelerated servers (including accelerated drivers in the SVGA server),
there are many chipset and card-specific options and settings. This program
does not know about some of these. On some configurations some of these settings must
be specified. Refer to the server man pages and chipset-specific READMEs.

Before continuing with this program, make sure you know the chipset and
amount of video memory on your video card. SuperProbe can help with this.
It is also helpful if you know what server you want to run.

Press enter to continue, or ctrl-c to abort.
```

TIP   You need to be the root user to successfully complete all the steps involved in configuring X Windows with xf86config.

NOTE   Xf86config presents a lot of dense text on the screen during the configuration process. The welcome screen is just the first example of this. It is a good idea to read everything thoroughly if you are not familiar with xf86config so that you are fully aware of the significance of the choices you make.

The first menu presented is the mouse menu shown in Figure 7.12. Select the correct option by typing the associated number and pressing Enter. You will then be presented with a series of mouse-related questions, which may include the following:

- "Do You Want to Enable ChordMiddle?" If you have a three-button Microsoft-compatible mouse made by Logitech, you can select Chord-Middle to make the middle button work. Otherwise, only the left and right mouse buttons will work.

- "Do You Want to Enable Emulate3Buttons?" This option should be enabled when you are using a two-button mouse and a two-button mouse protocol such as the Microsoft-compatible protocol. This allows you to emulate a middle button, which is necessary in some X Windows applications, by clicking the left and right mouse buttons together.

FIGURE 7.12:

The mouse protocol menu

```
First specify a mouse protocol type. Choose one from the following list:

   1.  Microsoft compatible (2-button protocol)
   2.  Mouse Systems (3-button protocol)
   3.  Bus Mouse
   4.  PS/2 Mouse
   5.  Logitech Mouse (serial, old type, Logitech protocol)
   6.  Logitech MouseMan (Microsoft compatible)
   7.  MM Series
   8.  MM HitTablet
   9.  Microsoft IntelliMouse
  10.  Acecad tablet

If you have a two-button mouse, it is most likely of type 1, and if you have
a three-button mouse, it can probably support both protocol 1 and 2. There are
two main varieties of the latter type: mice with a switch to select the
protocol, and mice that default to 1 and require a button to be held at
boot-time to select protocol 2. Some mice can be convinced to do 2 by sending
a special sequence to the serial port (see the ClearDTR/ClearRTS options).

Enter a protocol number:
```

The final question related to your mouse will be a request to enter the mouse device. If you are using the same mouse you used when you installed Red Hat Linux and you configured the mouse during installation in Chapter 4, "Installing Red Hat Linux 6," then you should enter **/dev/mouse**. Because this is the default, you can just press Enter here.

The next major section involves configuring your keyboard. The first question is, "Do You Want to Use XKB?" XKB is a new addition to X Windows that simplifies defining the keyboard layout for particular languages and keyboard types. It is recommended that you enable this option.

If you choose to enable XKB, the next screen will be a menu of possible keyboard types, as shown in Figure 7.13.

```
List of preconfigured keymaps:

 1  Standard 101-key, US encoding
 2  Microsoft Natural, US encoding
 3  KeyTronic FlexPro, US encoding
 4  Standard 101-key, US encoding with ISO9995-3 extensions
 5  Standard 101-key, German encoding
 6  Standard 101-key, French encoding
 7  Standard 101-key, Thai encoding
 8  Standard 101-key, Swiss/German encoding
 9  Standard 101-key, Swiss/French encoding
10  None of the above

Enter a number to choose the keymap.
```

Choose the keyboard that most closely matches yours. The Standard 101-key keyboard is the likeliest candidate for most North American computers. If none of the options fits, choose None of the Above. This choice leads to a submenu where you can choose from another series of standard keyboard models. Once you select a keyboard from this list, you will be presented with a screen from which to choose the country where the keyboard was purchased. The list of countries extends beyond one screen, and you can use the Enter key to cycle to the next screen of countries.

If you opt not to choose the XKB option, then things should work fine for a standard North American English keyboard. Non-English keyboards and non-standard keyboards, however, will require manual configuration, which is discussed in Chapter 12, "Advanced X Windows Configuration."

If you don't enable XKB, you will be presented with another option: "Do You Want to Enable Special Bindings for the Alt Keys to Allow Non-ASCII Characters to Be Entered?" For now, you might want to answer **No** to this option. You do not need this enabled for most standard software, and if in the future you obtain software that depends on this option, you can quickly run xf86config to enable it.

After configuring your keyboard, the next step is to specify the horizontal and vertical sync ranges for your monitor. The first menu presented is the horizontal sync range menu shown in Figure 7.14.

FIGURE 7.14:

The horizontal sync range menu

```
You must indicate the horizontal sync range of your monitor. You can either
select one of the predefined ranges below that correspond to industry-
standard monitor types, or give a specific range.

It is VERY IMPORTANT that you do not specify a monitor type with a horizontal
sync range that is beyond the capabilities of your monitor. If in doubt,
choose a conservative setting.

    hsync in kHz; monitor type with characteristic modes
 1  31.5; Standard VGA, 640x480 @ 60 Hz
 2  31.5 - 35.1; Super VGA, 800x600 @ 56 Hz
 3  31.5, 35.5; 8514 Compatible, 1024x768 @ 87 Hz interlaced (no 800x600)
 4  31.5, 35.15, 35.5; Super VGA, 1024x768 @ 87 Hz interlaced, 800x600 @ 56 Hz
 5  31.5 - 37.9; Extended Super VGA, 800x600 @ 60 Hz, 640x480 @ 72 Hz
 6  31.5 - 48.5; Non-Interlaced SVGA, 1024x768 @ 60 Hz, 800x600 @ 72 Hz
 7  31.5 - 57.0; High Frequency SVGA, 1024x768 @ 70 Hz
 8  31.5 - 64.3; Monitor that can do 1280x1024 @ 60 Hz
 9  31.5 - 79.0; Monitor that can do 1280x1024 @ 74 Hz
10  31.5 - 82.0; Monitor that can do 1280x1024 @ 76 Hz
11  Enter your own horizontal sync range

Enter your choice (1-11): █
```

If you don't find an exact match for your horizontal sync range and you have the range for your monitor on hand, select Enter Your Own Horizontal Sync Range and provide the correct range. If you don't have access to this information, choose a conservative value. For an average 15-inch multisync monitor, try the Super VGA or Extended Super VGA setting. For a low-end 14-inch monitor, it is probably safest to select Standard VGA.

Next, you need to specify the vertical sync range for your monitor. Xf86config presents a small number of options, but you can select Enter Your Own Vertical Sync Range to specify the range for your monitor. If you don't know the range for your monitor, it is probably safest to choose the lowest and smallest range, generally 50–70 in most versions of XFree86.

Once you have specified this monitor data, xf86config asks you to specify an identifier for your monitor, the monitor's maker, and the model name or number. These do not actually affect the configuration or performance of XFree86, but they provide an easy way to identify the monitor definition in your XFree86 configuration file if you need to refer to it in the future.

Once you have all your monitor information entered, you need to specify your video card or chipset. The first screen asks if you want to look at a database of known cards and chips to make your selection. If you choose to do this, a menu of known cards appears, similar to Figure 7.15.

FIGURE 7.15:

The video card menu

```
 0  2 the Max MAXColor S3 Trio64V+          S3 Trio64V+
 1  3DLabs Oxygen GMX                       PERMEDIA 2
 2  928Movie                                S3 928
 3  AGX (generic)                           AGX-014/15/16
 4  ALG-5434(E)                             CL-GD5434
 5  ASUS 3Dexplorer                         RIVA128
 6  ASUS PCI-AV264CT                        ATI-Mach64
 7  ASUS PCI-V264CT                         ATI-Mach64
 8  ASUS Video Magic PCI V864               S3 864
 9  ASUS Video Magic PCI VT64               S3 Trio64
10  AT25                                    Alliance AT3D
11  AT3D                                    Alliance AT3D
12  ATI 3D Pro Turbo                        ATI-Mach64
13  ATI 3D Pro Turbo PC2TV                  ATI-Mach64
14  ATI 3D Xpression                        ATI-Mach64
15  ATI 3D Xpression+                       ATI-Mach64
16  ATI 3D Xpression+ PC2TV                 ATI-Mach64
17  ATI 8514 Ultra (no VGA)                 ATI-Mach8
Enter a number to choose the corresponding card definition.
Press enter for the next page, q to continue configuration.
```

You can press Enter to page forward through the menus, and at any time you can type the number of a specific card and press Enter to select it. If you find that there isn't a match for your card, simply enter **q** to skip this phase.

The next screen allows you to choose which server to use. By default, you are offered four choices:

- Mono

- VGA16

- SVGA

- Accelerated (all other servers)

If you selected a card from the card database, a fifth option is offered based on that selection. The fifth option is actually a repeat of one of the four other options, as appropriate to your card selection. If you selected a card in the early step, then select the fifth option to make sure you use the appropriate server.

WARNING   Whatever server you select, it needs to be one of the servers you installed in the installation section earlier in this chapter. If it isn't one of those servers, you need to go back and install the appropriate server before proceeding. Otherwise, your X Windows system will be configured to use a server that doesn't exist on your computer.

Once you have selected a server, you are asked if you want xf86config to create a symbolic link to the server. It is important to answer **Yes** to this question. What this option does is link the filename `/usr/bin/X11/X` to the server you selected so that, regardless of which server you are running, this filename can be used to access it.

After you set the symbolic link, a menu screen appears like the one in Figure 7.16. Here you have to select the amount of video memory on your video card.

FIGURE 7.16:

The video memory menu

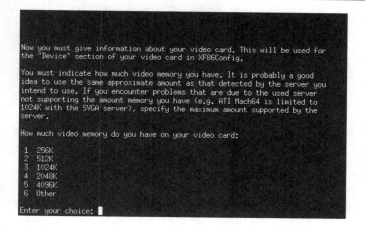

Once you have selected an amount of video memory, you are asked to provide an identifier, maker, and model for your video card. As with your monitor, these entries have nothing to do with the proper functioning of your X Windows system, so you should enter something that you will recognize later if you ever need to manually edit your XFree86 configuration file.

The next menu, shown in Figure 7.17, allows you to select a clock chip for your card. It is generally a good idea to choose No Clockchip by pressing Enter, since most cards lack a clock chip. You should only select a clock chip if you know for certain that your card has one and you know the type of chip.

FIGURE 7.17:

The clock chip menu

```
A Clockchip line in the Device section forces the detection of a
programmable clock device. With a clockchip enabled, any required
clock can be programmed without requiring probing of clocks or a
Clocks line. Most cards don't have a programmable clock chip.
Choose from the following list:

 1  Chrontel 8391                                              ch8391
 2  ICD2061A and compatibles (ICS9161A, DCS2824)              icd2061a
 3  ICS2595                                                    ics2595
 4  ICS5342 (similar to SDAC, but not completely compatible)  ics5342
 5  ICS5341                                                    ics5341
 6  S3 GenDAC (86C708) and ICS5300 (autodetected)             s3gendac
 7  S3 SDAC (86C716)                                           s3_sdac
 8  STG 1703 (autodetected)                                    stg1703
 9  Sierra SC11412                                             sc11412
10  TI 3025 (autodetected)                                     ti3025
11  TI 3026 (autodetected)                                     ti3026
12  IBM RGB 51x/52x (autodetected)                             ibm_rgb5xx

Just press enter if you don't want a Clockchip setting.
What Clockchip setting do you want (1-12)?
```

If you don't choose a clock chip, the next screen asks Do You Want Me to Run 'X -probeonly' Now? This program will try to detect the clock information from your card that is needed when a clock chip is unavailable.

It is important to note, however, that not all cards can be probed successfully. If, earlier in the configuration, you selected a card that does not support probing from the card database, then xf86config warns you (on the line immediately preceding the question) not to probe. Heed the warning.

If you didn't choose a card from the card database, you won't know if your card supports probing unless you try it. If the probing fails, two possibilities can occur: either you will be given an error message like the one here:

```
X -probeonly call failed.
No Clocks line inserted.
```

or xf86config will crash completely and you will be returned to the command prompt. If the latter happens, you need to run xf86config again, and when you get to the question "Do You Want Me To Run 'X -probeonly' Now?" you need to answer **No**.

The next screen prompts you for your preferred video modes. X Windows allows you to specify multiple video modes and cycle through them without restarting the X Windows environment.

You should make sure not to accept default modes that exceed the capabilities of your card and monitor. For instance, a 14-inch monitor is unlikely to support 1280×1024 resolution, and a card with 512KB of video memory probably can't produce 24-bit color at any resolution.

To change video modes, first select the color bit depth you want to adjust the settings for. Once you do this, a menu appears that allows you to specify one or more resolutions for that bit depth. At the prompt, type the identification numbers of the resolutions you want, separating each number with a space, and press Enter when you are done.

This returns you to the main mode selection screen above. Repeat this process for each bit depth you need to adjust and then select The Modes Are OK, Continue.

The final question asks you if you should write the `xf86config` file in its default location. You are asked this so you can make sure you don't overwrite an old, working copy of your configuration file with a new one that might not work. If you have been using X Windows successfully and are trying to reconfigure it to slightly different settings, you may want to keep a copy of your old configuration file before you allow xf86config to write the new one.

If you answer **No** to the question, xf86config provides a series of alternate locations to write the file, as described in the following paragraphs.

First, you are asked if you want to write the file to the default location (usually `/usr/X11R6/lib/X11/XF86Config`). If you want to specify your own location for the file, answer **No**.

Next, you are asked if you want the file to be written in the current directory. If the current directory is a logical location (such as the root user's home directory or `/tmp`), then you can answer **Yes**. If you answer **No**, then you are finally prompted to supply the complete path and filename where you want the new configuration to be saved.

In order to use this configuration (once it is working to your satisfaction), you need to copy the file you have just saved to the correct location for the XFree86 configuration file, which for most versions of Linux is either `/etc/XF86Config` or `/etc/X11/XF86Config`. For Red Hat 6, the file should be `/etc/XF86Config`.

Another approach is to copy your current configuration file to a backup location before running xf86config; then, when you are asked if you want to overwrite the current configuration, you simply answer **Yes**. You will learn how to copy files in Chapter 14, "Working with Files," but a simple way to make a backup copy of the Red Hat 6 XFree86 configuration file is with the following command:

```
$ cp /etc/XF86Config /etc/XF86Config.keep
```

This command creates a copy of your existing configuration named `/etc/XF86Config.keep`.

Testing Your Configuration

Now that you have finished configuring X Windows, it is time to see if the configuration you created actually works. To do this, you need to try running X Windows. Red Hat Linux 6 comes with X Windows set up to run a default window manager and some default initial applications, so you should be ready to run once XFree86 is configured.

To start X Windows, use the following command:

```
$ startx
```

This starts X Windows running. If all goes well, a number of lines of information flash by on the screen, and then the screen switches to graphical mode and you see your default X Windows environment. This will probably look like the one in Figure 7.18.

FIGURE 7.18:

The default desktop in Red Hat Linux 6

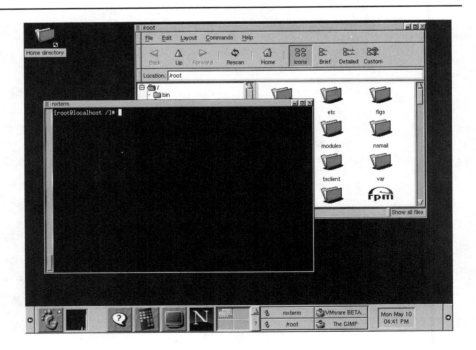

You can run X Windows as a regular user or as the root user for the purpose of verifying that it is working properly. But it is generally wise to run X Windows as a non-root user so that you minimize the chance of using X Windows applications to accidentally damage, erase, or change critical system files that only the root user has permission to modify.

The real problems begin if things don't work. Failure is usually indicated in one of three ways:

- You get an error message and are returned to the command prompt without your computer ever switching to graphical mode.

- You are switched to graphical mode but are left with a blank gray desktop, no window manager, and no functioning windows.

- You are switched to graphical mode but this is quickly exited and you are returned to the command prompt.

In the first case, this is likely an indication that XFree86 is not configured correctly. Unfortunately, the number of possible reasons for configuration failure is probably as large as the number of different hardware combinations that exist.

Here are a few tips that may help you get things working:

- Double-check your video card and monitor data.

- Try using smaller horizontal and vertical sync ranges.

- Try using a simpler server, such as the VGA16 rather than the SVGA server, or the SVGA server instead of a card-specific accelerated server.

If these attempts all fail, then you need to do some research into your specific problem. The best place to start is the XFree86 HOWTO file. You may already have this on your system if you have a fairly complete distribution. You can read this file in Red Hat Linux 6 by using the command

```
$ zless /usr/doc/HOWTO/ XFree86-HOWTO.gz
```

Alternately, you can read the HOWTO on the Web at `http://metalab.unc.edu/ mdw/HOWTO/XFree86-HOWTO.html`.

If you experience one of the other two problems (where your system switches to graphical mode but things don't quite work out), then the first step is to check the X Windows start-up configuration and your window manager configuration. Chapter 11, "Advanced X Windows Configuration," discusses these configurations in detail.

Looking Ahead

Now that you should have X Windows working, it is time to actually try your hand at using the X Windows environment for practical tasks. To do this, let's start with a look at GNOME, the GNU Object Model Environment.

GNOME is one of two competing standards emerging for the future of Linux graphical desktops. GNOME offers a fully integrated desktop environment for developing and running applications. GNOME is the default desktop in Red Hat Linux 6.

The next chapter looks at the basics of using X Windows with the GNOME desktop. Following that, Chapter 9, "Using Applications with GNOME and X Windows," discusses running GNOME and X Windows applications, including terminal emulators, file managers, graphics applications, and more. By the end of these two chapters, you should have enough experience and confidence to experiment with other available X Windows applications.

CHAPTER

EIGHT

8

Using GNOME and X Windows

- Starting X Windows and GNOME

- The GNOME Panel

- The GNOME Interface

Now that you have X Windows set up and running on your system, you will learn how to make use of the X Windows environment as it is designed in Red Hat Linux.

This chapter provides an overview on using the GNOME desktop. The GNOME desktop is sophisticated enough that it could easily warrant a small book of its own. Instead of providing a complete guide to using GNOME, the goal here is to provide you with enough familiarity that you will feel confident enough to experiment with GNOME. For users who have used Windows 95, 98, or NT, the basics of using GNOME should be quite straightforward.

Starting X Windows and GNOME

Because Red Hat comes preconfigured for GNOME, starting the desktop manager is as simple as starting the X Windows environment. As you learned in Chapter 7, "Installing and Configuring X Windows," begin by logging in as a user and then issue the command:

```
$ startx
```

This command starts X Windows and launches the GNOME desktop manager. Initially, this results in a screen similar to the one in Figure 8.1.

> **NOTE** Depending on how your Red Hat installation is configured, Red Hat may launch X Windows when you start your system and present a graphical login prompt. If this is the case, then GNOME automatically starts as soon as you log in and you don't need to use the `startx` command.

Manually Installing GNOME

By default, Red Hat Linux 6 will install the GNOME desktop environment. If, for some reason, you chose not to install GNOME or GNOME was not automatically installed, you will need to install GNOME manually.

Continued on next page

To do this, you need to install the following packages from the **RedHat/RPMS** directory of the Red Hat CD-ROM:

- `gnome-audio-1.0.0-6.noarch.rpm`
- `gnome-core-1.0.4-34.i386.rpm`
- `gnome-games-1.0.2-10.i386.rpm`
- `gnome-games-devel-1.0.2-10.i386.rpm`
- `gnome-libs-1.0.8-8.i386.rpm`
- `gnome-users-guide-1.0.5-4rh.noarch.rpm`
- `gnome-libs-devel-1.0.8-8.i386.rpm`
- `gnome-linuxconf-0.22-1.i386.rpm`
- `gnome-media-1.0.1-3.i386.rpm`
- `gnome-objc-1.0.2-4.i386.rpm`
- `gnome-core-devel-1.0.4-34.i386.rpm`
- `gnome-objc-devel-1.0.2-4.i386.rpm`
- `gnome-pim-1.0.7-2.i386.rpm`
- `gnome-pim-devel-1.0.7-2.i386.rpm`
- `gnome-utils-1.0.1-6.i386.rpm`

To install each of these packages, use the `rpm` command:

```
# rpm -i filename
```

Two main components load by default when GNOME loads: the main GNOME panel and an `xterm` window.

FIGURE 8.1:

The default GNOME
desktop in Red Hat
Linux 6.0

The GNOME Panel

The panel, shown in Figure 8.2, is displayed across the bottom of the screen. It includes a main System Menu button (the button with the stylized footprint at the far left), a small panel displaying the time and date at the far right, a pager and other buttons for default actions, and space to display buttons for each open window.

FIGURE 8.2:

The GNOME panel

In this panel, there are four open windows: VMWare BETA, nxterm, /root, and The GIMP. Clicking any of these buttons once opens the window if it had been temporarily minimized to the panel and brings the window to the front of all open windows.

Using the Main System Menu

The System menu works in the same way as the Start menu in Windows 95 and Windows NT 4. Clicking the Start menu pops up a menu like the one in Figure 8.3.

FIGURE 8.3:

The GNOME System menu

The System menu has several items on it:

Submenus   There are several submenus you can access from the System menu, each with a right arrow to the right of the submenu name. Each of these options opens a submenu containing programs that can be launched. The standard submenus are:

Applications   This submenu offers standard GNOME applications such as the GNOME calendar tool and the GNOME spreadsheet, Gnumeric.

Games   This submenu offers a set of X Windows and GNOME games.

Graphics   This submenu provides a handful of graphics tools for GNOME, including the acclaimed The GIMP image-editing software.

Internet   This submenu provides quick access to standard Internet tools, including Netscape Communicator and the GNOME FTP tool, Gftp.

Multimedia   This submenu offers a selection of multimedia tools, including a CD player and a volume control tool.

System   This submenu offers access to a few system tools, including a GNOME-based package management system for Red Hat RPM packages.

Settings   This submenu provides a collection of tools for configuring GNOME. Chapter 10, "Advanced GNOME Configuration," looks at these tools in more detail.

Utilities   This submenu provides access to commonly used GNOME and X Windows utilities, including xterm, a calculator, and a text file viewer.

Red Hat Menus   This submenu provides access to the standard Red Hat menus that were used in previous versions of Red Hat Linux that used fvwm95 as their default window manager.

KDE Menus   This submenu provides access to the standard KDE menus if you have installed KDE as an alternate desktop manager on your system.

Panel   This submenu provides tools for configuring your GNOME panel. Chapter 10, "Advanced GNOME Configuration," describes these tools in more detail.

File Manager   Selecting this menu entry launches the GNOME file manager, like the one shown in Figure 8.4. The GNOME file manager is discussed in more detail in Chapter 9, "Using Applications with GNOME and X Windows."

FIGURE 8.4:

The GNOME file manager

Help System   This option can be used to launch the GNOME help system. The help system is an HTML system using a built-in HTML browser, as shown in Figure 8.5. The GNOME help system provides comprehensive documentation on using GNOME, and you should refer there for detailed guidance on using GNOME.

Run Program   Use this option to run any program or application installed on your Linux system. Selecting this option opens the dialog box shown in Figure 8.6. Enter the path and name of the program and click the Run button to launch the application. Alternately, click the Browse button to choose the program to run from the file selection window shown in Figure 8.7.

FIGURE 8.5:

The GNOME Help System

FIGURE 8.6:

Running a program

FIGURE 8.7:

Choosing a program to run

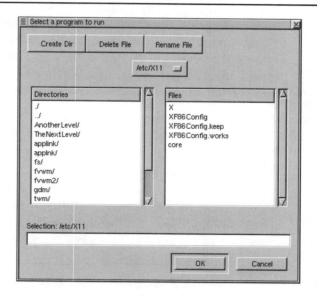

User Menus   As you will see in Chapter 10, "Advanced GNOME Configuration," users can define their own menus to appear in this section of the main System menu. By default, this section will be empty.

Lock Screen   This option lets you activate the screen saver with a password.

About GNOME   This option displays a dialog box containing information about the GNOME panel.

About GNOME   This option displays a dialog box containing information about your current GNOME session.

Log Out   This option allows you to log out and exit GNOME. If you start GNOME by logging in from a graphical login screen, then this option causes GNOME to exit and return to the login screen. If you start GNOME from a command-line console, you are returned to the command line.

Manipulating the GNOME Panel

One drawback of the GNOME panel for some users is that it takes up considerable screen space for users with small screens, such as those using notebooks or those with smaller 14- and 15-inch monitors. Luckily, there are several ways to alleviate this problem.

One option is to roll up the panel to a small rectangle. The standard panel sits horizontally across the bottom of the screen. You can roll up the panel into a small rectangle at the bottom-left corner of the screen by clicking the small left-arrow button at the left end of the panel. The panel disappears and only a small rectangle containing a right arrow remains. Clicking the right arrow unrolls the panel to fill the bottom of the screen.

Similarly, clicking the right arrow at the far-right side of the panel rolls up the panel to the bottom-right corner of the screen with only a left-arrow button visible. Clicking the left arrow unrolls the panel.

If this isn't sufficient and you find the arrows take up too much space, you can shrink the desktop real estate consumed by a rolled-up panel to almost nothing by eliminating the arrows from the buttons. To do this, right-click the background of the panel and select This Panel Properties from the menu that appears. This opens the Panel Properties dialog box for the panel, shown in Figure 8.8.

FIGURE 8.8:

The GNOME Panel Properties dialog box

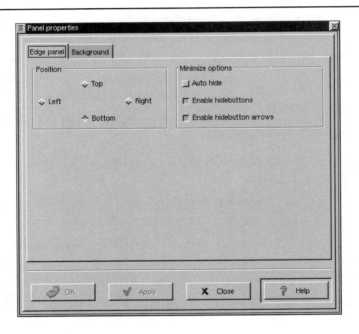

Here, you can deselect the Enable Hidebutton Arrows option and click the Apply button to remove the left and right arrows from the buttons at each end of the panel and make the button as narrow as possible.

Another useful option for reclaiming desktop space is to select the Auto Hide option in the Panel Properties dialog box and click the Apply button. This hides the panel, leaving visible only a narrow strip across the bottom of the screen. You need to move the mouse over this narrow strip for the entire panel to be made visible. As soon as you move the mouse pointer out of the panel, it automatically hides again, leaving only the small strip visible.

Another useful feature of the Panel Properties dialog box is that it gives you the ability to place the panel on a different edge of the screen than the default bottom edge. For instance, some users prefer to place the panel along the top, left, or right of the screen. You can do this by selecting the appropriate side in the Position section of the dialog box and clicking Apply.

Panel Applets

The GNOME panel is a highly customizable tool. One of its most powerful capabilities is to run small applets inside the panel.

GNOME includes numerous applets and provides an interface by which programmers can develop their own applets. Some of the applets included with GNOME on Red Hat Linux 6 are:

- A small scrambled-tile game
- Monitor applets to track battery usage, CPU load, and disk space
- A CD player applet
- An applet to check your inbox for new messages
- A clock applet
- A printer control applet
- A pager applet for providing virtual desktops

By default, the pager applet and the clock applet are displayed on the GNOME panel. Figure 8.9 shows the pager applet sitting next to the clock applet.

FIGURE 8.9:

The pager and clock applets

There are several types of actions you need to take with respect to panel applets:

- Adding applets to the panel
- Moving applets on the panel
- Changing applet properties
- Removing applets from the panel

Adding Applets to the Panel

Adding applets to the panel is fairly easy. To add an applet, right-click the background of the panel (as opposed to inside the space used by an applet, button, or menu). This causes a menu to appear. On this menu, there is a submenu called Add Applet which contains several submenus of applets that you can add to the panel. Simply select the desired applet and it is added to the panel.

Moving Applets on the Panel

Once an applet is on the panel, you may find that you want to move it to a different location on the panel as dictated by the way that you use the panel. To move an applet, right-click the applet itself and choose Move Applet from the menu that appears. Then, use the left mouse button to click and drag the applet to a new location on the applet. When you release the mouse button, the applet relocates to the indicated location.

Changing Applet Properties

Most applets have properties that you can configure to customize their behavior. These properties are controlled from a Properties dialog box that can be opened by right-clicking the applet and selecting Properties from the menu that appears.

Removing Applets from the Panel

The ability to remove applets from the panel once they are placed there is important. This makes it easy to experiment with the many applets included with GNOME and allows you to clean up your panel as it gets more cluttered. To remove an applet, right-click the applet and select Remove From Panel from the menu that appears.

Using the Pager Applet

This section discusses the pager applet as a way to highlight how to use applets and because the pager applet is a default applet on the GNOME panel. The pager is a small applet, like the one in Figure 8.10, that provides virtual desktops.

FIGURE 8.10:

The pager applet

The concept of virtual desktops is simple. Let's start with a basic example. If you have two virtual desktops, this is like having two monitors but only one power cable for those monitors. You could have two different sets of applications open, running, and displayed on the monitors and switch between these environments by switching the power cable between the monitors.

Virtual desktops provide similar functionality but without the delay, difficulty, and frustration of switching your power cable between two monitors. Each desktop in a virtual desktop system is like a brand-new work environment in which you can open windows and run applications. At the same time, these applications, regardless of which desktop they appear in, are running in the same X Windows session, which means you can cut and paste between them as if they were visually displayed on the same desktop.

The pager applet has two components:

- On the left side are four virtual desktops.

- On the right side are buttons representing the open applications on the current desktop.

You can switch desktops by clicking the left mouse button on any of the four squares on the pager. This immediately switches the displayed desktop to the one selected.

On the right of the virtual desktops is a space used to display buttons for all open windows on the current desktop. You can bring any window to the foreground by clicking its button.

Between the virtual desktop and the applications button is a small button with an up arrow. Clicking this button displays a menu of all open windows on all virtual desktops. You can click any application to switch to the desktop where that window is located and bring the window to the foreground.

The GNOME Interface

GNOME has many critical user interface elements. This section discusses the features of GNOME that allow you to manipulate windows and to work with the desktop.

Manipulating Windows

The windows in GNOME look a lot like their counterparts in Windows 95 and behave in much the same way. This is advantageous for Windows users, since it makes moving from Windows 95 or NT 4 to X Windows a simple process in terms of interacting with windows.

Let's take a look at the main window components: title bar, window action icons, window operations menu, and window border.

Title Bar

The title bar is displayed across the top of the window. It contains the name of the window, which in most cases is the name of the application that is displaying the window. In the case of an `nxterm` window, the title is `nxterm` by default (although it is possible to change it, as you will see later).

The title bar area serves several functional purposes in GNOME. As you might expect, you can click once with the left mouse button in the title bar to bring a window to the front of other open windows. (You can usually click anywhere in an open window to bring it to the front, though in some rare cases you will find it necessary to click in the title bar to do so.)

Clicking and dragging with the left mouse button allows you to move the window. When you release the left mouse button, the window remains in the new location.

Double-clicking the title bar minimizes the window to just the title bar, hiding the contents of the window but leaving the title bar visible. The title bar can continue to be used in the same way as when the window contents are visible, and double-clicking the title bar again redisplays the window contents. In GNOME terminology, this is known as *shading* and *unshading* the window.

Window Action Icons

The window action icons appear as a group of three icons in the top-right corner of most windows.

From left to right, these icons perform the following actions when single-clicked:

Minimize the Window   This action hides the window, leaving a button for it in the pager applet on the GNOME panel.

Maximize/Reset the Window   This icon acts as a toggle, switching the window between full screen (Maximize) and its original size before being maximized (Reset).

Close the Window   This action closes the window. In the case of multi-window applications, this does not act as a kill operation but leaves other windows in the application open.

Window Operations Menu

To the left of the title, in the top-left corner of the window, there's an icon that, when clicked, displays the window operations menu from the Start menu. This menu offers several options for controlling your windows. The commonly used menu options are:

Close   This option closes the active window.

Annihilate   This option closes the active window and kills the process that had the window open (which can close all windows of an application that supports multiple windows).

Iconify   This option hides the window, leaving it only as a button in the right section of the pager applet.

Raise   This option raises the window above all other open windows.

Lower   This option lowers the window, placing it behind all other open windows.

Shade/Unshade   This option toggles the window between the shaded and unshaded state. In the shaded state, only the title bar of the window is visible.

Stick/Unstick   This option toggles between sticking the window and unsticking it. Sticking the window means that as you switch between virtual desktops, the window moves with you rather than remaining only on a single desktop.

Desktop   You can use this submenu to move the current window to another desktop by specifying the direction in which to move the window (for instance, the window to the right of the current window).

For a full description of these and the other options on the Window Operations menu, consult the GNOME help system. You can access this by selecting Help System from the main GNOME menu.

Window Borders

Most windows have a border that is five pixels wide (a default value that can be changed, as you will see in the next chapter). This border is used to visually indicate the edge of the window as well as to allow users to resize a window.

It is possible to resize a window horizontally, vertically, or both. Simply click and drag anywhere on the border except the edges immediately adjacent to the title bar. As you drag outside the existing window border, the window resizes based on the location of the mouse pointer. Clicking the left and right sides allows you to resize horizontally; clicking the bottom edge allows vertical resizing; and clicking the bottom corners allows resizing vertically and horizontally in one action.

The GNOME Desktop

You probably noticed that the GNOME desktop contains a single icon when you first start GNOME. This icon is a folder with the name Home Directory. Double-clicking this icon opens the GNOME file manager and displays the current user's home directory in the file manager, as shown in Figure 8.11.

FIGURE 8.11:

The GNOME file manager

The GNOME file manager is discussed in depth in Chapter 9, "Using Applications with GNOME and X Windows." Right-clicking the GNOME desktop displays a menu that you can use for several purposes, including

- Opening a new GNOME file manager window
- Arranging the icons on the desktop
- Opening new terminal windows

For instance, choosing Arrange Icons rearranges the icons on your desktop into a clean grid pattern. This is useful if you keep a large number of icons on your desktop and they become disorganized and cluttered. The Create New Window option opens a new file manager window (in the same way as double-clicking the Home Directory folder icon on the desktop).

Looking Ahead

By now, you should be feeling fairly comfortable navigating your chosen X Windows environment. You can control basic options of GNOME, you can launch applications, and you can manipulate windows.

In the next chapter you will learn how to use some actual applications in GNOME. These applications include everything from simple applications such as terminal windows to utilities such as the GNOME file manager to high-end software such as The GIMP, a professional-quality image-editing package.

CHAPTER
NINE

Using Applications with GNOME and X Windows

- Using Xterm

- Customizing Xterm

- Managing Files with GNOME

- Graphics in X Windows

- X Windows Utilities

This chapter will take a look at some X Windows and GNOME applications and how they can be run and used within the GNOME desktop. These applications include xterm, the GNOME file manager (called Midnight Commander), a graphics program called The GIMP, and several X Windows utilities.

These applications have been selected based on one of two criteria: they are useful in everyday Linux operations, or they are representative of the power or range of many Linux applications.

This chapter should give you the confidence to begin experimenting with other X Windows applications.

Using *Xterm*

While X Windows puts a nice-looking and user-friendly face on Linux and allows the creation of fully graphical applications, the fact remains that as a Unix clone, Linux is a command line–oriented operating system.

Although it is possible to use Linux for everyday work without ever using the command prompt, to take advantage of the real power and flexibility of a Unix-like operating system, you need to make at least occasional forays into the world of the command line.

Fortunately, this doesn't mean abandoning the ease of X Windows. The xterm program provides a command prompt window that is fully integrated into the X Windows environment, with a scroll bar, a resizable window, and the ability to copy and paste with other X Windows applications—all features that a standard Linux console lacks.

The simplest way to launch an xterm window in Red Hat Linux 6 is to click the terminal icon on the default GNOME panel. Alternately, select Regular Xterm from the Utilities submenu of the System menu. In addition, the default Red Hat Linux 6 configuration launches an xterm window when you start X Windows with GNOME as your default desktop.

If you want to launch additional xterm windows, you can also do so from the command line of another xterm window using the command

```
$ xterm &
```

or, if you find that for some reason xterm isn't on your path, use the command

```
$ /usr/bin/X11/xterm &
```

By default, this opens a window that is 80 characters wide and 25 lines deep (the standard size of a Linux console) with a scroll bar down the left side. The window can be resized to provide more space for viewing information and working. Notice that in Red Hat Linux 6, the default color scheme for new xterm windows is white characters on a black background and the default title of the window is xterm.

Customizing *Xterm*

The xterm program is highly customizable. Among other things, you can change the following characteristics:

- The window's font
- The color scheme
- The default window size
- The placement of new windows on the screen
- The title of the window

This section will look at these options and describe how to use them when launching new xterm windows.

At first it might seem that this flexibility has no real value, but in reality it does. On different monitors, different color combinations produce the most readable text, so being able to change the color scheme is a valuable feature. Also, if you regularly use several xterm windows for different tasks (such as running Top for managing system performance, reading your e-mail, and managing your files), being able to quickly identify which window is currently being used for which task makes switching between open windows much easier.

Flags and Arguments: A Quick Unix Primer

Before going forward, you need a quick tutorial about how Unix commands work. A complete introduction to Unix and Unix commands as used in Linux comes in Chapter 13, "Introducing Linux Commands."

To execute a program (or command), you simply need to type the name of the program (and possibly the complete location of the program) and press the Enter key.

For instance, to launch xterm, you can use the command

```
$ xterm
```

or, if xterm is not on your path, use the command

```
$ /usr/bin/X11/xterm
```

But most programs either require or can accept information that alters the way they behave or provides information to be processed. Two types of information can be provided to a command: flags and arguments.

Arguments are information provided to the program to be processed; they can be anything from filenames to text to search for.

Flags are options that alter the behavior of a program. They appear after the command, separated by one or more spaces and preceded by a dash. For instance, the flag -help causes xterm to print out a help message:

```
$ xterm -help
```

```
usage:
        xterm -options ... -e command args
```

where *options* include:

```
    -help               print out this message
    -display display name   X server to contact
    -geometry geom          size (in characters) and position
    -/+rv                   turn on/off reverse video
    -bg color               background color
    -fg color               foreground color
    -bd color               border color
    -bw number              border width in pixels
    -fn fontname            normal text font
    -iconic                 start iconic
    -name string            client instance, icon, and title
                    ➡strings
```

Continued on next page

-title string	title string
-xrm resourcestring	additional resource
	➥specifications
-/+132	turn on/off column switch
	➥inhibiting
-/+ah	turn on/off always highlight
-/+ai	turn on/off active icon

Complex flags can also be created to provide information that the flag needs to function correctly. For instance, to set the xterm title, you use the –T flag, but you also need to provide the text that you want to appear in the title bar. The command

```
$ xterm -T Email
```

creates an xterm window with the word Email as the title.

Arguments, on the other hand, are not configuration options but information provided to a program to be processed. Arguments are not preceded by a hyphen as are flags. Arguments are often the names of files to be opened, processed, or edited—as in the following example, which indicates that the file testfile should be opened for editing with the editor emacs:

```
$ emacs testfile
```

Setting the Color Scheme

Using a variety of flags, it is possible to set almost all aspects of an xterm window's color scheme from border color to the color of the cursor. This section will look at the main elements of the color scheme: foreground color, background color, and cursor color.

Understanding X Windows Colors

Before looking at the specific flags used to set colors of an xterm window, you need to look at how colors are referred to in X Windows.

Colors in X Windows are specified in *RGB (red-green-blue)* format. RGB format consists of ordered triplets of numbers, with each number having a value from 0 to 255. The numbers represent the value of the red, green, and blue channels respectively, with 0 representing no color and 255 representing the highest possible value of the color.

Luckily, you don't need to figure out the color channel combinations to get your desired color. The work has already been done and is stored in a file that X Windows uses to map color names to their numerical triplets. This file, normally called `rgb.txt`, is usually found in the directory `/usr/X11R6/lib/X11/`.

A selected list of values in the Red Hat Linux 6 `rgb.txt` file appears here to make it easy to experiment with colors as you work through this section:

snow	GhostWhite	PapayaWhip	LemonChiffon
AliceBlue	LavenderBlush	MistyRose	white
DarkSlateGray	DimGray	gray	MidnightBlue
NavyBlue	SlateBlue	blue	SteelBlue
turquoise	cyan	DarkGreen	SeaGreen
LawnGreen	green	GreenYellow	DarkKhaki
LightYellow	yellow	gold	RosyBrown
IndianRed	sienna	beige	wheat
tan	chocolate	DarkSalmon	orange
tomato	red	DeepPink	pink
maroon	magenta	violet	orchid
purple	DarkCyan	DarkRed	LightGreen

NOTE Depending on the color depth of your video display and the applications you are running, you may find that the colors you use don't appear quite the way you expect. This is due to video card limitations and differences between systems.

Background and Foreground Colors

Setting background and foreground colors allows you to control the appearance of the text on your screen. Text appears in the foreground color while the background color, logically, is assigned to the background of the window.

The usual default xterm window is white text on a black background. Use the -fg and -bg flags to set the foreground and background colors:

```
$ xterm -fg black -bg white &
```

This command provides exactly the reverse color scheme of the default xterm window, causing the background to be set to white and the foreground to black. The result looks like Figure 9.1.

FIGURE 9.1:

Controlling the color scheme

> **NOTE**   The -bg and -fg flags are not specific to xterm. In fact, they are standard X Windows flags that can be used to change the color schemes of most X Windows applications.

Cursor Color

If you tried the last example for setting colors, you probably noticed that the cursor stayed the same color as the default xterm color scheme (pink in most Red Hat installations). You can change this color as well, using the -cr flag. For instance, if you want a dark blue cursor, you might use the command

```
$ xterm -bg black -fg white -cr MidnightBlue &
```

Setting the Window Size and Location

When you open an `xterm` window (or any other application's window, for that matter), the size of the window is set to a default size and the location of the window is determined by the configuration of your window manager (you will learn how this works in fvwm95 in the next chapter).

However, you can specify the exact size and placement of windows in X Windows using the `-geometry` flag. This flag is a standard X Windows flag (like `-bg` and `-fg`) and works with most X Windows programs.

The basic syntax of the flag is: `-geometry` *widthxheight+x+y*. The variables in this command are:

- *width* specifies the width of the window in pixels
- *height* specifies the height of the window in pixels
- *x* specifies the horizontal placement of the window as an offset in pixels from the left side of the display
- *y* specifies the vertical placement of the window as an offset in pixels from the top of the display

Xterm accepts the use of the `-geometry` flag but handles the information in a somewhat nonstandard way. When you think about it, specifying the height and width of a terminal window in pixels doesn't make a lot of sense. Instead, `xterm` interprets *width* and *height* as the number of columns and rows of characters to display, and sizes the window according to the font being used.

The default window size is 80 columns by 25 lines of characters. But what if you want a small 10-character by 10-character window to be placed 200 pixels from the left side of the screen and 300 pixels down from the top of the screen? You could use the command

```
$ xterm -geometry 10x10+200+300 &
```

to get a window like the one in Figure 9.2.

FIGURE 9.2:

Using the `-geometry` flag

By adding the -fg and -bg flags, you can also change the default color scheme at the same time you define the size of the window when it opens:

```
$ xterm -geometry 10x10+200+300 -fg DarkRed -bg cyan &
```

The result looks like Figure 9.3.

FIGURE 9.3:

Combining the -geometry
flag with the color flags

Setting the Window Title

As mentioned earlier, it is useful to be able to set the title of an xterm window to help identify what different windows are being used for. The easiest way to set the title is with the -T or -title flag (they are the same). The command

```
$ xterm -title Email &
```

creates an xterm window with the title Email, as would the command

```
$ xterm -T Email &
```

In order to create titles consisting of more than one word (in other words, containing spaces and other separators), you need to quote the title so that xterm knows which part of the command to treat as the title. If you prefer to use the title My Email, use the command

```
$ xterm -T "My Email" &
```

By default, the name of an xterm window in Red Hat Linux 6 is nxterm unless, as you will see below, an application is specified to run inside the xterm window when it opens.

Running an Application in an *Xterm* Window

While the purpose of an xterm window is to use the command line to execute commands, you may want certain character mode programs to run by default when you launch the xterm window. For instance, if you always keep Top running inside an xterm window while working, you might want to have Top launch when you open its xterm. This is done with the -e flag:

```
$ xterm -e top &
```

This command opens a window like the one in Figure 9.4.

When the program running inside the window quits, the xterm window closes.

It is important to note that the default window title when you use the -e flag is the name of the program launched with the -e flag.

Setting the Font

The default font used by xterm is usually quite readable and suited to the average monitor. But if you have a particularly large or small monitor or use an unusually low or high resolution, you may find it wise to change the font you use in your xterm windows.

In order to do this, use the -fn flag. But how do you refer to fonts? Fonts are referred to by names that can be as simple as 7x13 (which indicates 7 pixels wide and 12 pixels deep) or as complex as -sony-fixed-medium-r-normal—24-230-75-75-c-120-iso8859-1, which indicates the 24-point Latin character set, medium weight, Roman style font named fixed from the Sony font foundry.

X Windows offers a program, xlsfonts, that provides a list of available fonts on your X Windows system. To see a list of available fonts on your system, use the following command in an xterm window:

```
$ xlsfonts | more
```

The | more part of the command allows you to page through the long list of fonts (491 on my system) by hitting the space bar to move forward a page.

So, to choose the 10×20 font, use the command

```
$ xterm -fn 10x20 &
```

to get a window with a large font like the one in Figure 9.5.

FIGURE 9.5:

The 10x20 font

In theory, any of these fonts can be used with the -fn flag and the xterm command. In practice, though, this doesn't work. The nature of xterm is that it needs fixed-width fonts—that is, fonts in which all characters occupy the same amount of space regardless of their comparative sizes. In the world of Microsoft Windows, an example of a fixed-width font is Courier.

By contrast, many fonts are proportionally spaced. This means that a letter "i" takes up less space than a "w" because the latter is a wider letter. Xterm doesn't do a good job of handling these proportionally spaced fonts, as can be seen in Figure 9.6 where the selected font is from the Times family.

FIGURE 9.6:

Using a proportionally spaced font

Listed below are some of the common (and easy to type) fixed-width fonts that are available in the X Windows distribution included with Red Hat Linux 6:

5×7	6×13bold	7×14bold	9×15bold
5×8	6×9	8×13	10×20
6×10	7×13	8×13bold	12×24
6×12	7×13bold	8×16	
6×13	7×14	9×15	

If you want to experiment with other fonts, use xlsfonts to see a list of fonts, select a font, and then use the xfd command to display the font in a window. For instance, to display the Sony font -sony-fixed-medium-r-normal–24-230-75-75-c-120-iso8859-1 that you saw earlier, use the command

```
$ xfd -fn -sony-fixed-medium-r-normal–24-230-75-75-c-120-iso8859-1
```

Notice the use of the -fn flag to specify the font name. The font will be displayed in a window like the one in Figure 9.7.

FIGURE 9.7:

Displaying fonts with the
xfd command

Click the Quit button to close the window.

Other Features

Xterm offers many more features than the ones listed here. You can find out about them in the xterm man page. A man page provides information about how to use a specific program. To access the xterm man page, use the command

```
$ man xterm
```

in an xterm window. This command displays a man page like the one shown in Figure 9.8. Use the arrow keys to scroll through the man page.

FIGURE 9.8:

The xterm man page

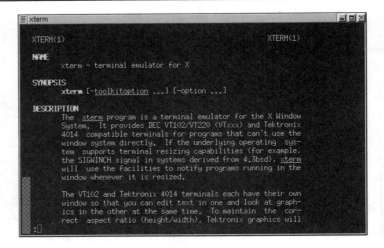

Managing Files with GNOME

Windows 3.1 users have the File Manager, Windows 95 users have the Explorer, and Mac OS users can make use of Finder. All of these programs provide facilities for managing files (including copying, moving, renaming, and deleting) as well as for launching applications.

In the X Windows world there has traditionally been no standard tool to provide these features. Numerous applications that call themselves file managers or desktop managers attempt to provide this functionality. You can find a selected list of file managers at http://www.xnet.com/~blatura/linapp2.html#file.

However, with the emergence of GNOME and KDE as alternate standards for the Linux desktop environment, the situation is stabilizing. Both GNOME and KDE offer standard file managers. On GNOME, the GNOME file manager, also known as the GNU Midnight Commander, provides a flexible, high-quality file management and browsing tool. This section will look at the GNOME file manager.

Launching the GNOME File Manager

The GNOME file manager can be launched by selecting File Manger from the default GNOME system menu. Alternatively, you can issue the command

```
$ gmc &
```

from the command line of an xterm window or, if you need to specify the complete path,

```
$ /usr/bin/gmc &
```

in a Red Hat Linux 6 installation. Gmc stands for GNU Midnight Commander.

The File Manager Window

The file manager window looks like the one in Figure 9.9.

FIGURE 9.9:

The GNOME file manager window

The window displays the contents of a single directory on your computer. By default, the directory displayed is the home directory of the user running the program. In Figure 9.9, user `armand` has run the file manager so the directory displayed is his home directory: `/home/armand`.

The window is divvied into three main sections:

- Directory tree (left side)
- Display pane (right side)
- Toolbar (across the top)

The Directory Tree

On the left side of the GNOME file manager's window is an expandable and collapsible directory of your Linux system. This directory tree is reminiscent of the one used in Windows Explorer in Windows 95, 98, and NT. The tree works in the same way as its Windows counterpart:

- Clicking a plus sign next to a directory name expands the segment of the tree to display the next level of subdirectories below the particular directory.

- Clicking a minus sign next to a directory name collapses the segment of the tree and hides all children of the particular directory.

- Clicking the name of the directory displays the contents of the directory in the pane on the right side of the file manager window.

The Display Pane

On the right side of the GNOME file manager's window is the display pane where the contents of the directory currently selected in the directory tree are displayed. In this pane, the default display format is to display each file as a full-sized icon. There are several types of icons that represent different types of files and other elements such as directories. The most important icons to familiarize yourself with are those representing directories, generic document, packages and archives, and HTML files.

NOTE

A full discussion of file types and the directory structure of Linux is provided in Chapter 14, "Working with Files." You already have a basic understanding of the Linux directory structure from the discussion provided in Chapter 4, "Installing Red Hat Linux 6."

The folder icon represents a directory and should be familiar to users of both Macintosh and Windows systems.

A blank piece of paper represents a generic document file such as a text file or a Microsoft Word file.

A piece of paper with the word HTML floating above it represents an HTML file.

Finally, the box icon represented packages and archives such as ZIP files.

The Toolbar

Across the top of the file manager window is a toolbar, which contains nine buttons:

Back   Returns the previously displayed directory.

Up   Changes to the parent directory of the current directory.

Forward Returns to the next directory in the history list (you have to have moved back using the Back button to be able to move forward).

Rescan Rescans the currently displayed directory and synchronizes the displayed files to those actually stored on disk. The display doesn't automatically update when changes are made by other programs to the contents of the currently displayed directory; you must use Rescan to reflect these changes in the file manager window.

Home Changes to the user's home directory.

Icons Switches the current display mode to large icons (this is the default mode when you first open the GNOME file manager).

Brief Switches the current display mode to a list of file and directory names with a small folder icon next to each directory name (as shown in Figure 9.10).

FIGURE 9.10:

Displaying a directory in Brief mode

Detailed Switches the current display mode to a detailed list including the name, size and modification time of the files or directories (as shown in Figure 9.11).

FIGURE 9.11:

Displaying a directory in
Detailed mode

Custom Switches the current display mode to a detailed list displaying customized statistical information specified by the user (as shown in Figure 9.12).

FIGURE 9.12:

Displaying a directory in
Custom mode

Important Menu Options

The GNOME file manager has five menus offering several commands and options. Let's take a quick look at some of the more commonly used menu options in the file manager. For complete documentation on the GNOME file manager, refer to the GNOME Help System by selecting Help System from the main GNOME system menu.

File ➢ New Window

The GNOME file manager allows you to have multiple windows open, each displaying a different directory. You can move files between open directories by dragging and dropping them between two GNOME file manager Windows.

File ➢ Copy

To copy a file to a new location, select the file in the display pane and then choose File ➢ Copy. A dialog box appears like the one in Figure 9.13. Click the Browse button to choose a destination directory or enter the destination path in the text field. By selecting Copy As a Background Process, a large copy operation (large directory with many files or one large file) is executed in the background, allowing you to return to other work with the GNOME file manager.

FIGURE 9.13:

Copying a file

An alternative way to copy a file is to right-click the file in the display pane and then choose Copy from the resulting pop-up menu.

File ➣ Delete

To delete a file, select the file in the display pane and then choose File ➣ Delete. A confirmation dialog box appears in which you can confirm the deletion of the file or cancel it. Once confirmed, the action is not reversible. An alternative way to delete a file is to right-click the file in the display pane and choose Delete from the resulting pop-up menu.

File ➣ Move

To move a file to a new location, select the file in the display pane and then choose File ➣ Move. A dialog box appears similar to the Copy dialog box shown in Figure 9.13. Here you can specify the destination and indicate if you want large move operations to be executed in the background. An alternative way to move a file is to right-click the file in the display pane and choose Move from the resulting pop-up menu.

Layout ➣ Sort By

To change the order in which files and directories are displayed in the display pane, select Layout ➣ Sort By. A dialog box appears like the one shown in Figure 9.14. In this dialog box, you can choose to sort files and directories by name, file type, size, or time of access or modification by selecting the relevant choice from the drop-down list. In addition, you can specify if the sorting should be case insensitive and you can reverse the normal sort order using the two check boxes in the lower part of the dialog box.

FIGURE 9.14:

Changing the sort order

Commands ➣ Find File

To find files on your computer, you can use the Commands ➣ Find File option in the GNOME file manager. The Find File dialog box shown in Figure 9.15 appears.

FIGURE 9.15:

Searching for a file

In this dialog box, you can specify three possible parameters:

- Where to start your search using the Start At field
- The filenames to search for using the Filename field
- Text to search for inside a file using the Content field

When specifying filenames, you can use wildcards. For instance, indicate gi* to search for all files starting with gi and *gi for all files ending in gi. When specifying the directory from which to start your search, you can specify an entire directory path (such as /home/username), a slash (/) for the top-level directory of your Linux system, or a dot (.) for the currently selected directory. Search results are displayed in a window like the one in Figure 9.16 as they are found.

FIGURE 9.16:

The results of a file search

Graphics in X Windows

So far, you have seen the most basic of X Windows applications in action: xterm and xfm. If this is all there was, it would reinforce the views of the naysayers who complain that X Windows doesn't have any applications, that Windows and the Mac OS are where the action is.

The reality, though, is that powerful, effective applications do exist for the X Windows environment. Even among the free tools out there are those that rival the features of commercial applications.

This section will look at two of the more popular Linux graphics applications: The GIMP and xv. Because these are both large programs with extensive feature sets, this section will just give you an overview of the applications and what they do, and then point to where complete information on the applications is available. Mastering an application like The GIMP, after all, would require a book in itself.

The GIMP

The GIMP (General Image Manipulation Program) is an attempt to offer the Linux community a freely available, full-featured image-editing package to rival the likes of Adobe Photoshop or Corel PhotoPaint. Figure 9.17 shows The GIMP running with several of its dialog boxes and tools open. The GIMP is designed to integrate tightly into GNOME and is considered the standard image-editing application for GNOME and a showcase of a high-powered GNOME application. GNOME is included as part of Red Hat Linux 6.

Offered under the GNU Public License, The GIMP is under constant development by Spencer Kimball and Peter Mattis at the University of California–Berkeley.

The GIMP includes all the tools expected of a full-featured image-editing package, including numerous brush types, special-effects filters, intelligent scissors, Bezier selection, layers, transparencies, and 24-bit image support.

The GIMP also provides a plug-in mechanism. Numerous plug-ins are freely available on the Internet to perform a variety of tasks, including despeckling, mapping to a sphere, creating mosaics, generating lens flares, and more.

In addition, the most recent version (1.0.4) includes a downloadable manual that provides the in-depth instruction and documentation often lacking in free software. This is all available from The GIMP Web site at www.gimp.org. The version included with Red Hat Linux 6 is 1.0.3.

Using The GIMP

Let's take just a quick look at using The GIMP. The GIMP is included on the CD-ROM as part of the standard Red Hat Linux 6 distribution. You can run it from an xterm window with the command

```
$ gimp &
```

or

```
$ /usr/bin/gimp &
```

Alternately, choose The GIMP from the Graphics submenu of the main GNOME system menu to start The GIMP.

The GIMP starts up by displaying its toolbar. This window, shown in Figure 9.18, offers access to a wide range of tools plus the main File menu.

FIGURE 9.18:

The GIMP toolbar

From the File menu, you can perform basic functions such as opening and closing images, creating new images, and opening and closing dialog boxes such as the color palette, the gradient editor, and the brush selector. When working on an actual image, right-clicking anywhere in the image brings up the complete menu for The GIMP like the one shown in Figure 9.19. From this menu, you can access all the features of The GIMP—special filters, layer controls, and more.

FIGURE 9.19:

The GIMP main menu

To learn the full set of The GIMP features, refer to the manual for the software that is on The GIMP's Web site, mentioned earlier.

Xv

Xv is one of the best-known and most widely used X Windows programs. This small but powerful program is distributed as shareware that is free for personal use. While not quite as widely distributable as the rest of Linux, it still can be found in most Linux distributions, and for good reason: for basic image manipulation in the Unix world, xv is the de facto standard.

Xv supports a wide range of image file formats, both the common ones you would expect (TIF, GIF, JPG, etc.) and lesser-known formats such as PNG. It can be used to convert images, perform screen and window captures, change color depth and resolution of images, crop images, and adjust the color maps of images. In addition, xv includes a handful of its own special-effects filters, such as embossing, oil painting, and despeckling.

Xv used to be included with Red Hat Linux. Now, with version 6, you need to download it yourself. The xv Web site is located at `http://www.trilon.com/ xv/`. There you will find several versions of xv including source code and pre-compiled binaries including a pre-built Red Hat package (`.rpm`) file. You can download and save this file and then install it using the command:

```
$ rpm -i filename
```

Once installed, you can launch xv with the command

```
$ xv &
```

or

```
$ /usr/bin/X11/xv &
```

Xv operations center around two windows: a viewer window and a controls window. When you launch xv, the viewer window appears with its logo image displayed, as in Figure 9.20.

Clicking with the right mouse button in the viewer window opens and displays the controls window shown in Figure 9.21.

FIGURE 9.20:

The viewer window with
the xv logo

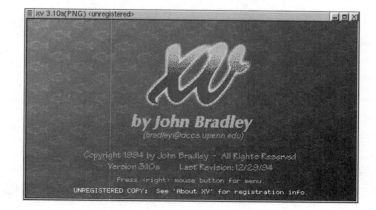

FIGURE 9.21:

The controls window

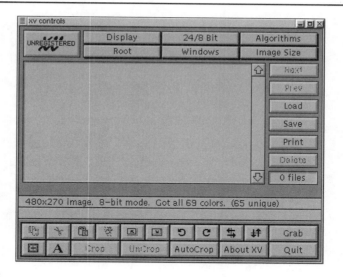

Almost everything in xv is done in the controls window. The viewer window
allows you to see the results of your work.

Let's take a quick look at some of the main tasks in xv: opening and saving images, cropping an image, and capturing a window to an image file. An HTML version of the xv documentation can be found on the Web on Shelly Johnson's Home Page at Rice University at `http://is.rice.edu/~shel/`. Follow the link for the xv documentation.

Opening Images

Opening images is done by clicking the Load button in the controls window. A dialog box like the one in Figure 9.22 appears.

This dialog box works in a vaguely Mac-like fashion. Above the list of files, you see the name of the current directory. You can click the directory name to get a list of its parent directories and, by selecting one of these, quickly change to that directory.

To open a file, simply select the filename and click the OK button (or you can simply double-click the filename). The file appears in the viewer window and the dialog box closes. If you check the Browse check box, the behavior of the dialog box changes slightly: when you click a file and then click OK, the file opens in the viewer window but the dialog box remains open. This allows you to look at different files to find the file you want. Once the correct file is displayed, simply click the Cancel button to close the dialog box.

Saving Images

The Save File dialog box shown in Figure 9.23 is similar to the Load File dialog box. Directory navigation works in the same fashion; you select existing filenames by clicking them in the file list, and clicking OK saves the current file to the name displayed in the Save File field.

FIGURE 9.23:

The xv Save window

If you want to save the image to a new filename, simply type the name you want in the field.

When saving an image, you also want to specify the type of image. In the top-right corner of the dialog box is the file format menu. By clicking this menu, you can view a list of available files. Select the file type you desire from the list. In addition, the color depth menu just below the file format menu presents any available color depth option for the file format you have selected.

Cropping an Image

Cropping an image is a simple process: select the area you want to crop to and press the Crop button in the controls window.

To select an area for cropping, drag out a rectangle with the left mouse button in the viewer window. Figure 9.24 shows an image displayed in the viewer window with a rectangle indicating where the user has dragged the mouse.

FIGURE 9.24:

Selecting a crop area

Once you have selected an area to crop, simply click the Crop button in the controls window. The result would be something like Figure 9.25 for the previous example.

FIGURE 9.25:

The result of cropping

If you don't like the results of your cropping, simply click the UnCrop button to undo the action.

Capturing a Window

One of the popular uses of xv is to create screen shots. If you want to capture an open window to an image file, you can do this using the Grab feature of xv.

Clicking the Grab button in the controls window opens the Grab dialog box like the one in Figure 9.26.

FIGURE 9.26:

The xv Grab window

There are two easy ways to grab the contents of a window: manually or automatically.

To manually grab the contents of a window, leave the Delay value set to zero seconds. Then click the Grab button. The next window you click in will be captured. The only caveat is this: the window needs to be unobscured. Any portion of any other window overlapping the selected window will also be captured.

To give you time to bring a window to the front before capturing, enter a suitable number of seconds in the delay field (4 or 5 should work well in most situations). This means that after clicking the Grab button, you have that number of seconds to work normally before xv enters the Grab mode. After the delay has expired, xv issues a distinct beep and then the next window you click is captured.

Automatic mode is similar to manual mode, with two differences. First, automatic grabbing requires a delay. Second, you need to click the AutoGrab button instead of the Grab button. You have the specified number of seconds to work normally (to get the desired window to the front and unobscured), and then xv issues the same beep and captures whichever window is underneath the mouse pointer at that time.

Once you have grabbed a window, the image of that window appears in the viewer window and you can save it like any other image in xv.

X Windows Utilities

Before closing this chapter, let's look at a few handy X Windows utilities and how to use them. These utilities are:

- gEdit
- xclock and oclock
- xcalc

Using *gEdit*

GEdit is a GNOME application that provides functionality similar to the Windows Notepad. You can use it to open and change the contents of plain text files, search and replace text, and create new files.

Admittedly, as Figure 9.27 shows, the gEdit interface is a bit spartan, but for quick editing of simple text files, it does the trick.

FIGURE 9.27:

The gEdit window

You can launch gEdit with the command

   $ **gedit &**

or, if gEdit is not on your path, with the command

   $ **/usr/bin/gedit &**

or you can select gEdit from the Applications submenu of the main GNOME system menu.

The interface is simple. Across the top is the toolbar with self-explanatory buttons for loading and saving files, cutting, copying and pasting, and searching for text.

To load an existing file, click the Open button or choose File ➢ Open. A dialog box appears where you can browse for and select a file to open. When a file is opened, it appears as shown in Figure 9.28.

FIGURE 9.28:

The results of loading a file

You can save a file you have opened by clicking the Save button on the toolbar or by choosing File ➢ Save.

The Find button on the toolbar brings up Search dialog box shown in Figure 9.29. You can also open this dialog box by choosing Edit ➢ Find.

FIGURE 9.29:

The search dialog box

Using this dialog box is relatively simple: fill in the text to search for and click the Search button. You can also indicate if you prefer to start your search at the beginning of the document or the current cursor position and whether or not the search should be considered case sensitive. Search and replace takes things one step further. You can open the Search and Replace dialog box by selecting Edit ➢ Replace. This dialog box looks like the Search dialog box except that it has an additional field for indicating the text to replace each found item with. In addition, you can indicate that you want to be prompted before replacing any text.

The other major feature of gEdit is the spell-checker that can be accessed from Plugins ➢ Spell Check. This is a simple but useful spell-checker, as shown in Figure 9.30.

FIGURE 9.30:

The gEdit spell-checker

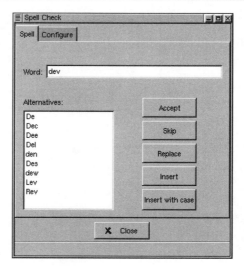

X Windows Clocks

You have probably noticed the clock that appears in the GNOME panel. Some users, though, like to see a larger digital or analog clock on their desktop.

This can be achieved using the `xclock` program. `Xclock` is a basic clock program that allows you to create an analog or digital clock. By default, `xclock` displays an analog clock, so the command

```
$ xclock &
```

or

```
$ /usr/bin/X11/xclock &
```

creates a window like the one in Figure 9.31.

FIGURE 9.31:

The default `xclock` style

The `-digital` flag causes `xclock` to display a digital clock like Figure 9.32.

FIGURE 9.32:

A digital xclock window

Wed May 27 22:23:52 1998

The `-digital` flag is not the only flag accepted by `xclock`. The `-hd` and `-hl` flags help create a more interesting visual display for an analog clock. The `-hd` flag is used to specify a color for the hands of the clock, and the `-hl` flag specifies the color for the outline of the hands of the clock. (Remember the discussion of RGB colors earlier. This is one instance where you would use RGB colors.

For example, the command

```
$ xclock -hd yellow -hl green &
```

creates a clock that has yellow hands with green outlines like Figure 9.33 (of course, this is hard to see in the black-and-reproduction you are looking at).

FIGURE 9.33:

Setting the color of the clock's hands

Notice the lack of contrast between the hands and the white face of the clock. This can be rectified with a standard X Windows flag: the -bg flag that you saw earlier in the discussion of xterm. By specifying a background color of black with

```
$ xclock -hd yellow -hl green -bg black &
```

you end up with something like Figure 9.34.

FIGURE 9.34:

Setting the background color

While the hands are now clearly visible, a new problem has arisen: the marks that indicate the points of the clock are now not visible, since they are black and they are drawn against a black background. These marks are considered part of the foreground, and their color can be changed with the standard X Windows -fg flag. The command

    $ xclock -hd yellow -hl green -bg black -fg cyan &

gives a result like Figure 9.35.

Using the GNOME Calculator

Finally, let's take a quick look at the GNOME calculator, the default GNOME calculator tool that should be available in every distribution of Linux that includes GNOME.

As you might expect by this point, you can run the GNOME Calculator with the command

    $ gcalc &

or with the command

    & /usr/bin/gcalc &

The GNOME calculator can also be opened by selecting Simple Calculator from the Utilities submenu of the main GNOME system menu.

The GNOME calculator window looks like Figure 9.36.

FIGURE 9.36:

The GNOME Calculator window

The calculator operates much as any standard scientific calculator does. It provides all the expected scientific functions, including trigonometric and logarithmic functions, plus a memory. The actual use of such a calculator and its functions is not really the subject of this chapter, and a full description of the meaning of these functions is best left to a mathematics text.

Looking Ahead

By now, you should be feeling fairly comfortable navigating your GNOME environment. You can control basic options of GNOME, you can launch applications, and you can manipulate windows.

As mentioned earlier, though, the power of both X Windows and GNOME comes from their flexibility and configurability.

The next chapter looks at how to go about configuring GNOME to meet your personal needs. This includes customizing the main GNOME panel, changing your desktop appearance and themes, and other common GNOME configuration tasks.

CHAPTER

TEN

Advanced GNOME Configuration

■ Using the GNOME Control Center

■ Configuring GNOME Panels

Now that you have learned to use GNOME and to run applications in the GNOME desktop environment, let's look at the advanced configuration options available in GNOME. At the center of GNOME configuration is the GNOME Control Center. From the GNOME Control Center, you can:

- Use a graphical interface to configure your desktop's background and theme

- Define multimedia properties for your system

- Fine-tune dialogs and other interface items

GNOME panels are the center of the user interface. GNOME panels have a separate configuration procedure that allows you to control the position, size, behavior, and other settings of the main GNOME panel as well as any additional panels you create.

This chapter will consider both aspects of GNOME configuration.

Using the GNOME Control Center

The GNOME Control Center can be accessed in two main ways:

- Click the Control Center button on the main GNOME Control Panel.

- Select the Settings ➤ GNOME Control Center option from the main GNOME system menu.

When you first launch the Control Center, a window appears like the one in Figure 10.1.

FIGURE 10.1:

The initial GNOME Control
Center window

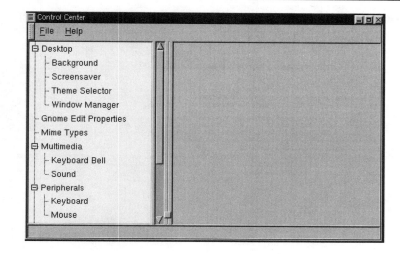

This window contains two main parts:

- The left side displays a heirarchichal tree of configuration options organized in four main categories: Desktop, Multimedia, Peripherals, and User Interface Options.

- The right side displays the controls for the particular section of the configuration tree that you have selected. For instance, in Figure 10.2, the Desktop Background section is displayed.

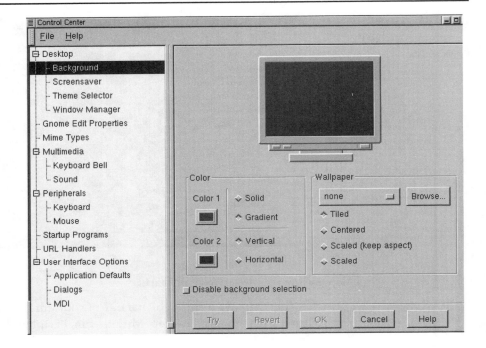

The Desktop Section

The Desktop section of the Control Center makes it possible to control several aspects of your desktop's appearance and behavior, including the background color and wallpaper, the screen saver, and your choice of desktop themes.

To control your background properties, choose the Background entry in the Desktop section in the left side of the Control Center window. In the right side of the window, the Desktop Background applet appears, as shown in Figure 10.3.

FIGURE 10.3:

Controlling the desktop
background

In this window, you can create three possible desktop backgrounds:

- A single solid color by selecting the Solid radio button and choosing a color for Color 1. You choose a color by clicking the color sample below the title Color 1 to open the color chooser window shown in Figure 10.4.

FIGURE 10.4:

The color chooser window

- A two-color gradient by selecting the Gradient radio button and choosing colors for both Color 1 and Color 2. This creates a gradient effect from the top to the bottom of the screen changing from Color 1 to Color 2. Alternatively, you can create a horizontal gradient from left to right by choosing the Horizontal radio button.

- A desktop wallpaper by clicking the Browse button and choosing an image from your hard disk to use as background wallpaper that you can choose to center on the desktop, tile repeatedly on the desktop, or scale to fill the desktop.

When you are finished changing your background settings, click the OK button to commit the changes.

To control your screen saver settings, select the Screen Saver entry in the Desktop section of the GNOME Control Center. In the right side of the GNOME Control Center window, the screen saver configuration applet shown in Figure 10.5 appears.

FIGURE 10.5:

Configuring your screen saver

In the top-left corner is a list of screen savers available on your system. To the right of this list, a small demonstration of your currently selected screen saver is displayed. Below this, you can indicate how many minutes of inactivity should pass before starting the screen saver and if a password is required. The Priority setting indicates how much of your computer's resources should be devoted to the screen saver. When the Priority is set to High, then any background process is denied access to computer resources in favor of smooth screen saver animations. By contrast, choosing a Low priority means that your background processes get priority in accessing system resources; the cost of this may be choppy screen saver graphics.

Finally, you can specify if power management should be able to power down your monitor while the screen saver is active and how many minutes to wait after starting the screen saver before powering the monitor down.

Again, once you have finished with your settings, click the OK button to save them.

Another useful feature of the Desktop section of the Control Center is the Theme Selector shown in Figure 10.6.

FIGURE 10.6:

The Theme Selector

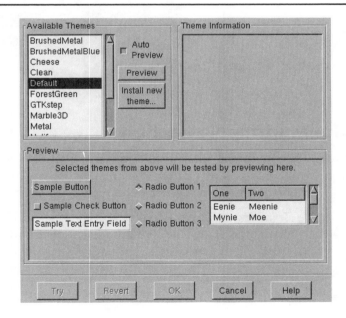

In this section, you can choose from a list of desktop themes in the top-left corner. These desktop themes define cohesive sets of window backgrounds, button styles, window styles, and color schemes. When you select a theme, a sample of the theme is displayed in the lower half of the applet, as shown in Figure 10.7 where the Odo theme is selected.

FIGURE 10.7:

Selecting the Odo theme

The Multimedia Section

The Multimedia section allows you to control two aspects of sound on your GNOME-based system: the sound and volume of the keyboard bell and the definition of sounds to play when different events occur.

To define the style and volume of the keyboard bell, select the Keyboard Bell entry. This displays the configuration applet shown in Figure 10.8.

FIGURE 10.8:

Controlling the
keyboard bell

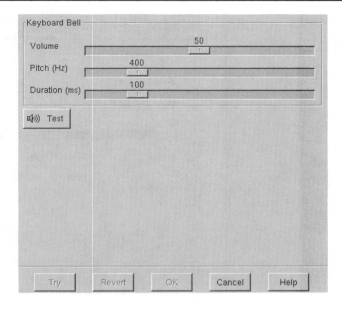

Using this entry, you can control the volume, pitch, and duration of the keyboard bell that sounds whenever the system wants to emit a beep. You can test your settings by clicking the Test button below the sliders.

To control the sounds to play for different system events, choose the Sound entry in the Multimedia section of the Control Center. This displays the sound configuration applet. This applet has two tabbed screens. The first, which is displayed by default, allows you to enable or disable GNOME support for sound and, if enabled, to enable or disable support for sounds for events. The second tab, labeled Sound Events, is shown in Figure 10.9.

FIGURE 10.9:

The Sound Events tab

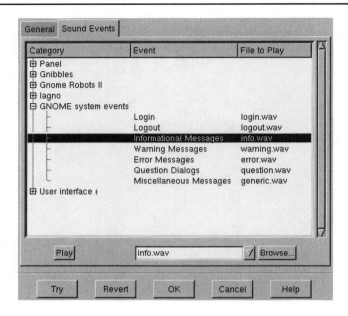

You can use the Sound Events tab to specify individual sound files (in the WAV format, which is common on Windows systems) to play for a wide range of sound events. The upper part of the screen shows a list of events and the currently assigned WAV file to play. If you select an event, you can test the current sound by clicking the Play button. Alternatively, you can select a new sound by clicking the Browse button and finding a different WAV file to use.

The Peripherals Section

The Peripherals section allows you to control basic aspects of keyboard and mouse behavior using the Keyboard and Mouse entries.

The Keyboard entry, shown in Figure 10.10, allows you to indicate if you want keyboard auto-repeat enabled and if you do, to specify the delay before repeating starts and how quickly characters should repeat. In addition, you can choose to enable a click sound to be played each time a key is pressed. If you enable keyboard clicks, you can control the volume of the click. Regardless of your settings, you can test them by putting the cursor in the Test Settings text field and typing any text.

FIGURE 10.10:

Configuring your keyboard

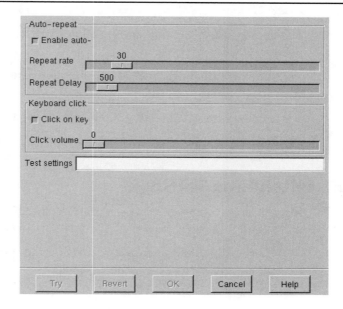

The mouse entry shown in Figure 10.11 allows you to indicate if the mouse user is left- or right-handed, effectively swapping the default behavior of the left and right mouse buttons, and to specify the mouse speed and responsiveness.

FIGURE 10.11:

Setting your mouse's behavior

The User Interface Options Section

The User Interface Options section allows you to control various aspects of your user interface, including:

- The default appearance of windows elements, such as menus and toolbars, for GNOME applications

- The way in which dialog box elements are displayed

- How multiple windows from the same application are handled

Miscellaneous Settings

In addition to these main sections, the GNOME Control Center offers a number of other configuration entries:

- GNOME Edit Properties: Use this entry to specify the default editor to use when editing text files with GNOME.

- Mime Types: Use this entry to associate file extensions with particular applications for opening, editing, and viewing files with the specified extension.

- Startup Programs: Use this entry to specify programs that should start each time you start GNOME and X Windows.

For details on using these configuration settings along with other settings in the Control Center that haven't been discussed in detail in this chapter, consult the GNOME help system. You can access the GNOME help system by selecting Help System from the main GNOME system menu.

Configuring GNOME Panels

The center of the GNOME user interface is GNOME panels. GNOME creates a default panel when it first starts.

Users can create their own panels by choosing Panel ➤ Add New Panel ➤ Edge Panel from the main GNOME system menu on the default GNOME panel. You can also right-click the background of an existing panel and choose Add New Panel ➤ Edge Panel from the menu that appears. For the purposes of this chapter, you will work with the default GNOME panel.

The main configuration tasks you want to perform with a panel are:

- Adding a drawer
- Adding a logout button
- Adding a launcher
- Controlling panel properties

Adding a Drawer to a Panel

You add a drawer to a panel by right-clicking the background of the panel and choosing Add Drawer from the menu that appears.

Drawers appear on the panel and can be opened and closed. An open drawer can display and contain other icons, such as those for launching applications. When the drawer is closed, the icons are hidden. You can move icons and applets from a panel to the drawer by right-clicking the item you want to move to an open drawer and selecting Move Applet from the menu that appears and then clicking and dragging the item in question.

Adding a Logout Button to a Panel

Normally, you log out of GNOME by choosing Logout from the main GNOME menu. You can add a button to a panel, though, to allow for single-click logouts. To do this, right-click the background of the panel and choose Add Logout Button. A logout button is added to the panel.

Adding a New Launcher

The default GNOME panel contains several buttons that launch applications like Netscape Communicator and a terminal window. These are *launcher buttons*. You can create your own launcher button by right-clicking the background of the panel and selecting Add New Launcher from the menu that appears. This opens a dialog box like the one in Figure 10.12 for defining which application to launch.

FIGURE 10.12:

Defining a new application launcher

You need to provide at least a name for the launcher and the path and name of a GNOME or X Windows application as the command. You can also choose an icon for the launcher by clicking the button labeled No Icon to display a collection of icons to choose from.

If you want the launcher to start a console application (one that needs to run at the command line and inside a terminal window), select the Run In Terminal check box.

Controlling Panel Properties

If you right-click a panel's background and select This Panel Properties from the menu that appears, the Panel Properties dialog box shown in Figure 10.13 appears.

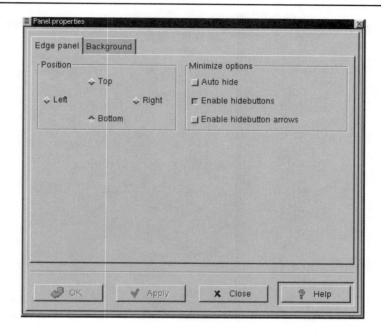

This dialog box contains two tabs. The Edge Panel tab allows control of the panels position on the screen, activation of the auto-hide features, and the state of the hide buttons at both ends of the panel. These features are described in Chapter 8, "Using GNOME."

The Background tab is shown in Figure 10.14. This screen allows you to define a background image or color for a panel. At the top of the screen, you can choose between a Standard, Pixmap, or Color background. A Standard background follows the theme or color scheme you have defined for GNOME, Pixmap uses a bitmap image as a background, and Color allows you to define a solid color for the background.

FIGURE 10.14:

The Panel Properties dialog
box, Background tab

If you select Pixmap, you can click the Browse button and choose an image file from the file selection dialog box that appears. You can choose to have the image either tiled on the background or stretched to fill the entire background (by selecting the Scale Image to Fit Panel check box).

If you select Color, you can click the Background Color button at the bottom of the tab to open a color selection window where you can choose a color for the background of the panel.

Looking Ahead

By now, you should feel fairly comfortable with GNOME and X Windows. In the next chapter, you will explore an alternate graphical user interface called KDE. You will learn the history of KDE, then move on to installing it. Once you have the KDE desktop up and running, you will explore its features and browse its file system. After you understand the basics of navigation, you will learn to configure KDE to suit your needs. By the end of the chapter you will be able to use KDE to view text and graphics, manage your time, and administer your Linux system.

CHAPTER
ELEVEN

11

Using KDE

- A History of the KDE Project

- Installing KDE

- Exploring the KDE Desktop

- Browsing the File System

- Configuring KDE

- Using KDE Utilities

One of the most promising developments in the user interface of Linux has been the K Desktop Environment (KDE). KDE is a complete graphical desktop environment developed from scratch. Although the GNOME development project is sponsored by Red Hat and is included with Red Hat Linux 6, KDE is included with Red Hat Linux 6.

A History of the KDE Project

As with most components of a complete Linux distribution, KDE was developed by a group of dedicated programmers who wanted to create something new and useful. The KDE Project was founded in October 1996 by Matthias Ettrich in Germany. Its original purpose was to create a powerful desktop environment for Linux and other Unix systems similar to the commercially available Common Desktop Environment (CDE) available for commercial Unix platforms such as Solaris. The end result has been a project much wider in scope than simply emulating CDE.

Contributors to the KDE Project include hundreds of developers around the world who communicate via e-mail and the occasional in-person conference. Individuals who want to participate in the development of KDE can work on the core components such as the window manager, the desktop panel, and other components, or they can create their own application for KDE, using the KDE-defined APIs.

Among the contributors to the KDE Project are translators, writers, user-interface designers, and multimedia specialists, in addition to systems and application programmers.

KDE doesn't replace the X Windows system on your Linux computer. Instead, KDE uses the X Windows system as a graphical base on which to build the Desktop.

If you've used other X window managers, such as fvwm, AfterStep, or even CDE, you may recognize that KDE includes its own window manager, called kwm. Part of the window manager functionality includes the ability to place icons on the Desktop background.

In addition to the kwm window manager, which provides core functionality for creating and managing on-screen windows, KDE includes a few key components such as a taskbar and a main menu that enable you to easily access applications.

Finally, a KDE distribution includes a large collection of applications such as standard utilities, system administration tools, and entertainment packages.

Reviewing a KDE Distribution

As with Linux, KDE uses the term "distribution" to describe a complete collection of desktop components and the default set of applications that accompany them.

A KDE distribution includes the following components:

- The graphical libraries used by all KDE applications

- The core KDE libraries, also used by all KDE applications

- A collection of support functions, used by most applications

- The base applications that define KDE, such as the window manager and the panel/taskbar programs

- Additional optional applications that can be installed on a running KDE system

As with most Linux-related projects, the source code to KDE is available for download and review. The KDE code is licensed under the OpenSource General Public License (GPL).

Writing KDE Applications

KDE was developed from ground zero to a full-featured desktop in about two years. This was possible only by using a pre-built commercial graphical toolkit called Qt, from Troll Tech in Oslo, Norway.

NOTE   By using Qt, KDE developers were able to focus on design issues for the desktop and immediately begin coding, rather than spending additional months or years creating a toolkit to standardize the interface.

Qt is a cross-platform graphical toolkit that forms the basis of the KDE Application Programming Interface. Any application written for KDE can use the Qt functionality. The result is that a complete KDE application can be created in only a few days.

Both Qt and KDE itself are written in C++, an object-oriented programming language. You can also write KDE applications in Python, a high-level object-oriented scripting language, or Perl.

Development tools for KDE applications are still in their early stages. A few simple tools such as the KAppTemplate (`http://home.sprintmail.com/~granroth/kapptemplate/`) are available to simplify the initial stages of application development. Other more robust tools are beginning to appear. Check the KDE Developer Web site for details on these tools (`http://developer.kde.org`).

KDE and Red Hat Linux 6

For Red Hat Linux 6, the files needed to run KDE are available with the distribution. If you installed KDE during the Red Hat installation process, then you already have KDE on your system. If not, you can find the RPM files you will need to use in the next section on the Red Hat Linux 6 CD-ROM at `/mnt/cdrom/RedHat/RPMS` (assuming you mounted the CD-ROM at `/mnt/cdrom`).

The KDE files on the Red Hat Linux 6 CD-ROM are named:

- `kdeadmin-1.1.1pre2-1.i386.rpm`
- `kdebase-1.1.1pre2-2.i386.rpm`
- `kdegames-1.1.1pre2-2.i386.rpm`
- `kdegraphics-1.1.1pre2-1.i386.rpm`
- `kdelibs-1.1.1pre2-2.i386.rpm`
- `kdemultimedia-1.1.1pre2-1.i386.rpm`

- `kdenetwork-1.1.1pre2-1.i386.rpm`

- `kdesupport-1.1.1pre2-1.i386.rpm`

- `kdeutils-1.1.1pre2-1.i386.rpm`

Starting KDE

In RedHat 6, the default desktop environment is GNOME. If you have installed your copy of RedHat Linux so that the default graphical login window is displayed, you can indicate that you want KDE to launch instead of GNOME before you log in. To do this, follow these steps:

1. Click the Options button.

2. Click the Sessions Sub-menu from the drop-down menu.

3. Select KDE from the list of possible desktops.

4. Login using your username and password.

When KDE starts, an initial screen appears, like the one in Figure 11.1.

FIGURE 11.1:

The initial KDE screen includes several Desktop icons and an open Help window.

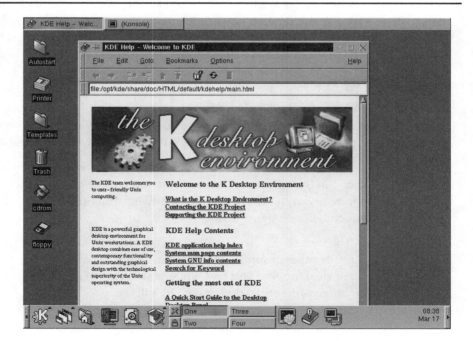

If you normally start X Windows by logging in at the console login prompt and then using the `startx` command to start X Windows, then you need to configure things so that KDE launches when you issue the `startx` command.

In this regard, you have two options:

- If you want to change the default desktop for every user, edit the global `XClients` file, which you can find at `/etc/X11/xinit/XClients`.

- If you want to change only your default desktop user, copy the global `XClients` file to your home directory, name the file `.XClients`, and then edit the file in your home directory. You can copy the file with the command:

```
$ cp /etc/X11/xinit/XClients ~/.XClients
```

In either case, you only need to make one change to the file. The fifth line should read:

```
PREFERRED=
```

Change this line so that it reads:

```
PREFERRED=startkde
```

Once you make this change and save it, X Windows should start with KDE as your desktop when you use the `startx` command. If you make this change to the global `XClients` files, then every user will have KDE as their default desktop.

Exiting KDE

When you're ready to exit KDE, select Log Out from the main menu. The screen is grayed and the KDE Log Out confirmation window appears. Choose OK to log out of KDE and shut down the X Windows system graphical environment.

If you have any windows open when you choose Log Out, those windows are listed in the KDE Log Out confirmation window. The confirmation window provides a warning to check to see if any information in those windows needs to be saved before logging out.

The next time you start KDE, it attempts to reopen those windows, launching KDE or other graphical applications that you were running to re-establish the same desktop that you had when you selected Log Out. Not all applications may be successfully restarted, but KDE will try.

NOTE   You can always exit KDE using the default keyboard method of exiting the X Windows system: hold down Ctrl+Alt and then press the Backspace key. However, this method should be used only for emergencies (such as if the graphics lock up), because it doesn't allow KDE to exit gracefully—you may lose some data if you use this keyboard method to exit KDE.

The status of your KDE environment, including information about the windows that you had open when you selected Log Out, is all saved in a hidden file in your home directory called `.kderc`. You can review this file if you'd like, but be careful about changing it, since you may confuse KDE the next time it launches.

NOTE   Information about the state of specific applications, such as the file manager or a networking utility, is not saved in `.kderc`, but rather in the application's configuration file, which is normally located in your home directory under `.kde/share/config`.

Using Kdm for Graphical Login

If you're accustomed to using xdm for a graphical login to your Linux system, you may want to try the kdm graphical login application provided with KDE.

The functioning of xdm and kdm is very similar, but kdm can be graphically configured using the KDE Control Center (described later in this chapter in the section, "Exploring the KDE Desktop").

TIP   To enable a graphical login, first make sure that the X Windows system is working, then change the `/etc/inittab` file to use run level 5 instead of 3. See the **inittab** man page for further information.

Changing from xdm to kdm is easy once you have KDE installed. Just open the `/etc/inittab` file in a text editor and locate the following line, which indicates what program should be launched to use the graphical (x) login:

```
x:5:respawn:/usr/bin/X11/xdm -nodaemon
```

Change this line to read as follows:

```
x:5:respawn:/opt/kde/bin/kdm -nodaemon
```

Now when you restart your system (or change run levels using the `telinit` command), the kdm graphical login is used.

Configuring Kdm

By using kdm, you can configure many features of the graphical login, including the greeting string, the icon in the dialog box, and the background color or wallpaper graphic displayed.

To configure kdm, follow these steps:

1. Log in to your Linux system using the graphical login dialog box.

2. Open the main menu by clicking the K icon in the lower left corner of the KDE screen.

3. Choose Settings ➢ Applications ➢ Login Manager.

The kdm configuration dialog box appears, as shown in Figure 11.2.

FIGURE 11.2:

Use this dialog box to configure the features of the kdm graphical login.

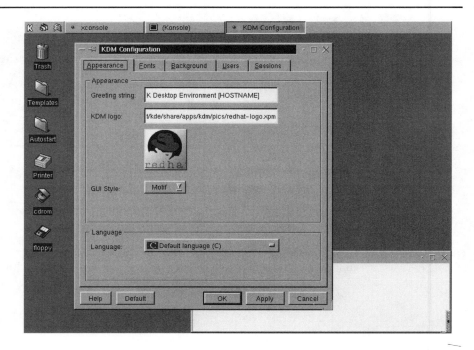

NOTE   You must be logged in as root to configure the kdm graphical login manager.

On the Appearances tab (shown in Figure 11.2) you can select the following items:

- The Greeting String used at the top of the graphical login window.

- The logo used within the login window.

- Normally, only three icons are displayed if you click the icon to change it. You can create or import any suitably sized icon. Place the icon in the directory /opt/kde/share/apps/kdm/pics and select it from this configuration dialog box.

- The GUI style (Motif or Windows).

- The language used for messages in the graphical login window.

The Fonts tab lets you define the text font used for the Greeting, Fail, and Standard messages. To change a font, choose which font you want to alter from the drop-down list and choose the Change Font button. A Select Font dialog box appears where you can select the font that you want.

The Background tab (shown in Figure 11.3) enables you to select a background color pattern or a background graphic image for the login screen.

If you prefer a colored background, you can select in the Color area of the dialog box:

- Solid color for a single color (the top of the two color bars)

- Horizontal blend for two colors blended side to side

- Vertical blend (the default) for two colors blended top to bottom

To select a single color, or the two colors for blending, click either of the color bars presented below the three color choices. A Select Color dialog box (shown in Figure 11.4) appears, where you can select the color that you want to use.

FIGURE 11.3:

From the Background tab, you select the colors or wallpaper graphics to use behind the kdm login window.

FIGURE 11.4:

The standard KDE Select Color dialog box lets you define the color that you want to use for the kdm background.

If you prefer to have a wallpaper graphic in the background of the login screen, you can select an image from the Wallpaper section of this dialog box.

Over 100 standard wallpaper graphics are provided with KDE 1.1. You can select any of these from the drop-down list.

If you have another graphic that you want to use as wallpaper, choose the Browse button and select it from the directory where you have the graphic image stored.

TIP   It's a good idea to copy the graphic file that you want to use as wallpaper to a standard KDE wallpaper directory so that you don't accidentally delete the file after specifying it as a KDE wallpaper. Standard directories would be `/opt/kde/share/wallpapers` or `.kde/share/wallpapers` in your home directory.

The wallpaper graphic can be placed in several different locations on your background by selecting among the buttons shown below the wallpaper selection drop-down list. Options include:

- Tile to use the wallpaper graphic as a repeating pattern across the entire background.

- Center to center a single copy of the wallpaper in the middle of the kdm screen—it might be mostly covered by the kdm login window in this case.

- Top Left to move the wallpaper to the upper left corner of the background.

NOTE   If you use a wallpaper option such as Tile or Scale, none of the background colors that you select will be visible. If you want to use only a background color without a wallpaper graphic, be sure to choose the None button below the wallpaper drop-down list.

The Users tab lets you configure which users are shown as icons within the login window. Any user shown as an icon in the login window can log in without typing their username. They only need to type their password.

The Sessions tab lets you specify how login sessions are defined. You shouldn't need to alter the Sessions tab because the standard settings are fine.

When you have defined the kdm options you want, choose OK to close the dialog box and save your settings. You'll see them the next time you log out of KDE.

Adding Other KDE Applications

When you install KDE, you have at your disposal a comprehensive set of utilities and entertainment programs, as described later in this chapter. However, many other KDE applications are available to meet the unique needs of your specific installation.

In particular, you may want to update to a newer version of a favorite KDE application, or download an application that wasn't included in the default KDE distribution.

KDE applications are often located on the author's Web site or FTP site, but they can also be accessed through the directory of all KDE applications that is maintained on the KDE Web site.

The regularly updated list of all KDE applications that can be obtained directly from the KDE Web site is stored at `http://www.kde.org/applications.html`. On this page, you'll find a table of applications, each with a short description and a link directly to the FTP download directory.

Examples of what you can find on this applications page include the following:

- Utility to configure bind (DNS)
- Additional sets of icons and color schemes (KDE themes)
- Video file player
- KDE-aware Telnet application
- ISDN line-management tool
- Laptop power-management utility
- User administration tool
- Dozens more games

Remember, these are in addition to the many KDE applications that you probably already have installed on your KDE system.

Unfortunately for new KDE users, almost all of these additional KDE applications are distributed as source code. In order to use them, you'll need to install the development packages and compile the source code on your Linux system.

This actually isn't very difficult. The problems arise for users who are not familiar with the development tools. In that case, resolving any error or warning messages that appear can be quite time-consuming.

Once you have the development libraries installed for KDE, Qt, and the X Windows system, you can prepare a source code tree that you have downloaded and unarchived using these simple commands:

```
# configure
# make
# make install
```

With these commands, the new application is compiled and placed in your KDE menus or binary directories so that you can immediately execute it. Some applications may require more complicated steps to compile and install them. In these cases, consult the README and installation files that are included with most applications to provide detailed instructions to get you started.

Exploring the KDE Desktop

Once you have KDE installed and running, you can start learning how to use it. The elements on the KDE Desktop are probably familiar to you. Figure 11.5 shows a blank KDE Desktop as it appears when you first start KDE. One program has also been started to show the Taskbar.

The elements you see on the Desktop are as follows:

- The background, which shows icons for programs and files that you want to have easily accessible (three icons are shown by default).

- The Panel, which is a bar of icons across the bottom of the screen (you can configure the location of the Panel). Clicking an icon launches a commonly used program.

- The Taskbar, which shows a button for each main application window that you have opened in KDE. Clicking a button brings that application's window forward.

- The main menu, which you view by clicking the K icon on the Panel. All of KDE's major functions are available from the main menu and its submenus.

FIGURE 11.5:

The initial KDE Desktop, with the main menu opened, the Panel below, and the initial Desktop icons visible.

You can explore many of KDE's applications by choosing items from the main menu or by clicking buttons on the Panel. Anytime you leave your mouse pointer sitting on a menu item or Panel button, a pop-up hint describes that item for you (see Figure 11.6).

FIGURE 11.6:

Pop-up hints identify each Panel button and menu item when you pause your mouse pointer over an item.

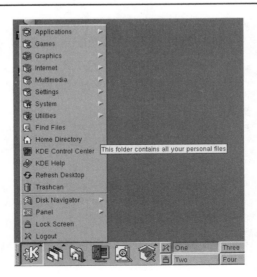

Launching KDE Applications

Start a couple of KDE applications to experiment with as you learn about the KDE graphical environment. The KDE text editor and a terminal emulator window provide a good starting point. Choose Utilities ➤ Terminal Emulator on the main menu to open a command line window. Next, choose Utilities ➤ Text Editor to open a graphical KDE text editor.

TIP
Once you have a terminal emulator window open, you can enter the name of any KDE program instead of selecting it from a menu or clicking a Panel icon. For example, you can launch the text editor by entering **kedit** at the command line.

Now try launching another terminal emulator window from the Panel by clicking the Terminal Emulator button, as shown below.

When you are running the KDE Desktop, KDE applications are special compared to other X Windows system graphical applications because they can interact with each other, use common graphical libraries to save system resources, and have the same look and feel.

Other graphical or text-based applications can also be used in KDE, of course. Some of the more popular graphical applications may be included in the KDE main menu under a Non-KDE Applications submenu.

You can also launch your favorite applications from a terminal emulator window in KDE, just as you would in any other window manager like fvwm or CDE.

To try this, enter a command like **xv** or **gimp** or **gs** in a KDE terminal emulator window. (The program name you choose will depend on what you have installed.)

TIP
One quick way to enter a command to start a program is to use the pop-up command window in KDE. To use this, press Alt+F2 and enter the command in the small pop-up window that appears.

Using Multiple Desktops

If you're familiar with other Linux window managers, you might have used the Pager program to manage multiple virtual desktops, each containing many open windows. In one virtual desktop, you might have your browser; in another, your word processor; in another, terminal windows where you edit code.

KDE uses the same idea to provide multiple visual workspaces for you. By default, KDE includes four Desktops, which you can switch between by clicking the Desktop name in the Panel, or by pressing Ctrl+F1 for Desktop One, Ctrl+F2 for Desktop Two, and so forth.

TIP   You can change the number of Desktops and rename them to fit how you use each one. Choose Settings ➤ Applications ➤ Panel and then select the Desktops tab to configure these options.

You can rotate between Desktops by holding down the Ctrl key and pressing Tab or Shift+Tab repeatedly.

Working with Application Windows

Working with application windows in KDE is similar to other graphical environments you may have worked with. The same methods of moving, resizing, and closing windows can be used in KDE.

When you have multiple windows open on your KDE Desktop, you can activate any window by clicking anywhere in the window.

TIP   The KDE *focus policy* determines which window is the active window in KDE. If you're accustomed to a particular type of focus, such as being able to type in whichever window your mouse pointer is in, you can alter the focus policy of KDE by choosing Settings ➤ Windows ➤ Properties and selecting a different focus policy.

KDE's multiple virtual Desktops can make it easy to work with many open windows at the same time, but you also have available other methods for switching between open application windows:

- The Taskbar displays a button for each open window. You can click a Taskbar button to activate that window and bring it to the front.

- You can hold the Alt key and press Tab or Shift+Tab repeatedly to rotate between the open windows, much as you would in Microsoft Windows.

- You can press Ctrl+Esc to open a list of windows in the current KDE session. From this list you can select any window to activate it and bring it to the front.

- You can also click the Window List icon on the Panel (or click the Taskbar if the Panel is closed) to see a list similar to that shown in the Ctrl+Esc window.

NOTE　Depending on how your KDE system is configured, some of these options may display a list of windows on the current Desktop rather than windows available on all session Desktops. Choose Settings ➢ Windows ➢ Advanced to review these options.

Browsing the File System

A big part of using any graphical system is accessing the files on your computer. Linux provides a completely integrated file manager to do this. In addition, you can directly access the file system from the KDE main menu using the Disk Navigator, though this method doesn't provide the interaction of a file manager window.

This section describes how to work with KDE file manager windows and the Disk Navigator menus.

Using File Manager Windows

The file manager in KDE is called kfm, for KDE File Manager. You'll often see this at the top of file manager windows as you work.

Although you can access the file manager from a command line, the easiest way to view your files is to begin with your home directory by choosing Home Directory from the main menu or by clicking the home directory icon on the Panel. A file manager window appears, as shown in Figure 11.7.

FIGURE 11.7:

The file manager window lets you view the contents of your home directory and browse to other directories.

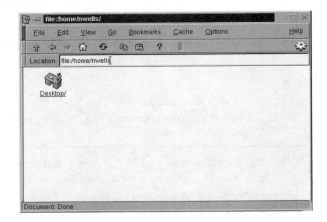

The default view of your file system uses large icons (assigned by KDE according to file type). You can see a toolbar and location line shown in the top of the file manager window.

Changing the view of these files to see more information is easy: choose another display option from the View menu, such as Long or Text View. You can also select Show Hidden Files on the View menu to see all the files in your home directory.

The Up-Arrow icon on the left end of the toolbar changes to the parent directory; clicking any directory opens that directory and displays its contents within the same file manager window. To open a new file manager window at the current location, choose File ➢ New Window or press Ctrl+N.

TIP You can also press the Home Directory button on the Panel several times to open several file manager windows. Having at least two open file manager windows can be convenient for drag-and-drop file copying or moving.

To move or copy a file or directory, click and drag any icon, dropping it in the directory where you want to move or copy it. (A pop-up menu lets you choose either move or copy.)

Anytime you click an icon in a file manager window, KDE attempts to launch that item. If it's a text file, for example, KDE opens it in the KDE text editor; graphics files appear in the graphics viewer. If KDE can't figure out what to do with the file, a small Open With dialog box appears where you can specify a program to use for launching the icon you clicked.

KDE Link files (described later in this section) and additional MIME types (choose File ➤ New ➤ MIME Type) are good methods to use when KDE doesn't recognize the type of file you want to launch.

Changing File Properties

Within a file manager window, you can alter any file or directory properties that you have access to. To view the file or directory properties, right-click any file or directory icon. From the pop-up menu that appears, choose Properties. A Properties dialog box, as shown in Figure 11.8, appears with several tabs that you can view and alter.

FIGURE 11.8:

The Properties dialog box lets you view and change information about objects in file manager windows.

NOTE

The specific tabs that appear in the Properties dialog box depend on the type of object that you are viewing. For example, KDE Link files (described later in this section), directories, and regular files all have different sets of properties.

You can also create new objects by using the New submenu (either from the right-click pop-up menu or the File menu). From the New submenu, you can create a new folder (subdirectory) or new information objects that KDE can use to access your system resources.

Browsing with the File Manager

The KDE file manager windows resemble Web browser windows, and in fact, they can be used to access any Web page. If you browse in your local file system to a directory that contains an `index.html` file, that file will be displayed rather than icons for the contents of the directory.

TIP   Deselect View ➤ HTML View to see the files in a directory instead of the HTML index of the directory.

While viewing any directory, you can click in the location field and enter a full Web URL, such as

`http://www.sybex.com`

or

`ftp://ftp.kde.org`

The appropriate Internet page will be downloaded and displayed in your file manager window.

NOTE   You can configure the browser features of the file manager windows to use a proxy server on your network. Choose Options ➤ Configure Browser within any open file manager window.

Using the Disk Navigator

File manager windows provide a great way to graphically manage files, but if you want to immediately launch a program or access a data file, file manager windows can seem a little slow. The Disk Navigator enables you to access any part of your file system using the KDE main menu, without ever opening a file manager window.

Of course, you can't drag and drop files between directories, or open Properties windows for items via the Disk Navigator menus, but for launching an application or opening a data file, the Disk Navigator is the perfect tool.

To access the Disk Navigator, choose Disk Navigator on the main menu. The Disk Navigator submenu has several sections:

- The Shared option lists file system resources that all users access, such as the root of the file system and the CD-ROM.

- The Personal option lists file system resources that you want to define yourself for easy access. You can add to this list by placing KDE Link files (see the next section) in the `.kde/share/apps/kdisknav` directory of your home directory.

- The Recent option lists directories that you have viewed recently and lists applications or data files that you have launched recently.

- The Home option opens a file manager window with your home directory, just like choosing Home Directory on the main menu.

- The Options option opens an Options dialog box where you can configure the operation of the Disk Navigator tools.

The usefulness of the Recent and Personal options should be obvious: you can access your most-visited subdirectories or programs using the Disk Navigator as a sort of bookmark to get there in just a couple of clicks.

To see how the Shared option can be used to view your file system, choose Disk Navigator ➤ Root/ on the main menu and spend a moment browsing through the submenus that appear, as illustrated in Figure 11.9.

- Whenever you move to a directory, the contents of that directory are displayed.

- Whenever you click a file, KDE attempts to launch or open that file.

FIGURE 11.9:

You can use the Disk Navigator submenus to browse through your entire file system without the need to open a file manager window.

For example, browse in the Disk Navigator menus to Root/≻opt/≻kde/
≻bin/≻kab. When you click kab, the KDE Address Book is launched.

Creating KDE Link Files

You've read a lot by now about KDE Link files. These files are small informational text files that describe a system resource so that KDE can use it.

For example, a KDE file that refers to your CD-ROM drive is part of the default KDE Desktop. This KDE Link file (and the icon associated with it) enables you to access the file system on your CD-ROM drive without ever using a command line. You can mount, unmount, and view the CD-ROM contents directly from the Desktop.

Fortunately, KDE lets you create these KDE Link files graphically.

If you want to see what a KDE Link file really looks like, go to the directory /opt/kde/share/applnk and open one of the files ending in .kdelnk in your text editor.

To create a new KDE Link file that refers to a graphical application such as the graphics viewer xv, follow these steps:

1. Open a file manager window to view your home directory.

2. Choose File ➤ New ➤ Application. A Naming dialog box appears.

3. Change the first part of the name shown to match your application, but don't change the .kdelnk file extension.

4. Choose OK. A new icon appears in your home directory with the name you gave the new application: KDE Link.

5. Right-click the new application icon and choose Properties. A Properties dialog box appears.

6. Choose the Execute tab (see Figure 11.10).

FIGURE 11.10:

On the Execute tab of the Properties dialog box of a KDE Link file, you define how to launch an application.

7. In the Execute field of the Execute tab, enter the command used to launch the program that you want to access using this KDE Link file.

TIP

You can store additional information about this application as well. For example, click the default icon to select a new icon, or choose the Application tab to define which data types this application can work with.

8. Click OK to close the Properties dialog box.

You've now created a KDE Link file. You can use this link to extend the KDE menus, add icons to your Desktop, auto-start applications, and add icons to your KDE Panel. The next section, "Configuring KDE," describes how to complete some of these tasks with a KDE Link file.

Configuring KDE

You've already seen many of the KDE configuration options as you've learned about the kdm graphical login program and some of the windowing options provided by KDE. These and many other settings can be configured using the KDE Control Center. Some of the most useful configuration options are described in this section.

Using the KDE Control Center

To start the KDE Control Center, choose KDE Control Center from the main menu or click the Control Center icon on the default Panel. The Control Center opens with a list of areas on the left side of the window. You can click any of these areas to open a list of configuration topics. When you click a topic, the right half of the screen changes to display those configuration options.

TIP   The items in the Control Center match the Settings submenus on the main menu. Depending on how much configuration you want to do, using the Control Center can be more convenient.

NOTE   Choosing Apply or OK in the Control Center activates your configuration changes, but doesn't close the Control Center window. To do that, choose File ➢ Exit or click the close button on the title bar.

Several dozen configuration options are included in the Control Center. The sections that follow describe how to work with a few of the most useful options for the average KDE user.

Changing the Look and Feel of KDE

Many of the Control Center pages are used to define the appearance and interface options of KDE. You've already seen a few of these, such as the Login Manager configuration, in previous sections of this chapter.

The most interesting interface configuration options are provided in the Applications and Desktop sections.

Under Applications, choose the Panel item to update how the Panel and Taskbar are arranged. From the four tabs in this section you can configure items such as the following:

- the screen location of the Panel and Taskbar

- the size of the Panel icons

- the arrangement of menu items on the main menu

- an auto-hide feature for the Panel and Taskbar

- the names and number of virtual desktops

You can use several of the Desktop section items to specify how your Desktop and background appear.

The Background tab, shown in Figure 11.11, enables you to define a background color and wallpaper, much as you can for the kdm login manager. Over 100 wallpaper graphics are included with KDE. Each Desktop can have a separate wallpaper and background color scheme.

On the Colors and Fonts tabs, you define the appearance of all the windows that KDE opens. Choosing a color scheme using the Colors tab (see Figure 11.12) is similar to choosing a color scheme in Microsoft Windows. In KDE, however, you can easily create additional color schemes or modify each window component (called a widget) individually.

FIGURE 11.11:

The Background tab of the Desktop section enables you to define background colors and wallpaper for each Desktop.

FIGURE 11.12:

The Colors tab defines a color scheme for all KDE windows.

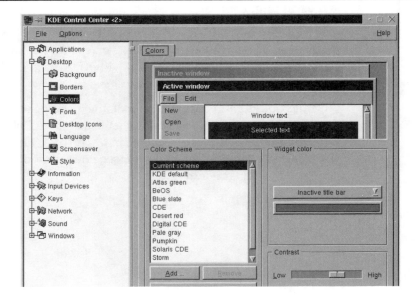

On the Screensaver tab (see Figure 11.13), you define a screen saver program that KDE will use when your system is inactive for a few minutes. KDE includes several dozen screen saver applications to choose from. Each one can be precisely configured by choosing the Setup button.

FIGURE 11.13:

Use the Screensaver tab to define and configure one of the KDE screensaver programs for use on your system.

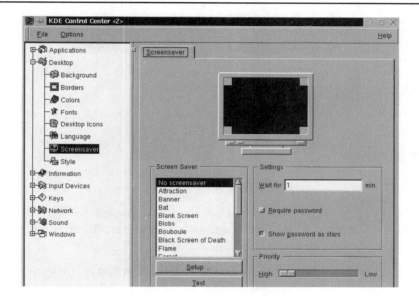

> **TIP**
>
> KDE also includes a Lock Screen option that requires your Linux password to restore the screen. To use this option when you step away from your computer, choose Lock Screen from the main menu, or click the small X icon on the Panel.

Many additional interface settings can be configured using the dialog boxes in the Windows section of the Control Center. These options are more advanced and will be of interest to only a few users. They include these settings:

- Altering how you use the keyboard to switch between open windows.

- Setting the window focus policy to match another preferred system (such as CDE).

- Changing the buttons included on the title bar of each KDE window.

- Changing the graphics image or color shading of the title bars.

- Setting performance options for resizing and moving windows.

Choosing Hardware Settings

Much of your Linux system cannot be accessed using the KDE Control Center. However, there are a few hardware settings related to your graphical system that can be configured using the Control Center.

In the Input Devices section, you can set up information about your keyboard and mouse.

- The Mouse tab defines whether you're using your mouse with your right or left hand, and how quickly you like to have the mouse move around the screen.

- The Keyboard tab defines the auto-repeat speed and volume of the keyboard clicking (this depends on your hardware itself, of course).

The International Keyboard tab lets you define which keyboard you are using among several dozen available and supported by the X Windows system, including languages such as Russian and Hebrew.

By selecting several keyboards that you might be working with (using the Add button on the General tab) you can switch between keyboard definitions as you work, making it easy to access different keys within various applications.

The keystrokes used to switch between keyboard definitions as you're working are shown on the General tab (see Figure 11.14). The normal mode of operation for the International Keyboard Handling feature is to display a small window on your Desktop or as part of the Panel. This window uses a two-character code to indicate the active keyboard. You can click this window or use the keyboard combination to switch to the alternate keyboards that you have selected for your system.

FIGURE 11.14:

The General tab of the International Keyboard dialog box defines which keyboards are accessible for KDE, using the keyboard switches shown.

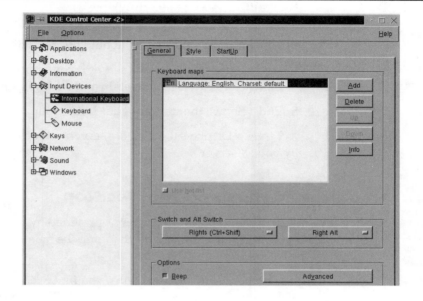

Gathering System Information

The Information section of the Control Center provides detailed statistics and technical information about your Linux system. The information in these tabs cannot be changed; it is provided for your review to learn about your system settings and status. The available tabs are

Devices   Lists the device types that Linux recognizes (not individual devices, however).

DMA-Channels   Lists the DMA memory access channels active on your system.

Interrupts   Shows the interrupts defined on your system (not all of them, however, so this may be of marginal value at this point).

IO-Ports   Shows the IO port addresses used on your system.

Memory   Displays a live memory usage screen, with second-by-second updates of your virtual and actual system memory usage.

PCI   Provides a report of all PCI device status.

Processor   Displays an information screen about your processor, with processor type, speed, and other information.

SCSI   Lists any information about your SCSI devices.

Samba Status   If the Samba server is configured and running, shows all users who are currently logged in and which Linux shares they are using.

Sound   Shows the status of your Linux sound system.

X-Server   Displays the version, server, color depth, and resolution used by your X server.

Updating Menus and the Desktop

In addition to the configuration options provided by the Control Center, you can update your KDE environment by changing the menus, the Desktop icons, and the Panel.

In order to update any of these items, you first need to create a KDE Link file to describe the item that you want to add to KDE. The section "Creating KDE Link Files" in this chapter described how to graphically create a KDE Link file.

Once you have a KDE Link file that represents a device or application, you can drag the icon for that file from the directory where you created it and drop it in several places to configure KDE:

- Drop the KDE Link file icon on the Panel to add the icon for that application or device to the Panel. (Right-click any Panel icon to rearrange or delete it from the Panel.)

- Drop the KDE Link file icon on the Autostart folder on your Desktop to make that application launch automatically each time to start KDE.

- Drop the KDE Link file icon on your KDE Desktop to have instant access to that device or application by clicking the icon at any time.

TIP   When you drop an icon on another folder, notice a small menu that allows you to copy, move, or link the file into the location. For KDE Link files, Copy is often the best choice so that you still have a copy of the file in the original location should you wish to place it somewhere else as well.

- Finally, you can drag and drop a KDE Link file to one of the directories that define the KDE menus. The application defined by the KDE Link file will then be part of the KDE menus.

  - If you're logged in as root, you can place a new KDE Link file in the directory /opt/kde/share/applnk to change the main KDE menu for all users.

  - If you're not logged in as root, drop the KDE Link file in the directory .kde/share/applnk to add it to a personal menu that will appear only for your user.

Using the KDE Utilities

KDE includes a number of standard utilities that you can use to view text and graphics, manage your projects, and administer your Linux system. This section describes just a few of the most popular utilities.

Viewing Text and Graphics

KDE includes a text editor, an image viewer, and an image-editing tool (similar to a paintbrush program). Launching these tools to edit a file or view a graphic is easy. When you're viewing the contents of a file manager window that contains a text file, just click the text file to open it within the KDE text editor (see Figure 11.15).

FIGURE 11.15:

KDE automatically opens the graphical text editor program whenever you click a text file icon in a file manager window.

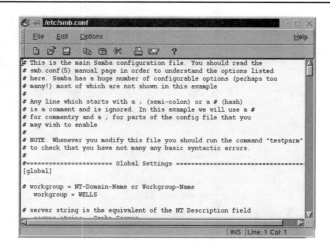

Similarly, you can view a graphic file by clicking its icon in any file manager window. If you want to use a different utility so you can edit the graphic instead of just viewing it, right-click the graphic file's icon and choose Open With.

When the Open With dialog box appears, enter the name of the program to use for editing the graphic file. Examples might be kpaint, xv, or gimp, depending on your preferred graphics tool.

Managing Your Time

Linux doesn't have a native copy of Microsoft Outlook or Project, but KDE does include a few tools to manage your time as you work.

KDE includes a time manager called KOrganizer, which includes an event calendar, prioritized task lists, scheduling, and so forth. You can access this tool by choosing Applications ➤ Organizer on the main menu.

Figure 11.16 contains the main KOrganizer screen. From this screen, you can move to different days, add to your task list, and schedule events based on different priorities.

FIGURE 11.16:

The KOrganizer program includes a calendar, task list, and various scheduling tools.

In addition to KOrganizer, KDE includes a time tracker, which enables you to start and stop a clock to track how much time you're spending on different projects that you work on. This tool is available by choosing Utilities ➤ Personal Time Tracker.

KDE also includes a simple Address Book utility. Use this program to record contact information and notes about friends or colleagues that you need to reach while working at your computer. The Address Book records several phone numbers, fax numbers, and numerous e-mail addresses for each person. To start the Address Book, choose Utilities ➤ Address Book.

Administering Your Linux System

KDE continues to add new system administration tools each month. Some of the most useful at this point allow you to manage your rpm packages, users and groups on your system, processes running on your system, and the System V initialization scripts of Linux.

These utilities are available either on the Utilities or System sections of the main menu.

You'll still need to work with some text configuration files for most Linux administration tasks, but using tools like KPackage makes it much easier to complete most tasks. To start KPackage, choose Utilities ➤ Kpackage. The main KPackage window appears and reads all the rpm package information for your system (see Figure 11.17).

FIGURE 11.17:

The main KPackage window lists all your installed rpm packages by category.

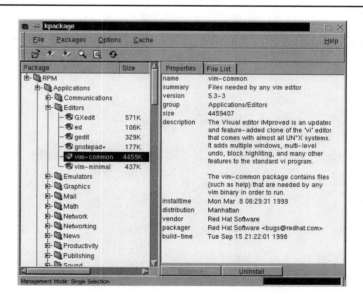

From this window, you can review installed packages, search for individual packages and files on your system, or install new rpm packages.

Looking Ahead

Now that you are more familiar with the variety of graphical Linux desktops, it's time to move on to more complex configurations of the X Windows environment.

The next chapter takes a look at how to go about configuring X Windows and the fvwm95 Window Manager to meet your personal needs and tastes. These tasks will include configuring the XFree86 server for special situations as well as configuring the entire fvwm95 interface from menu entries to icons to color schemes.

CHAPTER

TWELVE

12

Advanced X Windows Configuration

- The *XF86Config* File

- The X Windows Start-Up Sequence

- X Resources

As you have already seen in this part of the book, the X Windows environment provides a degree of flexibility and customizability not commonly found in many GUI-based operating systems. Of course, with this degree of flexibility comes some degree of complexity: to fully utilize the X Windows flexibility, you must use sometimes complex configuration methods.

This chapter will describe in detail the main components of X Windows and how they can be customized. It will start with the XF86Config file, which tells the X server how to behave. This file specifies everything from the type of video card and monitor in use (including the desired resolution and color depth) to the type of mouse and keyboard being used.

Once the X server is fully configured the way you like it, you will probably want to control how X Windows starts: what programs launch at start-up, what actions take place before X Windows loads, and how the Windows Manager gets launched. In addition, the X resources database provides a mechanism through which it is possible to control settings such as the colors and fonts used in windows and the behavior of windows in response to certain actions. These settings (and others) can be specified either globally or on a per-application basis.

The *XF86Config* File

The configuration of XFree86 is in the file XF86Config. This file usually can be found at /etc/XF86Config or /etc/X11/XF86Config, depending on your distribution of XFree86. Red Hat Linux 6 places the file in /etc/X11. With a fresh installation of XFree86, the configuration file can be found at /usr/X11R6/lib/ X11/XF86Config, but for ease of access, the file is usually put in one of the directories mentioned above instead of in this location.

If you don't know where your installation of XFree86 has placed this file, use the find command to find it:

```
# find / -name xf86config -print
```

The XF86Config file contains information pertinent to the operation of the X server, including keyboard definitions, mouse specifications, and monitor information. This file is generated by XFree86 configuration applications such as Xconfigurator and xf86config.

Sometimes, though, fine-tuning your X Windows environment can only be achieved by directly editing the XF86Config file with your favorite text editor. Refer back to Chapter 9, "Using Applications with GNOME," for an introduction to using GNOME's simple text editor.

The XF86Config file is broken down into seven main required sections:

- **Files**: This section specifies where XFree86 can find its supplementary files, such as fonts and the color table.

- **ServerFlags**: This section is used to enable and disable X server features, such as how to handle certain key sequences.

- **Keyboard**: This section specifies the keyboard protocol that controls how the key map is defined and other keyboard features, such as the repeat rate.

- **Pointer**: This section indicates the type of mouse being used, the device port occupied by the mouse, and the button behavior of the mouse.

- **Monitor**: This section defines the refresh rate and the resolution capabilities of your monitor.

- **Device**: These sections define available graphic devices (display adapters).

- **Screen**: These sections define the behavior of available X servers, such as the generic SVGA server, the monochrome server, and so on.

Files

The Files section is used to specify where certain critical files are located on your system. The following is a sample Files section without the comments:

> **NOTE**   In the XF86Config file, comments start with a hash mark (#) and continue to the end of the line. All the content contained in comments is ignored by XFree86.

```
Section "Files"

    RgbPath  "/usr/X11R6/lib/X11/rgb"

    FontPath "/usr/X11R6/lib/X11/fonts/misc/"
    FontPath "/usr/X11R6/lib/X11/fonts/75dpi/:unscaled"
    FontPath "/usr/X11R6/lib/X11/fonts/Type1/"
```

```
FontPath "/usr/X11R6/lib/X11/fonts/Speedo/"
FontPath "/usr/X11R6/lib/X11/fonts/75dpi/"

# ModulePath    "/usr/X11R6/lib/modules"

EndSection
```

There are several basic rules to note here that apply to the other six sections as well:

- Each section starts with a `Section` line.

- Each section ends with an `EndSection` line.

- On the `Section` line, the name of the section is specified in double quotes (in this case, `Section "Files"`).

There are three commonly used directives in this section, described in Table 12.1.

TABLE 12.1: Files Directives

Directive	Effect
RgbPath	This directive specifies the name of the RGB (red-green-blue) database without the `.txt` or `.db` extension. Generally, the default value can be left untouched unless you move or change the name of your RGB database (which is not a good idea, anyway, because several applications make use of the database and expect to find it in its normal location).
FontPath	This directive is used as many times as needed to specify where X Windows can find the installed X fonts on your system. Both scalable fonts and bitmap fonts can be indicated (the bitmap fonts, which can't be scaled, have `:unscaled` appended to the end of the directory). If you add new font directories to your system, you should add a `FontPath` directive for them here.
ModulePath	This directive is used on operating systems, like Linux, that support dynamically loaded modules. This directive indicates the path to look in for modules. With most versions of XFree86, this directive won't appear or will be commented out as in our example. The default path for modules is `/usr/X11R6/lib/modules`, and you only need to use this directive if you need to change this value.

ServerFlags

The `ServerFlags` section allows you to enable and disable some features of your X server. An example `ServerFlags` section, without comments, looks as follows:

```
Section "ServerFlags"

#  NoTrapSignals

#  DontZap

#  DontZoom

#  DisableVidModeExtension

#  AllowNonLocalXvidtune

#  DisableModInDev

#  AllowNonLocalModInDev

EndSection
```

Uncomment any of these directives that you want to activate; leave them commented (the usual default state) if you don't want them activated.

The directives in this example have the effects described in Table 12.2.

TABLE 12.2: ServerFlags Directives

Directive	Effect
NoTrapSignals	This directive is used for debugging purposes. When a signal indicating an error state is received, the server performs a core dump that dumps the contents of its section of memory to a file on the disk. This can cause instability in your system but is invaluable when debugging problems, particularly with beta and test versions of different X servers. You are best advised to leave this directive commented.
DontZap	Normally, the key combination Ctrl+Alt+Backspace causes X Windows to abort and returns you to the console. With this directive enabled, Ctrl+Alt+Backspace will be ignored and the key combination will be passed on to the current application for processing. You should uncomment this line only in those rare instances when you are running an application that needs to use this key combination to function properly.

Continued on next page

TABLE 12.2 CONTINUED: ServerFlags Directives

Directive	Effect
DontZoom	Normally, the key combination Ctrl+Alt+Keypad Plus cycles through available configured screen resolutions for your X server, increasing the resolution each time. Ctrl+Alt+Keypad Minus is similarly used to decrease the resolution. If these key combinations are needed for other purposes by an application, uncomment this line to have X Windows ignore these key combinations and pass them on to your application.
DisableVidModeExtension	This directive prevents tuning of your video display with the xvidtune client. (Xvidtune isn't discussed in this book; documentation for this program can be found by typing the command **man xvidtune** in an open **xterm** window.) There is no need to uncomment this entry, and you can leave it commented out by default.
AllowNonLocalXvidtune	Related to the previous directive, this directive allows nonlocal (in other words, out on the network somewhere) xvidtune clients to access your X Windows system. For security reasons, it is best to leave this directive disabled.
DisableModInDev	By enabling this directive, it becomes impossible to change keyboard and mouse settings dynamically while X Windows is running.
AllowNonLocalModInDev	Uncommenting this directive allows nonlocal computers to alter your keyboard and mouse settings. It is unwise to enable this directive unless you need to.

Keyboard

As you might expect, the Keyboard section specifies information pertinent to the functioning of your keyboard, including the keyboard type and protocol. A sample Keyboard section looks like this:

```
Section "Keyboard"

    Protocol "Standard"

    AutoRepeat    500 5

#   ServerNumLock

#   Xleds         1 2 3
```

```
#    LeftAlt         Meta
#    RightAlt        ModeShift
#    RightCtl        Compose
#    ScrollLock      ModeLock

     XkbDisable

#    XkbModel "pc102"
#    XkbModel "microsoft"

#    XkbLayout       "de"

#    XkbOptions      "ctrl:swapcaps"

#    XkbModel "pc101"
#    XkbLayout       "us"
#    XkbOptions      ""

     XkbKeymap       "xfree86(us)"

EndSection
```

This looks like a complicated section, but, as Table 12.3 describes, it is actually quite simple.

TABLE 12.3: Keyboard Directives

Directive	Effect
Protocol	There is only one valid value for this directive in Red Hat Linux 6: **Standard**. Make sure this directive is uncommented with the value assigned.
AutoRepeat	This directive is used to specify how long to wait while a key is pressed down before auto-repeat should start and how often the key should be repeated. All values are in milliseconds. In the previous example, **AutoRepeat 500 5** indicates that auto-repeat should start after a key has been held down for 500 milliseconds (half of a second) and then the key should repeat every 5 milliseconds.
ServerNumLock	Generally, this directive can remain commented out. It specifies that the server and not the application should handle processing of the NumLock key. This directive is only necessary for some older X Windows applications that require it. In a standard Linux distribution, you shouldn't need it.

Continued on next page

TABLE 12.3 CONTINUED: Keyboard Directives

Directive	Effect
Xleds	This directive specifies which keyboard LEDs can be controlled by the user using the **xset** command. It is probably a good idea to leave this line commented out, which is the default.
LeftAlt, RightAlt, RightCtl, and ScrollLock	X Windows originally ran on Unix workstations that had keyboards distinctly different from the standard PC keyboard. These keyboards included special keys such as Meta, ModeShift, Compose, and ModeLock. If you find that you need these keys to use your applications (which is not likely with most standard applications), then uncomment these directives.
XkbDisable	If this line is uncommented, then an extension to X Windows called XKB is disabled. When XKB is enabled (the directive is commented out), XKB determines the keyboard mapping using a series of directives, listed below. When XKB is disabled, the keyboard mapping used by the console is passed on to the X server. Generally, if you are using a non-English keyboard, you may get better recognition of some of your special keys if you use XKB. Most users using a standard U.S. English keyboard will probably find that they can disable XKB using this directive and everything will work fine.
•XkbModel	This directive is used when XKB is enabled to specify the keyboard model.
•XkbLayout	This directive is used when XKB is enabled to specify which keyboard layout to use.
•XkbOptions	This directive can be used when XKB is enabled to swap the position of your Caps-Lock and Ctrl keys. To do this, set the directive to the value **ctrl:swapcaps**.
•XkbKeymap	This directive is used when XKB is enabled to load a keyboard mapping definition.

Pointer

The Pointer section deals with mouse-related configuration. It is in the Pointer section that you set such information as the type of mouse you have, the port the mouse is connected to, and the behavior associated with different mouse buttons.

```
Section "Pointer"

    Protocol    "PS/2"
    Device      "/dev/psaux"

#   BaudRate    9600
#   SampleRate  150
```

```
        Emulate3Buttons
        Emulate3Timeout      50

    #   ChordMiddle

    EndSection
```

Let's take these entries line by line in Table 12.4.

TABLE 12.4: Pointer Directives

Directive	Effect
Protocol	This directive specifies the type of mouse you are using. Possible values include BusMouse for bus mice, PS/2 for PS/2-type mice, and a series of valid serial mice: GlidePoint, IntelliMouse, Logitech, Microsoft, MMHittab, MMSeries, MouseMan, MouseSystems, and ThinkingMouse. Generally, the two most common types of mice on today's PCs are PS/2 and Microsoft (the standard driver for serial mice).
Device	This directive is used to specify which device port your mouse is connected to. If you configured your mouse correctly when you installed your distribution, the device /dev/mouse will point to your mouse and you can use this. If /dev/mouse isn't configured to point to your mouse, specify /dev/psaux for the PS/2 mouse port, /dev/ttyS0 for COM1 in DOS and Windows, and /dev/ttyS1 for COM2 in DOS and Windows.
BaudRate	This directive is used for only a few Logitech-brand mice. Check your mouse's documentation.
SampleRate	This directive is used for only a few Logitech-brand mice. Check your mouse's documentation.
Emulate3Buttons	This directive should be used for two-button Microsoft-compatible mice. When uncommented, clicking the left and right mouse buttons at the same time will emulate the middle mouse button on a three-button mouse. Because X Windows relies on the presence of three mouse buttons, it is a good idea to enable this for a two-button Microsoft-compatible mouse.
Emulate3Timeout	This directive is used to specify how close in time the two mouse buttons must be clicked to be considered a simultaneous click; this value is only relevant when Emulate3Buttons is enabled. By default, the time is set to 50ms. If you find it hard to get the mouse buttons to click together, lengthen the time by assigning a higher value. This directive assumes the units are in milliseconds, and you should specify only the numeric value, not the units. In other words, Emulate3Timeout 100 is valid while Emulate3Timeout 100 ms is not.
ChordMiddle	This directive is used to enable the middle button on some three-button Logitech mice. If you have a Logitech mouse and your middle button is not working, try enabling this directive.

Monitor

So far, the configuration directives you have seen have mostly been self-explanatory and not difficult to use. When it comes to configuring video hardware such as monitors, things get more complicated. Let's consider the Monitor section from the sample configuration:

```
Section "Monitor"

Identifier   "monitor"
VendorName   "LG"
ModelName    "StudioWorks"

HorizSync    30-70
VertRefresh  50-160

# 640x400 @ 70 Hz, 31.5 kHz hsync
Modeline "640x400"     25.175 640  664  760   800    400  409  411  450
# 640x480 @ 60 Hz, 31.5 kHz hsync
Modeline "640x480"     25.175 640  664  760   800    480  491  493  525
# 800x600 @ 56 Hz, 35.15 kHz hsync
ModeLine "800x600"       36    800  824  896  1024    600  601  603  625
# 1024x768 @ 87 Hz interlaced, 35.5 kHz hsync
Modeline "1024x768"     44.9  1024 1048 1208 1264    768  776  784  817
➥Interlace

# 640x400 @ 85 Hz, 37.86 kHz hsync
Modeline "640x400"      31.5   640  672  736   832    400  401  404  445
➥-HSync +VSync
# 640x480 @ 72 Hz, 36.5 kHz hsync
Modeline "640x480"      31.5   640  680  720   864    480  488  491  521
# 640x480 @ 75 Hz, 37.50 kHz hsync
ModeLine  "640x480"     31.5   640  656  720   840    480  481  484  500
➥-HSync -VSync
# 800x600 @ 60 Hz, 37.8 kHz hsync
Modeline "800x600"       40    800  840  968  1056    600  601  605  628
➥+hsync +vsync

# 640x480 @ 85 Hz, 43.27 kHz hsync
Modeline "640x400"       36    640  696  752   832    480  481  484  509
➥-HSync -VSync
# 1152x864 @ 89 Hz interlaced, 44 kHz hsync
```

```
ModeLine "1152x864"     65     1152 1168 1384 1480    864  865  875  985
➥Interlace

# 800x600 @ 72 Hz, 48 kHz hsync
Modeline "800x600"      50     800  856  976 1040     600  637  643  666
➥+hsync +vsync
# 1024x768 @ 60 Hz, 48.4 kHz hsync
Modeline "1024x768"     65     1024 1032 1176 1344    768  771  777  806
➥-hsync -vsync

# 640x480 @ 100 Hz, 531 kHz hsync
Modeline "640x480"      45.8   640  672  768  864     480  488  494  530
➥-HSync -VSync
# 1152x864 @ 60 Hz, 53.5 kHz hsync
Modeline  "1152x864"    89.9   1152 1216 1472 1680    864  868  876  892
➥-HSync -VSync
# 800x600 @ 85 Hz, 55.84 kHz hsync
Modeline  "800x600"     60.75  800  864  928 1088     600  616  621  657
➥-HSync -VSync

# 1024x768 @ 70 Hz, 56.5 kHz hsync
Modeline "1024x768"     75     1024 1048 1184 1328    768  771  777  806
➥-hsync -vsync
# 1280x1024 @ 87 Hz interlaced, 51 kHz hsync
➥Modeline "1280x1024"   80     1280 1296 1512 1568   1024 1025 1037 1165
Interlace

EndSection
```

Table 12.5 describes the various directives for the `Monitor` section.

TABLE 12.5: Monitor Directives

Directive	Explanation
Identifier	This directive identifies with a user-assigned name the specifications for the monitor; this is used in other parts of the **XF86Config** file to refer to the monitor.
VendorName	This directive identifies the vendor of the monitor being defined. This value has no effect on the operation of XFree86, so it is best to assign a meaningful value that will help you identify the definition at a later date.

Continued on next page

TABLE 12.5 CONTINUED: Monitor Directives

Directive	Explanation
ModelName	This directive identifies the model of the monitor being defined. This value has no effect on the operation of XFree86, so it is best to assign a meaningful value that will help you identify the definition at a later date.
HorizSync	This directive specifies the horizontal sync range in kHz for your monitor. You may either specify a range as shown in the example or provide discrete values in a list with values separated by commas. It is essential that you consult your monitor's documentation and provide the correct values for your monitor. If you enter the incorrect values here, you have the potential to destroy or damage your monitor.
VertRefresh	This directive specifies the vertical refresh rates in Hz supported by your monitor. You may either specify a range as shown in the example or provide discrete values in a list with values separated by commas. It is essential that you consult your monitor's documentation and provide the correct values for your monitor. If you enter the incorrect values here, you have the potential to destroy or damage your monitor.
ModeLine	This directive specifies possible modes for your monitor. Modes combine a resolution with a refresh, a dot clock, and timings to determine how to display to the monitor. Any incompatible modes found in the **XF86Config** file are deleted by the X server when it tries to load them. However, getting the information correct for these lines is difficult at best. Generally, it is best to let your XFree86 configuration software create these lines for you and not to alter them.

Device

The XF86Config file generally can contain multiple Device sections. The Device sections describe the video cards that can be used by the X server. Usually the server can fill in most of this information, but it is wise to provide it manually so that mistakes aren't made. Because this information includes some highly technical specifications about your video hardware, you should let your XFree86 configuration software handle this section unless you really need to make these changes yourself.

Let's look at an example Device section:

```
Section "Device"
    Identifier  "Generic VGA"
    VendorName  "Unknown"
    BoardName   "Unknown"
    Chipset     "generic"
```

```
#     VideoRam    256

#     Clocks      25.2 28.3

EndSection
```

Table 12.6 describes the basic directives used in the Device section.

TABLE 12.6: Device Directives

Directive	Effect
Identifier	As in the **Monitor** section, this directive provides a name that can be used elsewhere in the **XF86Config** file to identify the video card.
VendorName	This directive doesn't affect the operation of the X server but helps you identify the hardware later.
BoardName	This directive also doesn't affect operation but is an aid in identifying the device definition.
Chipset	This directive identifies your video chipset. If XFree86 doesn't support your hardware, then the **generic** chipset will be used.
VideoRam	This directive specifies the amount of video memory available, in kilobytes. If you don't provide this information, the server will attempt to ascertain it directly from the video card.
Clocks	This directive specifies the clock settings for your video hardware. Don't edit this line by hand, but rather let your configuration software set it.
ClockChip	This directive specifies the clock chip being used by your video hardware, if it has one. If it does, there is no need to specify a **Clocks** line, since the clock chip will provide all the information.

Screen

The Screen section is used to bring together the information contained in your Monitor and Device sections. You can have multiple Screen sections.

The following is an example Screen section:

```
Section "Screen"
    Driver   "ACCEL"
    Device   "VideoCard"
    Monitor  "monitor"
```

```
    Subsection "Display"
        Depth       24
        Modes       "1024x768"
        ViewPort    0 0
    EndSubsection
    Subsection "Display"
        Depth       32
        Modes       "800x600"
        ViewPort    0 0
    EndSubsection
EndSection
```

The Screen section connects a chosen X server with a device and a monitor and then defines the accessible display modes (combinations of resolution and color depth). Table 12.7 describes the four main directives used in the Screen section:

TABLE 12.7: Screen Directives

Directive	Effect
Driver	This directive specifies one of four available drivers: SVGA, VGA2 (for generic VGA), MONO (for the monochrome X server), or ACCEL (for all the card-specific accelerated X servers).
Device	This directive specifies the name of a Device identifier.
Monitor	This directive specifies the name of a Monitor identifier.
DefaultColorDepth	This directive specifies the color depth used when a Depth directive in the Display section is not specified.

Display

In addition to these directives, a subsection called Display is also used in the Screen section. You can use multiple Display subsections to specify available video modes.

Let's analyze the first subsection from the previous example:

```
    Subsection "Display"
        Depth       24
        Modes       "1024x768"
```

```
        ViewPort 0 0
    EndSubsection
```

This Display subsection specifies three directives, as described in Table 12.8.

TABLE 12.8: Display Subsection Directives

Directive	Effect
Depth	This directive specifies the color depth of the display in the number of bits per pixel. For instance, 8-bit allows 256 colors, 16-bit allows 65,536, and 24-bit allows 16.7 million colors.
Modes	This directive specifies the resolution of the display. Common resolutions are 1024x768, 800x600, and 640x480.
ViewPort	This directive specifies the size of a possible virtual desktop. For instance, your 640x480 screen may be a window into a larger 1024x768 virtual display. As your mouse reaches the edge of the screen, the display will scroll until the edge of the virtual display. The ViewPort directive specifies the horizontal and vertical dimensions of the vertical desktop in pixels, but the values are separated by a space rather than by an x. The entry here, ViewPort 0 0, indicates that there is no virtual desktop.

The X Windows Start-Up Sequence

In addition to configuring your XFree86 server to provide the optimal display quality, you may want to configure the way in which your X Windows environment starts up. The two main files that allow each user to control their X Windows start-up sequence are .xinitrc and .Xclients. Both of these files sit in the user's home directory. They override system default files, which in Red Hat Linux 6 are /etc/X11/xinit/xinitrc and /etc/X11/xinit/Xclients.

The *.xinitrc* File

Xinit is a special program that is used to start the X server and an initial client program, usually a window manager. By default, startx first checks for the existence of the .xinitrc file in the user's home directory and runs xinit based on this file. If the user's .xinitrc file is not found, the system-wide xinitrc file

(/etc/X11/xinit/xinitrc in Red Hat Linux 6) is used by xinit. If neither of these is found, xinit will open a single xterm window after launching the X server.

The xinitrc or .xinitrc file is an executable shell script. You will learn about shells in Chapter 16, "Understanding the Shell." Accordingly, this chapter doesn't go into the details of the shell or shell scripts here; rather, it will quickly look at the default xinitrc file from a pre-release version of Red Hat Linux 6 to see what it does. (The lines are numbered to help make the discussion easier. The line numbers are not part of the actual file.)

```
 1:  #!/bin/sh
 2:  # (c) 1999 Red Hat Software, Inc.

 3:  userresources=$HOME/.Xresources
 4:  usermodmap=$HOME/.Xmodmap
 5:  sysresources=/usr/X11R6/lib/X11/xinit/.Xresources
 6:  sysmodmap=/usr/X11R6/lib/X11/xinit/.Xmodmap

 7:  # merge in defaults and keymaps

 8:  if [ -f $sysresources ]; then
 9:     xrdb -merge $sysresources
10:  fi

11:  if [ -f $sysmodmap ]; then
12:     xmodmap $sysmodmap
13:  fi

14:  if [ -f $userresources ]; then
15:     xrdb -merge $userresources
16:  fi

17:  if [ -f $usermodmap ]; then
18:     xmodmap $usermodmap
19:  fi

20:  if [ -z "$BROWSER" ] ; then
21:    # we need to find a browser on this system
22:    BROWSER=`which netscape`
23:    if [ -z "$BROWSER" ] || [ ! -e "$BROWSER" ] ; then
24:         # not found yet
25:         BROWSER=
26:    fi
27:  fi
```

```
28:  if [ -z "$BROWSER" ] ; then
29:   # we need to find a browser on this system
30:   BROWSER=`which lynx`
31:   if [ -z "$BROWSER" ] || [ ! -e "$BROWSER" ] ; then
32:        # not found yet
33:        BROWSER=
34:   else
35:        BROWSER="xterm -font 9x15 -e lynx"
36:   fi
37:  fi
38:  export BROWSER

39:  # The user may have their own clients they want to run.  If they
don't,
40:  # fall back to system defaults.

41:  if [ -f $HOME/.Xclients ]; then
42:   exec $HOME/.Xclients
43:  elif [ -f /etc/X11/xinit/Xclients ]; then
44:   exec /etc/X11/xinit/Xclients
45:  else
46:   # failsafe settings.  Although we should never get here
47:   # (we provide fallbacks in Xclients as well) it can't hurt.
48:   xclock -geometry 100x100-5+5 &
49:   xterm -geometry 80x50-50+150 &
50:   if [ -f /usr/bin/netscape -a -f /usr/doc/HTML/index.html ]; then
51:        netscape /usr/doc/HTML/index.html &
52:   fi
53:   if [ -f /usr/X11R6/bin/fvwm ]; then
54:        exec fvwm
55:   else
56:        exec twm
57:   fi
58:  fi
```

The following steps take place:

1. Lines 3 to 6: The locations of files needed throughout the script are set.

2. Lines 8 to 10: If a global Xresources file exists, apply it. (See the next section for a discussion of X resources.)

3. Lines 11 to 13: If a global key map file exists, apply the rules in the file.

4. Lines 14 to 16: If the user has a .Xresources file, apply it.

5. Lines 17 to 19: If the user has a keyboard map file, apply it.

6. Lines 20 to 27: These lines determine whether a Web browser exists on the system for later use in the script by checking for the existence of Netscape's browser.

7. Lines 28 to 37: If Netscape is not found, then check whether Lynx exists (Lynx is another Unix Web browser, discussed in Chapter 23, "Using the World Wide Web") and make it the default Web browser.

8. Lines 41 to 58: This is where you actually start running the first clients after the X server starts. First, the script checks whether the user has a .Xclients file. If this file exists, this file is executed to launch any clients specified in the file. If this file doesn't exist, then the script checks for the existence of the global Xclients file and, if it exists, executes it. Finally, if neither file exists, some default programs are launched, including xclock, two xterm windows, a Web browser, and, if available, either the fvwm or twm window manager.

The .Xclients File

As you noticed in the discussion of the xinitrc file, the user can override the global Xclients file with a .Xclients file in their home directory. In either case, in the Red Hat environment, xinit ends up calling one of these files to launch the initial clients after the X server has started.

Like xinitrc, this file is a shell script and follows all the pertinent rules for shell scripts. To understand the types of functions that Xclients can be used for, this section will look at the default Xclients file that shipped with a pre-release verion of Red Hat Linux 6 (line numbers have again been added):

```
1:  #!/bin/bash
2:  # (c) 1999 Red Hat Software, Inc.

3:  # by default, we run GNOME.
4:  GSESSION=`which gnome-session`
5:  if [ -f "$GSESSION" ]; then
6:  exec $GSESSION
7:  fi

8:  # if GNOME isn't installed, try KDE.
```

```
9:   STARTKDE=`which startkde`
10:  if [ -f "$STARTKDE" ]; then
11:  exec $STARTKDE
12:  fi

13:  # Last, try AnotherLevel

14:  # these files are left sitting around by TheNextLevel.
15:  rm -f $HOME/Xrootenv
16:  rm -f /tmp/fvwmrc* 2>/dev/null

17:  # First thing - check the user preferences
18:  if [ -f $HOME/.wm_style ] ; then
19:  WMSTYLE=`cat $HOME/.wm_style`
20:  case "$WMSTYLE" in
21:  Afterstep | AfterStep)
22:  exec /usr/X11R6/bin/RunWM –AfterStep
23:  ;;
24:  WindowMaker | Windowmaker | WMaker |  wmaker)
25:  exec /usr/X11R6/bin/RunWM –WindowMaker
26:  ;;
27:  Fvwm95 | fvwm95)
28:  exec /usr/X11R6/bin/RunWM –Fvwm95
29:  ;;
30:  Mwm | MWM | Lesstif)
31:  exec /usr/X11R6/bin/RunWM –FvwmMWM
32:  ;;
33:  esac
34:  fi

35:  # Argh! Nothing good is isntalled. Fall back to fvwm2 (win95-
style) or twm
36:  /usr/X11R6/bin/RunWM –Fvwm95 || {
37:  # gosh, neither fvwm95 nor fvwm2 is available;
38:  # fall back to failsafe settings
39:  xclock -geometry 100x100-5+5 &
40:  xterm -geometry 80x50-50+150 &
41:  if [ -f /usr/bin/netscape -a -f /usr/doc/HTML/index.html ]; then
42:  netscape /usr/doc/HTML/index.html &
43:  fi
44:  if [ -f /usr/X11R6/bin/fvwm ]; then
45:  exec fvwm
```

```
46:  else
47:  exec twm
48:  fi
49:  }
```

Let's break down the steps of this file as with `xinitrc`:

1. Lines 3 to 7: Check if GNOME is available and if it is, launch it and exit the script.

2. Lines 8 to 12: Check if KDE is available and if it is, launch it and exit the script.

3. Lines 15 to 16: Perform some cleanup by removing temporary files that may have been left behind the last time X Windows was run.

4. Lines 17 to 34: Check for a style for the AnotherLevel window manager and launch AnotherLevel with that style and exit the script.

5. Lines 35 to 49: Attempt to launch AnotherLevel with the Fvwm95 style. If that fails, launch `xclock`, `xterm`, and Netscape and then attempt to launch fvwm if it exists. If it doesn't exist, launch twm instead.

If you want to add your own clients to be run every time X Windows is started, you can copy the global `Xclients` file to your own `.Xclients` file in your home directory (Chapter 14, "Working with Files," describes file copying) and then edit it. The key to this process is to add the commands for the programs you want to run before the sections where the different window managers might be launched. The reason for this is that the **exec** keyword used to launch the different window managers causes the script to stop running as soon as the window manager is launched.

X Resources

The X resources database provides applications with preferences information that controls such attributes as colors and fonts, among others. X resources can be used by most X Windows applications to control almost every aspect of behavior that is controlled by command-line flags. With the X resources database, you can specify more suitable defaults than those that are standard for the application.

How X Resources Work

In order for this all to work, application-related information needs to be categorized so that only the appropriate applications are affected by X resources entries. This is done by grouping applications into classes. Most applications have their own classes; the documentation for the application specifies the class name. For example, `xload` belongs to the XLoad class and `xterm` belongs to the XTerm class. Where a number of similar applications exist, they often are part of the same class (`oclock` and `xclock` belong to the Clock class).

For each class, a standard set of resources allows you to specify such features as foreground and background colors (`foreground` and `background`), window size and placement (`geometry`), and default font (`font`). In addition, there are resource classes that group related resources. For instance, the Foreground class includes the `foreground` resource plus any additional foreground-related resources the application may have. Generally, though, you will not need to pay attention to individual resources and will only work with resource classes.

Setting X Resources with *.Xdefaults*

Setting X resources involves loading entries into the X resources database. These entries take the form:

```
<ApplicationClass>|<applicationName>*<ResourceClass>|<resourceName> :
<value>
```

In Linux man pages and other documentation, the vertical bar (or pipe character: |) is often used to represent "or." Therefore, in the example above, you can use either *<ApplicationClass>* or *<applicationName>* for the first entry, and *<ResourceClass>* or *<resourceName>* for the second entry.

These values are generally placed into the `.Xdefaults` file for user-specific resources. Let's look at a sample `.Xdefaults` file:

```
XTerm*background: Black
XTerm*foreground: Wheat
XTerm*cursorColor: Orchid
XTerm*reverseVideo: false
XTerm*scrollBar: true
XTerm*reverseWrap: true
XTerm*font: fixed
XTerm*fullCursor: true
```

```
XTerm*scrollTtyOutput: off
XTerm*scrollKey: on
XTerm*titleBar: false

xclock*Geometry: 100x100+100+100
xclock*Foreground: purple
xclock*Background: mauve
```

This .Xdefaults file sets X resources for both the XTerm class of applications and for the xclock application. For the XTerm class, you find resources setting the colors, the window properties (such as the presence of a scroll bar), and more. For xclock, you see color and geometry being set. The values being taken by these resources match the values that would have been provided to command-line flags such as -fg and -geometry where applicable.

Using the *xrdb* Command to Load X Resources

Normally, the .Xdefaults file is loaded when X Windows starts in the .xinitrc file. However, new values can be loaded into the database while X Windows is running by using the xrdb command. This is particularly useful for experimenting with values until you find just the combination you want.

In order to load the contents of .Xdefaults into the database, use the command

```
$ xrdb .Xdefaults
```

Looking Ahead

This chapter wrapped up the focus on X Windows. You will now move on to an area that is essential to gaining complete mastery of Linux: the command-line environment.

The next chapter describes the basics of Linux commands. It discusses how to work with files and directories on your disk drives. You will learn about the shell, which provides a powerful command-line environment in which to work, and you will learn how to use the Red Hat Control Panel to ease some of the more obscure aspects of Linux system configuration.

PART IV

Mastering the Essentials

CHAPTER

THIRTEEN

Introducing Linux Commands

- ■ What Is a Linux Command?

- ■ Executing a Linux Command

- ■ Common Linux Commands

In this chapter, you start your exploration of the Unix command-line environment. The command-line environment is where the heart and power of Linux lies. You have seen that X Windows provides quick and easy access to graphical applications that can make most users productive immediately. What is missing, though, is the ability to fully manipulate and work with your Linux system. This emerges when you begin to experiment with commands.

In this chapter, you'll learn to use some of the more common commands such as `ls`, `find`, and `grep`. Since these commands are found in most distributions, Unix users should immediately know what these and similar commands can do and what power they can provide in the hands of a knowledgeable user.

NOTE   For this chapter, you need to be using a Linux command line. You can get a command line in two ways: when your system boots, log in to one of the Linux virtual consoles, or, from X Windows, launch an **xterm** window.

What Is a Linux Command?

Before looking at specific commands, you need to understand exactly what is meant by the term "command."

Users coming from the DOS environment are probably familiar with the concept of commands that encompass core features of the operating system, such as `DIR`, `COPY`, and `ATTRIB`. These commands provided the basis on which more complicated actions could be built and from which sophisticated batch files could be written.

But in the DOS world, as in the world of many operating systems, the number of available commands is limited and generally static: users don't add new commands.

In the Unix world, and by extension in Linux, the concept is different. A command is any executable file. That is, a command consists of any file that is designed to be run, as opposed to files containing data or configuration information. This means that any executable file added to a system becomes a new command on the system.

Executing a Linux Command

From the discussions of launching X Windows applications, you probably already have a sense of how to execute a command. From the command prompt, simply type the name of a command:

    $ *command*

Or, if the command is not on your path, you type the complete path and name of the command, such as:

    $ **/usr/bin/***command*

NOTE   The concept of paths needs a little bit of explanation. Every user, when they log in, has a default path. The default path is a list of directories separated by colons. If a command is typed without its path indicated, then all the directories in the default path are checked, in order, for the file associated with the command. Chapter 16, "Understanding the Shell," provides complete details of how to set your path, and Chapter 14, "Working with Files," contains a full discussion of directories and paths.

TIP   To find out what your current path is, type the command **echo** **$PATH** at a command prompt and press the Enter key.

More complex ways of executing commands, including linking multiple commands together (called piping), are discussed in Chapter 16, "Understanding the Shell."

Common Linux Commands

The number of Linux commands that are available in a common Linux distribution like Red Hat Linux 6 is quite large. But on a day-to-day basis, even an advanced user will take advantage of only a small selection of these commands.

This section presents some of the most frequently used Linux commands. These commands cover a range of tasks, from moving around your directories to finding out what is running on your system to finding that file you thought was lost. The commands discussed in this section are:

- su
- pwd, cd, and ls
- more and less
- find and grep
- tar and gzip
- man

Su

The su command is one of the most basic, and is useful in many different tasks.

The su command is generally used to switch between different users. Consider an example: you are logged in as user1 and you need to switch to user2 to perform some work and then switch back to working as user1.

You could log out, log in as user2, do the work, log out again, and then log back in as user1, but that seems a little bit time-consuming. Alternately, you could log in as user1 in one virtual console and as user2 in another and switch back and forth. The problem with this is that you need to work with, and switch between, different screens.

A third option is to use the su command. If you are logged in as user1 and want to become user2, you simply type

```
$ su user2
```

and you are prompted for user2's password:

```
$ su user2
password:
```

When you finish working, enter the exit command to return to user1:

```
$ exit
```

Put together, a complete session should look like this:

```
[user1@localhost user1]$ su user2
Password:
[user2@localhost user1]$ exit
```

```
[user2@localhost user1]$ some commands
[user2@localhost user1]$ exit
exit
[user1@localhost user1]$
```

A common use of the su command is when you need to become the root user, called the superuser, to perform many administrative tasks, including creating and managing user accounts, performing network configuration, and configuring printers.

If you issue the su command with no username, you are prompted for the root password and, once this is provided, you are switched to working as the root user:

```
[user1@localhost user1]$ su
Password:
[root@localhost user1]#
```

If you are logged in as the root user, you can use su to become any user on the system without a password (hence the importance of keeping your root password safe from prying eyes). This is particularly useful for the system administrator who may need to become different users to debug problems but won't necessarily know other users' passwords. Note in the following example how using su to become user1 doesn't cause a prompt to display when the root user issues the command

```
[root@localhost /root]# su user1
[user1@localhost /root]$
```

The su command offers many other powerful features often used in advanced system administration tasks. You can learn about these from the su man page. See the section on the man command later in this chapter to learn how to read the su man page.

Pwd, Cd, and Ls

In Chapter 14, "Working with Files," you will be taking a deeper look at the pwd, cd, and ls commands. Put together, these commands provide the basic tools you need to work with your directories and files.

The pwd command (which stands for present working directory) is the most basic of the three commands. By typing the command and pressing Enter, you will be informed of which directory you are currently in:

```
$ pwd
/home/armand
```

In this case, the pwd command returns /home/armand as its answer. This tells you that you are in the home directory of the user armand (that's me).

The cd command does more than simply look at the current state of things: it actually changes the state. The cd command allows you to change your current directory to any accessible directory on the system.

For instance, consider the previous example where the current directory is /home/armand. Using the cd command, you could change to a subdirectory of the armand home directory called wordfiles:

```
$ cd wordfiles
$ pwd
/home/armand/wordfiles
```

Typing the pwd command after you change directories confirms that you ended up where you wanted to be.

Similarly, you could change to the system's temporary directory, /tmp, with the following command:

```
$ cd /tmp
$ pwd
/tmp
```

Finally, the ls command can be used to view the contents of the current directory. For instance, if you use the ls command to view the contents of the armand home directory, the result looks like this:

```
$ ls
2341ch11a.doc                   dead.letter     scmp-jpc.bak
DISKCOPY.COM                    foo             svgalib-1.2.11-4.i386.rpm
DRWEBDEM.IMG                    foo.html        test.txt
Xconfigurator-3.26-1.i386.rpm   mail            wabi
Xrootenv                        nsmail          xserver-wrapper-1.1-1.i386.rpm
armand                          scmp-jpc
```

Notice how the files or directory names are displayed in multiple columns and the width of the columns is determined by the width of the longest name.

In addition to listing the contents of the current directory, it is possible to list the contents of any accessible directory on the system. For instance, to list the contents of the directory /usr, you enter the command ls /usr:

```
$ ls /usr
X11        doc                 i486-linuxaout   lib       sbin
X11R6      dt                  ibase            libexec   share
X386       etc                 include          local     spool
bin        games               info             man       src
dict       i486-linux-libc5    interbase        openwin   tmp
```

As mentioned above, notice how the number and width of columns in the listing depends on the length of the largest name being displayed.

Of course, you probably are wondering what use a list like this really is. There is no information to tell you which names indicate files and which names indicate subdirectories, or what size the files are.

This information can be determined by using an extension of the ls command: ls -l. (To understand the command's structure, refer to the complete discussion of the ls command in Chapter 14, "Working with Files.") Used in the armand home directory, ls -l produces these results:

```
$ ls -l
total 1807
-rw-r--r--  1 armand    armand      52224 Apr 24 23:00 2341ch11a.doc
-rw-r--r--  1 armand    armand      24325 May  9 16:06 DISKCOPY.COM
-rw-r--r--  1 armand    armand    1474979 May  9 16:06 DRWEBDEM.IMG
-rw-r--r--  1 armand    armand      52313 Jan 21 18:04 Xconfigurator-
➥3.26-1.i386.rpm
-rw-r--r--  1 armand    armand        396 May 19 23:09 Xrootenv
drwx------  2 armand    armand       1024 May 17 09:55 armand
-rw-------  1 armand    armand      10572 May 18 22:29 dead.letter
-rw-------  1 armand    root         1455 Apr 24 21:38 foo
-rw-r--r--  1 armand    armand       2646 May  7 07:32 foo.html
drwx------  2 armand    armand       1024 Jun  4 07:12 mail
drwx------  2 armand    armand       1024 May 17 09:56 nsmail
-rw-r--r--  1 armand    armand       4288 May 14 22:17 scmp-jpc
-rw-r--r--  1 armand    armand       4289 May 14 22:12 scmp-jpc.bak
-rw-r--r--  1 armand    armand     195341 Mar 25 17:32 svgalib-1.2.11-
➥ 4.i386.rpm
-rw-rw-r--  1 armand    armand         94 May 17 11:44 test.txt
drwxr-xr-x  5 armand    armand       1024 May 19 23:07 wabi
-rw-r--r--  1 armand    armand       4493 Feb  4 15:31 xserver-wrapper-
➥ 1.1-1.i386.rpm
```

Note that each file contains reference information. The most important pieces of information are to the immediate left of each filename: the date of last modification of the file or directory and, in the case of files, the size of the file in bytes to the left of the date (so, for instance, a 1024 byte file is a 1KB file).

At the far left of each line, you will also notice that directories are indicated by the letter d while files are generally indicated with a simple hyphen (-). For instance, scmp-jpc is a file:

```
-rw-r-r-   1 armand   armand      4288 May 14 22:17 scmp-jpc
```

while mail is a directory:

```
drwx--   2 armand   armand      1024 Jun  4 07:12 mail
```

More and Less

The more and less commands are closely related and provide similar functionality, and the great irony is that less provides more capabilities than more.

The basic purpose of both commands is to display long files or lists of text one screen or window at a time, allowing users to page down through the text and, in some cases, move back up through the text. Both also provide capabilities to search the text being displayed.

This is useful in many instances, including when you want to look quickly at a long text file without having to open it in an editor like xedit and to view particularly long directory listings.

More

Let's start with the more command. The more command is fairly basic, allowing users to move forward a line or a screen at a time through a large body of text as well as search that text.

For instance, if you have a large text file called textfile, you could view it a page at a time with the following command:

```
$ more textfile
```

After pressing Enter, you see the first screen of the file with the text –More– displayed on the last line of the screen. Pressing the space bar jumps forward a full screen length, while pressing the Enter key moves forward one line at a time. When you reach the end of the body of text, you are returned to the command prompt.

To search forward through the file, enter a slash (/) followed by the word or phrase you want to search for and then press Enter. The display jumps forward to the first occurrence of the word or phrase being searched for and displays the occurrence near the top of the screen. You can repeat the same search by entering **n** after the first search, avoiding the need to type the same word or phrase repeatedly.

In addition to using more to view the contents of a file, you can pass along the results of another command to more using piping (a technique discussed in detail in Chapter 16, "Understanding the Shell").

For instance, on my system, using ls -l to view the contents of the /tmp directory produces results 237 lines long—many more lines than my largest xterm window can display. In order to be able to view the results of my ls -l command a window at a time, I need to pass the results to more:

```
$ ls -l /tmp | more
```

This command connects the ls -l command to the more command with a vertical pipe (usually Shift+\ on most English keyboards). The use of the pipe character is the source of the term "piping." The result of this piping is that more is used to display the results of the ls -l command, which means you can move down a screen or line at a time or search the results, just as you did earlier with the contents of a file.

> **NOTE**   Complete directions for using more are found in the more man page. Using a man page is discussed later in this chapter in the section on the man command.

Less

For all intents and purposes, the less command is a vastly improved version of the more command. In addition to the basic functions described previously (moving forward a screen or line at a time and searching), the following are some of the other actions that can be performed on a body of text:

- Jumping directly to a line
- Jumping directly to the beginning or end of the file
- Moving backward through a file
- Searching backward through a file

To jump directly to a line in a file, type the line number followed by the letter **g**. If you don't specify a line number and simply enter **g**, you will be jumped to the first line in the file. Entering the uppercase **G** works in much the same way except that without a line number specified, entering **G** jumps you to the last line of the body of text.

It is easy to move backward through a file using less. The up arrow moves up one line of text at a time and the down arrow moves down one line at a time. You can use Ctrl+B to jump backward one screen at a time.

Finally, entering a slash (/) followed by a word or phrase and then pressing Enter will search forward through the text being displayed, and entering a question mark (?) followed by a word or phrase and then pressing Enter will search backward through the text.

As with the more command, you can look at the less man page for details on all the features of the command. Using the man pages is discussed later in this chapter in the section on the man command.

Find and *Grep*

The find and grep commands are powerful tools for searching for files. This section only discusses their most basic uses because it would be easy to devote a full chapter to using these commands. If you want a full discussion of the commands, check their man pages once you learn to use the man command later in this chapter.

While both commands are used for searching, their purposes differ: find is used to search for files by any number of criteria, including name or date of creation. Grep is used to search the contents of files.

Find

If you used computers prior to buying this book, then you have probably faced the situation where you know you have created a file but can't remember where you put it. The find command is the Unix answer to this dilemma.

The command can be used to search for files by name, date of creation or modification, owner (usually the user who created the file), size of the file, and even type of the file. This section describes the most frequent use: searching for files by name.

The basic structure of the `find` command is

```
$ find starting-directory parameters actions
```

The starting directory specifies where to begin searching. For instance, specifying **/home** means only subdirectories of /home will be searched (in other words, only the user's home directories will be searched), while specifying **/** means everything will be searched.

The parameters are where you specify the criteria by which to search. In this case, you use the command -name *filename* to specify the file you are searching for.

The actions section indicates what action to take on found files. Generally, you will want to use the `-print` action, which indicates that the full name and path of the file should be displayed. Without this, the `find` command will perform the search indicated but will not display the results, which defeats the purpose.

Putting this together, if you want to search for all files named `foo` on your system, you could use the command

```
$ find / -name foo -print
```

In this case, the results look like this:

```
$ find / -name foo -print
/tmp/foo
/home/armand/foo
/home/tdanesh/foo
```

TIP   Notice that you attempted to search the entire system in the previous command. To do this effectively, you need to log in as the root user so that you can access all the directories on the system. If you don't, you will get `permission denied` errors every time `find` tries to search a directory for which you don't have permission.

It is also possible to search for partial filenames. For instance, if you know that the file you are looking for begins with `fo`, then you can use the expression `fo*` to indicate all files beginning with `fo` and ending with any combination:

```
$ find / -name 'fo*' -print
/tmp/foo
/var/lib/texmf/fonts
/usr/bin/font2c
/usr/bin/mh/folders
/usr/bin/mh/folder
/usr/bin/mh/forw
```

```
/usr/bin/formail
/usr/bin/fontexport
/usr/bin/fontimport
/usr/bin/fold
etc.
```

Notice the use of the single quotation marks around **fo***. When you use the *
character, it is important to place the single quote marks around the entire expression. Otherwise, find will give you an error:

```
$ find / -name fo* -print -mount
find: paths must precede expression
Usage: find [path...] [expression]
```

If the results being produced by the find command are too numerous to fit in one screen, you can use piping and the more command just like you did earlier with the ls -l command:

```
$ find / -name 'fo*' -print | more
```

Grep

Where find searched for a file by its name, type, or date, grep is used to look inside the contents of one or more files in an attempt to find the occurrence of a specific pattern of text inside the files.

Consider an example. You know that you created a text file that contains the word "radio" and stored it in your home directory. However, you have forgotten the name of the file and want to quickly check which files contain "radio." This is where grep comes in handy.

Assuming you are in your home directory, the following command searches for the word "radio" in each file in your home directory and produces results as follows:

```
$ grep radio *
ab.txt:This is a test of searching for the word radio.
pop.txt:On another radio station, he found that
```

Notice how the grep command returns one line for each occurrence of the word "radio" in a file. The name of the file is shown followed by a colon, which is followed by the complete text of the line where the word has appeared.

In general, the pattern for the grep command is

```
$ grep text-pattern file-list
```

The text pattern can be a simple word or phrase or a more complicated regular expression. (The use of regular expressions—a powerful method for searching for text patterns—with `grep` can be found in the `grep` man page.) The file list can take any form allowed by the shell. Consult Chapter 16, "Understanding the Shell," for a complete discussion of the types of expressions that constitute a file list.

Generally, though, you want to check either the contents of a single file, which takes the form

```
$ grep text-pattern file-name
```

or check the contents of all files in a directory using the command:

```
$ grep text-pattern *
```

where the * is an expression indicating that all files in the current directory should be searched.

In its simplest form, the text pattern is a single word or part of a word containing no spaces. If you want to search for a phrase, such as "is a test," you need to enclose the text pattern in quotation marks, as in the following example:

```
$ grep "is a test" *
ab.txt:This is a test of searching for the word radio.
```

Just as it is sometimes useful to pipe the results of a command through the `more` or `less` commands, the same is true for `grep`. Consider the situation where you want a listing of all files in the current directory with the modification date of May 12. You can find this information by piping `ls -l` through a `grep` command:

```
$ ls -l | grep "May 12"
-rw-r-r-    1 root     root        19197 May 12 21:17 rfbprotoheader.pdf
-rw-r-r-    1 root     root       110778 May 12 21:20 rfprotoA.zip
-rw-r-r-    1 root     root        17692 May 12 23:03 svnc-0.1.tar.gz
-rw-r-r-    1 root     root        25222 May 12 19:58 vnc-
➥ 3.3.1_javasrc.tgz
drwxr-xr-x 2 root     root         1024 May 12 21:49 vncjava
```

Tar and *Gzip*

Most users of other operating systems, including Windows 95 and the Mac OS, are familiar with the concept of *compressed archives*. A compressed archive is a single file that contains one or more files in a compressed form.

Compressed archives are often used to distribute software on the Internet, as is the case with the ZIP files common on the Internet. While Linux provides the unzip command to access the contents of ZIP archives, in the Unix world, tar archives are generally used to distribute software. These archives are then compressed using the gzip compression program, which compresses individual files.

Tar

The tar program was originally used to create system backups on tapes (or tape archives, hence "tar"). In its current form, it is widely used for creating archives of files for distribution.

Creating a tar archive is easy:

```
$ tar cvf tar-file-name file-list
```

This command creates a new archive specified by the filename tar-*file-name* (generally, tar files have a .tar extension) and then store all the files from the file list in this archive. The file list can follow any valid expression as outlined in Chapter 16, "Understanding the Shell." It is important to remember that this process copies the files into the archive so there is no danger that the original files will be deleted in the process.

Notice that the tar command is immediately followed by a series of options, in this case cvf. Each of these options is used to control different aspects of the behavior of the tar command:

- c specifies that you are creating an archive, as opposed to viewing an existing archive or extracting files from the archive.

- v indicates that the command should be run in verbose mode, which means that each filename will be displayed as it is copied into the archive.

- f means you are archiving to a file, as opposed to a tape drive.

For instance, if you want to archive all the .txt files in the current directory into an archive called text.tar, use the following command:

```
$ tar cvf text.tar *.txt
ab.txt
pop.txt
```

Notice how the filenames are listed as they are copied to the archive.

Sometimes you want to copy the entire contents of a directory into an archive. Luckily, `tar` copies all files and subdirectories in a directory into an archive if the directory is part of the file list. So if you have a directory called vnc and you want the entire contents of that directory to be copied to a new archive called vnc.tar, you could use the following command:

```
$ tar cvf vnc.tar vnc
```

and get the following results:

```
$ tar cvf vnc.tar vnc
vnc/
vnc/LICENSE.TXT
vnc/README
vnc/README.vncserver
vnc/Xvnc
vnc/classes/
vnc/classes/DesCipher.class
vnc/classes/animatedMemoryImageSource.class
vnc/classes/authenticationPanel.class
vnc/classes/clipboardFrame.class
vnc/classes/optionsFrame.class
vnc/classes/rfbProto.class
vnc/classes/vncCanvas.class
vnc/classes/vncviewer.class
vnc/classes/vncviewer.jar
vnc/vncpasswd
vnc/vncserver
vnc/vncviewer
```

Notice that the first line indicates the creation of the vnc directory in the archive and then the copying of the files in that directory into the archive.

If you have an existing archive, you will generally want to either view a listing of the contents of a file or extract the contents of a file.

To view the contents of an archive, you replace the c option with a t. So, to view the list of files in the vnc.tar archive you just created, you could use the following command:

```
$ tar tvf vnc.tar
drwxr-xr-x root/root            0 1998-05-16 23:55 vnc/
-rw-r--r-- root/root        18000 1998-01-23 16:52 vnc/LICENCE.TXT
-rw-r--r-- root/root         6142 1998-01-23 16:53 vnc/README
-r-r--r--  root/root          601 1998-01-23 16:28 vnc/README.vncserver
-r-xr-xr-x root/root      1286834 1998-01-23 13:00 vnc/Xvnc
drwxr-sr-x root/root            0 1998-01-23 16:24 vnc/classes/
-r--r--r-- root/root         7143 1998-01-23 16:24
➥vnc/classes/DesCipher.class
-r--r--r-- root/root         1329 1998-01-23 16:24 vnc/classes/animated
➥MemoryImageSource.class
-r--r--r-- root/root         2068 1998-01-23 16:24 vnc/classes/
➥authenticationPanel.class
-r--r--r-- root/root         1761 1998-01-23 16:24 vnc/classes/clipboard
➥Frame.class
-r--r--r-- root/root         3210 1998-01-23 16:24 vnc/classes/options
➥Frame.class
-r--r--r-- root/root         8309 1998-01-23 16:24
➥vnc/classes/rfbProto.class
-r--r--r-- root/root         7092 1998-01-23 16:24
➥vnc/classes/vncCanvas.class
-r--r--r-- root/root         7100 1998-01-23 16:24
➥vnc/classes/vncviewer.class
-r--r--r- root/root         20564 1998-01-23 16:24
➥vnc/classes/vncviewer.jar
-r-xr-xr-x root/root        11433 1998-01-23 13:00 vnc/vncpasswd
-r-xr-xr-x root/root        10795 1998-05-17 00:17 vnc/vncserver
-r-xr-xr-x root/root        49685 1998-01-23 13:00 vnc/vncviewer
```

Notice how the listing of files is in a complete form, similar to the way in which ls -l lists the contents of a directory.

To extract the contents of an archive into the current directory, replace the c or t with an x:

```
$ tar xvf vnc.tar
vnc/
vnc/LICENSE.TXT
vnc/README
```

```
vnc/README.vncserver
vnc/Xvnc
vnc/classes/
vnc/classes/DesCipher.class
vnc/classes/animatedMemoryImageSource.class
vnc/classes/authenticationPanel.class
vnc/classes/clipboardFrame.class
vnc/classes/optionsFrame.class
vnc/classes/rfbProto.class
vnc/classes/vncCanvas.class
vnc/classes/vncviewer.class
vnc/classes/vncviewer.jar
vnc/vncpasswd
vnc/vncserver
vnc/vncviewer
```

Gzip

While `tar` is useful for archiving files, it doesn't perform any compression in the previous examples. Compression in Linux is generally achieved with the `gzip` command.

Unlike Windows ZIP archives, which compress many files into a single compressed archive, `gzip` simply compresses individual files without compressing them into an archive.

For instance, if you have a particularly large file called `test.pdf` that you won't use for some time and you want to compress it to save disk space, use the `gzip` command:

```
$ gzip test.pdf
```

This command compresses the file and adds a `.gz` extension to the end of the filename, changing the name to `test.pdf.gz`.

Before compression, `ls -l` shows us the file size is 110,778 bytes:

```
-rw-r-r-   1 root     root        110778 Jun  5 16:54 test.pdf
```

After compression, the size has dropped to 83,729 bytes:

```
-rw-r-r-   1 root     root         83729 Jun  5 16:54 test.pdf.gz
```

As with most commands described in this chapter, you can use any valid shell file expression to list more than one file. For instance,

```
$ gzip *
```

compresses all files in the current directory (but not those in subdirectories).

Uncompressing *gzip* Files To uncompress a `gzip` file, you can use the `gzip` command with the `-d` option:

```
$ gzip -d test.pdf.gz
```

This uncompresses the file and removes the `.gz` extension, returning the file to its original uncompressed state with the name `test.pdf`.

An alternative command, `gunzip`, eliminates the need to use the `-d` option:

```
$ gunzip test.pdf.gz
```

Combining *gzip* and *tar* Because early versions of the `tar` command did not compress archives, this was typically done using `gzip`, as shown in the following example:

```
$ tar cvf text.tar *.txt
ab.txt
pop.txt
$ gzip text.tar
```

produces a compressed archive called `text.tar.gz`.

To access the contents of this archive, uncompress the archive and then use `tar`:

```
$ gunzip text.tar.gz
$ tar tvf text.tar
-rw-r-r- root/root        48 1998-06-05 16:13 ab.txt
-rw-r-r- root/root         6 1998-06-05 16:13 pop.txt
```

Recent versions of the `tar` command, including those shipped with all current distributions, provide a method for directly accessing and creating `gzip`-compressed `tar` archives.

By simply adding a z option to any of the `tar` commands discussed earlier, you can create a compressed archive without the need for a second command. For instance,

```
$ tar czvf vnc.tar.gz vnc
vnc/
vnc/LICENSE.TXT
vnc/README
vnc/README.vncserver
```

```
vnc/Xvnc
vnc/classes/
vnc/classes/DesCipher.class
vnc/classes/animatedMemoryImageSource.class
vnc/classes/authenticationPanel.class
vnc/classes/clipboardFrame.class
vnc/classes/optionsFrame.class
vnc/classes/rfbProto.class
vnc/classes/vncCanvas.class
vnc/classes/vncviewer.class
vnc/classes/vncviewer.jar
vnc/vncpasswd
vnc/vncserver
vnc/vncviewer
```

creates a compressed version of the vnc.tar archive,

```
$ tar tzvf text.tar.gz
-rw-r-r- root/root          48 1998-06-05 16:13 ab.txt
-rw-r-r- root/root           6 1998-06-05 16:13 pop.txt
```

displays the contents of the compressed text.tar.gz archive, and

```
$ tar xzvf text.tar.gz
ab.txt
pop.txt
```

extracts the contents of the archive.

NOTE   Full details of the tar and gzip commands and their options can be found in the man pages for those commands.

Man and Xman

Throughout this chapter, you have seen references to *man pages*. These are manual pages that are provided in a standard format with most Linux software. Almost all the commands that ship with the Red Hat Linux 6 distribution include man pages.

Using the man command in its most basic form, you can read any existing man page:

```
$ man command-name
```

This displays the man page for the specified command and allows you to scroll through it and search it the same way as when you are using the less command to display text.

If the specified man page cannot be found, you get the following error:

```
$ man non-existent-man-page
No manual entry for non-existent-man-page
```

Since you already are familiar with X Windows, you have an alternative to using the man command to view man pages: the xman program.

To launch xman, use

```
$ xman &
```

or

```
$ /usr/bin/X11/xman &
```

This will display the initial xman window like the one in Figure 13.1.

FIGURE 13.1:

The initial xman window

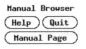

From here, you can press the Manual Page button to display the main xman window, shown in Figure 13.2.

The main area of the window is used to display the text of the currently selected man page. Initially xman's help file is displayed. The window has two menus: Options and Sections.

The Options menu, shown in Figure 13.3, allows you to switch between listings of man pages (Display Directory) and the contents of the current man page (Display Manual Page), in addition to searching the contents of the current man page. The Help option displays the complete help file for xman, which provides detailed instructions on using xman.

You are more interested in the Sections menu, shown in Figure 13.4, since this is where you begin the process of finding the man page you want to read.

FIGURE 13.2:

The main xman window

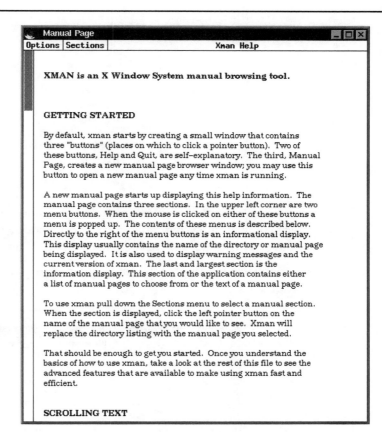

FIGURE 13.3:

A schematic view of the
Flight data structure and
the code that references it

Xman Options

Display Directory
Display Manual Page
Help
Search
Show Both Screens
Remove This Manpage
Open New Manpage
Show Version
Quit

FIGURE 13.4:

The Sections menu

Xman Sections

(1) User Commands
(2) System Calls
(3) Subroutines
(4) Devices
(5) File Formats
(6) Games
(7) Miscellaneous
(8) Sys. Administration
(l) Local
(n) New

As you can see, the manual pages are divided into eight main categories, including user commands, system calls, and so on. Choosing one of these sections brings up a directory listing for the section like the one shown in Figure 13.5.

By double-clicking any of the command names, you can read the man page for that command.

FIGURE 13.5:

A directory listing

```
Manual Page                                                          _ □ ✕
Options | Sections |              Directory of: (1) User Commands
AnotherLevel    Mail          a2p            addftinfo      addr2line
afm2tfm         afmtodit      ali            allcm          alldc
allneeded       amslatex      amstex         anno           answer
append_db       apropos       ar             arch           as
ascii-xfr       ash           at             atq            atrm
audiocompose    audiosend     aumix          autoexpect     awk
basename        bash          batch          bc             bggen
bibtex          biff          bison          bru            bsh
buildhash       burst         byacc          c++filt        cal
captoinfo(m)    cardinfo      cat            cccp           cdp
chage           chattr        checkalias     chfn           chgrp
chmod           chown         chroot         chsh           chvt
ci              cjpeg         cksum          clear          cleardbdir
co              col           colcrt         colrm          column
comm            comp          compress       configure      cp
cpio            cpp           cproto         createdb       createuser
crontab         cryptdir      csplit         cu             cut
date            dc            dd             ddate          deallocvt
decryptdir      depmod        destroydb      destroyuser    df
dialog          dig           dircolors      dirname        dislocate
dist            djpeg         dnsdomainname  dnsquery       doexec
domainname      dos           du             dumpkeys       dvilj
dvips           dvired        dvitype        echo           ed
egrep           eject         elm            elmalias       env
eqn             etex          exmh           expand         expect
expectk         expr          extcompose     false          fastmail
fax2ps          fax2tiff      fgrep          file           find
findaffix       finger        flex           fmt            fold
folder          fontexport    fontimport     formail        forw
free            frm           ftp            ftpcount       ftpwho
funzip          fuser         g++            gawk           gcc
gdb             geqn          getfilename    getopt         getty
gftodvi         gftopk        gftype         ghostscript    gif2tiff
gindxbib        glookbib      gnroff         gpasswd        gperf
gpic            gpm           gpm-root       gprof          grefer
grep            grodvi        groff          grog           grolj4
grops           grotty        groups         gs             gsftopk
```

Looking Ahead

In this chapter, you've taken your first big step toward becoming real Linux users by delving into the world of the command line.

Until now you have focused on X Windows and its capabilities, but the real heart of any Unix-like operating system lies in the command line.

In the next chapter, you will learn about the powerful commands provided by Linux for working with files and directories. You will build on the commands (such as ls) discussed in this chapter and explore creating directories and other advanced tasks.

CHAPTER
FOURTEEN

Working with Files

- Copying and Deleting Files

- Moving and Renaming Files

- Creating Files

- Creating Symbolic Links

- A Quick Introduction to Filename Expansion

In the last chapter, you got a glimpse of what's involved in using Linux. You saw how all commands are actually separate programs stored in separate files. You even began to learn how to manipulate files by seeing the various ways that the ls command can be used to display lists of files.

In this chapter, you are going to take a detailed look at the commands used to further manipulate files and directories, including copying, deleting, moving, renaming, and creating. This chapter wraps up with a quick look at filename expansion—that is, wildcards like the commonly used asterisks in DOS and Windows.

Copying and Deleting Files

Probably the two most common file manipulation tasks are copying and moving files. You will regularly find yourself replicating files all over your disk drive or copying files to floppy disks, the latter for backup purposes or to "transmit" files using the cheapest of all networking methods: your feet. Similarly, the average PC user at some point will run short of disk space and will strike out in search of files to delete in order to free up precious disk space and avoid investing in a new hard drive.

Copying Files

Anyone with even brief experience using DOS or the DOS prompt in any version of Windows is probably aware that clicking, dragging, and dropping is not the only way to copy files. In fact, DOS's copy command offers additional features, such as wildcards, that can make it quicker, easier, and more powerful to use than File Manager or Windows Explorer.

Similarly, in the Linux world, the cp command (normally found at /bin/cp) is used for copying and provides a powerful tool for copy operations.

Basic Copying

Obviously, the most basic uses of the cp command are to copy a file from one place to another or to make a duplicate file in the same directory. For instance, if you want to copy a file (ThisFile) in the current directory to a second file (to be called ThisFile-Acopy) in the same directory, enter the following command:

```
$ cp ThisFile ThisFile-Acopy
```

Using `ls  -l` to look at a directory listing of the files, you would find two files with identical sizes but different date stamps. The new file has a date stamp indicating when the copy operation took place: it is a new, separate file. Changes to `ThisFile-Acopy` do not affect the original `ThisFile` file.

Similarly, to make a copy of `ThisFile` in the `/tmp` directory (perhaps to share the file with another user), use the following command:

```
$ cp ThisFile /tmp
```

and if you want to copy `ThisFile` to `/tmp` but give the new file a different name, enter

```
$ cp ThisFile /tmp/NewFileName
```

Don't Overwrite That File

The scary thing about Linux distributions is that it is easy to accidentally overwrite a file by copying over an existing file. Consider the situation where `ThisFile` and `NewFile` both exist and you issue the command

```
$ cp ThisFile NewFile
```

Using this command, the contents of `NewFile` are overwritten by a copy of `ThisFile` and lost forever (unless you are disciplined about backing up your system).

To avoid this difficulty, you can use the `-i` flag of the **cp** command, which forces the system to confirm any file it will overwrite when copying. Then, you see a prompt like this when attempting to copy:

```
$ cp -i ThisFile NewFile
cp: overwrite `ThisFile'?
```

If you want to protect yourself, you can create an alias for the **cp** command. By issuing the command

```
$ alias cp='cp -i'
```

you are defining an alias so that any time you issue the **cp** command, you are in fact issuing the command `cp  -i`. In this way, you are always prompted before overwriting a file while copying. As you will learn later in Chapter 16, "Understanding the Shell," you can configure the Bash shell using the `.bashrc` file to ensure that every time you log in, this alias is set. (The shell controls the command-line environment in which you work, but more about that later.)

Continued on next page

Luckily, this alias is set by default when you log in as the superuser, or root. This is especially important because making a small mistake as the root user can have drastic consequences for the whole system. Using this default can help prevent major disasters.

Copying Multiple Files in One Command

One of the drawbacks of the DOS copy command is that it could only copy one file or file expression at a time. For instance, use the command

```
$ copy file /temp
```

to copy a single file to /temp, or enter the command

```
$ copy *.txt /temp
```

to copy all text files in the current directory to /temp. But if there are three separate files you want to copy, you need to use three commands; similarly, if you want to copy all text files and all executable files in the current directory, you need to use two commands.

The Linux cp command, however, makes this process a bit easier. The cp command can take more than the two arguments in the DOS version of the command. Instead, you can pass multiple arguments to the command and the last argument is treated as the destination and all preceding files are copied to the destination.

Let's look at an example. Suppose you want to copy the files FileOne, FileTwo, and FileThree in the current directory to /tmp. Obviously, you could issue three commands:

```
$ cp FileOne /tmp
$ cp FileTwo /tmp
$ cp FileThree /tmp
```

However, you can bundle this all together into one command, making the process easier:

```
$ cp FileOne FileTwo FileThree /tmp
```

Similarly, you can add wildcards to the mix and copy large numbers of files in one command. For instance, the command

```
$ cp *.txt *.doc *.bak /tmp
```

copies all files with any one of three extensions in one command.

When copying multiple files in this way, it is important to remember that the last argument must be a directory, since it is impossible to copy two or more files into a single file. If you forget to make the last argument a directory, then you will get an error message like this one:

```
cp: when copying multiple files, last argument must be a
➥directory. Try `cp –help' for more information.
```

If you want to copy an entire directory and all its subdirectories, you can use the -R flag of the cp command. This command indicates that you want to recursively copy a directory. If a subdirectory called SomeDir exists in the current directory and you want to copy SomeDir in its entirety to a subdirectory in /tmp, then use the command

```
$ cp -R SomeDir /tmp
```

to create a directory /tmp/SomeDir as a copy of the SomeDir subdirectory in the current directory.

Advanced Copying

The cp command offers several advanced features that extend it beyond simple copying of files and directories. These capabilities include preserving the state of original files in their copies and alternate methods to protect existing files while copying.

Making Copies as Close to the Originals as Possible

Take a close look at the copies you make. Notice that certain characteristics of the copied files bear little resemblance to the original files. These characteristics include the file ownership, permissions, date stamps, and symbolic links. Let's consider these one by one.

When you copy a file, the resulting file is normally owned by the copier as opposed to the creator of the original file. Let's say that user1 has created a file called TheFile and put it in /tmp for user2 to copy to their home directory. If you look at the file listing, the file looks something like this:

```
-rw-r-r-   1 user1    users      16992 Apr  5 12:10 TheFile
```

After user2 copies the file with the command

```
$ cp /tmp/TheFile ~/NewFile
```

the resulting file has a new ownership, that of the copier (user2):

```
-rw-rw-r-  1 user2    users      16992 Apr  5 13:10 NewFile
```

Similarly, when a file is created in a directory, it has a set of default permissions assigned to it. When copying a file, the copy will have the permissions set to the default for the destination directory rather than retaining the permissions of the original file. Notice in this example the change in permission between the original file and the new copy. The original file was only group readable but the copy is also group writable. A change has also occurred to the date of the copy, reflecting the date and time when the copy was made instead of the date stamp of the original file.

There are times, however, when you want to retain the original owner, date, and permissions of files when they are copied. Let's say, for example, that the root account is being used to copy a set of files to a removable hard disk for storage in a vault. Unlike a regular tape backup, which requires other tools, this type of backup can be done with the cp command. However, it is important that a backup like this matches the original as closely as possible. Luckily, the cp command provides the -p flag, which preserves these attributes. Using the previous example, if the command used was

```
$ cp -p /tmp/TheFile ~
```

then the resulting file would match the original quite closely:

```
-rw-r-r-   1 user1    users      16992 Apr  5 12:10 TheFile
```

Another sticky problem in copying files is how to handle symbolic links. As you learned in the previous chapter, a symbolic link provides a pointer to a file from another location. In this way, you can pretend that a file is in more than one place at once. If you try to access the link, Linux actually accesses the file that the link points to.

Normally, when you copy a symbolic link, the resulting file is a copy of the file pointed to by the link instead of a new link to the same file. For instance, if

TheFile had been a symbolic link as in this example

```
lrwxrwxrwx   1 user1    users          16992 Apr  5 12:10 TheFile ->
➥OtherFile
-rw-r—r—  1 user1    users             1 Apr  5 11:10 OtherFile
```

then issuing the following cp command

```
$ cp /tmp/TheFile ~/NewFile
```

results in a file that is a copy of OtherFile:

```
-rw-rw-r—  1 user2    users          16992 Apr  5 13:10 NewFile
```

But what if you want to copy the link instead of the file itself? What if you want the result to look as follows:

```
lrwxrwxrwx   1 user2    users             2 Apr  5 13:10 NewFile -
➥>/tmp/OtherFile
```

Well, once again the cp command has a flag to address the situation: the -d flag, which indicates not to dereference the symbolic link. Simply use the command

```
$ cp -d /tmp/TheFile ~/NewFile
```

to get the desired result.

Having said all this, it is time to put it all together. What if you want to use the cp command to create a useful backup copy of an existing directory and all its subdirectories? Using the combination of these two flags and a recursive copy, you can do this. For instance,

```
$ cp -pdR TheDirectory /backups
```

creates an exact copy of TheDirectory in the directory /backups/TheDirectory. But the cp command provides a simplified way to achieve this: the -a flag, which indicates that you want an archive of a directory. It is a quick way to indicate the three flags -pdR:

```
$ cp -a TheDirectory /backups
```

Preventing Mistakes

As you saw earlier, one way to prevent mistakes is to use the -i flag, which forces interactive prompting before overwriting occurs in the course of copying files or directories. Other methods are available to provide different degrees of protection.

One method is to use the -b flag to cause the cp command to create a backup copy of any file about to be overwritten. By default, the backup copy has the original filename with a tilde (~) after it. So, if you copy `FileOne` to `FileTwo` using the command

```
$ cp -b FileOne FileTwo
```

and `FileTwo` already exists, then a backup is made of the original `FileTwo` called `FileTwo~`.

It is possible to alter the way in which the `cp` command names the backup files by using two different flags: `-S` and `-V`. The `-S` flag allows you to change the character used in backup names from the default tilde to something else. For instance,

```
$ cp -b -S _ FileOne FileTwo
```

results in a backup filename `FileTwo_`.

The `-V` flag provides even more flexibility, allowing the user to specify one of three types of backup naming schemes:

- `t` or `numbered`: Create sequentially numbered backups. If an existing numbered backup file exists, then the new backup file created is numbered sequentially after the existing backup file; the resulting filenames look like `FileName.~Number~` (for example, `FileName.~2~` or `FileName.~11~`).

- `nil` or `existing`: If a numbered backup file already exists, then create a numbered backup; otherwise, create a regular simple backup file.

- `never` or `simple`: Create a simple backup file using the default tilde or alternative character indicated by the `-S` flag.

For instance, to create a numbered backup in the example above, use the command

```
$ cp -b -V t FileOne FileTwo
```

or

```
$ cp -b -V numbered FileOne FileTwo
```

Similarly, both of the following commands create simple backup files:

```
$ cp -b -V never FileOne FileTwo
```

and

```
$ cp -b -V simple FileOne FileTwo
```

Alternative Flags

You may have noticed that this section covered a lot of flags for the cp command. Sometimes it is difficult to remember the flags. Fortunately, there are long forms for most of these flags that may make them easier to remember:

Short Form	Alternate Long Form
-I	—interactive
-R	—recursive
-p	—preserve
-d	—no-dereference
-a	—archive
-b	—backup
-S	—suffix
-V	—version-control

While the long forms may seem more intuitive at first, ultimately any regular Linux user will use the short forms. The long forms involve too much typing for frequent use. For instance, consider the following complex cp command:

```
$ cp -i -b -V simple -S _ -R ThisDir /tmp
```

If you use the long form of these flags, you end up with the following command:

```
$ cp —interactive —backup —version-control simple —suffix _ —recursive
➡ThisDir /tmp
```

Sure, this command is more readable at first glance, but do you really want to type this simply to copy a directory?

Deleting Files

As it does for copying files, Linux provides a powerful command for deleting files: rm, found at /bin/rm.

In its simplest form, rm allows you to delete one or more files in the current directory. The command

```
$ rm ThisFile
```

deletes the file ThisFile in the current directory, and

```
$ rm *.txt
```

removes all files with the .txt extension in the current directory.

As with copying, it is possible to provide multiple arguments to the rm command and all referenced files will be deleted. For instance,

```
$ rm ThisFile *.txt
```

performs the same action as the previous two commands combined.

Like the cp command, this can be extremely useful and potentially dangerous. After all, what happens if, wanting to delete a backup of a document, someone accidentally issues the command

```
$ rm thesis.doc
```

instead of

```
$ rm thesis.bak
```

This is a potential nightmare, and as unlikely as it sounds, it happens all the time, resulting in unnecessary work and headaches.

For this reason, it is wise to use the same -i flag for the rm command because it provides the prompts to avoid disastrous mistakes:

```
$ rm -i thesis.doc
rm: remove `thesis.doc'?
```

You can also create an alias for rm, making this the default behavior:

```
$ alias rm='rm-i'
```

Deleting Whole Directories

Users frequently want to delete entire directories. Consider, for instance, a directory created after unzipping a software archive downloaded from the Internet. After you have finished installing and testing the software, you will probably want to delete the entire directory. This is done using the -r flag. For instance, to remove a directory called TempInstall, you would use:

```
$ rm -r TempInstall
```

Of course, if you have been following along in this chapter, you probably have an alias for the `rm` command, forcing it to prompt you for every deletion. This can become very tedious for big directories:

```
$ rm -r TempInstall
rm: descend directory `tempInstall'? y
rm: remove `TempInstall/File1'? y
rm: remove `TempInstall/File2'? y
...
rm: remove directory `TempInstall'? y
```

Just imagine if there were hundreds of files. Responding to prompts for each one would be impractical. In these instances, when you are absolutely certain that you want to delete a whole directory, you should use the -f flag of the `rm` command. This flag forces deletions, even when you have already indicated interactive operation with the -i flag in your alias:

```
$ rm -rf TempInstall
```

A Reminder...

Care needs to be taken when using the −f flag. While it is powerful, it can be extremely dangerous.

The superuser's account is configured so that the default alias for the `rm` command is `rm -i`. This is critically important, because even a seemingly small mistake can be disastrous. If the alias weren't being used, just consider what would happen if, in attempting to delete the /tmp directory, a space made its way in between the / and `tmp`:

```
$ rm -r / tmp
```

This would actually delete all the files and directories on the disk. This is why the alias for `rm -i` is so essential.

Similarly, using the -f flag requires great care when working as the superuser and underscores the need to limit your use of the superuser account to only essential tasks. After all,

```
$ rm -rf / tmp
```

would be just as dangerous if you did have the right alias in place.

Moving and Renaming Files

Moving files and renaming files are closely linked, and therefore they are treated together in this section. Unlike the DOS and Macintosh worlds, where renaming and moving are distinct actions, in the Linux environment renaming a file is just a special case of moving a file.

The Basic Move Operation

Let's start by considering the basic move operation:

```
$ mv FileOne /tmp
```

This command moves the file called FileOne from the current directory to the /tmp directory.

Moving *and* Renaming

Similarly, it is possible to move the file to the /tmp directory and change the name of the file using the following command:

```
$ mv FileOne /tmp/NewFileName
```

By using this concept, you can rename a file. Simply move a file from its existing name to a new name in the same directory:

```
$ mv FileOne NewFileName
```

See how moving and renaming are one and the same?

Moving More Than Just One File

As when copying files, it is possible to move multiple files in one step because the mv command can accept more than two arguments and the last argument serves as the destination directory of the move. (As with copying, you can't move multiple files to a file; the last argument must be a directory.) Consider the situation where you want to move all files in the current directory with the extension .bak, .tmp, or .old to /tmp. Use the command:

```
$ mv *.bak *.tmp *.old /tmp
```

This simple command moves all the specified files to the destination (/tmp) in one operation.

It is also possible to move entire directories with the mv command without using any special flags. If there is a subdirectory named TheDir in the current directory and you want to move it so it becomes a subdirectory under /tmp, you use the mv command just as you did earlier for files:

```
$ mv TheDir/ /tmp
```

Similarly, if you want TheDir to become a directory in the root directory called NewDir, you can use the following command:

```
$ mv TheDir/ /NewDir
```

NOTE   As with cp and rm, it is wise to set an alias for mv to mv -i to ensure that you don't accidentally overwrite files when moving. You can do this with $ alias mv= 'mv -i'. This is set by default for the superuser account.

Creating Files

You have already learned several ways to create files. After all, you create files when you copy files. You create files when you move files. Other obvious ways of creating files include creating a word processing document, saving an e-mail attachment, or making a screen capture.

However, there are cases where it is necessary to create a new file, even if the file is empty and has a length of zero. The most obvious instance of this would be in cases where a script needs to create a file to indicate a special state. The best example of this is a programming technique called *file locking*. If a script opens a file to make changes, it also creates a special file called a *lock file* that indicates to other programs and scripts that the current file is opened for editing and is therefore unavailable to be changed. Once the script closes the file, it deletes the lock file to make the file once again available.

In order to be able to create these lock files quickly and efficiently without exacting excessive disk space requirements, you need a shortcut method to signify an empty file of a specified name. This is achieved with the `touch` command. This command creates a file. For instance,

```
$ touch NewFile
```

creates a new file of zero length with the name `NewFile`:

```
-rw-rw-r-   1 armand    armand          0 Apr  6 21:06 NewFile
```

Another common use of the `touch` command is to change the modification date stamp of an existing file. Many programs depend on the date stamp of files they are working with to determine what action to take. The `touch` command lets you change the modification date of a file without opening and editing the file.

Creating Symbolic Links

In addition to creating files, there are times when it is necessary to create symbolic links. *Symbolic links* (which are simply pointers to a real file in another location) are usually used by system administrators and application developers. Consider a programmer who has several versions of a program that is under development. The current version for testing may be `prog5`, `prog8`, or `prog10`, depending on how far along the development is. In order to ensure that the latest version is always being executed during testing, the programmer can create a symbolic link from `prog` to the latest version. By doing this, executing `prog` always executes the desired revision of the application.

There are two possible approaches to creating a symbolic link. The first is to use the `ln` command with the `-s` flag to indicate a symbolic link. This command takes two arguments: the file to be linked to and the location and name of the symbolic link to that file.

For instance, to create a link to `/bin/cp` in the current directory, `MyCopy`, you use the command

```
$ ln -s /bin/cp MyCopy
```

Using `ls -l` to see the listing of `MyCopy` shows us a symbolic link:

```
lrwxrwxrwx   1 armand    armand          7 Apr  6 22:50 MyCopy ->
↪/bin/cp
```

Another, far less common, way to create a symbolic link is to use the `cp` command with the `-s` flag:

```
$ cp -s /bin/cp MyCopy
```

A Quick Introduction to Filename Expansion

Before closing out this chapter, you need to take a quick look at an important subject: *filename expansion*. Chapter 16 covers filename expansion in more detail when discussing the Unix shell, but since you have already seen examples of filename expansion in this chapter, this section will put it in context.

Filename expansion refers to a special syntax that can be used to expand a compact expression into a list of one or more file or directory names. The simple examples you have seen in this chapter involve the use of the asterisk (*) to represent zero or more characters. For instance, the expression `*.txt` could match any of the following filenames:

- `.txt`
- `a.txt`
- `file.txt`
- `txt.txt`

The default Bash shell provides a rich syntax for filename expansion. This book will explore the Bash shell later, but a few of the more useful symbols are outlined below:

- ?: Matches any single character, so `file.?` would match `file.c` but not `file.txt`.

- [*CharacterList*]: Matches any single character in the character list, so `file.[abc]` would match `file.a`, `file.b`, and `file.c` but not `file.d` or `file.txt`.

Looking Ahead

You've come a long way. You now know how to use X Windows and have begun to delve into the real depths of Linux: the command line and the shell. You learned about some of the major programs available in the command prompt environment and are able to manipulate files in sophisticated ways using concise and powerful commands.

The next step, which you will take in the next chapter, is to learn to perform some important system configuration and management tasks using two tools: LinuxConf and Red Hat Linux's Control Panel utility. These functions include setting up printers for use in Linux, managing users, and more.

CHAPTER

FIFTEEN

Using LinuxConf and the Control Panel for System Configuration

- Launching the Control Panel

- Control Panel Features

- Configuring Printers

- Setting the Time and Date

- Configuring a Modem

- Other Control Panel Features

- Launching LinuxConf

- Managing Users and Groups

While avid Linux power users and system administrators will want to roll up their sleeves and get down to the business of hand-editing the files that control the behavior of their systems, the everyday computer user who wants to use Linux as a productivity tool may find this a daunting and overwhelming proposition.

In fact, the thought of having to hand-edit configuration files is so daunting that it may be one of the leading reasons why Linux is seen as user-unfriendly and Windows is perceived as user-friendly.

However, Red Hat has long strived to integrate tools into their distribution of Linux that help shield the user from dealing with the underlying configuration of a basic Linux workstation.

At the center of these tools are the Control Panel and, in Red Hat Linux 6, LinuxConf. Like its namesake in the Windows world, the Red Hat Control Panel provides facilities to perform the most common system management tasks through easy-to-use graphical dialog boxes and windows. LinuxConf provides an alternative graphical interface for system management.

The two tools provide different but overlapping features. Among the tasks you can perform with the combination of the Control Panel and LinuxConf are

- Adding users and groups
- Managing printers
- Configuring networks
- Handling installation and removal of software packages

This chapter takes a close look at the most frequently used features of the Control Panel and LinuxConf.

Launching the Control Panel

If you have a relatively complete installation of Red Hat Linux 6, then you already have all the files on your system required to run the Control Panel. The best way to find out if everything necessary is installed is to use the Red Hat package management system.

First, check to see if the Control Panel is installed at all by using the command:

```
$ rpm -qa | grep control
```

This should produce a result like

```
control-panel-3.11-2
```

if Control Panel is installed.

If you find the package is not installed (rpm will tell you this quite clearly: control-panel is not installed), use rpm to install the package:

```
$ rpm -i control-panel-3.11-2.i386.rpm
```

assuming you are in the RedHat/RPMS subdirectory on the Red Hat CD-ROM.

If you are missing any required packages, rpm will inform you, and you can install them using the same rpm command in order to make sure that the Control Panel will work. Some of the packages that are commonly missing are modemtool, printtool, and netcfg. These provide the actual individual modules that allow the Control Panel to do its magic.

Once you are sure the Control Panel is installed, try to run it. There are two things to keep in mind about the Control Panel:

- It requires X Windows to run.

- It must be run by the root user because it attempts to edit system configuration files that only the root user should have permission to alter.

To launch the Control Panel, from an xterm window, issue the command

```
$ control-panel
```

and the application should run. The full path of the Control Panel is normally /usr/bin/control-panel. If it launches successfully, you should see the Control Panel windows like the one shown in Figure 15.1.

Control Panel Features

Once you have the Control Panel running, there are a few features to look at. First, notice that the application runs in a vertical mode. If you prefer a horizontal Control Panel, you can choose Change Orientation from the File menu, shown in Figure 15.2.

Choosing Change Orientation changes the Control Panel window to look like the one in Figure 15.3.

FIGURE 15.3:

A horizontal Control Panel window

The Control Panel window consists of numerous icons representing functions. For instance, the icon pictured in Figure 15.4 represents Network Configuration. Holding the mouse over each icon for a few seconds displays small help balloons indicating the meaning of each icon.

FIGURE 15.4:

The User and Group Configuration icon

To launch the Control Panel applet associated with a given icon, simply click the icon once. For instance, clicking the icon in Figure 15.4 once launches the Network Configurator applet pictured in Figure 15.5.

FIGURE 15.5:

The Network Configurator applet

Configuring Printers

Probably one of the more intimidating configuration tasks in Unix is trying to get a printer working—especially a PCL printer—by manually editing the necessary system configuration files.

Red Hat has done an admirable job of making this task manageable (if not exactly easy) using the Print System Manager applet of the Red Hat Linux Control Panel. To launch the Print System Manager, click the icon shown in Figure 15.6. This brings up the Print System Manager, as shown in Figure 15.7.

FIGURE 15.6:

Click this icon to launch the Print System Manager.

FIGURE 15.7:

The Print System Manager

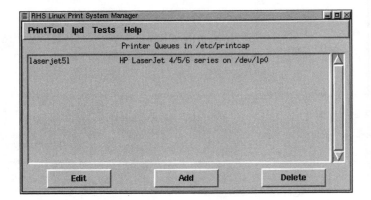

The Print System Manager consists of four menus (PrintTool, lpd, Tests, and Help), a list of existing printers, and three function buttons (Edit, Add, and Delete).

The PrintTool Menu

The PrintTool menu provides three options: Reload, About, and Quit.

The Reload option is used to reload the system's `printcap` file, found at `/etc/printcap`. This is the configuration file where the system stores all configuration information for all installed printers and remote printers on the system. This allows you to refresh the display of available printers should the `printcap` file be changed manually or by another program while the Print System Manager is running.

The About option does exactly what you might expect; it presents a dialog box with some detailed information about the Print System Manager. This dialog box looks like the one in Figure 15.8.

FIGURE 15.8:

The About dialog box

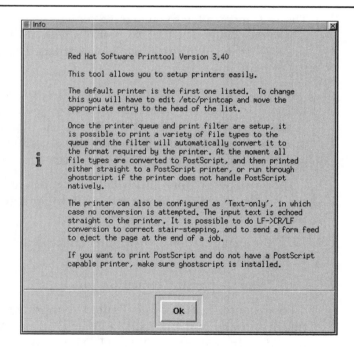

```
Info                                                                    X

          Red Hat Software Printtool Version 3.40

          This tool allows you to setup printers easily.

          The default printer is the first one listed.  To change
          this you will have to edit /etc/printcap and move the
          appropriate entry to the head of the list.

          Once the printer queue and print filter are setup, it
          is possible to print a variety of file types to the
          queue and the filter will automatically convert it to
          the format required by the printer. At the moment all
          file types are converted to PostScript, and then printed
          either straight to a PostScript printer, or run through
          ghostscript if the printer does not handle PostScript
          natively.

          The printer can also be configured as 'Text-only', in which
          case no conversion is attempted. The input text is echoed
          straight to the printer. It is possible to do LF->CR/LF
          conversion to correct stair-stepping, and to send a form feed
          to eject the page at the end of a job.

          If you want to print PostScript and do not have a PostScript
          capable printer, make sure ghostscript is installed.


                                 Ok
```

Finally, the Quit option quits without any confirmation. Unlike the User Configurator, when you make changes in the Print System Manager, they are immediately written to the relevant system configuration files.

The Lpd Menu

The lpd menu contains a single option: Restart lpd.

When you make changes to the printer setup on your system—whether those changes involve adding new printer queues, deleting existing printers, or changing the configuration of printers—they don't take effect until the line printer daemon, known as lpd, is restarted.

Lpd is a system program that runs in the background and handles the spooling of print jobs for all printers configured on a Linux system. To get lpd to look at its configuration files for new information requires that the program be restarted.

The Tests Menu

The Tests menu allows you to test a configured printer by sending sample print jobs to the printer. The first two tests print an ASCII or PostScript test file to the printer selected in the list of available printers. This tests the configuration of the printer.

If a job fails to print, test that you have the printer configured and connected to the correct serial or parallel port on your system. You can use the third menu option, Print a Test File Directly to the Port, to bypass the lpd-managed printer queue and send data directly to the printer's configured port to see if the physical connection is correct and on the port expected by lpd.

The usefulness of this quickly becomes apparent. For instance, if you print a test PostScript file to a printer and it fails to print, two possible things could be wrong:

- The configuration of the printer queue in question is incorrect (a software problem).
- There is a physical connection problem.

For instance, if you have configured your printer to be connected to /dev/lp0 (the first printer port, normally LPT1: in DOS and Windows) but have connected it to /dev/lp1 (normally LPT2: in DOS and Windows), then printing test pages will fail. Or you may have a bad printer cable, which can cause a print job to fail.

Using the Direct to Port test tells you whether the problem is in the hardware or in the software. If you print directly to the port and the text prints, then you know the printer is connected correctly to the port indicated in the printer queue configuration. This means that you only need to debug the configuration of the queue to solve any printing problems.

The Help Menu

The Help menu provides access to two help screens:

General Help   Offers general guidance about using the Print System Manager.

Troubleshooting   Offers useful pointers about solving printing difficulties.

The Edit Button

If you select an existing printer and click the Edit button, a dialog box appears like the one in Figure 15.9.

FIGURE 15.9:

The Edit Local Printer Entry dialog box

This dialog box displays the relevant properties of the specified printer queue, including the name(s) of the printer, the spool directory, any limit on the size of print jobs, the port where the printer is connected, and the input filter. In addition, this dialog box indicates whether headers should be suppressed when printing to this printer. For a remote printer, the Edit dialog box looks a little different, showing the host name and queue name of the printer on the remote host instead of the port where the printer is connected. This looks like Figure 15.10.

FIGURE 15.10:

Editing a remote printer

Printer Names

You can give any name to a printer queue that doesn't include spaces—letters and numbers are best. If you want to give a printer more than one name, separate the names with the pipe symbol (|).

You might want to create more than one name for the default printer on your system, for instance. By default, the commands used to print and query a printer look for a printer named lp when none is specified. This is considered the default printer of the system.

But most users prefer to name their printers with names that reflect some useful information about the printer, such as the printer type or its location. For the default printer, then, you might want to use two names such as laserjet51|lp.

Spool Directory

The spool directory is the location on your system where print jobs are stored while in the queue waiting to be sent to the printer. Normally, this location is a subdirectory under the directory /var/spool/lpd with the same name as the first name given the printer.

By default, the Print System Manager copies the first name of a printer to the Spool Directory field so that a printer named laserjet51 has a spool directory of /var/spool/lpd/laserjet51. Normally you should leave the default unless there is a compelling reason to change the location, such as disk space limitations.

File Limit

The File Limit field specifies any limit on the size of print jobs in kilobytes. This can be especially useful in two instances:

1. When a printer has an extremely small memory and sending large jobs to the printer can leave it in an error state and inaccessible. This is especially critical in a situation where a printer is being shared on a network and the error state might go unnoticed for some time while people assume the jobs they are sending to the printer are being printed.

2. When disk space is limited and a large print job can cause the partition or disk containing the spool directories to quickly fill up.

In these cases, specify any limits in kilobytes in this field. If you want to place no limit on the size of print jobs, enter 0 in this field.

Printer Device

This field is used to indicate which device to send print jobs to. Table 15.1 indicates which Linux devices map to which DOS devices and what type of port they are.

TABLE 15.1: Linux Devices and DOS Devices

Linux Device	DOS Device on a Typical System	Port Type
/dev/lp0	LPT1:	Parallel
/dev/lp1	LPT2:	Parallel
/dev/lp2	LPT3:	Parallel
/dev/ttyS0	COM1:	Serial
/dev/ttyS1	COM2:	Serial
/dev/ttyS2	COM3:	Serial
/dev/ttyS3	COM4:	Serial

Note that the numbering of devices differs from DOS and Windows. Linux numbering starts at 0 where DOS and Windows start at 1. Also, there is another subtle difference. In Linux, the first available printer port will be /dev/lp0. But, in DOS and Windows, LPT1: is tied to a specific port. If that port is unavailable, LPT2: does not become LPT1:. But in Linux, if you have two ports and you remove the port associated with /dev/lp0 from the system, the port which used to be accessed with /dev/lp1 will shift to /dev/lp0.

Remote Host and Queue

The Print System Manager handles remote network printers as well as local printers. In the Unix and Linux world, a remote printer is handled in essentially the same way as a local printer. A queue exists on the local machine with its own spool directory. But instead of indicating a device for the printer, the Print System Manager specifies a remote host and remote queue name, and files sit in the local queue until they can be sent to the print queue on the remote host.

Given this, it is easy to configure remote printers. When editing a remote printer, you see Remote Host and Remote Queue fields instead of the Printer Device field.

Let's consider an example. A printer in the Finance department connected to a Linux system is called Finance. On this system, the printer queue for the local printer might be called lj4p, indicating that the printer is a LaserJet 4P.

If you wanted to create a print queue on your own Linux system pointing to that remote printer, you might want to call the print queue finance-printer, since you also have a LaserJet 4P and using a similar name would be confusing.

In this example, the printer name on your system would be finance-printer, on the remote host it would be finance, and the remote queue would be lj4p.

Input Filter

Generally speaking, Linux programs that offer printing capabilities send one of two types of data to a printer queue: ASCII or PostScript. Depending on your printer, however, one or the other or both of these types of data might be inappropriate. For instance, a PostScript printer won't print a plain ASCII file and a PCL printer won't print a PostScript file.

In order to address this problem, you need to use input filters. Input filters are generally programs or scripts that can translate a variety of file formats including ASCII, PostScript, pictures, and more, into the right format for a printer. When you edit a printer queue entry, the Input Filter field displays the filter in a special format such as *auto* - LaserJet4 for a LaserJet 4–compatible printer.

Luckily, the Print System Manager provides a graphical interface for selecting the correct input filter for your printer. Simply click the Select button next to the Input Filter field, and a dialog box like the one in Figure 15.11 appears.

FIGURE 15.11:

The Configure Filter dialog box

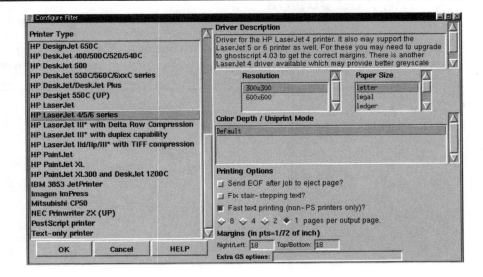

The Configure Filter dialog box offers a selection of printer types, including the popular dot matrix, ink jet, and laser printers. If you select the closest printer to the one you are using, it often works. For instance, owners of HP LaserJet 6 series printers can select HP LaserJet 4/5/6 Series, which is actually a LaserJet 4 series filter that usually works with newer models.

Once you select the appropriate filter, you can configure details such as default resolution, paper size, and more. Generally, aside from the Resolution, Paper Size, and Color Depth entries, the default entries selected when you choose an input filter are the best ones for your printer.

Suppress Headers

Selecting the Suppress Headers option turns off the printing of header pages. Header pages are used in a networked environment to indicate who printed a given document and are helpful in sorting print jobs. However, some printers have trouble with the header pages. If you experience difficulty because of header pages, deselect this option.

The Add Button

As you might expect, adding a new printer is closely related to editing an existing printer. When you click the Add button, a dialog box appears like the one in Figure 15.12 asking you what type of printer queue you wish to create.

FIGURE 15.12:

Adding a printer

Select the correct type (local or remote) and then click OK to get a dialog box like the one in Figure 15.13 or Figure 15.14.

FIGURE 15.13:

Adding a local printer

FIGURE 15.14:

Adding a remote printer

These dialog boxes look like the ones used to edit local and remote printers and work in the same way. You need to fill in the correct information for your printer and click OK to add the printer.

The Delete Button

Deleting a printer is a fairly simple process. Select the appropriate printer from the list of available printers and click the Delete button. A confirmation dialog box like the one in Figure 15.15 will come up.

FIGURE 15.15:

The Delete Printer confirmation dialog box

If you want to delete the printer, click Continue; otherwise, click Cancel. If you choose to delete a printer, you are reminded to delete the spool directory manually. There is no requirement to do so, but doing this keeps your system well organized and uncluttered by unneeded directories.

Remember, as soon as you click Continue to delete a printer, it is removed from the necessary configuration file. There is no second chance after that.

Working with Windows Printers

You may have noticed the reference to LAN Manager Printers in the Add dialog box. These are printers shared by a Windows 95 or NT system that use standard Windows networking and the Server Message Block (SMB) protocol. When adding this type of printer, a dialog box appears like the one in Figure 15.16.

The critical differences here are the need to know the host name of the server, the IP address of the server, and the username and password of the shared printer. If you want to integrate a Linux system into an existing Windows network with shared printers, you can get this information from your Windows network system administrator.

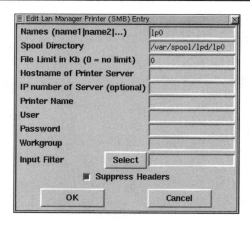

Setting the Time and Date

The Control Panel lets you set the system time and date using the Time Machine. You can launch the Time Machine by clicking the icon shown in Figure 15.17. The Time Machine window looks like Figure 15.18.

FIGURE 15.17:

The Time Machine icon

The time and date are displayed at the top of the window. You can click any part of the time or date (the hour, the minutes, the seconds, the month, the day, or the year) and adjust it using the arrows. When you make these changes, the system clock doesn't update; you can reset the time to the system clock's time by clicking the Reset Time button. If you prefer to view the time in 24-hour format in the Time Machine, select the 24 Hour Time option. This option has no impact on the time stored in the system clock since the system clock doesn't make the distinction between 12- and 24-hour clocks.

FIGURE 15.18:

The Time Machine window

After changing the time here, you can change the time of the system clock by clicking Set System Clock. A warning screen appears like the one in Figure 15.19.

FIGURE 15.19:

System time change warning

The warning suggests that you reboot your system immediately after changing the system time or else risk system instability. This is not an idle threat. There are system processes that rely on the system clock and can get confused by changes in the clock. If you aren't in a position to reboot your system when you are changing the time, it is best to put off changing the time until you plan to shut down your system.

If you still want to change the system time once the warning is displayed, click Continue and the system clock will be updated.

Configuring a Modem

The Control Panel provides a simple modem configuration applet that is accessed by clicking the icon shown in Figure 15.20. This brings up the Configure Modem window, as shown in Figure 15.21.

FIGURE 15.20:

The Configure Modem icon

FIGURE 15.21:

The Configure Modem window

This window offers very little to choose from: you can simply select the port your modem is connected to or, in the case of an internal modem, configured to use. This creates the necessary link so that programs that expect the modem to be on the device /dev/modem can find your modem.

This setting is independent of the configuration of programs that use the modem for accessing the Internet or faxing. These programs are discussed in later chapters such as Chapter 22, "Connecting Linux to the Internet."

Other Control Panel Features

You probably have noticed that many of the Control Panel icons are not discussed in this chapter. These icons bring up tools for performing advanced system configuration that requires deeper knowledge of system administration. Some of these will be discussed in the appropriate sections of this book, including the Network Configurator, which is discussed in Chapter 21, "Understanding Linux Networking."

Launching LinuxConf

LinuxConf can be launched in two ways: from the Control Panel or from the command line.

To launch LinuxConf from the Control Panel, click the last icon in the Control Panel, shown in Figure 15.22.

FIGURE 15.22:

The LinuxConf icon in the Control Panel

Alternately, you can type the following command at the command prompt in an `xterm` window:

```
# linuxconf
```

As with the Control Panel, you need to launch LinuxConf as the root user so that it has the necessary permissions to make changes to your system configuration. When LinuxConf first launches, a window appears like the one in Figure 15.23.

LinuxConf can be used to control many different aspects of your Linux environment, including your network configuration and user and group management. These different sections of LinuxConf can be chosen from the expandable tree hierarchy in the left pane of the window. This expandable and collapsible tree works in much the same way as the tree for navigator files and directories in the Windows 98 and NT Explorer.

FIGURE 15.23:

The LinuxConf window

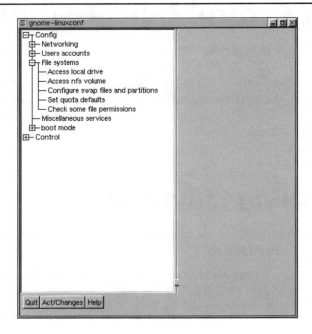

Managing Users and Groups

This section focuses on using LinuxConf to manage users and groups.

User and group management facilities can be found under the Config ➤ Users Accounts ➤ Normal section of the selection tree at the left of the LinuxConf window.

Managing Users

To manage users, select Config ➤ Users Accounts ➤ Normal User Accounts in LinuxConf. This opens the default user management screen shown in Figure 15.24. This screen lists details of existing users and includes a row of function buttons immediately below the list of users.

FIGURE 15.24:

Use the list of users and the row of function buttons to manage users.

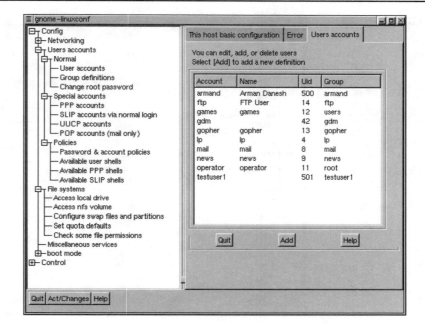

Using this screen, it is possible to

- Add new users
- Edit properties of existing users or view their current properties
- Lock and unlock users
- Permanently remove users from the system

Adding a New User

To add a new user, click the Add button. The User Account Creation screen shown in Figure 15.25 appears. Most of the information fields in the dialog box are empty, waiting for you to enter information about the new user. When you are done entering the information as outlined here, click the Accept button to create the user.

FIGURE 15.25:

Adding a new user

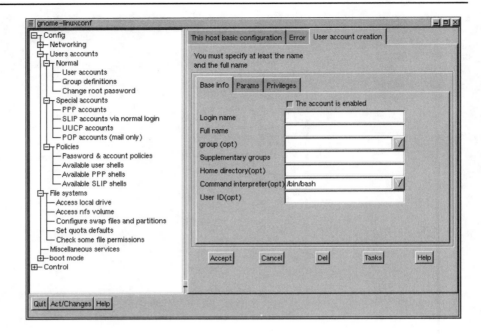

Login Name The first field in the box is the Login Name field. In this field, enter the username of the user, the name the user types to log in to the system, not their complete name. These usernames should not contain spaces and should start with a letter or number.

For instance, for a user named Arman Danesh you might choose any of the following usernames:

- armand
- adanesh
- arman
- danesh
- arman_danesh
- ArmanDanesh

because they all relate in some way to the name of the user.

Full Name The Full Name field is where you enter the full name of the user. The full name is used, for example, in constructing the From line of the user's e-mails, including both the e-mail address of the user, which is derived from the username, and the full name of the user.

Group and Supplementary Groups The group field allows you to assign a user to a specific default group. If left blank, Red Hat Linux gives the user a unique group with a group ID number corresponding to that user's user ID number.

You are probably best off not changing the preselected numbers that will be assigned by LinuxConf.

The Supplementary Groups field can be used to assign a new user to additional groups for security and access control purposes. On most small systems and networks, this won't prove necessary.

Home Directory The Home Directory field indicates the full path of the user's home directory. By default, on a Red Hat Linux system this is a subdirectory of the /home directory, and the directory name is the same as the username. In fact, once you enter the username in the User Name field, LinuxConf automatically uses it to assign a default home directory under /home. You can override this default by providing and alternate directory path in the Home Directory field.

For example, the home directory for a user with the username armand would be /home/armand. Unless you have a large multiuser server or are implementing a custom scheme for placing home directories on your system, leave the default entry as is.

Command Interpreter The Command Interpreter field is used to indicate the user's default shell, which governs the way in which the user's command-line environment functions. (To learn about different shells and their features, see Chapter 16, "Understanding the Shell.")

The default shell for all new users in Red Hat Linux is the Bash shell. Clicking the drop-down menu next to the Command Interpreter field produces a list of alternate shells, including variations on Bash such as the Ash shell, or the C-Shell and the Enhanced C-Shell (/bin/tcsh). Normally, it is not necessary to change the default shell.

Creating the User Once you are finished providing the necessary information for a new user, click the Accept button to add the user. Once you click Accept, you are prompted twice for a password for the user (you are prompted twice because of the need to confirm the password). The password prompt looks like the one in Figure 15.26.

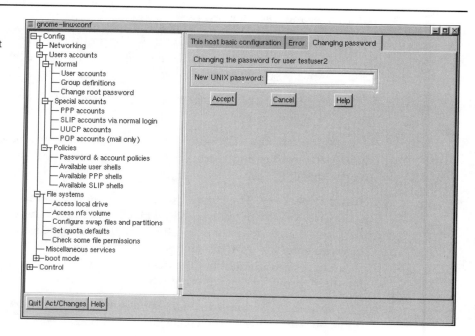

Once you have entered the password twice and clicked Accept each time, the main user management screen shown in Figure 15.24 reappears and the new user now appears on the list of current users.

Editing or Viewing a User

To view the details or change the information for a user, simply click their name in the list of users in the main user management screen. A screen box appears like the one in Figure 15.27. This screen box looks the same as the one you saw when you tried to add a new user, with one major difference: all the fields contain information relating to the user selected from the list. You can use this form to change any information about the user.

FIGURE 15.27:

Viewing and editing a user

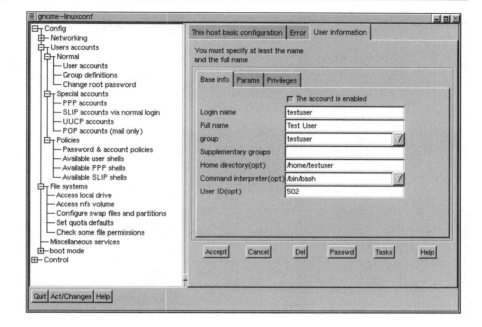

If you make changes to a user and want to commit those changes to the user list, simply click Accept. Otherwise, click Cancel to exit the dialog box without saving the changes.

Enabling and Disabling Users

Enabling and disabling users is a useful concept. The idea behind disabling a user is to temporarily deactivate the user's account without permanently removing it from the system. This allows the user to be reinstated later. Examples of when this type of functionality is used might include an Internet Service Provider (ISP) who temporarily suspends access privileges when a user has not paid their access charges.

To disable a user's account, simply click the user in the user list and deselect The Account is Enabled. When you accept the changes, the user's account is disabled.

Enabling a User To enable a disabled user, simply click the user's name in the user list and select The Account is Enabled in the edit screen for that user. Next, click Accept to commit the changes and enable the user's account.

Deleting a User The final option in managing users is to delete a user from the system. Once done, you can only bring a user back by recreating the user's account. To delete a user, click the user in the user list to open the edit screen for that user. Next, click the Del button at the bottom of the edit screen. A confirmation screen appears like the one in Figure 15.28.

FIGURE 15.28:

The Delete User confirmation screen

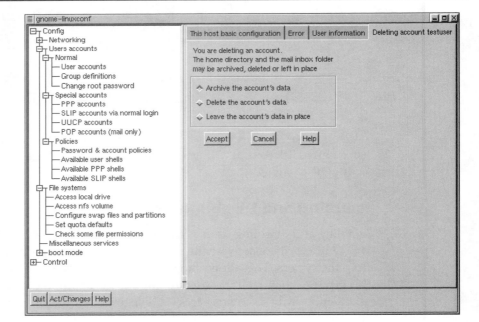

On the Delete User confirmation screen, you have three options:

Archive the Account's Data The data from the user's account (home directory, quotas, etc.) will be archived and compressed for later access.

Delete the Account's Data   The data from the user's account will be permanently deleted.

Leave the Account's Data in Place   The data from the user's account will be left untouched even though the user account will no longer exist.

Select your desired option and click Accept to delete the user.

Managing Groups

The second aspect of managing users and groups is to work with groups. To switch to group management, select Config ➢ Users Accounts ➢ Normal ➢ Group Definitions in the left pane of the LinuxConf window. When managing groups, you work with a groups list and a row of function buttons like those in Figure 15.29. Groups are discussed in detail in Chapter 17, "General System Administration."

FIGURE 15.29:

Group management

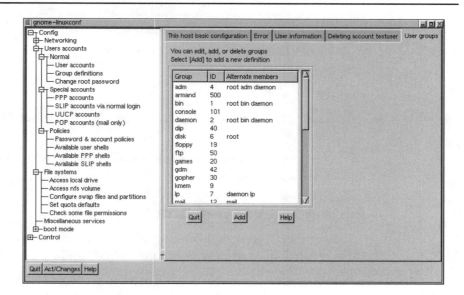

Adding Groups

To add a new group to the groups list, simply click Add. A screen appears like the one in Figure 15.30.

FIGURE 15.30:

Adding a group

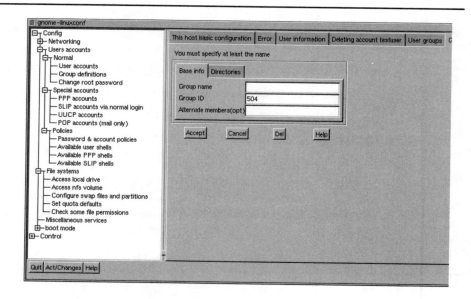

This looks like a scaled-down version of the screen used for adding users to the system. Here you can

- Assign a group name.

- Select a GID for the group if you don't like the default group provided by the system.

- Assign alternate users as members of the group with a list of users in the Alternate Members field with a space between each user.

Editing and Viewing Groups

To edit or view a group's details, simply click the group in the groups list of the main group management screen to get a window like the one in Figure 15.31.

Notice that the screen box looks like it did when you added a group, except that here all the data is filled in. You can change the GID or user list for a group.

FIGURE 15.31:

Editing and viewing a group

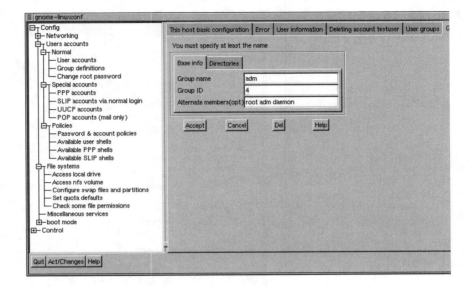

Saving and Quitting

After finishing any configuration tasks with LinuxConf, it is necessary to quit and save your changes. To do so, click Quit at the bottom left corner of the LinuxConf window. The confirmation screen shown in Figure 15.32 appears.

On the confirmation screen you can choose to

- Apply the changes you have made.

- Preview what will be done before applying the changes.

- Cancel the decision to quit from LinuxConf by clicking the Don't Quit button.

To commit the changes you have made, click the Activate the Changes button and then click Quit to close LinuxConf.

FIGURE 15.32:

Quitting from LinuxConf

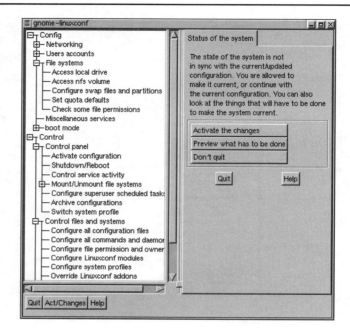

Looking Ahead

This chapter has given you a grounding in how to configure some of the most basic components of your system—components that you will use every day, such as printers, modems, users, and groups.

With this knowledge and your basic grasp of Unix and managing Linux files, you are ready to delve into the world of the shell. The shell is the program that provides you with the powerful command-line environment that is loved by the Unix guru but feared by the Linux novice.

The next chapter will take a look at the role played by the shell, compare many of the available shells (including the ever-popular Bash and C shells), and then take a deeper look at Bash, the default shell of almost every Linux distribution.

CHAPTER
SIXTEEN

Understanding the Shell

- Comparing Shells

- Overview of the Bash Shell

Now that you have learned some basic Unix commands, it is important to understand the command-line environment you are using to enter them. This command-line environment is known as the *shell*—a command interpreter, similar to the DOS prompt in Windows 3.1 and Windows 98, that allows you to type commands, launch programs, and manipulate files.

Unlike the Windows world where the DOS prompt is a fixed environment with limited flexibility, Unix shells are small application programs that run as processes when you log in and provide a variety of command-line interface features and capabilities to suit different users and applications.

In the Unix world, and by extension in Linux, there are numerous shells to choose from. Each shell offers you a different set of features and capabilities and most offer their own scripting languages, which allow you to create sophisticated, self-executing programs similar to—but more powerful than—DOS batch files (with the familiar .BAT extension).

First, this chapter will give you an overview of the major Unix shells, including the Bourne Shell, the C Shell, and the Korn Shell, and then you will get an in-depth look at the Bourne Again Shell, known as Bash, which is the default shell installed with most Linux distributions.

Comparing Shells

The earliest Unix shell was very limited, with no history list, no command-line editing, and no job control. It was with the emergence of the Bourne Shell and the C Shell in the 1970s that shells began to garner serious attention in the Unix world. Today there is a plethora of shells available to Unix users, with a wide variety of unique features distinguishing them from each other.

There are two main classes of shell—those that derive their essential syntax and design from the Bourne Shell and those that base their model on the C Shell. Before taking a close look at the Bourne Again Shell—the default shell that ships with most Linux distributions—let's take a quick look at some of the major Unix shells.

TIP   If you want to keep track of the latest developments in the world of Unix shells, consider subscribing to the `comp.unix.shell` newsgroup.

Bourne Shell (*sh*)

The Bourne Shell (sh) is seen by many as the original Unix shell. In many ways it is rather limited, lacking features such as a history list and command-line editing. But as the original Unix shell, many features of the Bourne Shell, including its core command set, are found in many modern shells. It is rare, however, to find modern systems that use the Bourne Shell as their default shell. Instead, the Bourne Again Shell or the Enhanced C Shell are commonly found in most Linux distributions.

The Bourne Shell is well known for introducing many key shell concepts, such as the ability to test programs for success or failure status when they exit, which allows for sophisticated scripting. This concept is now standard in all Unix shells.

C Shell (*csh*)

The C Shell (csh) was an early Unix shell that was developed to provide a command set and scripting environment derived from the syntax of the popular C programming language. Like the early Bourne Shell, the C Shell lacked some important features, such as command-line editing. Still, the C Shell introduced many key ideas, including command aliases and command histories. An Enhanced C Shell (tcsh), which adds command-line editing and other features found in Bash, is usually shipped with most Linux distributions as an alternate shell.

The C Shell is generally hailed for introducing several key concepts that today are found even in shells based on the Bourne Shell. These include the idea that certain shell functions, such as arithmetic calculations and comparison testing, can be performed by the shell itself. In the case of the Bourne Shell, these tasks require calling external programs.

Bourne Again Shell (*bash*)

The Bourne Again Shell (bash) is the most common shell installed with Linux distributions. Known as Bash, this shell is based on the Bourne Shell (as the name implies) but provides a broad additional feature set including command-line editing, a history list, and filename completion. With Bash, it is possible to write sophisticated shell scripts using a Bourne Shell–like syntax. As the most common Linux shell, Bash is the focus of most of this chapter and is the default shell being used in all examples in this book.

Korn Shell (*ksh*)

The Korn Shell (ksh) is another of the family of shells that is derived from the original Bourne Shell. By some counts, the Korn Shell is the most popular Unix shell in use; however, it is generally not the default shell on most Linux systems. The Korn Shell was probably the first to introduce many of the popular features you now see in Bash, including command-line editing. The Korn Shell was also one of the first shells to bring many features introduced in the C Shell into the Bourne Shell world.

Other Shells

There are numerous other shells available, all of which provide their own unique command-line interfaces. None of these, however, is sufficiently popular or well known to be shipped with most Linux distributions. These shells include the Adventure Shell (ash), a subset of the Bourne Shell; Extensible Shell (es), which provides a completely reprogrammable shell environment; ERGO Shell (esh), a shell that aims to provide a more ergonomic, structured approach to a shell; and Z Shell (zsh), which, like Bash, brings together features from several shells and is similar to the Korn Shell.

TIP   An excellent source of alternate shells for your Linux system is at the SunSite Linux archive. In their Shells directory at `ftp://metalab.unc.edu/pub/Linux/ system/shells/`, you will find all the shells listed here as well as a collection of less common shells such as `lsh`, `pash`, and `pdksh`.

Experimenting with Different Shells

At this point, you are probably wondering how you can try out these different shells without making them your default shell. You can do this by simply executing the shell as a program from within your default shell. For instance, the Enhanced C Shell comes preinstalled even though Bash is set up to be the default shell for all users. If you want to try out `tcsh`, you just need to enter the command

```
$ tcsh
```

This command assumes `tcsh` is on your path; if not, you need to include the appropriate path to the shell, such as `/bin/tcsh`. Once you do this, the Enhanced C Shell executes and you are switched to that shell. Simply typing `exit` returns you to your default shell.

On most Linux systems, you will find a symbolic link from `/bin/sh` to `/bin/tcsh`, so using the command

```
$ csh
```

also launches the Enhanced C Shell.

If you plan to experiment with different shells, you can use this technique to try them all out before switching your default shell. In order to change the default shell that executes when you log in to your system, you need to change your entry in the Unix password file. You can do this using the `chsh` command.

Consider a user `someuser` whose default shell is currently `/bin/bash` (the Bourne Again Shell). Their current entry in the Unix password file might look like:

```
someuser::790:103:Some User:/home/someuser:/bin/bash
```

In this password entry, the last section specifies the shell as `/bin/bash`. Running the command

```
$ chsh -s /bin/tcsh someuser
```

changes the shell for `someuser` to `/bin/tcsh`. The resulting entry for someuser in the Unix password file would be

```
someuser::790:103:Some User:/home/someuser:/bin/tcsh
```

and the next time they log in, Enhanced C Shell would be their shell instead of the Bourne Again Shell.

Overview of the Bash Shell

Now let's take a closer look at Linux's most common shell, the Bash shell. As the first step to learning where the Bash shell fits into the Linux universe, it is important to understand the whole login process. When you log in at the `Login:` prompt, several things take place. The first of these is the launching of your shell (in this case Bash), followed by the execution of any configuration file you may have created for your personal Bash environment.

In order to provide a personalized configuration to Bash, you need to create a file called `.bashrc` in your home directory. This is a simple text file that is executed by Bash whenever you launch the shell—generally, when you log in.

The `.bashrc` file can contain any legitimate combination of commands and Bash functions that you would type at the normal Bash prompt, as well as sophisticated scripting commands.

It is in the `.bashrc` file that you can configure the behavior of Bash, set environment variables such as your path, and launch any programs that you may want to launch every time you run the Bash shell. The following commands make up a simple `.bashrc` file that creates a customized prompt, sets a command alias called `which`, and assigns some environment variables:

```
PS1="[\u@\h \W]\\$ "
alias which="type -path"
export PATH=$PATH:.:~/bin
export EDITOR=emacs
```

There are several major features of the Bash shell at play in this seemingly small example, including:

- Setting of environment variables
- Command aliases
- Pattern expansion

All of these will be discussed in the rest of this chapter, along with the following major features of the Bash shell:

- Input and output redirection
- Filename completion
- Full command-line editing
- Command history list
- Job control

Setting Environment Variables in Bash

Each shell has its own syntax for the setting of environment variables. In Bash, this is generally done in two steps:

1. Set the value of a variable.

2. Export the variable to the environment.

For instance, if you want to assign emacs as your default text editor, you might set the EDITOR environment variable with the command

```
$ EDITOR=emacs
```

and export it with

```
$ export EDITOR
```

The two steps can also be combined into a single step where you assign a value to EDITOR and export EDITOR in one command:

```
$ export EDITOR=emacs
```

As you will learn in greater detail when pattern expansion is discussed, the value of environment variables can be accessed by adding a $ at the beginning of the name of the variable in a Bash command. In this way, you can add information to the current value of an environment variable. For instance, if the PATH variable currently contains

```
/bin:/usr/bin:/usr/X11R6/bin
```

you can add /usr/local/bin to the path by using the following command:

```
$ export PATH=$PATH:/usr/local/bin
```

Notice how this command uses $PATH to include the current value of the PATH variable in the new value of the PATH variable. The resulting value of the variable would be

```
/bin:/usr/bin:/usr/X11R6/bin:/usr/local/bin
```

Input and Output Redirection

One of the most useful concepts in the Unix world is that of standard input and standard output. Often, non-interactive programs receive their input data through the standard input—usually the keyboard. Similarly, they display their results to the standard output—usually the screen.

However, most shells provide the ability to redirect standard input and output, which allows you to build complex command combinations out of multiple commands and data files. As you saw in the last chapter, the use of the pipe (|) allows the redirection of standard output to standard input. For instance, in the command

```
$ ls -l | more
```

the output of the `ls -l` command is not displayed to standard output but is instead redirected to the standard input of the `more` command. The `more` command processes this redirected input and then displays the results to the standard output.

There is another way to redirect standard input and output in Bash: using the < and > redirection symbols. For instance, consider a situation where you want to save a directory listing to a file for later processing. You can use the > symbol to redirect the standard output:

```
$ ls -l > filelist
```

This command saves the output of the `ls -l` command in a file called `filelist`. Similarly, if you want to use the contents of a file as the standard input for a command, you use the < symbol:

```
$ mail user@juxta.com < filelist
```

This command causes the contents of the file `filelist` to be used as the input data for the `mail` command, effectively causing the contents of the file to be used as the body of the resulting e-mail message.

Filename Completion

Sometimes called word completion, filename completion is a simple but very useful concept. It works like this: if you type enough characters to uniquely identify a file, command, or directory name, Bash can complete the rest of the name. Consider if you typed

```
$ /usr/lo
```

On most systems, `/usr/lo` will uniquely identify the directory `/usr/local/`. By simply pressing the Tab key, Bash attempts to complete the name. If only one file, command, or directory begins with `/usr/lo`, then Bash completes the name for you, in this case filling in the text to read `/usr/local/`.

Of course, there are going to be times when you don't provide enough information for Bash to know how to complete a name. In this situation, the shell is able to provide you with all possible alternatives to match the name you are trying to complete. For instance, if you type

`$ /usr/l`

`/usr/local/` and `/usr/lib/` would usually be matched. If you press Tab, then Bash is confused—it doesn't know which name to complete with, and so it cannot complete the name. If you press Tab a second time, Bash displays all the possible alternatives, as follows:

`lib         local`

You are free to type enough characters to uniquely identify the name you want and then press Tab again. In the example above, if you type an additional **o** and then press Tab, Bash completes the name as `/usr/local/`.

By now you are probably asking: What happens if I want to type a filename in the local directory or somewhere else on my path without providing the complete path to the file? Can Bash complete filenames for me then? Luckily, the answer is "yes." If you attempt to complete a file or directory name without providing a complete path, as in the case of

`$ gr`

Bash searches the path for names that match the entered characters. For most systems, the previous example will match only a few commands, including `grep` and `groff`, and Bash will present you with a list of possible alternatives:

`grep      groff      grotty`

If you want the command `grep`, all you would need to do is type **e** and then press Tab again, and Bash completes the command name for you.

Command Alias

Command aliasing is a powerful feature of the Bash shell that allows you to define your own custom commands. For instance, if you regularly check all running processes on your system, you might use a command like

`$ ps -aux | more`

Rather than needing to type **ps -aux | more** whenever you want to check all the processes running on your system, you can save yourself unnecessary keystrokes by defining an alias using Bash's built-in `alias` command.

In this example, let's say you want to create an alias called psa to use whenever you want to check all the running processes. You could define this alias using the following command:

```
$ alias psa="ps -aux | more"
```

Once you do this, typing **psa** at the Bash prompt executes the command ps -aux | more. The alias remains in place until the end of your current Bash session. When you log out and Bash exits, the aliases you have defined are lost.

If you want to create permanent command aliases, you should set the aliases in your .bashrc file using the same method you used earlier to make emacs the default text editor.

In addition to providing a way to create shortcuts to commonly used commands, command aliasing can be used to protect yourself from major mistakes. For instance, if you are logged in as the root user, normal use of the cp, mv, and rm commands can be quite dangerous. One mistake can overwrite or erase files, directories, or whole file systems without your realizing it. For this reason, the Bash shells of the root account are configured to have the following set of default aliases:

```
alias cp='cp -i'
alias mv='mv -i'
alias rm='rm -i'
```

In all these cases, the -i flag forces the command to interactively prompt the user for all actions it takes to overwrite or erase files. In order to cause the commands to run without prompting for each action, the user has to explicitly ask for this with the appropriate flags (for instance, rm -f).

Command-Line Editing

One feature of Bash that was missing in some earlier shells such as the Bourne Shell and the C Shell is the ability to edit a command line. Without this feature, once you type a sequence of characters on the command line, you are not free to go back to that sequence—your only choice is to delete all the characters back to the one you want to edit, fix the character, and then retype the rest of the line. For instance, if you had typed:

```
$ /usr/kocal/bin/mycommand
```

and subsequently realized that koca1 had to be loca1, you would have had to delete all the way back to the k, replace the k with an 1, and then retype the rest of the line. Needless to say, this is a rather inefficient way to work.

For this reason, most modern shells, including Bash, provide full command-line editing. This allows you to use the arrow keys to move through the current line, delete and insert characters as needed, and press Enter to execute the command without moving the cursor to the end of the line. By default, Bash has insertion turned on, so if you type new characters, they are inserted at the cursor rather than overwriting existing characters.

Bash provides several useful key shortcuts to speed up editing, especially with long command lines. Table 16.1 highlights these shortcuts.

TABLE 16.1: Useful Command-Line Editing Key Shortcuts

Keystroke	Action
Ctrl+A	Jump to the start of the line.
Ctrl+E	Jump to the end of the line.
Ctrl+B	Move back one character.
Ctrl+F	Move forward one character.
Esc, B	Move back one word.
Esc, F	Move forward one word.
Ctrl+L	Clear the screen and display the current command as the first line of the screen.
Ctrl+D	Delete the character at the current cursor position.
Backspace	Delete the character to the left of the cursor.
Ctrl+T	Transpose the character to the left of the cursor with the character at the current cursor position.
Esc, T	Transpose the word to the left of the cursor with the word at the current cursor position.
Esc, U	Uppercase the current word.
Esc, L	Lowercase the current word.
Esc, C	Capitalize the current word.
Ctrl+K	Delete from the current cursor position to the end of the line.

If you are familiar with the emacs editor, you will notice that many of the above keystrokes are the same as the ones you use in emacs. This is because the default editing mode of Bash is designed to use emacs-like commands. Alternatives include a vi-like mode, but since familiarity with vi and its more obscure style of editing is generally limited to programmers and advanced system administrators, this book won't discuss how to use the vi editing mode in this book.

The list of commands in Table 16.1 represents only a small portion of all the editing commands available in Bash. It covers the core set of editing functions needed by most users to become efficient with Bash. If you want to delve more deeply into the editing functions of Bash, you should read the READLINE section of the bash man page, which you can find by typing **man bash** at the shell prompt.

Command History List

The idea behind the command history list is really rather simple. Every command you execute (by pressing Enter instead of Ctrl+C) is added to a history list buffer, which you can access in reverse order starting with the most recent command executed and ending with the least.

To access the history list, the simplest method is to press the up arrow key to cycle through the history list until you find the command you are looking for.

The history list is most often used for two purposes:

- Fixing mistakenly entered commands

- Repeating commands many times during a session

Let's address the first application of the history list. Let's say you have just tried to view the contents of the file testfile by typing

```
$ moer testfile
```

When you press Enter, an error message is generated along the lines of

```
bash: moer: command not found.
```

To quickly correct and execute the command, you could simply hit the up arrow key to recall the last command, change moer to more using the command-line editing functions discussed above, and press Enter to view the file.

Similarly, let's consider the situation where you are experimenting with the configuration for a program you are installing. You might want to repeat the process of editing the configuration file and executing the program several times. You can do this by using the history list to repeatedly perform each step of this two-step process.

A quick method to access commands on the history list is to use the ! symbol. By typing ! followed by the first few letters of a command in the history list, the most recent command starting with the specified letters will be executed.

For instance, if you previously used the command

```
$ ps -aux | grep httpd | more
```

and you want to execute the same command again, typing the command

```
$ !ps
```

executes the previous command as long as no other ps command had been used after ps -aux | grep httpd | more was used. Using !ps executes the most recent command starting with ps in the history list.

As with command-line editing, there are some advanced key shortcuts to perform more advanced functions with the command history list. Table 16.2 outlines these keystrokes.

TABLE 16.2: Command History Key Shortcuts

Keystroke	Action
Ctrl+P	Move to the previous command in the history list.
Ctrl+N	Move to the next command in the history list.
Esc, <	Jump to the top of the history list (the least recent command).
Esc, >	Jump to the end of the history list (the most recent command).
Ctrl+R	Reverse-search through the history list.
Ctrl+O	Execute the current line and fetch the next line in the history list for editing and executing.

The most interesting of these is Ctrl+R, which allows you to search backwards through the history list in a dynamic, interactive fashion. As you start to type a command, Bash displays the most recent command that matches what you have typed so far. The more you type, the more you narrow down your search to the command you are looking for.

Let's say you want to execute a complicated `find` command you have already executed once. You could use Ctrl+R to start a reverse search. When you do this, Bash presents an interactive search prompt:

```
(reverse-i-search)`':
```

As you type the letters in the `find` command, Bash finds the most recent command that has a match for the currently entered string. For instance, just typing **f** might bring up

```
(reverse-i-search)`f': pico info/.signature
```

and continuing on to typing **fi** might produce

```
(reverse-i-search)`fi': rm -rf StarOffice-3.1
```

until finally typing **fin** displays

```
(reverse-i-search)`fi': find / -name 'foo' -print
```

which is the command you are looking for. You can now press Enter to execute that command.

Job Control

The concept of job control is particularly useful in Linux given the multitasking nature of the operating system. Using job control, it is possible to use a single shell to execute and control multiple programs running simultaneously.

Normally, when you execute a command, it runs in the foreground. That is, the shell executes the command and the prompt doesn't return until the command is finished. In the case of interactive programs such `emacs`, this means the program takes over the screen or window where the shell is running and only when you quit the program does the command prompt become available again. In the case of non-interactive programs such as `find`, the program runs and, even if it displays nothing on the screen, the command prompt is not returned until the program finishes.

Consider the following command:

```
$ find / -name '*.tmp' -print > templist
```

This command searches the entire directory structure of a Linux system for files with the .tmp extension and prints all of those filenames to the standard output. With the previous command, the output is redirected to a file called templist that can be used for later processing. This means that nothing is printed to the display—but you still won't be able to run other commands while find is running.

Such a limitation runs against the very notion of multitasking. There should be a way to start the find command and then continue with other work while find finishes running.

This is where the idea of running a program in the background comes into play. Rather than running it in the foreground, thus preventing the simultaneous execution of other commands, placing a job in the background allows the command to run while the user issues new commands at the command prompt.

The easiest way to place a job in the background is to add an ampersand (&) to the end of the command when you run it. This character tells Bash to run the command in the background and immediately gives you a new command prompt. To put the find command in the background, use the following command:

```
$ find / -name '*.tmp' -print > templist &
```

Once you press Enter to execute this command, you are immediately presented with a new command prompt; at the same time, find begins executing.

Using Bash's jobs command, it is possible to track the jobs that are running in the background. Using jobs might produce results like:

```
$ jobs
[1]+  Running                 find / -name '*.tmp' -print >templist &
```

Here, the jobs command returns results telling us that there is one background (note the &) job running, and that the first job running is find / -name '*.tmp' -print >templist &.

If you have several jobs running in the background, you might get results such as

```
[1]-  Running                 find / -name '*.tmp' -print >templist &
[2]+  Running                 ls -lR / >dirlist &
```

from the jobs command.

If you have already started a program in the foreground and want to put it in the background, you can do so. The key shortcut Ctrl+Z is interpreted by Bash as a request to temporarily suspend the current process. For instance, if the `find` command in the previous example is running in the foreground and you type Ctrl+Z, the process is temporarily stopped. Entering the `jobs` command at this point produces a result like this:

```
[1]+  Stopped                 find / -name '*.tmp' -print >templist
```

Notice how the status of the job is `Stopped` instead of `Running`. You can then place the job in the background with the `bg` command

```
$ bg 1
```

where 1 specifies the number of the job. If there is only one stopped job, it is not necessary to specify the job number, and

```
$ bg
```

places the single stopped job in the background. Once a stopped job is placed in the background, typing **jobs** produces a result showing the job as `Running`.

Sometimes it is useful to temporarily suspend a job without placing it in the background. This is particularly true when you are using an interactive application such as `emacs` or another text editor and want to run one or more commands and then return to your editing. Instead of completely quitting from the editor, it is easier to use Ctrl+Z to stop the editor job, execute your desired commands, and then return the stopped job to the foreground. By their nature, though, interactive applications are not well suited to being run in the background, and they are best left stopped while they are not in use.

To send a stopped job (or a background job) to the foreground, you can use the `fg` command. For instance, if you were running `emacs` but stopped it with Ctrl+Z, executed some commands, and now you want to return to `emacs`, you can use

```
$ fg
```

If you have one or more stopped or background jobs, it is best to specify the job number when you enter the `fg` command. If your `emacs` command was job 2, then the command

```
$ fg 2
```

returns it to the foreground, and you could continue editing.

Finally, there may be times when you want to terminate or kill a stopped or background job. The `kill` command can be used to kill a command on the basis of a process ID (PID). Use the `ps` command to find out the process ID (check the `ps` man page for details) or to directly kill stopped and background jobs in Bash.

For instance, if you have two background jobs and the `jobs` command produces

```
[1]-  Running          find / -name '*.tmp' -print >templist &
[2]+  Running          ls -lR / >dirlist &
[3]+  Stopped          emacs somefile
```

then you can kill the `ls` command using the `kill` command, like this:

```
$ kill %2
```

Notice that, unlike killing a PID, killing a job requires that a percent sign (%) appear before the job number. Without the percent sign, `kill` would attempt to kill the process with the PID of 2 rather than job 2 in the current shell. This is an important distinction because the job number and the PID of a job are extremely unlikely ever to be the same.

Consider the following example: You already have a background process running in your shell and you start a new one as job 2. When you launch this new job, the system automatically assigns the job a PID from a list of PIDs. This number might be 100, 999, or 25,678. Generally, small PIDs (especially those below 100) are used up by all types of system processes that start when Linux boots and stay running until you shut the computer off. Therefore, it is unlikely that the PID of your job will match the job number.

Pattern Expansion

One of the strengths of many modern shells, including Bash, is the ability to use powerful patterns to specify one or more commands or files.

Let's consider a simple example to illustrate the concept. Normally, if you use the command

```
$ ls -l
```

you get a full listing of all files in the current directory. Suppose you want to find a specific file and all you know is that the filename starts with the letter z. Then the command

```
$ ls -l z*
```

can be used. Here, you pass z* as an argument. The pattern z* says to list any file whose filename starts with z followed by zero or more characters. This is the same function of the * that any DOS or Windows user is probably familiar with. What really happens here is that Bash builds a list of all filenames starting with z and then replaces z* with this list, effectively passing all filenames as arguments to the ls -l command.

Unlike DOS and the Windows DOS prompt, however, Bash offers a greater pattern of possibilities for the simple * symbol.

Pathname Expansion

One form of pattern expansion is *pathname expansion.* In addition to the *, you can use up to two other major special symbols to expand pathnames, as shown in Table 16.3:

TABLE 16.3: Pathname Expansion in Bash

Symbol	Description
?	Match any single character.
[...]	Match one of the characters enclosed in the brackets.
[A-F]	Match any single character that falls between the first character and the second.
[^...] or [!...]	Match any single character other than those specified in the brackets.
[^A-F] or [!A-F]	Match any single character other than those that fall between the first character and the second.

Let's look at some examples.

Suppose you want to list all files whose names are three letters long and start with a and end with z. You can use the command

```
$ ls -l a?z
```

Similarly, if you want to match any files whose names simply start with a and end with z, you can use the command

```
$ ls -l a*z
```

The difference is that the ? matches exactly one character in the first example, forcing the filename to be three characters long. In the second example, the * matches zero or more characters, meaning the filename could be two or more characters in length.

Next, consider the situation where you want to see a listing of all files starting with the letters a, b, c, or d. You can use the command

```
$ ls -l a* b* c* d*
```

but this is rather inefficient and becomes cumbersome when you want to see files starting with more letters. To make the process easier, you can use the command

```
$ ls -l [abcd]*
```

which tells you to list any file starting with one of a, b, c, or d followed by zero or more characters.

However, because a, b, c, and d are a continuous sequence of letters, you can use the command

```
$ ls -l [a-d]*
```

making the pattern even more concise.

Finally, you need to consider the case where you want to exclude a particular character or pattern and include all others. Consider cases where you are producing a compressed archive of all the home directories on a system for backup purposes. Let's say that, for whatever reason, you want to produce an archive of all home directories except those starting with the letter m. You can use the command

```
$ tar czvf home.tar.gz /home/[a-1]* /home/[n-z]*
```

However, you can make things easier with the command

```
$ tar czvf home.tar.gz /home/[!m]*
```

which indicates that all home directories starting with any letter except m should be processed by this command.

Taking things one step further, you can exclude all directories starting with the letters m, n and o by using

```
$ tar czvf home.tar.gz /home/[^mno]*
```

or

```
$ tar czvf home.tar.gz /home/[!m-o]*
```

Brace Expansion

Closely related to the pathname expansion is *brace expansion*. Brace expansion provides a method by which it is possible to expand an expression regardless of whether the names being generated actually exist as files or directories at all.

An example of a brace expression is the command

```
$ mkdir testdir{1,2,3,4}
```

which causes the directories `testdir1`, `testdir2`, `testdir3`, and `testdir4` to be created.

Here each element in the braces is separated by a comma, and one by one these elements are used to produce the resulting names. Unlike the [...] expressions you saw earlier, the use of a comma means that the elements between the braces can be more than one character in length:

```
$ mkdir testdir{01,02,03,04}
```

It is important to keep in mind that a brace expression must contain at least one comma.

An interesting feature of both pathname expansion and brace expansion is that they can be used within another brace expression. This is possible because the first expansion to take place is brace expansion.

Consider the following example:

```
$ mkdir newdir/{firstdir,firstdir/dir{01,02}}
```

This command creates the following directories:

```
firstdir
firstdir/dir01
firstdir/dir02
```

Here you used the brace expression {01,02} inside the outer brace expression.

Similarly, you can use any of the pathname expansion symbols inside a brace. The command

```
$ chmod 644 testfile.{tx?,bak,0[0-9]}
```

changes the permissions on a series of files including any file matching the expression `testfile.tx?`, `testfile.bak`, and `testfile0` through `testfile9`.

Command Substitution

Finally, let's take a look at *command substitution,* another form of pattern expansion. In some ways this is similar to piping commands together, but the difference is that in piping, the standard output of a command is passed to the standard input of another command. With command substitution, though, the standard output of one command becomes an argument or parameter to another command.

For instance, consider an example where you want to compress all files that have a .bak extension. You can get a list of all these files by using the following command:

```
$ find / -name '*.bak' -print
```

Using the **exec** flag of the find command you can compress all the files in question:

```
$ find / -name '*.bak' -exec gzip {} \;
```

The other option is to use command substitution, as in the following command:

```
$ gzip `find / -name '*.bak' -print`
```

Here the find command is contained in backwards single quotes. These quotes indicate that the results of the command should be used as part of the command line, in this case as arguments to the gzip command.

An alternative to the backward single quotes is the following form, which has the same meaning and gets the same result:

```
$ gzip $(find / -name '*.bak' -print)
```

The main difference between these two forms is the meaning of the special character \. In the latter example, no characters have special meanings, while in the former example, the backslash retains special meaning except when followed by $, `, or \.

NOTE   In addition to the types of expansion described here, there are other types of expansion available in Bash. These are outlined in detail in the **bash** man page. However, the pattern expansion forms in this chapter provide a lot of power. If you find yourself needing more powerful pattern and expansion abilities, check out the man page using the command **man bash**.

Looking Ahead

Now that you are shell power users and can perform lots of nifty magic in the world of Bash, it is time to move on to working with real, productive applications in Linux.

In the next chapter, you are going to learn about the essential tasks of system administration. These include managing users and groups of users as well as scheduling tasks for automated execution and controlling the way in which a Linux system boots.

CHAPTER
SEVENTEEN

17

General System Administration

- Managing Users

- Managing Groups

- System Start-Up

- Scheduling Jobs with *Crond*

- Managing Logs

This chapter will describe some of the basic administrative tasks that are necessary for maintaining a working Linux system.

Fundamental to any Linux system, from a network server to a home computer shared by family members, is user management. This runs the gamut from creating new user accounts to changing user passwords to ensuring that a user's home directory is just the way you, as the system administrator, want it when the user's account is created.

On even a moderately sophisticated system, user access to system resources will be governed on both a per-user basis and a per-group basis, where a group consists of a number of users associated in a common organizational entity with a single name. Linux provides facilities to associate users in groups and to use these groups to manage access to system resources.

Another administrative essential—one that is crucial to taking full advantage of Linux—is the automation of tasks, both at start-up and on a scheduled basis. Linux's notion of run levels provides a powerful mechanism to specify what will occur at what point in the start-up process (and in the shutdown process as well). And the Unix Cron facility offers a mechanism to schedule one-time jobs as well as operations that are repeated daily, weekly, monthly, or yearly.

Finally, Linux provides sophisticated logging capabilities that make it possible to know exactly what is happening on your system. Of course, for logs to be of use, they need regular management. After all, if your log contains one year's worth of entries, it becomes too large to be useful for analysis or for quickly tracking down problems or potential problems.

Managing Users

Chapter 15, "Using LinuxConf and the Control Panel for System Configuration," introduced you to user management when it described Red Hat Linux 6's Control Panel. However, the Control Panel is not universally available in all distributions of Linux, and to fully master the administration of Linux you must learn to manage users without this tool.

Creating Users

Creation of users in Linux is done through `useradd` (generally found in `/usr/sbin/`; it may be called `adduser` on some systems). The version of `useradd` shipped with Red Hat Linux 6 is a highly complex tool that can make the creation of new user accounts exceptionally easy. Let's start with the simplest example and work up to more complicated cases. The simplest case is to create a user with all the default settings. For instance, to create a new user called `testuser1`, you simply type

```
# useradd testuser1
```

This command creates the user by performing the following actions:

- Creating an entry for the user in the `/etc/passwd` file without a password. In Red Hat Linux 6, a password needs to be assigned before the user is able to log in.

- Assigning a user ID to the user. In Red Hat Linux 6, the default is to use the smallest number greater than 500 that is greater than all other users' IDs.

- Adding the user to the appropriate group. In Red Hat Linux 6, this means creating a group for the user to which only that user belongs.

- Creating a home directory for the user (at `/home/testuser1` on most Linux systems) and copying the contents of `/etc/skel` to the home directory. Skeleton directories are discussed in more detail in the section "Setting Up Default Home Directories" later in this chapter.

NOTE On Red Hat Linux 6 systems, the default behavior to create users' home directories is automatically specified in the file `/etc/login.defs` and is generally true by default. To force `useradd` to create the home directory regardless of the entry in `/etc/login.defs`, add the –m flag: `# useradd -m testuser`.

Using the `useradd` command to add users leaves the system administrator free to assign a password for the user, utilizing the techniques described in the section, "Changing Passwords."

What happens, though, if you want to override the system defaults for assignment of the user ID? Consider an organization where Red Hat Linux user IDs are based on the individual's corporate identification number. In this case, you will want to force the assignment of a particular ID. This is done with the -u flag:

```
# useradd -u 10001 testuser1
```

This creates the account for testuser1 with the assigned user ID of 10001.

Similarly, what if you want to force the assignment of a particular group to the user as their default group? For instance, if testuser1 should be assigned to the collective group named users rather than to an individual group as is the default in Red Hat Linux, you could use the -g flag:

```
# useradd -g users testuser1
```

Let's go a step further and assume that testuser1 should belong to the groups group1 and group2 in addition to the default group of users. You could create the user as indicated and then manually add them to the groups, as shown later in the section on managing groups. But useradd offers the -G flag, which allows you to specify additional groups to add the new user to when the account is created:

```
# useradd -g users -G group1,group2 testuser1
```

Finally, to specify an alternate home directory for a user, use the -d flag:

```
# useradd -d /other/home/directory testuser1
```

Changing *Useradd* Defaults

There are some defaults used by useradd that you may want to override every time you create a user. For example, you may want all home directories to be created in /users instead of /home. Similarly, you may want all new users to belong to the default group users instead of their own private groups.

These defaults can be reset using the -D flag of the useradd command and several supplementary flags. The -D flag indicates that the command should not create a new user but should assign new defaults.

The -D flag is used in conjunction with supplementary flags. Here you will see how to use the -b and -g flags for resetting the default home directory path and default group, respectively.

To set the default home directory path to /users, use the command

useradd -D -b /users

Similarly, to set the default group for all new users to users, use the command

useradd -D -g users

These commands can be combined into one command:

useradd -D -b /users -g users

Changing Passwords

Changing passwords is accomplished with the passwd command. Any user can change their password by simply typing the command at the prompt. They will be asked to enter their current password, followed by their new password twice for confirmation:

```
$ passwd
Changing password for test
(current) UNIX password:
New UNIX password:
Retype new UNIX password:
passwd: all authentication tokens updated successfully
```

In many versions of Linux, the passwd command checks to see if a password is too short, too simple, too similar to the username, or too similar to the previous password. An invalid password produces errors like these:

```
$ passwd
Changing password for test
(current) UNIX password:
New UNIX password:
BAD PASSWORD: it does not contain enough DIFFERENT characters
New UNIX password:
BAD PASSWORD: it is too short
New UNIX password:
BAD PASSWORD: is too simple
passwd: Authentication token manipulation error
```

WARNING   With some versions of the `passwd` command, the type of protection against invalid passwords described in this section can be circumvented if the user is stubborn enough and keeps supplying the same password. Eventually the `passwd` program gives up and accepts the password.

The root user has the power to change any user's password by supplying the username as an argument to the `passwd` program. In this case, the only prompts are to enter the new password twice:

```
# passwd test
New UNIX password:
Retype new UNIX password:
passwd: all authentication tokens updated successfully
```

Setting Up Default Home Directories

You've probably noticed a reference to skeleton directories earlier in the section, "Creating Users." By default, every user is given a home directory, usually in the `/home` directory. When the user's account is created, their home directory is created and populated with a default set of files. This default set of files is copied from the `/etc/skel` directory, which contains the skeleton directory for new home directories.

In order to include a file in every new home directory, simply create the file and place it in `/etc/skel` with the same name you would want it to have in users' home directories. All users added after you place the file there will find the file in their home directories when their accounts are created.

Removing Users

Deleting users is a parallel process to adding users: you use the `userdel` command. Fortunately, though, this command is far simpler to use than the `useradd` command. To delete a user's account and remove their entry from relevant system files such as `/etc/passwd`, simply provide the username as an argument:

```
# userdel username
```

The problem here is that the user's files are not deleted. To delete the user's home directory at the same time, provide the `-r` flag:

```
# userdel -r username
```

This leaves one other issue: What if the user owned files elsewhere on the system that need to be deleted? This can be achieved by using the `find` command after deleting the user. In order to do this, make note of the user's user ID from the password file before deleting the user, and then use the `find` command:

```
# find / -type f -uid 503 -print -exec rm {} \;
```

Let's break the components of this command down:

- The forward slash (/) indicates that the command should search the entire directory structure from the top level.

- `-type f` indicates that the command should only find files.

- `-uid 503` indicates that only files owned by the user with ID 503 should be returned. (This number should be substituted with the user ID of the user you are deleting.)

- `-print` indicates that the filenames should be printed as they are found so that you can track the progress of the command.

- `-exec rm {} \;` indicates that the command `rm` should be performed on every file found, effectively removing the files.

WARNING   Great care needs to be taken when using the `find` command described above. Because it runs as the root user, a mistake in typing the command or in the ownership of files on your system could cause critical data to be lost. Use `find` only if the user is likely to own files outside their home directory.

Managing Groups

Managing groups—collections of associated users—is as simple as managing users and parallels the user management process. As with user management, Linux provides commands to automate the creation and modification of groups.

NOTE   On some systems, these commands may behave differently than described in this section, so you should check the documentation if you are not using the copy of Red Hat Linux included with this book.

Creating Groups

You can add new groups to your system using the `groupadd` command (this command is called `addgroup` on some distributions). To create a group, simply provide the group name as an argument:

```
# groupadd groupname
```

The group is created and assigned a new user number based on the following rule from the man page for `groupadd`: "The default is to use the smallest ID value greater than 500 and greater than every other group."

If you want to specify the group number, simply use the `-g` flag to indicate the number:

```
# groupadd -g 503 groupname
```

This should produce an entry similar to the following in `/etc/group`:

```
groupname::503:
```

This entry shows an empty group with the specified name and group ID.

Adding Users to Groups

Unfortunately, there is no standard program available to easily add users to a group. In order to do this, the easiest thing is to directly edit the file `/etc/group`. Each line in this file represents the definition for a group and takes the form

```
groupname::password:groupid:userlist
```

The components of this line are as follows:

- The *groupname* entry is the name of the group.

- The *password* entry represents an encrypted password for the group; passwords generally are not applied to groups, so this is usually blank.

- The *groupid* is the numeric ID for the group and should be unique for the group.

- The *userlist* entry is a comma-separated list of users who belong to the group. For instance, if user1, user2, and user3 all belong to the group named group1 whose group ID is 505, the entry for the group would look like:

```
group1::505:user1,user2,user3
```

If you want to add users to an existing group, simply edit the file /etc/group with your favorite text editor and add the usernames to the end of the user list, separating each user with a comma.

Deleting Groups

Deleting groups is achieved with the groupdel command. This command is truly simple; no flags or options are available. Simply provide the group name to delete as an argument, and the group will be deleted, as follows:

```
# groupdel groupname
```

For all its simplicity, though, there are some caveats:

1. Files belonging to the group won't be deleted or have their group changed.

2. If the group serves as the primary group for a user (in other words, is indicated as the user's group in the password file), the group won't be deleted.

The first issue can be handled much as you dealt with deleting a user's files once the user had been deleted. First, you note the group ID of the group you are deleting (this can be found in the /etc/group file). Once the group is deleted with groupdel, you use the find command to change the group ownership of all files that belonged to the deleted group:

```
# find / -type f -gid 503 -print -exec chgrp newgroupname {} \;
```

This find command will find all files belonging to the group whose ID is 503 and then use the chgrp command to change the group ownership of the file to the group named *newgroupname*.

System Start-Up

One area that is a mystery to many Unix users (as opposed to system administrators) is the boot sequence, when all those arcane messages flash by on the screen.

NOTE   Start-up messages are saved in the system log file /var/log/messages. Log files are discussed later in this chapter.

What Happens During Booting?

The boot cycle is really simpler than the boot-time messages suggest. Basically, there are two stages to the boot process:

1. Booting the kernel. During this phase, the kernel loads into memory and prints messages as it initializes each device driver.

2. Executing the program init. After the kernel finishes loading and initializing devices, the program init runs. Init handles the launching of all programs, including essential system daemons and other software that is specified to load at boot time.

The *Init* Program

This section will take a closer look at the init program because it is here that you are able to easily customize which programs load during the boot cycle. init has the job of launching new processes and restarting other processes when they exit. A perfect example of this is the set of processes that provide the virtual login consoles in Linux. On most Linux systems, six of these are initially loaded at boot time. When you log out of a console window, that process dies and init starts a new one so that six console windows are always available.

The rules that govern the operation of the init program are stored in the file /etc/inittab. Red Hat Linux 6's /etc/inittab file looks like this:

```
#
# inittab       This file describes how the INIT process should set up
#               the system in a certain run-level.
#
# Author:       Miquel van Smoorenburg, <miquels@drinkel.nl.mugnet.org>
#               Modified for RHS Linux by Marc Ewing and Donnie Barnes
#

# Default runlevel. The runlevels used by RHS are:
#   0 - halt (Do NOT set initdefault to this)
#   1 - Single user mode
#   2 - Multiuser, without NFS (The same as 3, if you do not have
➥networking)
#   3 - Full multiuser mode
#   4 - unused
#   5 - X11
#   6 - reboot (Do NOT set initdefault to this)
```

```
#
id:3:initdefault:

# System initialization.
si::sysinit:/etc/rc.d/rc.sysinit

l0:0:wait:/etc/rc.d/rc 0
l1:1:wait:/etc/rc.d/rc 1
l2:2:wait:/etc/rc.d/rc 2
l3:3:wait:/etc/rc.d/rc 3
l4:4:wait:/etc/rc.d/rc 4
l5:5:wait:/etc/rc.d/rc 5
l6:6:wait:/etc/rc.d/rc 6

# Things to run in every runlevel.
ud::once:/sbin/update

# Trap CTRL-ALT-DELETE
ca::ctrlaltdel:/sbin/shutdown -t3 -r now

# When our UPS tells us power has failed, assume we have a few minutes
# of power left.  Schedule a shutdown for 2 minutes from now.
# This does, of course, assume you have powerd installed and your
# UPS connected and working correctly.
pf::powerfail:/sbin/shutdown -f -h +2 "Power Failure; System Shutting
➡Down"

# If power was restored before the shutdown kicked in, cancel it.
pr:12345:powerokwait:/sbin/shutdown -c "Power Restored; Shutdown
➡Cancelled"


# Run gettys in standard runlevels
1:12345:respawn:/sbin/mingetty tty1
2:2345:respawn:/sbin/mingetty tty2
3:2345:respawn:/sbin/mingetty tty3
4:2345:respawn:/sbin/mingetty tty4
5:2345:respawn:/sbin/mingetty tty5
6:2345:respawn:/sbin/mingetty tty6


# Run xdm in runlevel 5
# xdm is now a separate service
# x:5:respawn:/usr/bin/X11/xdm -nodaemon
```

While it is not important to learn how to write your own inittab file, it is useful to understand what this file is telling us.

Linux has a system of *run levels*. A run level is a number that identifies the current state of the system and which processes init should run and keep running in that system state. In the inittab file, the first entry specifies the default run level that loads at boot time. In the previous example, it is a multiuser console mode, run level 3. Then, each entry in the inittab file specifies which run level it applies to in the second field of the entry (each field is separated by a colon). So, for run level 3, the following lines are relevant:

```
l3:3:wait:/etc/rc.d/rc 3
1:12345:respawn:/sbin/mingetty tty1
2:2345:respawn:/sbin/mingetty tty2
3:2345:respawn:/sbin/mingetty tty3
4:2345:respawn:/sbin/mingetty tty4
5:2345:respawn:/sbin/mingetty tty5
6:2345:respawn:/sbin/mingetty tty6
```

The last six lines set up the six virtual consoles provided in Linux. The first line runs the start-up script /etc/rc.d/rc 3. This will run all the scripts contained in the directory /etc/rc.d/rc3.d. These scripts represent programs that need to start at system initialization, such as sendmail, PCMCIA services, the printer daemon, and crond. Generally, you will not want to edit these scripts or change them; they are the system defaults.

What is important to note is that the last script in rc3.d to be executed will be the S99local script. This script is actually a link to the file /etc/rc.d/rc.local; it is here that you can put any custom start-up programs that you want to launch at boot time.

On other Linux systems, the structure of /etc/inittab may differ, as will the organization of the /etc/rc.d directory. In all systems, however, the file /etc/rc.d/rc.local represents the file in which you can add your own start-up commands.

Using the *Rc.local* File

The default Red Hat Linux 6 rc.local file sets up the login prompt and does nothing else:

```
#!/bin/sh

# This script will be executed *after* all the other init scripts.
```

```
# You can put your own initialization stuff in here if you don't
# want to do the full Sys V style init stuff.

if [ -f /etc/redhat-release ]; then
    R=$(cat /etc/redhat-release)

    arch=$(uname -m)
    a="a"
    case "_$arch" in
      _a*) a="an";;
      _i*) a="an";;
    esac

    # This will overwrite /etc/issue at every boot.  So, make any
➥changes you
    # want to make to /etc/issue here or you will lose them when you
➥reboot.
    echo "" > /etc/issue
    echo "$R" >> /etc/issue
    echo "Kernel $(uname -r) on $a $(uname -m)" >> /etc/issue

    cp -f /etc/issue /etc/issue.net
    echo >> /etc/issue
fi
```

This may look complicated, but it is actually quite simple. The steps here are:

1. Identify the Red Hat Linux release being used.

2. Identify the hardware architecture (such as i386 for Intel or axp for Alpha).

3. Store the contents of the login prompt in /etc/issue; this file is displayed at each console prompt.

Because the rc.local file is a standard shell script, you can do anything here that is legitimate in a shell script, including assigning environment variables and launching programs. For instance, on one system I manage, we launch a database daemon in our rc.local file with the following command:

```
# /usr/local/Minerva/bin/msqld &
```

Feel free to use the rc.local file to add any start-up programs that you want to run. For instance, if you want to receive an e-mail every time a particular machine on the network finishes booting, you can use the rc.local file on the machine in question to run the command

```
# /bin/mail -s "I have booted — machinename" username@some.domain
```

to send a quick mail message to *username@some.domain* with the subject line I have booted–*machinename*.

Shutting Down

Closely related to system start-up is system shutdown. In Linux, as in all other multitasking operating systems, it is essential to shut down your system cleanly in order to prevent corruption of data stored on attached hard disk drives. Generally, this is done by the root user with the shutdown command:

```
# shutdown -h now
```

The use of the now argument tells the program to shut down the system immediately. The –h flag tells the system to halt after shutting down. When you see the message System Halted, it is safe to power off your computer.

Closely related to the shutdown command is the reboot command, which cleanly shuts down the system and then reboots it. Hitting the key combination Ctrl+Alt+Delete invokes the reboot command.

Scheduling Jobs with *Crond*

One of the great strengths of a multiuser server-class operating system like Linux is that much can happen in an unattended manner. If you use Linux as a mail server, Web server, or FTP server, unattended activity occurs every time one of these applications answers incoming connections and requests for service. Similarly, individual users and the system administrator can configure Linux to perform prescheduled tasks in an unattended manner.

This activity is achieved through the facility of a daemon called crond. This daemon is standard and is generally installed to start every time the system boots.

How *Crond* Works

The way in which crond works is amazingly simple. Once crond starts (generally at boot time), it wakes up every minute and checks whether any jobs have been scheduled to run during that minute. If so, the job is executed and the resulting output is sent by e-mail to the user who scheduled the job.

Because `crond` checks the date stamps on its configuration files every minute, any changes to schedules are noted without the necessity of restarting the `crond` process.

Scheduling Jobs

Scheduling jobs is an easy matter. All scheduled jobs are stored in an individual configuration file (known as a `crontab` file) for the user, with each line representing a job that has been scheduled.

Let's start by looking at the format of `crontab` file entries before moving on to how to edit the `crontab` file to create scheduled jobs.

Each entry takes the form

`time-date command`

The *time-date* entry consists of five numeric fields, each separated by spaces, which indicate when a job should be run. The five fields (in order) are:

- Minute: Possible values are 0–59.

- Hour: Possible values are 0–23.

- Day of month: Possible values are 0–31.

- Month: Possible values are 0–12 (or the first three letters of the month's name).

- Day of week: Possible values are 0–7 where both 0 and 7 represent Sunday (or the first three letters of the day's name).

For all these fields, several rules provide flexibility:

- Ranges of numbers can be used. For instance, 1-3 in the hour field says to schedule the command for 1:00 A.M., 2:00 A.M., and 3:00 A.M. Similarly, 2-4 in the day of the week field schedules the job for Tuesday, Wednesday, and Thursday.

- Ranges can be stepped through in increments greater than one. For instance, to indicate every other hour from midnight to midnight, use the range 0-23 and combine it with the step of 2, separating them with slashes: 0-23/2.

- An asterisk (*) indicates the entire range for a field from smallest value to largest value. Thus, * in the day of the month field is the same as 0-31 and in the day of the week field is the same as 0-7.

Sample Times and Dates

Let's take a look at some example time-date fields:

0 1 * * *	This field indicates a job that should run every day at 1:00 A.M.
30 14 * * 0	This field indicates a job that should run every Monday at 2:30 P.M.
0 12 1 * *	This field indicates a job that should run at noon on the first day of every month.
0 12 * 1 mon	This field indicates a job that should run at noon on every Monday in January every year.
0 12 2 feb *	This field indicates a job that should run at noon on February 2 every year.

The Command Field

The time-date field is separated from the command field by one or more spaces and runs until the end of the line. The commands are processed by the /bin/sh shell.

For instance, the crontab entry

```
0 1 * * *    /usr/local/bin/backup
```

causes the program /usr/local/bin/backup to execute daily at 1:00 A.M.

Sometimes commands (such as the mail command) require information to be entered through the standard input. This is achieved using percent signs (%). The first percent sign marks the start of standard input, and each subsequent percent sign serves as a new line character in the standard input.

So the crontab entry

```
30 14 * * fri    /bin/mail -s "TGIF" armand@landegg.edu%Thank God It's
➥Friday%%Me.
```

sends the following e-mail message:

```
Thank God It's Friday

Me.
```

to armand@landegg.edu each Friday afternoon at 2:30 P.M.

Editing the *Crontab* File

You can edit your crontab file with the crontab command. Two approaches are available: create a file containing all the entries desired in the crontab file and then load it with the crontab command or edit the crontab file directly with the crontab command.

Loading Entries from a File　In order to load entries from a file, it is first necessary to create a file (using your favorite text editor) containing all the entries you wish to have appear in your crontab file. A sample file might contain two entries as follows:

```
0 1 * * *      /usr/local/bin/backup
30 14 * * fri        /bin/mail -s "TGIF" armand@landegg.edu%Thank God
➡It's Friday%%Me.
```

This file needs to be saved, under a suitable name such as cronjobs.

Once the file is created and saved, it can be loaded into a user's crontab file by issuing the command:

```
$ crontab cronjobs
```

The contents of cronjobs overwrites any current entries in the crontab file for the user. Using this method, any user can manipulate their own crontab file.

The root user has special privileges that allow them to edit the crontab entries for any user. Using the -u flag, the root user can specify that another user's crontab file, rather than the root user's crontab file, should be altered. For instance, the command

```
# crontab -u username cronjobs
```

loads the file cronjobs as the crontab file for the user username.

Editing *Crontab* Files Directly　Instead of creating a separate file and loading it into the crontab file, the crontab command provides the -e flag, which allows the user to edit the crontab file directly.

By default, crontab -e attempts to edit the crontab file using the vi editor. The vi editor is a powerful but hard-to-master editor popular among longtime

Unix users. If you prefer to use another editor, such as xedit, you need to set the value of the EDITOR environment variable to this program:

```
$ export EDITOR=xedit
```

Then the command

```
$ crontab -e
```

opens the crontab file for editing using the specified editor, as shown in Figure 17.1.

FIGURE 17.1:

Editing the crontab file
with xedit

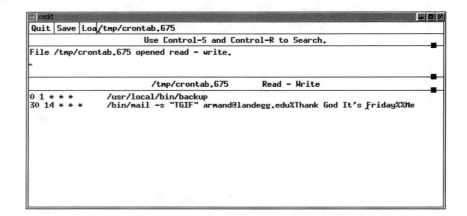

As when you load a file into the crontab file using the -u flag, the root user can directly edit another user's crontab file:

```
$ crontab -u username -e
```

Viewing the Contents of the *Crontab* File In order to view the contents of the crontab file, simply use the -l flag:

```
$ crontab -l
# DO NOT EDIT THIS FILE - edit the master and reinstall.
# (/tmp/crontab.555 installed on Mon Jul 13 00:07:05 1998)
# (Cron version - $Id: crontab.c,v 2.13 1994/01/17 03:20:37 vixie Exp
➡$)
0 1 * * *        /usr/local/bin/backup
30 14 * * fri    /bin/mail -s "TGIF" armand@landegg.edu%Thank God It's
➡Friday%%Me
```

Notice that the crontab file has several comment lines at the beginning that start with the hash mark (#).

As with editing the crontab file, the root user can view the contents of any user's crontab file with the -u flag:

```
# crontab -u username -l
```

Removing the *Crontab* File In order to erase the contents of a user's crontab file, the user can use the -r flag:

```
$ crontab -r
```

Similarly, the root user can clear any user's crontab file with the -u flag:

```
# crontab -u username -r
```

Managing Logs

One of the benefits of Linux and all forms of Unix is that they provide standardized mechanisms for the logging of activity from the numerous daemons and programs running on the system. These logs can be used to debug system problems as well as track usage of the system, covering everything from possible security breaches to advanced warning of possible hardware failure.

For example, the following extract of the main Red Hat Linux 6 system log file (/var/log/messages) provides numerous pieces of information from a two-minute period:

```
Apr 16 03:55:29 localhost login: ROOT LOGIN ON tty1
Apr 16 03:55:58 localhost syslog: Warning - secret file /etc/paus has
➥world and/or group access
Apr 16 03:55:58 localhost kernel: CSLIP: code copyright 1989 Regents of
➥the University of California
Apr 16 03:55:58 localhost kernel: PPP: version 2.2 (dynamic channel
➥allocation)
Apr 16 03:55:58 localhost kernel: PPP Dynamic channel allocation code
➥copyright 1995 Caldera, Inc.
Apr 16 03:55:58 localhost kernel: PPP line discipline registered.
Apr 16 03:55:58 localhost kernel: registered device ppp0
Apr 16 03:55:58 localhost pppd[207]: pppd 2.2 started by root, uid 0
Apr 16 03:55:59 localhost chat[208]: send (ATDT8447077^M)
Apr 16 03:56:00 localhost chat[208]: expect (CONNECT)
Apr 16 03:56:32 localhost chat[208]: ATDT8447077^M^M
Apr 16 03:56:32 localhost pppd[207]: Serial connection established.
Apr 16 03:56:32 localhost chat[208]: CONNECT - got it
```

```
Apr 16 03:56:32 localhost chat[208]: send (^M)
Apr 16 03:56:33 localhost pppd[207]: Using interface ppp0
Apr 16 03:56:33 localhost pppd[207]: Connect: ppp0 <-> /dev/cua1
Apr 16 03:56:36 localhost pppd[207]: Remote message:
Apr 16 03:56:36 localhost pppd[207]: local  IP address 194.209.60.112
Apr 16 03:56:36 localhost pppd[207]: remote IP address 194.209.60.97
```

What exactly do you learn here? The login program informs you that the root user has logged in, you have a warning about the security of information in a file that should be secure, you see the kernel loading its PPP module successfully, and you see the pppd process establish a connection to the Internet.

What Gets Logged?

It is important to make a distinction between different types of logs in a Linux system. Basically, there are two types of logs: system logs and application logs. This section looks at system logs because all systems have them. Application-specific logs are dependent on the applications being run and how these applications are configured to generate their logs.

In the system logs, you are likely to find messages and warnings from the kernel that include information about modules that have loaded, data from the sendmail daemon that provides a trail of the messages that have been processed in the system, and messages about the success or failure of authentication (login) attempts.

System logs are generated by the syslogd daemon, which loads at boot time. The daemon accesses messages at eight levels of severity from various system processes such as the kernel, the mail system, user programs configured to use syslogd, and authentication programs such as the login program.

These levels of messages are, in order of increasing severity:

- debug
- info
- notice
- warning
- err
- crit
- alert
- emerg

These levels are used in the /etc/syslog.conf file to tell syslogd where to create logs for different types of information. The /etc/syslog.conf file contains multiple entries, one on each line, each containing two fields separated by one or more spaces: a facility-level list and a log file location.

The facility-level list is a semicolon-separated list of facility-level pairs. Facilities are indicated by facility names such as mail, kern (for the kernel), user (for user programs), and auth (for authentication programs). Sample facility-level pairs include:

- mail.err: errors generated by the mail daemon

- *.info: all information messages

- kern.emerg: emergency messages from the kernel

Let's look at the default /etc/syslog.conf file that is included with Red Hat Linux 6 to get a sense of how this works:

```
# Log all kernel messages to the console.
# Logging much else clutters up the screen.
#kern.*                                          /dev/console

# Log anything (except mail) of level info or higher.
# Don't log private authentication messages!
*.info;mail.none;authpriv.none                   /var/log/messages

# The authpriv file has restricted access.
authpriv.*                                       /var/log/secure

# Log all the mail messages in one place.
mail.*                                           /var/log/maillog

# Everybody gets emergency messages, plus log them on another
# machine.
*.emerg                                                *

# Save mail and news errors of level err and higher in a
# special file.
uucp,news.crit                                   /var/log/spooler
```

The first important line is

```
*.info;mail.none;authpriv.none                   /var/log/messages
```

This line logs information messages from all facilities except mail and authentication (hence, `mail.none;authpriv.none`) to the file `/var/log/message`. This is followed by

`authpriv.*`   `/var/log/secure`

which places all authentication messages in `/var/log/secure`.

Next you find the following line, which specifies that all mail log messages should be placed in `/var/log/maillog`:

`mail.*`   `/var/log/maillog`

followed by

`uucp,news.crit`   `/var/log/spooler`

which logs certain mail- and news-related messages to `/var/log/spooler`.

The first thing you will probably notice is that log messages are separated into different files. The goals behind this practice are to keep the size of each log manageable and to keep the information in each log related so that tracking down log messages is easy. If every message of every level from every facility ended up in a single log file, the information would be practically useless because the volume of information in the file would be unmanageable.

If you want to change your logging strategy by editing `/etc/syslog.conf`, you can do this by editing the `syslog.conf` file and then telling `syslogd` to reload the configuration with the command

`# kill -HUP `cat /var/run/syslogd.pid``

Notice the use of the back quotes. These indicate that the command they contain should be executed and the resulting standard output should be provided as an argument to the `kill -HUP` command. The -HUP flag of the `kill` command indicates that the process should reread its configuration but keep running.

Rotating Logs

In order for logs to remain useful, they need to be rotated on a regular basis. This allows the size of the logs to be manageable and clears them of old information that is no longer of particular value. Also, because the size of logs will continue to grow, rotating them frees up the disk space they are using.

The simplest strategy for rotating logs is to remove them and restart syslogd. When syslogd restarts, it will create a new, empty log file to replace any that have been removed. For instance, the following commands:

```
# rm /var/log/messages
# kill -HUP `cat /var/run/syslogd.pid`
```

remove the /var/log/messages file and restart syslogd to create a new, empty /var/log/messages file.

This strategy of removing files works well on a single-user or home system where historical logs may not serve a valuable purpose. On multiuser servers, however, historical information is of particular value, especially for tracking possible security breaches. In this case, the strategy may be slightly different. For instance, to keep one generation of historical logs, you can move the current logs to a new filename and then restart syslogd to create a new current log file:

```
# mv /var/log/messages /var/log/messages.1
# kill -HUP `cat /var/run/syslogd.pid`
```

Similarly, if you want to create two generations of historical log files, you need to move the first-generation files to the second-generation filename and then move the current logs to the first-generation filename:

```
# mv /var/log/messages.1 /var/log/messages.2
# mv /var/log/messages /var/log/messages.1
# kill -HUP `cat /var/run/syslogd.pid`
```

On most systems, you may want to automate this procedure, running it every week at a set time. To do this, you first need to create a script that performs the necessary actions to rotate your log files. For instance, on a Red Hat Linux 6 server where you keep one generation of logs, the script would look something like this:

```
#!/bin/sh

mv /var/log/messages /var/log/messages.1
mv /var/log/secure /var/log/secure.1
mv /var/log/maillog /var/log/maillog.1
mv /var/log/spooler /var/log/spooler.1
kill -HUP `cat /var/run/syslogd.pid`
```

This script file needs to be created with a text editor in a logical location (such as /usr/local/bin/newlogs) and then made into an executable file:

```
# chmod 755 /usr/local/bin/newlogs
```

Next, you need to edit the root user's crontab file, using the methods described earlier in this chapter, and add an appropriate entry. For instance, to run the script every Sunday morning at 12:01 A.M., you would use the entry:

```
1 12 * * sun /usr/local/bin/newlogs
```

Looking Ahead

In this chapter, you have learned a handful of useful system administration tasks relating to users, scheduling, and logs.

The next chapter describes how to configure and use two of the most popular PC peripherals: printers and modems.

You will learn how to configure both PostScript and PCL printers, and you will discover the mechanics of the Unix print spool systems.

The next chapter also discusses modem configuration, and you'll get to experiment with the minicom program to test and use your modems.

Using Peripherals

- ■ Printers

- ■ Modems

This chapter will explain how to configure the two most common types of peripherals: printers and modems. You will get an understanding of how Linux ports work, take a look at the files that control the Linux printing system, and become acquainted with minicom, a standard Linux terminal emulator that you can use to access your modem.

Printers

In Chapter 15, "Using LinuxConf and the Control Panel for System Configuration," you learned how to easily configure printers in Red Hat Linux 6 using the Control Panel. This chapter will discuss the basics of configuring printers manually. A good reference for this process is the Printing HOWTO at `http://metalab .unc.edu/mdw/HOWTO/Printing-HOWTO.html`.

What Printer to Use

Before discussing configuration of printers in Linux, let's take a quick look at which printers work with Linux and how to go about using them.

First, though, a word of warning: printers that use the Windows Printing System (also called *GDI printers*) generally cannot be used with Linux. These printers are essentially "dumb" printers that require the computer to do the job of preparing à document for printing and rely on specialized Windows software provided by the printer manufacturer. You are best off avoiding a GDI printer for use in Linux.

Having said that, most other printers are supported as follows:

- PostScript printers: Most Unix software generates PostScript output for printing, so your best choice is a PostScript printer. Of course, low-end laser printers and inkjet printers don't support PostScript.

- Non-PostScript printers supported by GhostScript: If your printer doesn't support PostScript but supports the Printer Control Language (PCL), it is probably supported by the GhostScript application, a software-based PostScript interpreter. To see if your printer is supported, check the GhostScript home page at `http://www.cs.wisc.edu/~ghost/`. Table 18.1 contains a partial list of printers supported by GhostScript.

TABLE 18.1: Printers Supported by GhostScript

Canon BubbleJet BJ10e	HP DeskJet 682C
Canon BubbleJet BJ200	HP DeskJet 683C
Canon BubbleJet BJC-210 (41)	HP DeskJet 693C
Canon BubbleJet BJC-240 (3.33, 43)	HP DeskJet 694C
Canon BubbleJet BJC-250 (5.10)	HP DeskJet 850
Canon BubbleJet BJC-70 (5.10)	HP DeskJet 855
Canon BubbleJet BJC-600	HP DeskJet 870Cse
Canon BubbleJet BJC-4000	HP DeskJet 870Cxi
Canon BubbleJet BJC-4100	HP DeskJet 890C
Canon BubbleJet BJC-4200	HP DeskJet 672C
Canon BubbleJet BJC-4300	HP DeskJet 680
Canon BubbleJet BJC-4550	HP DeskJet 1100C
Canon BJC-210	HP DeskJet 500C
Canon MultiPASS C2500 color printer/fax/copier	HP DeskJet 510
Canon BJC-240	HP DeskJet 520
Canon BJC-70	HP LaserJet 5
Canon BubbleJet BJC-800	HP LaserJet 5L
Canon BubbleJet BJC-7000	HP LaserJet 6L
HP DeskJet	Oki OL410ex LED printer
HP DeskJet Plus	NEC SuperScript 860
HP DeskJet 500	HP PaintJet XL300
HP DeskJet Portable	HP DeskJet 1200C
HP DeskJet 400	HP DeskJet 1600C
HP DeskJet 500C	Ricoh 4081 laser printer
HP DeskJet 540C	Ricoh 6000 laser printer

Continued on next page

TABLE 18.1 CONTINUED: Printers Supported by GhostScript

HP DeskJet 690C	Epson Stylus Color
HP DeskJet 693C	Epson Stylus Color II
HP DeskJet 550C	Epson Stylus 500
HP DeskJet 560C	Epson Stylus 600
HP DeskJet 600	Epson Stylus 800
HP DeskJet 660C	

The *Printcap* File

The printcap file is found in the /etc directory and is the core of Linux printer configuration. This file contains entries for each printer that is available to your Linux system. When the Linux printer daemon, lpd, is loaded (generally at boot time), it looks at this file to learn about the printers it will be managing.

A basic entry in the printcap file is as follows:

```
# LOCAL
djet500lp|dj|deskjet:\
     :sd=/var/spool/lpd/dj:\
     :mx#0:
     :lp=/dev/lp0:\
     :sh:
```

Each entry contains numerous fields separated by colons. If the entry needs to span more than one line, the backslash indicates that the entry continues on the next line.

This example has a printer with three possible names: djet500lp, dj, and deskjet. This printer has a spool directory at /var/spool/lpd/dj where lpd can store temporary files while they are waiting to be printed. The printer is connected to the first parallel port (/dev/lp0) and no header pages should be printed (sh). This all might seem very cryptic, and to a certain extent it is. The printcap file can take literally dozens of different fields. These are outlined in the printcap man page:

```
$ man printcap
```

If this information was all that was needed to get a printer to work, configuring your printers wouldn't be so bad. But lpd is essentially stupid. With an entry like the one above, whatever data is provided to lpd is sent directly to the printer. If the data provided is not understood by the printer, you will get gibberish or nothing in return. Consider the following possible problems:

- An ASCII text file sent to a PostScript printer does not print.

- An ASCII text file sent to a PCL printer does not print with the correct formatting unless the control codes in the file are adjusted.

- A PostScript file sent to a PCL printer prints as a long list of PostScript commands instead of the actual page image defined by the commands.

These are just some of the problems encountered when printing using a barebones printcap entry like the one outlined above. They can be resolved by the use of print filters.

Print Filters

Print filters are special programs or scripts that process data before it is sent to the printer. For instance, if you have a PCL printer, you could write one script to process ASCII text before sending it to the printer so it will appear in correct format, and another script to send PostScript data through GhostScript to generate correct PCL output. But if you do this manually, you need to have multiple printer entries in the printcap file, one for each type of filter you plan to make available:

```
# PCL Printer with ASCII filter
ascii-pcl:\
     :sd=/var/spool/lpd/ascii-pcl:\
     :mx#0:
     :lp=/dev/lp0:\
     :sh:\
     :if=/var/spool/lpd/ascii-pcl/filter

# PCL Printer with PostScript filter
ps-pcl:\
     :sd=/var/spool/lpd/ps-pcl:\
     :mx#0:
     :lp=/dev/lp0:\
     :sh:\
     :if=/var/spool/lpd/ps-pcl/filter
```

```
# PCL Printer with no filter
pcl:\
      :sd=/var/spool/lpd/pcl:\
      :mx#0:
      :lp=/dev/lp0:\
      :sh:\
```

These filters would generate the correct output, but they would add complications to the printing process. Users would need to know what type of output is being generated by their application (plain text, PostScript, or PCL) and then select the correct printer accordingly. There might also be confusion because the filters suggest that there are three physical printers available when there is really only one.

These difficulties are addressed by *magic filters*. Magic filters, which are available for downloading from the Internet, handle all the `printcap` configuration for most supported printers and provide filters that can determine the type of data being sent to the printer and perform the correct filtering on that basis.

The APS Print Filter System

The leading magic filter package is the APS Print Filter system. You can download the latest version of the APS Print Filters from `ftp://metalab.unc.edu/pub/Linux/system/printing/`. At the time of this writing, two versions of the APS Print Filters were available on the SunSite FTP server: 4.9.1 and 4.9.9. This chapter works with version 4.91, and the file to download is `aps-491.tgz`. The operations discussed here should work with version 4.9.9 as well.

To install the software, use the `tar` command to uncompress and extract the archive in a logical location, such as `/usr/local`. You need to create a directory in which to store the uncompressed files. The following commands assume you have downloaded the original archive in `/tmp`:

NOTE   You need to perform these steps as the root user.

```
# cd /usr/local
# mkdir apsfilter
# cd apsfilter
# tar /tmp/tzvf aps-491.tgz
```

To configure APS to work with your printer, the next step is to run the `setup` script that comes with the package:

```
# ./SETUP
```

This brings up a welcome screen. Press Enter and the setup script presents its first question:

```
For which printer type do you want to setup apsfilter...

    1 - for a Postscript printer
    2 - for HP Deskjets
    3 - for another printer who doesn't support the Postscript language
```

At this prompt, select the type of printer you are installing; this section will describe each printer type in turn.

PostScript Printers

If you choose to install a PostScript printer, the process is relatively easy. The next question is about the resolution of your printer:

```
Very fine, you have a real PS printer...Please select a printer
driver that fits your PS-printers resolution:

 [ PS_300dpi PS_400dpi PS_600dpi PS_800dpi ]
```

Here you need to select the appropriate option by typing the complete name presented. For instance, if you have a 600 dpi laser printer, type **PS_600dpi** and press Enter.

The next question is about the color capabilities of your printer:

```
Is your printer a  (c)olor printer
             or a  (m)ono printer ?
```

Type **c** or **m** as appropriate. For most PostScript laser printers, monochrome is the right choice.

Once you have selected the color status of your printer, you need to indicate the default paper you are using:

```
What paper form do you use (i.e.: a3, a4, letter,...)
See /usr/local/apsfilter/doc/paper for valid sizes...
Note: enter the paper form in lowercase letters:
```

In the U.S., this will usually be letter (or on occasion, legal); outside the U.S. the most likely size is a4.

The next question asks about the port you are using to connect the printer to your computer:

```
Do you have a (s)erial or a (p)arallel printer interface ?
```

Any respectable printer sold today uses the parallel interface, so unless you are using an extremely old printer or are trying to get some Macintosh printers to work with your PC, you should type **p** and press Enter.

Now you need to specify the Linux device that is associated with your printer:

```
What's the device name for your parallel printer interface ?
For Linux Systems with kernel <= 1.1.X :)
Device Name Major Minor  I/O address!
/dev/lp0    6     0      0x3bc (1. parallel device)
/dev/lp1    6     1      0x378 (2. parallel device)
/dev/lp2    6     2      0x278 (3. parallel device)

type in the full path name, i.e.: /dev/lp0:
```

As discussed earlier, LPT1: on DOS normally maps to /dev/lp0, and LPT2: in DOS is usually the same as /dev/lp1.

Following this, the setup program creates several files and then prompts you to press Enter after being presented with different pieces of information about your configuration. As it continues the job of configuring your print system, the setup program periodically displays screens of information that you should read so you'll understand what's happening.

Finally, you are greeted with the message

```
We made it!
```

and returned to the command prompt.

Hewlett-Packard DeskJet Printers

Configuring a Hewlett-Packard (HP) DeskJet printer is subtly different than configuring a PostScript printer. After selecting this type of printer, a list of DeskJet printers appears.

You can use the up and down arrow keys to scroll through the list. Once you have finished reading the list and identified a likely printer, type **Q** to exit the list and return to the main part of the setup script. A prompt appears like this:

```
which printer driver do you want to use ?

-------------------------
cdjmono         *1    300, 300,   1, 4, 0, 1
cdeskjet        *1    300, 300,   3, 4, 2, 1
cdjcolor        *1    300, 300,  24, 4, 2, 1
cdj500          *1    300, 300, bpp, 4, 2, 1
cdj550          *1    300, 300, bpp, 0, 2, 1
deskjet         +     300, 300,   1, -  -  -
djet500         +     300, 300,   1, -  -  -
djet500c        *2    300, 300,   3, -, 1, 1

-------------------------


Perhaps good choices are:
For a HP Deskjet  (b&w):     deskjet
For a Deskjet 500 (b&w):     djet500
For a color Deskjet:         cdeskjet

What driver do you want for your deskjet ?
```

Select the appropriate driver and press Enter. From there, the setup script continues on to ask you about the color capabilities of your printer, your default paper size, the type of connection being used, and the Linux device associated with your printer, just as it did for a PostScript printer.

Other Non-PostScript Printers

If you choose the third type of printer, configuration is subtly different again. Here you are presented with a list of printer drivers to choose from:

```
Select one of the following gs(1) printer driver ...

[ appledmp bj10e bj200 declj250 eps9high epson epsonc escp2
   ibmpro jetp3852 la50 la75 laserjet lbp8 lj250 ljet2p ljet3
   ljet4 ljet4l ljetplus ln03 m8510 necp6 nwp533 oki182 paintjet
   pj pjxl pjxl300 r4081 sparc t4693d2 t4693d4 t4693d8 tek4696
   gs V3.X: st800 ]

Do you need a more verbose description of the printer
drivers ? y/n ?
```

If you see a driver that clearly matches your printer, type **n** and press Enter to move on to the selection prompt. Otherwise, type **y** to view a detailed description of the drivers (use the up and down arrow keys to scroll through the list) and type **Q** when you are done to move on to the following prompt:

```
[ appledmp bj10e bj200 declj250 eps9high epson epsonc escp2
   ibmpro jetp3852 la50 la75 laserjet lbp8 lj250 ljet2p ljet3
   ljet4 ljet4l ljetplus ln03 m8510 necp6 nwp533 oki182 paintjet
   pj pjxl pjxl300 r4081 sparc t4693d2 t4693d4 t4693d8 tek4696
   gs V3.X: st800 ]

Which printer driver do you want ?
```

Enter the driver name and press Enter to make your selection.

From there, the setup script continues on to ask you about the color capabilities of your printer, your default paper size, the type of connection being used, and the Linux device associated with your printer, just as it did for a PostScript printer.

After Configuration

After configuration, you should have a `printcap` file that looks something like this:

```
# LABEL apsfilter
# apsfilter setup Mon Jul 27 17:17:05 CEST 1998
#
# APS_BASEDIR:/usr/local/apsfilter
```

```
#
#
ascii|lp1|escp2-a4-ascii-mono|escp2 ascii mono:\
        :lp=/dev/lp1:\
          :sd=/usr/spool/escp2-a4-ascii-mono:\
          :lf=/usr/spool/escp2-a4-ascii-mono/log:\
          :af=/usr/spool/escp2-a4-ascii-mono/acct:\
          :if=/usr/local/apsfilter/filter/aps-escp2-a4-ascii-mono:\
          :mx#0:\
          :sh:
#
lp|lp2|escp2-a4-auto-mono|escp2 auto mono:\
          :lp=/dev/lp1:\
          :sd=/usr/spool/escp2-a4-auto-mono:\
          :lf=/usr/spool/escp2-a4-auto-mono/log:\
          :af=/usr/spool/escp2-a4-auto-mono/acct:\
          :if=/usr/local/apsfilter/filter/aps-escp2-a4-auto-mono:\
          :mx#0:\
          :sh:
#
lp3|escp2-a4-ascii-color|escp2 ascii color:\
          :lp=/dev/lp1:\
          :sd=/usr/spool/escp2-a4-ascii-color:\
          :lf=/usr/spool/escp2-a4-ascii-color/log:\
          :af=/usr/spool/escp2-a4-ascii-color/acct:\
          :if=/usr/local/apsfilter/filter/aps-escp2-a4-ascii-color:\
          :mx#0:\
          :sh:
#
lp4|escp2-a4-auto-color|escp2 auto color:\
          :lp=/dev/lp1:\
          :sd=/usr/spool/escp2-a4-auto-color:\
          :lf=/usr/spool/escp2-a4-auto-color/log:\
          :af=/usr/spool/escp2-a4-auto-color/acct:\
          :if=/usr/local/apsfilter/filter/aps-escp2-a4-auto-color:\
          :mx#0:\
          :sh:
#
raw|lp5|escp2-a4-raw|escp2 auto raw:\
          :lp=/dev/lp1:\
          :sd=/usr/spool/escp2-raw:\
          :lf=/usr/spool/escp2-raw/log:\
```

```
:af=/usr/spool/escp2-raw/acct:\
:if=/usr/local/apsfilter/filter/aps-escp2-a4-raw:\
:mx#0:\
:sh:
```

Regardless of the printer you configure for use with Linux, the APS filter system always makes the following three print queues available:

- ascii: a queue that is exclusively for printing plain text files

- lp: an automatic filter that will detect the file type and process it accordingly

- raw: an unfiltered print queue that can be used if the software you are using generates output in the native format required by your printer

Printing

Now you are ready to print. You can do this with the lpr command. The -P flag specifies which printer queue to use. For instance, the command

```
$ lpr -Pascii /etc/printcap
```

prints the printcap file out through the plain text print queue, while

```
$ lpr -Plp /etc/printcap
```

prints the same file through the automatic filter.

Modems

Modems are among the simplest types of peripherals to get working in Linux. Generally, external modems can be plugged into an available serial port and be expected to work, while standard internal modems should be equally easy to get up and running under Linux.

NOTE   Not all internal modems are supported under Linux. If you have one, try it. If you are buying a new modem, it is probably worth the extra cost to buy an external one. If you must purchase an internal modem, be sure it is not a "win modem," which uses specialized Windows software to implement flow control.

This section will look at how Linux handles ports, since this is essential to the understanding of Linux modem management, and then will describe some simple ways to use your modem.

Understanding Linux Ports

In the Linux environment, every physical peripheral or connection port is associated with one or more files in the special directory /dev. This includes hard disk drives, CD-ROM drives, parallel ports, and serial ports.

The concept behind this is easy to understand. Let's look at hard drives as an example.

Each IDE hard drive is named hdx, where x is a letter starting with a for the first drive on the primary IDE bus, b for the second drive on the primary IDE bus, c for the first drive on the secondary IDE bus, and so on. Thus, the secondary master drive is associated with /dev/hdc.

In addition, each partition on the drive is associated with a /dev entry. The second partition on the primary slave drive, for instance, is /dev/hdb2, while the first partition of the secondary master drive is /dev/hdc1.

Parallel Ports and Linux

So far, this is a simple concept.

Let's consider parallel ports. In the DOS and Windows world, parallel ports are referred to as LPT1:, LPT2:, LPT3:, and so on. On most PCs, there is generally only one parallel port, so you usually only have to deal with LPT1:.

In the Linux world, the parallel ports correspond to the device files lpx, where x is the number of the port. Here is where the crucial difference lies: Linux starts counting the ports at 0 instead of 1, so LPT1: is usually /dev/lp0 and LPT2: would then be /dev/lp1. There may be cases where you have only one port available in DOS and this is not LPT1:. In these cases, this port is mapped to /dev/lp0; /dev/lp0 is always the first available parallel port and /dev/lp1 the second available port.

Now, on to serial ports. You need to fully understand all of this to understand how to get your modems working.

Serial Ports and Linux

In Linux, serial ports are generally each associated with two device files: one for outgoing connections and one for incoming connections. Let's start with outgoing connections: these are ttySx, where x is a number starting from 0. So DOS's COM1: maps to /dev/ttyS0 in Linux and COM2: to /dev/ttyS1.

Simple, right?

NOTE   It isn't uncommon for a link to be maintained from **/dev/modem** to the serial port device for the modem. In this way, the modem can be referred to through the device **/dev/modem**.

NOTE   In older versions of Linux, serial ports were also associated with another device file for incoming connections: **cuax**, where x is a number starting from 0. Therefore, **COM1:** would have been both **/dev/ttyS0** and **/dev/cua0**, while **COM4:** was both **/dev/ttyS3** and **/dev/cua3**. In current versions of Linux, only **/dev/ttySx** is used. Support for **/dev/cuax** is provided only for backward compatibility and should not be used. Eventually, **/dev/cuax** will not be supported.

Getting Your Modem Ready

In order for a modem to work properly, it must meet several criteria:

- It must be properly connected to the PC.
- It must be using a dedicated serial port.
- It must not have an IRQ or I/O address conflict with another device.

Connecting a Modem to Your PC

Connecting a modem is fairly simple. If you have an external modem, you need to connect it to one of your existing serial ports. If you have no free ports, you need to consider purchasing a serial card; consult your PC or modem vendor about this. Generally, though, most PC users only need two external serial ports: one for their mouse and one for their modem. The usual practice is to connect your mouse to the first serial port (COM1:, /dev/ttyS0, /dev/cua0) and your modem to the second serial port (COM2:, /dev/ttyS1, /dev/cua1).

Internal modems usually need to be placed into a free slot inside your PC. If you are wary about opening your PC, then you may want to consider getting a technician from the store where you purchased your PC or modem to install the modem.

Choosing a Serial Port

When installing an external modem, you select a serial port by simply choosing which physical port to connect the modem to. In doing this, it is important to make sure that you have not installed an internal device that is using the same serial port. If you haven't installed any hardware inside your PC, consult your PC's documentation to see if there are any preinstalled internal devices that are using the same serial port as one of your external connections. Generally, though, unless you already have an internal modem installed, you aren't likely to have an internal device conflicting with one of your available external serial ports.

Installing an internal modem requires a bit more work. Most standard internal modems need to be configured to use a specific serial port in order to function. For instance, DIP switches or jumpers on the modem card are commonly used to specify a particular serial port. You need to consult your modem's documentation for instructions on how to do this.

As with external modems, you must make sure you don't choose a port that matches one already in use by an external device. For instance, you definitely wouldn't make your modem use the first serial port if you have a mouse connected to the external connector for this port. The third or fourth serial port is usually the best choice for an internal modem.

IRQs and I/O Addresses

Associated with each serial port is an interrupt request (IRQ) and an input/output (I/O) address. This is numerically specified information that ensures that your PC and operating system always know which physical device is providing data or information or is asking for the attention of the system.

Table 18.2 outlines the four common serial ports and their associated IRQs and I/O addresses.

TABLE 18.2: Serial Port IRQs and I/O Addresses

DOS Name	Linux device files	IRQ	I/O Address
COM1:	/dev/ttyS0	4	0x3f8
COM2:	/dev/ttyS1	3	0x2f8
COM3:	/dev/ttyS2	4	0x3e8
COM4:	/dev/ttyS3	3	0x2e8

Notice that the first and third ports share the same IRQ and the second and fourth ports also share the same IRQ. This poses certain issues that have to be considered. The fact that port 1 and port 3 share the same IRQ but have different I/O addresses basically means that they cannot be used simultaneously. That is, you can't have devices on these two ports (or on ports 2 and 4) that will need to be in use at the same time.

This means, for example, that you can't have a mouse on the first port and put a modem on the third port unless you will never be using the mouse while the modem is in use. If you use X Windows, this is a highly improbable scenario. Therefore, when installing an internal modem, you also need to take care not to create an IRQ conflict. If you use a mouse on the first serial port, then you will probably want to put your internal modem on the fourth port to eliminate all possible conflicts with your mouse.

Finally, there is one more consideration: internal modems often allow you to configure special IRQ and I/O addresses for the card that differ from the norms for the four serial ports. This should only be done if you have so many serial devices already on your system that you simply cannot make the modem work in any other way. In this situation, you will need to consult the serial devices HOWTO at `ftp://metalab.unc.edu/pub/Linux/docs/HOWTO/unmaintained/Serial-HOWTO` to get a stronger sense of how to do this safely and correctly in Linux.

Plug-and-Play Modems

The introduction of plug-and-play motherboards and internal cards with Windows 95 has caused some problems with other operating systems. Many plug-and-play devices (modems included) are often designed to work expressly with

Windows and are configured using special Windows 95 or 98 software that is not available in Linux. If you have a card like this, you usually have one of two options:

1. If you are lucky, after you configure the modem in Windows 95 or 98, you can reboot to Linux and the modem will retain its configuration.

2. If you are unlucky, the modem will need to be configured every time the computer is power-cycled and Windows will have to do this during the boot process. If this is the case, you need to start Linux from within Windows using `loadln` (see Chapter 5, "Special Installations," for more information about this) to start Linux without rebooting the system.

Generally, though, you are best off without a plug-and-play modem, and you should really consider spending the small amount of extra money required to get an external modem.

Software for Working with Your Modem

There are numerous types of software in Linux that you will be using with your modem. These include:

- minicom: a basic, text-based terminal emulation package

- seyon: an X Windows–based terminal emulation package

- pppd: a daemon used for establishing PPP connections to the Internet (see Chapter 22, "Connecting Linux to the Internet")

- efax: a collection of programs used for sending and receiving faxes (see Chapter 25, "Faxing from Linux")

The next section gives you a quick look at using minicom to make sure your modem is working properly.

Using Minicom to Test Your Modem

The first step to using minicom is to create a global configuration file. This is done by running minicom as the root user with the -s flag:

```
# minicom -s
```

This command launches the minicom configuration environment, as illustrated in Figure 18.1.

FIGURE 18.1:

Configuring minicom

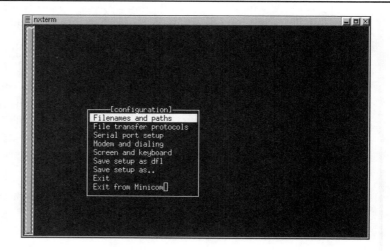

You can use the up and down arrow keys to move through the menu and the Enter key to select menu items.

The critical settings for testing your modem are under Serial Port Setup. Selecting this option displays the Serial Port Setup screen, shown in Figure 18.2.

FIGURE 18.2:

Configuring your serial port

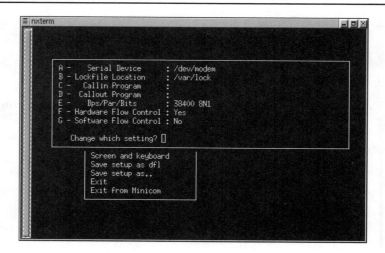

In order to change the values, select them by letter.

First, you need to set your serial device. This is done with choice A, Serial Device. You should change this location to the appropriate device file. For instance, if your modem is on the second serial port, you could set this to /dev/ttyS1 since you are using minicom for an outgoing connection.

You also need to configure option E, Bps/Par/Bits, to match your modem's settings and the settings required by the system you will be connecting to (usually an Internet provider's system). Option E displays the communication parameters screen, shown in Figure 18.3.

FIGURE 18.3:

Configuring communication parameters

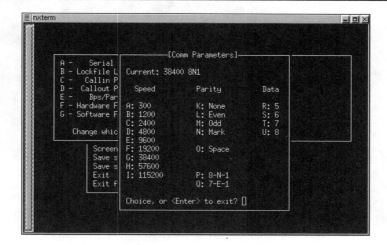

At the top of the screen, the current settings are shown. You can change the settings by selecting the appropriate letters.

For speed, you should choose your modem's top compressed connection speed. This is generally four times the speed of your modem. For instance, for a 14.4Kbps modem, this would be 57600bps; for a 28.8Kbps modem, this should be set to 115200bps. If you have a faster modem, choose 115200bps.

For parity and data bit, the norm for most connections today is no parity (option J), and 8 stop bits (option T). Confer with the administrator of the system you will be connecting to in order to determine the correct settings.

When you are done, press the Enter key to return to the Serial Port Setup screen. Pressing Enter at the Serial Port Setup screen returns you to the main menu.

This information should be sufficient to allow you to test your modem. Select Save Setup as Dfl to save the configuration as the default setting, and then select Exit to exit the setup screen and use minicom with the settings you have selected. This brings up the minicom terminal emulator, as shown in Figure 18.4.

FIGURE 18.4:

The main minicom screen

If you see an OK prompt, your modem should be configured correctly and working. You can test this further by typing **AT** and pressing Enter. You should get back an OK message:

```
AT
OK
```

If this works, you can try dialing into a system to see if you can connect:

ATDT1234567

If this works, you may hear the sound of a connection and then should see a connection message and possibly some messages or prompts from the remote system:

```
ATDT1234567
CONNECT 115200
```

If you have problems with any of these stages, then your modem's physical connection or configuration may be incorrect. In this case, refer to the serial devices HOWTO at ftp://metalab.unc.edu/pub/Linux/docs/HOWTO/unmaintained/ Serial-HOWTO for a detailed discussion of getting a modem to work with Linux.

Issues with ISDN Adapters

ISDN adapters can be a little problematic with Linux. The difficulties stem from the fact that internal and external adapters function in fundamentally different ways, and among internal adapters, there are distinctly different technological approaches.

External ISDN adapters are your best choice for a Linux system because external adapters mimic the behavior of external modems, making the use of them generally transparent to Linux.

Internal modems pose issues, though. Some internal modems emulate standard serial modems and others emulate standard network cards, and both can be made to work with Linux. There are those known not to work, however.

Consult the Linux ISDN page at `http://www.caliban.org/linux_isdn.html` for a detailed discussion of Linux and ISDN.

Looking Ahead

In the next chapter, you will learn about an area that most users find important: multimedia. You will see how to install and configure common multimedia peripherals such as sound cards, and you will take a quick tour through common Linux multimedia software.

CHAPTER

NINETEEN

Linux Multimedia

- Configuring Sound Blaster Cards

- Using XPlaycd

- Other Multimedia Applications

This chapter looks at an area of Linux that, unfortunately, is not as well developed as it is on competitive platforms such as Windows and the Mac OS: multimedia.

This chapter describes Red Hat Linux 6's built-in support for Sound Blaster cards and discusses how to configure the cards. Next, it discusses a representative multimedia application, XPlaycd, and then reviews other available multimedia applications.

Unfortunately, fully mastering multimedia for Linux can be somewhat complicated. You should consult the Linux Sound HOWTO at `http://www.linux-howto.com/ptHOWTO/Sound-HOWTO` for a detailed discussion of how to work with sound in Linux.

Configuring Sound Blaster Cards

Generally, Linux's support for sound cards has been sketchy. Strong support is provided for Sound Blaster cards and those cards that are compatible on a hardware register level with genuine Sound Blaster cards. Other cards that are labeled "compatible" don't work with the standard Sound Blaster drivers.

A collection of other drivers for sound cards can be found, but they all have their own quirks and unique ways of being configured, so this chapter will only address the Sound Blaster line of cards. The Linux Sound HOWTO mentioned above is a good reference if you find yourself facing another card on your Linux system.

Over time, the level of support for a broad range of sound cards has improved, and Red Hat Linux 6 supports a respectable selection of sound cards, although this support is by no means as complete as sound support in Windows 98.

Adding sound support may mean recompiling your kernel from source code. This is a task best reserved for expert Linux users. Making the right decisions in compiling the kernel is tricky, and taking a wrong step can render your system non-bootable and difficult to return to a working state.

For this reason, Red Hat has developed the Sound Blaster driver into a loadable module so it is possible to add Sound Blaster support to your Red Hat Linux 6 system without reconfiguring your kernel.

> **NOTE**
> In order to configure your card, you need to know all the relevant hardware settings of the card such as I/O port, IRQ, and DMA addresses. Consult your card's documentation for instructions on how to determine the settings of your card.

Using *Sndconfig*

Red Hat includes the `sndconfig` program for configuring the Sound Blaster module. To run the `sndconfig` program, type the command

    # sndconfig

at a command prompt in the console or an `xterm` window.

After an initial screen, a screen appears like the one in Figure 19.1. This screen asks you to identify your sound card type. You can select from a list of standard supported cards. If you think you have a proper hardware-compatible card, select the type of card it is supposed to be compatible with.

FIGURE 19.1:

Selecting a Sound
Blaster card

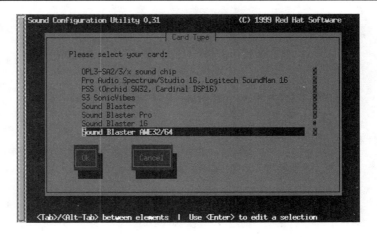

The next screen that appears depends on the type of card you select. That screen asks you to provide relevant hardware settings such as I/O port, IRQ, and DMA addresses for your card. Figure 19.2 shows this screen for a regular Sound Blaster card.

FIGURE 19.2:

Specifying hardware settings for a Sound Blaster card

Once you specify these settings, `sndconfig` adds the entries to the `/etc/conf.modules` file (and backs up your original `conf.modules` file) and then attempts to play a test sound.

In Case of Silence

If `sndconfig` fails to play a sound, then one of several things may be wrong.

First, check that your sound card is properly inserted in your PC and that your speakers are correctly plugged into the card and are turned on and have power.

If all these physical things are OK, then there are two likely sources of difficulty:

1. You have chosen the wrong card type or have provided the wrong hardware settings. Check all these details and try running `sndconfig` again.

2. Your card is not supported by the Red Hat Sound Blaster module. You need to consult the Linux Sound HOWTO for more details about Linux sound and building a new kernel with the correct driver for your card.

Using XPlaycd

One popular use of sound cards is to play audio CD-ROMs through the speakers of the sound card. You can do this with the XPlaycd program. This is an X Windows application that ships with Red Hat Linux 6 and provides a simple, graphical interface to your CD-ROM drive.

As Figure 19.3 shows, XPlaycd should be familiar to anyone with an audio CD player as part of their stereo.

FIGURE 19.3:

The XPlaycd window

From left to right, the control buttons in the top row perform the following functions:

Exit   Quits XPlaycd.

Open/Close   Alternately ejects and closes the CD tray for drives that support software-controlled eject.

Rewind   Scans backward through the current track in two-second intervals.

Play/Stop   Alternately plays and stops the current track.

Fast Forward   Scans forward through the current track in two-second intervals.

Pause/Continue   Alternately pauses and resumes playing.

Shuffle/Resort   Alternately plays tracks in a random order or returns tracks to their physical order.

Repeat   Continuously repeats the playlist.

Immediately below the Rewind button is the Back Track button. Pressing the Backtrack button once jumps to the start of the current track, and pressing it again moves back one track at a time. Immediately below the Fast Forward button is the Forward Track button, which jumps to the start of the next track.

The third row of controls is the volume control. You can control each channel separately or change both channels' values together. To change the setting of either volume bar, click to the left or the right of the current setting to move the bar one notch in the desired direction.

To move both bars in either direction, you need to click the desired side, but exactly between the two bars.

Finally, below the volume controls is the playlist. The playlist shows a small icon for each track, initially in numerical order. The Start icon is represented by a right arrow and the End icon is marked with a left arrow.

The playlist is played from the Start icon to the End icon, playing each track between the two icons as they appear on the playlist in order from left to right. You can click and drag any icon to the right or left to change its place on the playlist. Figure 19.4 shows an altered playlist in which all tracks are played, but not in their original order.

FIGURE 19.4:

A reordered playlist

By moving the Start and End icons, it is possible to create a playlist that excludes some of the tracks, as shown in Figure 19.5.

FIGURE 19.5:

Adjusting the start and end of the playlist

Other Multimedia Applications

While the availability of slick, fancy multimedia applications and games falls short of what is available on some other platforms, that hasn't prevented a healthy number of applications from being developed for Linux.

On the Linux Applications and Utilities page at `http://www.hongik.com/linux//linapp5.html#mm` you can find a list of many available multimedia applications for Linux. This section takes a brief look at a small selection of multimedia applications.

The GNOME CD Player

GNOME, the default desktop manager in Red Hat Linux 6, includes an integrated CD player, shown in Figure 19.6.

FIGURE 19.6:

The GNOME CD player

This CD player offers the standard functionality you might expect, centered around simple graphical control buttons similar to those in most PC-based CD players, as well as those in most physical CD players. Notably, this application contains a robust track editor to choose the order of tracks to play and offers other features such as keyboard controls that are missing in some Linux-based CD players.

MpegTV Player 1.0

This application, a U.S. $10 shareware application, is a real-time MPEG video/audio player for Linux and many other Unix platforms. It provides a simple, intuitive control panel that allows the user to control the playing of files, jump to any location in an open file, and adjust the volume. The software can be downloaded from `http://www.mpegtv.com/`.

Festival Speech Synthesis System

Currently in a state of development, the Festival speech synthesis system is designed to offer a powerful, multilingual (currently English, Spanish, and Welsh) speech synthesis system that can be used to convert text to speech and provides the necessary tools for application developers to add speech to their own software. The current release of the package is available at `http://www.cstr.ed.ac.uk/projects/festival/festival.html`.

MiXViews

MiXViews is an X Windows–based digital sound editor that is freely distributable. Multiple files can be displayed and edited, allowing for cutting and pasting between files and for applying sound modifications to the data. The MiXViews home page is at `http://www.ccmrc.ucsb.edu/~doug/htmls/MiXViews.html`.

MMaudio

MMaudio is an X Windows–based audio player that supports many popular formats including AU, WAV, and MPEG 1 files. The program can record and encode MPEG files and is capable of playing MPEG files directly off a Web server, thanks to its built-in MIME support. The software can be found at `http://www.powerweb.de/mpeg/unix.html`.

RealPlayer

The RealPlayer from RealNetworks is the popular player software for playing RealAudio and RealVideo files in real time, streamed across the Internet. Many of the popular Web-based, radio, television, and music sites use RealAudio and

RealVideo technology, and the RealPlayer is needed to view or listen to this content. Free and enhanced commercial versions of the player are available for download from `http://www.real.com/products/player/50player/index.html?src=404`.

FreePhone

FreePhone is an Internet audio-conferencing tool similar in concept to the Internet phone software that can be found for Windows and Macintosh systems. It is more than a one-to-one phone system; users can create unicast or multicast audio conferences. FreePhone supports a variety of popular audio compression systems and uses the Internet's multimedia Mbone backbone. The software is online at `http://www.inria.fr/rodeo/fphone/`.

Looking Ahead

This chapter looked at just the tip of the multimedia iceberg. Multimedia in the Linux environment can be technically demanding (as it can be in Windows as well), and a general book like this one can only offer a cursory look at the subject.

If you are using a supported card or a truly compatible one, you should now have it working with your Red Hat Linux system. You should have been able to download and test some multimedia applications and should feel at least comfortable with using multimedia applications in Linux.

If you really want to delve into multimedia and all its related specialties, such as sound and video editing, IP audio, and streaming media, you should start by consulting *The Linux Multimedia Guide* by Jeff Tranter and Andy Oram (O'Reilly & Associates, 1996).

The next chapter discusses an important, but advanced, subject: recompiling the Linux kernel. Recompiling the kernel can be necessary for a number of reasons, including adding support for devices such as sound cards, adding support for less common network protocols, or shrinking the size of the default kernel installed when you installed Linux. You will learn about the process of recompilation and review the major choices that you will need to make during recompilation.

CHAPTER

TWENTY

20

Recompiling the Linux Kernel

- ■ Why Change the Kernel?

- ■ Checking for Source Packages

- ■ Backing Up the Old Kernel

- ■ Configuring the New Kernel

- ■ Compiling and Running the New Kernel

Linux is one of the few operating systems where you can impact how your computer works at its core. Because Linux includes all of the source code to the kernel of the operating system, anything you can think of can be attempted in Linux. Of course, for most of us, that means reconfiguring the kernel with the tools provided, rather than modifying the C language source code files.

Nevertheless, hundreds of options settings are available as part of the standard kernel configuration utilities. This chapter describes how to use the kernel configuration tools to select options that you want included with your running Linux system and then describes how to recompile the kernel source code based on those options.

Red Hat doesn't install the kernel source code by default. You'll need to install it using the `rpm` command as described in this chapter before you can run the configuration tools or recompile the kernel.

Why Change the Kernel?

If you're new to Linux, you may be asking yourself, "Why on Earth would I want to recompile the kernel?" You may also be thinking that it's a very difficult process.

Linux is much more user-friendly than it was two or three years ago; advancements in the installation process, graphical interfaces, and hardware support have all made Linux accessible to those of us who aren't computer science gurus. In fact, the process of recompiling the kernel, described here, uses a menu-driven configuration interface and a single (long) command line to remake the kernel.

Programming Terms: Making, Building, and Compiling

As you read about working with the kernel, you'll see three terms used interchangeably: *remaking*, *rebuilding*, and *recompiling* the kernel. Although you can think of them as being synonymous, it's also helpful to understand what each of these terms really means.

Continued on next page

When you develop software in Linux (and in many other operating systems), you use a configuration file for your programming project that describes how the pieces of source code and all libraries fit together. This information is stored in a file called `Makefile`, which is used by the utility `make`. (You'll use the `make` utility several times later in this chapter.)

The process of actually converting the source code of a project into something the computer can use (a binary) is called *compilation*. The standard C language compilers for Linux, `gcc` or `egcs`, are used to compile source code.

However, because a programming project generally has dozens of separate components, the `make` utility checks the dates and times on each component, and only recompiles the components that have been updated since they were last compiled. This saves a great deal of time in creating a new version of a project when only part of the source code has been altered.

When you use the `make` utility, you can indicate that you want to recompile "from scratch" all of the components of your project. This is called a *build*.

So remaking the kernel, rebuilding the kernel, and recompiling the kernel all do similar things. And with several hundred thousand lines of source code, it still takes a while to complete, no matter what you call it.

Linux is highly "tunable"; you can refine its capabilities to meet your unique requirements. However, many of the features of Linux are not activated by default in the standard Linux kernel. This is true for several reasons.

The most important thing to understand is that every user makes trade-offs in their software. For example, when using a compression program, you can choose a faster compression time or choose a smaller compressed file.

In the same way, Linux kernels must make trade-offs. For example, you can have a smaller kernel or one that supports more hardware without additional configuration steps. Or you can have a system optimized for routing IP packets or for handling normal workstation tasks.

The kernel is configured to provide a good balance between kernel size, speed, and hardware support. This balance seeks to meet the needs of average users as the Linux vendor sees them. In this chapter, you will learn how to make your own decisions about which features are most important to your computing environment.

Learning About Modules

Kernel modules are a critical part of Linux. A kernel module allows you to add functionality to the core of Linux without recompiling the kernel source code. As you'll see later in this chapter, that's a great benefit.

For example, if you discover that you need to work with a special new SCSI interface card, you can load a kernel module to support it with a single command (using the `insmod` command). Previously, Linux would have required you to rebuild the kernel to include support for that SCSI device.

As the number of hardware devices supported by Linux has increased, kernel modules have allowed the Linux kernel to remain relatively small, while still allowing users to easily add support for the hardware that they own.

> **TIP**
>
> A big difference between Linux and some other operating systems is the ability to load or remove support for hardware, file systems, languages, and so forth without ever rebooting the system.

Table 20.1 contains a summary of the commands used with kernel modules. You can view the man page for any of these commands to see more information.

TABLE 20.1: Commands Used with Kernel Modules

Command	Description
`lsmod`	List all of the modules currently installed in the running kernel.
`insmod`	Insert a module into the running kernel. This command uses the module name and, optionally, additional parameters to define how the module behaves (for example, IRQ and address information for a hardware device).
`rmmod`	Remove a module from the running system. Be careful that you don't remove modules that are in use by other modules. (See the output of the `lsmod` command for details on dependencies of currently loaded modules.)
`depmod`	Create a dependencies file that can be used by the **modprobe** command to load a set of modules.
`modprobe`	Load the set of modules defined by the **depmod** command.

Other information about the modules on your Linux system is available by reviewing certain system files.

Because kernel modules are inserted into the running source code, they are stored as object code (already compiled). Each module has the file extension `.o`.

Check the following files:

- `/boot/module-info-2.2.5-15` contains per-module information that you can alter to reflect any specific settings of your hardware.

- `/lib/modules/2.2.5-15` contains several subdirectories that divide all of the available kernel modules on your system. For example, check the contents of the `cdrom` subdirectory to see all the modules available to support various CD-ROM drives.

Understanding Reasons to Recompile

If you're still wondering specifically why you would need to recompile your Linux kernel, the information in Table 20.2 should provide some insight. This table outlines some solutions to common problems you may encounter.

Of course, you may only need to rebuild the kernel for one of these reasons. But understanding why people work with the kernel will show you more about the flexibility of Linux.

TABLE 20.2:   Solutions to Problems Recompiling the Linux Kernel

Problem	Solution
You hear that your processor has a bug that could crash your system. Linux has a workaround, but you're using an older version.	Download the patch to the Linux kernel and remake the source code. In 20 minutes, the problem is solved.
You've purchased a new SCSI card that is supported in a Linux kernel module, but you can't boot the system from your SCSI hard disk unless the SCSI module is part of the default kernel.	Remake the kernel, indicating that the necessary SCSI support is built in rather than created as a module.
A security alert appears about problems with a Linux file system driver. A patch is available within hours.	Download the patch and remake your kernel to provide the most up-to-date security for your system.

Continued on next page

TABLE 20.2 CONTINUED: Solutions to Problems Recompiling the Linux Kernel

Problem	Solution
A new network card driver is available for your system. You download the source code from the vendor's Web site.	Remake the kernel so that the source code version for all modules matches your new network card module.
You purchased a commercial Linux product that had a 2.2.5 Linux kernel, but now you'd like the latest development kernel.	Download the kernel sources (they're fairly large, but not too big) and remake the kernel so you have the latest version of the kernel.
Users on your system are complaining that they can't access certain file systems unless they use a bunch of strange commands first (such as insmod, for example).	Remake the kernel with the needed file system support built in so that file systems of that type can be mounted without explicitly adding a kernel module.

Finding Out About Kernel Updates

The Linux kernel can change literally every day. Fortunately, when you're running a stable system, you generally don't care to follow all of those changes. In fact, most of the changes to Linux occur in the development version of the kernel, which isn't something you want to run a production system on anyway.

To keep up-to-date on happenings with the Linux kernel and related topics, plan to visit the following two Web sites regularly. Both sites are updated several times a day with new information:

- www.linuxhq.com: This site contains a large collection of information about the Linux kernel, with sections on the latest development and stable kernels, links to information resources, and many useful details about the Linux kernel.

- www.freshmeat.net: This site is a clearinghouse for announcements about releases of open source software and related topics. This site includes a searchable archive of release information. The Freshmeat site is not focused on the Linux kernel per se, but it includes information about kernel releases.

Checking for Source Packages

In order to recompile your Linux kernel, you must have the source code to the kernel installed on your system. The kernel source code on Red Hat is located in a single `rpm` package but is not installed by default. The package to check for is

```
kernel-source-2.2.5-15.i386.rpm
```

You can install this package using the `rpm` command after mounting the CD-ROM on which the source package is located:

```
rpm -Uvh kernel-source
```

> **NOTE**   Red Hat includes the kernel source code in an `rpm` package that is not marked as a "source code package" with the file extension `.src.rpm`. Don't be confused by this.

> **NOTE**   The kernel source package is not included on the Publisher's Edition of Red Hat Linux 6 which ships with this book, but it can be downloaded from http://www.redhat.com.

Checking for Tools

In addition to the source code itself, you must have a compiler available to rebuild the source code. The two tools you need are:

- The `make` utility
- The C language compiler, `gcc` or `egcs`

The exact versions of these utilities may vary from system to system. It's best if you have a recent version of the compiler, such as `gcc 2.7` or `egcs 1.1.2`.

To check for these utilities on your Linux system, use the following commands (the output from a Red Hat default installation is shown):

```
# rpm -q make
make-3.77-6
# rpm -q egcs
egcs-1.1.2-12
```

NOTE   The same commands should work on any system that uses **rpm** for software package management.

If you don't see these tools installed on your system, you'll need to use **rpm** or a similar utility to install them before proceeding with this chapter.

Backing Up the Old Kernel

Although the implication here is that rebuilding the Linux kernel is child's play, you should still take a few precautions before diving into the deep end of the pool. That means backing up your kernel and providing a method to reboot to the previous version of the kernel in case of problems.

Backing up the current kernel involves three steps:

1. Back up the source code tree for the kernel so you can recreate the current kernel if the configuration becomes corrupted.

2. Back up the kernel itself so you have a kernel to start your system with that you already know works.

3. Create a new boot loader entry so you can boot from the backup of your kernel.

Backing up the source code tree for your current kernel is simple. Just use a command such as the following **cp** command, which copies the entire kernel source code tree to a duplicate directory. (You can then copy it back to the original name if you need to use the backup.)

```
# cp /usr/src/linux / usr/src/linux.sav
```

Backing up the kernel itself is almost as simple; use a command like the following **cp** command. (Change it to match the exact kernel version you're running.)

```
# cp /boot/vmlinuz-2.2.5-15 /boot/vmlinuz-2.2.5-2.orig
```

TIP   When you rebuild the kernel, the existing kernel is saved with the file extension **.old**. However, that old kernel version is not automatically accessible to boot your system, which is the purpose of these steps.

The LILO boot loader that normally launches Linux from your hard drive is configured by pointing to a kernel file in your root file system. For example, you may see a line like this in your `/etc/lilo.conf` file:

```
image = /boot/vmlinuz-2.2.5
```

This line indicates the path and filename of the kernel to start.

Once you have created a backup of the kernel itself (in the previous step), you should also create another entry in `lilo.conf` so that you can start your Linux system with the old (proven) kernel.

To do this, follow these steps:

1. Find the section in the `/etc/lilo.conf` file that refers to your kernel image.

2. Make a copy of that entire section (usually about four or five lines of text).

3. In your copy, change two items:

    - Change the name of the kernel to the name of your backed-up kernel (with the `.orig` ending in the example).

    - Change the label field to something like `linux.original` or `linux-previous`.

4. Save your changes to `/etc/lilo.conf`.

5. Run the command `lilo` to add the new entry to your boot loader. As `lilo` runs, you see the different labels on screen as images are added to your boot loader.

The next time you reboot your system, press Tab at the LILO prompt to see the additional image you defined as a precaution before rebuilding your kernel.

Configuring the New Kernel

The interesting part of creating a new Linux kernel is setting up the new kernel configuration. This is the step in which you decide what the kernel will include, what it will not include, and so forth.

Linux includes three separate configuration utilities. Each one is suited to different preferences:

A command-line interface   A command-line interface asks questions one at a time about what you want to include in the kernel. This interface is convenient for those who are very familiar with the kernel, or who may have a script that processes the configuration information using this interface.

The command-line interface is also the choice for those who have very limited control over their screens, and therefore can't use the menu-based interface. The greatest disadvantage of the command-line interface is that you can't return to a previous question and review it or change your selection.

A character-based menu interface   This interface uses several levels of menus that you can explore, selecting options as you go, and return to any area.

A graphical, X-based interface   This interface is very similar to the character-based menu interface, but it is truly graphical. This is the most attractive interface, but it requires that you are running the X Windows system.

All three methods (command line, menus, or true graphical) create the same configuration file that is used by the make utility during the compilation/rebuilding process.

All three methods also include copious help information to answer your questions about specific options.

Understanding the Options

As you review the various options presented in any of the configuration methods (command line, menu, or graphical), you need to understand how each option can be applied to your Linux kernel.

The options are identified by different indicators, depending on which tool you use to configure the kernel, but the same options are available in each case. The configuration items fall in two groups:

- Module-capable
- Non-module-capable

If an option is not capable of being a loadable kernel module, then it must be either

- [*]   Part of the kernel, or
- [ ]   Not part of the kernel

The bracket indications above show how the selection of an option is shown in the menu-based configuration tool.

If an option is module-capable, you have three choices (again, these are shown as they would appear in the menu configuration tool; similar indications are shown in both of the other tools):

- < >   Not included, and not created as a module that can be loaded later.
- <*>   Included as part of the kernel, so that it doesn't have to be loaded later as a kernel; it's always part of the system.
- <M>   Included as a module, but not part of the kernel itself. Thus, this option can be added or removed from the running kernel at your discretion.

TIP

If you're having trouble changing an option, you may need to set another option first. For example, you must enable SCSI devices in general before you can select specific SCSI device support.

Once you have all the tools (`make` and `egcs`) and the source code installed, you are ready to start one of the configuration tools and configure your kernel.

Remember that you only need to use one of the three interfaces described in the following sections. Review each section briefly and decide which interface you want to use, based on the figures and descriptions given.

Starting the Command-Line Interface

To start the command-line interface, follow these steps:

1. Use the `su` command to obtain root access.

2. Change to the source code directory:

```
# cd  /usr/src/linux
```

3. Execute the following make command:

   # **make config**

   Almost immediately, you see the first configuration question. When you use the make config command, you are prompted to respond to a series of questions about the kernel. Figure 20.1 shows the first few questions.

FIGURE 20.1:

The most basic configuration option for the Linux kernel is make config, which asks you questions in a command-line format.

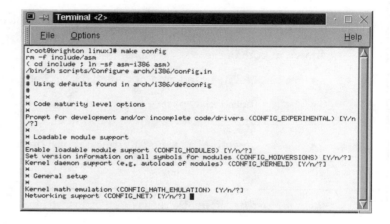

```
[root@brighton linux]# make config
rm -f include/asm
( cd include ; ln -sf asm-i386 asm)
/bin/sh scripts/Configure arch/i386/config.in
#
# Using defaults found in arch/i386/defconfig
#
*
* Code maturity level options
*
Prompt for development and/or incomplete code/drivers (CONFIG_EXPERIMENTAL) [Y/n
/?]
*
* Loadable module support
*
Enable loadable module support (CONFIG_MODULES) [Y/n/?]
Set version information on all symbols for modules (CONFIG_MODVERSIONS) [Y/n/?]
Kernel daemon support (e.g. autoload of modules) (CONFIG_KERNELD) [Y/n/?]
*
* General setup
*
Kernel math emulation (CONFIG_MATH_EMULATION) [Y/n/?]
Networking support (CONFIG_NET) [Y/n/?] █
```

> **TIP**
>
> The exact series of questions that you see depends on how you respond to questions as you go along.

If you want to select the default option for each question, simply press Enter. In each case, the default selection is shown as an uppercase letter. For example, you will see this question about networking:

    Networking support (CONFIG_NET) [Y/n/?]

If you press Enter, the default of Y, for Yes, is selected. For those options that can be defined as built in or as modules, the options appear as in this example:

    Kernel support for ELF binaries (CONFIG_BINFMT_ELF) [Y/m/n/?]

Many of the device-related questions present only M/n options, for [Module], or [Don't include].

For each question you see, you can enter a question mark, **?**, to see a screen of descriptive information. This information is usually very helpful in determining how to use the option.

TIP

The same help information is available in any of the three kernel configuration tools.

Three disadvantages of using this configuration option are:

- You have to answer more than 350 individual questions (depending on how you respond, the total number will vary).

- You can't back up and change a selection you've made without starting over.

- You can't easily see an overview of the options in various categories.

The advantages of using this configuration option include:

- Except for the Linux kernel source, you don't need other development packages to configure the kernel.

- You can create scripts to feed input to the configuration script for automated configurations.

The menu configuration option described in the next section provides an easier way for most people to review all of the kernel configuration parameters and create a kernel configuration file.

NOTE

If you need to end or cancel the configuration process before answering all of the questions, press Ctrl+C. An error message from the script appears and no configuration file is created.

Starting the Character-Based Menu Interface

To start the character-based menu interface, follow these steps:

1. Use the su command to obtain root access.

2. Change to the source code directory:

   ```
   # cd /usr/src/linux
   ```

3. Execute the following make command:

   ```
   # make menuconfig
   ```

The menu-based configuration tool requires a package named **ncurses**. **ncurses** is installed by default on most Linux systems, but if you see errors when you run the **make menuconfig** command, check that the **ncurses-devel rpm** is installed.

You see a collection of suspiciously confusing lines scroll down your screen as the make command compiles the menu-based configuration utility. You can ignore these lines; they are the output of the compiler and related programs. After a minute or two, you see the screen shown in Figure 20.2.

FIGURE 20.2:

You can configure the Linux kernel from this character-based menu interface.

The menu configuration option starts with a list of the categories in which you can select kernel options. To navigate this interface, remember the following keystrokes:

- Use the up and down arrow keys to move among the options listed in the menus.

- Type **M** to select a kernel option as a module (when applicable).

- Use the Tab key to move between the buttons shown below the list of kernel options: Select, Exit, and Help.

- Press Enter to choose a selected item, such as the Help button.

The three buttons below the option list have the following functions:

Select   Displays the submenu of options associated with the highlighted item.

Exit   Returns to the previous menu, finishing the configuration if selected from the highest level menu.

Help   Displays a help screen full of information about the highlighted menu option.

A sample help screen is shown in Figure 20.3.

FIGURE 20.3:

Help information is available for every kernel option by choosing the Help button.

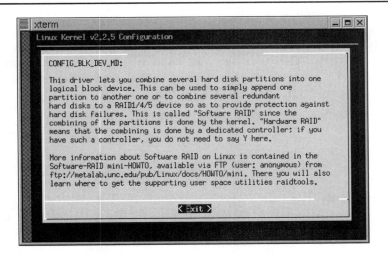

The kernel configuration tools described in this section are used to create a kernel configuration file that is used to rebuild the kernel. If you have once set up a kernel with all the options you prefer, you can save a copy of the configuration file for repeated use later.

This is done using the last two items on the main menu: "Save Configuration to an Alternate File" and "Load an Alternate Configuration File." Use the down arrow or Page Down key to scroll down to these items.

These last two items on the main menu provide the capability to save your configuration settings or load an existing configuration file:

- Use the Save Configuration Settings option to create a second copy of the kernel configuration file to reuse yourself or to pass on to another person.

WARNING Don't use the Save Configuration Settings option until you have completed the selection of all kernel options in the various menus.

- Use the Load Configuration File option if you have a configuration file that someone has given you or that you have saved previously. Loading such a file sets all the options so that you don't have to select any of the menu items unless you want to make further changes.

Items in the menu list that have submenus of options are displayed with an arrow on the right side of the item, for example, on the main menu, you see the following option:

```
General Setup   -->
```

When you view a menu item that actually sets a kernel option, you see the following options displayed to the left of the option, as described previously in this chapter (see also Figure 20.4):

- [*]   Part of the kernel, or

- [ ]   Not part of the kernel

- < >   Not included, and not created as a module that can be loaded later.

- <*>   Included as part of the kernel, so that it doesn't have to be loaded later as a kernel; it's always part of the system.

- <M>   Included as a module, but not part of the kernel itself. Thus, this option can be added or removed from the running kernel at your discretion.

FIGURE 20.4:

Individual options in the menuconfig tool are shown with selection brackets to the left of each item.

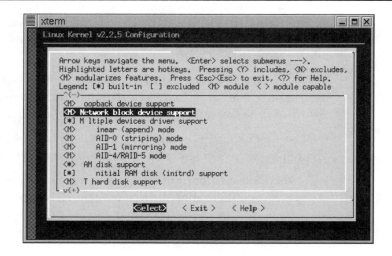

Depending on the screen that you're viewing the menus on, you should see a bold character as part of each line. You can type that character to select that option rather than using the arrow keys and the Select button.

The current state of each option is shown in the brackets to the left of that option. To change the selected option, type any of the following keys:

- **Y**   to include the feature in the kernel
- **M**   to create a module to support this feature (when a possibility)
- **N**   to not include the feature, nor make a module for it
- **?**   to display a help screen for the highlighted item

You can also press the space bar repeatedly to toggle between the available options for the highlighted item.

When you have reviewed and set all of the kernel options that you want to check, choose the Exit item on the main menu. A configuration appears asking if you want to save the updated kernel configuration file based on your selections (see Figure 20.5). Choose Yes to create the configuration file.

FIGURE 20.5:

After choosing configuration options, be sure to save a new configuration file as you exit the menu-based configuration tool.

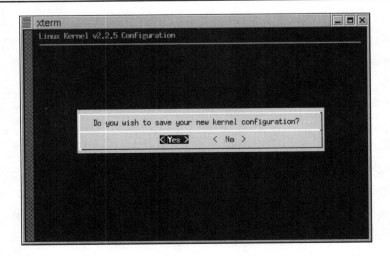

Starting the Graphical Interface

To start the graphical (X-based) kernel configuration interface, follow these steps:

1. Start the X Windows system (using any graphical environment or desktop that you prefer).

2. Open a terminal emulator (command line) window.

3. Use the `su` command to obtain root access.

4. Change to the source code directory:

   ```
   # cd /usr/src/linux
   ```

5. Execute this `make` command:

   ```
   # make xconfig
   ```

> **NOTE**   The X-based configuration tool requires a few X Windows system development packages. If you see errors when you run the `make xconfig` command, check that the appropriate development packages have been installed on your system.

As with the menu-based option, a series of lines scroll down your screen as the `make` command compiles the X-based configuration utility. These lines are the output of the compiler and related programs. After a minute or two, you see the main window of the X-based configuration utility, as shown in Figure 20.6.

FIGURE 20.6:

The graphical kernel configuration tool provides menus and buttons to select kernel options.

Using the X-based tool is very similar to using the menuconfig tool. You choose categories for features that you want to select or deselect. For each category, a dialog box appears in which you can choose to have a feature built in to the kernel, created as a loadable module, or not used at all. Figure 20.7 contains a sample of one of these dialog boxes.

FIGURE 20.7:

Dialog boxes similar to this one are used to select features in the X-based kernel configuration tool.

As you review different features, you can always select the Help button to the right of an item to see a help screen about that feature. (See Figure 20.8.) The information provided in these screens is the same as you would see in the command-line or menu-based configuration tools.

FIGURE 20.8:

Help information appears in separate windows when using the X-based configuration tool.

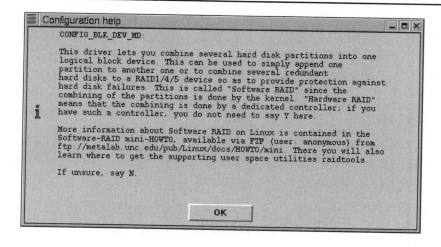

```
Configuration help                                              _ □ ×
CONFIG_BLK_DEV_MD:

This driver lets you combine several hard disk partitions into one
logical block device. This can be used to simply append one
partition to another one or to combine several redundant
hard disks to a RAID1/4/5 device so as to provide protection against
hard disk failures. This is called "Software RAID" since the
combining of the partitions is done by the kernel. "Hardware RAID"
means that the combining is done by a dedicated controller; if you
have such a controller, you do not need to say Y here.

More information about Software RAID on Linux is contained in the
Software-RAID mini-HOWTO, available via FTP (user: anonymous) from
ftp://metalab.unc.edu/pub/Linux/docs/HOWTO/mini. There you will also
learn where to get the supporting user space utilities raidtools.

If unsure, say N.

                              OK
```

One great advantage of using the X-based configuration tool when you're first working with new kernel configurations is that the graphical interface shows you dependencies between various options. For example, in the Block Devices section, you must enable the Multiple Device Driver Support option before the RAID support options can be built in to your kernel.

The menuconfig tool shows a dependency using indents on the menus, but the graphical tool disables the RAID options until you select the Multiple Device Driver Support option on which RAID depends. As a result, it is easier to understand relationships between modules and features by using the X-based configuration tool.

The options on the bottom of the X-based tool are similar to what you use in the menu-based tool:

Save and Exit   Create the kernel configuration file and close the configuration tool.

Quit Without Saving   Close the configuration tool, but don't create a kernel configuration file.

WARNING   If you don't create a kernel configuration file using one of the three tools described in this chapter, you can't rebuild the kernel.

Load Configuration   Load a previously saved configuration file (for use later on or to pass to a friend) that was stored under a name that you chose.

Store Configuration   To save a kernel configuration file (for use later on or to pass to a friend) under a name that you select. You must still use the Save and Exit option to create a kernel configuration file in the default location to be used immediately for kernel rebuilding.

Compiling and Running the New Kernel

Once your configuration is complete and a new configuration file has been created by the configuration option that you selected, you're ready to use the make command to rebuild your kernel.

The preferred commands vary slightly based on your Linux system, but are straightforward in every case.

Return to a command line after configuring the kernel and make sure you can leave your system running for a while to let the compilation proceed.

Rebuilding the kernel can take from 15 minutes to several hours, depending on your processor, memory, and other factors. Because of this, most people prefer to combine all of the commands to rebuild the kernel on a single command line, separated by semicolons, so that they execute one after another. By doing this, you can simply return to your system after a while and find the whole process completed.

Starting the Rebuild Process

The commands given here create a new kernel and also rebuild all the kernel modules, placing them in the correct system directories to be accessible to your kernel using standard module commands.

To rebuild the system, use these commands:

```
# make dep; make clean; make; make modules; make modules_install
```

TIP You can also enter each **make** command separately, entering the next command after each one has finished.

When you enter these commands, you see lines of information scrolling slowly down your screen as the make program enters different directories, starts the gcc or egcs compiler for various source code files, and links together pieces of the code.

Once the commands described previously have completed and you return to a command prompt, you have a new kernel that you can run your system on.

You need to move the newly created kernel to the standard location so it can be used. The command to do this is:

```
# cp /usr/src/linux/arch/i386/boot/zImage /boot/vmlinuz
```

TIP The name of the copied kernel image given here, vmlinuz, may include a kernel version number. The important point is that it must match the filename given in your /etc/lilo.conf file.

Testing the New Kernel

After you have moved your new kernel into the default position (as shown in the lilo.conf file), you can reboot your system to start the new kernel.

Once your Linux system has been rebooted, try the additional features that you specified in the kernel configuration. This might include things like:

- Comparing the size of the new kernel to the previous one. Also try the free command to see how much system memory is used.

- Mounting a file system or accessing a device without first loading a kernel module to support it (if you had built-in support for that service).

- Using a networking resource (such as IP aliases) that was not available in your original kernel.

You may also want to try the `uname` command to see the timestamp of your current kernel. This command verifies that the kernel you're running is the one that you rebuilt. Make sure that the date and time match when you rebuilt your kernel.

```
# uname  -v
#1 Tue Mar 9 23:27:39 MST 1999
```

NOTE   If the response from the `uname` command indicates that you are not running the new kernel, you may have a problem with your LILO boot loader. Check the information in the `/etc/lilo.conf` file to be sure that the correct kernel has been specified.

Looking Ahead

The next section of this book covers basic connectivity. The following chapters address a range of subjects related to connecting a stand-alone PC to the Internet, including the mechanics of establishing a PPP connection, browsing the World Wide Web with Linux, and sending and receiving e-mail with Linux.

In the next chapter, you will start this journey with a review of basic networking concepts as they apply to Linux. This will include a quick overview of TCP/IP, the protocol that makes the Internet work and is the basis for most Unix- and Linux-based networks.

PART V

Basic Connectivity

CHAPTER

TWENTY-ONE

21

Understanding Linux Networking

- TCP/IP Fundamentals

- TCP and UDP Services and Ports

- Routing Concepts

This part of the book dives into a topic that is of interest to most computer users these days: networking.

This chapter starts by considering the basic Linux networking concepts, including TCP/IP networks and routing. You will discover the basic concepts behind TCP/IP and the components of a TCP/IP configuration, such as IP addresses, netmasks, ports, and gateways. Then you will look at the types of services that typically run on the TCP/IP connection of a standard Linux system.

TCP/IP Fundamentals

This chapter discusses TCP/IP networks for a simple reason: in the world of Unix, TCP/IP networks are undoubtedly the standard.

When a type of network is discussed, such as TCP/IP, IPX/SPX, or SNA, you are really talking about the protocols, or languages, that are used to communicate between machines connected to the network. This is independent of the type of physical connection on which the network is built.

At a physical level, today's networks are built using a variety of Ethernet technologies, including 10-Base-2, 10-Base-T, and 100-Base-TX Ethernet, as well as fiber optic and other technologies. In fact, a TCP/IP network can be composed of components running on different types of network infrastructures: Ethernet components, components connected via telephone serial connections, and connections running on infrared transmitters and receivers. At the level of the network protocol, it doesn't matter what type of hardware and cabling is actually used to move the data around the network.

This abstraction, or separation, of the logical (the protocols) from the physical (the hardware and cabling) makes it possible to talk about networking without concern for the types of connections being made.

What Is TCP/IP?

Possibly because the genesis of the Internet occurred on a series of interconnected Unix systems, the networking standard for most Unix networks and for the Internet is the same: TCP/IP.

TCP/IP is a two-part name. TCP stands for Transmission Control Protocol and IP stands for Internet Protocol. Together, they make up one of the most pervasive networking protocols in use today.

This powerful combo allows the Internet to act as a global TCP/IP network. In fact, connecting a TCP/IP-based LAN to the Internet can be a simple job because the same technology is being used on the internal network (the LAN) and the external network (the Internet).

Taken separately, the job of IP is to act as the mechanism for routing and transmitting TCP packets (packages of information) as well as packets that use the User Datagram Protocol (UDP), a relative of TCP. TCP and UDP are the protocols utilized by programs such as FTP and Telnet to build meaningful packets to be shared across the network. TCP and UDP know nothing about the mechanics of delivering these packets across the network; they leave that work to IP.

The metaphor that is often used to explain the relationship is that of addressed envelopes and their contents. TCP and UDP packets are letters placed in envelopes with the destination address on the outside. IP then acts as the postal system, delivering the packet to the destination where the package is opened and handed back to TCP or UDP.

TCP/IP Configuration Essentials

In order to understand how TCP/IP is configured and networks are designed, it is important to understand some fundamental concepts:

- IP addresses
- Subnetworking and netmasks
- Broadcast addresses
- Gateway addresses
- Name servers

IP Addresses

In the world of TCP/IP, each machine (or host) connected to the network is assigned a unique address known as an *IP address*. An IP address is a four-part number that uniquely identifies the host. Each machine that has direct access to the Internet has a unique IP address. If you dial into the Internet through an

Internet service provider (ISP), for the duration of your connection you possess and use a unique IP address assigned to you by your ISP.

IP addresses are made up of four one-byte integer numbers separated by dots. A one-byte integer is any integer that can be represented by eight binary digits (eight binary digits, or bits, is one byte). This means each of the four parts of an IP address can take a value between 0 and 255. For instance, possible IP addresses include 194.148.43.194, 134.65.98, 23.98.45.23, and 65.87.99.254. Invalid IP addresses would include 194.148.43.294, 341.65.98, 222.98.145.256, and 230.980.450.230.

The total number of IP addresses available, then, is 256 to the power of 4, or 4,294,967,296. This may seem like a lot of addresses, but with the rate at which the Internet has grown in recent years and continues to grow, IP addresses are increasingly becoming rare commodities. Efforts are under way to upgrade the structure of IP addresses to consist of four 32-bit integers for a total of 340,282, 366,920,938,463,463,374,607,431,768,211,456 addresses, which is the total number of existing IP addresses to the power of 4.

As you might guess, over four billion addresses are not simply randomly used around the globe. Rather, they are assigned in chunks, known as networks, for use by organizations, ISPs, and other groups needing IP addresses for use on the Internet.

There are three types of TCP/IP networks available: Class A, Class B, and Class C networks.

- In a Class A network, the network is identified by the first byte of the IP addresses while the remaining three bytes identify specific machines on the network, for a total of 16,777,216 available addresses.

- In a Class B network, the network is identified by the first two bytes of the IP address while the remaining two bytes identify specific machines on the network, for a total of 65,536 machines.

- In a Class C network, the network is identified by the first three bytes of the IP address while the remaining byte identifies specific machines on the network, for a total of 256 machines.

For example, in a Class C network, the machine identified by the IP address 194.148.43.194 is machine 194 on the network 194.148.43. Similarly, on a Class B network, the machine 194.148.43.194 would be the machine 43.194 on the network 194.148.

It is not uncommon for organizations with large IP address needs to obtain a Class B network and then subdivide (subnetwork) it into 256 Class C networks. A perfect example of this is a large ISP that needs to provide Class C networks to its corporate clients and does this by dividing up a Class B network.

Subnetworking and Netmasks

There is a potential for confusion in this situation. How can a machine know what type of network it is on? If a machine has an IP address of 194.148.43.194, there is no immediately apparent way for it to know if it is on the Class A network 194, the Class B network 194.148, or the Class C network 194.148.43.

This situation is resolved by the use of a *network mask* (or *subnetwork mask*), also known as a *netmask* (or *subnetmask*). A netmask is another set of dot-separated one-byte integers that define which portion of the IP address identifies the network. This is done by combining the IP address and the netmask with a logical AND. Let's consider how this works with a simple eight-bit number.

If you have an eight-bit number of 194, its binary representation is:

11000010

To split this number in two, with the first four bits representing the network and the last four representing the host, then our netmask, when combined with this number using logical AND, needs to leave zeros in the last four bits and should ensure that the first four bits are left unchanged.

A logical AND operation follows this set of rules:

- 1 and 1 is 1
- 1 and 0 is 0
- 0 and 1 is 0
- 0 and 0 is 0

Each bit is matched with the corresponding bit in the same position.

Therefore, if you want to create a netmask that keeps the first four bits of an eight-bit number intact, the netmask, in binary form, would be as follows:

11110000

Consider the value of 194 from above:

11000010 and

```
11110000 is
11000000
```

Now, let's apply this to a more complex example of an actual IP address and network mask combination. Consider an IP address of 194.148.43.194. If you want a network mask to indicate a Class B network and its network address, you need to make all the bits in the first two bytes 1 (each byte will have a value of 255) and all the bits in the last two bytes 0 (each byte will have a value of 0). The end result is a netmask of 255.255.

Similarly, for a Class C address, the netmask would have the first three bytes set to 255 and the last to zero: 255.255.255.

The value returned by combining the netmask and the IP address is your network address. In the Class B example discussed previously, using logical AND to combine 194.148.43.194 and 255.255 produces a Class B network address of 194.148. Similarly, using the netmask of 255.255.255 produces a Class C network address of 194.148.43.

Because the network address of a Class C network uses up the first IP address (the one with 0 in the last byte), this IP address can't be used for an actual host on the network.

Broadcast Addresses

The *broadcast address* is a special address that can be used when sending information to all hosts on the network. Instead of sending a separate packet to each host, a single packet can be sent out and all machines listening can receive it (like radio or television signals).

The broadcast address is based on the network address with the host portions replaced by 255. So, for the Class B network 194.148, the broadcast address is 194.148.255.255, and for the Class C network 194.148.43, the broadcast address is 194.148.43.255.

As with the network address, the broadcast address is also reserved and can't be used for an actual host.

Therefore, counting out the network and broadcast addresses leaves an actual 254 available host addresses on a Class C network and 65,534 on a Class B network.

Gateway Addresses

As you will see later in the section on routing, a computer configured for the local network or subnetwork has no knowledge of how to communicate with machines on external networks (for instance, on the Internet).

A *gateway* is a machine that provides a route to the outside world. It generally has at least two network interfaces: one connected to the local network and one to the outside world. The gateway reroutes packets on and off the local network as appropriate.

For a host to connect to external networks, the gateway needs to know the IP address of at least one gateway off the local network.

Name Servers

While it is great to be able to communicate on the local and external networks, it is impractical for users to remember IP addresses for every machine they want to connect to.

This is resolved by the Domain Name System (DNS). DNS provides a mechanism to map domain names (such as bahai.org) and host names (www.bahai.org) into IP addresses for actual use. For each registered domain, there are at least two DNS servers responsible for answering lookup queries for hosts in the domain.

In addition, every host that wants to be able to resolve host names into IP addresses needs the services of at least one DNS server that can handle the task of contacting other DNS servers to get name lookup answers.

For this reason, when configuring TCP/IP, it is usually necessary to provide the IP address of at least one name server.

TCP and UDP Services and Ports

When two machines wish to use TCP/IP to communicate with each other, they generally specify the destination by using a combination of the IP address and a port. *Ports* are 16-bit integers that identify the service that is being used and that receives the data. Think of ports as the mailboxes in an apartment block.

Let's look at an example: the Web. A Linux Web server runs a process known as a *daemon* whose job it is to listen to a specific port for incoming Web connections. Widely used services such as TCP/IP, the Web, FTP, and e-mail all have well-known ports that daemons listen to for incoming connections. Table 21.1 lists common TCP and UDP ports.

TABLE 21.1: Common TCP and UDP Ports

Service Name	Port	Type	Description
FTP	21	TCP	File Transfer Protocol
Telnet	23	TCP	Telnet connections
SMTP	25	TCP	Simple Mail Transfer Protocol
Name	42	TCP	Domain Name System services
HTTP	80	TCP	Hypertext Transfer Protocol (World Wide Web)
POP3	110	TCP	Post Office Protocol 3 mail readers
IMAP	143	TCP	Internet Message Access Protocol mail readers

A more complete list of TCP and UDP services and ports can be found on the Internet at `http://www.con.wesleyan.edu/~triemer/network/docservs.html`.

Back to the Web example. Since port 80 is the default port for the Web, the Web daemon will listen on port 80 for an incoming connection. A Web client initiates a connection requesting a document on port 80.

When the daemon notices an incoming connection, it answers, and the daemon and client are able to communicate. However, if the daemon returns the document being requested on port 80, it will tie up port 80, preventing new incoming requests.

This is resolved by the fact that the Web client is dynamically assigned its own port and sends this port along to the Web daemon, allowing the Web daemon to return the document requested on the client's own port, thus leaving port 80 free for further incoming requests. This is how it is possible for a Web daemon to handle a large number of incoming requests while listening on a single port.

Routing Concepts

The discussion of gateways earlier in this chapter alluded to the notion of *routing*. Routing is the mechanism by which it is possible for the apparently chaotic Internet to work.

After all, when you use Netscape Communicator to connect to Yahoo's Web site, your machine knows nothing about the actual physical location of the Yahoo Web server. Still, your request somehow makes it to Yahoo and Yahoo's response finds its way back to you.

Let's start with a simple example of routing. You are connected to a small corporate local area network (LAN) that has an Internet connection. The Internet connection is made through a router connected to the corporate LAN and your company's leased line connection to its ISP. Figure 21.1 illustrates this network layout.

FIGURE 21.1:

A LAN connected to the Internet

Because your LAN has only a single connection to the outside world through the router, routing is a simple matter. Each machine on the Internet is configured with a default gateway that points to the router. Whenever a host on the LAN is trying to connect with a machine off the local network, it sends the packets to the router and the router is responsible for redirecting the information.

In this way, the entire outside world is a black box: all outward-bound information is simply sent to the router as if the router encapsulated the entire network beyond the LAN. The router has a simple decision to make. When it receives a packet, the router looks at the destination address. If the address is for the local LAN, the router sends it to the local LAN Ethernet; if the packet is addressed to any external address, the router simply sends it across the leased line to the ISP.

Let's take things a step further and enlarge the black box to include the ISP's network and its connection to the Internet, as shown in Figure 21.2.

Now things get a bit more interesting. Consider the ISP's LAN. Here you see two routers: Router A, which connects the ISP's LAN to the leased line to the local LAN and Router B, which connects the ISP's LAN to the leased-line connection to the Internet.

Since each network needs a default gateway, Router B becomes the default gateway: when a host on the ISP's LAN is trying to connect to a host not on the local LAN, and for which no known route exists, it sends the information to Router B.

But if the ISP only specifies Router B as the default gateway for machines on its LAN, then information destined for your local LAN is actually sent to Router B and from there out to the Internet. This problem is solved with the addition of a static route.

FIGURE 21.2:

The LAN and its ISP

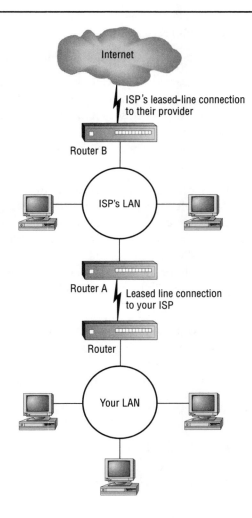

A static route specifies that information for a specific network or host should be sent to a different gateway than the default gateway. In this way, a static route can be defined for sending all traffic from the Internet provider for the local LAN to Router A. For hosts on the ISP's LAN, then, there is a series of three routing rules to follow:

1. If a packet is destined for a host on the local LAN, send it directly to the host.

2. If a packet is destined for the LAN connected via Router A, send the packet to Router A.

3. Send all packets not destined for the Router A LAN to Router B.

The process should be clear now. When an incoming packet destined for your network arrives, it comes from the Internet to Router B. Router B looks at the destination of the packet, sees it is for the LAN, and follows the static route, sending the packet to Router A. Router A looks at the destination of the packet, determines it is for the local LAN, and sends the packet directly to the destination host on your local LAN.

Routing can become extremely complex in large organizations with multiple sites, multiple LANs, and multiple connections to the Internet. In these cases, routing has to be carefully designed to ensure the most efficient routing of information in the most secure manner possible. For instance, two remote locations may have a leased-line connection between them in addition to their own connections to the Internet. It wouldn't make sense to route packets between these sites through the public Internet. This is both inefficient and an unnecessary security hole.

Complex routing of large networks is beyond the scope of this book and belongs in tomes dedicated to networking. The discussion in this chapter should provide sufficient background to understand the typical network routing environment in which most Linux users will find themselves.

Looking Ahead

In this chapter, you have learned the basic concepts of TCP/IP networking and routing.

Taking this theoretical knowledge into the realm of the practical, in the next chapter you will learn how to connect a Linux PC to the Internet through a dial-up PPP connection like those commonly offered by Internet providers.

In the chapters that follow, you will learn how to use specific Internet services such as the World Wide Web and e-mail from Linux.

CHAPTER

TWENTY-TWO

Connecting Linux to the Internet

- What Is PPP?

- Required Hardware and Software

- Your First PPP Connection

- Automating Your Internet Connection

The subject of connecting a Linux system (or any computer system, for that matter) to the Internet is a complex one and a subject that can require a thorough knowledge of that system's network environment.

Still, for many users, this process is simple enough that both X Windows and Linux work on the first attempt.

This chapter will start with a quick look at PPP and its role in the Internet world. It will review the hardware and software requirements for connecting to the Internet and then walk you through the mechanics of manually making a PPP connection. Finally, this chapter will wrap up by learning how to automate these connections.

What Is PPP?

Most Internet users are probably familiar with the acronym PPP, simply because the type of account they have with their Internet service provider (ISP) is a PPP account. Many users, though, really don't understand what PPP is all about.

PPP stands for *Point-to-Point Protocol* and is designed to provide a method by which TCP/IP is extended across an analog modem connection. In this way, when you are connected to the Internet using PPP, you become part of your ISP's network, you are an actual host on the Internet, and you have an IP address.

Traditionally, dial-up Internet connections were done using terminal software and Unix shell accounts on central servers. In this environment, the terminal software on the client system merely acted as a display for the server, and only the server really existed as a node on the Internet. This contrasts sharply with today's PPP connections, which bring the Internet right up to your modem.

The great flexibility of Internet connection technologies allows for a wide variety of PPP connection types. You can have PPP connections with fixed IP addresses or dynamic IP address assignments. Connections can use special authentication protocols such as PAP (Password Authentication Protocol) or can use standard text-based prompt-and-response mechanisms. Connections can be made manually or can be made automatically as needed.

This chapter will discuss the most common Internet connection scenario: connecting by modem to an ISP that offers PPP connections with dynamically assigned IP addresses.

Required Hardware and Software

In order to make PPP work properly, some preparation is needed. Hardware and software needs to be in place and configured before you can get PPP to work properly. Three key components need to be considered:

- A modem needs to be installed, configured, and working.
- PPP support needs to be compiled into the Linux kernel.
- PPP software needs to be installed.

The Modem

Because PPP is designed for dial-up connections, a modem is an essential piece of the PPP puzzle.

Chapter 18, "Using Peripherals," discussed modems and how to install them, test them, and get them working. Refer to that chapter to get your modem up and running and to make a test connection to be sure everything is in order.

To configure PPP, you need to know the speed of your modem connection and which device it uses in Linux (probably /dev/modem or one of /dev/ttyS0 through /dev/ttyS3).

PPP in the Kernel

The Linux kernel is designed to be highly flexible. It can be compiled to include (or exclude) support for numerous technologies ranging from serial mice right up to networking facilities such as PPP.

In order to make a PPP connection with Linux, it is necessary for the kernel to include PPP support. In Red Hat Linux the default kernel that is installed by the distribution has PPP support built right in.

You can check to see if support is there by watching the messages that scroll by while the operating system is booting. If you see a series of lines like these:

```
PPP: version 2.2 (dynamic channel allocation)
PPP Dynamic channel allocation code copyright 1995 Caldera, Inc.
PPP line discipline registered.
registered device ppp0
PPP: ppp line discipline successfully unregistered
```

then PPP is compiled into your kernel. If you find the messages scroll by too quickly, you can use the **dmesg** command to see the part of the start-up messages that should include the PPP messages:

```
$ dmesg | more
```

NOTE   If you find you need to recompile your kernel to include PPP support, refer to Chapter 20, "Recompiling the Linux Kernel," which discusses the steps involved in recompiling your kernel.

Installing PPP Software

Red Hat Linux 6 installs PPP software with a complete or default installation.

Two programs are used to establish a PPP connection: /usr/sbin/pppd and /usr/sbin/chat. In Red Hat Linux 6, these are part of the ppp -2.3.7-2 package, and you can see if these are installed by using the rpm command:

```
$ rpm -q ppp
ppp -2.3.7-2
```

If you find you are lacking either **pppd** or **chat**, you need to install a new set of PPP software before continuing.

Mount the Red Hat CD-ROM at a suitable location (such as /mnt/cdrom) and then install the package ppp-2.3.7-2.i386.rpm:

```
$ rpm -i ppp-2.3.7-2.i386.rpm
```

Alternately, you can download the latest sources for PPP from Metalab's Linux archive in the directory ftp://Metalab.unc.edu/pub/Linux/system/network/serial/ppp. The current version of PPP is 2.3.7 and the filename is ppp-2.3.7.tar.gz.

You need to expand the archive in a suitable location with the command

```
$ tar xzvf ppp-2.3.7.tar.gz
```

and then read through the README.linux file carefully. Installing a new PPP package involves not only compiling the software but also upgrading your Linux kernel source files and recompiling the Linux kernel to match the version of the PPP software being installed.

Describing the details of this process would take up a whole chapter, so it is best left to the documentation.

Your First PPP Connection

Now that you have the necessary software and hardware in place, you are ready to work out the details of your first connection. First, it is necessary to understand how things work.

In Linux, the PPP connection is made and maintained by **pppd**. But **pppd** assumes that a connection has already been made between your modem and your ISP's modem, that all the necessary logging in has taken place, and that the ISP's system is also trying to establish a PPP connection on top of the same modem connection.

This sounds like a lot of conditions, but it really isn't that bad. On almost every ISP, the connection process goes like this:

1. The modem connection is made.

2. The login process occurs.

3. Once the user is authenticated, the ISP begins to try to make a PPP connection by sending the IP address of the client to the client system.

The **pppd** program requires steps 1 and 2 to have occurred before number 3 gets under way.

Given this process, it is necessary to make a modem connection to the ISP before attempting to run **pppd**. Once the connection is made, the PPP connection can be established with **pppd**.

Making a PPP Connection

Fortunately, the pppd software is designed to bring things together and work with the chat program to handle the entire connection process.

Before attempting to connect, you need to gather some information:

- Are you assigned an IP address each time you connect, or do you have a permanently assigned IP address? Because most ISPs work on the basis of assigning a dynamic IP address with each connection, you will also work on this basis.

- How do you log in to your ISP? One option uses plain text prompt-and-response logins; the other uses a special authentication protocol called PAP. If you attempt to dial into your ISP with minicom or other terminal software and are presented with a login prompt of some sort, then you are logging in with plain text prompts. If you see random characters after connecting, or no characters at all, then you are probably using PAP authentication.

> **NOTE**   All the examples in this section assume that you are working as the root user on your machine. Because the process of connecting via PPP requires manipulation of interfaces and creation and deletion of network routes, the programs involved need to be run by the root user.

Connecting with Plain Text Prompts

Let's start with plain text prompts because they are a little easier to work with.

Because pppd by itself can take control of your modem device but cannot perform the actual dialing or logging in, you need a way to issue commands to the modem and provide the necessary login information. This is achieved with the chat program. The chat program allows you to create a conversational exchange.

For instance, the normal dialing process on a modem is to run a terminal editor and in an empty terminal window, type a dial command such as **ATDT12345678**. The response to this is usually a connect string such as CONNECT 9600, to which the user doesn't respond.

This exchange can be turned into a simple chat script:

```
"" ATDT1234567 CONNECT ""
```

This script is made up of two *expect-send pairs*: " " ATDT1234567 and CONNECT " ". An expect-send pair contains two pieces of information separated by a space. In the first pair, chat is told to expect nothing and in response to send back the string ATDT1234567. In other words, as soon as the script starts processing, the first action is to send the dial string. Next, the second pair is processed and chat is told to expect the string CONNECT and in response to do nothing. If this were the complete script, chat would finish at this point and exit.

Of course, your chat script needs to be a bit longer. In order to complete your chat script, you need to find out exactly what your login session looks like. You can do this by logging in with regular terminal software such as minicom.

Login prompts at most ISPs generally take the form of

```
Username:
Password:
```

or

```
Login:
Password:
```

Consider the first case as the example in this chapter. If you find your login prompts are different, substitute accordingly as you work through the section.

NOTE   It may be necessary for you to leave off the first letter of the prompts. This is because different operating systems handle the case of the first letter differently, and with some ISPs you can't be sure which operating system will be providing the prompt to you when you log in. By waiting for the ogin: or assword: your scripts will work regardless of the case of the first letter.

So, what is the next expect-send pair? After connecting, you are presented with a Username: prompt, in response to which you provide a username (let's say your username is "testuser"). The expect-send pair for this interaction would be Username: **testuser**.

Once a username is provided, you get a Password: prompt, to which you provide a password (let's assume this is "testpassword"). This produces the expect-send pair Password: **testpassword**.

For many ISPs this is sufficient, and PPP starts on the ISP's system after the correct password is entered. On a smaller number of systems, the ISP's computers present you with a command prompt at which you have to type a command to start PPP. In this case, you need to create an additional pair.

For this example, the complete chat script looks like this:

```
"" ATDT1234567 CONNECT "" Username: testuser Password: testpassword
```

To use this with the chat program (which is normally in /usr/sbin), you simply provide the script as an argument to chat:

```
/usr/sbin/chat "" ATDT1234567 CONNECT "" Username: testuser Password:
testpassword
```

Note, however, that you don't want to type this at the command line and press Enter. Without being integrated with pppd and provided access to the modem through that program, chat attempts to chat in the console. You can use this to test your script, though. Simply type the command at the command prompt. When you see ATDT1234567, type **CONNECT** and then type **Username:**. You should see testuser in response. Follow this by typing **Password:** and you should see testpassword in response.

NOTE   If you need to work out problems with your chat script, try adding the –v flag to your chat command. This causes the output of the script to appear in the system log, where you can analyze the results to find problems.

Once you have a working script, you need to integrate it with pppd. You are going to use a handful of pppd options to do this. (The pppd application takes many additional options, which can be found in the pppd man page.) The options you will use are the following:

connect   This option is employed to specify a program or command used to establish a connection on the serial line being utilized. In this case, you use the connect option to specify the chat program and its script.

noipdefault   The default behavior of pppd is to determine the IP address of the local machine on the basis of its host name. But if the ISP assigns a dynamic IP address, then the noipdefault is used to tell pppd to get the IP address from the remote machine to which it is connecting.

defaultroute   This option tells pppd to add a default route to the system's routing table, using the remote system as the default gateway. The entry is removed when the connection is broken.

The structure of the pppd command is:

```
$ pppd device-name device-speed options
```

If you are connecting with the device /dev/modem and the modem has a top compressed speed of 57600bps (in other words, a 14.4Kbps modem), then you use the following command to connect with the chat script:

```
$ pppd /dev/modem 57600 connect '/usr/sbin/chat "" ATDT1234567 CONNECT
"" Username: testuser Password: testpassword' noipdefault defaultroute
```

When this command is issued, the modem should dial and, after connecting, it will authenticate and establish a PPP connection. If this process is successful, two things should happen.

First, issuing the command ifconfig with no flags or arguments should return a list of interfaces including a PPP interface similar to this one:

```
ppp0      Link encap:Point-to-Point Protocol
          inet addr:194.209.60.101  P-t-P:194.209.60.97
Mask:255.255.255
          UP POINTOPOINT RUNNING  MTU:1500  Metric:1
          RX packets:10 errors:0 dropped:0 overruns:0
          TX packets:11 errors:0 dropped:0 overruns:0
```

Second, entries should be added to the routing table to create a default route through the remote machine (check for this using the route command with no flags or arguments):

```
Kernel IP routing table
Destination  Gateway      Genmask           Flags Metric Ref   Use Iface
du1.paus.ch  *            255.255.255.255   UH    0      0       0 ppp0
default      du1.paus.ch  0                 UG    0      0       0 ppp0
```

In this example, the du1.paus.ch is the remote machine in the PPP connection and is serving as the default gateway.

Connecting with PAP Authentication

Connecting with PAP authentication follows the same basic principles as the text prompt example you just worked through, except that the method of providing the username and password differs.

The first major difference is that you don't provide the username and password on the command line as part of a PAP script. Instead, you create entries in a special `secrets` file that is used during the PAP authentication process. In Red Hat Linux 6, this file is `/etc/ppp/pap-secrets`. By default, the permissions on this file make it readable and writable only by the root user. Other users do not have read access to this file.

The format of entries in the `secrets` file are:

```
username device/interface password
```

For instance, if you use the test username and password from the previous section, the entry might be:

```
testuser * testpassword
```

The * indicates that this password can be used for connections on any interface. If you have a single PPP interface (ppp0), you can limit the use of this password to that device by changing the entry:

```
testuser ppp0 testpassword
```

Comments in the `pap-secrets` file start with a hash mark (#).

Once your username and password are in the file, you need to write a new `chat` script. For most ISPs, as soon as the modem connection is established, PAP authentication can begin. Therefore, your `chat` script gets simpler:

```
"" ATDT12345678 CONNECT ""
```

This script dials the ISP and makes sure that a connect message is received before ending the `chat` program and proceeding on to authentication.

Finally, you need to introduce one more option for pppd: `user`. The `user` option indicates which PAP user from the `pap-secrets` file is to be authenticated. The end result is the following `pppd` command:

```
$ pppd /dev/modem 57600 connect '/usr/sbin/chat "" ATDT1234567
➥CONNECT'noipdefault defaultroute user testuser
```

As with the earlier text login example, you can check that everything is in order using `ifconfig` and `route`.

Once You Have a Connection

Once you have an Internet connection, you need to make sure you can fully connect to the Internet. To do this, you need to verify that your DNS services are properly configured to point to your ISP's nameserver.

This is done by editing two files: `/etc/host.conf` and `/etc/resolv.conf`. Both of these files are discussed more fully in Chapter 28, "Configuring Red Hat Linux 6 for an Ethernet Network." This section just covers the necessary basics of the files so that you can quickly get online.

The file `/etc/host.conf` should contain the following two lines:

```
order hosts,bind
multi on
```

This should be the default.

Next, `/etc/resolv.conf` should contain at least two lines:

```
search
nameserver 100.100.100.100
```

In your case, replace the IP address 100.100.100.100 with the IP address of your ISP's nameserver. Your ISP can provide this information. If your ISP provides you with a list of more than one nameserver, create a separate line for each nameserver, following the form of the `nameserver` line above:

```
search
nameserver 100.100.100.100
nameserver 200.200.200.200
```

Once this is done, you should be able to resolve names and thus access the Internet. You should also be able to run Internet software such as Netscape and FTP. These programs are discussed in later chapters, such as Chapter 23, "Accessing the World Wide Web."

Hanging Up

When you are finished using the Internet, you should hang up to reduce phone costs and online charges. To do this, you need to kill the `pppd` process.

You can find out the process ID of the pppd program using the ps command as the root user:

```
$ ps x | more
```

The entry for pppd should look something like

```
1316  a1 S    0:00 /usr/sbin/pppd /dev/cua1 115200 connect
/usr/sbin/chat "" AT
```

The first number is the process ID. You can kill this process with the kill command:

```
$ kill 1316
```

When pppd is killed, the modem should hang up.

Automating Your Internet Connection

While it is great to be able to establish PPP connections to the Internet, if you have to type the long pppd and chat commands each time you connect, the practicality of using Linux to connect to the Internet will be limited.

To improve the situation, you can create two scripts: one for dialing and one for hanging up. These two scripts are going to be called dial and hangup (logical choices, yes?). You will want to place these files in a directory on your path such as /usr/local/bin.

Because you haven't learned about scripting yet, these two scripts are presented here with a brief discussion so that you can get right down to using them. These scripts can be created in any text editor. It is important to make sure that lines that appear as one line here stay as one line in your files.

For the dial script, let's assume that the PAP example earlier in the chapter is the way you want to connect to the Internet.

Once you have created the scripts, you will want to make them executable with the chmod command:

```
$ chmod 700 dial hangup
```

The permission 700 makes the script readable, writable, and executable by the root user and no one else. This will work fine since you need to be running as root in order to make a PPP connection.

The *Dial* Script

The `dial` script should look like this:

```
#!/bin/sh
/usr/sbin/pppd /dev/modem 57600 connect \
'/usr/sbin/chat "" ATDT1234567 CONNECT' \
noipdefault defaultroute user testuser
```

The first line tells Linux to process the script through the Bourne Shell, which is at `/bin/sh`. Notice that the pppd command is split across three lines. This is done to make the script more readable and the individual lines shorter. The backslashes at the ends of the first and second lines indicate that the line breaks shouldn't be treated as line breaks and that the command continues on the next line of the file.

The *Hangup* Script

The hangup script should look like this:

```
#!/bin/sh
kill `cat /var/run/ppp0.pid`
```

As with the `dial` script, you start by specifying that the script should be processed with the Bourne Shell. Next, you kill the process in a slightly different way than you learned to before.

You are relying on the fact that the pppd process writes its process ID to a file that usually sits in `/var/run` on most modern Linux systems. The filename consists of the device name followed by a `.pid` extension. If you have only one modem and one PPP connection active at a time, you can assume the device is ppp0 and type **/var/run/ppp0.pid** directly into your script.

The cat command simply displays the contents of the ppp0.pid file on the standard output. You put the cat command in back quotes to pass the result of the cat command (which is the process ID of the pppd process) to the kill command.

But what happens if you have multiple PPP interfaces and want to be able to specify which one to hang up? A quick modification of the hangup script makes this possible:

```
#!/bin/sh
kill `cat /var/run/$1.pid`
```

Here, you have replaced ppp0 with $1. The $1 indicates that the value of the first argument to the script should be placed in this location. Now you can pass the interface name to the script as an argument. The command

```
$ hangup ppp1
```

hangs up the modem that is being used for the ppp1 interface.

Looking Ahead

In this chapter, you took a big step. You brought your Linux system from the isolation of a lone computer on a desktop and connected it to the world with a PPP connection.

In the next chapter, you will take advantage of this new capability and learn how to use Netscape Communicator, the premier Web browser and Internet client for the Linux platform.

Following that, in Chapter 24, you will look at the rich variety of e-mail software available for Linux so that you can choose the one that best supports your style of using e-mail.

CHAPTER

TWENTY-THREE

23

Using the World Wide Web

- An Overview of Linux Browsers

- Installing and Using Netscape Communicator

- Installing and Using Lynx

Now that you have your Linux system connected properly to the Internet, the first thing most of you will want to do is get out there and browse the World Wide Web.

This chapter takes a brief tour through the numerous Web browsers that are available for Linux, and then takes a closer look at three browsers: Xmosaic, Netscape Communicator, and Lynx.

Netscape Communicator is the latest version of the free Web browser and Internet client from Netscape. This full-featured package is available for Windows, Macintosh, and almost every conceivable Unix variant, including Linux.

Finally, this chapter will look at Lynx, the de facto standard in Unix text-based browsers. Lynx has a longer history than Netscape, going back to when Web technology was used to deliver small amounts of scientific information in a simple text-based hypertext system. Lynx has continued to evolve and ships with almost every distribution of Linux. While it lacks the fancy graphics and icon-driven interface of Netscape Communicator, for a quick way to go online, check some information, and go offline, nothing beats Lynx.

An Overview of Linux Browsers

There are several browsers available for the X Windows environment that work with Linux. These browsers range from the test platform Amaya, developed at the World Wide Web Consortium (W3C), to mainstream browsers such as Netscape. This section takes a quick look at some of these browsers so that you have a sense of the breadth of available Web software for Linux.

Amaya

Amaya is a Web browser developed by the W3C as a test bed for new Web protocols and data formats. Since this is the organization that maintains such standards as HTML and cascading style sheets (CSS)—both critical Web technologies—it makes sense that the Consortium should develop its own software as part of developing new standards for the World Wide Web.

Amaya is a combination Web browser and authoring tool that is supposed to support cascading style sheets and HTML, along with new graphics formats such as PNG. Amaya also includes a powerful mathematical expression editor.

Although Amaya offers leading-edge features, it does not support all the features of the Web that are currently supported by commercial browsers such as Netscape.

The Amaya home page is on the Web at `http://www.w3.org/Amaya/`. Figure 23.1 contains a sample Amaya window.

FIGURE 23.1:

The Amaya Web browser

Lynx

Lynx is the de facto standard for text browsers for the World Wide Web and is available for all versions of Unix, Windows 95 and NT, and DOS. Work is underway for a Macintosh version. The Lynx home page is available at `http://lynx.browser.org/`.

You may be wondering what possible use a text browser could be. In the Unix world, it has many uses:

- Browsing HTML documentation or the Web on a system without X Windows running, such as a server console or a character terminal connected to a Unix network

- Quickly accessing the Web to download information without inflicting the system load that launching Netscape or a similar graphical browser would have

- Accessing the Web from low-end hardware such as a 386 PC

Whatever the reason, Lynx has evolved into an ideal offline browser with the means to cope with most of the advanced features of the Web today, including a way to view a site using frames. Figure 23.2 shows Lynx running in an `xterm` window. Detailed coverage of Lynx is provided later in this chapter.

FIGURE 23.2:

The Lynx Web browser

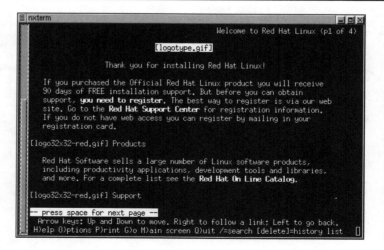

Xmosaic

The emergence of Mosaic from the labs of the National Center for Supercomputer Applications was the first indication that Web technology could mean more than a simple alternative to the omnipresent Gopher, which was the hypertext system of choice until the early 1990s.

Early versions of Mosaic ran in the X Windows environment of popular Unix systems such as Sun's. Users of the then-fledgling World Wide Web were dazzled by Mosaic's pages of combined graphics and text and the new, easy-to-navigate, mouse-driven interface.

While Mosaic is no longer under active development, the last release (version 2.6 in the case of X Windows) is still available at the Mosaic Web page at the University of Illinois at Urbana-Champaine, `http://www.ncsa.uiuc.edu/SDG/Software/Mosaic/`. Figure 23.3 provides a sense of what the early pioneers of the Web used as their browser of choice.

FIGURE 23.3:

The last version of Mosaic for X Windows

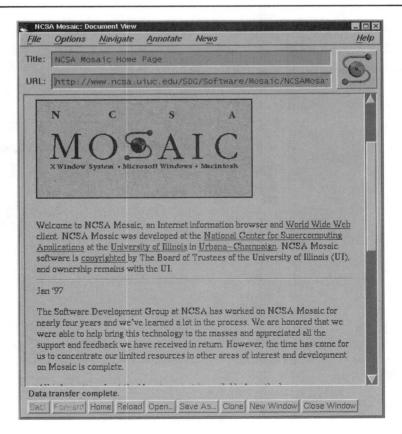

Netscape Communicator

Netscape Communicator, which includes the Navigator Web browser, can really be considered the flagship browser of the World Wide Web, and has been the source of many browser features that you now consider standard. While Microsoft can now be regarded as an equal competitor to Netscape in the Web browser market, Netscape still retains a large majority share by some counts, helped in part by the decision to release Communicator and its source code for free redistribution and alteration in early 1998.

In fact, at the time of this pricing policy change, Netscape highlighted Linux as an example of the open source model that Netscape was adopting for Communicator.

As would be expected, Netscape Communicator looks pretty much the same and behaves pretty much consistently on all the platforms it is available for, including Linux. Figure 23.4 shows Netscape Communicator for Linux. At first glance, it looks much the same as its Windows counterpart.

Netscape Communicator for Linux is discussed in detail later in this chapter.

FIGURE 23.4:

Netscape Communicator for Linux

Installing and Using Netscape Communicator

Netscape Communicator version 4.51 is included on the CD-ROM that accompanies this book. You can also download new copies of Communicator from Netscape's Web site at `http://home.netscape.com/`.

This section takes a quick look at installing Communicator in Linux, and then take a brief introductory tour of the software. This tour is not intended to provide a comprehensive guide to Communicator, but rather to provide enough information so that you can use it to get online. Netscape Communicator includes complete online help that has all the information needed to take full advantage of Communicator's features.

Installing from the CD-ROM

Netscape Communicator 4.51 is part of Red Hat Linux 6 and is likely to have been installed by default for most installations. If you find that Netscape is not on your system, you can install it from the CD-ROM that accompanies this book.

In order to install Communicator, you first must mount your CD-ROM to a logical location, such as /mnt/cdrom. Next, you want to use the rpm command to install the Netscape Communicator packages as follows:

```
$ rpm -i/mnt/cdrom/RedHat/RPMS/netscape-common-4.51-7.i386.rpm
$ rpm -i/mnt/cdrom/RedHat/RPMS/netscape-communicator-4.51-7.i386.rpm
```

These commands install the complete version of Netscape Communicator on your system. If you prefer to install only the Navigator component of Communicator and not the whole package, replace the second rpm command with

```
$ rpm -i/mnt/cdrom/RedHat/RPMS/netscape-navigator-4.51-7.i386.rpm
```

Installing from the Web

If you decide to download a newer version of Communicator from the Netscape Web site, installation will be somewhat different. At the time of this writing, the most recent version of Netscape Communicator was version 4.51 and was available as a compressed tar archive called communicator-v451-export.x86-unknown-linux2.tar.gz.

You need to download this archive to a temporary location, such as /tmp/. Next, create a temporary directory to hold the installation files, such as /tmp/netscape/, and then change directories (using the cd command) into this directory. Next, uncompress the archive with the command:

```
$ tar xzvf /tmp/communicator-v451-export.x86-unknown-linux2.tar.gz
```

This command creates several files in your temporary directory, including a README file and the ns-install script. You can proceed to install by running the installation script:

```
$ ./ns-install
```

From there, the procedure will be the same as if you were installing from the CD-ROM.

NOTE   If you download a newer version of Communicator than 4.51, there is the chance that the installation procedure is different than outlined here. In this case, check the installation files for a README file or an INSTALL file and take a look at the instructions in the file using the more command. When in doubt, accept the default options for all questions asked during installation, as this will help ensure that installation goes smoothly.

Accessing the World Wide Web

Accessing the Web with Communicator requires no additional preparation. Simply connect to the Internet (as outlined in the previous chapter) and then issue the command

```
$ /usr/bin/netscape-communicator
```

or whatever is appropriate for your installation to launch Communicator. A window appears similar to the one in Figure 23.5.

From here, Netscape works pretty much in the same way as it does on Windows or Macintosh computers.

FIGURE 23.5:

The initial Netscape Communicator window

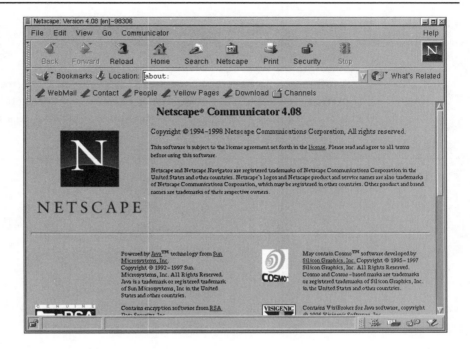

Red Hat Linux also ships with a stripped-down version of Communicator, called Netscape Navigator, which only provides a Web browser and doesn't include the mail or news reader that are part of Communicator. Netscape Navigator is not included on the Publisher's Edition of Red Hat Linux 6 that ships with this book, but it can be downloaded from `http://www.redhat.com`.

Opening a Web Page

You can open a Web page in several ways. The first is to type the URL of the desired page directly into the location field of the main window, as shown in Figure 23.6. As you can see in the figure, when you start typing a new URL in the location field, the name of the field changes to Go To, indicating that the URL being displayed is not the URL of the currently loaded document. When you press Enter, Communicator attempts to load the URL you have typed.

FIGURE 23.6:

The Location/Go To field

Another way to open a new page is to select Open Page from the File menu, as shown in Figure 23.7. This brings up the Open Page dialog box like the one in Figure 23.8. Simply type the URL you want to open and click the Open in Navigator button to open the Web page.

FIGURE 23.7:

The File menu

FIGURE 23.8:

The Open Page dialog box

Returning to Previous Pages

Returning to the previously viewed page is as simple as clicking the Back button in the Communicator toolbar. The toolbar is shown in Figure 23.9; the Back button is the first button at the left.

FIGURE 23.9:

The Communicator toolbar

You can also return to the previous page by choosing Back from the Go menu shown in Figure 23.10. The Go menu shows the history of documents you have viewed, and you can return to any displayed document by selecting it from the Go menu.

FIGURE 23.10:

The Go menu

Printing Pages

You can print Web pages from Communicator as long as you have already installed and configured a printer as discussed in Chapter 15, "Using LinuxConf and Control Panel for System Configuration," and Chapter 18, "Using Peripherals."

To print a displayed page, simply click the Print button in the toolbar or select Print from the File menu. This brings up a dialog box like the one in Figure 23.11.

FIGURE 23.11:

The Print dialog box

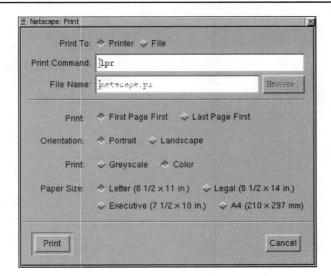

You can use this dialog box to print to a file or print to a configured printer queue.

Printing to a File Printing to a file causes Netscape to generate a PostScript image of the page being printed. The resulting file can be viewed with a PostScript viewer such as GhostScript, or can be used with software that can handle PostScript files (including word processors, graphics, and other applications) and sent directly to a printer at a later date.

To print to a file, select Print To, File at the top of the dialog box and then fill in the complete path and filename where you want Netscape to create the resulting file. All the other options are the same as printing to a printer (see below) and should be selected as appropriate, depending on the intended use of the resulting file.

Printing to a Print Queue To print to a printer queue, select Print To, Printer at the top of the dialog box. Next, enter the complete print command for your printer. For instance, if you want to print to a printer with a print queue called `laserjet5l`, enter the print command **`lpr -Plaserjet5l`** in the Print Command box. You may need to specify the full path of the `lpr` command, in which case your print command would be **`/usr/bin/lpr -Plaserjet5l`**. The `lpr` command is covered in detail in Chapter 18, "Using Peripherals."

The choice of printing First Page First or Last Page First depends on the way in which pages come out of your printer. Generally, if they come out face down, choose First Page First; if they come out face up, select Last Page First.

Choose your orientation based on the nature of the document you are printing. If the document is a tall document with lots of text, Portrait will probably look best. If the document has some wide images, try Landscape to see how things look.

Selecting the correct option of Greyscale or Color is important. If you have a black-and-white printer, you should select Greyscale; some black-and-white printers will produce unusable results if Color is selected, printing all colors as black and rendering documents unreadable. If you have a color printer, you can choose either option, depending on whether you want your final printout to be black and white or color.

Finally, choose the correct paper size to match the paper in your printer and click the Print button.

Using Help

Netscape Communicator includes complete online help for the software. The online help system is accessible by selecting the Help Contents entry in the Help menu, shown in Figure 23.12.

FIGURE 23.12:

The Help menu

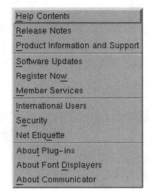

The Communicator Help window looks like the one shown in Figure 23.13.

FIGURE 23.13:

The Netscape NetHelp window

The help system includes a table of contents down the left side of the window. The text contains underlined hypertext links that allow you to quickly jump to the content of interest. In addition, you can click the Index button to view and search an index of the help contents.

Accessing Your E-Mail with Communicator

In addition to a Web browser, Netscape Communicator includes an integrated mail package, Messenger Mailbox, that you can use to read mail stored on POP or IMAP servers. In order to use the Messenger Mailbox, you first need to configure Communicator to know where to find your mail and how to send your mail.

Configuring Communicator for E-Mail

Communicator can be configured with the Preferences dialog box, accessed by selecting Preferences from the Edit menu. Figure 23.14 shows the Preferences dialog box when it is first opened.

FIGURE 23.14:

The Preferences dialog box

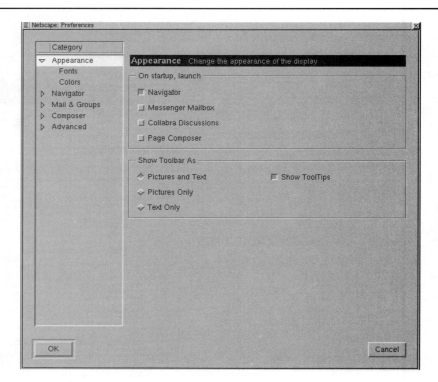

The Preferences dialog box contains numerous sections and subsections that are used to configure Communicator. To set up Communicator to read your mail, you need to open Mail & Groups by clicking the right-facing triangle next to its name. This opens the first configuration panel, as shown in Figure 23.15, and displays a submenu of configuration panels for the Mail & Groups section.

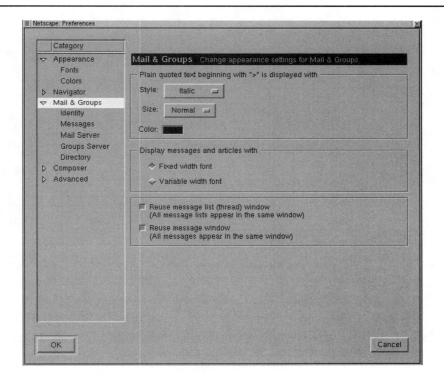

FIGURE 23.15:

The Mail & Groups section

In order to get your mail working, you need to use the Identity and Mail Server panels, at a minimum. The other panels provide configuration options that you may want to consider, but these are not essential to basic e-mail operation.

The Identity Panel   You use the Identity panel to configure the information (such as your e-mail address, name, and organization) that will appear on all e-mails you send. This panel is shown in Figure 23.16.

FIGURE 23.16:

The Identity panel

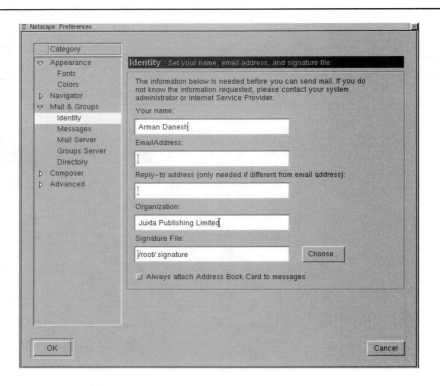

The fields that you really need to fill in are Your Name, which should contain your full name as you would wish mail recipients to see it, and Email Address, which should contain your complete e-mail address as it needs to appear on the From line of your e-mails.

Fill in the Reply-To Address field if the address that people should use to reply to your messages is different than the From line of your outgoing e-mails. You can also fill in the Organization field. This information will be included in the header of all e-mails you send and will be displayed in some mail readers, including Communicator.

The Signature File field specifies a file containing a signature to be appended at the end of all the e-mails you send. A signature is text that might include your name, address, and phone number, or other identifying information. This field can be left blank if you want no signature on outgoing e-mails.

The Mail Server Panel The Mail Server panel is used to tell Communicator how to find your inbox and how to send mail you compose. It looks like Figure 23.17.

FIGURE 23.17:

The Mail Server panel

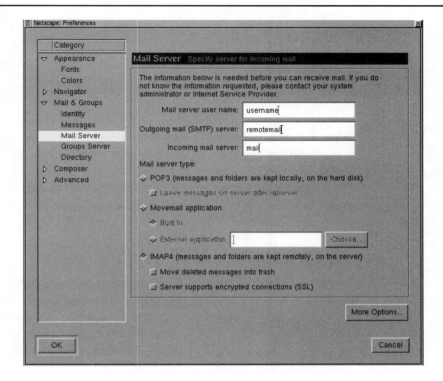

The information required by the Mail Server panel will generally be given to you by your ISP, or by your system administrator if you are on a corporate LAN.

The Mail Server User Name you need to specify is the name that identifies you to the mail server that has your inbox on it. This may not be the same as your e-mail address. The Outgoing Mail Server (the SMTP server) specifies the server that will route your outgoing Internet mail. In the case of many ISPs, this may be the same as the incoming mail server.

The choice of Mail Server Type depends on the type of mail server you are connecting to:

- If you are using an ISP, it will likely be a POP3 server. When first configuring Communicator to use a POP3 server, select Leave Messages on Server After Retrieval to make sure you don't lose any e-mails by misconfiguration or other problems with your Communicator setup.

- On a corporate LAN, you may find that you are accessing an IMAP4 server. The information for this type of server will be provided by your system administrator.

Finally, Communicator for Linux includes one mail server option that is not available on the Windows version of Communicator: the Movemail application. The Movemail application can be used if Sendmail or another mail transport agent is running on your system and delivering your mail to a local mailbox (which is normally found in `/var/spool/mail/`). In this case, you can use Communicator's built-in Movemail application to move mail from this type of Linux inbox into Communicator's Mailbox.

Reading Mail

Once you have configured Communicator for your mail account, you can read mail by clicking the Mailbox icon. This icon appears either in a component button bar docked in the bottom right corner of the main Communicator window (as in Figure 23.18) or in a floating component window (as in Figure 23.19). Alternately, you can select Messenger Mailbox from the Communicator menu shown in Figure 23.20.

FIGURE 23.18:

The docked Communicator component bar

FIGURE 23.19:

The floating Communicator
component bar

FIGURE 23.20:

The Communicator menu

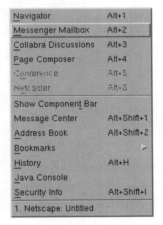

Any of these selections open the Mail & Discussions window shown in Figure 23.21.

The Mail & Discussions window consists of a menu and toolbar at the top, a message list pane showing the headers of messages in the mailbox currently being viewed, and a message pane showing the contents of the message currently selected in the message list.

If, after opening the Mail & Discussions window, you want to check your mail again, simply click the Get Msg button in the Mail & Discussions toolbar shown in Figure 23.22.

FIGURE 23.21:

The Mail & Discussions window

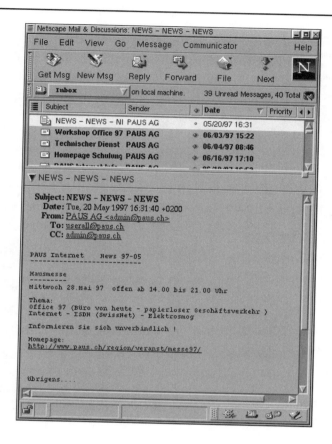

FIGURE 23.22:

The Mail & Discussions toolbar

Composing a New Message

You can compose a new message by selecting the New Msg button on the toolbar, as shown in Figure 23.22. A message composition window appears like the one in Figure 23.23. In this window you can fill in one or more recipients by pressing Enter after each recipient's name. Clicking the To at the left of each e-mail address allows you to select alternate modes of addressing a recipient, such as Cc and Bcc.

FIGURE 23.23:

The Message Composition window

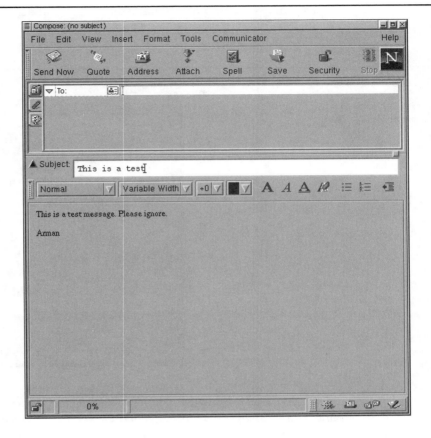

After filling in the recipients, subject, and message text, you have several options: you can add an attachment, you can spell-check the document, you can send the document immediately, or you can queue the document to send later.

Attaching a File In order to attach a file, simply click the Attach button on the Message Composition toolbar shown in Figure 23.24.

FIGURE 23.24:

The Message Composition toolbar

This produces a drop-down menu that lets you attach a file or Web page. If you choose File, a dialog box appears like the one in Figure 23.25, from which you can select the file to attach.

FIGURE 23.25:

Selecting a file to attach using the Attach File dialog box

After you attach a file, the recipient list pane switches to an attachment list pane. Figure 23.26 shows this changed view, with a file named `core` as the attachment. If you attach more files, more than one icon will appear.

If you want to switch back to the recipient list to add or remove recipients, simply select Address Pane from the View menu.

Spell-Checking   To spell-check your message before sending it, simply click the Spell button on the toolbar of the Message Composition window. This brings up the Spell Check dialog box shown in Figure 23.27. Each word that is not found in the system's dictionary will be presented to you with a list of suggestions. Click Replace to correct a misspelled word, Ignore to skip a word, or Learn to add a word to the dictionary.

FIGURE 23.26:

The attachment list

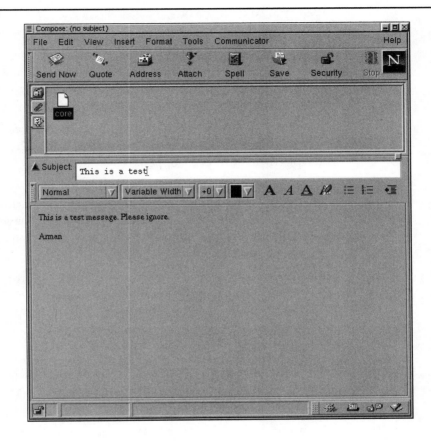

FIGURE 23.27:

The Spell Check dialog box

At any time during the process of spell-checking a message you can click the Stop button to cancel the operation.

Sending a Message Immediately If you are connected to the Internet (or are lucky enough to enjoy a dedicated Internet connection), you can send your messages as soon as you finish composing them by clicking the Send Now button on the toolbar of the Message Composition window.

This immediately connects to your outgoing mail server and delivers the message. Once this happens, you can't cancel a message. The message is en route to the recipients and can't be stopped.

Queuing a Message for Later Delivery Most users who connect to the Internet through an ISP will want to compose messages offline and then quickly connect to their ISP to send all the messages that they have written. You can do this with Netscape Communicator by selecting Send Later from the File menu when you are done composing the message.

Then, when you finally connect to the Internet, simply select Send Unsent Messages from the File menu of the main Mail & Discussions window to send all messages that are queued for delivery.

Replying to a Message

Replying to a message is closely related to composing a new message. Simply select the message you want to reply to in the Mail & Discussions window and then click the Reply button in the toolbar.

This brings up a pre-addressed Mail Composition window with the subject line preset and the text of the original message displayed if you selected the Automatically Quote Original Message when Replying option when configuring Communicator. By default, reply messages are addressed only to the sender of the original message. If you want to send a reply to the sender and all other recipients of the message, simply click and hold the Reply button. A drop-down menu like the one in Figure 23.28 appears, and you can select To Sender and All Recipients.

FIGURE 23.28:

The Reply drop-down menu

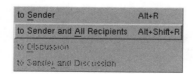

When you finish composing your reply, you can send it in the same way as described previously for a new message.

Installing and Using Lynx

The final browser this chapter will discuss is Lynx, by far the most common text browser in use in the Unix and Linux worlds. Lynx is included in most Linux distributions, among them the Red Hat distribution bundled with this book.

You can check whether Lynx is installed with the command

```
$ rpm -qa | grep lynx
```

If you find that Lynx is not installed, use rpm to install `lynx-2.8.1-11.i386.rpm` from the RedHat/RPMS subdirectory of the CD-ROM:

```
$ rpm -i lynx-2.8.1-11.i386.rpm
```

Once it is installed, you can find Lynx at `/usr/bin/lynx`.

Downloading a Newer Version

The version of Lynx included with this book is version 2.8.1. If you are interested in a newer version, check the Lynx home page at `http://lynx.browser.org/`. At the time of this writing, the most current version of Lynx was version 2.8.1.

Lynx comes as source code that you need to compile, but don't let this stop you from installing a newer version if you intend to make regular use of Lynx. The archive of version 2.8 is called `lynx2-8-1.zip`. Simply download it to a temporary location (such as `/tmp/`) and then take the following steps to compile and install this version of Lynx.

Compiling Lynx from Source Code

Once you have downloaded the archive, use the cd command to change to the `/tmp/` directory and then unzip the archive with the command:

```
$ unzip /tmp/lynx2-8-1.zip
```

This creates a subdirectory called `lynx2-8`. Change to this directory.

To start compiling Lynx, simply issue the command

```
$ make linux-ncurses
```

while in this directory. The `linux-ncurses` argument ensures that the correct options for Linux are set while compiling and that the `ncurses` library is used. The `ncurses` library, which provides a collection of functions for manipulating character-mode screens, is included with the distribution of Red Hat Linux 6 on the CD-ROM.

Once this is done, you should see a message informing you that Lynx has been successfully compiled. Next, issue the command

```
$ make install
```

to install the new Lynx binary file in `/usr/local/bin/`.

Starting Lynx

To use Lynx, you need to launch it in an `xterm` window or in a character console. If you launch Lynx without any arguments, Lynx attempts to load its default page. In the case of the binary version distributed with Red Hat Linux 6, this default page is an HTML documentation page that is installed with the operating system. If you compiled Lynx yourself, then this page is probably `http://lynx .browser.org/`.

Starting Lynx produces a screen like the one in Figure 23.29. It contains the local help file installed by Red Hat.

FIGURE 23.29:

Lynx with the Red Hat help file

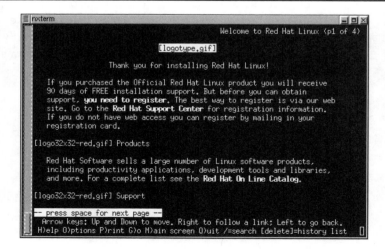

If you want to directly access a specific page or file when you launch Lynx, simply provide the page URL or the filename as an argument to Lynx using the command

```
$ lynx http://www.yahoo.com/
```

or the command

```
$ lynx /tmp/filename
```

Lynx also takes numerous flags that can alter its behavior. You can view the complete list with the −? argument:

```
$ lynx −?
```

Generally, however, you won't need to use any of these command-line arguments when browsing the Web with Lynx.

Opening a New Page

Notice that the bottom line of the Lynx screen displays the main key commands that you can use to browse the Web. To open a new page once Lynx is running, use the Go command by hitting the G key.

Lynx prompts you with the prompt

```
URL to Open:
```

Simply enter a URL and press Enter to open the page.

Following Links

Links in a document show up in bold text when running in an `xterm` window and as blue text when running in color mode in a console window. You can select a link to follow by using the Tab key to move forward through the links or the up and down arrows to move backward and forward through the links. The currently selected link will appear in reverse text in an `xterm` window or in red text in a console window.

Once you have selected a link to follow, press Enter or the right arrow key to follow the link. You can return to the previously visited page by using the left arrow key.

Viewing Images

If you are running Lynx in an `xterm` window, you can configure things so that you can view images embedded in pages in a separate window using the `xv` program.

In order to do this, you need to configure Lynx so that it knows to use `xv` to display images. You do this by editing the file `/etc/lynx.cfg` using your favorite text editor.

In this file, there are two lines that start with `#XLOADIMAGE_COMMAND`. One line appears under the header VMS and the other line appears under the header Unix. You will work with the one under the header Unix. Change this line to read

```
XLOADIMAGE_COMMAND:/usr/bin/X11/xv %s &
```

Notice that the pound sign (#) at the start of the line has been removed. This uncomments the line so that Lynx will pay attention to it when Lynx loads.

Once you have done this, save the changed file and launch Lynx. Next, you need to turn on the Images-As-Links mode. This is done with the asterisk (*). If you press this, all pages will now display images as links. Following one of these links causes the `xv` program to load and the image to be displayed in `xv`.

Online Help

You can access Lynx's online help with the key H. This connects to a Web site on the Internet containing the complete documentation for Lynx, so it is necessary to be connected to the Internet to access the online help system.

Looking Ahead

Now that you've managed to get online and browse the Web using Linux, you are ready to look at the full range of options for the other major Internet function: e-mail.

You have already reviewed one of the popular mail-reading applications, Netscape Communicator. But Communicator is only one of many alternatives.

Linux offers a broad range of mail clients, both commercial and free. These range from powerful (but complicated) prompt-oriented systems to comprehensive and lightweight character-mode mail readers (such as the well-known `Pine` and `Elm` packages) to graphical mail readers (such as `Xmail`).

The next chapter will take a broad look at the mail readers available for Linux and then take a closer look at some of the more common mail readers available.

CHAPTER

TWENTY-FOUR

Reading E-Mail

- ■ Local Versus Remote Mailboxes

- ■ Offline Mail Readers

- ■ Online Mail Program

This chapter will discuss the different approaches and programs available in Red Hat Linux 6 for reading, composing, and sending e-mail.

The discussion will start with a look at mailboxes. Most home users of the Internet have remote mailboxes maintained on the servers of their Internet service provider (ISP). But when they read the mail using a mail reader such as Eudora or Netscape Communicator's built-in mail reader, they permanently copy their messages into a mailbox created locally by their mail software.

Another approach is to read mail online. In this way, the mailbox remains on the server and is simply manipulated by the mail software without permanently creating a local mailbox as new mail is read.

This chapter will cover all approaches available in Linux for online and offline mail reading. It will move on to various types of mail software for offline reading and online access to a remote mailbox.

Local Versus Remote Mailboxes

The distinction between local and remote mailboxes may seem subtle and not a major issue, but this distinction is fundamental to understanding the various types of mail software in the Unix world.

In most Unix networks, users' mail is stored in local mailboxes in a format known as Berkeley Mail Folders (after the University of California at Berkeley where this type of folder originated). Unix mail systems such as Sendmail, which is responsible for routing incoming and outgoing mail, automatically store new messages in users' personal mailboxes in this standard format. Users can then use any of numerous standard Unix-based mail applications to read their mail, compose new messages, and organize their mailboxes.

All of this is available in the Linux world. All the common Unix mail tools are available for Linux, and, as you will see later in the book in the discussion of small business networks, the Berkeley Mail Folder with Sendmail and a Unix mail client is a common solution for providing users with e-mail capabilities.

But for a home user, mail generally sits in a mailbox on a remote server managed by their ISP. There is no way for software to access these remote folders as if they were local Berkeley Mail Folders. Instead, it is necessary to use mail software that speaks either the POP3 or IMAP4 protocol. These protocols provide different ways to access remote mailboxes.

POP3 Mail Servers

Most users of Windows- or Macintosh-based mail software who access mail that sits on an ISP's mail server probably use the POP3 protocol.

In the POP3 model, users connect to the Internet, download new mail from their mailboxes, and then optionally delete the original copy from the mailboxes on the remote server. This effectively creates a local mailbox that can be read offline. The local mailbox contains a complete copy of the contents of the original mailbox on the server. Users can read their messages, compose replies and new messages, and organize their mail while offline, and then reconnect to send messages they have composed and check for new mail.

This is a simple protocol and is a familiar one to most users. It is an ideal solution when the cost of online time is expensive or the amount of available bandwidth is limited. Because it is designed for working offline, POP3 is well suited to users with limited network access. But the simplicity of the protocol creates some fundamental limitations.

For instance, consider the user who needs to access a remote mailbox from two or more locations. It is possible to leave copies of all downloaded messages on the remote server using POP3. This would allow all messages to be downloaded using mail software on two different PCs in two different locations. But there is no way to know whether a message has been answered from the other location, and if a message is deleted off the remote server for any reason before it is downloaded to both locations, then one location has an incomplete mailbox.

Consider this scenario of a user who uses two PCs, one at home and one on the road. Both PCs are used to read mail from the same mailbox using POP3 mail software. First thing in the morning, the home PC is used to download the day's mail. There are 50 messages, including 33 junk messages. The user immediately deletes the junk messages, responds to 7 messages, and files 10 messages for later processing.

Later in the afternoon, this same user proceeds to access their mailbox using their portable system. They proceed to download their mail. The number of messages now numbers 58. This includes the 33 junk messages that were deleted on the home machine, the 7 messages that have been replied to, and the 10 messages kept for later processing, in addition to 8 new messages to be handled.

This situation, which is not uncommon, can lead to a lot of unnecessary repetition in trying to work with the same mail in two or more locations.

IMAP4 Mail Servers

One solution to this problem is an IMAP4 mail server.

In the IMAP model, mailboxes exist on remote servers and remain there. Users then open and access these mailboxes using their client applications, but instead of copying the messages to a local mailbox, they are simply manipulating the remote mailbox without ever creating a local copy.

IMAP offers several benefits to address the problems found in POP3 systems. This includes the ability to work with, and maintain, a single mailbox from multiple locations and computers. This is achieved by the fact that the mail remains in a single remote mailbox instead of replicating into multiple local mailboxes. If a user deletes a message from the mailbox from one location and then accesses the mailbox from another, the message won't be there.

However, the very nature of IMAP4—manipulating a remote mailbox—makes it necessary to work online to read, reply to, and process mail. Thus, IMAP4 is best suited to situations where a network connection is either permanent or essentially free. For instance, in a location with flat-rate Internet costs and flat-rate local phone costs, POP3 and IMAP4 mail connections would cost the same. But if a user is paying per-minute Internet and phone call costs, then IMAP4 will prove much more expensive than POP3.

In addition, not many ISPs give users access to their mailboxes through IMAP4 servers. IMAP4 systems are far more common in corporations and allow users to access their mailboxes at work and from home without the difficulties introduced by POP3 systems.

Offline Mail Readers

For most users, accessing a remote mailbox with POP3 is the right solution. This can be done using any of numerous available mail applications for Linux, including Netscape Communicator, which is available on the enclosed CD-ROM.

This section will look at Netscape Communicator because it is becoming one of the most popular graphical mail clients today and because users coming to Linux from the Windows and Macintosh platforms should already be familiar with Netscape's product. There are many other POP and IMAP mail readers available for Linux. You can check the Linux Applications and Utilities Page at `http://www.xnet.com/~blatura/linapps.html` for a list of alternative packages.

Netscape Communicator

It is fairly simple to configure Netscape Communicator to read your remote POP3 mailbox and to use it to compose messages offline and queue them. To launch Netscape Communicator, issue the command

```
$ /opt/netscape/netscape
```

from an xterm window, assuming that you installed Communicator in the default location (see the section about installing Netscape Communicator in Chapter 23, "Using the World Wide Web").

Configuring Netscape Communicator for E-Mail

Once Communicator is launched, you can configure its mail reader from the Preferences dialog box by following the steps in the section "Configuring Netscape Communicator for E-Mail" in Chapter 23.

Here you have the option of setting up a POP3 or IMAP4 mail server. This section will discuss using Netscape Communicator in a POP3 configuration. Configure your POP3 server in the Mail Server panel of the Preferences dialog box. Figure 24.1 shows a sample POP3 configuration.

FIGURE 24.1:

Configuring Netscape Communicator to read mail from a POP3 server

Mail Server User Name   The mail server user name is the name of your POP3 mail account. Generally, this will be the same as the part of your e-mail address before the @ symbol, although sometimes it can bear no relationship to the e-mail address. This value is generally specified by your e-mail provider.

Outgoing Mail Server   The outgoing mail server, also known as an *SMTP server*, indicates where to send outgoing messages (messages you are sending) for delivery. The name or address of the server is provided by your ISP. In the example in Figure 24.1, the ISP is different than the mailbox provider, and all outgoing mail is sent out via a server from the ISP (`remotemail`).

Incoming Mail Server   In the case of a POP3 configuration, this field should contain the name of the POP3 mail server where your mailbox sits. In this example, this server is with an e-mail provider (`mail`) that is different from the ISP. For most users with a normal Internet account, the ISP and e-mail provider are one and the same. The name of the server will be specified by the provider.

Mail Server Type   There are three choices of mail server type in Netscape Communicator:

- POP3   When your mail sits on a POP3 server

- Movemail   When your mail sits in a local Berkeley Mail Folder

- IMAP4   When your mail sits on an IMAP4 server

Each of these server types offers a selection of options for working with mail folders. In the case of POP3 mail, there is one option: Leave Messages on Server After Retrieval. This is useful especially when you access your mail from more than one location and don't want to miss mail at any location. If you only access your mailbox from one location, you probably want to deselect this option once you have tested that everything is working. Many ISPs impose disk space limitations on the size of inboxes, and if you don't delete messages after downloading them, your inbox on the server will grow without restriction.

More Options   Clicking the More Options button brings up a dialog box like the one in Figure 24.2.

The Local Mail Directory field indicates where Netscape should create its local mailboxes and folders. This is usually a subdirectory of a user's home directory called nsmail. For instance, for a user named joeb, Netscape defaults to /home/ joeb/nsmail/ as the local mail directory. You can, of course, change this value, but there is little reason to do so unless you have very specific and unique needs.

The IMAP4 options are not relevant to a POP3 configuration and can be left with their default settings. The last two options, however, are of interest to a POP3 user.

You can specify how often Communicator should automatically check for new mail. If you rarely connect to the Internet and are usually online for very short periods of time, you probably want to deselect this option so that you can check your mail manually.

Checking Remember My Mail Password means that you will only be prompted for your password the very first time you access your mailbox; from then on, Communicator remembers the password and you don't have to provide it again. This, of course, is a security risk if there is any chance of an unauthorized person using your computer. They will be able to access your inbox without providing a password.

As an alternative, you can leave this option unselected. Then you will be prompted for your mail password the first time you access your inbox after launching Communicator. Communicator remembers the password until you quit the program, and the next time you launch it to access your inbox, Communicator prompts you for your password again.

Reading Mail with Netscape Communicator

Once you have configured Netscape Communicator to access your mailbox, you are ready to try reading messages. But before you are able to access your mailbox, you need to do two things:

1. Connect to the Internet (follow the method discussed in Chapter 22).

2. Launch Netscape Communicator.

By default, Communicator launches with a Web browser window open. You can open the mailbox window in two ways:

1. Click the mailbox icon, which appears either in a floating toolbar

or in a smaller, fixed toolbar in the bottom right corner of the Communicator windows.

Both toolbars show a mailbox icon.

2. Select Messenger Mailbox from the Communicator menu (or press Alt+2), as shown in Figure 24.3.

FIGURE 24.3:

The Communicator menu

The mailbox window looks like the one in Figure 24.4.

FIGURE 24.4:

The Messenger Mailbox
window

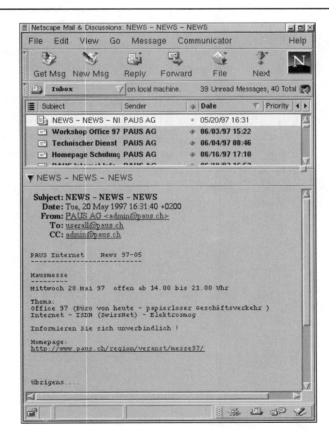

The mailbox window is divided into two distinct regions, one on the top and one on the bottom. The top pane displays the list of messages in the current folder. The information displayed includes the date, subject, sender, and size of the message. The bottom pane displays the contents of the current mail message.

Because Communicator supports HTML mail, a mail message formatted using HTML is displayed in the mailbox window just as if it were a Web page. Links are highlighted, as expected, and are clickable. Clicking a link opens the requested document in a browser window instead of in the mailbox window.

Composing Messages in Communicator

The flip side of reading messages is being able to compose new messages. Composing new messages is actually quite simple. Simply click the New Msg icon.

This brings up a message composition window like the one in Figure 24.5.

To address a message, simply fill in the address in the field next to the To field. Pressing the Enter key after the address creates a new, blank To field on the next line so that you can address your message to multiple recipients. If you want some of the recipients to receive the message as a carbon copy (the Cc field) or blind carbon copy (the Bcc field), click the down arrow key next to the To field for the addressee you wish to change. This brings up an address field menu where you can specify the correct option.

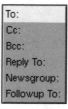

FIGURE 24.5:

The message composition
window

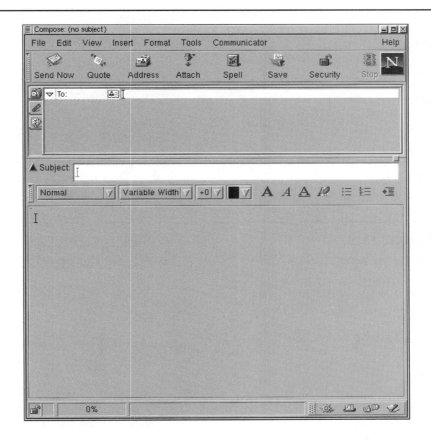

To add an attachment to your message, click the Attach button on the toolbar.

This displays the Attachment drop-down menu, where you can choose to attach a file or a Web page.

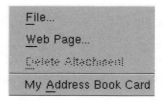

If you choose to attach a file, this opens the Attach file dialog box shown in Figure 24.6, where you can choose a file and click the Attach button.

FIGURE 24.6:

The Attach File dialog box

As shown in Figure 24.7, once you attach a file, the Attachments tab is displayed with an icon for your attachment.

FIGURE 24.7:

An attached file in the Attachments tab

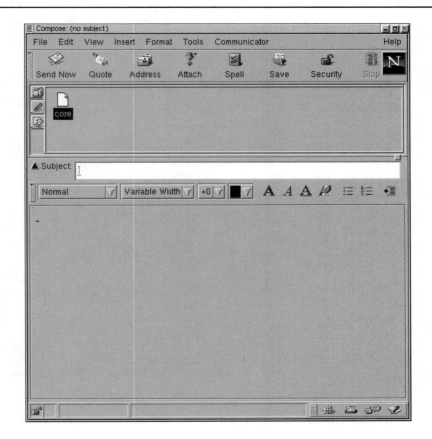

Type the subject of the message in the subject field and the body of the message in the large text editing area, as shown in the completed message in Figrue 24.8.

FIGURE 24.8:

A completed message

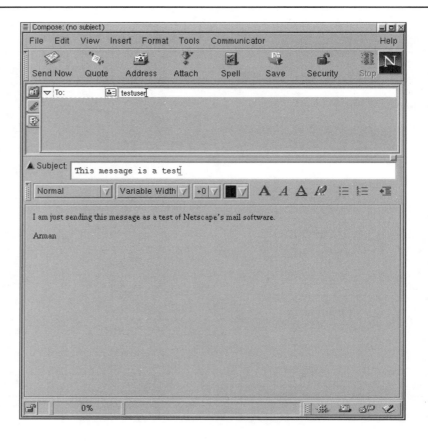

Finally, click the Send Now button to send the message (assuming you are connected to the Internet when you finish composing the message).

Queuing Messages   Usually, users with a POP3 mail connection to an Internet provider want to compose their messages while offline, queuing them for later delivery when they connect to their ISP. This is achieved quite easily. Once a message is composed, instead of clicking the Send Now button on the composition window's toolbar, simply select Send Later from the File menu shown in Figure 24.9. This queues the message for later delivery.

The message composition file menu

Once you have finished composing your messages, connect to the Internet, and from the main Messenger Mailbox window, select Send Unsent Messages from the File menu shown in Figure 24.10.

The Messenger Mailbox's file menu

Any unsent, queued messages are sent.

Replying to Messages and Forwarding Messages Closely related to composing new messages are replying to messages and forwarding messages to other people.

Let's start with replying, since it is the more common activity for most people. To reply to a message, select the message in your mailbox and then click the Reply button on the toolbar.

This brings up a pre-addressed message composition window like the one in Figure 24.11. If you have configured Netscape Communicator to do so, the window will include the contents of the original message in the message body pane.

FIGURE 24.11:

Replying to a message

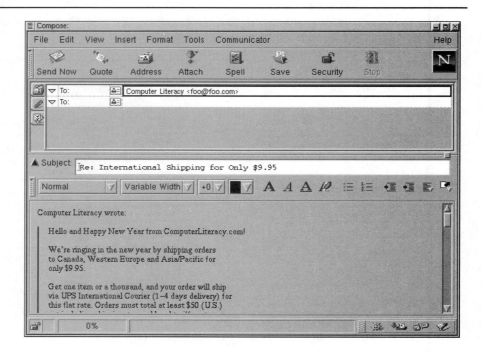

Similarly, to forward a message, select the message and click the Forward button.

This brings up an unaddressed mail-composition window with the selected message attached to your message as shown in Figure 24.12. Note that the subject line indicates a forwarded message.

FIGURE 24.12:

Forwarding a message

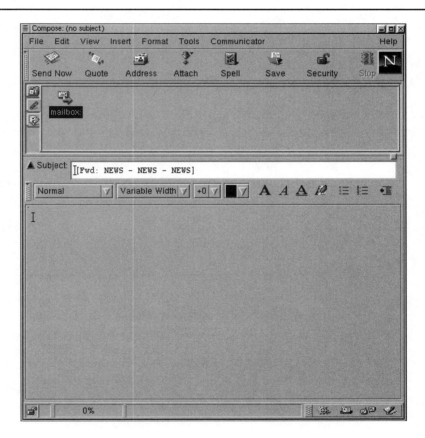

Online Mail Programs

This section describes those mail programs whose primary purpose is to read local Unix mailboxes; some mail programs can access IMAP4 servers as well. What distinguishes these from the offline software like Netscape Communicator is that they are designed to send messages at the time they are composed, rather than queuing them for later delivery. This is not uncommon on Unix systems: even on a system that is not connected to the Internet, you can run a mail server that handles the job of queuing messages for all users and sending them when a connection is periodically established. As far as the mail client software is concerned, you are always connected to the Internet, so the mail client can send a message immediately by passing it over to a mail server.

Pine and *Elm*

In the Unix world, and by extension in the Linux world, the two most common mail programs are `pine` and `elm`. These programs are both designed to work in a character-based environment, so they can be used at the console or in an `xterm` window. They are both designed to read local Berkeley Mail inboxes, and both are highly flexible with a large number of configurable options.

NOTE An interesting bit of history: `elm` predates `pine`. `Pine` was written to make some aspects of `elm` easier to handle for the average user. `Pine` is known to stand for "Pine Is Not Elm."

Both `elm` and `pine` are commonly found in universities, where many students still have shell accounts to access e-mail. Because of space limitations, this section takes a close look at only one, of these programs: `pine`. The choice of `pine` versus `elm` is a highly subjective one, and many diehard Linux and Unix users may argue that `elm` should be presented instead of `pine`.

The logic behind my choice is this: both `elm` and `pine` are powerful packages, neither superior to the other. Most users are now likely to use graphical packages such as Netscape Communicator to manage their mail, since today's average PC is more than capable of running processing-intensive graphical applications of that type. To give users a sense of these traditional (and still popular) Unix mail programs, I chose `pine` because it is somewhat more user-friendly for a newcomer to Linux. And at the university where I worked as a system administrator, all users use `pine` as their mail application, and this has proven to be quite a successful choice.

Using *Pine*

At first glance, `pine` may seem very complicated, but in reality it isn't. For the average user who wants to send and receive e-mail, `pine` is quite easy to use.

Most Linux systems will include `pine` already installed if the complete suite of networking applications was selected during the installation process. If yours doesn't, you can find `pine` at `http://www.washington.edu/pine/`. The version of `pine` included with Red Hat Linux 6 is version 4.10.

Simply type the command

```
$ pine
```

to launch the program. The default configuration on most Linux systems should work without any tweaking.

When it first launches, `pine` will present its default main menu, as shown in Figure 24.13.

FIGURE 24.13:

The pine main menu

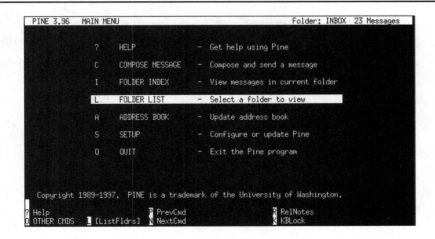

The `pine` screen contains four main areas:

- The top line presents the version number of `pine` that you are running, the name of the currently open folder (`INBOX` when `pine` first starts), and, if applicable, the current message being read, along with the total number of messages in the folder.

- The bottom two lines present the more common commands accessible from the current screen. These commands change as the context dictates.

- The line above the menus is where pine displays prompts asking the user for input (Figure 24.14 provides an example of how this line is used) as well as information messages for the user.

- The rest of the screen represents the main work area.

FIGURE 24.14:

A user prompt

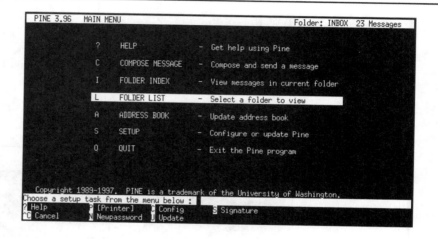

From the main menu, there are four main options:

C (COMPOSE MESSAGE) This option is used to compose and send a new message; this option can also be accessed when viewing the contents of a mail folder.

I (FOLDER INDEX) This option is used to view the contents of the current folder (as displayed on the top line of the screen).

L (FOLDER LIST) This option is used to view a list of available folders.

A (ADDRESS BOOK) This option is used to access the address book.

Let's discuss the first two options. All the options are documented fully in pine's online help, which is available from the main menu with the HELP command (the ? key).

Opening and Working in a Folder Index To open a folder index, use the up or down arrow keys to select the FOLDER INDEX option and press the Enter key. Alternately, type **I**. This opens an index of the current folder (initially the inbox), as shown in Figure 24.15.

FIGURE 24.15:

A folder index

In the folder index, the top line of the display shows the currently selected message, the number of messages in the folder, and the status of the message (such as NEW for a new, unread message or ANS for an answered message).

Each message in the inbox is presented on a single line showing, from left to right, the status of the message (N for new, A for answered, D for deleted), the number of the message, the date the message was received, the sender of the message, the size of the message in bytes, and, finally, the subject line of the message.

To select a message, use the up and down arrow keys until the desired message is highlighted. Alternately, use the P key to move to the previous message or the N key to move to the next message.

To delete the currently selected message, type **D**. This marks the message for deletion and changes the status indication for that message to show that it has been marked for deletion. The message won't be deleted, however, until you quit pine. Until then, you can undelete the message by selecting it and typing **U**.

If you have a folder index that is longer than one screen, you can move through it quickly using the space bar to jump down a page and the hyphen key to jump up a page. In addition, you can jump directly to a specific message using its message number. Type **J** and, when prompted, enter the message number and press Enter.

To read a message in a folder, simply select the message and press Enter or type **V** to view the message. The message is displayed as shown in Figure 24.16.

FIGURE 24.16:

Viewing a message

While viewing a message, you can continue to type **P** and **N** to move through messages in the folder, and you can type **D** and **U** to delete and undelete messages.

If the message is more than one screen long, you can use the space bar to move down a screen and the hyphen key to move up a screen.

To return to the main menu from the folder index or while viewing a message, simply type **M**.

Composing a Message   You can start composing a message from the main menu or while viewing a folder index or a message. To do this, simply type **C** (from the main menu, you can also select the COMPOSE MESSAGE option and press Enter). A blank message form appears like the one in Figure 24.17.

This screen is divided into two parts, one above the Message Text dividing line and one below. Above the dividing line you can specify the recipients, the subject, and other details; below the line, you enter the message. You can move between sections and fields using the up and down arrow keys.

FIGURE 24.17:

The message composition screen

The To and Cc fields can take any number of e-mail addresses separated by commas. When the cursor leaves the field, the display refreshes to show each address on a separate line, as in Figure 24.18.

FIGURE 24.18:

Multiple message recipients

If you want to send a blind carbon copy, you can expand the available message header fields by pressing Ctrl+R while the cursor is in the header (not in the body of the message text). This calls up the rich headers feature, as shown in Figure 24.19.

FIGURE 24.19:

Rich headers

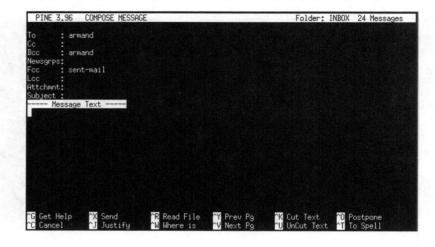

Here you will find a Bcc field for sending blind carbon copies of e-mail messages. The other fields provide more obscure functions such as specifying an alternate location for storing a copy of the outgoing message or copying the message to a newsgroup as a posting.

Below the Message Text divider, you can type the body of your message. Figure 24.20 shows a completed message.

FIGURE 24.20:

A completed message

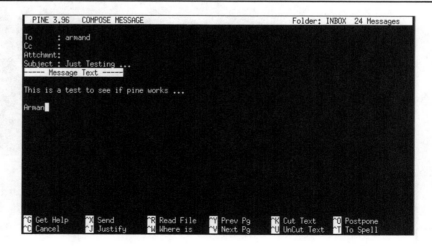

Once you are finished, you have two choices: you can send the message or you can cancel it. To send the message, type Ctrl+X; you are prompted to confirm that you want to send the message, to which you can answer **y** for yes or **n** for no. To cancel the message, type Ctrl+C; again, you are prompted to confirm that you want to cancel the message. Once the message is canceled, you won't be able to recover its contents.

The *Pico* Editor

When you are editing messages in `pine`, you are using its integrated text editor called `pico`. The following commands should help you use `pico` effectively:

- Ctrl+V: page down
- Ctrl+Y: page up
- Ctrl+K: cut a line of text
- Ctrl+U: uncut (paste) cut text
- Ctrl+A: jump to the start of a line
- Ctrl+E: jump to the end of a line
- Ctrl+J: justify (adjust the layout of) the current paragraph

Cutting and pasting of text requires some explanation. When you type Ctrl+K, a single line of text is cut and placed in a buffer in memory. If you type Ctrl+K to cut multiple lines in succession (these have to be continuous lines in the document), then all the lines are copied into the buffer. Ctrl+U, to uncut text, copies the entire contents of the buffer to the current cursor location but does not clear the contents of the buffer. In other words, you can paste multiple copies of cut text back into your messages.

Replying to and Forwarding Messages   Replying to messages and forwarding them to other recipients is much the same as composing a new message. To reply to a message, select the message and type **R** (from the folder index or while viewing the message). You are prompted with one or two questions:

- Include Original Message in Reply?   If you answer affirmatively to this question, the entire contents of the message you are replying to will appear in your reply.

- Reply to All Recipients?   This question appears if there are multiple recipients of the original message (either on the To field or the Cc field). If you answer **Y** for Yes, then everyone who received the message will receive your response. If you answer **N** for No, then only the person who sent the message will receive your response.

Next, a message composition screen appears with the appropriate recipients, subject line, and any necessary body text already in place. An example of this is shown in Figure 24.21.

FIGURE 24.21:

Replying to a message

Just as you did when composing a new message, type Ctrl+X to send your reply and type Ctrl+C to cancel it.

Forwarding a message is similar to sending one: select the message and type **F**. A message composition window appears like the one in Figure 24.22, with the text of the message in place and a subject line that indicates that this is a forwarded message.

Forwarding a message

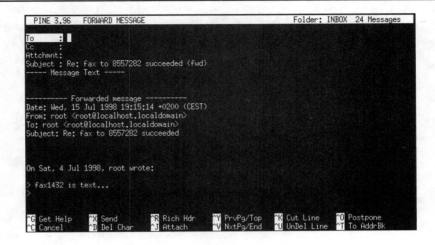

```
 PINE 3.96    FORWARD MESSAGE                          Folder: INBOX  24 Messages
To      :  █
Cc      :
Attchmnt:
Subject : Re: fax to 8557282 succeeded (fwd)
----- Message Text -----


---------- Forwarded message ----------
Date: Wed, 15 Jul 1998 19:15:14 +0200 (CEST)
From: root <root@localhost.localdomain>
To: root <root@localhost.localdomain>
Subject: Re: fax to 8557282 succeeded


On Sat, 4 Jul 1998, root wrote:

> fax1432 is text...
>



^G Get Help   ^X Send      ^R Rich Hdr   ^Y PrvPg/Top  ^K Cut Line   ^O Postpone
^C Cancel     ^D Del Char   ^J Attach     ^V NxtPg/End  ^U UnDel Line ^T To AddrBk
```

Looking Ahead

You now know how to perform the two most common Internet operations: browsing the Web and sending and receiving e-mail.

However, there is one more very popular use of modems to be discussed: faxing.

The next chapter will look at the software that allows you to send, receive, and print faxes on a Linux system. Among other tasks, you will learn how to send faxes in the same way that you print from your applications and how to set up an automated fax reception system.

CHAPTER

TWENTY-FIVE

25

Faxing from Linux

- Linux Fax Software

- Efax for Linux

You've already learned about the use of modems to establish network connections, mostly with the goal of accessing the Internet and its myriad services. This chapter will look at the other popular use of modems: sending and receiving faxes.

There are several fax software packages available for Linux. As would be expected in the Linux and Unix world, at their heart these fax packages are powerful, fast command-line tools that make it possible to send a large variety of documents by fax and to build fax services into automated processes.

On top of this, it is possible with many fax packages for Linux to extend these command-line tools to allow faxing through the print features of some applications, or to allow users to send faxes in the same way that they send e-mail.

In this chapter, you will take a broad look at Linux faxing and consider the major fax packages. Then you learn in detail about efax, a common fax package that is found in the Red Hat Linux 6 distribution accompanying this book.

Linux Fax Software

In the Linux world, and in the Unix world in general, there are only a few main software packages for sending and receiving faxes: efax, NetFax, mgetty+sendfax, and HylaFax.

Of all these, efax is generally considered the easiest to configure and install because it is ideally suited to a single-user system. For many home users of Linux, efax will suffice.

As a basic package, of course, efax doesn't have many of the sophisticated features that make HylaFax and NetFax well suited to multiuser network environments. Nonetheless, efax offers sufficient capabilities to meet the needs of all but the most demanding single and small office users.

Efax for Linux

Efax is almost the de facto standard fax software for Linux, because it ships with many Linux distributions (including the version of Red Hat Linux 6 on the enclosed CD-ROM). This chapter focuses on using efax for Linux.

> **TIP**
>
> If you are interested in other fax packages for Linux, see the listing at the Linux Applications and Utilities page at `http://www.xnet.com/~blatura/linapp4 .html#comm`.

> **NOTE**
>
> The discussion in this chapter assumes that you have a functioning fax modem installed in your system. Chapter 18, "Using Peripherals," discusses how to configure a modem for use with Linux, and you should follow those guidelines to make sure that your modem is properly configured.

Installing Efax in Linux

The first step to getting fax capabilities up and running on your system is to make sure you have the efax software installed on your system. If you have installed the version of Linux included with this book, you may already have the software installed. You can check this with the rpm command:

```
$ rpm -qv efax
```

If efax is installed, then rpm informs you by displaying the name of the efax package, such as efax-0.8a-11. If the package is not installed, then rpm will inform you with a message similar to this:

```
package efax is not installed.
```

If efax is not installed, then you have two choices:

- Install it from the Red Hat Linux 6 CD-ROM.

- Download and install it from the Internet.

Installing Efax from the Red Hat CD-ROM

If you have installed Red Hat Linux from the CD-ROM accompanying this book and want to install the version of efax that comes with the distribution, you need to mount your CD-ROM at your standard location—typically at /mnt/cdrom—using the mount command. (This example assumes that the CD-ROM is the device /dev/hdc):

```
$ mount /dev/hdc /mnt/cdrom
```

Once the CD-ROM is mounted, you need to use rpm to install the package efax-0.8a-11.i386.rpm:

```
$ rpm -i /mnt/cdrom/RedHat/RPMS/efax-0.8a-11.i386.rpm
```

Downloading and Installing Efax from the Internet

If you want to install the latest version of efax, you can obtain it by FTP from ftp://metalab.unc.edu/pub/Linux/apps/serialcomm/fax/. At the time of this writing, the most recent version of the software is version 0.9 and the name of the file to be downloaded is efax09.tar.gz.

Once you have downloaded the file, use the tar command to unarchive the files into a temporary location:

```
$ tar xzvf efax09.tar.gz
```

Next, change your working directory to the temporary one where you unarchived the files and, as the root user, issue the following command:

```
$ make
```

This causes the efax software to be compiled.

Assuming that there are no errors during compilation (a safe assumption, since efax is a fairly simple program), you can install efax to its default location using the command

```
$ make install
```

For full instructions regarding the compilation and installation of the efax software, read the README file included with the distribution.

Configuring Efax for Linux

Before sending your first fax, you need to specify a few parameters that will allow efax to function properly. In order to do this, you need to edit the file /usr/bin/fax and set certain information:

- Find the line that starts with FROM and set the value to your phone number (e.g., FROM="+1 212 555 1212").

- Find the line starting with CLASS and set the class of the fax modem to match the specifications of your modem (either CLASS=1 or CLASS=2).

- Find the line starting with PAGE and set the default page size for your country (probably PAGE=letter, PAGE=legal, or PAGE=a4).

When editing the file, note that lines starting with a hash mark (#) are comments and do not affect the configuration. You can comment out an existing line with a hash mark and add in your own variation on the line so that you can easily switch back to the default configuration.

This is the minimum configuration needed to run efax for Linux.

Sending Your First Fax

The efax package has three main components: efax, efix, and fax.

1. Efax is the core of the system. It sends and receives faxes to and from files in the standard fax file format: Group 3 compressed TIFF files. You can't use efax to send a text file or a PostScript file or any other type of file without first converting it to the necessary Group 3 compressed TIFF file format needed for faxing.

2. The efix program is used for conversion purposes, providing the ability to convert files to and from text, bitmap, and the fax TIFF format. By combining efax and efix, it is possible to send many images and text files as faxes.

3. The fax program provides an integrated layer from which it is possible to create, send, receive, view, and print faxes. This program integrates efax, efix, and other Linux components to provide fairly complete Linux faxing functionality.

In order to learn how to send and receive faxes with efax, let's focus on the fax program, since it brings together all the functionality you need.

Sending Faxes

The fax program makes it easy to send a fax from a text file or a PostScript file. For the purposes of sending, the syntax of the fax command is

```
$ fax send options number file
```

There are three available options that can be used when sending a fax:

-l Use low resolution (96 dots per inch).

-v Provide verbose messages and program status.

-m Assume the phone number has already been dialed (in which case the phone number should not be provided).

The phone number should be provided in the same form that you would use to dial it. For instance, if you want to dial the local phone number 555-1212, you could use 5551212 or 555-1212 as the phone number entry. If you need to dial 9 for an outside line, then use 95551212 or 9-5551212 or 9-555-1212.

Let's take an example. Suppose you have a text file called `textfile` in the directory /tmp and you want to send it as a low-resolution fax to the number 123-4567, using 9 to access an outside line. To do this, you use the command:

```
$ fax send -l 9-123-4567 /tmp/textfile
```

Given a text file containing the following text:

```
FAX TRANSMISSION:

TO: Arman Danesh

FROM: Arman Danesh

NOTE:

This is a test of the efax package. Using the fax command, we can send
text files as faxes.
```

this produces a fax that looks like the one in Figure 25.1.

FIGURE 25.1:

A sample efax fax

```
FAX TRANSMISSION:

TO: Arman Danesh

FROM: Arman Danesh

NOTE:

This is a test of the efax package. Using the fax command, we can send
text files as faxes.
```

Sending Multiple Files As One Fax

In addition to sending a single file as a fax, you can use `fax` to send multiple files as a single fax. For instance, if you want to send the contents of `/tmp/textfile` followed by the contents of another text file called `/tmp/textfile2`, use the command

```
$ fax send 9-123-4567 /tmp/textfile /tmp/textfile2
```

to send the files in the specified order.

> **NOTE**   You can only combine multiple text files in this way. If you try to combine a Post-Script file with text files or with another PostScript file, the process will not work.

But what if you want to send the pages out of order or only send some of the pages in a file? To do this, you need to first convert the file into a fax-formatted TIFF file. Each page of the fax is then placed in a separate file, and you can choose which pages to send by faxing only those files.

Here you utilize the `fax` program's ability to create fax-formatted files. For instance, if you have a PostScript file called `/tmp/psfile` that is three pages long, you can convert it into three fax-formatted TIFF files using the command:

```
$ fax make /tmp/psfile
```

The resulting pages are contained in three separate files named `/tmp/psfile01`, `/tmp/psfile02`, and `/tmp/psfile03`.

When you convert a file into fax format, the resulting pages retain the same name as the original file with three-digit, numerically ordered extensions. For instance, the file `test.txt` would create fax pages named `test.txt01`, `test.txt02`, and so on.

The only option available to you when using `fax make` is to choose low-resolution mode using the `-1` option:

```
$ fax make -1 /tmp/psfile
```

Back to the three-page document you converted earlier. If you want to send the third page followed by the first and not send the second page, use the command

```
$ fax send /tmp/psfile03 /tmp/psfile01
```

Sending a Fax by Printing

While it is great to be able to send faxes using the `fax` command, this isn't very useful when it comes to printing from applications such as Netscape, Word-Perfect, or Applix Words.

NOTE   Of course, if you have only one modem and are using this to browse the Internet with Netscape, you won't be able to send a fax from Netscape as long as the modem is being used to connect to the Internet.

For instance, consider the Netscape example. It is possible to print from Netscape to a file, generating a PostScript file as a result. But sending the page as a fax adds a second step to the process, requiring that the user switch to the command line to send the file as a fax.

Unfortunately, this isn't quite as simple as faxing from Windows or Macintosh applications, where faxing is generally as simple as printing.

Fortunately, it is possible to create a special printer device in Linux that uses efax to send the file being printed as a fax.

The process is fairly simple. The `lpd` printing system allows for input filters to be specified. If an input filter is specified for a printer queue, then the file being sent to the queue is sent to an input filter before being placed in the queue. If the filter doesn't return any data but instead faxes the file, the job is never sent to a printer.

There are three steps to setting up the necessary printer queue for printing to the fax modem:

1.   Configuring the printer queue

2.   Setting up the `faxlpr` script

3.   Preparing the spool directory

All of this preparation needs to be done as the root user on your system.

Configuring the Printer Queue

You can set up the printer queue for faxing using the printer configuration Control Panel applet. This applet is discussed in Chapter 18, "Using Peripherals."

When you create the queue, take the following steps:

1. Make sure the printer queue is configured as a local printer queue.

2. Set the spool directory to /var/spool/fax.

3. Set the printer device to /dev/null.

4. Set the input filter to /usr/bin/faxlpr.

5. Make sure that headers are not being suppressed.

Figure 25.2 shows how the printer configuration dialog should look for a fax queue named fax.

FIGURE 25.2:

Configuration of a fax printer queue

If you prefer to edit your printer configuration file manually, you can edit /etc/printcap and add the following entry:

```
fax:\
        :sd=/var/spool/fax:\
        :lp=/dev/null:\
        :if=/usr/bin/faxlpr:
```

This entry specifies the name of the queue as fax, sets the spool directory to /var/spool/fax, sets the print device to /dev/null, and sets the input filter to /usr/bin/faxlpr.

Finally, restart the lpd daemon using the printer configuration Control Panel applet or by killing and restarting /usr/sbin/lpd.

Setting Up the *Faxlpr* Script

The fax program is actually a highly flexible shell script. When the script is called by its regular name (fax), it assumes that the command is coming from the command line and behaves accordingly. If the script is called by an alternate name (faxlpr), the script assumes it is being asked to send a fax via an lpd printer queue.

In order to prepare for this, you need to create a link to /usr/bin/fax called faxlpr:

```
$ ln /usr/bin/fax /usr/bin/faxlpr
```

Next, you need to make some simple alterations in the faxlpr file. You have to do this because of problems inherent in the version of efax that ships with Red Hat Linux 6 (the version included with this book).

Use your favorite editor to edit the file /usr/bin/faxlpr and find the following pair of lines, which should appear around line 596 in the file:

```
0) echo "$1" | mail -s "fax to $num succeeded" $user@$host - ;;
*) echo "$1" | mail -s "fax to $num failed   " $user@$host - ;;
```

You need to edit these lines to remove the dash near the end of the line:

```
0) echo "$1" | mail -s "fax to $num succeeded" $user@$host ;;
*) echo "$1" | mail -s "fax to $num failed   " $user@$host ;;
```

Preparing the Spool Directory

The final step in preparing to use a printer queue to send faxes is to prepare the spool directory, /var/spool/fax.

First, check that the directory exists by using ls /var/spool and see if the fax subdirectory is there. The installation of efax should create this directory, so it should be there.

Next, set the permissions on the directory to world read and write so that any user can send a fax:

```
$ chmod 777 /var/spool/fax
```

Finally, create a lock file and give it the appropriate permissions:

```
$ touch /var/spool/fax/lock ; chmod 644 /var/spool/fax/lock
```

Sending Faxes Through the Print Queue

Once this is all done, you are ready to send your first fax using the lpd system. Just as you could print a file using the lpr command, now you can fax a text or PostScript file in the same way. The only new notion is that you use the -J argument of the lpr command to specify the phone number to send the fax to.

For instance, if you have a file called /tmp/testfile that you want to fax to 555-1212 using the print queue called fax, you could use the command

```
$ lpr -Pfax -J 5551212 /tmp/testfile
```

The lpd daemon passes the file over to the input filter (faxlpr), which attempts to fax the file. Following the attempt, faxlpr sends the user transmitting the fax an e-mail indicating the success or failure of the process.

You can print in this way from any program that allows you to specify options to the lpr command and that generates PostScript output (including, but not limited to, Netscape Communicator, WordPerfect for Linux, and StarOffice for OpenLinux).

Receiving Faxes

Receiving faxes is a fairly straightforward process. There are three ways in which you can arrange to receive a fax: manually, automatically for a specific incoming call, or automatically for all incoming calls.

Manually Receiving a Fax

To manually receive a fax, you need to tell the modem to answer the telephone and receive the fax once the phone is ringing. This is done with the receive option of the fax command.

If the line is ringing and you know the call is an incoming fax, you simply need to issue the command

```
$ fax receive
```

to receive the fax.

With the fax receive command, you can specify a filename for the incoming fax. Each page of the fax is saved in separate files with sequentially numbered extensions (001, 002, 003, etc.). For instance, if you receive a three-page fax with the command

```
$ fax receive testfax
```

the resulting fax is stored in three files named testfax01, testfax02, and testfax03. To view the fax, use the fax view command, described later in this section.

If you don't specify a filename for the incoming fax, then the `fax` command builds a 10-digit filename derived from the date and time the fax is received. For instance, a fax received on December 24 at 9:52:35 P.M. will be saved in a series of files names 122409523501, 122409523502, 122409523503, etc.

Faxes are stored in the default /var/spool/fax directory. You can view the contents of the fax spool directory with the `fax queue` command:

```
$ fax queue

Fax files in /var/spool/fax :

-rw-r-r-   1 root      root          247 Jul  2 17:49 070217485701
-rw-r-r-   1 root      root          247 Jul  2 17:59 070217584201
-rw-r-r-   1 root      root          247 Jul  4 17:14 070417133001
```

To view these faxes, use the `fax view` command while running X Windows:

```
$ fax view 070417133001
```

This command causes the fax to be filtered and displayed by the xv program, as shown in Figure 25.3.

Printing is equally simple using the `fax print` command:

```
$ fax print 070417133001
```

This command prints the same fax to the default printer queue, usually called `lp`.

FIGURE 25.3:

A fax displayed in xv

Automatically Receiving a Fax for a Specific Call

If you are expecting that the next phone call you receive will be an incoming fax, you can set things up so that the fax program will wait for the call, answer the phone, receive the fax, hang up, and then exit. To do this, you use the answer option of the fax command:

```
$ fax answer
```

The fax program starts, sits and waits patiently for the phone to ring, and then answers after the second ring. As with fax receive, the incoming fax is stored using the date to generate a filename. The incoming fax can be viewed and printed using the fax view and fax print commands.

Automatically Receiving All Incoming Faxes

If your fax modem is connected to a dedicated phone line that you want to use for incoming faxes, you can make the fax program continually monitor the line for incoming faxes while still allowing outgoing calls.

Using the wait option of the fax command causes the program to run as a daemon waiting for incoming calls to the fax modem:

```
$ fax wait
```

This works by having fax wait run as a daemon. The daemon runs fax answer to wait for a call. When fax answer exits (usually because an incoming fax has been received or a call has been answered), the daemon starts fax answer again to continue waiting for the next call.

This process can be monitored using the status option:

```
$ fax status
USER      PID %CPU %MEM  SIZE   RSS TTY STAT START   TIME COMMAND
root      721 0  0.7   936   456 p0 S <  17:28   0:00 /usr/bin/efax
-d/dev/

from: /var/spool/fax/modem.721

efax: 28:14 opened /dev/modem
efax: 28:16 waiting for activity
```

You can also specify a number of seconds after the fax status command, which causes the status display to be updated continually at the interval that has been specified. To cause the status to be displayed every five seconds, use the following command:

```
$ fax status 5
USER        PID %CPU %MEM  SIZE   RSS TTY STAT START   TIME COMMAND
root        721  0  0.7   936   456  p0 S <  17:28   0:00 /usr/bin/efax
-d/dev/

from: /var/spool/fax/modem.721

efax: 28:14 opened /dev/modem
efax: 28:16 waiting for activity
--------
USER        PID %CPU %MEM  SIZE   RSS TTY STAT START   TIME COMMAND
root        721  0  0.7   936   456  p0 S <  17:28   0:00 /usr/bin/efax
-d/dev/

from: /var/spool/fax/modem.721

efax: 28:14 opened /dev/modem
efax: 28:16 waiting for activity
efax: 31:00 activity detected
--------
etc.
```

Luckily, the `fax wait` daemon doesn't lock the modem, so you can continue sending faxes (for instance, using `fax send`) while the daemon is running.

If you want your system to answer faxes all the time, you can consider putting the command `fax wait` in your `/etc/rc.d/rc.local` start-up file so that the daemon runs every time you launch Linux.

If you need to stop the answering daemon, you can use the command

```
$ fax stop
```

to kill the daemon. When the last `fax answer` process dies (or is killed by you), then all automatic answering ceases.

Looking Ahead

By now you should feel comfortable sending and receiving faxes using your Linux system.

The next section of the book moves into a whole new area: Linux in the small office/home office (SOHO) environment. You will learn how to install Linux in a network environment and how to examine basic network configuration. Then you will move on to a discussion of the types of services Linux can be used for in a SOHO environment, including mail server, intranet Web server, and file server for UNIX, Windows, and Novell networks.

PART VI

Using Linux in the Small Office/ Home Office (SOHO)

CHAPTER

TWENTY-SIX

26

Where to Use Linux in the SOHO

- Linux As a File Server

- Linux As a Print Server

- Linux As a Database Server

- Linux As an Intranet Server

- Linux As an Applications Server

- Linux As a Router

- Linux As a Workstation

At this point, the book is going to shift its focus. By now you have a firm grasp of using Linux on a stand-alone workstation, and perhaps even use Linux as your preferred operating system at home to access the Internet, surf the Web, compose e-mails and letters, and more.

Still, Linux's real home is in a networked world. Perhaps you run a small office at home with two PCs that you want networked. Linux makes a great file and print server in most networks. Perhaps in your business you are thinking about setting up an intranet. Linux provides an inexpensive way to move your business into an intranet environment by offering powerful Web and database servers.

If you want to connect a network of PCs to the Internet, Linux can be an excellent router. In many cases, it is far less costly to use a Linux computer as a router than to purchase a hardware router to connect your network to the world.

Finally, if you find that your current Windows-based desktops lack the performance or stability you would like to see on your home or office network, Linux as a workstation operating system may be the answer to your problems. It is possible to access both Windows and Unix applications from within Linux, network with other Unix, Windows, and Novell network systems, and easily share files and data with the rest of the world without worrying about bothersome crashes.

This chapter takes a quick look at these uses of the Linux operating system for small offices and home offices (commonly known as SOHO) where the cost of deploying expensive commercial solutions may be prohibitive.

Linux As a File Server

Perhaps the most fundamental need on a small network is a file server. File servers supply common places to store data, thus allowing shared files to be accessed by all users who need them and providing centralized locations for backing up files (thereby eliminating the need for daily data backups on each workstation on a network).

On a Windows or Novell network, this is generally done in one of two ways:

- Using dedicated file servers
- Using peer-to-peer networks

Dedicated File Servers

A *dedicated file server* is a system that is not used as a workstation but is set up as a central file server for the network. Users at different workstations or computers on the network can access directories on the file server as if these are directories or disk drives on their own computers.

Dedicated file servers offer the advantage of centralizing the management of shared data and the backup process, but they cost more than peer-to-peer networks. They also offer the benefit of being able to set up network access control policies for confidential, core, or shared data to ensure that unauthorized users don't have easy access to the information.

Linux is ideally suited to run as a low-cost file server for a small network. Linux can act as a file server to Unix, Windows, and Novell networks, making it an easily deployed universal file server for a network containing different types of computers and workstations. In addition, the stability and true multitasking capabilities of Linux make it a better choice than some other well-known options (such as Windows 95 or 98) when a robust file server solution is needed.

Chapter 29, "Integrating Red Hat Linux 6 in Windows and Novell Networks," discusses how to set up Linux as a file server.

Peer-to-Peer File Sharing

In a *peer-to-peer network*, there is no central file server. Instead, each user decides which directories and drives on their PC should be shared on the network and what level of access control to impose. In this way, each workstation or computer on the network becomes a small file server.

While there is a flexibility to this approach, allowing users to decide what data to share and with whom, there are also drawbacks. These include no centralized management of file sharing and access control policies, no centralized location for the backing up of critical data, and a performance impact on a user's desktop when several other individuals on the network are accessing shared files on that user's PC.

Linux can act as a reasonable peer-to-peer file server because of its ability to share with multiple types of networks. In addition, the true multitasking abilities of Linux mitigate much of the impact on performance when multiple users access files on a PC being used for other work.

Ultimately, though, the low cost of setting up a Linux-based dedicated file server for a small network makes the dedicated file server approach more attractive because of the management and centralized backup benefits it provides.

Linux As a Print Server

In addition to file servers, print servers are another component of the network. Generally, a dedicated file server also plays the role of offering print services to the network, serving double duty.

It is not uncommon to find print services provided in both a centralized, dedicated fashion and the peer-to-peer method on the same network. Some users who use a printer heavily may warrant their own printers at their desks, while others who use the printers less frequently may share a printer located in a common area. Often, a user with a dedicated printer shares it on the network so that other users can print documents for his or her attention directly to the dedicated printer rather than to the common shared printer.

Linux, of course, can work in both environments. Linux supports a healthy range of printers, including most PostScript and HP-compatible PCL printers. In addition, its printer-sharing options include the ability to share printers on Unix, Windows, and Novell networks.

Chapter 29, "Integrating Red Hat Linux 6 in Windows and Novell Networks," discusses how to set up Linux as a print server.

Linux As a Database Server

Like most Unix platforms, Linux has long had a wide selection of free database packages available for it, including Postgress and mSQL.

In 1998, though, major commercial database vendors gave Linux a boost in the database market by announcing and releasing Linux versions of their products. These vendors included Oracle, Sybase, and Informix, who have long produced commercial database packages for use on commercial Unix and Windows NT servers.

Where Linux once provided an attractive alternative for file servers and Web servers in an organization, Linux can now be deployed as a robust, scalable database platform for an organization using standard, widely used relational database systems.

As mentioned later, combining a Linux-powered database with a Linux-powered Web server allows Linux to serve as a complete intranet server solution.

Linux As an Intranet Server

If you follow the computing trends today, you have probably heard a lot about *intranets:* internal corporate networks that use Internet technology such as TCP/IP, Web browsers, and Internet-standard e-mail to share information and applications within an organization.

Many articles that discuss intranets and the hardware and software used to deploy them depict intranets as expensive endeavors only suited to large corporations and organizations. This couldn't be further from the truth.

Even in small offices, an intranet can provide a convenient way to publish information to be read by all employees through a Web browser. With a little forethought, some of the paperwork in your office can be eliminated by introducing electronic, online, Web-based forms for everything from leave requests to expense report submissions.

In addition, if you have small databases scattered across your organization, each used on a daily basis by different users, an intranet can provide a common means by which occasional users of the data can access the information in a database without needing full access to the database tools used to create, maintain, and update the data. By integrating the database with an intranet Web server, simple Web-based forms can be used to query the database.

Linux, which offers a wealth of powerful and flexible Web servers as well as fully functional relational database systems, can allow the creation of an intranet server without the cost involved in deploying Windows NT, a commercial database such as Oracle, and an expensive Web database integration tool. There are even some free tools for Linux that make it relatively easy to produce intranet programs and applications that make use of your corporate databases.

Chapter 32, "Building Your Own Web Server," discusses the basics of getting a Linux-based intranet server up and running.

Linux As an Applications Server

Unlike Windows NT as a server platform, Linux is by nature designed to act as both a file/print/intranet server and a full-fledged applications server.

With an applications server, applications actually run on the server and are only displayed on a terminal or workstation, using the X Windows protocol or a terminal connection such as Telnet. In a typical Windows network, the applications run on the desktop and the data is stored on the server and accessed there.

For some types of applications and in some situations, centralizing the running of applications can bring both performance and management benefits.

If you are running a Windows or Novell network, a Linux system can act as an applications server for several purposes:

- Running character-based programs such as powerful Unix mail software

- Running a custom-designed, character-based database interface to a centralized Linux database

- Accessing custom in-house applications, such as a corporate telephone book, designed to run in a Unix shell

If you install an X server on a Windows desktop, you can even deliver centrally managed X Windows applications to the desktop while running the applications on a Linux applications server.

Where budgets are low, Linux can create full-fledged GUI networks without the hardware or software expense of running Windows 95 or 98, or NT. For instance, I have deployed a 10-desktop network running Linux exclusively. The desktops are all 486-class machines with 8MB of RAM. It would be exceptionally difficult to run Windows plus Microsoft Office on them, and the cost for the necessary software licenses would run over U.S. $300 per desktop.

But with Linux on their older hardware, these systems can act as simple X terminals, displaying applications that run on a single applications server. In this case, the applications server is a Pentium 200MHz system with just 96MB of RAM. The only software license fee needed here is the cost of the desired Unix office suite for the number of concurrent users who will use the software.

A network like this can provide performance to the user that feels like a low-end Pentium system with 16MB of RAM running Windows 95 or 98. All of the management of software, user accounts, backups, and system maintenance can be done centrally on one or two servers.

Of course, this type of solution takes a fundamental strategic decision: not to use popular Windows-based productivity applications. But where cost is of the essence or the availability of modern hardware is limited, Linux makes a strong candidate for an organization-wide computing platform.

Linux As a Router

The concept of a router is simple: where two or more networks need to be connected, a router is the device that makes it possible to communicate between the networks.

Routers come in all shapes and sizes, from software-based routers running on Windows NT servers to hardware routers from well-known vendors such as Cisco. Routers can connect to networks in different ways, using technology ranging from regular modems to Ethernet cards to ISDN connections.

Let's consider an example: an office with a small network that is connected to the Internet by an ISDN connection. That is, a small company has a single dial-up ISDN connection to the Internet but has a network of two or more computers that would like to share the connection.

A router for this situation offers a single Ethernet connection connected to the local network and a single ISDN modem connection connected to the phone line. All computers on the network send all packets to the router. The router decides if the packet is destined for another location on the local network or for an outside address (in other words, somewhere on the Internet). Figure 26.1 contains a diagram of this network.

FIGURE 26.1:

A typical Ethernet-to-ISDN
routing diagram

All local packets are sent by the router back out on the Ethernet connection to
the local network. If a packet is destined for the outside world, an ISDN connection is established, the information is sent, and, after a specified period of non-
use, the connection is dropped.

Similar routing situations include connecting two separate Ethernet networks
through a router that has two or more Ethernet connections, as illustrated in Figure 26.2, or connecting a local Ethernet network to the Internet through a leased
line connection such as a T1 connection.

FIGURE 26.2:

Connecting two Ethernet networks with routers

Linux has all the features needed to act as a router:

- Support for multiple Ethernet cards

- Support for ISDN and regular modems

- Support for IP forwarding (the means by which packets can be received, analyzed, and rerouted by the Linux-based router)

In fact, for small Ethernet-to-Ethernet interconnectivity or Ethernet-to-ISDN Internet routing, a Linux-based solution can be far less expensive than dedicated hardware routers, and once it is properly configured can be very reliable.

Chapter 31, "Security and Red Hat Linux 6 As an Inexpensive Router," discusses using Linux as a router.

Linux As a Workstation

A final use of Linux in a small office environment is as the actual desktop operating system. If the application base available in Linux is suitable to the work of the office, then Linux-based desktops provide the following advantages:

- Stability and performance
- Full remote management by the network administrator
- Full network backup capabilities
- Lower cost of ownership in comparison with Windows-based desktops

Where money is available, high-powered Linux workstations can offer speed rivaling that of the more expensive Windows-based systems. Linux also offers peer-to-peer networking that is more robust and offers better performance than is seen on many systems, especially those running Windows 95 or 98.

Also, as mentioned in the previous section, Linux can enable low-end or old hardware that can't run the latest Windows software to become full-fledged X terminals, providing performance on obsolete desktop hardware that feels like that of a low-end Pentium system.

Looking Ahead

This chapter used broad brushstrokes to paint a picture of the ways in which Linux can be used in a small home or office network environment.

The next chapters of this book will cover this topic in more detail. You will start by learning how to install Linux in an Ethernet network environment, move on to learning about Linux in different capacities, as a file server, as a print server, as a router, and as an intranet server. Then you'll consider the advanced system administration techniques you can use to get the most out of your office Linux systems.

The next chapter looks at specific points of installing Linux in a networked environment.

# CHAPTER TWENTY-SEVEN

Installing Red Hat Linux 6 for the SOHO

- Choosing Packages for a LAN Installation

- Configuring Network Support During Installation

- Installing from a Network Source

In this chapter, you will move from considering principles that apply to Linux in the often-isolated context of a home workstation to examining another common role for Linux: as a desktop or server operating system in a local area network (LAN).

In fact, Linux has an increasingly important role to play in the small-office, home-office (SOHO) market, where Linux can deliver enterprise-class networking capabilities at a fraction of the cost of commercial Unix solutions.

Linux can easily be configured to work with most LANs and brings with it a wide range of tools, including Web servers, mail servers, and news servers, all essential components of successful intranet solutions.

Choosing Packages for a LAN Installation

An important piece of a network puzzle is consideration of which software packages to install on a networked Linux system.

If, as discussed in Chapter 4, "Installing Red Hat Linux 6," you find yourself unable to install all Red Hat Linux 6 components on your system, consider the guidelines listed in Table 27.1 when selecting packages to install on your network-enabled system.

T A B L E 2 7 . 1 : Suggested Packages for Different Network Installations

Type of System	Packages to Install
Networked Workstation	Mail/WWW/News tools Networked workstation NFS server SMB (Samba) connectivity
Network Management Workstation	*Everything for a networked workstation plus:* IPX/NetWare connectivity (if needed) Network management workstation
Network Server	*Everything for a network management workstation plus:* Anonymous FTP/Gopher server Print server News server Web server DNS nameserver Postgress (SQL) server (if needed)

Configuring Network Support During Installation

During the Linux installation process, you will get a chance to configure LAN support for your Linux system. While Chapter 28, "Configuring Red Hat Linux 6 for an Ethernet Network," discusses how to configure an existing Linux system to communicate on a LAN, this is generally easier to do during the installation process.

In order for LAN configuration to work, you need to have a network card already installed in your computer before you install Linux. This is important because the installation program will attempt to communicate with the card when networking is being configured.

Regardless of what media you choose to install from (CD-ROM, hard disk partition, or network mount), you will have a chance to configure your network environment. Normally, you are given the option to configure your network following installation of the Linux files. In Chapter 4, "Installing Red Hat Linux 6," you were instructed not to configure LAN support when prompted. However, in the case of a networked system, you need to answer "Yes" at this prompt. Once you do, you need to provide information in a minimum of four screens to fully configure your network.

NOTE   Much of the information requested during the network configuration process is covered in Chapter 21, "Understanding Linux Networking," and Chapter 28, "Configuring Red Hat Linux 6 for an Ethernet Network." These discussions include definitions of such terms as IP address, network mask, and nameserver.

Choosing a Network Interface Card

The first step to configuring your network is to select a network interface from the provided list of network cards, which is the first screen you should see during the configuration process. Most popular cards are supported, so you should find a reasonable match on the list.

Once you have selected a network card, you may be asked to indicate how the card's settings should be determined. The two options are Specify Options and Autoprobe. Autoprobe causes Linux to attempt to determine the settings of the card automatically. With many cards this will succeed. With some cards, though, this can fail or even cause your system to freeze, making it necessary to start the Linux installation process again. If autoprobing doesn't work for your card, you need to specify the card's settings manually. When you select Specify Options, a screen appears asking for information specific to the card you have selected.

Selecting a Boot Protocol

Once the card's settings are determined, you need to indicate how the system will obtain its network identity, including IP address, nameserver, and other crucial settings. This is done using the Boot Protocols screen. The three options on this screen are:

- Static IP Address
- BOOTP
- DHCP

With the Static IP Address option, all network configuration information is stored locally. The BOOTP or DHCP option allows your system to acquire its network configuration information from a server at boot time instead of storing information locally (and having to change the information locally when configuration changes are required).

Unless you know that you should be using DHCP or BOOTP to configure your network, it is necessary to choose Static IP Address. With this option, you can manually specify all the information necessary to make your system talk successfully with the rest of your LAN.

Configuring Your Network

Having chosen to configure your network settings manually, you will see the next two screens.

In the first screen, you are asked for the following information:

- IP address
- Network mask
- Default gateway
- Primary nameserver

If you don't know the correct values for these entries, consult your network administrator. For any LAN connected to the Internet, a default gateway and a primary nameserver are essential. For isolated networks, you may not need a gateway or a nameserver, so these fields can be left blank if your network administrator indicates they are not needed.

In the second screen, you have the opportunity to provide the following supplementary network configuration information:

Domain Name   This is the domain name of your network. This is essential for Internet-connected networks but may not be needed for isolated LANs that do not use the Domain Name System (DNS) for resolving host names.

Host Name   This is the fully qualified host name for your machine. In the case of systems on LANs where a domain name was specified, this value includes the host name of the machine as well as the domain name.

Secondary and Tertiary Nameservers   Many networks and systems connected to the Internet use more than one nameserver to ensure reliability of their domain name system. If you use two or three nameservers, enter the second and third servers' IP addresses in these two fields.

Once these screens are completed, your network is installed and configured. When your system reboots after the installation, you should find that it is configured correctly to work with your LAN.

Installing from a Network Source

If your system is connected to a LAN during the installation process, then it is possible to install Red Hat Linux 6 from a source image located on a server on the network. Examples of this include installing from an NFS source or installing from an FTP source.

In order to install from a network source, you need to use a different boot disk than you used in Chapter 4, "Installing Red Hat Linux 6." You can create this boot disk from the `bootnet.img` disk image file, which is located in the `images` directory of the Red Hat Linux 6 CD-ROM. Refer to Chapter 3, "Getting Ready to Install Red Hat Linux 6," for a discussion of creating boot disks from the Linux CD-ROM.

Installing from an NFS Source

In a Unix network, it is most common for the image to exist on a Network File System (NFS) server, which is the norm for sharing resources in Unix and Linux operating systems.

If your Red Hat Linux 6 CD-ROM is being made available from an NFS server on your network, you can use the boot install disk to install from this source.

When prompted for the source for your installation, instead of choosing Local CD-ROM, simply select NFS Image. You are immediately prompted to configure your network as outlined previously, and then the NFS Setup screen appears.

In this screen you need to provide two pieces of information: the IP address (or host name) of the NFS server you want to use and the path on the server where the Red Hat Linux 6 source image is located.

For instance, if your Red Hat Linux 6 CD-ROM is mounted on the NFS server at /mnt/cdrom and the NFS server has the IP address 10.10.10.1, you should enter **10.10.10.1** as the NFS server name and **/mnt/cdrom** as the Red Hat Directory.

The rest of the installation procedure should proceed in the same way as when you install from a local CD-ROM drive.

Installing from an FTP Source

As an alternative, you can install Linux from an FTP server. Using this option, you have two choices:

- Install from an FTP server on your LAN.

- Install from the Red Hat FTP server on the Internet. (Keep in mind that this could prove painfully slow unless you have a fast, dedicated Internet connection.)

If you want to use the FTP option, you need to select FTP at the point where you selected SMB Image and NFS Image in the previous two sections. As with the SMB option, using FTP to install Linux requires the supplementary installation disk.

You are prompted to configure your network once you have finished configuring disk partitions and selecting your swap partition. After the network is configured, the FTP Setup window appears. In this window, you can provide three pieces of information:

FTP Site Name   This is the name of the FTP server you plan to use. If you want to install from the Red Hat FTP server, use `ftp.redhat.com`.

Red Hat Directory   This is the directory on the FTP server where the Red Hat source files are located. To install Red Hat Linux 6 from the Red Hat FTP server, use `/pub/redhat/redhat-6/i386/`.

Use Non-Anonymous FTP or Proxy   Select this option if you are required to log in to the FTP server you plan to use or if your site is connected to the Internet through a proxy server and you plan to install Linux from the Red Hat FTP site.

If you select the last option, then another screen appears after you select OK on the FTP Setup screen. This supplementary screen, the Further FTP Setup screen, allows you to provide the account name and password you need to use for non-anonymous FTP, as well as the host name or IP address of your proxy server if those are required to access the Internet.

Looking Ahead

Now that you have installed a networked Linux system, you are going to look at the details of Linux Ethernet configuration. This information will allow you to install existing non-networked Linux systems onto an Ethernet LAN or reconfigure existing network configurations as needed.

Once you have learned these details, you will spend much of the rest of the book looking at some of the roles that Linux can play in a small intranet, including:

- Serving as an inexpensive router or firewall

- Acting as an intranet Web server

- Handling e-mail services for your network

CHAPTER

TWENTY-EIGHT

28

Configuring Red Hat Linux 6 for an Ethernet Network

- Preparing and Configuring the Network

- Testing Your Network

- Manual Network Configuration

- Sharing Files on a Unix Network

- Basic Network Security

In Chapter 27, "Installing Red Hat Linux 6 for the SOHO," you learned how to install Linux on a computer and connect it to a TCP/IP Ethernet network in the process.

In this chapter, you will learn how to configure an already-installed Linux system to connect to a Linux network. These steps including preparing your PC for a network, configuring the network, and testing the network. This chapter covers the entire process.

Preparing and Configuring the Network

As you saw in the last chapter, there are two main steps that need to be taken to get your network working:

- Installing and setting up a network card

- Setting up your TCP/IP parameters

This chapter will look at how to configure these essentials after Linux has been installed. This process can be used to install new PCs onto the network or to change the configuration of current PCs.

Installing and Setting Up a Network Card

Installing and setting up a network card is highly dependent on the type of network card you plan to use. You should consult the discussion of network cards in Chapter 27, "Installing Red Hat Linux 6 for the SOHO," to decide what type of card to use and what information is needed to configure it properly with Linux.

Having selected a card (this chapter assumes you select an EtherWORKS 3c59x class card, such as the 3Com Etherlink III card), you need to first install the hardware according to the instructions that come with the card and then restart your computer and let Linux load.

Having done this, log in as the root user and start X Windows. You will use the Control Panel for network configuration in this chapter; therefore you need to start the Control Panel as outlined in Chapter 15, "Using LinuxConf and the Control Panel for System Configuration," using the `control-panel` command.

In the Control Panel, single-click the kernel daemon configuration icon

to launch the kernel daemon configuration applet shown in Figure 28.1.

FIGURE 28.1:

The kernel daemon configuration window

This window displays any installed kernel modules. These kernel modules represent support for devices that, instead of being compiled into the kernel, are loaded at boot time or later. In addition to Ethernet cards, these devices can include SCSI cards, CD-ROM drives, and other hardware.

If you are adding a new Ethernet card to your system, click the Add button to get the Choose Module Type dialog box shown in Figure 28.2. Here you can click the Module Types to produce a drop-down list of device types. For Ethernet cards, choose the eth device type, which is the Linux abbreviation for Ethernet.

FIGURE 28.2:

The Choose Module Type dialog box

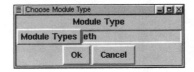

Having done this, the Define Module dialog box shown in Figure 28.3 appears. In this box, you need to specify the exact device name and type of hardware being used. Click the Which Module Type button to drop down a list of Ethernet device names such as eth0, eth1, and eth2. Generally, the first Ethernet card in a system is eth0, the second is eth1, and so on. If you are installing a new card in a system that previously had no Ethernet card, choose eth0.

FIGURE 28.3:

The Define Module dialog box

Next, click the Which Module button to select the type of Ethernet card you are installing from a list of available cards. In your case, you should select 3c59x.

A dialog box appears asking you to provide any configuration information necessary for your card. In some cases, this includes the IRQ and base I/O address of the card. Consult your card's manual for information about how to determine and set your card's hardware configuration. In the case of your chosen card, you are offered the chance to provide additional arguments; these are not necessary for a standard installation, so just click the Done button and your new card appears in the Kernel Configurator dialog box as shown in Figure 28.4.

FIGURE 28.4:

Adding a new Ethernet card

The final step to installing a new Ethernet card is to restart the kerneld process, which forces kerneld to load any configuration information related to the card. In order to do this, simply click the Restart Kernel button.

Checking Whether the Module Loaded

Verifying the configuration is not the easiest task. Until you try to make the network work in the next section, there is no quick way to see if your Ethernet card is configured correctly. But you can check whether the module will load by manually using the `insmod` command to install a loadable kernel module.

In order to do this, either go to a console command line or open an `xterm` window as the root user. First, you need to change your current directory to the following:

```
$ cd /lib/modules/2.2.5-15/net/
```

This command assumes you have installed the Red Hat Linux 6 distribution that shipped with this book and have not upgraded the kernel. In this case, the kernel version is `2.25`, which is reflected in the path of the directory.

Once you are in the correct directory, load your desired module (in this case, for the 3c59x series of cards) with the `insmod` command:

```
$ insmod 3c59x.o
```

Notice that the filenames for the modules have a `.o` extension.

If successfully configured, your card loads and a series of messages are generated by the driver. In the case of your chosen card, the messages will look something like this:

```
3c59x.c:v0.46C 10/14/97 Donald Becker
http://cesdis.gsfc.nasa.gov/linux/drivers/vortex.html
loading device 'eth0'...
etho: 3Com 3c905 Boomerang 100baseTx at 0x1440, 00:60:08:71:ad:8c, IRQ 11
    8k word-wide RAM 3:5 Rx:Tx split, autoselect/MII interface.
eth0: MII transceiver found at address 24.
eth0: Overriding PCI latency timer (CFLT) setting of 64, new value is 248.
```

If no errors appear, then the module has loaded successfully and your card should be configured just fine. If you continue to experience trouble configuring your network card, refer to the Ethernet HOWTO at `http://metalab.unc.edu/mdw/HOWTO/Ethernet-HOWTO.html`.

Setting Up Your TCP/IP Parameters

The next step is to set up your TCP/IP parameters using the network configuration applet, which is accessed using the network configuration icon in the Control Panel.

The network configuration window looks like the one shown in Figure 28.5.

FIGURE 28.5:

The Network Configurator dialog box

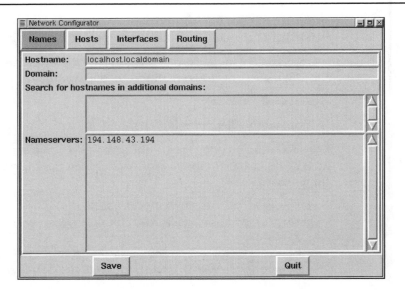

In this dialog box you specify critical information about your system in relation to the network it is connected to. This information includes

- The name and address of your machine

- The names and addresses of other machines on your network

- How each available network interface should be used

- How to correctly route traffic so that it reaches its destination

If you are connecting to an existing network, much of the information needed for this section will come from your network's administrator. If you plan to deploy your own network from scratch, it is a good idea to read up on the fundamentals of TCP/IP networking and network design.

The first step is to configure your computer's name and nameserver. This is done in the Names panel, which is displayed by default when you open the network configuration dialog box. Figure 28.5 shows this default panel.

Three main pieces of information need to be provided in the Names panel:

- Your complete host name: This includes the name of your machine plus the complete domain name in which the machine exists. For instance, the machine `foobar` in the domain `foo.com` would have the host name `foobar.foo.com`.

- The domain in which your machine exists: This is the latter part of the host; in the example above, this would be `foo.com`.

- Your nameservers: This is a list, one per line, of machines that provide domain name services to your network. Domain name services allow you to look up the names of systems on internal and external networks (such as the Internet) but are not used on all networks. If you need to provide a list of nameservers, list them as IP addresses. The job of the nameserver is to convert names into IP addresses, and if you provide the list of nameservers as names and not addresses, your system won't be able to look up the name of the nameserver in order to connect to it.

The next step involves the host table for your machine. The host table, which actually is kept in the file `/etc/hosts`, is the simplest form of name lookup. The host table file contains lists of names and their associated IP addresses. In small networks that don't run their own domain nameservers, it is common for the host table to contain the names and addresses of all machines on the network. At a minimum, though, a machine connected to a local area network needs two entries:

- A local host entry

- An entry with the machine's name and IP address

To add an entry to the list, click the Add button. A dialog box appears like the one in Figure 28.6.

FIGURE 28.6:

Adding a host

In this dialog box, there are three fields that you can fill in. At the very least, fill in the IP address and the complete name of the machine that you are configuring (such as `foobar.foo.com`). In the Nicknames field, you can enter alternative names for the machine separated by spaces. Frequently, system administrators place the unqualified host name (in the case of `foobar.foo.com` the unqualified name is `foobar`) in this field. When you are finished, click the Done button.

Editing entries in the host table is similar to adding new entries. Select an existing entry and then click the Edit button to get a dialog box like the one in Figure 28.7.

FIGURE 28.7:

Editing the host table

Here you find the same three fields as when you were adding a new entry to the host table. Once you finish editing the contents of the entry, click the Done button to commit the changes to the host table.

The next panel is where you configure the network interfaces on your system. Interfaces can include modem-based PPP connections, Ethernet connections through an Ethernet card, and even Token Ring connections. By default, this table should include at least one entry, called `lo` (this is the local loopback entry and is needed for Linux to work without a network present). Each interface is associated with an IP address.

The first step to adding a new interface (assuming yours isn't there) is to click the Add button. A dialog box appears like the one in Figure 28.8, where you can select the type of interface you are adding.

FIGURE 28.8:

The Choose Interface Type dialog box

In the case of a LAN, select the same type of device that you did earlier when setting up the module for your network card. This will probably be an Ethernet interface.

After clicking OK, a dialog box appears where you can configure the properties of the interface. In the case of an Ethernet interface, this looks like the one in Figure 28.9.

FIGURE 28.9:

Configuring an Ethernet interface

At the very least, you need to provide the IP address of the interface and a netmask for the network. If you have only one network interface, then the IP address should be the same one you entered for the machine in the Names and Hosts panels. The other available options are:

- Activate Interface at Boot Time: Select this if you want the network to be enabled every time you boot your computer; if you don't select this, you will need to enable your network manually. It is usually preferable to select this option for an Ethernet LAN connection.

- Allow Any User to (De)activate Interface: Normally, only the root user can activate or deactivate a network interface. Allowing any user to do so is particularly useful for dial-up interfaces, such as PPP, where any user may want or need to dial out to establish a network connection. If you are dealing strictly with an Ethernet LAN connection and are activating the interface at boot time, then you probably won't need to enable this feature.

- Interface Configuration Protocol: On some networks, special servers provide network workstations with the information they need to operate on the network. This makes it easier to configure your workstation because instead of performing the complete network configuration, you can allow the computer to obtain its configuration from the server every time the network interface is activated. If your network uses BOOTP or DHCP for this purpose, select the option here. If your network doesn't use a boot protocol such as BOOTP or DHCP, select None.

The final piece of the network configuration puzzle is the setting of routes. Click the Routing button at the top of the window to display the routing table panel shown in Figure 28.10.

The routing table is used to tell the computer how to direct data that is destined for different locations on the network. In the case of a small LAN that is not connected to another LAN or to an external network such as the Internet, configuration of routes can be an easy job.

FIGURE 28.10:

The routing table panel

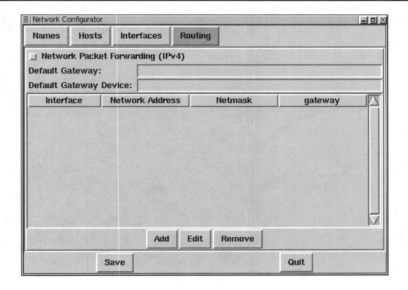

If your network uses a default gateway, you may be able to simply indicate the IP address of the default gateway and the network device on your system that is used to send information to the gateway (if you have a single Ethernet card, this should be the device eth0). If you have multiple interfaces (such as more than one Ethernet card), you can specify when to use these devices by creating static routes.

For example, let's say your computer has two Ethernet cards, one attached to your main corporate network (eth0) and another connected to a small network you are using to test some software (eth1). Your routing configuration would indicate that your default gateway device should be eth0, and a static route for your test network should use eth1, as shown in Figure 28.11.

FIGURE 28.11:

Using static routes

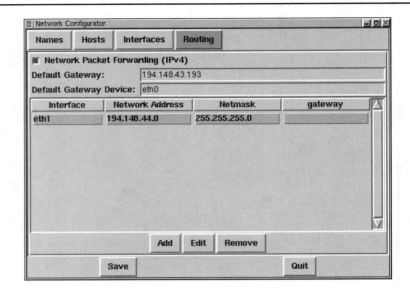

It is not uncommon to include a static route for the local Ethernet network you are connected to.

Testing the Network

The next step is to test your network connection to make sure everything is healthy.

First, you need to test basic network connectivity. You can do this with the `ping` command, which allows you to send a query to a specific IP address to see if any machine is currently on and alive at the address.

Let's use a fictional network with IP addresses in the range of 194.148.43 to 194.148.43.255. You are configuring your workstation to act as 194.148.43.100. On your network is a file server with the IP address 194.148.43.10. If your network is correctly configured, at the very least you should be able to talk to this server. Test this with the command

```
$ ping 194.148.43.10
```

If you get back the errors

```
ping: sendto: Network is unreachable
ping: wrote 194.148.43.10 64 chars, ret=-1
ping: sendto: Network is unreachable
ping: wrote 194.148.43.10 64 chars, ret=-1
etc.
```

then you immediately know that you have a problem with the configuration of your Ethernet card's driver module or a basic configuration error such as the wrong IP address or netmask for the device. You should go back and review these settings to make sure they are correct. First, check that the module for the Ethernet card is loading successfully; once it is, double-check your IP address and netmask entries.

Once you can ping on the local network, you need to see if your default gateway and access to networks outside your local network are functional. You can do this by using ping for an external IP address. If you don't know the IP address of any external system, you can skip this step or ask your system administrator for an appropriate IP address to test.

Just as you did before, use the ping command:

```
$ ping 194.148.8.10
```

If this succeeds, then your routing is correctly set up and you can access external networks through your default gateway.

The final step is to see if name lookups are working. To test this, you can use the nslookup command to try to look up a host name using your default DNS server. For instance, you can try looking up www.yahoo.com:

```
$ nslookup www.yahoo.com
```

If successful, the nslookup command should produce results that look like this:

```
Server:   du1.paus.ch
Address:  194.209.60.97

Name:     www5.yahoo.com
Address:  204.71.177.70
Aliases:  www.yahoo.com
```

Notice that the name and address of the nameserver being used are displayed (you can use this to confirm you have configured your DNS services correctly), and then the results of the name lookup are provided.

Assuming all three of these steps work, then you probably have a fully functional network connection. If not, you may want to refer to the networking HOWTO document at /usr/doc/HOWTO/NET-3-HOWTO.gz:

```
$ zless /usr/doc/HOWTO/NET-3-HOWTO.gz
```

Manual Network Configuration

This section will describe a series of steps that can be taken to configure your network. These steps assume you have your Ethernet card's module loaded.

Setting Up the Interface

The first step is to activate the network interface you want to use. If you are trying to activate eth0 as IP address 100.100.100.10, then you can use the ifconfig command to activate the interface:

```
$ ifconfig eth0 100.100.100.10 netmask 255.255.255 up
```

This command tells the system to assign the IP address 100.100.100.10 and the netmask 255.255.255 to the eth0 interface, and then activates the interface with the up argument.

To test whether the interface has been successfully activated, you can use the ifconfig command without any parameters or arguments to see a list of enabled interfaces like the one that follows:

```
eth0      Link encap:10Mbps Ethernet  HWaddr 00:C0:F0:0D:76:5A
          inet addr:100.100.100.10  Bcast:100.100.100.255
➡Mask:255.255.255
          UP BROADCAST RUNNING MULTICAST  MTU:1500  Metric:1
          RX packets:11239889 errors:0 dropped:0 overruns:0
          TX packets:16384520 errors:3 dropped:0 overruns:0
          Interrupt:3 Base address:0x300
```

```
lo          Link encap:Local Loopback
            inet addr:127.1  Bcast:127.255.255.255  Mask:255
            UP BROADCAST LOOPBACK RUNNING  MTU:3584  Metric:1
            RX packets:2142848 errors:0 dropped:0 overruns:0
            TX packets:2142848 errors:0 dropped:0 overruns:0
```

This list generally contains at least a loopback device (device `lo`) plus any network devices you have enabled. In this case, you are looking for the `eth0` interface. Red Hat sets things up to configure a loopback device at boot time. To keep your system running happily, make sure you have a local loopback device configured. If `lo` is not set up on your system, you can configure it with the following `ifconfig` command:

```
$ ifconfig lo 127.1 up
```

Setting Up a Nameserver

The next step is to set up your nameserver. In order to do this, you need to edit the file `/etc/resolv.conf` using your favorite text editor. This file tells the system everything it needs to know to go out and find the address for host names.

Generally, you want at least two lines in your `resolv.conf` file such as:

```
domain landegg.edu
nameserver 194.148.43.194
```

The `domain` line specifies the domain name of the local system. If your machine is being placed on a network whose domain is `foo.bar`, then this line should read `domain foo.bar`. The second line specifies the IP address of the primary nameserver that you will be using. This may be a machine on your local network, a server running at your Internet service provider (ISP), or a public nameserver on the Internet. Your network administrator can provide you with this information.

Many sites use multiple nameservers for redundancy. If one is down or not available for some reason, users should still be able to look up names using the alternate servers. You can specify multiple servers by including multiple `nameserver` lines in `resolv.conf`:

```
domain landegg.edu
nameserver 194.148.43.194
nameserver 194.148.43.196
nameserver 194.148.8.10
nameserver 194.148.1.10
```

In a situation like this, the first listed server will be the first tried when looking up a name. If this attempt fails, Linux moves on to the second machine on the list and so on. If all listed nameservers fail to respond to the query, then Linux gives up and the attempted name lookup fails.

Setting Up a Local Hosts File

While it is theoretically possible to use a DNS nameserver to look up every name, including those of hosts on the local network, this is hugely inefficient. As an alternative to using a nameserver to look up the names of machines on moderately sized networks, you can use a local hosts file to perform these lookups.

A local hosts file sits on your system and contains a list matching IP addresses with host names. To enable a local hosts file, you first need to edit the file /etc/ host.conf with your favorite text editor. This file tells Linux how to go about looking up names, and needs to contain the following two lines to enable a local hosts file:

```
order hosts,bind
multi on
```

The first line says that when a name is being looked up, first check the local hosts file (hosts) and then check the DNS (bind stands for Berkeley Internet Name Daemon) by following the instructions in /etc/resolv.conf.

Next, you need to create the local hosts file, which is called /etc/hosts. Edit this file with your favorite text editor and create a one-line entry for each host being listed. The entry should take the following form:

```
IP_Address hostname alias alias alias ...
```

Each section of the line (IP address, host name, and alias) can be separated by one or more spaces. Comment lines begin with a hash mark (#) and can be used to structure and explain the entries in larger hosts files.

Let's consider an example. The following four entries are taken from a hosts file:

```
194.148.43.194     serv1.landegg.edu
194.148.43.195     apps.landegg.edu        apps
194.148.43.196     serv3.landegg.edu       serv3     www.landegg.edu
194.148.43.215     office15.landegg.edu    office15
```

Notice that all lines start with the IP address and then provide a host name and any aliases for the host. Aliases are not required. In addition, notice that for many machines, the aliases include a short form of the host name without the complete domain name. This is done so that you can access machines on the local network without having to type the complete host name with domain name. In this example, apps.landegg.edu can be accessed locally as apps, and office15.landegg.edu as office15.

Setting Up Routes

The final step is to set up the necessary routes that allow you to talk to the network and the rest of the world. Basically, for each interface you need a routing entry that tells Linux what network is connected on that interface. In addition, you need an entry specifying a default gateway if your network is connected through a gateway to other non-local networks.

Let's start with the loopback device. Use the route command to specify that the local machine is accessed through the loopback device:

```
$ route add -host 127.1 lo
```

This command says that the host 127.1 (the local host) should be accessed through the device lo.

Next, let's consider our eth0 device from earlier in this section. This device connects the PC to a network with the network address 100.100.100 and a netmask of 255.255.255. Use the route command again to tell Linux to send all information for the local network out on the eth0 interface:

```
$ route add -net 100.100.100 netmask 255.255.255 eth0
```

Finally, use the route command once more to specify the default gateway that can be used to access remote networks. If your default gateway is at the IP address 100.100.100.1, use the following command:

```
$ route add default gw 100.100.100.1 eth0
```

This indicates that the default gateway (gw) is at the address 100.100.100.1 and can be accessed by sending information destined for the gateway out through the eth0 interface.

Finally, check all your routing entries by using the route command with no parameters or arguments. This should return a routing table like this:

```
Kernel IP routing table
Destination    Gateway          Genmask          Flags Metric Ref Use Iface
100.100.100    *                255.255.255   U     0      0    317 eth0
127       *              255      U     0       0    6 lo
default       100.100.100.1  0              UG    0       0    2605 eth0
```

Automating Network Configuration at Boot Time

By now, you should have a fully functional network connection. However, it would be laborious to have to type all of those commands each time you start your Linux system.

Luckily, you can place all the needed ifconfig and route commands into one of the system's start-up scripts, such as /etc/rc.d/rc.local. In the case of the examples used here, you could add the following lines to your rc.local file using a text editor:

```
/sbin/ifconfig eth0 100.100.100.10 netmask 255.255.255 up
/sbin/ifconfig lo 127.1 up
/sbin/route add -host 127.1 lo
/sbin/route add -net 100.100.100 netmask 255.255.255 eth0
/sbin/route add default gw 100.100.100.1 eth0
```

Sharing Files on a Unix Network

Now that you have your Linux system talking with other machines on a local TCP/IP network, let's look at one of the most basic networking tasks: sharing files. In the Unix and Linux world, this is generally done using NFS, the Network File System.

Sharing takes place in two directions:

- Accessing directories and files on other hosts on the network that have been shared

- Sharing files and directories on your PC for other users on the network to access

Accessing Remote File Systems

Accessing remote files and directories is done using the `mount` command. The command takes the form

```
$ mount remote-directory-name local-directory
```

where the remote directory is specified with the form *hostname:/directory-name*, and the *local-directory* is an existing directory, preferably empty, that becomes the location through which the remote directory is accessed.

Let's consider an example. Suppose you want to access the directory `/test/dir` on the machine `foo.bar` on your local network; the directory has been made available for remote mounting via NFS. You have an empty directory called `/foo` on your machine, which will be the mount point for the remote directory.

To assign this directory, you use the `mount` command:

```
$ mount foo.bar:/test/dir /foo
```

This command says to mount the directory `/test/dir` on machine `foo.bar` to the local directory `/foo`. Once this is done, you have access to the files and subdirectories in the remote directory on the basis of the file permissions assigned to the files. Listing the contents of `/foo` actually lists the contents of `/test/dir` on `foo.bar`.

WARNING There is one caveat to the NFS system. On your local system, the root user has godlike power to open, read, or erase a file anywhere on the system regardless of who created or owns the file. But in a remotely mounted directory, root has severe restrictions under the NFS model: it can only access files and directories for which explicit permission has been granted.

Mounting Remote Directories at Boot Time

If there are remote directories that you frequently use, you probably want them to mount automatically at boot time. To do this, you can use LinuxConf. To do this, start LinuxConf with the `linuxconf` command, and select Config ➢ Filesystems ➢ Access NFS Volume from the list of configuration screens. This screen contains a list of current NFS mounts, if any. Click the Add button to display the Add NFS Mount screen shown in Figure 28.12.

FIGURE 28.12:

The Add NFS Mount dialog box

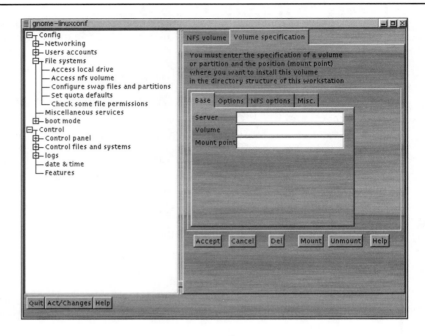

To enter the remote mount example used above, enter **foo.bar** for Server, **/test/dir** for Volume, and **/foo** for Mount Point. If you want the mount to occur automatically at boot time, select the Options tab and make sure the Not Mount at Boot Time option is not selected. Finally, click the Accept button to complete configuration of the automatic mount.

This procedure adds an entry to the /etc/fstab file similar to the following:

```
foo.bar:/test/dir   /foo   nfs   exec,dev,rw 1 1
```

If you want to manually create an automatic mount to mount at boot time, you can add a similar entry to /etc/fstab on your system using a text editor.

Sharing Directories on the Network

The flip side of the whole equation is sharing your files and directories with users on the network. After all, before you mounted the remote file system on the machine foo.bar in the last section, foo.bar had to make the directory available to the network.

Exporting directories with NFS requires the use of two daemons, `/usr/sbin/rpc.nfsd` and `/usr/sbin/rpc.mountd`, plus one configuration file, `/etc/exports`. The files `rpc.mountd` and `rpc.nfsd` should be installed on most systems. If they're not on your system, you can install them from the enclosed Red Hat Linux 6 CD-ROM from the RPM file `knfsd-981204-3.i386`.

The first step to sharing a directory on the network is to edit `/etc/exports` using a text editor and add one entry for each directory being shared. The entries take the form

```
/directory host (options)
```

The following is a sample `/etc/exports` file from the man page for `/etc/exports`:

```
# sample /etc/exports file
/                  master(rw) trusty(rw,no_root_squash)
/projects          proj*.local.domain(rw)
/usr               *.local.domain(ro)
/home/joe          pc001(rw,all_squash,anonuid=150,anongid=100)
/pub               (ro,insecure,all_squash)
/pub/private       (noaccess)
```

Let's break this file down line by line:

- Line 1: This is a comment line, as indicated by a hash mark (#), and is ignored.

- Line 2: Two machines are being given different levels of access to the `/` directory: `master` with read and write permission (the `rw` option), and `trusty` with read and write permission enabled and permission for the root user to have full access to all the files and subdirectories being exported (the `no_root_squash` option). In other words, a root user on `trusty` has the same permissions as root on the local system.

- Line 3: Any host whose name starts with `proj` and is part of the domain `local.domain` is given read and write access to the directory `/projects`.

- Line 4: Any host in the domain `local.domain` has read-only (the `ro` option) access to `/usr`.

- Line 5: The host `pc001` is being given read and write access to the directory `/home/joe`. All users accessing this mount from `pc001` are treated as the anonymous user (the `all_squash` option), and the anonymous user is considered to have a user ID of 150 and group ID of 150 (the `anonuid=150` and `anongid=150` options).

- Line 6: The directory `/pub` is being made available to all hosts with access to the exporting system. Access is granted on a read-only basis, with all users treated as anonymous users. The `insecure` option allows clients that don't use a reserved TCP/IP port for NFS to access the mount.

- Line 7: Access is denied (the `noaccess` option) to all hosts for the directory `/pub/private`.

Other options for the `/etc/exports` file can be found in the `exports` man page, which is accessed with the command

```
$ man exports
```

Once you have specified your exported directories in `/etc/exports`, you need to restart the `rpc.nfsd` and `rpc.mountd` processes (which usually run at boot time). First, use `ps` to check the process IDs of the two processes:

```
$ ps aux | grep rpc.nfsd
root 1103  0.2  0.8  872  508  ?  S  22:25  0:00 /usr/sbin/rpc.nfsd
$ ps aux | grep rpc.mountd
root 1105  0  0.7  836  500  ?  S  22:25  0:00 /usr/sbin/rpc.mountd
```

Next, kill and restart the processes:

```
$ kill 1103 1105; /usr/sbin/rpc.nfsd; /usr/sbin/rpc.mountd
```

Your new exports are made available on the network for remote users to access.

Basic Network Security

While it is great to be able to connect to a network and access all of its resources, this does present a security risk. Luckily, Linux provides a basic mechanism that gives some control over which machines on the network can actually attempt to connect to services on your Linux system.

The basic security mechanism consists of two files: `/etc/hosts.allow` and `/etc/hosts.deny`. Together, these files are part of a three-part basic security chain:

1. Allow access to any daemon-client combination in `hosts.allow`.

2. Deny access to any daemon-client combination in `hosts.deny`.

3. Grant access to everyone else.

By default, there are no entries in `hosts.allow` or `hosts.deny`, so the default is option 3: anyone can attempt to connect to the system. Of course, this doesn't prevent individual services such as Telnet and FTP from requiring further authentication, but it also doesn't prevent those initial probing attempts to connect that can be the start of many hackers' joyrides through unknown systems.

Creating entries for `hosts.allow` and `hosts.deny` is straightforward:

```
Daemon_List: Client_List
```

Any entry like this specifies which network daemons (e.g., `ftpd`, `in.telnetd`, `in.rshd`) should allow connections from which hosts (in `hosts.allow`) or deny connections from which hosts (in `hosts.deny`). Any network daemon can be listed. For instance, the entry

```
ftp: host1
```

in the file `hosts.allow` allows incoming FTP connections from the specified host, `host1`.

A few special keywords help make things easy, preventing the necessity of listing all daemons and clients individually. The ALL keyword can match any client or any daemon. For instance, the entry

```
ALL: ALL
```

in `hosts.allow` allows any type of access from any client, while the same entry in `hosts.deny` stops all access.

The EXCEPT keyword allows exceptions in a network that is otherwise thrown wide open by ALL. For instance, the entry

```
ALL EXCEPT ftpd: ALL
```

in `hosts.deny` denies access to all clients accessing all services except FTP services. Similarly,

```
ALL: .local.domain EXCEPT foo.local.domain
```

in `hosts.allow` allows access to all services to any machine in the domain `local.domain` (note the necessary "." in front of `local.domain`) except `foo.local.domain`.

Finally, the LOCAL keyword makes it easy to provide access to all machines in the local domain:

```
ALL: LOCAL
```

in `hosts.allow` allows any type of access from machines in the local domain.

The `hosts.allow` and `hosts.deny` files can take a very rich set of entries that provide more finely grained control than most users need. This is detailed in the man page for `hosts.allow`:

```
$ man hosts.allow
```

Looking Ahead

In this chapter, you learned the basics of connecting a Linux PC to an Ethernet network using TCP/IP. This allows Linux to communicate easily with other Unix systems on the network, including other Linux systems.

However, fully integrating your Linux system with Windows and Novell networks requires more work. In the next chapter, you will take a look at the basics of integrating your Linux system with Windows and Novell.

CHAPTER
TWENTY-NINE

Integrating Red Hat Linux 6 in Windows and Novell Networks

- Sharing Linux Files and Printers with Windows Networks

- Accessing Windows Network Files and Printers from Linux Systems

- Connecting Linux to a Novell Network

This chapter will examine the capabilities of Linux that make it an attractive addition to many existing intranet networks.

If your organization is running a standard Windows network, Linux is able to step in and play the role of an effective, efficient, and powerful file and print server. With a price-point far lower than Windows NT and stability that exceeds that of Windows 95 and Windows 98, Linux may be the ideal file and print server for budget-conscious offices that need to share files between Windows desktops on a network.

Working from the other direction, Linux can also access files on Windows file servers as if they are local hard disks on the Linux system. This serves any number of purposes. For instance, suppose you run a Linux-based Web server but your Web developer performs development on a Windows system. The Linux Web server could automatically connect to a pre-specified directory on the Windows development system and copy new files onto the Web server, preventing any need to manually update the Web server's content.

Next, this chapter will look at the integration of a Linux system into a Novell network. These tools are not as well developed and robust as those available for integration with Windows networks, but this chapter will discuss the Novell options and point you to sources of information on the subject.

Sharing Linux Files and Printers with Windows Networks

The most common method of Linux-Windows network integration is to make a Linux system act as a file and print server to Windows clients on the network. This is achieved through the use of Samba. Samba is a collection of software that makes Linux capable of the SMB (Server Message Block) protocol that is the basis of Windows network file and print sharing. Possible clients to a Linux-based SMB server include LAN Manager, Windows NT, OS/2, and other Linux systems.

Installing Samba

If you are running the version of Red Hat Linux that comes with this book, you may already have installed Samba when you installed Linux. You can check this using the `rpm` command:

```
$ rpm -q samba
```

If you find that Samba is not installed, you can install it from the Red Hat CD-ROM by mounting the CD-ROM to a logical location (such as /mnt/cdrom) and then using `rpm` to install the file `samba-2.0.3-8.i386.rpm`:

```
# rpm -i /mnt/cdrom/ samba-2.0.3-8.i386.rpm
```

Installing Samba from the Internet

If you want the latest version of Samba available, you can download the latest Samba source code from `ftp://ftp.samba.org/pub/samba/`.

Once you download the file, you need to extract the compressed archives and read the documentation for instructions about how to compile and install Samba from the source code. Because these procedures can change from version to version, they aren't included here.

Alternatively, if you are wary of compiling from the source code, the easiest approach is to install the binaries that came with Red Hat Linux 6.

What Gets Installed

When you install Samba, several files are installed, including:

- `/usr/sbin/smbd`: The Samba server that handles connections from clients
- `/usr/sbin/nmbd`: The NetBIOS server that allows clients to locate servers on a Windows network
- `/usr/bin/smbclient`: A basic Samba client for accessing SMB servers
- `/etc/smb.conf`: The Samba configuration file

Configuring Samba

The entire Samba configuration is contained in the file /etc/smb.conf. The smb.conf file consists of multiple entries that contain a header followed by multiple parameters. For instance, the following entry shares the /tmp directory on the network:

```
[temp]
    comment = Temporary file space
    path = /tmp
    read only = no
    public = yes
```

Notice that the header is contained in square brackets ([tmp]), that each parameter is on a separate line, and that the structure of parameters is parameter = value.

The *[global]* Section

Most smb.conf files start with a [global] section that defines some essential parameters that affect the overall behavior of Samba. Common parameters in the [global] section include:

- printing: Specifies the type of print system being used; on Linux systems, this should be bsd.

- printcap name: Specifies the location of the printcap file; generally, this is /etc/printcap.

- load printers: Should be set to yes if you will be sharing printers.

- guest account: Indicates which Linux user to use for attempted guest connections; most Linux administrators will make this nobody because of its extremely limited privileges.

- lock directory: Indicates where to place lock files for file locking. This is usually /var/lock/samba; this directory must exist and be world readable (use chmod 755 /var/lock/samba to make it world readable).

- share modes: Specifies whether multiple users can share the same file. This should be set to yes to ensure that the necessary locking mechanisms are used to protect the integrity of shared files.

- workgroup: Indicates the Windows workgroup or domain to which the Samba server belongs.

- security: Specifies how to authenticate users for access to system resources; when set to user, Samba authenticates out of the local Unix password file. If this parameter is set to server, Samba authenticates from a Windows NT domain server specified by the password server parameter.

Consider the following [global] section in the smb.conf file of the Landegg Academy server that I manage:

```
[global]
    printing = bsd
    printcap name = /etc/printcap
    load printers = yes
    guest account = nobody
    lock directory = /var/lock/samba
    share modes = yes
    workgroup = testgroup
    security = user
```

This section specifies the type of printing system used in Landegg, sets up the guest account to use the Linux user nobody, points to a lock directory, makes the server part of the testgroup Windows workgroup, and specifies that Samba should use the local Unix password file for authentication.

The *[homes]* Section

The [homes] section is used to specify how to share users' home directories to the Windows network. Without this section, users' home directories need to be shared individually, as you will see later.

Consider the following [homes] section comes from a smb.conf file:

```
[homes]
    comment = Home Directories
    browseable = no
    read only = no
    preserve case = yes
    short preserve case = yes
    create mode = 0750
```

The `comment` parameter provides additional information about the section but doesn't affect its operation. The `browseable` parameter is used to indicate whether other users can browse the directory; setting it to **no** limits access to those users with permission. The `read only` parameter is set to **no** so that users can both read and write files in their home directories. The `preserve case` and `short preserve case` parameters ensure that case-insensitive Windows systems do not change the case of letters in filenames, because Linux is case sensitive. Finally, the `create mode` parameter specifies what permission to give to files created by users connected through Samba; in this example, **0750** indicates that the files should be readable, writable, and executable by the owner, readable and executable by the file's group, and off-limits to everyone else.

In order for a user to access their home directory from a Windows system, they use their username for the share name. For instance, for the user `username` to access their home directory on `smbserv`, they would access the share \\smbserv\username.

The *[printers]* Section

As the [`homes`] section was used to share all users' home directories, the [`printers`] section is used to share all Linux printers to the Windows network.

Table 29.1 outlines common parameters in the [`printers`] section.

TABLE 29.1: [Printers] Section Parameters

Parameter	Description
comment	Provides information about the section but does not affect operation.
path	Specifies the spool path; you may want to create your own spool directory for Samba and point there. (For instance, Red Hat Linux creates /var/spool/samba and points there.)
browseable	As with the home directories, setting this to **no** ensures that only users with permission can browse the printers.
printable	This should be set to **yes**, otherwise printing won't work. (How does one print to a non-printable printer?)
public	If set to **yes**, then the guest account can print; on many networks, it is wise to set this to **no** to prevent excessive printing by guest users.
writable	Printers are not writable, so this should be **no**.
create mode	This specifies the permissions on spool files created during printing; this is often set to **0700**.

Put together, these can be used to produce a fairly common [printers] section like the default Red Hat Linux one shown in the following example:

```
[printers]
    comment = All Printers
    path = /var/spool/samba
    browseable = no
    printable = yes
    public = no
    writable = no
    create mode = 0700
```

Accessing Linux printers from Windows works the same way as with directories. The share name is the Linux printer name in the printcap file. For instance, to access the printer printername on smbserv, Windows users should access \\smbserv\printername.

Sharing a Directory for Public Access

Sometimes it is necessary to create a publicly accessible directory that is accessible by all users and is read only. The directory can be set up to share information centrally in a way that prevents users from altering the information.

Consider the following entry:

```
[public]
    path = /public/directory
    public = yes
    read only = yes
    printable = no
```

This entry creates a share named public that is accessible by all users (hence, public = yes) but is read only (hence, read only = yes).

Consider another example: sharing /tmp as a publicly accessible temporary directory that can be read and written to by all users. This can be achieved with the following entry:

```
[temp]
    path = /tmp
    read only = no
    public = yes
```

Sharing a Directory for Private Access

In addition to sharing directories for public access, it is sometimes necessary to create shared directories accessible by a limited number of users.

Consider a situation where you want to share the directory /private/directory as the share named private. Suppose, as well, that this directory is only to be accessible by three users: user1, user2, and user3. This could be achieved with an entry similar to the following:

```
[private]
    path = /private/directory
    valid users = user1 user2 user3
    public = no
    writable = yes
    printable = no
    create mask = 0765
```

Notice the use of a new parameter: valid users. This parameter takes as its value a list of users with permission to access the resource, with spaces separating the usernames.

Note, as well, that public is set to no to prevent unwanted prying eyes and writable is set to yes so that it is a fully writable resource.

Putting It All Together

Now, let's put this all together into a complete smb.conf file. There are two things to note here:

- Blank lines are ignored.

- Comment lines start with a semicolon or a hash mark (#) and continue to the end of the line.

Our completed file looks like this:

```
; Sample smb.conf

; Global Settings
[global]
    printing = bsd
    printcap name = /etc/printcap
    load printers = yes
; The guest user is nobody
```

```
   guest account = nobody
   lock directory = /var/lock/samba
   share modes = yes
   workgroup = testgroup
   security = user

; Export All Home Directories to the Network
[homes]
   comment = Home Directories
   browseable = no
   read only = no
   preserve case = yes
   short preserve case = yes
   create mode = 0750

; Make All Printers Accessible on the Network
[printers]
   comment = All Printers
   path = /var/spool/samba
   browseable = no
   printable = yes
   public = no
   writable = no
   create mode = 0700

; Create Public read-only Directory
[public]
   path = /public/directory
   public = yes
   read only = yes
   printable = no

; Provide a Public Temporary Directory
[temp]
   path = /tmp
   read only = no
   public = yes

; Export a Private Workspace for user1, user2 and user3
[private]
   path = /private/directory
   valid users = user1 user2 user3
```

```
public = no
writable = yes
printable = no
create mask = 0765
```

Running Samba

If your network is running on TCP/IP, configuration is complete and you are ready to run Samba. However, if you have a NetBIOS network, you need to perform one more step. In the file /etc/services, look for the following lines (and if they aren't there, add them):

```
netbios-ns      137/tcp                   # NETBIOS Name Service
netbios-ns      137/udp
netbios-dgm     138/tcp                   # NETBIOS Datagram Service
netbios-dgm     138/udp
netbios-ssn     139/tcp                   # NETBIOS session service
netbios-ssn     139/udp
```

Now that you have Samba configured, it is time to run the software. By default, the Red Hat Linux version of Samba is installed to start at boot time so that it is always available. In addition, the system script /etc/rc.d/init.d/smb can be used to manually start and stop Samba.

For example, you can start Samba with the command

```
# /etc/rc.d/init.d/smb start
```

and stop it with the command

```
# /etc/rc.d/init.d/smb stop
```

The following two commands can be used on the command line by the root user to manually start Samba.

```
/usr/sbin/smbd -D
/usr/sbin/nmbd -D
```

Without a handy system script to stop Samba, you will probably have to use a brute-force combination of ps and kill to stop Samba:

```
# ps aux | grep smbd
root      929  0.0  1.0  1112   664  ?  S   13:47   0:00
/usr/sbin/smbd -D
# ps aux | grep nmbd
root      931  0.0  0.9   976   608  ?  S   13:47   0:00
/usr/sbin/nmbd -D
# kill 929 931
```

Accessing Windows Network Files and Printers from Linux Systems

The flip side of this procedure is for Linux to be able to access SMB shared files and printers. There are several ways in which this can be achieved. The simplest way involves use of two client programs that come with the Samba installation: smbclient and smbprint.

While this approach works, it is somewhat limited, particularly for file access. Smbclient provides an FTP-like way in which to access a remote share. Of course, this doesn't allow use of regular Unix commands such as cp and mv to manipulate files and, thus, prevents access to shares from other applications (unlike NFS-mounted remote file systems, which appear as local file systems to Linux applications).

This problem is effectively addressed using an alternative method: the smbfs package, which allows SMB shared file systems to be mounted on Linux, as NFS file systems and local file systems are.

Using *Smbclient*

The smbclient program is normally installed in /usr/bin. The program can be used to move files to and from shared resources on an SMB server using an FTP-like interface.

The first step to using `smbclient` is to establish a connection to a resource on the SMB server. In its simplest form, the command looks like this:

```
$ smbclient \\server\resourcename
```

Of course, things are rarely that simple. If you need to provide a password, for instance, to access a protected resource, your command gets somewhat more complicated:

```
$ smbclient \\server\resourcename password
```

In addition to this, there are several flags that alter the way in which `smbclient` connects to the server. The major flags are outlined in Table 29.2.

TABLE 29.2: Common Smbclient Flags

Flag	Effect
-L *host*	This flag displays a list of services available on a server specified by `host`; when using this flag, a resource does not need to be specified.
-I *IP_address*	This flag is useful when the address for the named server can't be looked up; it forces `smbclient` to assume the machine is at the specified IP address.
-N	This flag suppresses the password prompt. It is especially useful when a resource doesn't require a password; if this flag is not specified when a password is not required, the user is still prompted for a password and must press Enter to supply a null password.
-U *username*	Using this flag, you can specify the username to use to connect to a resource. Without this flag, the server uses the content of the USER or LOGNAME environment variables; if these are empty, no username is provided to the server. You can send a password along to the server by putting a percent sign (%) after the username and following it by the password: -U *username%password*.
-W *workgroup*	This flag specifies which workgroup is to be used when connecting to the server.
-T *tar options*	This flag allows you to move data into or out of a `tar` file on the local Linux system. For instance, `-Tx backup.tar` restores files from `backup.tar` to the remote share, while `-Tc backup.tar` creates a `tar` file called `backup.tar` that contains all files and directories in the remote share.

By way of example, let's build a `smbclient` command based on this information:

```
$ smbclient \\server\resourcename -U username%password -W workgroup
```

This command attempts to connect to resourcename on server in the workgroup named workgroup, with the user username using the password password.

Available Operations for File Resources

Once connected to a file resource, there are a number of commands available for moving data back and forth. These are outlined in Table 29.3.

TABLE 29.3: File Operation Commands

Operation	Description
cd *directory*	Changes to another directory on the SMB shared resource.
del *file*	Deletes the specified file on the server. (You can also use the **rm** command).
dir	Displays the current directory listing from the server. (You can also use the **ls** command).
get *file*	Gets the specified file from the remote server and saves it with the same name in the current directory on the local system; optionally, you can specify a different name for the file on the local system: **get** *file localfilename*.
lcd *directory*	Changes to the specified directory on the local system.
mget *filemask*	Gets all files on the remote server matching the specified filemask.
mkdir *directory*	Makes the specified directory on the remote server. (You can also use the **md** command).
mput *filemask*	Puts all files in the local directory matching the specified filemask into the current directory on the remote server.
prompt	Toggles prompting on and off for multiple file operations (**mput** and **mget**). When on, users are prompted for each file copied.
put *file*	Copies the specified file in the current local directory to the current directory on the remote server and keeps the name of the file the same; the name of the file on the remote server can also be changed: **put** *file remotefilename*.
quit	Exits **smbclient**. (You can also use the **exit** command.)
recurse	Toggles directory recursion on and off for multiple file operations (**mput** and **mget**). When on, the commands search through all directories under the current directory when copying files.
rmdir *directory*	Removes the specified directory from the remote server. (You can also use the **rd** command).

Let's look at some examples:

- To change the local directory to the subdirectory foo, use the command lcd foo.

- To change the remote directory to the directory ../foo, use the command cd ../foo.

- To copy the file foo in the local directory to the remote share and give the copy the name newfoo, use the command put foo newfoo.

- To get all files ending in .txt from the remote share's current directory, use the command mget *.txt.

- To create a new directory on the remote share called foo, use the command mkdir foo.

Available Operations for Printer Resources

When you use smbclient to connect to a printer resource, the following commands are available for working with the printer:

print file   Prints the specified file using the current resource based on the mode specified by printmode.

printmode option   Sets the printer mode based on the specified option; possible options are graphics or text, where graphics mode indicates any binary data.

queue   Displays the current status of the remote print queue.

quit (or **exit**)   Exits smbclient.

Of course, this is a little cumbersome. If someone wants to print a text file, they can't simply print it from the application they used to create it the way they might normally do with a Unix print queue. Instead, they need to connect to the printer with smbclient and then issue the command printmode text, followed by print *filename*. Printing more complicated print formats gets even more difficult.

For instance, what if the remote printer is a PCL printer and the software being used only generates PostScript output (as is often the case in the Unix world)? In that case, the user needs to print to a file, pass this file through gs to convert it to PCL, connect the printer with smbclient, set the print mode, and then print the file. This is a lot of work.

Luckily, smbprint helps to solve this problem.

Using *Smbprint*

The smbprint script is a tool that makes it possible to print using smbclient via a standard Unix print queue. Smbprint makes printing to remote SMB printer resources virtually seamless for users.

With most Samba installations, you will find the script at /usr/bin/smbprint.

In order to use this script, you need to create a printcap entry for the remote printer and create a configuration file that indicates where the printer is.

First, the printcap entry:

```
queuename:\
        :sd=/var/spool/samba:\
        :af=/var/spool/samba/accountingfile:\
        :if=/usr/bin/smbprint:\
        :mx=0:\
        :lp=/dev/null:
```

Let's look at the important entries here:

sd=/var/spool/samba   Specifies the spool directory.

af=/var/spool/samba/accountingfile   Specifies the accounting file. This file should be in the same directory as the configuration file, probably in your spool directory.

if=/usr/bin/smbprint   Specifies that the input filter should be smbprint.

lp=/dev/null   Indicates that the printer is not physically connected to the machine where the printcap file exists.

Next, you need to create a configuration file called .config in the same directory as your accounting file. This file contains three entries and looks like this:

```
server=SERVERNAME
service=PRINTERNAME
password="password"
```

Once this is done, most files should be printable using the lpr command:

```
$ lpr -P queuename filename
```

Because this is the way applications like Netscape Communicator handle printing, this configuration will work for many printers and applications.

Using *Smbfs*

The smbfs package allows the direct mounting of SMB shares to Linux in the same way that NFS volumes are mounted by Linux. Usage of smbfs is fairly straightforward once it is installed.

If you are using Red Hat Linux 6, then smbfs should be installed with Samba.

NOTE   If your installation doesn't have smbfs, you can download the latest version of smbfs from the Linux LAN Web page at http://samba.SerNet.DE/linux-lan/. This is a source distribution that can be difficult to install because it may require recompilation of the Linux kernel in order to work. To make things easier, try to find the binary version of smbfs that comes with Red Hat Linux 6.

Using *Submount*

At the core of the smbfs system is the smbmount program. The smbmount program is the tool you use to mount SMB shares to your Linux system.

At its most basic, smbmount takes the form:

```
# smbmount //servername/resourcename mountpoint
```

As with the mount command, the mount point must be an existing directory (which can be, and probably should be, empty) on your system. Forward slashes are used instead of back slashes in the specification of SMB shares to avoid problems using back slashes in some shells.

WARNING   There is one caveat here: smbmount doesn't use NetBIOS to look up the server name. Therefore, if the SMB server name is different than the TCP/IP host name for the server, things won't work. In this situation, use the Unix host name for the server in question.

The submount command can be followed by several options, the more common of which are outlined in Table 29.4.

TABLE 29.4: Submount Flags

Flag	Explanation
-n	Suppresses the password prompt where none is required.
-P password	Provides a password where one is required.
-s server name	If the NetBIOS is different than the Unix host name, use the Unix host name to specify the resource and then provide the NetBIOS name with the -s flag.
-c client name	If the local client's NetBIOS name and Unix host name are different, specify the NetBIOS name here.
-U username	Specifies the username to be used in accessing the SMB resource.
-D domain name	Specifies the SMB domain to use in accessing the resource.

For example, to mount the resource testdir on the SMB server smbserv to the local directory /smbdir as user user1 using the password testpass, you would use the command:

```
# smbmount //smbserv/testdir /smbdir -U user1 -P testpass
```

Complete documentation for the smbmount command is in the smbmount man page (man smbmount).

Connecting Linux to a Novell Network

The world of NetWare-Linux integration is far less robust than Windows-Linux integration. For that reason, this section will only discuss available options without going into the details of implementation.

In the realm of freely available software, a fairly limited Novell NetWare client package called ncpfs is available, as is a still-beta NetWare server product called mars_nwe. Both of these products are limited as to the versions of NetWare they support and the types of NetWare products they can interact with. Both are included with Red Hat Linux 6.

Together, ncpfs and mars_nwe provide the closest thing to a complete free Linux NetWare solution. Both are available for download from the Linux LAN Web page at http://samba.SerNet.DE/linux-lan/.

Both products have limitations, however. For example:

- Both are only NetWare 3.*x* bindery compatible.

- Ncpfs is not backward compatible with NetWare 2.*x* servers.

- Ncpfs does not work with some NetWare-compatible servers, such as Windows NT 3.51.

Looking Ahead

In this chapter, you learned how to integrate Linux into Windows intranets, enabling file sharing between Linux and Windows.

In the next chapter, you will take a look at an important topic in today's corporate world: the ability to run DOS and Windows software in Linux.

To a surprising extent, Linux is able to support DOS applications using its dosemu software. On top of that, efforts are under way, albeit still at an early stage, to write a Windows emulator called Wine that is capable of running 16-bit and 32-bit Windows applications. Although not ready for deployment as a tool for day-to-day work in a corporate environment, Wine can currently run Microsoft Word and other popular Windows applications. Chapter 30 discusses the features and uses of these two compatibility packages.

In addition, Chapter 30 will look at Wabi, a Windows emulation environment created by Sun Microsystems for the Solaris operating system and ported to Linux by Caldera. Wabi offers stable, reliable Windows 3.1 emulation and the certified ability to run dozens of popular Windows 3.1 applications.

C H A P T E R
T H I R T Y

Red Hat Linux 6 and DOS/Windows

- Running DOS Applications in Linux

- Windows with Wabi

- Why Not Wine?

- The Future of Wine

- Running a Virtual Machine with VMware

One of the biggest arguments against using Linux as a day-to-day operating system for productivity tasks such as word processing is that there is a lack of applications for Linux. Add to that the inability to run Windows applications (at least OS/2 can do that, right?) and Linux is just an oddity, a curious example of great technology with poor marketing.

The problem with this argument is that Linux *can* in fact run the majority of DOS applications and many Windows applications, and there is promise of even wider ranging Windows compatibility.

DOS support has been available for Linux for some time, and numerous popular DOS applications can be run under Linux with little effort.

Also, several efforts are currently under way to provide complete Windows compatibility within the Linux environment. Commercially, Sun Microsystems' Wabi environment has been ported to Linux by Caldera and is available at a very reasonable cost. But, in true Linux spirit, a team of Linux developers has taken up the task of delivering a freely available, better-than-commercial Windows compatibility package called Wine.

This chapter discusses all three endeavors: DOS emulation, Wabi, and Wine. In addition, this chapter will look at a new entry to the field called VMware, a virtual machine technology capable of running almost any PC operating system on top of a Linux system.

Running DOS Applications in Linux

Support for DOS applications is the strongest compatibility offering in Linux and is included with most Linux distributions.

Red Hat Linux 6 ships with the DOS emulation application DOSEmu. Under the DOSEmu environment, it is possible to install and run DOS, including recent versions such as DOS 6.2, and then run most DOS applications. There are limitations, of course, including those that affect some graphics and font operations, but overall, things work well.

In addition, a DOS environment can run inside a separate window in X Windows, making it easy to run DOS applications next to Linux programs.

Among the features offered by DOSEmu are the following:

- The ability for multiple users to run DOS applications simultaneously
- The ability to mount Unix directories to specific drive letters in the DOS environment
- The ability to print to Unix printer spools

Running DOSEmu

There are numerous configurations that can be used to run DOSEmu in Linux. These include:

- Booting DOS from a floppy disk
- Booting DOS from a disk image
- Booting DOS from a separate partition

For the sake of simplicity, and to get a glimpse into how the software works, this chapter only looks at booting DOS from a disk image. Advanced configurations, including booting from other media, are well covered in the documentation, which for Red Hat Linux 6 can be found at `/usr/doc/dosemu-0.99.10/`.

NOTE   Detailed information and documentation for DOSEmu is available at `http://www.suse.com/dosemu/`. You can also download the latest version of DOSEmu, with complete installation instructions, from this site.

NOTE   The publisher's edition of Red hat Linux 6 included with this book does not include some components of the full edition for space reasons. This includes DOSEmu. The installation files for DOSEmu can be downloaded from `http://www.redhat.com`.

In order to get DOS running, it is necessary to have a configuration file called `/etc/dosemu.conf`. This is a highly complex file that has extensive documentation.

However, Red Hat Linux 6 makes things easy, coming with a preconfigured disk image file and a `dosemu.conf` file designed to boot from that disk image. The disk image itself is located at `/var/lib/dosemu/hdimage`. It contains a free variant of DOS called FreeDOS and provides many useful commands and utilities, including `fdisk`, `format`, `unix2dos`, and `lredir` (a utility for redirecting Linux directories to DOS drive letters).

To get a sense of what is involved in configuring a typical DOSEmu environment, the following is the contents of the default Red Hat Linux 6 `dosemu.conf` file:

```
#####################################################################
➡#######
# This file is /etc/dosemu.conf, included by
➡/var/lib/dosemu/global.conf
#
# Linux DOSEMU configuration  for parser versions >= 3 (dosemu-
➡0.97.1)
#
# ./doc/README.txt (chapter 2.) contains a description of the syntax
# and the usage of dosemu.conf.
#
#
# Access rights are defined in
#
#       /etc/dosemu.users
#
#####################################################################
➡#######


# Notes for editing this section:
#
#    In     $_xxx = (n)     n is a numerical or boolean value
#                 =       =
#    In     $_zzz = "s"     s is a string
#
# Please edit only between the brackets and quotes and keep the rest
➡intact.
```

```
#         ^^^^^^^^^^^^^^^^^^^^^^^^^^^^^^^^^^^^^^^^^^^^^
➡^^^^^^^^^^^^^^^^^^^^^^^

$_debug = "-a"            # same format as -D commandline option
                         # (but without the -D in front)
$_features= ""           # list of temporary hacks, see release notes in
                         # the file ChangeLog. e.g "0:1 2:0", which
➡means
                         # to set feature_0 to 1 and feature_2 to 0.
$_timint = (on)          # emulate INT08 type timer interrupts
$_mathco = (on)          # or off
$_cpu = (80386)          # CPU emulation, valid values:  80[345]86

$_rdtsc = (off)          # if possible use Pentium cycle counter
$_cpuspeed = (0)         # 0 = calibrated by dosemu, else given
➡(e.g.166.666)
$_pci = (off)

$_xms = (1024)           # in Kbyte
$_ems = (1024)           # in Kbyte
$_ems_frame = (0xe000)
$_dpmi = (off)           # in Kbyte
$_dosmem = (640)         # in Kbyte, < 640
$_hardware_ram = ""      # list of segment values/ranges such as
                         # "0xc8000 range 0xcc000,0xcffff"

$_secure ="ngd"          # secure for: n (normal users), g (guest), d
➡(dexe)
                         # empty string: depending on 'restricted'
                         # "0": always insecure (not recommended)
$_odd_hosts = ""         # black list such as "lucifer.hell.com
➡billy.the.cat"
$_diskless_hosts=""      # black list such as "hacker1 newbee gateway1"

$_emusys = ""            # empty or 3 char., config.sys   -> config.XXX
$_emubat = ""            # empty or 3 char., autoexec.bat ->
➡autoexec.XXX
$_emuini = ""            # empty or 3 char., system.ini   -> system.XXX

$_hogthreshold = (1)     # 0 == all CPU power to DOSEMU
$_irqpassing = ""        # list of IRQ number (2-15) to pass to DOS such
➡as
```

```
                                 # "3 8 10"
    $_speaker = ""               # or "native" or "emulated"


    $_term_char_set = ""         # Global code page and character set selection.
                                 # "" == automatic, else: ibm, latin, latin1,
    latin2


    $_term_color = (on)          # terminal with color support
    $_term_updfreq = (4)         # time between refreshs (units: 20 == 1 second)
    $_escchar = (30)             # 30 == Ctrl-^, special-sequence prefix

    $_rawkeyboard = (0)          # bypass normal keyboard input, maybe dangerous
    $_layout = "us"              # one of: finnish(-latin1), de(-latin1), be,
    ➥it, us

                                 # uk, dk(-latin1), keyb-no, no-latin1, dvorak,
    ➥po

                                 # sg(-latin1), fr(-latin1), sf(-latin1), es(-
    ➥latin1)

                                 # sw, hu(-latin2), hu-cwi, keyb-user
                                 # hr-cp852, hr-latin2
    $_keybint = (on)             # emulate PCish keyboard interrupt


    $_X_updfreq = (5)            # time between refreshs (units: 20 == 1 second)
    $_X_title = "DOS in a BOX"   # Title in the top bar of the window
    $_X_icon_name = "xdos"       # Text for icon, when minimized
    $_X_keycode = (off)          # on == translate keybord via dosemu keytables
    $_X_blinkrate = (8)          # blink rate for the cursor
    $_X_font = ""                # basename from /usr/X11R6/lib/X11/fonts/misc/*
                                 # (without extension) e.g. "vga"
    $_X_mitshm = (on)            # Use shared memory extensions
    $_X_sharecmap = (off)        # share the colormap with other applications
    $_X_fixed_aspect = (on)      # Set fixed aspect for resize the graphics
    ➥window
    $_X_aspect_43 = (on)         # Always use an aspect ratio of 4:3 for
    ➥graphics
    $_X_lin_filt = (off)         # Use linear filtering for >15 bpp
    ➥interpolation
    $_X_bilin_filt = (off)       # Use bi-linear filtering for >15 bpp
    ➥interpolation
```

```
$_X_mode13fact = (2)      # initial size factor for video mode 0x13
➥(320x200)
$_X_winsize = ""          # "x,y" of initial windows size (defaults to
➥float)
$_X_gamma = (1)           # gamma correction
$_X_vgaemu_memsize = (1024)   # size (in Kbytes) of the frame buffer
➥for emulated vga
$_X_lfb = (on)            # use linear frame buffer in VESA modes
$_X_pm_interface = (on)   # use protected mode interface for VESA modes
$_X_mgrab_key = ""        # KeySym name to activate mouse grab, empty ==
➥off
$_X_vesamode = ""         # "xres,yres ... xres,yres"
                          # List of vesamodes to add. The list has to
➥contain
                          # SPACE separated "xres,yres" pairs


$_video = "vga"           # one of: plainvga, vga, ega, mda, mga, cga
$_console = (0)           # use 'console' video
$_graphics = (0)          # use the cards BIOS to set graphics
$_videoportaccess = (1)   # allow videoportaccess when 'graphics' enabled
$_vbios_seg = (0xc000)    # set the address of your VBIOS (e.g. 0xe000)
$_vbios_size = (0x10000)  # set the size of your BIOS (e.g. 0x8000)
$_vmemsize = (1024)       # size of regen buffer
$_chipset = ""            # one of: plainvga, trident, et4000, diamond,
➥avance
                          # cirrus, matrox, wdvga, paradise, ati, s3
$_dualmon = (0)           # if you have one vga _plus_ one hgc (2
➥monitors)


$_vbootfloppy = ""        # if you want to boot from a virtual floppy:
                          # file name of the floppy image under
➥/var/lib/dosemu
                          # e.g. "floppyimage" disables $_hdimage
                          #      "floppyimage +hd" does _not_ disable
$_hdimage
$_floppy_a ="threeinch"   # or "fiveinch" or "atapi" or empty, if not
➥existing
                          # optionally the device may be appended such as
                          # "threeinch:/dev/fd0"
```

```
$_floppy_b = ""              # dito for B:

$_hdimage = "hdimage.first" # list of hdimages under /var/lib/dosemu
                             # assigned in this order such as
                             # "hdimage_c hdimage_d hdimage_e"
                             # If the name begins with '/dev/', then partion
                             # access is done instead of virtual hdimage
➥such as
                             # "/dev/hda1" or "/dev/hda1:ro" for readonly
                             # Currently mounted devices and swap are
➥refused.
                             # Hdimages and devices may be mixed such as
                             # "hdimage_c /dev/hda1 /dev/hda3:ro"
                             # Note: 'wholedisk' is _not_ supported.
$_hdimage_r = $_hdimage # hdimages for 'restricted access (if
➥different)

$_aspi = ""                  # list of generic SCSI devices to make
➥available
                             # for the builtin aspi driver (format of an
➥entry
                             # is 'device:type:mappedtarget' such as
                             # "sg2:WORM sg3:Sequential-Access:6 sg4:CD-ROM"
➥or
                             # "sg2:4 sg3:1:6 sg4:5" (which are equal)

$_com1 = ""                  # e.g. "/dev/mouse" or "/dev/cua0"
$_com2 = ""                  # e.g. "/dev/modem" or "/dev/cua1"
$_com3 = ""                  # dito               "/dev/cua2"
$_com4 = ""                  # dito               "/dev/cua3"
$_ttylocks = ""              # Lock directory (e.g. "/var/lock")
                             # default ("") is /usr/spool/uucp

$_mouse = ""                 # one of: microsoft, mousesystems, logitech,
➥mmseries
                             # mouseman, hitachi, busmouse, ps2
$_mouse_dev = ""             # one of: com1, com2, com3, com4 or /dev/mouse
$_mouse_flags = ""           # list of none or one or more of:
                             # "emulate3buttons cleardtr"
```

```
$_mouse_baud = (0)        # baudrate, 0 == don't set

$_printer = "lp"          # list of (/etc/printcap) printer names to
➡appear as
                          # LPT1, LPT2, LPT3 (not all are needed, empty
➡for none)
$_printer_timeout = (20)# idle time in seconds before spooling out

$_ports = ""              # list of portnumbers such as "0x1ce 0x1cf
➡0x238"
                          # or "0x1ce range 0x280,0x29f 310"
                          # or "range 0x1a0,(0x1a0+15)"

$_ipxsupport = (off)      # or on
$_novell_hack = (off)
$_vnet = (off)            # 'on' for packet-multi (used by dosnet)

$_sound = (off)           # sound support on/off
$_sb_base = (0x220)
$_sb_irq = (5)
$_sb_dma = (1)
$_sb_dsp = "/dev/dsp"
$_sb_mixer = "/dev/mixer"
$_mpu_base = "0x330"
```

Launching DOS

The simplest way to run DOSEmu is using the dos command from the console or inside an xterm window. When you issue the command

```
$ dos
```

DOSEmu loads and boots from the specified boot device in /etc/dosemu.conf. By default, in Red Hat Linux 6, this means booting from the provided disk image file. Figure 30.1 shows the DOS prompt in an xterm window after the dos command has been issued.

FIGURE 30.1:

Running DOS in an xterm window

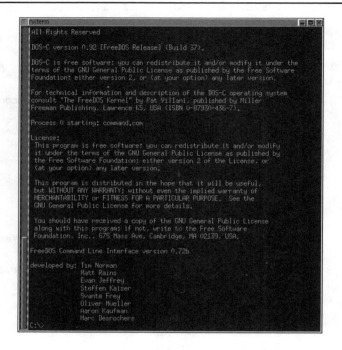

Once DOS is running, you can use standard DOS commands and syntax to run programs from floppy disks or, as you will see later in this chapter, to run applications contained in redirected directories.

Launching DOS in a Separate X Window

In addition to running DOS in the current window, DOS can be launched in its own window when running X Windows. You can do this by running the command

```
$ xdos
```

The xdos command is actually a link to the main dos binary file. Running the program through the xdos link has the same effect as the command

```
$ dos -X
```

Running DOS in its own X window produces results like those in Figure 30.2.

FIGURE 30.2:

Running DOS in its own
X window

Useful DOSEmu Commands

The disk image that comes with DOSEmu, which Red Hat Linux 6 boots from by default, contains several useful commands and utilities including those outlined in the following table. These commands and many others can be found in the c:\bin and c:\dosemu directories when running DOSEmu using the default disk image.

TABLE 30.1: Selected DOSEmu Commands

Command	Description
eject.com	Ejects the CD-ROM drive.
emumouse.com	Tunes the DOSEmu mouse driver.
exitemu.com	Exits DOSEmu.
lredir.com	Redirects a Unix directory to a DOS drive letter.
unix.com	Executes a Linux command from within DOSEmu.

Mounting Directories with *Lredir*

For DOSEmu to be useful, it needs to do more than work with disk images or floppy disks. It must be able to access parts of the Linux directory structure as if they were DOS disk drives. This ability allows your DOS environment to access data and applications that are stored on any existing DOS or Linux partitions or hard drives on your system.

The first step of the process takes place before the DOSEmu environment is launched: you need to make sure that the partitions you want to access are mounted at a logical location in your Linux directory structure. For instance, if you have an existing DOS partition, you could mount it at /dos.

Once all the directories and partitions you want to make available are accessible in Linux, you can start your DOS environment with

```
$ dos
```

or

```
$ xdos
```

Once DOS is running, use the lredir command to redirect Linux directories to DOS drive letters. The basic syntax of the lredir command is:

```
$ lredir driveletter: linux\fs/linuxdirectory
```

This command causes the specified Linux directory to be made available in DOS using the specified drive letter. For instance, to make a DOS partition mounted as /dos in Linux available in your DOSEmu environment as D:, use the command

```
$ lredir D: linux\fs/dos
```

> **NOTE** Lredir is in the c:\dosemu directory when using the default disk image from Red Hat. If this directory is not on your path, either use the complete path for the command (c:\dosemu\lredir) or make c:\dosemu your current director.

Another useful application of lredir is to make users' home directories available to them on a pre-specified DOS drive letter. To do this, use the following variation on the lredir command you just saw:

```
$ lredir E: linux\fs\${HOME}
```

In this command, a user's home directory is obtained from the Linux environment variable HOME, where Red Hat stores the current user's home directory.

Finally, if you are booting initially from the provided disk image but want all booting from the loading of the config.sys file onward to occur from another location (such as a mounted DOS partition), you can use a simple two-step trick:

1. Edit the config.sys file on the initial disk image that is used to boot the DOSEmu environment. Make the following line the first line of the file (assuming the DOS partition is mounted under Linux at /dos):

   ```
   install=c:\dosemu\lredir.exe c: linux\fs/dos
   ```

2. Make sure the config.sys files on the disk image and the DOS partition are identical. This means including the line from step 1 in the config.sys file on your DOS partition.

Now, before executing the rest of config.sys and then autoexec.bat, the disk image is unmounted and the DOS partition is redirected to C: in the DOS environment.

Windows with Wabi

While it is great to be able to run DOS applications, for most users, the ability to run at least a handful of major Windows applications is more important than being able to run the majority of DOS applications.

Two main solutions are available for doing this: Wabi, which this section will discuss, and Wine, which is discussed in the next section.

Wabi is a product that originated with Sun Microsystems, which developed it as a way to run Windows 3.1 and critical Windows 3.1 applications on their Sun

Solaris platform. The program has since been ported to Linux and is available from Caldera (`http://www.calderasystems.com`). You don't need to use Caldera's OpenLinux to run Wabi; it should work fine on most other modern Linux distributions. In fact, 75 percent of this book was written using Microsoft Word 6 for Windows running through Wabi on a Red Hat Linux 6 system (the other 25 percent used Wine instead of Wabi to run Word 6, but you'll hear about that later).

NOTE   It is important to note that Wabi, unlike most software for Linux described in this book, is a commercial product. That means it is not available for free download from the Internet and must be purchased.

This section will describe the capabilities of Wabi. If you are interested in more information, visit the Caldera Web site mentioned previously. The software comes with a manual and clear installation instructions.

How Wabi Works

The concept behind Wabi is really quite simple: it translates Microsoft Windows' calls into X Windows and Linux calls, displaying windows and applications that look strikingly similar to Windows 3.1 in the X Windows environment. Figure 30.3 shows an X Windows desktop with an `xterm` window overlapping Windows' Program Manager.

Luckily, because both Windows and Linux with Wabi run on Intel's x86 processors, the vast majority of commands in a Windows program (which are general x86 instructions, not Windows specific) can be sent directly to the processor for processing. It is only those Windows-specific calls that Wabi has to handle in a special way, converting them to the appropriate Linux or X Windows instructions and requests.

Wabi allows copying and pasting between Windows applications and X Windows applications, supports object linking and embedding between Windows applications, supports Windows sockets networking, and can access the PC's serial and parallel ports.

FIGURE 30.3:

Wabi and X Windows can
co-exist

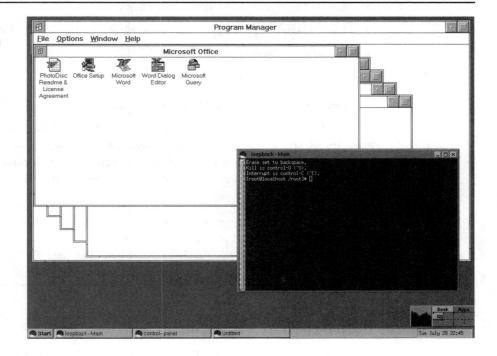

In some ways, though, Wabi provides even better Windows than Windows 3.1 itself. Because Wabi is running in the true multiuser, multitasking environment of Linux, it allows the following benefits that are missing in Windows 3.1:

- True multitasking of Windows applications
- Capability for multiple users to run Windows applications simultaneously on the same system
- Remote display of Windows applications (using the X Windows environment)

In addition, Wabi supports a useful drive-mapping capability in which any mounted Linux directory can be mapped to any drive letter under Windows, giving Wabi users access to their important Linux files.

Limitations of Wabi

Of course, Wabi is not a perfect environment. Several limitations make Wabi unsuitable for some potential users. These limitations include the following:

- Lack of support for MIDI audio devices

- Lack of support for NetWare networks
- Lack of support for applications requiring Windows VGA display drivers
- Inability to format floppy disks
- Lack of support for virtual device drivers
- Lack of support for Adobe Type Manager

In addition, Wabi cannot run the 32-bit Windows applications popular in Windows 95, 98, and NT, which limits its usefulness to older versions of popular applications. Sun Microsystems is no longer actively developing Wabi, so it is unlikely to have support for newer Windows applications in the future.

> **NOTE** It is also important to note that Wabi is not a Windows emulator. A licensed copy of Windows 3.1 and the original installation disks are necessary to complete the Wabi installation process. You need to use these disks to install Windows 3.1 on your Linux system.

Wabi Application Support

Wabi is designed to provide full support for a list of certified applications. For a complete list, you can visit the Caldera Wabi Web page at `http://www.caldera-systems.com/products/wabi`. The current list of supported applications include those shown in the following table.

TABLE 30.2: Wabi-Supported Windows 3.1 Applications

Application	Versions
CorelDRAW!	3, 4
Harvard Graphics	2, 3
Lotus 1-2-3	4, 5
Lotus Ami Pro	3.1
Lotus cc:Mail client	23, 2.2
Lotus Approach	2.1, 32

Continued on next page

TABLE 30.2 CONTINUED: Wabi-Supported Windows 3.1 Applications

Application	Versions
Lotus Freelance Graphics	21, 2.1
Lotus Notes client	3c, 3.3
Lotus SmartSuite	3.1, 4
Lotus WordPro	96
Microsoft Access	2
Microsoft Excel	4, 5
Microsoft Mail client	3.2
Microsoft Office	4.3
Microsoft PowerPoint	3, 4
Microsoft Project	3, 4
Microsoft Schedule+	1
Microsoft Word	2, 6
PageMaker	4, 5
Paradox	4.5, 5
Procomm Plus	12, 2.11
Quattro Pro	5, 6
Quicken	3, 4
Quicken Deluxe	4
WordPerfect	6a, 6.1

In addition to the list of certified applications, there are numerous other applications that are known to run in Wabi, but that are not certified by Sun Microsystems or Caldera.

Why Not Wine?

Wine is a completely different product than Wabi for two reasons: it is not commercial and it aims to provide a completely free environment in which to run Windows applications on Linux systems.

The latter point is especially significant. While current development versions of Wine still rely on an existing Windows installation for some of the Windows system files, the goal of the project is to provide a complete alternative: If you install Wine on your Linux system, you won't need to install any version of Windows to run Windows applications.

As is typical of many open-source Linux applications, Wine is under constant development and revision and is considered pre-release software. In fact, the release notes for Wine indicate that the software is considered development code, and should be used with caution. The Wine home page is at `http://www.winehq.com/`; new releases of Wine happen frequently and you can always get the latest version from this Web site.

The compilation, configuration, and installation of Wine reflect this early development phase. Even so, it is possible to get some heavy-duty Windows applications, including Word 6, to run under Wine (25 percent of this book was written this way).

The Future of Wine

The Wine team has a lot of plans for the Wine project that make it significant. These plans include:

- Being able to run Windows 3.1, 95, 98, and NT software on major PC Unix platforms, including Linux, FreeBSD, OpenBSD, and Solaris.

- Being able to run Windows applications without having an installed, licensed version of Windows available. Wine plans to provide a complete alternative set of system DLLs that are free of Microsoft code. You can still use your original Windows system DLLs if you have them, but they won't be required when Wine is finished. Planned support includes:

  - Partial DirectX support for Windows games

- Full GDI support

- Support for native Windows 16-bit printer drivers

- Support for Winsock networking

- Support for scanners

- Limited support for Unicode

- Support for multiple languages

Wine is officially alpha developers-only code, and is not yet suitable for general use. Nevertheless, many people find it useful to run many different Windows applications in Linux, with some versions of Wine supporting a surprising range of Windows applications.

Running a Virtual Machine with VMware

During the writing this book, a new possibility for running Windows software became available: VMware for Linux (`www.VMware.com`).

VMware is a virtual machine technology. What it does is create a virtual computer which uses all of your existing PC's resources to provide a complete virtual computer running inside of a window into which you can install practically any operating system that would normally run directly on your PC's hardware.

The first release of VMware can run DOS, Windows 3.1, Windows 95, Windows 98, any flavor of Windows NT 4, plus popular Unix distributions for PCs such as FreeBSD and Linux. Because you are installing and running the real operating system in what appears to the operating system to be a full-blown hardware PC, compatibility is almost never an issue. This provides a powerful way to run multiple operating systems on your Linux system for development, testing, and compatibility purposes. You can even run multiple instances of VMware at the same time, each running a different operating system.

Of course, powerful hardware is an issue. To get reasonable performance, you need fast Pentium II or Pentium III CPUs and a lot of memory since Linux and any client operating systems you run with VMware will have to share the available memory.

By way of example, the system I used to write this book has VMware installed and I use it to run Windows NT Workstation 4, Windows 3.11 for Workgroups and other distributions of Linux, when I need to check details of those distributions for different writing projects.

Looking Ahead

In this chapter, you learned about several available paths for running your existing Windows and DOS applications in Linux. With each passing week, support for Windows and DOS applications under Linux improves and it may not be too long before most off-the-shelf Windows applications can be run fairly successfully on a well-configured Linux system.

The next chapter will look at an interesting topic: how to use Linux as an inexpensive router. As a robust networking operating system, Linux is ideally suited to act as a router for a small network, connecting it to the Internet through a regular modem or ISDN connection or connecting to another LAN as an inter-LAN router.

Specifically, you will consider a typical example for many small offices: connecting an entire LAN to the Internet on a dial-up connection that provides only one real IP address.

Security and Red Hat Linux 6 As an Inexpensive Router

- Basic Security Issues

- Creating a Linux-Based Router

This chapter will address two related topics: security and connecting networks to the Internet.

You will learn about Linux security at several levels, first considering how to keep individual Linux systems secured and then discussing the broader issue of keeping a LAN secure when it is connected to the Internet.

In addition, you will take a look at the Linux Router Project, which allows you to use a single floppy disk containing a special distribution of Linux to create a Linux-based router that can act as a gateway between your network and your existing Internet connection.

Basic Security Issues

The area of computer security is a huge one that cannot be addressed adequately in a single chapter of a book. In fact, entire books are devoted to only small areas of computer and network security.

Given the scope of the subject, this section discusses computer security in general and points out the basic concepts that you can consider applying to your specific circumstances.

Securing a Stand-Alone System

If you have a stand-alone Linux system, your security needs are the most basic. Because the system is not connected to a LAN and, assuming that you connect to the Internet through a modem, is not left connected permanently or for long periods of time, your security concerns are relatively minor.

Still, there are some fundamental security issues that you should address:

- Make sure your passwords are sufficiently complex that they can't be guessed or cracked easily. This includes combining letters and numbers and other characters into non-word passwords. Passwords should also be changed frequently. It is especially important that your root password be a non-word, complex password that is changed regularly. (A complex passwords includes combinations of uppercase and lowercase letters as well as numbers and punctuation to make it difficult to guess)

- Make sure your computer is kept physically secure. If it contains important data, don't leave it in an unlocked office while you go to lunch. Similarly, don't walk out of the office and leave the system logged in, especially if you have logged in as the root user at the console or in a terminal window.

- Do not create unnecessary user accounts. If only two people use the system on a regular basis, create accounts only for those users and not for anyone else. This makes it easier to keep track of who is using the system and where any security violations originate.

- Most important of all, do not share passwords (user or root), even with people who are authorized to use the system on a regular basis. Especially keep the root password secure. All it takes is the wrong user obtaining the root password and you could find all the data on your system erased one day.

- Because no system can be completely secure, consider encrypting important data. There are many tools for doing this, including PGP encryption. A step-by-step guide to PGP encryption can be found on the Internet at the Linux Focus Web site at `http://mercury.chem.pitt.edu/~angel/LinuxFocus/English/November1997/article7.html`.

Securing a Linux System on a LAN

The instant you connect your Linux system to a LAN, new security issues appear. After all, even if you follow all the rules outlined previously for a stand-alone system (which you should also follow when the system is on a LAN), it is still possible for the intent hacker to gain access to your Linux system by exploiting any number of security weaknesses via the network.

Two simple policies can help minimize this problem:

- Do not run unnecessary network services. If you do not need to allow users to telnet into your system, make sure the Telnet daemon (probably `/usr/sbin/in.telnetd`) is not installed and there is no entry for the daemon in `/etc/inetd.conf`. Similarly, if your machine does not act as a mail server, consider not running the `sendmail` daemon, which can open up several unwanted security holes. The same rules go for most network services: FTP, finger, news, DNS, and many others. Only run those network service daemons that are necessary to connect to the network and perform the tasks that you are using your Linux system for.

- Make effective use of /etc/hosts.allow and /etc/hosts.deny, which are discussed in Chapter 28, "Configuring Red Hat Linux 6 for an Ethernet Network." Not only should you deny access from all IP addresses to all the services you chose not to run in the previous point, but you should be sure you are only allowing incoming access to services that you are running to hosts with permission to use those services. For instance, if you are running an FTP server to allow incoming FTP access by only two users, allow just those two systems access to the FTP service instead of allowing any user on your LAN to make an FTP connection.

Keeping Your Network Secure

Even if you keep your Linux system fairly secure on your LAN, if your LAN is connected to the Internet, the rest of your network is open to a wide range of possible security threats and attacks.

Keeping a network secure is a large job and requires detailed knowledge of network security. Fundamentally, though, there are two main techniques (and many variations on them) for ensuring at least minimal network security.

Remember that your network will be connected to the Internet through some type of router that has the job of moving data on and off the LAN as appropriate. Generally, a router can provide some level of security to ensure that the most malicious attacks cannot infiltrate your LAN.

Router-level protection is usually provided in one of two ways:

Using a packet-filtering firewall *Packet filtering* is a process that every router is capable of performing. Whenever a packet of information from the Internet is received by the router and is destined for a system on the LAN, the originating IP address, the destination IP address, and the port of the connection are examined and compared to a table to determine whether the packet is allowed into the LAN. If the packet is not allowed, it essentially vanishes into the ether. In this way, connections from specific hosts, to specific hosts, or for specific ports (or any combination of these) can be allowed or denied.

Using a proxy firewall A *proxy firewall* is a different approach because it prevents direct connections between the machines inside the firewall and those on the Internet. If a host on your LAN makes a connection to a host on the Internet, it actually connects to the proxy system and then the proxy system makes the actual connection to the system on the Internet, serving as the relay for all data traveling back and forth. Similarly, if you allow any incoming connections to your LAN, the proxy plays the same role of middleman. In addition to keeping the LAN and the Internet totally separate, the proxy firewall has capabilities similar to a packet-filtering firewall. It can be configured to allow only certain types of traffic through the firewall in either direction, or to deny connections on the basis of several variables, including originating IP address, destination IP address, and port being used.

To really understand the fundamentals of network security, you should read the Linux Security HOWTO at `http://metalab.unc.edu/LDP/HOWTO/ Security-HOWTO.html`.

A Linux system can easily be configured to act as a router between your LAN and the Internet, providing connections over standard analog phone modems or ISDN lines. This router can also be configured to act as a packet-filtering or proxy firewall as well. Setting up a Linux-based router generally costs less than buying complete hardware router solutions and offers more security options than do many hardware-based routers.

Creating a Linux-Based Router

This section will walk you through the steps for creating a Linux-based router using the Linux Router Project's distribution of Linux.

Designed as a minimalist Linux installation, the Linux Router Project's distribution of Linux can fit on a single 1.44MB floppy disk for most sites and provides all the components needed to route between two Ethernet LANs or between an Ethernet LAN and the Internet via PPP. With add-on modules, support is available for additional hardware for WAN connections. Other features such as SNMP management are also available.

The benefit of setting up a router using the Linux Router Project's Linux distribution instead of full-scale versions of Linux such as Red Hat is that all the hard work has been done for you. You won't need to make the effort to identify what needs to be installed to get routing to work. In addition, the software includes a simple, menu-driven configuration system that allows you to check that everything that needs configuration is done.

The Linux Router Project software is available on the Web site for this book at `http://linux.juxta.com/`. For complete information, updates, and add-ons for the router distribution, visit the Linux Documentation Project Web site at `http://www.linuxrouter.org/`.

What You Will Create

You will use the Linux Router Project software to create a router that serves as a firewall, protecting the private areas of your LAN from the Internet. This procedure that you will follow makes two assumptions:

- You have an existing Internet connection, most likely through a leased line and an existing router or through an ISDN connection and an ISDN router.

- You want to allow some incoming access to servers on your network. For instance, you may have a Web server that the public should be able to access, but you don't want any incoming access to the sensitive file, application, and database servers on the rest of your network.

Given these assumptions, your network arrangement will resemble Figure 31.1.

FIGURE 31.1:

A typical firewall-protected network

Notice that the router connecting you to the outside world provides looser protection than does the router between your unsecure and secure networks. This means that, at the worst, only the systems sitting on your unsecure network are directly open to possible attacks from outside. Because your second router, between the unsecure and secure LANs, does not allow incoming connections into the secure network, your systems are—as far as this is possible in a networked environment— safe from outside attack.

It is this second router, between the unsecure and secure LANs, that you will implement using the Linux Router Project software.

Getting Ready

To prepare the Linux Router Project floppy disk, you need a blank floppy disk. (Any data on the floppy disk will be erased, so be sure there is nothing there that you want to keep). The following instructions assume you are creating the disk from within an existing Linux system.

1. Download the Linux image file and save it in a convenient location, for instance, /tmp/disk.img.

2. Change your current directory to the directory containing the downloaded file with a command such as cd/tmp.

3. Copy the disk image file to your floppy disk using a dd command like this: dd if=disk.img of=/dev/fd0.

Once this is done, you have a boot floppy disk for the Linux Router Project distribution.

Be sure you have sufficient hardware to run the router. While a 386SX with 8MB of RAM can function as a router and a 486DX2 66MHz with 12MB of RAM will be respectable, these days you really want to run a Pentium 100MHz or faster system with at least 16MB of RAM. No hard drive is needed, just a floppy drive to boot from. If you want to add many add-ons to your Linux Router Project configuration, then the software may exceed the size of your floppy disk, in which case consider booting from a hard disk or a bootable Zip drive and increasing your RAM to 32MB. Details of how to boot from other media can be found on the Linux Router Project home page.

The PC needs to have two Ethernet cards. One will be used to connect to the unsecure network and the other will connect to the secure network.

The Operating Environment

Before starting the Linux router software, let's define the environment in which the router will run so that the configuration you perform later makes sense.

First, you need to determine IP addresses. Your unsecure network will use the addresses 200.200.200.0 through 200.200.200.255 with the netmask 255.255.255.0. The router connecting the network to the outside world is at 200.200.200.1, and the router you will build has the IP address 200.200.200.254 on the unsecure side of the router. These are genuine IP addresses in that the rest of the Internet knows they exist and they are unique on the Internet. If your router to the external world allows it, machines on the Internet can communicate directly with any host on the unsecure LAN.

Your secure network will use the addresses 10.10.10.0 through 10.10.10.255 with the netmask 255.255.255.0. The router connecting the secure and unsecure LANs will use the IP address 10.10.10.1 on the secure side of the router. These are fake, or non-routable, IP addresses. The rest of the world doesn't know about the existence of hosts on the internal network, and no direct communication is possible with hosts on the internal network; your router, in its firewall role, hides the existence of the secure network from the rest of the world (including your unsecure network).

In the router you are building, the device `eth0` will be connected to the unsecure LAN (with IP address 200.200.200.254) and the device `eth1` will be connected to the secure LAN (with the IP address 10.10.10.1).

You will allow only outgoing connections from the secure LAN—no incoming connections. What's more, you will use a feature of the Linux kernel known as *IP masquerading* in order to implement a security feature known as *network address translation*. Under network address translation, the router not only handles the work of routing data into and out of the secure LAN but, when a machine inside the secure LAN makes a connection through the router, it also hides the IP address of that machine and translates it into an address on the unsecure LAN. In this way, the connection cannot be traced back to the real IP address of the host, thus helping to hide the existence of hosts on the secure network from the rest of the world.

Because the secure network uses non-routable IP addresses, the hosts on your unsecure network do not know about the existence of hosts on that network and cannot attempt to communicate with them. Similarly, the router connecting the unsecure network to the Internet doesn't know about the existence of the internal, secure network and so will never route packets directly to hosts on the internal network.

Starting the Linux Router

To boot your computer as a Linux-based router, simply insert the floppy disk and restart your computer. Your computer should boot from the floppy disk.

The Linux Router Project software then creates a RAM disk and loads the contents of the boot disk into the RAM disk. Then the entire router runs from RAM. Any configuration changes you make can be saved back to the boot disk so that the next time you boot, your configuration is retained.

After you boot, you are prompted to log in. Log in as the root user with no password and the Linux router software starts, presenting you with a configuration menu. Let's walk through the steps to get a minimal network running as described previously:

1. Basic settings: Configuration of the IP addresses, network masks, and routes of the two Ethernet cards

2. Basic security: Configuration of the network security needed to implement network address translation

3. Further configuration: Configuration of additional network parameters, such as nameservers and host tables

The menus are entirely numeric and are accessed by typing the number of a selection and pressing Enter. For instance, typing 1 for Network Settings on the main configuration menu causes the network settings submenu to be displayed. Selecting an entry on a submenu opens the file for editing (for configuration purposes) in a simple editor. To use the editor effectively, you really only need to know how to save (press Ctrl+W and then press Enter to confirm the filename) and quit (press Ctrl+C). You can use the editor to do more than this, but you are only going to perform basic editing tasks here.

Configuring Basic Network Settings

The first thing to do is configure your basic network settings: tell your router who you are, which interface is connected to which network, and so on.

To do this, you need to edit the main network settings file, option 1 on the network settings submenu (accessed by selecting option 1 on the main configuration menu). The main network settings file opens in the editor.

First, you need to assign IP addresses and network masks to your Ethernet cards. Find the lines

```
#IF0=eth0
IPADDR0=192.168.1.1;          NETMASK0=255.255.255.0
BROADCAST0=192.168.1.255      NETWORK0=192.168.1.0
```

Change them to the correct settings for eth0 and activate the interface by removing the # from the first line:

```
IF0=eth0
IPADDR0=200.200.200.254;       NETMASK0=255.255.255.0
BROADCAST0=200.200.200.255     NETWORK0=200.200.200.0
```

Next, find the lines

```
#IF0=eth1
IPADDR0=192.168.2.1;          NETMASK0=255.255.255.0
BROADCAST0=192.168.2.255      NETWORK0=192.168.2.0
```

and likewise change them to the correct settings for eth1 (your internal, secure network) and remove the hash mark:

```
IF0=eth1
IPADDR0=10.10.10.1;           NETMASK0=255.255.255.0
BROADCAST0=10.10.10.255       NETWORK0=10.10.10.0
```

These steps configure the respective Ethernet cards in the router to communicate with their assigned networks. (Make sure the Ethernet cards are physically connected to the correct networks.)

Other sections of the configuration file set up default routes without requiring additional configuration.

Setting Up Basic Security

Basic security setup takes place in the same file as basic network setup, so for this reason you haven't saved the file yet.

First, an overview of the default setting. The router is configured by default to deny all traffic across the router. In addition, *IP spoofing*—where an external host pretends to be a host on the secure network by feigning the same IP addresses—is monitored and prevented.

What you need to do is use network address translation to explicitly allow outgoing traffic from the secure network. To do this, find the section of the file called IP Masquerade (aka NAT) and uncomment the first entry:

```
#[ "IF$" ] && ipfwadm -F -a -m -S "$NETWORK1"/24 -D 0.0.0.0/0
```

Without going into the syntax of ipfwadm (which you can find at http://kac.poliod.hu/cgi-bin/dwww?type=man&location=/usr/man/man8/ipfwadm.8.gz), note that this command does the following:

- Enables IP forwarding for outgoing connections from the secure network to the outside world.

- Enables IP masquerading so that the source address of all outbound connections is the external IP address of the router, rather than the original host address on the secure network.

- Handles all return connections to make sure that data in response to an outgoing connection is returned to the correct host.

Now you can save the file (Ctrl+W) and quit the editor (Ctrl+C).

Further Network Configuration

There are other network settings that you would be wise to configure. They include:

- Giving the router a host name (number 2 on the network settings submenu)

- Providing a host table (number 3 on the network settings submenu)

- Providing a correct resolv.conf file (number 6 on the network settings submenu)

Configuration of these settings should be straightforward on the basis of what you learned in Chapter 28, "Configuring Red Hat Linux 6 for an Ethernet Network."

A final note: the hosts.allow and hosts.deny files are designed to protect the router itself from unwanted attack by denying attempts to log in to the router remotely across the network. In other words, the router needs to be configured at the console rather than through a network login. It is probably wise to leave these files unchanged.

Saving Your Changes

Once you have configured the router, it is necessary to save your changes back to the boot floppy. You can do this by choosing b from the main configuration menu. You are backing up the etc module because you have changed files in the /etc directory only. You can do this by selecting 2 from the backup menu.

After writing the changes back to the boot floppy, you are ready to reboot your system to enable your new configuration. Now you should have a functioning router serving as a basic firewall.

Going Further

Using these basic principles, it is possible to work with the Linux Router Project distribution to implement (among other things) more advanced routers that support ISDN connections, dial-up PPP users, and leased-line Internet connections. These all require additional combinations of modules and system-specific configuration. More information is available on the Linux Router Project Web site at http://www.linuxrouter.org.

Looking Ahead

In this chapter, you saw how flexible Linux is, allowing you to turn a PC into not just a powerful workstation or network server, but also a router and a security firewall.

In the next chapter, you will continue your look at Linux in a networked environment with a detailed discussion of how to use Linux as an intranet Web server. Linux is an increasingly popular platform for Internet and intranet Web servers because of the availability of high-performance, industry-standard Web server software that can be run on inexpensive hardware.

In fact, the reliability and speed of Linux Web servers makes them popular in many circumstances where high-cost, commercial Web server solutions could have been used.

If you don't have a background in Web development or design, the chapter still provides the basic knowledge you need to begin setting up your own Web server in your organization.

PART VII

Using Red Hat Linux 6 As a Web, Database, and E-Mail Server

CHAPTER

THIRTY-TWO

Building Your Own Web Server

- What is a Web Server?

- Linux Web Servers

- Installing Apache

- Configuring Apache

- Managing Your Web Server

- Building a Web Site

You've come a long way in your study of Linux and you are now ready to look at one of the most popular applications of Linux: using the operating system as the basis for small and medium-sized Web servers.

In fact, Linux is widely used for deploying Web servers for a number of reasons:

- It provides the flexibility and manageability of Unix.
- It costs little or nothing to set up and run.
- It provides a strong breadth of tools for building fairly sophisticated Web sites.

This chapter will cover the basics of turning a Linux PC into a Web server for an intranet or Internet site. It starts with an overview of the job played by a Web server and then examines some of the major Web servers available for Linux.

You then get detailed information about installing, configuring, and managing the Apache Web server, arguably the most popular Web server on the Internet and the one that currently ships with Red Hat Linux 6.

This chapter closes by taking a guided tour through the building of a simple Web site using Apache. By the end of the chapter, you should be in a position to create your own Web site using Linux and Apache and feel confident enough to experiment with other Web servers available for Linux.

What Is a Web Server?

If you have used the Web at all, you have probably heard the term "Web server" bandied about, but may not have a clear picture of what a Web server does.

While it is often the case that a term serves a dual purpose, referring to physical machines as well as the software they run, "Web server" correctly refers to the software that can be run to answer requests from Web clients such as Web browsers.

Web server software is designed to serve a simple purpose: to answer requests from clients, using the Hypertext Transfer Protocol (HTTP), for documents available from the Web site being handled by that software.

What happens is this: The client requests a document using a URL; the Web server receives the request, maps the URL to a physical file on the system (which could be an HTML file or any one of numerous other file types), and then, after making sure that the client has permission to retrieve the file, returns the file to the client. In addition, the Web server generally keeps logs of who has requested which documents and how many times requests were made, allowing for the production of statistics used to determine how popular Web sites are.

More Than Just Retrieving Files

The description above is overly simplistic, but that explanation serves to describe the work done by the majority of Web servers most of the time.

Of course, as you browse the Web, you quickly become aware that the Web is more than simply a set of static documents that a Web server sends to Web browsers on request. Forms can be used to request information from the server or provide information to the organization running the server. Products can be ordered, credit cards can be verified, and many other types of transactions can take place.

In order for all this interactivity to occur, modern Web servers must do more than simply answer HTTP requests. Web servers generally provide two mechanisms for interactions:

- The Common Gateway Interface (CGI)
- Server application program interfaces (APIs)

The Common Gateway Interface (CGI)

CGI is the most widely deployed method for adding interactivity to a Web server. Under the CGI model, a very simple extension is added to the HTTP protocol for requesting static files.

CGI provides a standardized method for causing a program to be run on the server and for data from a form to be passed to the program for processing. These programs can be written in almost any programming or scripting language—C, Perl, and Java are commonly used.

When a user requests a CGI program—possibly by submitting a form or by clicking a link to the program—the Web server passes the user's data to the CGI program and waits for the program to return data. Any data returned by the program is passed straight back to the client in the same way that the contents of a static file are returned to a browser. It is the program's job to produce valid content to be returned to the browser and to handle all contingencies so that valid content is returned to the client.

Overall, the CGI concept has worked quite well. The simplicity of the way data is passed from the server to the CGI program, and the way in which the program needs to build the data it returns to the server, means that simple CGI programs can be written with little programming experience.

In addition, it is easy to change and test CGI programs, since popular scripting languages such as Perl can be used to write them.

The standard nature of the CGI interface also means that a CGI script or program written for one Linux Web server will likely function without alteration on any other Linux Web server—and possibly on any other Unix server—if it is written using a language commonly found in all operating systems.

Still, for all its advantages, CGI suffers from some serious drawbacks that make it unattractive for some Web sites. Its two main weaknesses pertain to security and speed.

Since the emergence of the Web, significant security holes in the CGI interface have been discovered that, if a script is poorly written, can allow a system running a Web server to be completely accessible to a knowledgeable hacker. This makes CGI less than desirable where the security of the data on the Web server is paramount, as it would be on most corporate Internet and intranet servers—and especially on sites offering online financial transactions and credit card sales.

In addition, the CGI interface is not very efficient. The Web server runs one or more processes that answer client requests. The browser then starts child processes for the CGI program, passing data to this new process and waiting for it to finish. On a busy site, this can lead to large numbers of new processes needing to start in short periods of time, especially where CGI scripts are being heavily used. Each request for a CGI program leads to a separate process for each request.

This is a highly inefficient way to process large amounts of data and requests, and it's the reason why many leading Web servers have implemented their own APIs for writing server-side programs.

Application Program Interfaces

APIs provide a way to write programs that integrate tightly into the Web server and generally don't require new processes for each request.

API has enabled the development of Web-based applications that are capable of handling large numbers of requests as compared to similar CGI-based solutions. In addition, API-based solutions have been the subject of less criticism with regard to security.

API-based programs can generally do the same jobs as CGI programs do, such as processing information provided in forms, accessing data in databases, and verifying credit cards.

The biggest disadvantage of server APIs is that they commit an application to a particular Web server. Moving an application to a new server can require significant reprogramming, and with a large application this can be impractical.

Just remember that a server needs to be well tested with regard to security, performance, and flexibility before you deploy a large application on it using the server's built-in API.

Linux Web Servers

The Unix world is where the Web emerged, so it isn't surprising that Unix platforms enjoy the broadest choice of available Web servers.

As with most things in the Unix world, this same range of Web servers is available for Linux. The majority of Linux Web servers are free. The most well-known Linux Web servers are:

- NCSA httpd
- Apache
- AOLserver
- Boa
- WN
- W3C/Cern

In addition to these free servers, there are several commercial alternatives available for Linux, including:

- FastTrack
- Java Web Server
- Stronghold
- Zeus

Apache

By some counts, Apache is the most widely used Web server software. Standing for "A Patchy Server," Apache grew out of efforts to patch NCSA httpd, one of the original Web servers, to fix some problems and add functionality.

Since then, Apache has emerged as the non-commercial server of choice for Unix systems. More recently, it has been ported to Windows and can be used as a Web server on Windows NT systems.

Apache offers numerous features that make it attractive for Unix system administrators. Besides using a configuration based on the original NCSA httpd configuration files, Apache is available in full source code and is collectively developed, like many other popular applications for the Linux environment.

Apache offers its own API, which can be used as an alternative to CGI (which is also supported by Apache). In addition, the API can be used to produce plug-in modules that serve numerous purposes. Among the available modules are:

- Alternative authentication systems, including authentication from NIS authentication servers or from LDAP (Lightweight Directory Access Protocol) databases

- Server-side scripting environments that serve the same function as Microsoft Active Server Pages or Netscape LiveWire, including PHP/FI and HeiTML

- Modules designed to improve the performance of traditional CGI. For instance, the FastCGI module uses shortcuts to minimize the time it takes to execute a CGI program and return the results. The Perl module allows Perl scripts to run in a single process and to be compiled on first execution only, making Perl-based CGI perform almost as fast as compiled CGI programs and some API-based Web applications.

The original source code for the latest version of Apache is available from www.apache.org, along with precompiled binaries for many different systems including Linux. Apache is included as the default Web server installed with Red Hat Linux 6.

NCSA Httpd

NCSA httpd is one of the two original Web servers (along with the Cern Web server) upon which the Web was first built. NCSA httpd comes out of the National Center for Supercomputer Applications at the University of Illinois at Urbana-Champaign, which is also the home of Mosaic, the original graphical Web browser that launched the Web onto the road to widespread popularity.

NCSA httpd offers a core set of functions designed to meet the needs of all but the most demanding of Web sites. These features include built-in support for multiple hosts, Basic and Digest authentication, directory-level access controls, server-side includes, and full CGI support.

The original source code and precompiled binaries for NCSA httpd are available from `hoohoo.ncsa.uiuc.edu`.

AOLserver

AOLserver has an interesting history, moving from a commercial offering in 1995 to one of the most full-featured free servers currently available.

AOLserver started its life as NaviPress, one of the first commercial servers available. In late 1995, AOL acquired the company producing NaviPress and began to use the server internally. In early 1997, AOL released the server as a free product for distribution on the Internet.

At the time of this writing, the latest release (2.2) of AOLserver included the following features:

- Built-in full-text indexing for offering a search function on a Web site
- A built-in API that is accessible from C and the Tcl scripting language
- Full CGI and server-side include support
- Server-side dynamic page functionality similar to Microsoft's Active Server Pages
- Database connectivity for building database-driven dynamic applications without needing third-party Web-database integration tools

AOLserver can be downloaded from the AOLserver Web site at `www.aolserver.com/server/index.html`.

W3C/Cern

The Cern Web server was one of the first Web servers to be created. After all, the Web was born at Cern, and the Cern server was the platform for this fledgling Web.

Now the server is distributed as a public-domain server by the World Wide Web Consortium (W3C), the Internet standards body that defines such standards as HTML and cascading style sheets.

In terms of overall features, the Cern server doesn't have a lot in it to recommend it against today's crop of servers. Many of today's free servers are derived from the NCSA server and follow its style of configuration and management. Cern is decidedly different from these, and many Webmasters prefer the NCSA approach.

Probably the most compelling feature of the W3C server is that it can perform the role of both a Web server and a proxy server, allowing users behind a firewall to access the Internet. The server continues to be used as a proxy by many sites.

The W3C maintains a page about the server at `www.w3.org/Daemon`.

WN

This chapter's survey of free servers is now moving toward less commonly used servers. Still, these niche market servers help you to see the diversity possible in Web server technology and features.

WN is another freely available server with unique features that set it apart from other Web servers. For instance, WN allows full text searching of what the developer refers to as a *logical HTML document*: a document that consists of more than one file. In addition, users can search files on the server and easily obtain matching documents. Users can also download a single logical document made up of multiple linked documents, making it easy for them to print files that are structured as a series of small documents.

Another unique feature of the WN server is its ability to serve up conditional documents. That is, it is possible to create a single document with definitions that cause the correct version to be sent to a client on the basis of such variables as the IP address of the client or the browser version of the client.

The security model of the WN server also sets it apart from the likes of Apache and the NCSA httpd Web server. In the latter servers, the default action is to serve a file unless permission is specifically denied. With WN, no file is served unless permission is specifically granted for the file. This potentially makes the server more secure and provides finer-grained control over access to files.

You can get a copy of WN at `hopf.math.nwu.edu`.

Boa

The last free Web server in our survey is the Boa server. This is a little-known server that is still in a pre-1 release as of the writing of this book.

Boa is included here to show that servers can be small, simple, and basic and still serve a useful role. Boa offers very basic functionality and less fine-grained access control than Apache or WN.

But Boa is designed in a way that makes it potentially faster than almost any other available Web server for Linux. In fact, the creators of Boa claim that the server is twice as fast as Apache, although more real-world testing on large Web sites is needed to prove this claim.

Boa achieves this performance gain through a single-tasking design. Where traditional Web servers create multiple processes to listen for requests, and then create a process to handle each request, the Boa server runs as a single process and handles all the processing and juggling of multiple requests internally rather than allowing the operating system's multitasking mechanism. Boa only spawns a child process when a CGI request is made.

You can learn more about Boa at `www.boa.org`.

Stronghold

Stronghold is probably one of the best-known commercial Web servers for Linux. Stronghold is a commercially available version of Apache that offers full support as well as a feature lacking in the free version of the server: SSL support.

SSL support, or support for the Secure Sockets Layer, is necessary for creating the secure browser-server links used in online shopping applications, or for anywhere data moving from client to server and back needs to be encrypted and hidden from prying eyes.

Stronghold provides all the tools you need to set up a secure server, including Certificate Authority tools. With a Certificate Authority you can, if necessary, issue digital certificates approved by a third-party certificate authority such as VeriSign.

In addition, since Stronghold comes with full source code, you can use it for everything you use Apache for, including compiling in Apache modules and writing your own modules.

Stronghold is distributed by C2 Software, which is on the Web at `www.int.c2.net`.

FastTrack

FastTrack is one of Netscape's well-known families of Web servers. Unfortunately, until its recent decision to release its browser and browser source code into the public domain, Netscape never had any interest in developing Web servers for noncommercial operating systems such as Linux.

Instead, for less popular operating systems, Netscape would license their servers to other companies, which would port the server. In the case of Linux, the FastTrack server has been ported by Caldera, which sells the server and bundles it with some versions of their OpenLinux product.

FastTrack is an easy-to-manage Web server. All configuration and administration is done through Web-based forms. These forms allow a Webmaster to do everything from creating users to controlling access to files at the directory level.

FastTrack provides support for server-side includes, CGI, and Netscape's own API for developing applications. In addition, FastTrack can support Netscape's server-side JavaScript development environment, LiveWire.

The server is also capable of being used as a secure server using SSL technology.

TIP   If you want to learn more about the Linux version of FastTrack or want to place an order, contact Caldera at `www.calderasystems.com`.

Java Web Server

The Java Web Server from Sun's JavaSoft division is a unique Web server on this list. Instead of being developed specifically for Linux, the Java Web Server is developed fully in Java and can theoretically run on any platform with a Java Virtual Machine.

The Java Web Server offers numerous features that make it a competitive commercial offering, including a server applet framework for writing applications without falling back on CGI, and full support for SSL so that the server can be used in secure applications such as online storefronts.

To help improve performance, it is possible to produce compiled pages that contain both HTML and program code. For statistical purposes, user sessions can be tracked in programs using a built-in server tracking mechanism.

You can read the complete specifications of the Java Web Server at the JavaSoft home page at www.javasoft.com.

Zeus

The final Web server discussed in this survey is the Zeus Web server.

Zeus is a Web server for Unix and Windows NT. It offers built-in clustering support, which clearly positions it as a potential choice for high-volume sites. With clustering, it is possible to serve a single Web address from multiple Web servers. This allows the load of requests to be distributed over a group of servers and it means that more simultaneous hits can be handled.

In addition, Zeus offers support for ISAPI, the API from Microsoft's Internet Information Server, and offers this support on Unix as well as Windows NT. Zeus also supports Java servlets like those used in the Java Web Server, and offers integrated database connectivity using the JDBC standard for accessing databases.

Perhaps most interesting is that Zeus offers SSL with full 128-bit encryption worldwide. Because the U.S. government limits the export of 128-bit encryption technology, the majority of secure products being exported by U.S. companies have offered only watered-down 40-bit encryption. Most reported occurrences of people cracking the encryption of products such as Netscape have involved the 40-bit encryption versions of products.

Zeus information is available at www.zeus.co.uk.

Installing Apache

The rest of this chapter will take a detailed look at the Apache Web server, for two reasons:

1. The Apache server is the default Web server that ships with Red Hat Linux (including Red Hat Linux 6 on the CD-ROM accompanying this book).

2. Since Apache is the most popular Web server currently on the Internet, it will most likely be the Web server you want to use.

If you performed a reasonably complete installation when you set up your Linux system, in all likelihood you already have Apache installed. There are several ways you can check this. You can use the `rpm` command:

```
$ rpm -qa | grep apache
```

If you have Apache installed, you should get back a result like:

```
apache-1.3.6-7
```

If you get back an indication that Apache is installed, you can skip forward to the section titled "Configuring Apache."

Installing Apache from the Red Hat CD-ROM

The simplest way to install Apache is from the Red Hat CD-ROM that comes with this book. In order to do this, simply mount the CD-ROM (normally at `/mnt/cdrom`) and then `cd` to the directory `/mnt/cdrom/RedHat/RPMS`. (If you mounted your CD-ROM somewhere other than `/mnt/cdrom`, you need to change to the appropriate directory based on your mount point.) This directory contains all the rpm files for the complete Red Hat Linux distribution. Here you simply use `rpm` to install the package:

```
$ rpm -i apache-1.3.6-7.rpm
```

Downloading the Latest Version of Apache

If you plan to run a mission-critical or high-volume Web server, you may want to download the latest version of Apache from www.apache.org (see Figure 32.1). By using the latest version, you can be sure that small bugs that wouldn't affect the average site won't come to plague your more complex or heavily used site.

FIGURE 32.1:

The Apache Web site

All discussion of configuration and management of Apache assumes that you are using the version of Apache on the Red Hat CD-ROM included with this book. Generally, new versions of Apache are backward compatible. That is, the configuration files you look at in this chapter should work with newer versions of Apache.

When downloading Apache from the Apache Web site, you have the option to download either the original source code or precompiled binary files for Linux. While there are compelling reasons to use the source code version, especially if you plan to develop programs using the Apache API or you want to build extra modules into your server, you should download the precompiled binaries to set up a Web site with the basic Apache feature set. This book won't discuss compiling your own copy of Apache, since this requires a much deeper discussion of Web servers than can be provided in a single chapter.

If you want to obtain the latest binary distribution from Apache, point your browser to the Apache Web site (`www.apache.org`) and select the Download link there. This leads to a directory of files and a link called Binaries. After following the Binaries link, select your operating system (in our case, Linux). Here you will find a list of available files. At the time of writing, this list was as follows:

```
apache_1.3.1-sparc-whatever-linux.README
apache_1.3.1-sparc-whatever-linux.tar.gz
apache_1.3.6-armv41-whatever-linux2.README
apache_1.3.6-armv41-whatever-linux2.tar.gz
apache_1.3.6-i586-whatever-linux2.README
apache_1.3.6-i586-whatever-linux2.tar.gz
apache_1.3.6-i686-whatever-linux2.README
apache_1.3.6-i686-whatever-linux2.tar.gz
apache_1.3.6-mips-whatever-linux2.README
apache_1.3.6-mips-whatever-linux2.tar.gz
apache_1.3.6-sparc-whatever-linux2.README
apache_1.3.6-sparc-whatever-linux2.tar.gz
```

From these filenames, notice that the current version is Apache 1.3.6. The i586 and i686 designations indicate that the package has been compiled with optimizations for either Pentium- or Pentium II-class processors.

The README files are text files; it is a good idea to read them before downloading. The .gz files are compressed using the gzip utility. Once you have your chosen package downloaded, expand the file in a temporary location. You can use the command

```
$ tar xzvf apache-file-name
```

to expand the archive into a subdirectory of the current directory. In this case, the subdirectory is called apache_1.3.6, but this may be different depending on the version of Apache that is available when you download the binaries. Inside this directory is the complete source code for the version you have downloaded, along with sample configuration files and full documentation in HTML format.

In order to install the binaries you have downloaded, you need to run the install-bindist.sh installation script from the top-level directory of the expanded archive:

```
$ install-bindist.sh
```

By default, this command installs the Apache server in /usr/local/etc. This differs from Red Hat, which places the configuration files in /etc/httpd/conf and makes `/home/httpd/html` the root directory for Web documents. This chapter assumes the Red Hat defaults since this is what you will find if you install Apache from the CD-ROM included with the book.

The binary Apache distributions include complete instructions for compiling the application from the included source code, so if you find that the binaries you have downloaded are not working as expected (perhaps because of problems such as incompatible libraries in your version of Linux), you may want to follow those instructions and try building your own Apache binaries.

Configuring Apache

Prior to version 1.3.6, Apache was configured using three main configuration files: `httpd.conf`, `srm.conf`, and `access.conf`. In the standard Red Hat installation of Apache, these files are found at `/etc/httpd/conf/`, although this location can easily be changed (as you will see later when this chapter discusses starting the Apache Web server). From version 1.3.6, these three files are combined into a single file: `httpd.conf`. This combined file combines the purposes of all three files and the content is essentially the same as the original three files combined.

The roles of these three configuration files are not very clearly defined and there is some overlap, but essentially they are used as follows:

- `httpd.conf`: This file is used to set general settings such as the port number used by the server as well as to load modules into the server when it starts. This file also indicates the location of the `srm.conf` and `access.conf` files.

- `srm.conf`: This file sets other general settings such as the root document tree of the server and the rules related to CGI programs.

- `access.conf`: This file can be used to set access control restrictions for the server or for specific directories.

Let's discuss the handful of major settings that any Webmaster should consider before running Apache on an open Web server. In these examples, you will use the Apache 1.3.4 server that was included in a pre-release version of Red Hat Linux 6. This version of Apache uses the three separate configuration files.

Httpd.conf

The structure of the httpd.conf file is fairly straightforward. Below is a listing from a sample Web site:

```
##
## httpd.conf - Apache HTTP server configuration file
##

# This is the main server configuration file. See URL
➥http://www.apache.org/
# for instructions.

# Do NOT simply read the instructions in here without understanding
# what they do, if you are unsure consult the online docs. You have
➥been
# warned.

# Originally by Rob McCool

# Dynamic Shared Object (DSO) Support
#
# To be able to use the functionality of a module which was built as a
DSO you
# have to place corresponding `LoadModule' lines at this location so
➥the
# directives contained in it are actually available _before_ they are
used.
# Please read the file README.DSO in the Apache 1.3 distribution for
➥more
# details about the DSO mechanism and run `httpd -l' for the list of
➥already
# built-in (statically linked and thus always available) modules in
➥your httpd
# binary.
#
# Example:
# LoadModule foo_module libexec/mod_foo.so
#
# Documentation for modules is in "/home/httpd/manual/mod" in HTML
➥format.
```

```
#LoadModule mmap_static_module modules/mod_mmap_static.so
LoadModule env_module          modules/mod_env.so
LoadModule config_log_module   modules/mod_log_config.so
LoadModule agent_log_module    modules/mod_log_agent.so
LoadModule referer_log_module  modules/mod_log_referer.so
#LoadModule mime_magic_module   modules/mod_mime_magic.so
LoadModule mime_module         modules/mod_mime.so
LoadModule negotiation_module  modules/mod_negotiation.so
LoadModule status_module       modules/mod_status.so
LoadModule info_module         modules/mod_info.so
LoadModule includes_module     modules/mod_include.so
LoadModule autoindex_module    modules/mod_autoindex.so
LoadModule dir_module          modules/mod_dir.so
LoadModule cgi_module          modules/mod_cgi.so
LoadModule asis_module         modules/mod_asis.so
LoadModule imap_module         modules/mod_imap.so
LoadModule action_module       modules/mod_actions.so
#LoadModule speling_module      modules/mod_speling.so
LoadModule userdir_module      modules/mod_userdir.so
LoadModule proxy_module        modules/libproxy.so
LoadModule alias_module        modules/mod_alias.so
LoadModule rewrite_module      modules/mod_rewrite.so
LoadModule access_module       modules/mod_access.so
LoadModule auth_module         modules/mod_auth.so
LoadModule anon_auth_module    modules/mod_auth_anon.so
#LoadModule dbm_auth_module      modules/mod_auth_dbm.so
LoadModule db_auth_module      modules/mod_auth_db.so
LoadModule digest_module       modules/mod_digest.so
#LoadModule cern_meta_module    modules/mod_cern_meta.so
LoadModule expires_module      modules/mod_expires.so
LoadModule headers_module      modules/mod_headers.so
LoadModule usertrack_module    modules/mod_usertrack.so
#LoadModule example_module      modules/mod_example.so
#LoadModule unique_id_module    modules/mod_unique_id.so
LoadModule setenvif_module     modules/mod_setenvif.so

# Extra Modules
#LoadModule php_module          modules/mod_php.so
#LoadModule php3_module         modules/libphp3.so
#LoadModule perl_module         modules/libperl.so
```

```
#   Reconstruction of the complete module list from all available
➡modules
#   (static and shared ones) to achieve correct module execution order.
#   [WHENEVER YOU CHANGE THE LOADMODULE SECTION ABOVE UPDATE THIS, TOO]
ClearModuleList
#AddModule mod_mmap_static.c
AddModule mod_env.c
AddModule mod_log_config.c
AddModule mod_log_agent.c
AddModule mod_log_referer.c
#AddModule mod_mime_magic.c
AddModule mod_mime.c
AddModule mod_negotiation.c
AddModule mod_status.c
AddModule mod_info.c
AddModule mod_include.c
AddModule mod_autoindex.c
AddModule mod_dir.c
AddModule mod_cgi.c
AddModule mod_asis.c
AddModule mod_imap.c
AddModule mod_actions.c
#AddModule mod_speling.c
AddModule mod_userdir.c
AddModule mod_proxy.c
AddModule mod_alias.c
AddModule mod_rewrite.c
AddModule mod_access.c
AddModule mod_auth.c
AddModule mod_auth_anon.c
#AddModule mod_auth_dbm.c
AddModule mod_auth_db.c
AddModule mod_digest.c
#AddModule mod_cern_meta.c
AddModule mod_expires.c
AddModule mod_headers.c
AddModule mod_usertrack.c
#AddModule mod_example.c
#AddModule mod_unique_id.c
AddModule mod_so.c
AddModule mod_setenvif.c
```

```
# Extra Modules
#AddModule mod_php.c
#AddModule mod_php3.c
#AddModule mod_perl.c

# ServerType is either inetd, or standalone.

ServerType standalone

# If you are running from inetd, go to "ServerAdmin".

# Port: The port the standalone listens to. For ports < 1023, you will
# need httpd to be run as root initially.

Port 80

# HostnameLookups: Log the names of clients or just their IP numbers
#    e.g.   www.apache.org (on) or 204.62.129.132 (off)
# The default is off because it'd be overall better for the net if
➥people
# had to knowingly turn this feature on.

HostnameLookups off

# If you wish httpd to run as a different user or group, you must run
# httpd as root initially and it will switch.

# User/Group: The name (or #number) of the user/group to run httpd as.
#   On SCO (ODT 3) use User nouser and Group nogroup
#   On HPUX you may not be able to use shared memory as nobody, and the
#   suggested workaround is to create a user www and use that user.
#   NOTE that some kernels refuse to setgid(Group) or semctl(IPC_SET)
#   when the value of (unsigned)Group is above 60000;
#   don't use Group nobody on these systems!

User nobody
Group nobody

# ServerAdmin: Your address, where problems with the server should be
# e-mailed.

ServerAdmin user1@juxta.com
```

```
# ServerRoot: The directory the server's config, error, and log files
# are kept in.
# NOTE!  If you intend to place this on a NFS (or otherwise network)
# mounted filesystem then please read the LockFile documentation,
# you will save yourself a lot of trouble.

ServerRoot /etc/httpd

# BindAddress: You can support virtual hosts with this option. This
➥option
# is used to tell the server which IP address to listen to. It can
➥either
# contain "*", an IP address, or a fully qualified Internet domain
➥name.
# See also the VirtualHost directive.

#BindAddress *

# ErrorLog: The location of the error log file. If this does not start
# with /, ServerRoot is prepended to it.

ErrorLog logs/error_log

# LogLevel: Control the number of messages logged to the error_log.
# Possible values include: debug, info, notice, warn, error, crit,
# alert, emerg.

LogLevel warn

# The following directives define some format nicknames for use with
# a CustomLog directive (see below).

LogFormat "%h %l %u %t \"%r\" %>s %b \"%{Referer}i\" \"%{User-
➥Agent}i\"" combined
LogFormat "%h %l %u %t \"%r\" %>s %b" common
LogFormat "%{Referer}i -> %U" referer
LogFormat "%{User-agent}i" agent

# The location of the access logfile (Common Logfile Format).
# If this does not start with /, ServerRoot is prepended to it.
```

```
CustomLog logs/access_log common

# If you would like to have an agent and referer logfile uncomment the
# following directives.

#CustomLog logs/referer_log referer
#CustomLog logs/agent_log agent

# If you prefer a single logfile with access, agent and referer
➥information
# (Combined Logfile Format) you can use the following directive.

#CustomLog logs/access_log combined

# PidFile: The file the server should log its pid to
PidFile /var/run/httpd.pid

# ScoreBoardFile: File used to store internal server process
➥information.
# Not all architectures require this.  But if yours does (you'll know
➥because
# this file is created when you run Apache) then you *must* ensure that
# no two invocations of Apache share the same scoreboard file.
ScoreBoardFile /var/run/httpd.scoreboard

# The LockFile directive sets the path to the lockfile used when Apache
# is compiled with either USE_FCNTL_SERIALIZED_ACCEPT or
# USE_FLOCK_SERIALIZED_ACCEPT. This directive should normally be left
➥at
# its default value. The main reason for changing it is if the logs
# directory is NFS mounted, since the lockfile MUST BE STORED ON A
➥LOCAL
# DISK. The PID of the main server process is automatically appended to
# the filename.
#
#LockFile /var/lock/httpd.lock

# ServerName allows you to set a host name which is sent back to
➥clients for
# your server if it's different than the one the program would get
➥(i.e. use
# "www" instead of the host's real name).
```

```
#
# Note: You cannot just invent host names and hope they work. The name
➥you
# define here must be a valid DNS name for your host. If you don't
➥understand
# this, ask your network administrator.

ServerName linux.juxta.com

# UseCanonicalName:  (new for 1.3)  With this setting turned on,
➥whenever
# Apache needs to construct a self-referencing URL (a url that refers
➥back
# to the server the response is coming from) it will use ServerName and
# Port to form a "canonical" name.  With this setting off, Apache will
# use the hostname:port that the client supplied, when possible.  This
# also affects SERVER_NAME and SERVER_PORT in CGIs.
UseCanonicalName on

# CacheNegotiatedDocs: By default, Apache sends Pragma: no-cache with
➥each
# document that was negotiated on the basis of content. This asks proxy
# servers not to cache the document. Uncommenting the following line
➥disables
# this behavior, and proxies will be allowed to cache the documents.

#CacheNegotiatedDocs

# Timeout: The number of seconds before receives and sends time out

Timeout 300

# KeepAlive: Whether or not to allow persistent connections (more than
# one request per connection). Set to "Off" to deactivate.

KeepAlive On

# MaxKeepAliveRequests: The maximum number of requests to allow
# during a persistent connection. Set to 0 to allow an unlimited
➥amount.
# We reccomend you leave this number high, for maximum performance.
```

```
MaxKeepAliveRequests 100

# KeepAliveTimeout: Number of seconds to wait for the next request

KeepAliveTimeout 15

# Server-pool size regulation.  Rather than making you guess how many
# server processes you need, Apache dynamically adapts to the load it
# sees -- that is, it tries to maintain enough server processes to
# handle the current load, plus a few spare servers to handle transient
# load spikes (e.g., multiple simultaneous requests from a single
# Netscape browser).

# It does this by periodically checking how many servers are waiting
# for a request.  If there are fewer than MinSpareServers, it creates
# a new spare.  If there are more than MaxSpareServers, some of the
# spares die off.  These values are probably OK for most sites --

MinSpareServers 8
MaxSpareServers 20

# Number of servers to start -- should be a reasonable ballpark figure.

StartServers 10

# Limit on total number of servers running, i.e., limit on the number
# of clients who can simultaneously connect -- if this limit is ever
# reached, clients will be LOCKED OUT, so it should NOT BE SET TOO LOW.
# It is intended mainly as a brake to keep a runaway server from taking
# Unix with it as it spirals down...

MaxClients 150

# MaxRequestsPerChild: the number of requests each child process is
#  allowed to process before the child dies.
#  The child will exit so as to avoid problems after prolonged use when
#  Apache (and maybe the libraries it uses) leak.  On most systems,
➥this
#  isn't really needed, but a few (such as Solaris) do have notable
➥leaks
#  in the libraries.
```

```
MaxRequestsPerChild 100

# Proxy Server directives. Uncomment the following line to
# enable the proxy server:

#ProxyRequests On

# To enable the cache as well, edit and uncomment the following lines:

#CacheRoot /var/cache/httpd
#CacheSize 5
#CacheGcInterval 4
#CacheMaxExpire 24
#CacheLastModifiedFactor 0.1
#CacheDefaultExpire 1
#NoCache a_domain.com another_domain.edu joes.garage_sale.com

# Listen: Allows you to bind Apache to specific IP addresses and/or
# ports, in addition to the default. See also the VirtualHost command

#Listen 3000
#Listen 12.34.56.78:80

# VirtualHost: Allows the daemon to respond to requests for more than
➥one
# server address, if your server machine is configured to accept IP
➥packets
# for multiple addresses. This can be accomplished with the ifconfig
# alias flag, or through kernel patches like VIF.

# Any httpd.conf or srm.conf directive may go into a VirtualHost
➥command.
# See also the BindAddress entry.

#<VirtualHost host.some_domain.com>
#ServerAdmin webmaster@host.some_domain.com
#DocumentRoot /www/docs/host.some_domain.com
#ServerName host.some_domain.com
#ErrorLog logs/host.some_domain.com-error_log
#TransferLog logs/host.some_domain.com-access_log
#</VirtualHost>
```

The first thing you should notice is that this file consists of comments and actual configuration entries. Comments are preceded by the hash mark (#). Configuration entries consist of an entry name followed by an entry value.

Loading Modules

Let's look at the more important entries and sections in the `httpd.conf` file. The first main section consists of a series of `LoadModule` directives followed by a series of `AddModule` directives. Apache's functionality is created and extended through the use of modules. In earlier versions of Apache, these modules were combined into the executable Apache `httpd` file. With version 1.3 of Apache, it is now possible to create modules that load at the time the server starts.

Because most of these modules are configured through directives in one of the three configuration files, it is important that all relevant modules are loaded before any other directives occur in the `httpd.conf` file (which loads first before `srm.conf` and `access.conf`).

For most basic installations, the default module list is fine and you won't need to change it. If you need to extend or change the functionality of your Web server, consult the on-line Apache documentation at `www.apache.org` for more information on adding loadable modules and using the `LoadModule` and `AddModule` directives.

ServerType

The first directive you will learn about is `ServerType`. The Apache server can run in two ways: in a `standalone` mode with its own processes listening for connections or in `inetd`, which you saw in the section on networking. In the `inetd` mode, `inetd` listens for connections and then starts an Apache process when a connection comes. If this is your first time running a Web server, you are best off running Apache in `standalone` mode unless you are familiar with `inetd` and have compelling reasons for running the server in this way.

Port

The second important entry is the `Port` entry. By default, a Web server is supposed to run on port 80. When a browser requests a URL without a port, it assumes that the URL is being requested from a server on port 80.

Because of the vulnerability of processes running below port 1024, if you are running a Web server that is not being made publicly available on the Internet and want to avoid the risks associated with these ports, you can try running the server on a port above 1024. Common ports for these types of Web servers are 8000 and 8080, but you can choose any free port.

User and *Group*

The User and Group entries are critical entries because they affect the very security of your system. Normally, the httpd process is fired by the root account, but this process does not listen for connections. Rather, this process launches one or more child processes as the user and group (which are specified by name or ID number) indicated with these configuration directives.

This is done because all processes fired by the Web server, including CGI programs, would otherwise be run as root. This would pose a huge security risk, especially if a poorly written CGI script leaves a large security hole. By running the Web server and its related children as a user with limited power, it is possible to limit these security holes.

The normal operation is to run the Web server as nobody with a group of nobody or #-1. I generally use user nobody and group nobody, since they are easily identifiable when reading the configuration file. This user has limited privileges on the system, and potential hackers can wreak only limited havoc if a CGI script lets them into the system.

ServerRoot

ServerRoot is used to indicate the base directory where configuration files and logs for the server can be found. Red Hat sets this up in the directory /etc/httpd. Inside this directory is a conf directory containing the three configuration files plus a logs directory as a link to /var/logs/httpd.

You are free to move the directory anywhere on your system to match the style of management you are using. However, it is usually easiest to keep things where your distribution of Linux puts them.

ServerName

The ServerName configuration directive identifies the host name returned to clients with the pages they request. This is one of the legitimate names for your

Web server as identified in a DNS record or host table on your network. In an intranet environment, you can define a host name in host tables using NIS, or in the DNS server for your site. For an Internet Web server, you should make sure that the name you indicate here is a valid name in your domain's DNS record. If you aren't sure, consult with your domain name records manager.

In the case of the example file, ServerName is linux.juxta.com.

ServerAdmin

This directive indicates the e-mail address of the administrator of the Web site. When the server generates an automated error message, such as one indicating that a page is not found, then this e-mail address is usually added to the page indicating who to contact to report the problem.

Make sure that this is a valid address and that the address is the correct one for the server's administrator.

Srm.conf

The srm.conf file has the same basic structure as the httpd.conf file. The srm.conf file for linux.juxta.com is shown here:

```
##
## srm.conf - Apache HTTP server configuration file
##

# With this document, you define the name space that users see of your
➥http
# server.  This file also defines server settings which affect how
➥requests are
# serviced, and how results should be formatted.

# See the tutorials at http://www.apache.org/ for
# more information.

# Originally by Rob McCool; Adapted for Apache


# DocumentRoot: The directory out of which you will serve your
```

```
# documents. By default, all requests are taken from this directory,
➥but
# symbolic links and aliases may be used to point to other locations.

DocumentRoot /home/httpd/html

# UserDir: The name of the directory which is appended onto a user's
➥home
# directory if a ~user request is recieved.

UserDir public_html

# DirectoryIndex: Name of the file or files to use as a pre-written
➥HTML
# directory index.  Separate multiple entries with spaces.

DirectoryIndex index.html index.htm index.shtml

# FancyIndexing is whether you want fancy directory indexing or
➥standard

FancyIndexing on

# AddIcon tells the server which icon to show for different files or
➥filename
# extensions

AddIconByEncoding (CMP,/icons/compressed.gif) x-compress x-gzip

AddIconByType (TXT,/icons/text.gif) text/*
AddIconByType (IMG,/icons/image2.gif) image/*
AddIconByType (SND,/icons/sound2.gif) audio/*
AddIconByType (VID,/icons/movie.gif) video/*

AddIcon /icons/binary.gif .bin .exe
AddIcon /icons/binhex.gif .hqx
AddIcon /icons/tar.gif .tar
AddIcon /icons/world2.gif .wrl .wrl.gz .vrml .vrm .iv
AddIcon /icons/compressed.gif .Z .z .tgz .gz .zip
AddIcon /icons/a.gif .ps .ai .eps
AddIcon /icons/layout.gif .html .shtml .htm .pdf
AddIcon /icons/text.gif .txt
```

```
AddIcon /icons/c.gif .c
AddIcon /icons/p.gif .pl .py
AddIcon /icons/f.gif .for
AddIcon /icons/dvi.gif .dvi
AddIcon /icons/uuencoded.gif .uu
AddIcon /icons/script.gif .conf .sh .shar .csh .ksh .tcl
AddIcon /icons/tex.gif .tex
AddIcon /icons/bomb.gif core

AddIcon /icons/back.gif ..
AddIcon /icons/hand.right.gif README
AddIcon /icons/folder.gif ^^DIRECTORY^^
AddIcon /icons/blank.gif ^^BLANKICON^^

# DefaultIcon is which icon to show for files which do not have an icon
# explicitly set.

DefaultIcon /icons/unknown.gif

# AddDescription allows you to place a short description after a file
➥in
# server-generated indexes.
# Format: AddDescription "description" filename

# ReadmeName is the name of the README file the server will look for by
# default. Format: ReadmeName name
#
# The server will first look for name.html, include it if found, and it
➥will
# then look for name and include it as plaintext if found.
#
# HeaderName is the name of a file which should be prepended to
# directory indexes.

ReadmeName README
HeaderName HEADER

# IndexIgnore is a set of filenames which directory indexing should
➥ignore
# Format: IndexIgnore name1 name2...

IndexIgnore .??* *~ *# HEADER* README* RCS
```

```
# AccessFileName: The name of the file to look for in each directory
# for access control information.

AccessFileName .htaccess

# TypesConfig describes where the mime.types file (or equivalent) is
# to be found.

TypesConfig /etc/mime.types

# DefaultType is the default MIME type for documents which the server
# cannot find the type of from filename extensions.

DefaultType text/plain

# AddEncoding allows you to have certain browsers (Mosaic/X 2.1+)
➥uncompress
# information on the fly. Note: Not all browsers support this.

AddEncoding x-compress Z
AddEncoding x-gzip gz

# AddLanguage allows you to specify the language of a document. You can
# then use content negotiation to give a browser a file in a language
# it can understand.  Note that the suffix does not have to be the same
# as the language keyword -- those with documents in Polish (whose
# net-standard language code is pl) may wish to use "AddLanguage pl
➥.po"
# to avoid the ambiguity with the common suffix for perl scripts.

AddLanguage en .en
AddLanguage fr .fr
AddLanguage de .de
AddLanguage da .da
AddLanguage el .el
AddLanguage it .it

# LanguagePriority allows you to give precedence to some languages
# in case of a tie during content negotiation.
# Just list the languages in decreasing order of preference.

LanguagePriority en fr de
```

```
# Redirect allows you to tell clients about documents which used to
➡exist in
# your server's namespace, but do not anymore. This allows you to tell
➡the
# clients where to look for the relocated document.
# Format: Redirect fakename url


# Aliases: Add here as many aliases as you need (with no limit). The
➡format is
# Alias fakename realname

# Note that if you include a trailing / on fakename then the server
➡will
# require it to be present in the URL.  So "/icons" isn't aliased in
➡this
# example.

Alias /icons/ /home/httpd/icons/

# ScriptAlias: This controls which directories contain server scripts.
# Format: ScriptAlias fakename realname

ScriptAlias /cgi-bin/ /home/httpd/cgi-bin/

# If you want to use server side includes, or CGI outside
# ScriptAliased directories, uncomment the following lines.

# AddType allows you to tweak mime.types without actually editing it,
➡or to
# make certain files to be certain types.
# Format: AddType type/subtype ext1

# For example, the PHP3 module (not part of the Apache distribution)
# will typically use:
#AddType application/x-httpd-php3 .php3
#AddType application/x-httpd-php3-source .phps
# The following is for PHP/FI (PHP2):
#AddType application/x-httpd-php .phtml


# AddHandler allows you to map certain file extensions to "handlers",
```

```
# actions unrelated to filetype. These can be either built into the
➡server
# or added with the Action command (see below)
# Format: AddHandler action-name ext1

# To use CGI scripts:
AddHandler cgi-script .cgi

# To use server-parsed HTML files
AddType text/html .shtml
AddHandler server-parsed .shtml

# Uncomment the following line to enable Apache's send-asis HTTP file
# feature
#AddHandler send-as-is asis

# If you wish to use server-parsed imagemap files, use
AddHandler imap-file map

# To enable type maps, you might want to use
#AddHandler type-map var

# To enable the perl module (if you have it installed), uncomment
# the following section
#
#Alias /perl/ /home/httpd/perl/
#<Location /perl>
#SetHandler perl-script
#PerlHandler Apache::Registry
#Options +ExecCGI
#</Location>

# Action lets you define media types that will execute a script
➡whenever
# a matching file is called. This eliminates the need for repeated URL
# pathnames for oft-used CGI file processors.
# Format: Action media/type /cgi-script/location
# Format: Action handler-name /cgi-script/location

# MetaDir: specifies the name of the directory in which Apache can find
# meta information files. These files contain additional HTTP headers
# to include when sending the document
```

```
#MetaDir .web

# MetaSuffix: specifies the file name suffix for the file containing
➥the
# meta information.

#MetaSuffix .meta

# Customizable error response (Apache style)
#   these come in three flavors
#
#     1) plain text
#ErrorDocument 500 "The server made a boo boo.
#   n.b.  the (") marks it as text, it does not get output
#
#     2) local redirects
#ErrorDocument 404 /missing.html
#   to redirect to local url /missing.html
#ErrorDocument 404 /cgi-bin/missing_handler.pl
#   n.b. can redirect to a script or a document using server-side-
➥includes.
#
#     3) external redirects
#ErrorDocument 402 http://some.other_server.com/subscription_info.html
#

# mod_mime_magic allows the server to use various hints from the file
➥itself
# to determine its type.
#MimeMagicFile /etc/httpd/conf/magic

# The following directives disable keepalives and HTTP header flushes.
# The first directive disables it for Netscape 2.x and browsers which
# spoof it. There are known problems with these.
# The second directive is for Microsoft Internet Explorer 4b2
# which has a broken HTTP/1.1 implementation and does not properly
# support keepalive when it is used on 301 or 302 (redirect) responses.

BrowserMatch "Mozilla/2" nokeepalive
BrowserMatch "MSIE 4\b2;" nokeepalive downgrade-1 force-response-1.0

# The following directive disables HTTP/1.1 responses to browsers which
```

```
# are in violation of the HTTP/1 spec by not being able to grok a
# basic 1.1 response.

BrowserMatch "RealPlayer 4\" force-response-1
BrowserMatch "Java/1\" force-response-1
BrowserMatch "JDK/1\" force-response-1
```

DocumentRoot

The DocumentRoot configuration entry specifies where the root directory for html files is located. In the case of Red Hat Linux, the default is usually set to /home/ httpd/html, and I have kept this setting for linux.juxta.com. Thus, the file /home/httpd/html/file.html would be accessed using the URL http://linux .juxta.com/file.html.

UserDir

UserDir is a directive that is useful when a Webmaster wants to enable each user on the system to have their own personal Web site that they manage through a directory in their home directory. This directive indicates the name of the subdirectory in their home directory that should be considered as their Web directory.

The norm is to use public_html. So, if the user testuser has a directory /home/ testuser/public_html, then this directory can be accessed via the Web using the URL http://servername/~testuser.

DirectoryIndex

DirectoryIndex is an important directive in that it indicates which files should be considered default files. This is how it is possible for a URL such as http:// www.juxta.com/ to access the correct file.

For instance, in the sample srm.conf file above, there are three entries given for the Directory Index: index.html, index.htm, and index.shtml. This means that for any URL that doesn't specify a filename and only gives a directory, the server will first try to return index.html from the specified directory. If that file is missing, index.htm is returned; if that file is missing, index.shtml is sent back to the client.

If no file match is found, the server either returns a directory listing or an error message based on other configuration options.

AccessFileName

AccessFileName is used to specify the filename that contains access control information for a given directory. As you will see later when the access.conf file is discussed and when you build your sample Web site, it is possible to store access control information in the access.conf file or in files in each directory.

The sample file indicates that if a file .htaccess exists in a directory, then that file contains access control information for the directory.

ScriptAlias

It is important to set the ScriptAlias directive so that you can set up a directory to store CGI programs and scripts. ScriptAlias specifies which directory is used for CGI scripts and what the URL is for that directory. Unless other permissions are given to run CGI programs on the basis of file extensions (as you will see in the next section's discussion of the AddHandler directive), this is the only directory where you can place CGI programs.

For instance, the sample file used the following directive:

```
ScriptAlias /cgi-bin/ /home/httpd/cgi-bin
```

This line indicates that the URL http://linux.juxta.com/cgi-bin/ points to /home/httpd/cgi-bin/. In this directory, files are considered CGI scripts and the server attempts to execute the files instead of returning them directly to the requesting client.

AddHandler and *AddType*

The AddHandler and AddType directives really need to be considered together.

AddHandler allows files with a specified extension to be mapped to a particular action, which can be a built-in action in the server (such as running CGI programs) or an external action that generally invokes a special program outside the server and passes the file in question through that program.

AddType creates a new MIME type for a specific extension. MIME types are important in informing the client how to handle a file. For instance, if a file is passed with MIME type text/plain to the browser, the browser won't attempt to interpret the file for any HTML code it contains, while a MIME type of text/html causes the browser to process the file it receives as an HTML file.

Two of the main uses of these directives are to allow the execution of CGI scripts outside the specified CGI script directory and to enable server-parsed HTML, which allows special tags embedded in an HTML file to be processed by the server before it returns the page to the client.

Enabling CGI Scripts   You can use the AddHandler directive to enable CGI processing outside the specified CGI directory. The sample srm.conf file, uses the directive

```
AddHandler cgi-script .cgi
```

to indicate that any file with the extension .cgi that is found outside the specified CGI directory should be treated as a CGI program and handled in that way. Without this directive, a CGI script found outside the CGI directory is not processed as a CGI program; instead, the contents of the file are simply returned to the client. Generally, this means that the user sees the actual program code of a script rather than the results of running a script.

Enabling Server-Parsed HTML   Both the AddHandler and AddType directives are used to enable server-parsed HTML. The normal usage for Apache is:

```
AddType text/html .shtml
AddHandler server-parsed .shtml
```

Here AddType ensures that the results of a server-parsed HTML file (those with the extension .shtml) are viewed as HTML by the client browser and are displayed as such.

The AddHandler line indicates that files with the extension .shtml should be handled by the server-parsed action of the server. This effectively enables server-parsed HTML for .shtml files.

Access.conf

The role of access.conf is a little bit different than httpd.conf and srm.conf. This file defines when, where, and by whom certain types of actions are allowed. It can be used for a number of purposes, including to specify access restrictions and to limit where scripts can be executed (overriding the settings in srm.conf).

```
##
## access.conf - Apache HTTP server configuration file
##
```

```
# access.conf: Global access configuration
# Online docs at http://www.apache.org/

# This file defines server settings which affect which types of
➥services
# are allowed, and in what circumstances.

# Each directory to which Apache has access, can be configured with
➥respect
# to which services and features are allowed and/or disabled in that
# directory (and its subdirectories).

# Originally by Rob McCool

# First, we configure the "default" to be a very restrictive set of
# permissions.

<Directory />
Options None
AllowOverride None
</Directory>

# Note that from this point forward you must specifically allow
# particular features to be enabled - so if something's not working as
# you might expect, make sure that you have specifically enabled it
# below.

# This should be changed to whatever you set DocumentRoot to.

<Directory /home/httpd/html>

# This may also be "None", "All", or any combination of "Indexes",
# "Includes", "FollowSymLinks", "ExecCGI", or "MultiViews".

# Note that "MultiViews" must be named *explicitly* -- "Options All"
# doesn't give it to you.

Options Includes

# This controls which options the .htaccess files in directories can
# override. Can also be "All", or any combination of "Options",
➥"FileInfo",
# "AuthConfig", and "Limit"
```

```
AllowOverride All

# Controls who can get stuff from this server.

order allow,deny
allow from all

</Directory>

# /home/httpd/cgi-bin should be changed to whatever your ScriptAliased
# CGI directory exists, if you have that configured.

<Directory /home/httpd/cgi-bin>
AllowOverride None
Options ExecCGI
</Directory>

# Allow server status reports, with the URL of
➥http://servername/server-status
# Change the ".your_domain.com" to match your domain to enable.

#<Location /server-status>
#SetHandler server-status

#order deny,allow
#deny from all
#allow from .your_domain.com
#</Location>

# There have been reports of people trying to abuse an old bug from
➥pre-1.1
# days.  This bug involved a CGI script distributed as a part of
➥Apache.
# By uncommenting these lines you can redirect these attacks to a
➥logging
# script on phf.apache.org.  Or, you can record them yourself, using
➥the script
# support/phf_abuse_log.cgi.

#<Location /cgi-bin/phf*>
#deny from all
#ErrorDocument 403 http://phf.apache.org/phf_abuse_log.cgi
```

```
#</Location>

# You may place any other directories or locations you wish to have
# access information for after this one.
```

At a minimum, the access.conf file needs to set up the necessary permissions to enable the root HTML directory and the CGI directory. You will usually find it easier to implement access control for specific directories using .htaccess files located in the directories in question. As you saw in the section discussing the srm.conf file previously, you must enable this directory-level access control file for it to work.

The next section will discuss how to set up access.conf to enable the HTML and CGI directories.

Enabling the HTML Directory

The code below is the section of the sample access.conf dealing with the HTML document root directory, without any comments.

```
<Directory /home/httpd/html>
Options Includes
AllowOverride All
order allow,deny
allow from all
</Directory>
```

The structure of the entry is to enclose the necessary directives inside opening and closing <Directory> and </Directory> tags. The opening tag specifies the directory that all directives between the tags should apply to, in this case /home/httpd/html.

Inside the <Directory> and </Directory> tags, notice four directives.

The Options directive is used to indicate what special actions can be taken on the files contained in the directory and its subdirectories. Possible values include None, All, Indexes, Includes, FollowSymLinks, ExecCGI, and MultiViews. Commonly used values for HTML directories are None when only normal HTML files and images appear on a site and Includes when you plan to enable server-parsed HTML. (Some server-parsed HTML files offer the capability to include other files in the contents of a file, and this value allows this action to occur.)

The next directive is the `AllowOverride` entry, which indicates how much power a local `.htaccess` file has to override entries in the global `access.conf` file. Possible values include `None`, `All`, `Options`, `FileInfo`, `AuthConfig`, and `Limit`. For instance, the `Options` value limits the `.htaccess` file to overriding the `Options` directive. On servers where the Webmaster has good control over all content, it is usually easiest to allow full right to override. When you run a server with multiple users controlling their own directories' content, it may be wise to limit the power of these users to override global access configuration.

Finally, the `order` and `allow` directives go together to control who has access to pages in the directory. Here, `order allow,deny` indicates that first the `allow` directive should be used, and if that directive doesn't allow the user to obtain the file in question then any `deny` directive should be applied.

Normally, when you are not applying access control you will want to use `order allow,deny`. When you are attempting to implement access controls, `order deny,allow` is the best entry (as you will see later when you build your small sample Web site with access control).

Following the `order` directive is the `allow` directive, which indicates that all users should be allowed access. If you want to fully understand how to deny users, you should read the Apache documentation available online at `http://www.apache.org/`.

Enabling the CGI Directory

Things look a little bit different with the CGI directory entry:

```
<Directory /home/httpd/cgi-bin>
AllowOverride None
Options ExecCGI
</Directory>
```

Notice that all overrides have been disallowed. This is generally a wise idea, since CGI is a security hole even on a well-configured system and it is prudent to prevent all possible security mistakes with CGI directories.

Managing Your Web Server

In addition to being able to start and stop your Web server, once you have your Web server up and running there are a few tasks that you will need to do occasionally to make sure your server continues to run without incident. These steps include creating and deleting users and groups, protecting directories by using access control, and maintaining the server logs so that they continue to be useful.

Starting and Stopping Apache

If you installed Apache when you installed Red Hat, then your start-up files have been set up to start Apache at boot time. This occurs in the file /etc/rc.d/init .d/httpd. This file is an executable script that takes two possible arguments: start and stop. If you are planning to use the version of Apache included with your Red Hat installation and don't plan to move the location of the configuration files, then you can start and stop your Web server manually, using the command

```
# /etc/rc.d/init.d/httpd start
```

to start the server and using the command

```
# /etc/rc.d/init.d/httpd stop
```

to stop the server.

NOTE   All starting and stopping of your Web server needs to be done by the root user so that the main server process can change users to launch child processes to listen for connections.

However, if you want to install your own binaries or compile new binaries from source code, or if you wish to change the location of the configuration files, you will need to know how to invoke the httpd command by hand.

Usually, httpd is found in /usr/sbin/. Two flags are available:

- -f specifies the location of the httpd.conf file.
- -d specifies the server root, overriding the configuration file.

Usually, using -f is sufficient since ServerRoot is specified in httpd.conf. For instance, if you keep your configuration files in /home/httpd/conf, then you can issue the command

```
# /usr/sbin/httpd -f /home/httpd/conf/httpd.conf
```

to start the server.

If you want to stop your server manually and you started it yourself without using /etc/rc.d/init.d/httpd, you need to know the correct process ID

(PID) for the server. You can determine the PID of the server by using the `ps` command:

```
# ps -aux | grep httpd
```

This command produces a list of processes similar to the one shown here:

```
nobody    545   0.1   3.8   1104   572   ?   S   17:52   0:00 /usr/sbin/httpd
nobody    546   0.0   3.8   1104   572   ?   S   17:52   0:00 /usr/sbin/httpd
nobody    547   0.2   3.8   1104   572   ?   S   17:52   0:00 /usr/sbin/httpd
nobody    548   0.1   3.8   1104   572   ?   S   17:52   0:00 /usr/sbin/httpd
nobody    549   0.0   3.8   1104   572   ?   S   17:52   0:00 /usr/sbin/httpd
nobody    550   0.3   3.8   1104   572   ?   S   17:52   0:00 /usr/sbin/httpd
root      544   0.5   4     1104   592   ?   S   17:52   0:00 /usr/sbin/httpd
```

Notice that all the processes are owned by nobody, except for one owned by root. This is the parent process of all the httpd processes, and this is the one that needs to be stopped, in this case with the command

```
# kill 544
```

Managing Users and Groups

As you will see in the next section on protecting directories, one main method of protection is by username and password, restricting access to a specified list of users who must correctly provide their username and password to gain access to a protected directory.

Creating users is straightforward and is done using the command htpasswd, which, in the default installation of Apache that comes with Red Hat Linux, is found at /usr/bin/htpasswd. This program is used both to create a password file and to create individual users.

The password file serves as the repository for usernames and encrypted passwords, which can then be used by Apache for access control.

You create the password file the first time you create a user, using the command

```
# htpasswd -c filename username
```

Using this command, the file specified by *filename* is created and the first user is added to the file. The -c flag indicates that the file needs to be created. You can store your password file anywhere that is accessible by the Apache Web server. A good place to store it is with your configuration files. For instance, the command

```
# htpasswd -c /etc/httpd/conf/users user1
```

creates a `users` file in the same directory as the other Apache configuration files and would create the user user1.

When you issue the previous command, you are prompted to enter the password for the user twice to make sure it has been entered correctly. Then the password is encrypted and stored in `/etc/httpd/conf/users`. The entry looks like this:

```
user1:N31mVAxFtivO
```

The format of the entries is the username followed by a colon followed by the encrypted password. Each user entry is on a separate line.

While it looks like the passwords in the system password file (`/etc/passwd`) and the Apache password file are encrypted in the same way, the encryption process used by `htpasswd` is different and you can't simply copy encrypted passwords from `/etc/passwd` to create your Apache password file.

To add additional users once the file is created, simply use the `htpasswd` command without the `-c` flag:

```
$ htpasswd /etc/httpd/conf/users user2
```

This command adds the user `user2`, again evoking two prompts for the password. The resulting password file would contain two entries:

```
user1:N31mVAxFtivO.
user2:WROTrbH6.3pPk
```

In addition to creating users, you usually want to create groups. Groups associate multiple users together under a single name, making it easier to address related users when configuring access control for directories.

To create groups, make a `groups` file by simply editing the file using a text editor such as `pico` or `emacs`. You should probably place the `groups` file in the same directory as your `users` file. (In the sample site used in this book, you use `/etc/httpd/conf/groups`.) This file contains one or more entries, each on a separate line, with the format:

```
groupname: username1 username2 username3 ...
```

For instance, to create a group called authors with the two users you created previously as members, use the entry:

```
authors: user1 user2
```

Protecting Directories with Access Control

As noted previously in the section about access.conf, it is possible to configure access control on a directory-by-directory basis. Normally, this is done by creating a file called .htaccess in the directory you want to protect and then placing the necessary configuration directives in the file.

The main directives used in this file for access control purposes are as follows:

- AuthGroupFile
- AuthUserFile
- AuthName
- AuthType
- require
- order
- deny
- allow

AuthUserFile and *AuthGroupFile*

These directives are used to specify the location of the users and group files you learned to create in the last section. In the sample, these directives would read

```
AuthUserFile /etc/httpd/conf/users
AuthGroupFile /etc/httpd/conf/groups
```

These directives are important because without them, the server won't know where to look for the users and their passwords.

AuthName

AuthName is used to specify the domain of the authentication. Ultimately, this is a prompt that is displayed to the users so they know which username and password to provide. For instance,

```
AuthName Authors Only
```

displays an `Authors Only` prompt to the user when asking for username and password.

Require

The `require` directive is used in limiting access for users and groups. The directive can be used to restrict access to all users in the password file, to a list of specific users, or to a list of specific groups.

To restrict access to any existing user, use the directive

```
require valid-user
```

To restrict access to specific users, use the format

```
require user username1 username2 username3 ...
```

Finally, to restrict to a group, use the entry

```
require group groupname1 groupname2 groupname3 ...
```

Order

The `order` directive is used in conjunction with the `deny` and `allow` entries to control access based on host rather than user. Using `order`, `deny`, and `allow`, it is possible to permit access only to specified hosts by IP address or host name.

The `order` directive specifies the order in which the `deny` and `allow` directives should be applied. For instance,

```
order allow,deny
```

says that the `allow` directive should be applied first, and if the client host does not fall within those specified by the directive, then the `deny` directive should be applied.

Similarly,

```
order deny,allow
```

reverses the order, testing the deny directive first.

Deny

The deny directive specifies which hosts should be denied access to a directory. Possible values include all, a partial host name, or a partial or full IP address. For instance,

```
deny from all
```

means that all hosts are denied. Similarly,

```
deny from .juxta.com
```

denies access to all hosts in the juxta.com domain. With IP addresses, the format is the same:

```
deny from 194.148.43.195
```

The directive denies access to the specified host.

Allow

The allow directive is the opposite of the deny directive, specifying which hosts should be allowed access to the directory in question. It takes the same possible values as the deny directive.

Putting It All Together

Let's consider now how this all fits together with two examples: enabling access by group and allowing access by domain name.

Enabling Access by Group The following sample .htaccess file enables access to the specific directory only for users in the group authors:

```
AuthName Authors Only
AuthUserFile /etc/httpd/conf/users
AuthGroupFile /etc/httpd/conf/groups
require group authors
```

Notice that this sample specifies an AuthName for the prompt, identifies the password and group file, and then indicates that a user must be part of the group authors in order to access the directory.

Enabling Access by Domain Name The following sample .htaccess file enables access to the specific directory only to users accessing the Web site from hosts in the juxta.com domain:

```
order allow,deny
allow from .juxta.com
deny from all
```

In this sample, notice the order of allow and deny. The logic works like this: When a host accesses a directory, the host's domain is first compared to the domain juxta.com. If the host falls within the specified domain, access is granted. If the host does not, the deny directive is looked at and, because it indicates that all hosts should be denied access, the host in question is denied access.

Maintaining Logs

The final management function to consider is log management. Apache produces two important logs: an access log and an error log. Together, these provide information vital for several functions, including debugging buggy CGI scripts and producing statistical access reports with detailed information about usage patterns for your Web site.

However, left on their own, these log files will continue to grow, reaching extremely large sizes. As their size grows, their value decreases as it becomes more difficult to process the volumes of data they contain.

For this reason, it is wise to establish a schedule for rotating your logs. Rotating logs means saving the existing version to an archive and starting afresh with a new, empty log. Depending on how many hits you receive, the ideal frequency for rotating logs can be anything from monthly to weekly to daily.

In order to rotate logs, you use the rotatelogs utility that comes with the Apache distribution. By default, Red Hat Linux installs this at /usr/sbin/rotatelogs. In order to use the program, you need to add an entry to httpd.conf:

```
TransferLog "|/usr/sbin/rotatelogs /some/location/file time"
```

The entry `/some/location/file` provides a base filename for the rotated logs. A number indicating the system time at which the log starts is appended to the filename. The `time` parameter specifies in seconds how often to rotate the logs.

Building a Web Site

Now that you have your Web site configured and running smoothly, let's create a small sample Web site that shows how to deploy content for the Web.

The site that you are going to build will be the information for a small publishing company you will call On The Web Publishers. This site will offer a list of new titles, general information about the publisher, a contact form, and a password-protected section exclusively for the use of authors with contracts with the publisher.

All together, this will let you create a site that includes HTML and images, uses CGI programming, and implements access control for the password-protected section of the site.

First, you need to identify the structure of your site, as we see in Figure 32.2.

FIGURE 32.2:

The structure of your
Web site

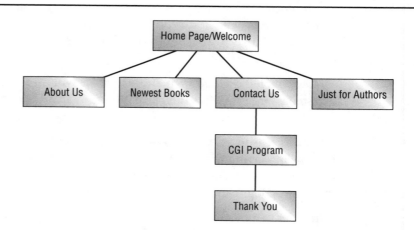

Having done this, you need to create the necessary files to implement this structure. Assuming the configuration used in the sections earlier in this chapter, the root document tree for HTML files is at `/home/httpd/html`, and the CGI directory is at /home/httpd/cgi-bin. Therefore, your directory and file tree for the site might include the following files:

```
/home/httpd/html/index.html
/home/httpd/html/about/index.html
/home/httpd/html/books/index.html
/home/httpd/html/contact/index.html
/home/httpd/html/authors/index.html
/home/httpd/cgi-bin/formmail
```

With the exception of the last file, which will be discussed shortly, all these files are HTML files. Any supporting images that are used by the HTML files can be placed in the same directory as the HTML files, but to keep things clean, many Webmasters prefer to place all their images in another directory. In your case, that directory could be:

```
/home/httpd/html/images/
```

Since you aren't learning HTML in this chapter, let's just look at two of the HTML files as examples of how they might be written. Let's start with the main home page at /home/httpd/html/index.html. In your example, the source code for this file would be:

```
<HTML>

    <HEAD>
    <TITLE>On the Web Publishers</TITLE>
    </HEAD>

    <BODY BGCOLOR=lightcyan TEXT=midnightblue>

    <DIV ALIGN=CENTER>
        <A HREF="/"><IMG SRC="/images/logo.gif" BORDER=0></A>
        <TABLE BORDER=0 CELLPADDING=5 CELLSPACING=5
            BGCOLOR=lightpink>
        <TR>
            <TD ALIGN=CENTER><A HREF="about">ABOUT
                US</A></TD>
            <TD ALIGN=CENTER><A HREF="books">OUR
                BOOKS</A></TD>
            <TD ALIGN=CENTER><A HREF="contact">CONTACT
                US</A></TD>
            <TD ALIGN=CENTER><A HREF="authors">JUST FOR
                AUTHORS</A></TD>
```

```
            </TR>
          </TABLE>
      </DIV>

      <FONT SIZE=5>W</F>elcome to <STRONG>On the Web
      Publishers</STRONG>. We offer the finest in
      on-line electronic books at reasonable prices.
      Check out what we have to offer ...

      <UL>
      <LI><A HREF="about">Learn about what we do</A>
      <LI><A HREF="books">See what books we offer</A>
      <LI><A HREF="contact">Contact us</A>
      </UL>

      </BODY>

  </HTML>
```

This file would produce results like those in Figure 32.3.

FIGURE 32.3:

The main home page

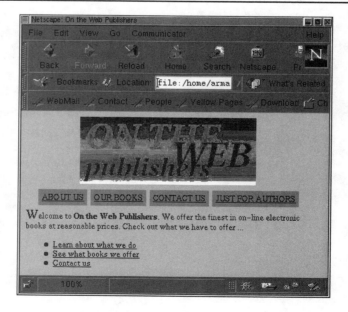

The other pages would have similar-looking source code, with the exception of the contact form at /home/httpd/html/contact/index.html. This page would look like Figure 32.4, which is produced by the following source code:

```
<HTML>

    <HEAD>
    <TITLE>On the Web Publishers</TITLE>
    </HEAD>

    <BODY BGCOLOR=lightcyan TEXT=midnightblue>

    <DIV ALIGN=CENTER>
        <A HREF="/"><IMG SRC="/images/logo.gif" BORDER=0></A>
        <TABLE BORDER=0 CELLPADDING=5 CELLSPACING=5
            BGCOLOR=lightpink>
        <TR>
            <TD ALIGN=CENTER><A HREF="/about">ABOUT
                US</A></TD>
            <TD ALIGN=CENTER><A HREF="/books">OUR
                BOOKS</A></TD>
            <TD ALIGN=CENTER BGCOLOR=yellow>CONTACT
                US</TD>
            <TD ALIGN=CENTER><A HREF="/authors">JUST FOR
                AUTHORS</A></TD>
        </TR>
        </TABLE>

        <H1>Drop Us A Line ...</H1>
    </DIV>

    <TABLE ALIGN=CENTER><TR><TD>
    <FORM METHOD=POST ACTION="/cgi-bin/formmail">
    <INPUT TYPE=TEXT WIDTH=30 NAME=name> Name<BR>
    <INPUT TYPE=TEXT WIDTH=30 NAME=address> Address<BR>
    <INPUT TYPE=TEXT WIDTH=30 NAME=city> City<BR>
    <INPUT TYPE=TEXT WIDTH=30 NAME=state> State<BR>
    <INPUT TYPE=TEXT WIDTH=30 NAME=zip> Zip/Post Code<BR>
    <INPUT TYPE=TEXT WIDTH=30 NAME=country> Country<BR>
    <INPUT TYPE=TEXT WIDTH=30 NAME=email> E-mail<BR>
    Comments:<BR>
    <TEXTAREA ROWS=10 COLS=30 NAME=comments
```

```
        WRAP=HARD></TEXTAREA><BR>
<INPUT TYPE=SUBMIT VALUE="Send Comments">
</FORM>
</TD></TR></TABLE>

</BODY>

</HTML>
```

FIGURE 32.4:

The contact form

What makes this page special is that it includes a form and a reference to a CGI program that processes the data in the form. The program you are using in this case is called formmail, a freely available CGI script written in Perl, which takes the contents of a form and mails them to a predefined mail address. In this way, the contact information from the form can be e-mailed to the bookstore's main e-mail address.

Formmail is written by Matthew M. Wright and is available at `http://www` `.worldwidemart.com/scripts/formmail.shtml`. Even though this chapter doesn't discuss Perl or CGI programming, the source code is presented here so you can see how simple it is to create basic CGI programs with little effort:

```perl
#!/usr/bin/perl
#########################################################################
➥#######
# FormMail                        Version 1.6
#
# Copyright 1995-1997 Matt Wright mattw@worldwidemart.com
#
# Created 06/09/95               Last Modified 05/02/97
#
# Matt's Script Archive, Inc.:    http://www.worldwidemart.com/scripts/
#
#########################################################################
➥#######
# COPYRIGHT NOTICE
#
# Copyright 1995-1997 Matthew M. Wright  All Rights Reserved.
#
#
#
# FormMail may be used and modified free of charge by anyone so long as
➥this #
# copyright notice and the comments above remain intact.  By using this
#
# code you agree to indemnify Matthew M. Wright from any liability that
#
# might arise from its use.
#
#
#
# Selling the code for this program without prior written consent is
#
# expressly forbidden.  In other words, please ask first before you try
➥and
# make money off of my program.
#
#
#
```

```
# Obtain permission before redistributing this software over the
➥Internet or #
# in any other medium.  In all cases copyright and header must remain
➥intact #
###########################################################################
➥#######
# Define Variables
#
#     Detailed Information Found In README File.
#

# $mailprog defines the location of your sendmail program on your unix
#
# system.
#

$mailprog = '/usr/lib/sendmail';

# @referers allows forms to be located only on servers which are
➥defined       #
# in this field.  This security fix from the last version which allowed
#
# anyone on any server to use your FormMail script on their web site.
#

@referers = ('linux.juxta.com');

# Done
#
###########################################################################
➥#######

# Check Referring URL
&check_url;

# Retrieve Date
&get_date;

# Parse Form Contents
&parse_form;

# Check Required Fields
```

```
    &check_required;

    # Return HTML Page or Redirect User
    &return_html;

    # Send E-Mail
    &send_mail;

sub check_url {

    # Localize the check_referer flag which determines if user is
➡valid.     #
    local($check_referer) = 0;

    # If a referring URL was specified, for each valid referer, make
➡sure     #
    # that a valid referring URL was passed to FormMail.
➡#

    if ($ENV{'HTTP_REFERER'}) {
        foreach $referer (@referers) {
            if ($ENV{'HTTP_REFERER'} =~ m|https?://([^/]*)$referer|i) {
                $check_referer = 1;
                last;
            }
        }
    }
    else {
        $check_referer = 1;
    }

    # If the HTTP_REFERER was invalid, send back an error.
➡#
    if ($check_referer != 1) { &error('bad_referer') }
}

sub get_date {

    # Define arrays for the day of the week and month of the year.
➡#
    @days   = ('Sunday','Monday','Tuesday','Wednesday',
               'Thursday','Friday','Saturday');
```

```
    @months =
('January','February','March','April','May','June','July',
            'August','September','October','November','December');

    # Get the current time and format the hour, minutes and seconds.
➡Add     #
    # 1900 to the year to get the full 4 digit year.
➡#
    ($sec,$min,$hour,$mday,$mon,$year,$wday) =
➡(localtime(time))[0,1,2,3,4,5,6];
    $time = sprintf("%02d:%02d:%02d",$hour,$min,$sec);
    $year += 1900;

    # Format the date.
➡#
    $date = "$days[$wday], $months[$mon] $mday, $year at $time";

}

sub parse_form {

    # Define the configuration associative array.
➡#
    %Config = ('recipient','',          'subject','',
               'email','',              'realname','',
               'redirect','',           'bgcolor','',
               'background','',          'link_color','',
               'vlink_color','',        'text_color','',
               'alink_color','',        'title','',
               'sort','',               'print_config','',
               'required','',           'env_report','',
               'return_link_title','',  'return_link_url','',
               'print_blank_fields','', 'missing_fields_redirect','');

    # Determine the form's REQUEST_METHOD (GET or POST) and split the
➡form    #
    # fields up into their name-value pairs.  If the REQUEST_METHOD was
➡#
    # not GET or POST, send an error.
➡#
    if ($ENV{'REQUEST_METHOD'} eq 'GET') {
        # Split the name-value pairs
```

```
        @pairs = split(/&/, $ENV{'QUERY_STRING'});
    }
    elsif ($ENV{'REQUEST_METHOD'} eq 'POST') {
        # Get the input
        read(STDIN, $buffer, $ENV{'CONTENT_LENGTH'});

        # Split the name-value pairs
        @pairs = split(/&/, $buffer);
    }
    else {
        &error('request_method');
    }

    # For each name-value pair:
➥#
    foreach $pair (@pairs) {

        # Split the pair up into individual variables.
➥#
        local($name, $value) = split(/=/, $pair);

        # Decode the form encoding on the name and value variables.
➥#
        $name =~ tr/+/ /;
        $name =~ s/%([a-fA-F0-9][a-fA-F0-9])/pack("C", hex($1))/eg;

        $value =~ tr/+/ /;
        $value =~ s/%([a-fA-F0-9][a-fA-F0-9])/pack("C", hex($1))/eg;

        # If they try to include server side includes, erase them, so
➥they
        # aren't a security risk if the html gets returned.  Another
        # security hole plugged up.
        $value =~ s/<!-(.|\n)*->//g;

        # If the field name has been specified in the %Config array, it
➥will #
        # return a 1 for defined($Config{$name}}) and we should
➥associate    #
        # this value with the appropriate configuration variable.  If
➥this    #
```

```
          # is not a configuration form field, put it into the
➥associative     #
          # array %Form, appending the value with a ', ' if there is
➥already a #
          # value present.  We also save the order of the form fields in
➥the    #
          # @Field_Order array so we can use this order for the generic
➥sort.   #
          if (defined($Config{$name})) {
              $Config{$name} = $value;
          }
          else {
              if ($Form{$name} && $value) {
                  $Form{$name} = "$Form{$name}, $value";
              }
              elsif ($value) {
                  push(@Field_Order,$name);
                  $Form{$name} = $value;
              }
          }
      }

   # The next six lines remove any extra spaces or new lines from the
➥#
   # configuration variables, which may have been caused if your
➥editor     #
   # wraps lines after a certain length or if you used spaces between
➥field #
   # names or environment variables.
#
   $Config{'required'} =~ s/(\s+|\n)?,(\s+|\n)?/,/g;
   $Config{'required'} =~ s/(\s+)?\n+(\s+)?//g;
   $Config{'env_report'} =~ s/(\s+|\n)?,(\s+|\n)?/,/g;
   $Config{'env_report'} =~ s/(\s+)?\n+(\s+)?//g;
   $Config{'print_config'} =~ s/(\s+|\n)?,(\s+|\n)?/,/g;
   $Config{'print_config'} =~ s/(\s+)?\n+(\s+)?//g;

   # Split the configuration variables into individual field names.
➥#
   @Required = split(/,/,$Config{'required'});
   @Env_Report = split(/,/,$Config{'env_report'});
   @Print_Config = split(/,/,$Config{'print_config'});
}
```

```perl
sub check_required {

    # Localize the variables used in this subroutine.
➡#
    local($require, @error);

    if (!$Config{'recipient'}) {
        if (!defined(%Form)) { &error('bad_referer') }
        else                 { &error('no_recipient') }
    }

    # For each require field defined in the form:
➡#
    foreach $require (@Required) {

        # If the required field is the email field, the syntax of the
➡email  #
        # address if checked to make sure it passes a valid syntax.
➡#
        if ($require eq 'email' && !&check_email($Config{$require})) {
            push(@error,$require);
        }

        # Otherwise, if the required field is a configuration field and
➡it    #
        # has no value or has been filled in with a space, send an
➡error.   #
        elsif (defined($Config{$require})) {
            if (!$Config{$require}) {
                push(@error,$require);
            }
        }

        # If it is a regular form field which has not been filled in or
➡#
        # filled in with a space, flag it as an error field.
➡#
        elsif (!$Form{$require}) {
            push(@error,$require);
        }
    }
```

```perl
    # If any error fields have been found, send error message to the
➥user.   #
    if (@error) { &error('missing_fields', @error) }
}

sub return_html {
    # Local variables used in this subroutine initialized.
➥#
    local($key,$sort_order,$sorted_field);

    # If redirect option is used, print the redirectional location
➥header.   #
    if ($Config{'redirect'}) {
        print "Location: $Config{'redirect'}\n\n";
    }

    # Otherwise, begin printing the response page.
➥#
    else {

        # Print HTTP header and opening HTML tags.
➥#
        print "Content-type: text/html\n\n";
        print "<html>\n <head>\n";

        # Print out title of page
➥#
        if ($Config{'title'}) { print "
➥<title>$Config{'title'}</title>\n" }
        else                  { print "  <title>Thank You</title>\n"
}

        print " </head>\n <body";

        # Get Body Tag Attributes
➥#
        &body_attributes;

        # Close Body Tag
➥#
        print ">\n  <center>\n";
```

```
        # Print custom or generic title.
➥#
        if ($Config{'title'}) { print "    <h1>$Config{'title'}</h1>\n"
}
        else { print "    <h1>Thank You For Filling Out This
➥Form</h1>\n" }

        print "</center>\n";

        print "Below is what you submitted to $Config{'recipient'} on
➥";
        print "$date<p><hr size=1 width=75\%><p>\n";

        # Sort alphabetically if specified:
➥#
        if ($Config{'sort'} eq 'alphabetic') {
            foreach $field (sort keys %Form) {

                # If the field has a value or the print blank fields
➥option  #
                # is turned on, print out the form field and value.
➥#
                if ($Config{'print_blank_fields'} || $Form{$field}) {
                    print "<b>$field:</b> $Form{$field}<p>\n";
                }
            }
        }

        # If a sort order is specified, sort the form fields based on
➥that.  #
        elsif ($Config{'sort'} =~ /^order:.*,.*/) {

            # Set the temporary $sort_order variable to the sorting
➥order,   #
            # remove extraneous line breaks and spaces, remove the
➥order:   #
            # directive and split the sort fields into an array.
➥#
            $sort_order = $Config{'sort'};
            $sort_order =~ s/(\s+|\n)?,(\s+|\n)?/,/g;
            $sort_order =~ s/(\s+)?\n+(\s+)?//g;
            $sort_order =~ s/order://;
            @sorted_fields = split(/,/, $sort_order);
```

```
            # For each sorted field, if it has a value or the print
➡blank    #
            # fields option is turned on print the form field and
➡value.     #
            foreach $sorted_field (@sorted_fields) {
                if ($Config{'print_blank_fields'} ||
➡$Form{$sorted_field}) {
                    print "<b>$sorted_field:</b>
➡$Form{$sorted_field}<p>\n";
                }
            }
        }

        # Otherwise, default to the order in which the fields were
➡sent.    #
        else {

            # For each form field, if it has a value or the print blank
➡#
            # fields option is turned on print the form field and
➡value.     #
            foreach $field (@Field_Order) {
                if ($Config{'print_blank_fields'} || $Form{$field}) {
                    print "<b>$field:</b> $Form{$field}<p>\n";
                }
            }
        }

        print "<p><hr size=1 width=75%><p>\n";

        # Check for a Return Link and print one if found.
➡#
        if ($Config{'return_link_url'} && $Config{'return_link_title'})
{
            print "<ul>\n";
            print "<li><a href=\"$Config{'return_link_url'}\">
➡$Config{'return_link_title'}</a>\n";
            print "</ul>\n";
        }

        # Print the page footer.
➡#
```

```
        print <<"(END HTML FOOTER)";
        <hr size=1 width=75%><p>
        <center><font size=-1><a
href="http://www.worldwidemart.com/scripts/formmail.shtml">FormMail</a>
V1.6 &copy; 1995 -1997  Matt Wright<br>
A Free Product of <a
href="http://www.worldwidemart.com/scripts/">Matt's Script Archive,
Inc.</a></font></center>
        </body>
        </html>
(END HTML FOOTER)
    }
}

sub send_mail {
    # Localize variables used in this subroutine.
➥#
    local($print_config,$key,$sort_order,$sorted_field,$env_report);

    # Open The Mail Program
    open(MAIL,"|$mailprog -t");

    print MAIL "To: $Config{'recipient'}\n";
    print MAIL "From: $Config{'email'} ($Config{'realname'})\n";

    # Check for Message Subject
    if ($Config{'subject'}) { print MAIL "Subject:
➥$Config{'subject'}\n\n" }
    else                    { print MAIL "Subject: WWW Form
➥Submission\n\n" }

    print MAIL "Below is the result of your feedback form.  It was
➥submitted by\n";
    print MAIL "$Config{'realname'} ($Config{'email'}) on $date\n";
    print MAIL "-" x 75 . "\n\n";

    if (@Print_Config) {
        foreach $print_config (@Print_Config) {
            if ($Config{$print_config}) {
                print MAIL "$print_config: $Config{$print_config}\n\n";
            }
        }
    }
```

```
        # Sort alphabetically if specified:
➡#
        if ($Config{'sort'} eq 'alphabetic') {
            foreach $field (sort keys %Form) {

                # If the field has a value or the print blank fields option
➡#
                # is turned on, print out the form field and value.
➡#
                if ($Config{'print_blank_fields'} || $Form{$field} ||
                    $Form{$field} eq '0') {
                    print MAIL "$field: $Form{$field}\n\n";
                }
            }
        }

        # If a sort order is specified, sort the form fields based on that.
➡#
        elsif ($Config{'sort'} =~ /^order:.*,.*/) {

            # Remove extraneous line breaks and spaces, remove the order:
➡#
            # directive and split the sort fields into an array.
➡#
            $Config{'sort'} =~ s/(\s+|\n)?,(\s+|\n)?/,/g;
            $Config{'sort'} =~ s/(\s+)?\n+(\s+)?//g;
            $Config{'sort'} =~ s/order://;
            @sorted_fields = split(/,/, $Config{'sort'});

            # For each sorted field, if it has a value or the print blank
➡#
            # fields option is turned on print the form field and value.
➡#
            foreach $sorted_field (@sorted_fields) {
                if ($Config{'print_blank_fields'} || $Form{$sorted_field}
➡||
                    $Form{$sorted_field} eq '0') {
                    print MAIL "$sorted_field: $Form{$sorted_field}\n\n";
                }
            }
        }
```

```
    # Otherwise, default to the order in which the fields were sent.
➥#
    else {

        # For each form field, if it has a value or the print blank
➥#
        # fields option is turned on print the form field and value.
➥#
        foreach $field (@Field_Order) {
            if ($Config{'print_blank_fields'} || $Form{$field} ||
                $Form{$field} eq '0') {
                print MAIL "$field: $Form{$field}\n\n";
            }
        }
    }

    print MAIL "-" x 75 . "\n\n";

    # Send any specified Environment Variables to recipient.
➥#
    foreach $env_report (@Env_Report) {
        if ($ENV{$env_report}) {
            print MAIL "$env_report: $ENV{$env_report}\n";
        }
    }

    close (MAIL);
}

sub check_email {
    # Initialize local email variable with input to subroutine.
➥#
    $email = $_[0];

    # If the e-mail address contains:
➥#
    if ($email =~ /(@.*@)|(\.\.)|(@\.)|(\.@)|(^\.)/ ||

        # the e-mail address contains an invalid syntax.  Or, if the
➥#
        # syntax does not match the following regular expression
➥pattern    #
```

```
        # it fails basic syntax verification.
➡#

        $email !~ /^.+\@(\[?)[a-zA-Z0-9\-\.]+\.([a-zA-Z]{2,3}|
➡[0-9]{1,3})(\]?)$/) {

        # Basic syntax requires:  one or more characters before the @
➡sign,  #
        # followed by an optional '[', then any number of letters,
➡numbers,  #
        # dashes or periods (valid domain/IP characters) ending in a
➡period  #
        # and then 2 or 3 letters (for domain suffixes) or 1 to 3
➡numbers   #
        # (for IP addresses).  An ending bracket is also allowed as it
➡is   #
        # valid syntax to have an email address like:
➡user@[255.255.255]    #

        # Return a false value, since the e-mail address did not pass
➡valid  #
        # syntax.
➡#
        return 0;
    }

    else {

        # Return a true value, e-mail verification passed.
➡#
        return 1;
    }
}

sub body_attributes {
    # Check for Background Color
    if ($Config{'bgcolor'}) { print " bgcolor=\"$Config{'bgcolor'}\"" }

    # Check for Background Image
    if ($Config{'background'}) { print " ① background=\"$Config
➡{'background'}\"" }
```

```
    # Check for Link Color
    if ($Config{'link_color'}) { print "
➥link=\"$Config{'link_color'}\"" }

    # Check for Visited Link Color
    if ($Config{'vlink_color'}) { print "
➥vlink=\"$Config{'vlink_color'}\"" }

    # Check for Active Link Color
    if ($Config{'alink_color'}) { print "
➥alink=\"$Config{'alink_color'}\"" }

    # Check for Body Text Color
    if ($Config{'text_color'}) { print "
➥text=\"$Config{'text_color'}\"" }
}

sub error {
    # Localize variables and assign subroutine input.
➥#
    local($error,@error_fields) = @_;
    local($host,$missing_field,$missing_field_list);

    if ($error eq 'bad_referer') {
        if ($ENV{'HTTP_REFERER'} =~ m|^https?://([\w\.]+)|i) {
            $host = $1;
            print <<"(END ERROR HTML)";
Content-type: text/html

<html>
 <head>
  <title>Bad Referrer - Access Denied</title>
 </head>
 <body bgcolor=#FFFFFF text=#000000>
  <center>
   <table border=0 width=600 bgcolor=#9C9C9C>
    <tr><th><font size=+2>Bad Referrer - Access Denied</font></th></tr>
   </table>
   <table border=0 width=600 bgcolor=#CFCFCF>
    <tr><td>The form attempting to use
     <a href="http://www.worldwidemart.com/scripts/formmail.shtml">
➥FormMail</a>
```

```
       resides at <tt>$ENV{'HTTP_REFERER'}</tt>, which is not allowed to
➥access
       this cgi script.<p>

       If you are attempting to configure FormMail to run with this form,
➥you need
       to add the following to \@referers, explained in detail in the
➥README file.<p>

       Add <tt>'$host'</tt> to your <tt><b>\@referers</b></tt> array.<hr
➥size=1>
       <center><font size=-1>
        <a
href="http://www.worldwidemart.com/scripts/formmail.shtml">FormMail</a>
V1.6 &copy; 1995 - 1997  Matt Wright<br>
        A Free Product of <a
href="http://www.worldwidemart.com/scripts/">Matt's Script Archive,
Inc.</a>
       </font></center>
      </td></tr>
     </table>
    </center>
   </body>
  </html>
(END ERROR HTML)
          }
          else {
              print <<"(END ERROR HTML)";
Content-type: text/html

<html>
  <head>
   <title>FormMail v1.6</title>
  </head>
  <body bgcolor=#FFFFFF text=#000000>
   <center>
    <table border=0 width=600 bgcolor=#9C9C9C>
     <tr><th><font size=+2>FormMail</font></th></tr>
    </table>
    <table border=0 width=600 bgcolor=#CFCFCF>
     <tr><th><tt><font size=+1>Copyright 1995 - 1997 Matt Wright<br>
         Version 1.6 - Released May 02, 1997<br>
```

```
        A Free Product of <a
href="http://www.worldwidemart.com/scripts/">Matt's Script Archive,
        Inc.</a></font></tt></th></tr>
   </table>
  </center>
 </body>
</html>
(END ERROR HTML)
        }
    }

    elsif ($error eq 'request_method') {
            print <<"(END ERROR HTML)";
Content-type: text/html

<html>
 <head>
  <title>Error: Request Method</title>
 </head>
 <body bgcolor=#FFFFFF text=#000000>
  <center>
   <table border=0 width=600 bgcolor=#9C9C9C>
    <tr><th><font size=+2>Error: Request Method</font></th></tr>
   </table>
   <table border=0 width=600 bgcolor=#CFCFCF>
    <tr><td>The Request Method of the Form you submitted did not match
     either <tt>GET</tt> or <tt>POST</tt>.  Please check the form and
➥make sure the
     <tt>method=</tt> statement is in upper case and matches
<tt>GET</tt> or <tt>POST</tt>.<p>

     <center><font size=-1>
      <a
href="http://www.worldwidemart.com/scripts/formmail.shtml">
➥ForMail</a> V1.6 &copy; 1995 - 1997  Matt Wright<br>
      A Free Product of <a
href="http://www.worldwidemart.com/scripts/">Matt's Script Archive,
➥Inc.</a>
     </font></center>
    </td></tr>
   </table>
  </center>
```

```
  </body>
</html>
(END ERROR HTML)
    }


    elsif ($error eq 'no_recipient') {
            print <<"(END ERROR HTML)";
Content-type: text/html

<html>
 <head>
  <title>Error: No Recipient</title>
 </head>
 <body bgcolor=#FFFFFF text=#000000>
  <center>
   <table border=0 width=600 bgcolor=#9C9C9C>
    <tr><th><font size=+2>Error: No Recipient</font></th></tr>
   </table>
   <table border=0 width=600 bgcolor=#CFCFCF>
    <tr><td>No Recipient was specified in the data sent to FormMail.
➥Please
    make sure you have filled in the 'recipient' form field with an
➥e-mail
    address.  More information on filling in recipient form fields can
➥be
    found in the README file.<hr size=1>

    <center><font size=-1>
     <a
href="http://www.worldwidemart.com/scripts/formmail.shtml">FormMail
➥</a> V1.6 &copy; 1995 - 1997  Matt Wright<br>
     A Free Product of <a
href="http://www.worldwidemart.com/scripts/">Matt's Script Archive,
➥Inc.</a>
    </font></center>
   </td></tr>
  </table>
 </center>
 </body>
</html>
(END ERROR HTML)
    }
```

```
        elsif ($error eq 'missing_fields') {
            if ($Config{'missing_fields_redirect'}) {
                print "Location: $Config{'missing_fields_redirect'}\n\n";
            }
            else {
                foreach $missing_field (@error_fields) {
                    $missing_field_list .= "        <li>$missing_field\n";
                }

                print <<"(END ERROR HTML)";
Content-type: text/html

<html>
 <head>
  <title>Error: Blank Fields</title>
 </head>
  <center>
   <table border=0 width=600 bgcolor=#9C9C9C>
    <tr><th><font size=+2>Error: Blank Fields</font></th></tr>
   </table>
   <table border=0 width=600 bgcolor=#CFCFCF>
    <tr><td>The following fields were left blank in your submission
➥form:<p>
     <ul>
$missing_field_list
    </ul><br>

    These fields must be filled in before you can successfully ①submit
➥the form.<p>
    Please use your browser's back button to return to the form ①and
➥try again.<hr size=1>
    <center><font size=-1>
     <a
href="http://www.worldwidemart.com/scripts/formmail.shtml">FormMail
➥</a> V1.6 &copy; 1995 - 1997  Matt Wright<br>
     A Free Product of <a
href="http://www.worldwidemart.com/scripts/">Matt's Script Archive,
➥Inc.</a>
    </font></center>
   </td></tr>
  </table>
 </center>
```

```
   </body>
   </html>
   (END ERROR HTML)
           }
       }
       exit;
}
```

What is important to note is that this program is designed to return an HTML page to the user, indicating that the contact information in the form has been processed or indicating an error, if there was one. This is an important component of all CGI programs: they should either return valid data to the browser (such as HTML or the contents of an image file) or they should redirect the browser to a valid URL.

The `formmail` program offers many other features, such as the ability to set the subject line of e-mails and ensure that the script is not abused by users on other Web sites. Full details are available at the Web site for the program.

The last important piece of your Web site is to create access restrictions for the directory `/home/httpd/html/authors/` so that only authorized users have access to the files in this directory. To do this requires a two-step process. First, you need to create a users file with the necessary users in it, as you did in the last section on protecting directories with access control.

You create access restrictions for all users you wish to give access to the directory. Second, you want to create a group—let's call it `authors`—to make the job of managing access to the directory easier. You create this group by adding an entry for the group to your Web server's `group` file that looks like:

```
authors: author1 author2 author3
```

This entry assumes that there are three users being given access to the directory.

Finally, you need to create a `.htaccess` file called `/home/httpd/html/authors/` ("`Auth`" in these directives refers to authentication, not to our authors group):

```
AuthName Just For Authors
AuthType Basic
AuthUserFile /etc/httpd/conf/users
AuthGroupFile /etc/httpd/conf/groups
require group authors
```

The contents of this file are fairly straightforward. AuthName specifies the prompt presented to the user, which you can see in Figure 32.5. AuthUserFile tells the server where to find the list of valid usernames and passwords, just as AuthGroupFile tells the server where the list of valid groups is. Finally, the require directive indicates that only members of the group authors should be given access to the directory.

FIGURE 32.5:

The user prompt box

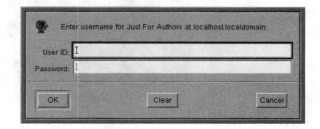

Now, when a user tries to access the directory in question for the first time in a session, they see an authentication dialog box displayed by their browser, like the one in Figure 32.6 produced by Netscape Communicator.

FIGURE 32.6:

An authentication dialog box in Netscape Communicator

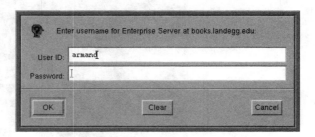

By default, if a user fails to authenticate properly, they receive a page like the one in Figure 32.7. In order to provide a customized page indicating failure like the one shown here, you can edit the srm.conf file to indicate a custom error message by adding the following entry to the file:

```
ErrorDocument 401 /error.html
```

This entry indicates that when error 401 (Authorization Required) occurs, the server should return the indicated URL instead of the default message. Now when a user fails to authenticate, they will receive the page shown in Figure 32.8.

FIGURE 32.7:

The standard error page when a user fails to authenticate

FIGURE 32.8:

A customized error page

NOTE   All the files for this sample site are on the CD-ROM included with this book. In addition, you can see this site on the Web site for this book at **linux .juxta.com/OnTheWeb**. This Web site is running using the Apache Web server on a Red Hat Linux system.

Looking Ahead

This chapter showed you how the Linux operating system provides a flexible tool as a network server, in this case a Web server.

The next chapter examines another important role that Linux can play: the job of a mail server. A mail server handles the processing of all the incoming and outgoing mail for a network, deciding which messages are destined for internal users and directing these messages to the users' mailboxes, and directing messages bound for external networks onto the Internet for delivery.

Setting up a mail server can be a daunting task in a Unix environment, especially using the Sendmail program, which is the dominant Linux mail server. Still, for many networks the job is manageable and, once it is done, a Linux mail server can be relied on to deliver high volumes of messages with little day-to-day administration.

CHAPTER

THIRTY-THREE

Red Hat Linux 6 as a Mail Server: The Power of Sendmail

- The Concept of a Mail Transport Agent

- Sendmail as the Foremost MTA

- Configuring Sendmail with M4

In this chapter, you are going to learn how to turn Linux into an organizational mail server using the Sendmail Mail Transport Agent.

The need for a mail server arises when you begin to connect together multiple desktops on a network and want to provide e-mail services to them. Using Sendmail, it is possible to configure a Linux system to act as the mail server for internal messages as well as for outgoing and incoming messages to and from the Internet.

This chapter will first consider the concept of a mail transport agent (MTA), and then take a quick look at Sendmail, the foremost MTA in the Unix world, and some alternative MTAs. Finally, you will get down to the business of configuring Sendmail.

The Concept of a Mail Transport Agent

Normally, when users think of e-mail systems, they think of the software they use to read, compose, and send messages. This may be Netscape Communicator's mail module, Eudora, Pegasus Mail, or `pine`, but in all cases these programs are simply an interface to the back-end systems that really do the work of routing and delivering mail.

In none of these cases does the user's software actually handle delivery of outgoing mail or receipt of incoming mail. These programs are mail user agents (MUAs). There are numerous MUAs, and their job is to provide the user interface to the world of e-mail.

Behind these MUAs are the mail transport agents. MTAs handle the job of delivering, receiving, and routing mail messages. Generally, they all adhere to certain standard protocols (such as the Simple Mail Transport Protocol, known as SMTP) that make up the Internet's e-mail system (and the e-mail system of almost every Unix-based network).

This distinction between an MUA and an MTA is an important one. In order to set up a mail server for an organization or any other network of computers, it is necessary to work with mail transport agents.

Sendmail as the Foremost MTA

There is little doubt that in the Unix world, the foremost MTA is the Sendmail program. This program defines the mail system you are familiar with on the Internet, providing the addressing structure you all know (*username@some.domain*) and the features you have come to expect (such as automatic mail-forwarding).

In its dominance, Sendmail has grown to be the most powerful and complex Unix MTA available. In fact, configuration and management of a Sendmail system can be so complex in a large organization that an entire book is dedicated to the subject of designing a Sendmail system, configuring it, and keeping it running happily.

This chapter will focus its attention on the configuration and use of Sendmail, since this is the default MTA included with Red Hat Linux and since it is so common on Unix networks.

TIP   This chapter only gives a cursory look at Sendmail and how to configure it. To gain deeper insight into the subject, visit the Web site **www.sendmail.org**.

First, though, let's take a brief survey of some of the alternative MTAs available for Linux.

Smail

Sendmail may be the dominant Unix mail transport agent, but in the Linux world, smail is widely used as an MTA. Its configuration can be easier than Sendmail's (though not always), and it offers similar features, including SMTP support and UUCP support, that make it well-suited to an online mail server configuration.

Red Hat Linux 6 uses Sendmail as its default MTA and doesn't include the smail package. You can download the latest version of smail from `ftp://ftp.uu.net/networking/mail/smail/`.

Qmail

Qmail is a an alternative to Sendmail that hasn't garnered the same fame as smail but has several features that make it a strong contender in the MTA arena.

The author of qmail has made security a stated priority for the package. Over the years, Sendmail has had a number of security bugs exposed, though they have always been closed subsequently. The qmail philosophy is to do everything possible to avoid hidden holes because mail is a perpetually running service and therefore constantly open to hacking attempts.

Qmail also tries to make the delivery process as reliable as possible, with an inbox format that is safer than most from corruption should a system crash occur while a message is being delivered to the inbox.

To top it off, qmail brings together features that are kept in separate applications in traditional MTAs: forwarding, aliasing, mailing lists, load management, and more.

The qmail home page is at `http://www.qmail.org/top.html`.

Configuring Sendmail with M4

As mentioned earlier, configuration of Sendmail can be a daunting task for even an experienced Unix system administrator. Mastering the intricacies of the system can take years.

Sendmail's configuration is stored in `/etc/sendmail.cf`, and just a look at the default configuration file that ships with Red Hat Linux 6 shows the complexity of the configuration.

If you look through this file, notice that it contains a large number of extremely cryptic rules that define the behavior of Sendmail. To expect anyone other than an expert in Sendmail to configure a basic system would be unreasonable if it were necessary to manually create and edit this type of configuration file.

Luckily, Sendmail provides a facility for creating a configuration file: a program called m4. M4 allows you to produce much simpler configuration files. M4 then processes these files and converts them into full-fledged Sendmail configuration files. All but the most knowledgeable users should create their Sendmail configurations in this manner.

NOTE   You can find a discussion of m4 Sendmail configuration in the README file included with the configuration files at `/usr/lib/sendmail-cf/README`. For examples of how to configure Sendmail using m4, see `/usr/lib/sendmail-cf/cf`.

This section will start by installing the necessary Sendmail configuration files for m4 to work and then look at the configuration of an online mail server.

Installing the Sendmail Configuration Files

The Sendmail configuration files are not installed by default when you install Red Hat Linux 6. Installing the files is easy. Mount the CD-ROM that comes with this book to a convenient location (such as /mnt/cdrom) and use rpm to install the file sendmail-cf-8.9.3-1.i386.rpm:

```
$ rpm -i /mnt/cdrom/RedHat/RPMS/sendmail-cf-8.9.3-10.i386.rpm
```

Creating an Online Mail Server

Now you can look at the configuration file for an online mail server. You do this because online mail servers are a little bit easier to configure and understand than offline servers.

NOTE   Even though the m4 system eases Sendmail configuration, the number of options is still immense. Only those options that appear in the configuration files are discussed in this chapter.

An online mail server is a mail server for a network that is fully connected to the Internet by a dedicated line. When someone outside the network directs a mail message to a user on the local network, it can be delivered directly, and when a user on the network sends a message, it is sent immediately.

In your case, you need to configure Sendmail to direct incoming messages to users' mailboxes and to immediately attempt to deliver messages sent by users. Messages are only queued for later delivery if there is a problem delivering a message, such as a failure in the Internet connection while attempting to deliver the message.

Our m4 configuration file looks something like this:

```
include(`../m4/cf.m4')
OSTYPE(`linux')
undefine(`UUCP_RELAY')
undefine(`BITNET_RELAY')
FEATURE(redirect)
FEATURE(always_add_domain)
MAILER(local)
MAILER(smtp)
```

Let's break this down line by line.

Line 1: `include(`../m4/cf.m4')`   These are the generic configuration files needed to build a Sendmail configuration file.

Line 2: `OSTYPE(`linux')`   Your operating system type is defined as Linux so that the appropriate defaults are set.

Line 3: `undefine(`UUCP_RELAY')`   By not defining a UUCP relay, you are indicating that there is no host to receive UUCP-directed mail and that UUCP recipients must be directly connected. Given that UUCP mail was designed for the era when most networks were not directly connected, most sites will leave UUCP_RELAY undefined.

Line 4: `undefine(`BITNET_RELAY')`   Because you are not connected to the Bitnet network, leave this undefined; addresses using the Bitnet format will not work.

Line 5: `FEATURE(redirect)`   If set, any mail addressed to `address.REDIRECT` is rejected with a message indicating the user's new address. In this way, when a user leaves, their new address can be aliased to their old address with `.REDIRECT` appended.

Line 6: `FEATURE(always_add_domain)`   This feature ensures that the From line always contains the local domain so that messages can be replied to by the recipients.

Line 7: `MAILER(local)`   Local mailer support allows Sendmail to deliver mail to local Unix mailboxes.

Line 8: `MAILER(smtp)`   SMTP mailer support allows Sendmail to send messages directly to recipient mail servers. This works in a system where the server is connected to the Internet and DNS services are available.

To create your Sendmail configuration file from the m4 configuration file, you need to create the m4 file in the directory `/usr/lib/sendmail-cf/cf`. In this case, let's call the file `online.mc`. The extension `.mc` is the generally accepted one for m4 configuration files.

Next, change the directory to `/usr/lib/sendmail-cf/cf` and issue this command:

```
$ m4 online.mc > online.cf
```

This command processes the file using m4 and generates a Sendmail configuration file called `online.cf`.

The next step is to make a backup of your existing `sendmail.cf` file and then replace it with the one you just created. This needs to be done by the root user:

```
# cp /etc/sendmail.cf /etc/sendmail.cf.keep
# cp online.cf /etc/sendmail.cf
```

The last and final step is to restart the Sendmail daemon:

```
# killall -HUP sendmail
```

The `killall` command sends the specified signal to all processes running the named program, in this case Sendmail.

When the Sendmail daemon starts at boot time, it will now load your new configuration file. If you want to load Sendmail manually, use the command:

```
# sendmail -bd
```

By default, the Sendmail daemon loads at boot time in most distributions of Linux unless you choose to disable it. You can use the `sendmail -bd` command in your `rc.local` file if you need to add Sendmail to your boot cycle.

TIP   If you plan to run a large Sendmail site, then the book *Sendmail* by Bryan Costales and Eric Allman from O'Reilly & Associates (2nd ed., 1997) is the definitive reference. Be prepared for a long read, though.

Looking Ahead

This chapter wraps up the main body of this book by covering the basics of setting up your own mail server using Linux. With this knowledge in hand, plus the experience you now have in using, configuring, and managing Linux systems, you should be able to perform every computing task you need to do using Linux.

The rest of this book consists of several appendixes, many of which you will find helpful in your daily use of Linux. In particular, "Linux Command Reference" (Appendix C) provides a quick guide to the syntax of major Linux commands, many of which you will find yourself using on a regular basis.

In addition, refer to Appendix B, "Sources of Linux Information," for useful resources for expanding your Linux knowledge and skills. Linux is a vast terrain that cannot be mastered quickly. Even the most adept Linux experts find themselves learning new tricks, secrets, and skills on an almost daily basis. Don't be afraid to do the same. More importantly, don't be afraid to ask questions in the Linux newsgroups or of the authors of popular Linux applications. Most often, the authors are more than happy to provide guidance, insight, and advice to fledgling Linux users. After all, it is in the interest of Linux developers and users to foster knowledge, awareness, and skill among the growing community of Linux users.

APPENDIX
A

Linux Around the World (Non-English Linux Distributions)

Linux in Croatian

MicroLinux

MicroLinux is a small Croatian-language distribution that is designed to sit on a DOS partition. This makes it convenient for users who can't repartition their Windows 95 systems and need to run both Windows (or DOS) and Linux.

```
HULK - Hrvatska udruga Linux korisnika
WWW: http://linux.hr/
```

Linux in French

Kheops Linux

Logiciels du Soleil from France produces Kheops Linux, a French version of the Red Hat Linux distributions. Version 5.2 of Red Hat in French is currently available.

```
Logiciels du Soleil
1 rue Pasqualini
F-06800 Cagnes sur mer
France
E-mail: kheops@linux-kheops.com
WWW: http://www.linux-kheops.com/
```

MNIS Linux

MNIS produces a French distribution of Linux known as MNIS Linux. MNIS Linux is billed as a PC-based X workstation and includes unique features such as the K Desktop Environment.

```
MNIS
28, rue Mahias
F-92100 Boulogne
France
E-mail: info@mnis.fr
WWW: http://www.mnis.fr/
```

S.u.S.E. Linux

S.u.S.E. Linux was originally available in both English and German. Now, a French version is available that closely matches the English version 6, with similar extras like S.u.S.E.'s set of extra servers for XFree86 and a good set of demo commercial software for Linux.

```
S.u.S.E.
Gesellschaft für Software und Systementwicklung mbH
Gebhardtstraße 2
D-90762 Fürth
Germany
E-mail: info@suse.de
WWW: http://www.suse.de
```

Linux in German

Delix DLD Linux

Delix produces DLD Linux (which stands for Deutsche Linux Distribution) as well as selling other Linux products, including Red Hat Linux, Xi Graphics' Accelerated X servers, and the Common Desktop Environment (CDE). DLD includes a commercial X server, Red Hat's RPM package management system, the Adabas-D database, and more. The current version of DLD Linux is version 6.

```
Delix Computer GmbH
E-mail: info@delix.de
WWW: http://www.delix.de/
```

Eagle Linux

Eagle Linux is a German Linux distribution for the Motorola 68000 series processors with specific installation support for Amiga computers. Support is provided for most popular Amiga models and most Amiga hardware and peripherals.

```
Media Computer Products GmbH
Altenbergstrasse 7
D-71549 Auenwald
Germany
WWW: http://www.eagle-cp.com/www/m68k.html
```

S.u.S.E. Linux

S.u.S.E. Linux is available in English, German, French, and Italian, but the Germany-based company makes the German-speaking market its primary focus. The German version of the distribution closely matches the English product, with similar extras like S.u.S.E.'s set of extra servers for XFree86 and a good set of demo commercial software for Linux.

```
S.u.S.E.
Gesellschaft für Software und Systementwicklung mbH
Gebhardtstraße 2
D-90762 Fürth
Germany
E-mail: info@suse.de
WWW: http://www.suse.de
```

Linux in Italian

S.u.S.E. Linux

S.u.S.E. Linux was originally available in both English and German. Now, an Italian version is available that closely matches the English version 6, with similar extras like S.u.S.E.'s set of extra servers for XFree86 and a good set of demo commercial software for Linux.

```
S.u.S.E.
Gesellschaft für Software und Systementwicklung mbH
Gebhardtstraße 2
D-90762 Fürth
Germany
E-mail: info@suse.de
WWW: http://www.suse.de
```

Linux in Japanese

Debian JP Linux

The Debian JP Project is an attempt to provide a Japanese installer and Japanese packages for the standard Debian Linux distribution. This is an ongoing effort, with work being done in translation and package development.

```
The Debian JP Project
WWW: http://www.debian.or.jp/index.html
```

Linux in Portuguese

Conectiva Linux

Conectiva Linux is a Portuguese version of Red Hat Linux produced by Conectiva Informática in Brazil. At the time of this writing, the current distribution of Conectiva Linux is version 3.

```
Conectiva Informática
Rua Prof. Rubens Elke Braga, 558
Parolin
Brazil
E-mail: info@conectiva.com.br
WWW: http://www.conectiva.com.br/
```

Linux in Russian

Open Kernel: Linux

Open Kernel: Linux from UrbanSoft is a Russian distribution based on Red Hat Linux, which offers Russian console fonts, a Russian X Windows environment, and additional Russian packages that are not part of the standard Red Hat environment. The current version is derived from Red Hat 5.2.

```
UrbanSoft
E-mail: info@usoft.spb.ru
WWW: http://www.usoft.spb.ru/
```

Linux in Spanish

Eurielec Linux

Eurielec Linux is yet another non-English Linux distribution based on Red Hat Linux, this time in Spanish. Eurielec Linux version 2.1 is based on the latest Red Hat Linux 5.1.

```
Eurielec - ETSI Telecomunicacion
WWW: http://www.etsit.upm.es/~eurielec/
```

APPENDIX

B

Sources of Linux Information

This appendix lists Internet resources where you can find additional Linux-related information, download or purchase Linux distributions, and ask for help. By no means is this intended to reflect a complete list of Linux resources on the Internet; it is more a record of the sites I have found useful around the Internet in my years using Linux.

General Information

Just Linux	http://www.justlinux.com/
Linux Documentation Project	http://metalab.unc.edu/mdw/
Linux Frequently Asked Questions with Answers	http://www.cl.cam.ac.uk/users/iwj10/linux-faq/index.html
Linux Hardware	http://www.fokus.gmd.de/linux/linux-hardware.html
linux-howto.com	http://www.linux-howto.com/
Linux Information Sheet	ftp://rtfm.mit.edu/pub/usenet-by-hierarchy/comp/os/linux/answers/linux/info-sheet
Linux Installation and Getting Started	http://metalab.unc.edu/mdw/LDP/gs/gs.html
Linux International	http://www.li.org/
Linux Journal	http://www.ssc.com/lj/index.html
Linux Meta FAQ	ftp://rtfm.mit.edu/pub/usenet-by-hierarchy/comp/os/linux/answers/linux/meta-faq
Linux NOW!	http://www.linuxnow.com/
Linux Online	http://www.linux.org/
The Linux Resources	http://www.linuxresources.com/
The Linux Software Review	http://karlsberg.usask.ca/~slg/lsr/lsr.html
Linux System Administrators' Guide	http://linuxwww.db.erau.edu/SAG/index.html

Linux User Group Registry | http://www.linux.org/users/index.html

The Linux Web Ring | http://nll.interl.net/lwr/

Slashdot | http://www.slashdot.org/

The Network Administrators' Guide | http://www.uni-tuebingen.de/zdv/projekte/linux/books/nag/nag.html

Woven Goods for Linux | http://www.fokus.gmd.de/linux/

Linux Professional Certifications | http://www.digitalmetrics.com

Linux Distributions

Caldera OpenLinux | http://www.calderasystems.com/

Conectiva Linux (Portuguese) | http://www.conectiva.com.br/

Debian/GNU Linux | http://www.debian.org/

Delix Linux (German) | http://delix.de/

DLX Linux | http://www.wu-wien.ac.at/usr/h93/h9301726/dlx.html

Eagle Linux (German, for Motorola 680x0 chips) | http://www.eagle-cp.com/www/m68k.html

Eurielex Linux (Spanish) | http://www.etsit.upm.es/~eurielec/redhat/index.html

Hal 91 | http://home.sol.no/~okolaas/hal91.html

Kheops Linux (French) | http://www.linux-kheops.com/

LinuxPPC (for PowerPC chips) | http://www.linuxppc.org/

Linux Pro Plus | http://www.linuxmall.com/Allprod/lxcdr.html

LinuxWare | http://www.trans-am.com/

MkLinux (for the Power Macintosh) | http://www.mklinux.apple.com/

MNIS Linux (French) | http://www.mnis.fr/

Red Hat Linux | http://www.redhat.com/

Slackware Linux	`http://www.slackware.org/`
Stampede Linux	`http://www.stampede.org/`
S.u.S.E. Linux (German and English)	`http://www.suse.com/`
TurboLinux	`http://www.turbolinux.com/`

Mailing Lists and Newsgroups

alt.os.linux	`news:alt.os.linux`
comp.os.linux.admin	`news:comp.os.linux.admin`
comp.os.linux.advocacy	`news:comp.os.linux.advocacy`
comp.os.linux.announce	`news:comp.os.linux.announce`
comp.os.linux.answers	`news:comp.os.linux.answers`
comp.os.linux.development	`news:comp.os.linux.development`
comp.os.linux.development.apps	`news:comp.os.linux.development.apps`
comp.os.linux.development.system	`news:comp.os.linux.development.system`
comp.os.linux.hardware	`news:comp.os.linux.hardware`
comp.os.linux.help	`news:comp.os.linux.help`
comp.os.linux.misc	`news:comp.os.linux.misc`
comp.os.linux.networking	`news:comp.os.linux.networking`
comp.os.linux.setup	`news:comp.os.linux.setup`
comp.os.linux.x	`news:comp.os.linux.x`
Linux Mailing Lists	`http://oslab.snu.ac.kr/~djshin/linux/mail-list/index.shtml`
LinuxWWW Mailing List Archives	`http://linuxwww.db.erau.edu/mail_archives/`

Non-Intel Platforms

ERAU SparcLinux Archive	`http://linuxwww.db.erau.edu/`
Linux Alpha FTP Archive	`http://gatekeeper.dec.com/pub/DEC/Linux-Alpha/`
Linux for BeBox	`http://www.guru.dircon.co.uk/belinux/`
Linux for Sparc Processors	`http://www.geog.ubc.ca/s_linux.html`
Linux/m68k for Macintosh	`http://www.mac.linux-m68k.org/`
The Linux/m68k Home Pages	`http://www.clark.net/pub/lawrencc/linux/index.html`
MkArchive	`http://ftp.sunet.se/pub/os/Linux/` `mklinux/mkarchive/info/index.html`
SGI-Linux	`http://linus.linux.sgi.com/`

Non-English Sites

EPC Home Page (Spanish)	`http://www.arrakis.es/~epujol/linux/`
Linux (Czech)	`http://www.linux.cz/`
Linux - Viel Unix für wenig Geld (German)	`http://www.uni-tuebingen.de/zdv/` `projekte/linux/`
Linux Indonesia (Indonesian)	`http://www.linux.or.id/`

Places to Purchase Linux CD-ROMs

CD-ROM Shop	`http://www.cdromshop.com/`
CheapBytes	`http://www.cheapbytes.com/`
The Computer Underground	`http://www.tcu-inc.com/`
I-Link	`http://i-linkcom.com/software.html`

InfoMagic	`http://www.infomagic.com/`
Just Computers	`http://www.justcomp.com/`
Linux Central	`http://linuxcentral.com/`
Linux Mall	`http://www.linuxmall.com/`
Universal CD-ROM	`http://www.bigmall.com/`
Walnut Creek	`http://www.cdrom.com/`

Places to Download Linux and Linux Files

BLINUX's FTP Site	`ftp://leb.net/pub/blinux/`
Caldera's FTP Site	`ftp://ftp.caldera.com/pub/`
Debian's FTP Site	`ftp://ftp.debian.org/`
Freshmeat.net	`http://www.freshmeat.net/`
Georgia Tech's Linux Archive	`ftp://ftp.cc.gatech.edu/pub/linux/`
Linux Applications	`http://www.linuxapps.com/`
Linux Applications and Utilties for New Users	`http://www.ameritech.net/users/dbarber/index.html`
Linux Applications and Utilities Page	`http://www.hongik.com/linux//linapps.html`
Linux Kernel Archives	`ftp://ftp.kernel.org/`
Linux Software Map	`http://www.linux.org/apps/lsm.html`
Red Hat's FTP Site	`ftp://ftp.redhat.com/pub/`
UNC's Linux Archive	`ftp://metalab.unc.edu/pub/Linux/`
Walnut Creek's FTP Site	`ftp://wcarchive.cdrom.com/pub/linux/`
Woven Goods for Linux's Software Page	`http://www.fokus.gmd.de/linux/linux-softw.html`

X Windows

MetroLink	http://www.metrolink.com/
XFree86 Project	http://www.xfree86.org/
Xi Graphics	http://www.xinside.com/

APPENDIX

C

Linux Command Reference

This appendix provides a guide to using the common Linux commands and utilities found in the following directories in most Red Hat Linux installations:

- /bin
- /sbin
- /usr/bin
- /usr/sbin

The approach taken here is to provide a quick reference to the syntax and common options for many major Linux commands. More details about these commands and about commands not listed here are generally found in the man pages for the commands (accessed by typing man *command*).

By no means should this appendix be considered a complete guide to all options, flags, and arguments for every Linux command. Instead, it is designed to get you started using common and important commands in their most common forms. In all cases, you can consult the relevant man page of a command to learn further details about that command.

This appendix presents the overall syntax of commands using the style found in standard Linux man pages, and then provides a description of the command followed by a description of major flags and arguments.

In order to keep this appendix to a reasonable size, most interactive programs, daemons, and Red Hat–specific commands have been excluded. Even so, there are almost 200 commands covered in this appendix.

Commands appear in alphabetical order.

Commands Covered in This Appendix

The following commands are covered in this reference:

arch	atrm	biff	chgrp
at	badblocks	cal	chkconfig
atd	batch	cat	chmod
atq	bc	checkalias	chown

clear	grep	listalias	mkdir
compress	groupadd	ln	mkdosfs
cp	groupdel	loadkeys	mke2fs
crontab	groupmod	logger	mkfs
cryptdir	groups	login	mkpasswd
date	grpck	logname	mkswap
dc	gunzip	logrotate	mlabel
decryptdir	gzexe	lpd	mmd
depmod	gzip	lpq	mmove
df	halt	lpr	modprobe
dir	head	lprm	more
dmesg	hostname	ls	mount
dnsdomainname	id	lsdev	mrd
dnsquery	ifconfig	lsmod	mren
domainname	ifdown	mail	mtype
du	ifport	mailq	mv
e2fsck	ifup	mailto	netstat
echo	insmod	man	newgrp
egrep	kbd_mode	mattrib	newusers
false	kbdrate	mbadblocks	nisdomainname
fdisk	kill	mcd	nslookup
fgrep	killall	mcopy	passwd
file	ksyms	mdel	paste
find	last	mdeltree	pathchk
finger	ldd	mdir	pidof
free	less	messages	ping
gpasswd	lilo	mformat	pppstats

ps	route	tar	uudecode
pwck	rsh	timeconfig	uuencode
pwconv	runlevel	timed	vipw
pwd	rup	timedc	vmstat
pwunconv	rusers	top	w
quota	rwho	touch	wc
quotacheck	rwhod	traceroute	whereis
quotaoff	setclock	true	which
quotaon	setkeycodes	umount	whoami
rcp	showkey	uname	ypdomainname
rdate	showmount	uncompress	zcat
rdist	shutdown	unzip	zgrep
repquota	sort	uptime	zip
rlogin	statserial	useradd	zipgrep
rm	su	userdel	zipinfo
rmdir	sync	usermod	zmore
rmmod	tail	users	znew

arch

Description	Displays the architecture of the machine on which Linux is running. For instance, i586 represents a Pentium-based system, i486 represents an 80486-based computer, and axp represents Linux running on an Alpha-based computer.
Syntax	arch
Important Flags and Options	None

at

Description	Schedules commands to be executed at a specific time. User is prompted for the commands, or the commands can be provided from a file. Each job is added to a schedule queue and is provided a job number.
Syntax	`at [-q queue] [-f filename] [-1] [-m] [-d job [job ...]] TIME`
Important Flags and Options	• `-d job`: Deletes a job specified by job number.
	• `-f filename`: Reads commands to be scheduled from the specified file rather than prompting for the commands.
	• `-1`: Displays commands in the schedule queue (the TIME argument is ignored).
	• `-m`: E-mails the user who scheduled the job once the job is finished, and includes any generated output in the body of the message.
	• `-q queue`: Specifies the queue to operate on. Queues are specified with a single letter (a-z or A-Z). By default, the a queue is used for **at** and related commands.
Notes	Specifying times: Several options exist for specifying time, including these:
	• *HH:MM* specifies the hour and minutes, such as 11:15 or 22:30. AM and PM suffixes are allowed, as in 11:15AM or 11:30PM.
	• midnight (24:00 or 12:00PM), noon (12:00), and teatime (16:00) are reserved words specifying the times indicated.
	• *MMDDYY*, *MM/DD/YY*, or *DD.MM.YY* can be used to indicate specific dates, as in 022598 or 25.02.98.
	• now specifies the current time.
	• tomorrow specifies the next day.
	• Using a + can specify offsets in minutes, hours, days, or weeks from a specified time. For instance, to schedule a command for noon two days from the current day, you could use noon + 2 days.

atd

Description	Daemon that runs jobs scheduled for later execution by programs such as **at** and **batch**.
Syntax	`atd [-1 load] [-b interval]`
Important Flags and Options	• `-b interval`: Indicates the minimum interval in seconds between the start of two batch jobs. By default, this is 60 seconds.
	• `-1 load`: Specifies a load limit over which scheduled batch jobs will not be run. By default, this load is 0.8.

atq

Description	Displays jobs scheduled by the command **at** that are in the schedule queue. This is the same as **at -l**.
Syntax	`atq [-q queue]`
Important Flags and Options	• **-q** *queue*: Specifies the queue to operate on. Queues are specified with a single letter (**a-z** or **A-Z**). By default, the **a** queue is used for **at** and related commands.

atrm

Description	Removes specified jobs from the **at** schedule queue. This is the same as **at -d**.
Syntax	`atrm job [job ...]`
Important Flags and Options	None

badblocks

Description	Checks a device (usually a hard disk) for bad blocks.
Syntax	`badblocks [-o filename] [-w] device blocks-count`
Important Flags and Options	• **-o** *filename*: Specifies a file where results should be written instead of displaying them on the standard output. • **-w**: Uses a write test, instead of a read-only test, in which data is written to each block of the device and then reread from the block.
Notes	You should specify the device using the full Linux device path, such as **/dev/hda2** or **/dev/sdb3**. The number of blocks on the device is essential (this information can be determined using **fdisk**).
Warnings	Do not use the **-w** flag on devices that contain important data. Data stored on devices that are checked with the **-w** flag will get erased during the checking process.

batch

Description	Schedules commands to be executed at a specified time as long as system load levels permit. User is prompted for the commands, or the commands can be provided from a file. Each job is added to a schedule queue and is provided a job number.
Syntax	`batch [-q queue] [-f filename] [-m] TIME`

Important Flags and Options	• -f *filename*: Reads commands to be scheduled from the specified file rather than prompting for the commands.
	• -m: E-mails the user who scheduled the job once the job is finished and includes any generated output in the body of the message.
	• -q *queue*: Specifies the queue to operate on. Queues are specified with a single letter (a-z or A-Z). By default, the b queue is used for **batch**.
Notes	Specifying times: Several options exist for specifying time, including these:
	• *HH:MM* specifies the hour and minutes, such as 11:15 or 22:30. AM and PM suffixes are allowed, as in 11:15AM or 11:30PM.
	• **midnight** (24:00 or 12:00PM), **noon** (12:00), and **teatime** (16:00) are reserved words specifying the times indicated.
	• *MMDDYY*, *MM/DD/YY*, or *DD.MM.YY* can be used to indicate specific dates, as in 022598 or 25.02.98.
	• **now** specifies the current time.
	• **tomorrow** specifies the next day.
	• Using a + can specify offsets in **minutes**, **hours**, **days**, or **weeks** from a specified time. For instance, to schedule a command for noon two days from the current day, you could use **noon + 2 days**.

bc

Description	An interactive, arbitrary-precision calculator. Processes all expressions in specified files as well as prompting user to provide expressions for evaluation.
Syntax	bc [*file* ...]
Important Flags and Options	None
Notes	The syntax of expressions used by **bc** is largely based on the C programming language. Refer to the **bc** man page for details.
	Expressions in files provided as arguments are processed before presenting a prompt to the user for entering additional expressions to be processed.

biff

Description	Notifies users when new mail arrives and indicates who sent the message.
Syntax	biff [ny]
Important Flags and Options	• n: Disables mail arrival notification when it is enabled.
	• y: Enables mail arrival notification when it is disabled.

cal

Description	Displays a calendar for a month or an entire year. If no month or year is specified, the current month's calendar is displayed.
Syntax	`cal [-j] [-y] [month [year]]`
Important Flags and Options	• `-j`: Specifies that Julian dates should be used instead of Gregorian dates.
	• `-y`: Displays a yearly calendar instead of a monthly calendar.
Notes	A single numeric argument specifies a year between the year 1 and the year 9999 (years must be complete--e.g., 1998, not 98). With two arguments, the first specifies the month numerically from 1 to 12 and the second specifies the year from 1 to 9999.

cat

Description	Combines one or more files and displays them on the standard output. If no files are given, then the standard input is written to the standard output.
Syntax	`cat [--benstvAET] [--number] [--number-nonblank] [--squeeze-blank]` ➥`[--show-nonprinting] [--show-ends] [--show-tabs] [--show-all]` ➥`[file ...]`
Important Flags and Options	• `-A/--show-all`: Displays a $ at the end of each line, tab characters as ^I, and control characters preceded by a ^. This is the same as the combination of -v, -T, and -E.
	• `-b/--number-nonblank`: Causes all non-blank lines to appear numbered. Numbering starts at 1.
	• `-e`: Displays a $ at the end of each line and control characters preceded by a ^. This is the same as the combination of -v and -E.
	• `-E/--show-ends`: Displays a $ at the end of each line.
	• `-n/--number`: Causes all lines to appear numbered. Numbering starts at 1.
	• `-s/--squeeze-blank`: Replaces sequences of multiple blank lines with single blank lines when displayed.
	• `-t`: Displays tab characters as ^I and control characters preceded by a ^. This is the same as the combination of -v and -T.
	• `-T/--show-tabs`: Displays tab characters as ^I.
	• `-v/--show-nonprinting`: Displays control characters preceded by a ^.

checkalias

Description	Checks the user's file and then the system alias file in order to see if a specified alias is defined.
Syntax	`checkalias alias[, alias,...]`
Important Flags and Options	None

chgrp

Description	Changes the group ownership of one or more files or directories.
Syntax	`chgrp [-Rcfv] [--recursive] [--changes] [--silent] [--quiet]` `➥[--verbose] group filename ...`
Important Flags and Options	• `-c/--changes`: Displays the names of only those files whose ownership is being changed.
	• `-f/--silent/--quiet`: Suppresses display of error messages when a file's ownership cannot be changed.
	• `-R/--recursive`: Recursively changes the ownership of all files in all subdirectories of any directory that has its ownership changed.
	• `-v/--verbose`: Displays the results of all ownership changes.
Notes	The group can be specified either by name or by group ID.

chkconfig

Description	Manipulates or displays settings for system run levels.
Syntax	`chkconfig -list [name]`
	`chkconfig -add name`
	`chkconfig -del name`
	`chkconfig <on	off	reset> [--level levels]`
	`chkconfig [--level levels] name`
Important Flags and Options	• `--add name`: Adds a new service for management by **chkconfig** and checks that the necessary start and kill entries exist. If entries are missing, they are created.
	• `--del name`: Deletes the named service from management; any links to it are also deleted.

- `--level [levels]`: Specifies numerically which run level a named service should belong to.

- `--list name`: Lists all services that `chkconfig` knows about and any relevant information about them. If a named service is specified, only information about that service is displayed.

- `off`: When specified after the service name, the service's status for the specified run level is changed to a stopped state. If no run level is specified, then this option affects run levels 3, 4, and 5.

- `on`: When specified after the service name, the service's status for the specified run level is changed to a started state. If no run level is specified, then this option affects run levels 3, 4, and 5.

- `reset`: When specified after the service name, the service's status for the specified run level is set to the default status indicated by the `init` script. If no run level is specified, then this option affects all run levels.

chmod

Description	Changes the access permissions of one or more files or directories.
Syntax	`chmod [-Rcfv] [--recursive] [--changes] [--silent] [--quiet]` ➥`[--verbose] mode file ...`
Important Flags and Options	

- `-c/--changes`: Displays the names of only those files whose permissions are being changed.

- `-f/--silent/--quiet`: Suppresses display of error messages when a file's permissions cannot be changed.

- `-R/--recursive`: Recursively changes the permissions of all files in all subdirectories of any directory that has its permissions changed.

- `-v/--verbose`: Displays the results of all permission changes.

Notes

Modes can be specified in two ways: symbolically and numerically. When done symbolically, modes take the form [ugoa][[+-=][rwxXstugo ...]. The first element ([ugoa]) represents the users whose permissions are being affected (u=user who owns the file or directory, g=all members of the group that owns the file or directory, o=anyone who is not the owner or in the owner group, a=all users). The + symbol means that the specified modes should be added to already specified permissions, the – symbol means the specified modes should be removed from existing permissions, and the = symbol means that the specified modes should replace existing permissions. There are many different permissions that can be specified in the third element of the mode, including **r** for read permissions, **w** for write permissions, and **x** for execute permissions.

Full details of symbolic and numeric modes appear in the **chmod** man page.

chown

Description	Changes the user and/or group ownership of one or more files or directories.
Syntax	`chown [-Rcfv] [--recursive] [--changes] [--silent] [--quiet]` `➡[--verbose] [user][:.][group]` *file* `...`
Important Flags and Options	• `-c/--changes`: Displays the names of only those files whose ownership is being changed.
	• `-f/--silent/--quiet`: Suppresses display of error messages when a file's ownership cannot be changed.
	• `-R/--recursive`: Recursively changes the ownership of all files in all subdirectories of any directory that has its ownership changed.
	• `-v/--verbose`: Displays the results of all ownership changes.
Notes	The user and group can be specified either by name or by IDs. User and group can be combined in several ways:
	• The user followed by a dot or colon followed by a group changes both the user and group ownerships to those specified.
	• The user followed by a dot or colon and no group changes the user ownership as specified and changes the group ownership to the specified user's login group.
	• If the colon or dot and group are specified without a user, then only group ownership is changed. This is the same as `chgrp`.
	• If the user is not followed by a dot or colon, then only the user ownership is changed.

clear

Description	Clears the terminal screen and resets the prompt and cursor location to the first line of the screen.
Syntax	`clear`
Important Flags and Options	None

compress

Description	Compresses files or the standard input using Lempel-Ziv compression.
Syntax	`compress [-f] [-v] [-c] [-r] [`*file* `...]`

Important Flags and Options

- -c: Returns compressed data on standard output rather than to a file as is the default when compressing a file.

- -f: Forces compression of hard-linked files, which are ignored by default.

- -r: Operates recursively. If a directory is specified as an argument, then compresses all files within that directory and in its subdirectories.

- -v: Displays the percentage reduction in size for each file compressed.

Notes

When compressing files, the **compress** command replaces the original file with a file whose name has a .Z prefix but otherwise remains unchanged. This behavior is overridden by the -c flag. If no files are specified, the standard input is compressed and the results are returned through standard output.

cp

Description

Copies files and directories.

Syntax

cp [-a] [--archive] [-b] [--backup] [-d] [--no-dereference] [-f]
➥[--force] [-i] [--interactive] [1] [--link] [-p] [--preserve]
➥[-R] [--recursive] [-s] [--symbolic-link] [-u] [--update] *source*
destination

cp [*options*] *source* ... *destination*

Important Flags and Options

- -a/--archive: Copies files and directories recursively, maintaining symbolic links as links and preserving ownership and permissions of the original files. This is the same as -dpR.

- -b/--backup: Makes backup copies of files before the original files are overwritten.

- -d/--no-dereference: Copies links as links rather than copying the files to which the links point.

- -f/--force: Forces removal of existing destination files that need to be overwritten.

- -i/--interactive: Prompts before overwriting existing destination files.

- -1/--link: Makes hard links instead of copying files. This applies only to files, not to directories.

- -p/--preserve: Preserves the ownership and permissions of the original files.

- -R/--recursive: Recursively copies directories. That is, for every source directory specified, every file in the directory and all its subdirectories are copied while retaining the matching directory structure.

- -s/--symbolic-link: Makes symbolic links instead of copying files. Source files must be specified with full paths.

- -u/--update: Replaces only those destination files that have older modification times than the corresponding source files.

Warnings

Care needs to be taken with the -f flag when working as the root user. Making a mistake can cause important system files to be overwritten because the root user generally has write permission for all files and directories.

crontab

Description	Displays or alters a user's Cron table (`crontab`). The Cron table specifies scheduled actions that are executed by the Cron daemon.
Syntax	`crontab [-u user] file`
	`crontab [-u user] { -l|-r| -e }`
Important Flags and Options	• `-e`: Edits the `crontab` file of the user executing the command or the user specified by the `-u` flag. The editor invoked is specified by the **EDITOR** environment variable.
	• `-l`: Displays the contents of the `crontab` file of the user executing the command or the user specified by the `-u` flag.
	• `-r`: Deletes the `crontab` file of the user executing the command or the user specified by the `-u` flag.
	• `-u user`: Specifies which user's `crontab` file to work with if it is not the same user as the one executing the command. This flag can only be used by the root user.
Notes	The format of entries in `crontab` files is discussed in Chapter 17, "General System Administration."

cryptdir

Description	Encrypts all files in a specified directory. If no directory is specified, then all files in the current directory are encrypted.
Syntax	`cryptdir [directory]`
Important Flags and Options	None
Notes	When encrypting files, you will be prompted twice for a password. This password is needed to decrypt files. Encrypted files will have the `.crypt` extensions added to their names. Use `decryptdir` to decrypt the files.

date

Description	Displays or sets the current system date and time.
Syntax	`date [-u] [--universal] [MMDDhhmm[[CC]YY][.ss]]`
Important Flags and Options	• `-u/--universal`: Displays the time in Greenwich Mean Time (also known as Coordinated Universal Time).

Notes If a date and time are provided as an argument, this is done entirely with numbers where the two-digit elements shown previously represent the following values:

- *MM*: month
- *DD*: day of the month
- *hh*: hour
- *mm*: minute
- *CC*: century (first two digits of the year)
- *YY*: last two digits of the year
- *ss*: seconds

Keep in mind that only the root user can set the system clock.

dc

Description An interactive, arbitrary-precision, reverse-polish notation calculator. Processes all expressions in specified files as well as prompting user to provide expressions for evaluation.

Syntax `dc [file ...]`

Important Flags and Options None

Notes Detailed syntax of expressions used by **dc** is documented in the **dc** man page. Expressions in files provided as arguments are processed before presenting a prompt to the user for entering additional expressions to be processed.

decryptdir

Description Decrypts all files in a specified directory. If no directory is specified, then all files in the current directory are encrypted. Files must have been encrypted with the `encryptdir` command.

Syntax `cryptdir [directory]`

Important Flags and Options None

Notes You will be prompted for a password when decrypting files. You need to provide the same password that was used when encrypting the files, or the process will fail.

depmod

Description	Returns module dependencies on the standard output. These can be stored in a file and then used by **modprobe** for installing loadable modules.
Syntax	depmod *module1*.o *module2*.o ...
Important Flags and Options	None

df

Description	Displays free space on one or more mounted disks or partitions. If no files (or directories) are specified, then the free space on all mounted file systems is displayed. If filenames are specified, then the free space for the file system containing each file is displayed.
Syntax	df [-T] [-t *fstype*] [-x *fstype*] [--all] [--inodes] [--type=*fstype*] ➥[--exclude-type=*fstype*] [--print-type] [*filename* ...]
Important Flags and Options	• -t/--type=*fstype*: Displays information only for file systems of the specified type.
	• -T/--print-type: Displays the file system type for each file system reported.
	• -x/--exclude-type=*fstype*: Does not report information for file systems of the specified type.

dir

Description	Displays a listing of the files in a specified directory, in alphabetical order unless otherwise specified. By default, displays the contents of the current directory unless another directory is specified.
Syntax	dir [-acCGlnrRStuU] [--all] [--no-group] [--numeric-uid-gid] ➥[--reverse] [--recursive] [file ...]
Important Flags and Options	• -a/--all: Shows all entries, including those whose names start with ".".
	• -c: Sorts by the creation time of the file and, when displaying complete file information (with the -l flag), displays the creation time.
	• -C: Displays entries in columns.
	• -G/--no-group: Prevents display of group information.
	• -l: Displays files with long listing format.
	• -n/--numeric-uid-gid: Lists user IDs and group IDs (UIDs and GIDs) instead of names.
	• -r/--reverse: Reverses order of entries when sorting.

- -R/--recursive: Recursively lists contents of subdirectories.
- -S: Sorts files by size.
- -t: Sorts by the modification time of the file and, when displaying complete file information (with the -1 flag), displays the modification time.
- -u: Sorts by the last access time of the file and, when displaying complete file information (with the -1 flag), displays the last access time.
- -U: Displays entries in their directory order rather than sorted.

dmesg

Description	Displays or manipulates the kernel ring buffer. This is where many bootup messages are kept.
Syntax	dmesg [-c]
Important Flags and Options	-c: Clears the ring buffer after displaying the contents.

dnsdomainname

Description	Displays the system's DNS domain name based on its fully qualified domain name.
Syntax	Domainname [-f *filename*] [--file *filename*]
Important Flags and Options	-f/--file *filename*: Specifies a file from which to read the host name.

dnsquery

Description	Queries DNS servers to look up information about a specified host.
Syntax	dnsquery [-n *nameserver*] [-t *type*] [-c *class*] [-r *retry*] ➥[-p *retryperiod*] host
Important Flags and Options	• -c *class*: Specifies the class of records being searched for.
	• -n *nameserver*: Specifies the name server to use for the query. If not specified, then uses the default name server.
	• -p *retryperiod*: Specifies how long to wait before assuming the server is not responding.
	• -r *retry*: Specifies the number of times to retry the query if the server is not responding.
	• -t *type*: Specifies the type of query to make.

Notes

When specifying the type of query, possible types include:

- **A**: Looks up the address only.
- **NS**: Finds the name server for the host.
- **CNAME**: Finds the canonical name for the host.
- **PTR**: Finds the domain name pointer.
- **SOA**: Finds the start of the authority record for the host.
- **MX**: Finds the mail exchanges for the domain.
- **ANY**: Finds anything and everything that can be found (this is the default behavior).

When specifying classes of information, possible classes include:

- **IN**: Internet (This is the default and you probably won't want to change it.)
- **HS**: Hesiod
- **CHAOS**: Chaos
- **ANY**: Any

domainname

Description

Displays or sets the system's NIS domain name. Without arguments or flags, the default behavior is to display the current NIS domain name.

Syntax

`domainname [-F file] [--file file] [name]`

Important Flags and Options

- `-F/--file file`: Indicates that the domain name should be set based on the contents of the specified file instead of expecting it as an argument on the command line.

du

Description

Displays a report of disk space usage for each specified file or directory as well as all subdirectories of specified directories. By default, displays information for all files and directories in the current directory.

Syntax

`du [-abcksx] [--all] [--bytes] [--total] [--kilobytes] [--summarize]`
➥`[--one-file-system] [file ...]`

Important Flags and Options

- `-a/--all`: Displays usage information for files and directories.
- `-b/--bytes`: Displays usage information in bytes.

- -c/--total: Displays a total usage figure for all.

- -k/--kilobytes: Displays usage information in kilobytes.

- -s/--summarize: Displays a total for each argument and does not display individual information for each file or subdirectory inside a directory.

- -x/--one-file-system: Skips directories that are not part of the current file system.

e2fsck

Description	Checks the state of a Linux second extended file system. This is the default file system used for Linux partitions.
Syntax	`e2fsck [-cfnpy] [-B blocksize] device`
Important Flags and Options	

- -B blocksize: Specifies a specific block size to use in searching for the superblock. By default, the program will search at various different block sizes until it finds the superblock.

- -c: Causes the **badblocks** program to be run and marks any bad blocks accordingly.

- -f: Forces checking of file systems that outwardly seem clean.

- -n: Opens the file system in a read-only state and answers "no" to all prompts to take action.

- -p: Forces automatic repairing without prompts.

- -y: Assumes an answer of "yes" to all questions.

Notes	The device to be checked should be specified using the complete Linux device path, such as **/dev/hda1** or **/dev/sdb3**. It is advisable that the file system not be mounted or, if you need to check the root file system or a file system that must be mounted, that this be done in single-user mode.

echo

Description	Displays a line of text, optionally without a trailing new line (a new line is included by default).
Syntax	`echo [-ne] [string ...]`
Important Flags and Options	

- -e: Enables interpretation of backslashed special characters in the string.

- -n: Disables output of a trailing new line.

Notes   Backslashed special characters include:

- \b: backspace

- \f: form feed

- \n: new line

- \r: carriage return

- \t: horizontal tab

- \\: backslash

egrep

Description   Searches files for lines matching a specified pattern and displays the lines. The pattern is interpreted as an extended regular expression.

Syntax   egrep [-bCciLlnvwx] [-*number*] [-e *pattern*] [-f file] [--byte-offset]
�➥[--context] [--count] [--regexp=*pattern*] [--file=*file*] [--ignore=*case*]
➥[--files-without-match] [--files-with-match] [--line-number]
➥[--revert-match] [--word-regexp] [--line-regexp] [*pattern*] *file*
➥[*file* ...]

Important Flags and Options
- -*number*: Displays matching lines with the specified number of lines of leading and trailing context.

- -b/--**byte**-offset: Prints the byte offset of the match before each line.

- -c/--**count**: Instead of displaying matching lines, simply outputs a count of the total number of lines matching the expressions (when combined with -v, displays the total count of non-matching lines).

- -C/--**context**: Displays matching lines with two lines of leading and trailing context (this is the same as −2).

- -e pattern/--regexp=*pattern*: Uses the specified regular expression rather than one provided as an argument.

- -f file/--file=*file*: Uses the regular expression found in the specified file rather than one supplied as an argument.

- -i/--**ignore**=case: Ignores case in both the pattern and the files being searched.

- -l/--files-with-matches: Instead of displaying each matched line, simply displays the name of each file that contains at least one match for the regular expression.

- -L/--files-without-match: Instead of displaying each matched line, simply displays the name of each file that contains no matches for the regular expressions.

- -n/--line-number: Prefixes each output line with its line number in the file.

- -v/--revert-match: Displays non-matching lines instead of matching lines.

- -w/--word-regexp: Displays only those lines with matches for the regular expression that are complete words.

- -x/--line-regexp: Displays only those lines with matches for the regular expression that are complete lines.

Notes The syntax of regular expressions used by **egrep** can be found in the **egrep** man page.

false

Description Does nothing and returns a failure exit status.

Syntax `false`

Important Flags and Options None

fdisk

Description Provides tools for manipulating partition tables. By default, **fdisk** starts ready to work with the current device unless a different device is specified as an argument.

Syntax `fdisk [-l] [-s partition] [device]`

Important Flags and Options

- -l: Lists the partition tables for **/dev/hda**, **/dev/hdb**, and **/dev/sda** through **/dev/sdh** and then exits.

- -s partition: Returns the size of the specified partition on the standard output and exits.

fgrep

Description Searches files for lines matching a specified pattern and displays the lines. The pattern is interpreted as a list of fixed strings as opposed to regular expressions. Strings are separated by new lines and any of the strings can be matched.

Syntax `fgrep [-bCciLlnvwx] [-number] [-e pattern] [-f file] [--byte-offset]`
`➡[--context] [--count] [--regexp=pattern] [--file=file] [--ignore=case]`
`➡[--files-without-match] [--files-with-match] [--line-number]`
`➡[--revert-match] [--word-regexp] [--line-regexp] [pattern] file`
`➡[file ...]`

Important Flags and Options

- -number: Displays matching lines with the specified number of lines of leading and trailing context.

- -b/--byte-offset: Prints the byte offset of the match before each line.

- **-c/--count**: Instead of displaying matching lines, simply outputs a count of the total number of lines matching the expressions (when combined with -v, displays the total count of non-matching lines).

- **-C/--context**: Displays matching lines with two lines of leading and trailing context (this is the same as -2).

- **-e pattern/--regexp=pattern**: Uses the specified pattern rather than one provided as an argument.

- **-f file/--file=file**: Uses the pattern found in the specified file rather than one supplied as an argument.

- **-i/--ignore=case**: Ignores case in both the pattern and the files being searched.

- **-l/--files-with-matches**: Instead of displaying each matched line, simply displays the name of each file that contains at least one match for the pattern.

- **-L/--files-without-match**: Instead of displaying each matched line, simply displays the name of each file that contains no matches for the pattern.

- **-n/--line-number**: Prefixes each output line with its line number in the file.

- **-v/--revert-match**: Displays non-matching lines instead of matching lines.

- **-w/--word-regexp**: Displays only those lines with matches for the pattern that are complete words.

- **-x/--line-regexp**: Displays only those lines with matches for the pattern that are complete lines.

file

Description	Determines and displays the type of files.
Syntax	`file [-zL] [-f file] file ...`
Important Flags and Options	

- **-f file**: Reads the list of files to be checked from the specified file. These will be checked before checking files provided as arguments.

- **-L**: Causes symbolic links to be followed.

- **-z**: Attempts to look at the type of files inside compressed files.

find

Description	Looks for files below the specified paths that match all the criteria indicated by the command-line options and takes any action indicated by those options. If no paths are specified, the search takes place below the current directory.

Syntax	`find [`*`path`* `...] [`*`options`*`]`
Important Flags and Options	• `-amin` *`minutes`*: Looks for files last accessed the specified number of minutes ago.

• `-anewer` *`file`*: Looks for files that were accessed more recently than the specified file was modified.

• `-atime` *`days`*: Looks for files last accessed the specified number of 24-hour periods ago.

• `-cmin` *`minutes`*: Looks for files whose status was last changed the specified number of minutes ago.

• `-cnewer` *`file`*: Looks for files whose status was last changed more recently than the specified file was modified.

• `-ctime` *`days`*: Looks for files whose status was changed the specified number of 24-hour periods ago.

• `-empty`: Looks for empty files or directories.

• `-exec` *`command`* `\;`: Executes the specified command. The string { } is replaced by the currently found filename and the command is repeated for each found filename.

• `-gid` *`gid`*: Looks for files with the specified numeric GID.

• `-group` *`group`*: Looks for files belonging to the named group.

• `-ilname` *`pattern`*: Looks for symbolic links whose names match the specified pattern in a case-insensitive manner.

• `-iname` *`pattern`*: Looks for files whose names match the specified pattern in a case-insensitive manner.

• `-ipath` *`pattern`*: Looks for files whose path matches the specified pattern in a case-insensitive manner.

• `-lname` *`pattern`*: Looks for symbolic links whose names match the specified pattern in a case-sensitive manner.

• `-maxdepth` *`levels`*: Descends at most the specified numbers of levels below the specified paths.

• `-mindepth` *`levels`*: Descends at least the specified number of levels below the specified paths before starting testing.

• `-mmin` *`minutes`*: Looks for files that were last modified the specified number of minutes ago.

• `-mount`: Does not descend any directories that are on other file systems than the current one.

• `-mtime` *`days`*: Looks for files that were last modified the specified number of 24-hour periods previously.

• `-name` *`pattern`*: Looks for files whose names match the specified pattern in a case-sensitive manner.

• `-newer` *`file`*: Looks for files modified more recently than the specified file.

- **-nogroup**: Looks for files whose numeric GID does not correspond to any existing group.

- **-nouser**: Looks for files whose numeric UID does not correspond to any existing user.

- **-ok** *command* **\;**: Executes the specified command for each file found after prompting the user. The string { } is replaced by the currently replaced filename.

- **-path**: Looks for files whose path matches the specified pattern in a case-sensitive manner.

- **-perm** *mode*: Looks for files whose permissions exactly match the specified mode. If *+mode* is used, then matches any of the specified permission bits; if *-mode* is used, then matches all of the specified permission bits.

- **-print**: Prints the full filename of all found files.

- **-regex** *pattern*: Looks for files whose names match the specified regular expression.

- **-size** *size*[bckw]: Looks for files of the specified size in the specified units. Units include **b** (512-byte blocks), **c** (bytes), **k** (kilobytes), and **w** (2-byte words).

- **-type** *type*: Looks for files that match the specified type. Types include **d** (directories), **f** (regular files), and **l** (symbolic links).

- **-uid** *uid*: Looks for files with the specified UID.

- **-user** *username*: Looks for files owned by the specified username or UID.

Notes	When providing numeric time information such as minutes and days, normally the match must be exact. Preceding the number with a + matches any value greater than the specified number and preceding a value with a – matches any value less than the number.

finger

Description	Looks up specified information about a user on the local system or remote systems. Users are specified on local systems by their username or their first or last name and on remote systems as *username@host*. With no users specified for the local system, all users logged in to the current system are listed. If a host with no username is provided in the form *@host*, then a list of all users logged into the remote system is displayed.
Syntax	`finger [user ...]`
Important Flags and Options	None

free

Description	Displays a report of free and used memory.
Syntax	`free [-b|-k|-m] [-s delay] [-t]`
Important Flags and Options	• `-b`: Displays the amount of memory in bytes.
	• `-k`: Displays the amount of memory in kilobytes (this is the default).
	• `-m`: Displays the amount of memory in megabytes.
	• `-s delay`: Displays continued reports separated by the specified delay in seconds.
	• `-t`: Displays an extra line containing totals.

gpasswd

Description	Administers the `/etc/group` file. Without flags, **gpasswd** allows changing of the specified group's password.
Syntax	`gpasswd group`
	`gpasswd -a user group`
	`gpasswd -d user group`
	`gpasswd -R group`
	`gpasswd -r group`
	`gpasswd [-M user,...] group`
Important Flags and Options	• `-a user`: Adds a user to the group.
	• `-d user:` Removes a user from the group.
	• `-M user,...`: Specifies one or more users who are members of the group.
	• `-r`: Removes the group password.
	• `-R`: Disables access to the group through the **newgrp** command.

grep

Description	Searches files for lines matching a specified pattern and displays the lines.

Syntax	`grep [-bCcEFGiLlnvwx] [-number] [-e pattern] [-f file] [--basic-`
	`➥regexp] [--byte-offset} [--extended-regexp] [--fixed-strings]`
	`➥[--byte-offset] [--context] [--count] [--regexp=pattern]`
	`➥[--file=file] [--ignore=case] [--files-without-match]`
	`➥[--files-with-match] [--line-number] [--revert-match]`
	`➥[--word-regexp] [--line-regexp] [pattern] file [file ...]`

Important Flags and Options	• `-number`: Displays matching lines with the specified number of lines of leading and trailing context.
	• `-b/--byte`-offset: Prints the byte offset of the match before each line.
	• `-c/--count`: Instead of displaying matching lines, simply outputs a count of the total number of lines matching the expressions (when combined with -v, displays the total count of non-matching lines).
	• `-C/--context`: Displays matching lines with two lines of leading and trailing context (this is the same as -2).
	• `-e pattern/--regexp=pattern`: Uses the specified pattern rather than one provided as an argument.
	• `-E/--extended-regexp`: Treats the pattern as an extended regular expression (similar to **egrep**).
	• `-f file/--file=file`: Uses the pattern found in the specified file rather than one supplied as an argument.
	• `-F/--fixed-strings`: Treats the pattern as a list of new line separated strings, one of which must match. This is the same as **fgrep**.
	• `-G/--basic-regexp`: Treats the pattern as a basic regular expression.
	• `-i/--ignore=case`: Ignores case in both the pattern and the files being searched.
	• `-l/--files-with-matches`: Instead of displaying each matched line, simply displays the name of each file that contains at least one match for the patterns.
	• `-L/--files-without-match`: Instead of displaying each matched line, simply displays the name of each file that contains no matches for the patterns.
	• `-n/--line-number`: Prefixes each output line with its line number in the file.
	• `-v/--revert-match`: Displays non-matching lines instead of matching lines.
	• `-w/--word-regexp`: Displays only those lines with matches for the patterns that are complete words.
	• `-x/--line-regexp`: Displays only those lines with matches for the patterns that are complete lines.
Notes	The syntax of regular expressions used by **grep** can be found in the **grep** man page.

groupadd

Description	Creates a new group.
Syntax	`groupadd [-g gid [-o]] [-r] [-f] group`
Important Flags and Options	• `-f`: Prevents the program from exiting when trying to add a group that already exists. In this case, the group won't be altered.
	• `-g gid`: Uses the specified GID for the group instead of automatically assigning a value.
	• `-o`: Indicates that group IDs do not need to be unique.
	• `-r`: Adds a system account with a group ID lower than 499.

groupdel

Description	Deletes a group.
Syntax	`groupdel group`
Important Flags and Options	None

groupmod

Description	Modifies an existing group.
Syntax	`groupmod [-g gid [-o]] [-n groupname] group`
Important Flags and Options	• `-g gid`: Changes the group ID of the specified group to the new GID. This value must be unique unless `-o` is specified.
	• `-n groupname`: Changes the group name of the specified group to the new group name.
	• `-o`: Indicates that group IDs do not need to be unique.

groups

Description	Prints the groups that one or more users belongs to. If no user is specified, then displays the groups that the user running the command belongs to.
Syntax	`groups [username ...]`
Important Flags and Options	None

grpck

Description	Checks the integrity of a group file such as **/etc/group** or **/etc/gshadow**. If no files are specified, then the default files are checked.
Syntax	`grpck [-r] [group shadow]`
Important Flags and Options	• `-r`: Operates in read-only mode, not allowing any alterations to be made to the files.

gunzip

Description	Decompresses files compressed with the **gzip** command (as well as the **compress** command and the **zip** command).
Syntax	`gunzip [-cflrt] [--stdout] [--to-stdout] [--force] [--list]` ➥`[--recursive] [--test] [name ...]`
Important Flags and Options	• `-c/--stdout/--to-stdout`: Writes output to standard output, keeping original file unchanged. By default, **gunzip** replaces the original compressed files with the uncompressed versions of the files. • `-f/--force`: Forces decompression even when a corresponding file already exists and will be overwritten by the decompressed file. • `-l/--list`: Lists files in the compressed file without decompressing. • `-r/--recursive`: Decompresses recursively, descending the directory structure and decompressing all files in subdirectories of directories named on the command line as arguments. • `-t/--test`: Tests the integrity of compressed files.

gzexe

Description	Creates an executable compressed file. If you compress a binary file or script with **gzexe**, then you can run it as if it were uncompressed. The file will simply uncompress into memory and execute, leaving the compressed version on your hard drive.
Syntax	`gzexe [-d] [name ...]`
Important Flags and Options	• `-d`: Uncompresses the specified file or files rather than compressing them.
Notes	When you compress a file named *filename*, the original, uncompressed file will be copied to *filename~* and the compressed file will retain the name *filename*. Once you have tested the compressed executable to see that it works, you can then delete the uncompressed copy.

gzip

Description	Compresses files using Lempel-Ziv encoding. The resulting file generally replaces the original, uncompressed file and will have a `.gz` extension.
Syntax	`gzip [-cdflrt] [--decompress] [--uncompress] [--stdout] [--to-stdout]` ➥`[--force] [--list] [--recursive] [--test] [name ...]`
Important Flags and Options	

- `-c/--stdout/--to-stdout`: Writes output to standard output, keeping original file unchanged. By default, `gzip` replaces the original, uncompressed files with the compressed versions of the files.

- `-d/--decompress/--uncompress`: Decompresses the specified files, like `gunzip`, rather than compressing them.

- `-f/--force`: Forces compression even when a corresponding file already exists and will be overwritten by the compressed file.

- `-l/--list`: Lists files in a compressed file.

- `-r/--recursive`: Compresses recursively, descending the directory structure and compressing all files in subdirectories of directories named on the command line as arguments.

- `-t/--test`: Tests the integrity of compressed files.

halt

Description	Halts the system. If the system is not in run level 0 or 6, this is done by calling the `shutdown` program.
Syntax	`halt [-n] [-w] [-d] [-f] [-i]`
Important Flags and Options	

- `-d`: Doesn't log the halt to `/var/log/wtmp`. By default, the halt is noted in this file.

- `-f`: Forces a halt or reboot without calling `shutdown`.

- `-i`: Shuts down network interfaces before halting.

- `-n`: Doesn't sync the file systems before halting.

- `-w`: Writes a record of a halt to `/var/log/wtmp` but doesn't actually halt the system.

Warnings	Care needs to be taken with this command. The `-n` flag, halting the system without syncing the disks, is of special concern because failing to sync the file systems before unmounting them can corrupt the data stored on them.

head

Description	Displays the first part of one or more files. By default, unless otherwise specified, the first 10 lines of each file are displayed. If no filenames are provided, then reads data from the standard input and displays the first section of the data, following the same rules as for files.
Syntax	`head [-c number[bkm]] [-n number] [-qv] [--bytes number[bkm]]` `➥[--lines number] [--quiet] [--silent] [file ...]`
Important Flags and Options	• `-c/--bytes number`: Displays the specified number of bytes from the start of each file. Optionally, the number can be followed by **b** for 512-byte blocks, **k** for kilobytes, and **m** for megabytes.
	• `-n/--lines number`: Displays the specified number of lines from the start of each file.
	• `-q/--quiet/--silent`: Prevents printing of filename headers when multiple files are being processed.

hostname

Description	Displays or sets the system's host name. If no flags or arguments are given, then the host name of the system is displayed.
Syntax	`hostname [-a] [--alias] [-d] [--domain] [-f] [--fqdn] [-i]` `➥[--ip-address][--long] [-s] [--short] [-y] [--yp] [--nis]`
Important Flags and Options	• `-a/--alias`: Displays the alias name of the host if available.
	• `-d/--domain`: Displays the DNS domain name of the host.
	• `-f/--fqdn/--long`: Displays the fully qualified domain name of the host.
	• `-i/--ip-address`: Displays the IP address of the host.
	• `-s/--short`: Displays the host name without the domain name.
	• `-y/--yp/--nis`: Displays the NIS domain name of the system.

id

Description	Displays real and effective user and group ID information for a specified user. If no user is specified, then prints the information for the user running **id**.
Syntax	`id [-gnruG] [--group] [--name] [--real] [--user] [--groups] [username]`

Important Flags and Options

- −g/−−**group**: Prints only the group ID.

- −G/−−**groups**: Prints only the supplementary groups.

- −n/−−**name**: Prints the user or group name instead of the ID number. Used in conjunction with −**u**, −**g**, or −**G**.

- −r/−−**real**: Prints the real user or group ID instead of the effective ones. Used in conjunction with −**u**, −**g**, or −**G**.

- −u/−−**user**: Prints only the user ID.

ifconfig

Description

Configures a network interface, or displays its status if no options are provided. If no arguments are provided, the current state of all interfaces is displayed.

Syntax

ifconfig *interface options address*

Important Flags and Options

- *interface*: Specifies the name of the network interface (e.g., **eth0** or **eth1**).

- **up**: Activates the specified interface.

- **down**: Deactivates the specified interface.

- **netmask** *address*: Sets the network mask for the interface.

- **broadcast** *address*: Sets the broadcast address for the interface.

- **pointtopoint** *address*: Enables point-to-point mode for an interface, implying a direct link between two machines. Also sets the address for the other end of the link.

- *address*: Specifies the host name or IP address for the interface. This is required.

ifdown

Description

Disables a specified interface, such as **eth0** or **eth1**.

Syntax

ifdown *interface*

Important Flags and Options

None

ifport

Description	Sets the transceiver type for a specified network interface.
Syntax	`ifport interface type`
Important Flags and Options	• *type*: Specifies transceiver type. Possible types include: **auto** (automatic selection); **10baseT** (twisted-pair Ethernet); **10base2** (coaxial-cable Ethernet); **aui** (AUI interface Ethernet); **100baseT** (twisted-pair Fast Ethernet).

ifup

Description	Enables a specified interface, such as **eth0** or **eth1**.
Syntax	`ifup interface`
Important Flags and Options	None

insmod

Description	Installs a loadable module into the current kernel.
Syntax	`insmod [-fpsxX] [-o module_name] object_file [symbol=value ...]`
Important Flags and Options	• `-f`: Tries to load the module even if the version of the kernel and the expected kernel version do not match.
	• `-o module`: Explicitly names the module instead of basing the name on the object file for the module.
	• `-p`: Probes the module to make sure it is loaded.
	• `-s`: Logs activity to the system log daemon rather than standard output.
	• `-x`: Doesn't export the module's external symbols.
	• `-X`: Exports the module's external symbols (this is the default).

kbd_mode

Description	Displays or sets the keyboard mode.
Syntax	`kbd_mode [-a|-u|-k|-s]`

Important Flags and Options
- -a: Sets the keyboard to ASCII (XLATE) mode.
- -k: Sets the keyboard to keycode (MEDIUMRAW) mode.
- -s: Sets the keyboard to scanmode (RAW) mode.
- -u: Sets the keyboard to UTF-8 (UNICODE) mode.

kbdrate

Description
Sets the repeat rate and delay time for the keyboard.

Syntax
`kbdrate [-r rate] [-d milliseconds]`

Important Flags and Options
- -d *milliseconds*: Sets the delay (before repeating) to the specified number of milliseconds.
- -r *cps*: Sets the repeat rate to the specified number of characters per second. Not all values are possible. You should select from the following values: 2.0, 2.1, 2.3, 2.5, 2.7, 3.0, 3.3, 3.7, 4.0, 4.3, 4.6, 5.0, 5.5, 6.0, 6.7, 7.5, 8.0, 8.6, 9.2, 10.0, 10.9, 12.0, 13.3, 15.0, 16.0, 17.1, 18.5, 20.0, 21.8, 24.0, 26.7, 30.0.

kill

Description
Sends a kill signal to one or more running processes.

Syntax
`kill [-s signal|-p] pid ...`

`kill -l`

Important Flags and Options
- -l: Displays a list of signal names.
- -p: Prints the process ID of a specified process rather than sending it a signal.
- -s *signal*: Sends the specified signal to the specified processes.
- *pid*: Specifies either the ID of a process or its name. When specifying processes by name, all processes with the specified name will receive the signal.

killall

Description
Sends a signal to all processes sharing a common process name.

Syntax
`killall [-eiw] [-signal] process ...`

`killall -l`

Important Flags and Options

- **-e**: Forces the program to send the signal to only exact matches for process names longer than 15 characters.
- **-i**: Asks for confirmation before sending the signal to each process.
- **-l**: Displays a list of signal names.
- **-w**: Waits for all killed processes to die. This means `killall` may wait indefinitely if a process fails to die.

ksyms

Description

Displays information about exported kernel symbols, including the address, name, and defining module.

Syntax

`ksyms [-a] [-m]`

Important Flags and Options

- **-a**: Displays all symbols, including those from the actual kernel.
- **-m**: Displays module information, including the address and size of the module.

last

Description

Displays a history of user logins and logouts based on the contents of `/var/log/wtmp`. If a specific tty such as **tty0** or **tty1** is specified, then only logins to that tty are displayed.

Syntax

`last [-R] [-number] [-n number] [-adx] [name ...] [tty ...]`

Important Flags and Options

- **-a**: Forces the host name to be displayed in the last column.
- **-d**: In the case of remote logins, displays all IP addresses as host names.
- **-n** *number*/**-number**: Indicates how many lines of history to display.
- **-R**: Suppresses the display of the host name in the report.
- **-x**: Causes system shutdown and run level changes to be displayed along with logins and logouts.

ldd

Description

Displays shared library dependencies for one or more programs.

Syntax

`ldd [-dr] program ...`

Important Flags and Options
- **-d**: Reports missing functions after performing relocations.
- **-r**: Reports missing data objects and functions after performing relocations.

less

Description

Displays a text file one screen at a time while allowing searching and backward scrolling.

Syntax

`less [-aeEGiINrsS] file ...`

Important Flags and Options
- **-a**: Causes searching to start after the last line on the screen. By default, searches include visible text.
- **-e**: Causes **less** to exit the second time it encounters the end of a file. Otherwise, users must quit with the "**q**" command.
- **-E**: Causes **less** to exit the first time it encounters the end of a file.
- **-G**: Suppresses highlighting of strings found by a search.
- **-i**: Causes searches to be case insensitive. This is ignored if the search pattern includes uppercase letters.
- **-I**: Causes searches to be case insensitive even when the search pattern contains uppercase letters.
- **-N**: Causes a line number to be displayed at the beginning of each line.
- **-r**: Causes raw control characters to be displayed using caret notation (e.g., Ctrl+A is ^A).
- **-s**: Squeezes consecutive blank lines into a single blank line.
- **-S**: Chops lines wider than the screen rather than wrapping them to the next line.

lilo

Description

Installs the Linux boot loader.

Syntax

`lilo [C file] [-d deciseconds] [-q] [-D label] [-u device]`

Important Flags and Options
- **-C file**: Specifies a specific configuration file to use in loading the boot loader. The default configuration file is `/etc/lilo.conf`.
- **-d deciseconds**: Indicates the number of deciseconds to wait at the LILO prompt during booting before loading the default kernel.
- **-D label**: Uses the kernel with the specified label as the default kernel rather than the first kernel in the configuration file.

- -q: Displays the currently mapped files listing the kernels to be booted.
- -u *device*: Uninstalls the boot loader for the specified device.

listalias

Description | Displays user and system aliases. If a regular expression is provided, then only aliases that match the expression are displayed.

Syntax | listalias [-s|-u] [*regular-expression*]

Important Flags and Options
- -s: Displays only system aliases.
- -u: Displays only user aliases.

ln

Description | Makes links between files. When the last argument is a directory, then each of the other source files specified is linked into a file with the same name in the specified directory.

Syntax | ln [-bis] [--backup] [--interactive] [--symbolic] *source* [*destination*]

ln [-bis] [--backup] [--interactive] [--symbolic] *source* ... *directory*

Important Flags and Options
- -b/--backup: Makes backups of files that are being removed.
- -i/--interactive: Prompts when it is necessary to remove a destination file.
- -s/--symbolic: Makes symbolic links instead of hard links.

loadkeys

Description | Loads compose key translation tables from one or more specified files. If no files are specified, the information is read from the standard input.

Syntax | loadkeys [-c --clearcompose] [-d --default] [-m --mktable]
➥[-s --clearstrings] [*file* ...]

Important Flags and Options
- -c/--clearcompose: Clears the current accent table before loading new entries. If no entries are found, the table will be empty.
- -d/--default: Loads the default keymap.
- -m/--mktable: Prints a table on standard output of the current mappings.
- -s/--clearstring: Clears the kernel string table.

logger

Description	Places entries in the system log. If no messages are specified and no input file is provided, then the standard input is logged to the system log.
Syntax	`logger [-is] [-f file] [-p priority] [-t tag] [message ...]`
Important Flags and Options	

- `-f file`: Logs the specified file to the system log.

- `-i`: Places the process ID of the process making the entry with each line in the log file.

- `-p priority`: Indicates the priority of the log entry.

- `-s`: Logs the message to standard error in addition to the system log.

- `-t tag`: Marks every line in the log entry with the specified tag.

login

Description	Log in to the system.
Syntax	`login username`
Important Flags and Options	None

logname

Description	Displays a user's username.
Syntax	`logname`
Important Flags and Options	None

logrotate

Description	Rotates log files, mailing the current file and then compressing it for archiving.
Syntax	`logrotate [-s|--state file] configfile`
Important Flags and Options	

- `-s/--state file`: Uses the specified state file instead of the default `/var/lib/logrotate.status`.

lpd

Description	Runs the line printer spooler daemon to control printing to attached and remote printers. If a port number is specified, it overrides the default port to listen to for incoming requests.
Syntax	`lpr [-l] [port]`
Important Flags and Options	• `-l`: Logs valid network requests.

lpq

Description	Examines and displays the current status of a printer spool queue. If no printer is specified, then the default printer is queried. Normally, all jobs for the queried printer are displayed unless specific job numbers are given. If users are specified, only these users' print jobs will be displayed for the queried printer.
Syntax	`lpq [-l] [-Pprinter] [job, ...] [user, ...]`
Important Flags and Options	• `-l`: Prints all information about the files composing the job entry instead of just what will fit on one line. • `-Pprinter`: Queries the specified printer.

lpr

Description	Prints one or more files to the specified printer spool. If no files are indicated, then the standard input is sent to the printer spool. If no printer is specified, data will be sent to the default printer.
Syntax	`lpr [-Pprinter] [-#number] [-C class] [-J job] [-i [numcols]]` `➡[-hlmrs] [file ...]`
Important Flags and Options	• `-#number`: Specifies the number of copies to print of each file. The default is one copy. • `-C class`: Prints the specified class name instead of the host name on the header page. • `-h`: Suppresses the printing of a header page. • `-i [numcols]`: Indicates that output should be indented by the number of blanks specified, or by 8 characters if no number is indicated. • `-J job`: Prints the specified job name instead of the filename on the header page.

- **-l**: Allows control characters to be printed while suppressing page breaks.

- **-m**: Sends an e-mail to the user when the print job is finished.

- **-Pprinter**: Prints to the specified printer.

- **-r**: Removes files after printing them.

- **-s**: Creates a symbolic link to the file being printed rather than copying the file to the spool directory. This is useful when printing extremely large files.

lprm

Description

Deletes one or more jobs from a specified print queue. If no printer is specified, it attempts to remove the jobs from the default print queue. If a username is specified, all jobs owned by the user are removed, unless specific jobs are indicated.

Syntax

lprm [-Pprinter] [*job* ...] [*user* ...]

Important Flags and Options

- **-Pprinter**: Deletes jobs from the specified printer spool queue.

ls

Description

Displays a listing of files and directories. If no file or directory is specified, then the current directory's contents are displayed. By default, contents are sorted alphabetically.

Syntax

```
ls [-acdlrRsStuX] [--all] [--time=ctime] [--time=status] [--directory]
➡[--format=long] [--format=verbose] [--reverse] [--recursive] [--size]
➡[--sort-size] [--sort=time] [--time=atime] [--time=access]
➡[--time=use][--sort=extension] [file|directory ...]
```

Important Flags and Options

- **-a/--all**: Lists all files in the directory, including those that start with ".".

- **-c/--time=ctime,--time=status**: Sorts entries by the change time of the files.

- **-d/--directory**: Lists directory names only, without showing directory contents. By default, directory contents are listed.

- **-l/--format=long/--format=verbose**: Lists files in long format, including file type, permissions, owner, and size.

- **-r/--reverse**: Displays files in reverse order.

- **-R/--recursive**: Lists the content of all subdirectories recursively.

- **-s/--size**: Displays the size of files, in kilobytes.

- **-S/--sort=size**: Sorts entries by file size starting with the largest file.

- **-t/--sort=time**: Sorts entries by timestamp starting with the newest files.

- -u/--time=atime/--time=access/--time=use: Sorts entries by the last access time.
- -X/--sort=extension: Sorts files by file extension in alphabetical order.

lsdev

Description	Displays information about installed hardware.
Syntax	lsdev
Important Flags and Options	None

lsmod

Description	Displays a list of loaded modules.
Syntax	lsmod
Important Flags and Options	None

mail

Description	Sends and receives e-mails. The user will be prompted for the text of the message unless it is provided through the standard input. Also, other information such as the subject can be provided as a flag when sending messages, or the program can prompt for the information. If no options or arguments are specified, the current user's mailbox is opened for reading.
Syntax	mail [-s *subject*] [-c *address*,...] [-b *address*,...] *address*
	mail -f [*mailbox*]
	mail -u [*user*]
Important Flags and Options	• -b *address*,...: Indicates a list of addresses that should receive blind carbon copies of outgoing messages.
	• -c *address*,...: Indicates a list of addresses that should receive a carbon copy of outgoing messages.
	• -f [*mailbox*]: Reads mail from your inbox or the mailbox specified.
	• -s *subject*: Specifies the subject line of outgoing messages.
	• -u *user*: Opens the specified user's inbox for reading.
Notes	The mechanics of using mail to read messages is discussed in the mail man page.

mailq

Description	Displays the contents of the outgoing mail queue.
Syntax	`mailq`
Important Flags and Options	None

mailto

Description	Sends an e-mail to one or more recipients. If no recipients are indicated on the command line, the user will be prompted for the recipients. If no standard input is provided, then the user is prompted for the content of the message.
Syntax	`mailto [-a character-set] [-c address,...] [-s subject]` `➥[recipient ...]`
Important Flags and Options	• `-a character-set`: Specifies an alternate character set, such as ISO-8859-8. The default is US-ASCII. • `-c address,...`: Specifies carbon-copy addresses. • `-s subject`: Specifies the subject line of the message. If the subject is more than one word, enclose it in quotation marks.
Notes	To finish composing a message, use Ctrl+D or type **a .** alone on a blank line.

man

Description	Displays the manual page for a specified command.
Syntax	`Man command`
Important Flags and Options	*command*: Specifies the command whose manual page is to be displayed.

mattrib

Description	Changes the attributes of a file on an MS-DOS file system such as a DOS floppy disk. This is similar to the DOS **ATTRIB** command.
Syntax	`mattrib [-a|+a] [-h|+h] [-r|+r] [-s|+s] msdosfile [msdosfile ...]`
Important Flags and Options	• +a|-a: Sets or unsets the archive bit. • +h|-h: Sets or unsets the hidden bit.

- +r | -r: Sets or unsets the read-only bit.
- +s | -s: Sets or unsets the system bit.

Notes

Use the + before an option to set a bit and the – to unset a bit.

mbadblocks

Description

Tests a DOS floppy disk for bad blocks. If any are found, they are marked in the disk's FAT.

Syntax

mbadblocks *drive:*

Important Flags and Options

None

mcd

Description

Changes the directory on an MS-DOS file system such as a floppy disk. If no argument is provided, then the current device and directory are displayed. Similar to the DOS **CD** command.

Syntax

mcd [*msdosdirectory*]

Important Flags and Options

None

mcopy

Description

Copies files in both directions between Unix and MS-DOS file systems such as floppy disks. Multiple files can be copied to a single directory when the directory is the last argument. Using a DOS drive designator such as **a:** implies a DOS file; otherwise a Unix file system is assumed. With only a single DOS file as an argument, this file will be copied to the current Unix directory. Similar to the DOS **COPY** command.

Syntax

mcopy [-tnm] *sourcefile targetfile*

mcopy [-tnm] *sourcefile* [*sourcefile* ...] *targetdirectory*

mcopy [-tnm] *MSDOSsourcefile*

Important Flags and Options

- -m: Preserves file modification times when copying.
- -n: Does not ask for confirmation when overwriting Unix files.
- -t: Converts text files between Unix and DOS text files while copying.

mdel

Description	Deletes files on an MS-DOS floppy disk. Similar to the DOS **DEL** command.
Syntax	mdel *msdosfile* [*msdosfile* ...]
Important Flags and Options	None

mdeltree

Description	Deletes one or more MS-DOS directories. Similar to the DOS **DELTREE** command.
Syntax	mdeltree *msdosdirectory* [*msdosdirectory* ...]
Important Flags and Options	None

mdir

Description	Displays the contents of a directory on an MS-DOS file system such as a floppy disk. If specific files are indicated, then only those files are listed. Similar to the DOS **DIR** command.
Syntax	mdir [-w] *msdosdirectory*
	mdir [-a] [-f] [-w] *msdosfile* [*msdosfile* ...]
Important Flags and Options	• -a: Lists hidden files as well as regular files.
	• -f: Displays files without listing total free space at the end of the listing.
	• -w: Displays files in wide output.

messages

Description	Displays a count of the number of messages in the user's inbox or, if named, in a specific mail folder.
Syntax	messages [*folder*]
Important Flags and Options	None

mformat

Description   Formats an MS-DOS floppy disk. Similar to the DOS **FORMAT** command.

Syntax   `mformat` *drive:*

Important Flags and Options   None

mkdir

Description   Creates one or more directories.

Syntax   `mkdir [-p] [-m` *mode*`] [--parents] [--mode=`*mode*`]` *directory* `...`

Important Flags and Options
- **-m/--mode** *mode*: Sets the mode for the created directory using the same symbolic notation as the **chmod** command. If this is not specified, the default mode is assigned to the directory.

- **-p/--parents**: Ensures that the parents of the specified directory exist and creates any missing parent directories needed.

mkdosfs

Description   Formats an MS-DOS file system on a specified device.

Syntax   `mkdosfs [-c] [-F` *fatsize*`] [-n` *name*`]` *device*

Important Flags and Options
- **-c**: Checks for bad blocks before formatting.

- **-F** *fatsize*: Indicates the type of file allocation to create. This can be either **12** for a 12-bit FAT or **16** for a 16-bit FAT. The program will select the best option for you, usually **16**.

- **-n** *name*: Sets the volume label to the specified name. The name can be up to 11 characters long. With no name, the volume label will not be set.

mke2fs

Description   Formats a Linux second extended file system.

Syntax   `mke2fs [-c] [-m` *percentage*`] [-L` *label*`]` *device*

Important Flags and Options
- **-c**: Checks for bad blocks before formatting.

- -L *label*: Sets the volume label as specified.

- -m *percentage*: Specifies the percentage of blocks to reserve for the superuser. This is set to 5 percent by default.

mkfs

Description	Creates a file system (similar to formatting a drive in DOS). Optionally, the number of blocks for the file system can be specified.
Syntax	`mkfs [-t fstype] [-c] [-l file] device [blocks]`
Important Flags and Options	

- -c: Checks the device for bad blocks before formatting.

- -l *file*: Reads the bad block list for the device from the specified file.

- -t *fstype*: Specifies the type of file system that should be created. The default file system type is minix if no other alternative can be found for the device in /etc/fstab.

mkpasswd

Description	Generates a random password and optionally assigns it to a user.
Syntax	`mkpasswd [-2] [-l number] [-d number] [-c number] [-C number]` ➥`[-p file] [user]`
Important Flags and Options	

- -2: Forces characters to alternate between the right and left hand when typing on a standard U.S. keyboard.

- -c *number*: Specifies the minimum number of lowercase letters in the password.

- -C *number*: Specifies the minimum number of uppercase letters in the password.

- -d *number*: Specifies the minimum number of digits in the password.

- -l *number*: Specifies the number of characters in the password.

- -p *file*: Specifies the program to use to set the password. By default, this is /etc/yppaswwd, or, if that is missing, /bin/passwd.

Notes	The use of the -2 flag makes it harder for the casual observer to see what is being typed by a user. But this can make it easier for a password-guessing program to guess the password.

mkswap

Description	Sets up a device as a swap area. The size of the file system can be specified in blocks if desired.
Syntax	`mkswap [-c] device [blocks]`
Important Flags and Options	• `-c`: Checks the device for bad blocks before creating the swap file system.
Notes	It is also possible to create swap files instead of swap partitions. Consult the `mkswap` man page for more information.

mlabel

Description	Labels an MS-DOS file system such as a floppy disk. If the label is not provided, the user is prompted for the label.
Syntax	`mlabel [-cs] drive:label`
Important Flags and Options	• `-c`: Clears the current label without any prompt to the user.
	• `-s`: Displays the current label.

mmd

Description	Makes one or more directories on an MS-DOS file system such as a floppy disk.
Syntax	`mmd msdosdirectory [msdosdirectory ...]`
Important Flags and Options	None

mmove

Description	Moves (also renames) MS-DOS files or directories. If the last argument is a directory, then all source files are moved into the target directory.
Syntax	`mmove sourcefile targetfile`
	`mmove sourcefile [sourcefile ...] targetdirectory`
Important Flags and Options	None

modprobe

Description	Loads one or more loadable modules, based on a pattern or a specified module object file.
Syntax	`modprobe module.o [symbol=value ...]`
	`modprobe -t tag pattern`
	`modprobe -a -t tag pattern`
	`modprobe -l [-t tag] pattern`
	`modprobe -r module`
	`modprobe -c`
Important Flags and Options	• `-a`: Loads all modules rather than the first module that loads successfully.
	• `-c`: Displays configuration information.
	• `-l`: Lists all modules of a specified type.
	• `-r module`: Unloads the specified module stack.
	• `-t tag`: Loads only modules marked with the specified tag.

more

Description	Displays one or more files screen-by-screen and allows for searching and jumping to an arbitrary location in the file.
Syntax	`more [-dlfs] [-number] [+number] [file ...]`
Important Flags and Options	• `-number`: Sets the number of lines per screen.
	• `+number`: Specifies the line to start on when displaying.
	• `-d`: Prompts the user at the end of each screen.
	• `-f`: Causes long lines not to be folded and to be counted as a single line.
	• `-l`: Prevents Ctrl+L from being treated as a form feed.
	• `-s`: Squeezes multiple blank lines into a single blank line.
Notes	For details of the commands that can be used when viewing files, consult the **more** man page.

mount

Description	Mounts a file system to a specified directory.
Syntax	`mount -a [-rw] [-t vfstype]`
	`mount [-rw] [-o options [,...]] device|dir`
	`mount [-rw] [-t vfstype] [-o options] device dir`
Important Flags and Options	• `-a`: Mounts all file systems in `/etc/fstab`. If a type is specified with `-t`, then only the file systems in `/etc/fstab` of the specified type will be loaded.
	• `-o`: See Note below.
	• `-r`: Mounts the file system in read-only mode. This is the same as `-o ro`.
	• `-t fstype`: Indicates the file system type.
	• `-w`: Mounts the file system in read-write mode. This is the same as `-o rw`.
Notes	Possible file system types for the `-t` flag include:

Minix	vfat	ufs
ext	proc	romfs
ext2	nfs	sysv
xiafs	iso9660	xenix
hpfs	smbfs	coherent
msdos	ncpfs	
umsdos	affs	

For a list of options for the `-o` flag, consult the **mount** man page, which provides detailed descriptions of the various options available.

mrd

Description	Removes one or more MS-DOS directories.
Syntax	`mrd msdosdirectory [msdosdirectory ...]`
Important Flags and Options	None

mren

Description

Renames an MS-DOS file. Similar to the DOS **REN** command, except that it can rename directories as well.

Syntax

`mren oldname newname`

Important Flags and Options

None

mtype

Description

Displays the contents of one or more MS-DOS files. Similar to the DOS **TYPE** command.

Syntax

`mtype [-ts] msdosfile [msdosfile ...]`

Important Flags and Options

- `-s`: Removes the high bit from data.

- `-t`: Translates DOS text files to Unix text files before displaying them.

mv

Description

Renames and moves files. When a directory is the last argument, move all other specified files into that directory.

Syntax

`mv [-bfiu] [--backup] [--force] [--interactive] [--update]`
➥`{source destination|source ... directory}`

Important Flags and Options

- `-b/--backup`: Makes a backup of files that are being moved.

- `-f/--force`: Removes existing files that are about to be overwritten by the move without prompting.

- `-i/--interactive`: Prompts before overwriting any existing files.

- `-u/--update`: Does not overwrite an existing file if it has the same or newer modification time.

netstat

Description

Displays network status information, including connections, routing tables, and interface statistics. When no options are provided, a list of active sockets will be displayed.

Syntax	`netstat [-Mnrs] [-c] [-i interface] [--interface interface]` `➥[--masquerade] [--route] [--statistics]`
Important Flags and Options	• `-c`: Displays the select information every second until Ctrl+C interrupts it.
	• `-i [interface]/--interface [interface]`: Displays information about a specified interface, or all interfaces if none is specified.
	• `-M/--masquerade`: Displays a list of masqueraded sessions.
	• `-n`: Shows numerical addresses instead of their host, port, or user names.
	• `-r/--route`: Displays the kernel routing tables.
	• `-s/--statistics`: Displays network statistics.

newgrp

Description	Logs the user into a new group, changing the user's group ID. If no group is specified, the group ID is changed to the user's login group ID.
Syntax	`newgrp [group]`
Important Flags and Options	None

newusers

Description	Reads a file containing a list of new users and creates the users. If no file is specified, the user information should be provided from standard input.
Syntax	`newusers [file]`
Important Flags and Options	None
Notes	The format of the file read by the **newusers** command is the same as the `/etc/passwd` file with the following exceptions:

- Passwords should not be encrypted. They will be encrypted when the user's account is created.
- If the group specified does not exist, the new group will be created.
- If the user's home directory doesn't exist, a new one will be created; if a directory with that name already exists, the ownership will be changed to that of the new user.
- Because this file will contain decrypted passwords, it is essential that it be kept secure at all times.

nisdomainname

Description	Displays the current NIS domain name.
Syntax	`nisdomainname`
Important Flags and Options	None

nslookup

Description	Queries a DNS name server. Can be run in interactive mode. If no host name is provided, then the program enters interactive mode. By default, the DNS server specified in `/etc/resolv.conf` is used unless another is specified. If you want to specify a server but not look up a specified host, you must provide a – in place of the host.
Syntax	`nslookup [host|-[server]]`
Important Flags and Options	None
Notes	For instructions on the commands available in interactive mode, see the `nslookup` man page.

passwd

Description	Changes a user's password. When run by the root user, it can be used to change a specific user's password by providing the username as an argument.
Syntax	`passwd [username]`
Important Flags and Options	None

paste

Description	Merges corresponding lines from one or more files. Prints sequentially corresponding lines on the same line, separated by a tab with a new line ending the line. If no filenames are provided, input is taken from the standard input.
Syntax	`paste [-s] [-d delim-list] [--serial] [--delimiters list] [file ...]`
Important Flags and Options	• `-d/--delimiters list`: Specifies a delimiter to use instead of the default tab character. If more than one character is in the list, then the characters will be used consecutively, returning to the first character in the list after the final character has been used.
	• `-s/--serial`: Pastes the lines of one file followed by the lines from the next file, rather than one line from each file.

pathchk

Description	Checks the validity and portability of filenames. Specifically, checks that all directories in the path of the file have appropriate execute permission and that the length of each component of the path and filename is no larger than the maximum length for a filename component.
Syntax	`pathchk [-p] [--portability] file ...`
Important Flags and Options	• `-p`/`--portability`: Tests the length of each filename against POSIX.1 standards instead of the length limitations of the actual file system. Checks are also made for the portability of the characters used in the filename.

pidof

Description	Finds the process IDs of one or more named programs and displays the PIDs.
Syntax	`pidof [-s] [-x] [-o pid] [-o pid ...] program [program ...]`
Important Flags and Options	• `-o pid`: Omits the specified process ID from the list returned.
	• `-s`: Returns only a single PID.
	• `-x`: Returns the PIDs of shells running named scripts as well as named programs.

ping

Description	Sends echo request packets to a network host to see if it is accessible on the network.
Syntax	`ping [-R] [-c number] [-d] [-i seconds] host`
Important Flags and Options	• `-c number`: Stops sending packets after the specified number of packets have been sent.
	• `-d`: Outputs packets as fast as they come back or 100 times per second. The greater number will be generated. This option can only be used by the root user because it can generate extremely high volumes of network traffic. Care should be taken when using this option.
	• `-i seconds`: Specifies the number of seconds to wait between sending each packet. The default is one second. This option cannot be used along with the `-f` option.
	• `-R`: Records the route the packet takes and displays the route buffer of packets that have returned.

pppstats

Description	Displays statistics of PPP activities.
Syntax	`pppstats [-a] [-v] [-r] [-z] [-c count] [-w secs] [interface]`
Important Flags and Options	None

ps

Description

Displays status reports for currently running processes. Given a specific process ID as an argument, **ps** displays information about that particular process. Without options or arguments, **ps** displays the current user's processes.

Syntax

`ps [lumaxwrf] [txx] [pid ...]`

Important Flags and Options

- a: Shows processes owned by other users in addition to the current user's processes.

- f: Displays processes in a tree showing which processes are children of which other processes.

- l: Displays information in long format.

- m: Displays memory information in the report.

- r: Displays only processes that are running.

- txx: Displays only those processes controlled by the tty specified by **xx**.

- u: Displays information in user format that includes the user name and start time of the format.

- w: Displays information in wide output mode, which prevents the truncation of commands to fit them on one line. For each w included as an option, an additional line is provided for displaying commands. Up to 100 w options may be used.

- x: Shows processes without a controlling terminal (this is useful for seeing daemons that were launched during the boot process and are still running.

pwck

Description

Checks the password file for errors and problems. The format of all entries is checked to be sure that valid information appears in each field. In addition, duplicate entries are found and the user is given the chance to delete poorly formatted or duplicate entries. If no password or shadow files are specified, the default `/etc/passwd` and `/etc/shadow` are used.

Syntax	`pwck [-r] [`*`passwordfile shadowfile`*`]`
Important Flags and Options	• `-r`: Executes in read-only mode so that no changes are made to the password file but the checks are done.

pwconv

Description	Copies entries from a password file to a shadow file, merging them with the existing shadow file. The new password file will be called **npasswd** and the new shadow file will be called **nshadow**.
Syntax	**pwconv**
Important Flags and Options	None

pwd

Description	Displays the name of the current directory.
Syntax	**pwd**
Important Flags and Options	None

pwunconv

Description	Restores a password from a shadow password file. The new password file will be called **npasswd**.
Syntax	**pwunconv**
Important Flags and Options	None

quota

Description	Displays a user's disk usage quota information. The root user can indicate specific users and groups and get reports about them. Non-root users can only view information about their own account and the groups to which they belong.
Syntax	`quota [-guv] [`*`user`*`|`*`group`*`]`

Important Flags and Options
- -g: Prints group quota for the groups that the user belongs to.
- -u: This is the default flag, causing the display of quota information for the user.
- -v: Displays quotas for file systems where no storage is allocated.

quotacheck

Description

Scans a file system for disk usage by a user or group and outputs the results to two quota files: `quota.user` and `quota.group`.

Syntax

`quotacheck [-g] [-u] [-a|filesystem]`

Important Flags and Options
- -a: Checks all file systems in the `/etc/fstab` file.
- -g: Checks for the files and directories used by a particular group ID.
- -u: Checks for the files and directory used by a particular user ID.

quotaoff

Description

Disables disk usage quotas for one or more file systems.

Syntax

`quotaoff [-g] [-u] [-a|filesystem ...]`

Important Flags and Options
- -a: Disables quotas for all file systems in `/etc/fstab`.
- -g: Disables group quotas for the specified file systems.
- -u: Disables user quotas for the specified file systems.

quotaon

Description

Enables disk usage quotas for one or more file systems.

Syntax

`quotaon [-g] [-u] [-a|filesystem ...]`

Important Flags and Options
- -a: Enables quotas for all file systems in `/etc/fstab`.
- -g: Enables group quotas for the specified file systems.
- -u: Enables user quotas for the specified file systems.

rcp

Description	Remote-copies one or more files between two systems. If the final argument is a directory, all other file arguments are copied to that directory.
Syntax	`rcp [-px] file ...`
Important Flags and Options	• `-p`: Preserves modification times and modes of the source file whenever possible.
	• `-x`: Turns on DES encryption for all copies.
Notes	Remote files and directories are specified with the form *remoteuser@remote-host:/path/to/file*.

rdate

Description	Retrieves the current time from one or more hosts on the network and displays the returned time.
Syntax	`rdate [-p] [-s] host ...`
Important Flags and Options	• `-p`: Displays the time returned from the remote system (this is the default behavior).
	• `-s`: Sets the local system's time based on the time retrieved from the network. This can only be used by the root user.

rdist

Description	Remotely distributes files in order to maintain identical copies on several hosts, preserving ownership, mode, and modification time wherever possible. If no destination directory is specified on the remote host, then the source files will be placed in the same location on the remote system.
Syntax	`rdist -c file|directory ... [login@]host[:directory]`
Important Flags and Options	• `-c`: Specifies a list of files to distribute to the remote system.
Notes	**Rdist** allows for controlling distribution from configuration files. This enables many more flags and options to be used. Consult the `rdist` man page for a complete description of this tool.

repquota

Description	Displays a summary of disk usage quotas for one or more file systems.
Syntax	`repquota [-gu] [-a|filesystem ...]`
Important Flags and Options	• `-a`: Displays reports for all file systems in `/etc/fstab`.
	• `-g`: Displays a report of group usage quotas for the specified file systems.
	• `-u`: Displays a report of user usage quotas for the specified file systems.

rlogin

Description	Logs in to a remote host.
Syntax	`rlogin [-Kx] [-l username] host`
Important Flags and Options	• `-K`: Turns off all Kerberos authentication.
	• `-l username`: Indicates that the connection should be logged in under the specified username rather than the user running `rlogin`.
	• `-x`: Turns on DES encryption for all data sent while logged in to the remote system.

rm

Description	Deletes one or more files or directories.
Syntax	`rm [-firR] [--force] [--interactive] [--recursive] file|directory ...`
Important Flags and Options	• `-f/--force`: Does not prompt the user for permission to delete files. This is dangerous if used as the root user.
	• `-i/--interactive`: Always prompts the user before deleting each file.
	• `-r/-R/--recursive`: Recursively removes the content of directories.

rmdir

Description	Deletes empty directories.
Syntax	`rmdir [-p] [--parents] directory ...`
Important Flags and Options	• `-p/--parents`: Removes the directory as well as all parents explicitly indicated on the command line as long as deleting the directory causes the parent to become empty.

rmmod

Description	Unloads one or more loaded modules.
Syntax	`rmmod [-as] module ...`
Important Flags and Options	• `-a`: Removes all unused modules.
	• `-s`: Sends all output to the system log instead of the display.

route

Description	Displays or alters the IP routing table. When no options are provided, the routing table is displayed.
Syntax	`route add [-net|-host] targetaddress [netmask Nm] [gw Gw] [[dev] If]`
	`route del [-net|-host] targetaddress [gw Gw] [netmask Nm] [[dev] If]`
Important Flags and Options	• `add`: Indicates that a route is being added.
	• `del`: Indicates that a route is being deleted.
	• `[dev] If`: Forces the route to be connected to the specified interface.
	• `gw Gw`: Specifies the gateway for the route.
	• `-host`: Indicates the target is a host.
	• `-net`: Indicates the target is a network.
	• `netmask Nm`: Specifies the netmask for the route.

rsh

Description	Opens a shell on a remote system. If a command is provided, the command is executed on the remote host, the results are returned, and the connection is terminated.
Syntax	`rsh [-Kx] [-l username] hostname [command]`
Important Flags and Options	• `-K`: Disables Kerberos authentication.
	• `-l username`: Attempts to connect to the remote host as a different user than the one running `rsh`.
	• `-x`: Enables DES encryption for all data sent between the two hosts.

runlevel

Description	Displays the current and previous run level of the system.
Syntax	`runlevel`
Important Flags and Options	None

rup

Description	Displays the status of one or more remote systems. If no host is specified, then the status of all machines on the local network is displayed.
Syntax	`rup [-dhlt] [host ...]`
Important Flags and Options	• `-d`: Displays the local time on each host.
	• `-h`: Sorts the entries by host name.
	• `-l`: Sorts the entries by load average.
	• `-t`: Sorts the entries by up time.

rusers

Description	Displays who is logged on to one or more machines on the local network. If no host is indicated, then all users logged in to all machines on the local network are displayed.
Syntax	`rusers [-l] [hostname ...]`
Important Flags and Options	• `-l`: Displays results in a long format, including username, host name, tty being used by the user, and the time of login, among other information.

rwho

Description	Displays a list of users logged into all machines on the local network.
Syntax	**rwho**
Important Flags and Options	None

rwhod

Description	Answers incoming requests from the **rwho** client.
Syntax	**rwhod**
Important Flags and Options	None

setclock

Description	Sets the computer's hardware clock to the value of the current system clock.
Syntax	**setclock**
Important Flags and Options	None

setkeycodes

Description	Loads key mappings into the scancode-to-keycode mapping table. Arguments are provided in pairs with the first argument being the scancode for a key and the second being the keycode to be associated with it.
Syntax	**setkeycodes** *scancode keycode* ...
Important Flags and Options	None
Notes	To understand how to specify scancodes and keycodes, consult the **setkeycodes** man page.

showkey

Description	Displays scancodes and keycodes generated by the keyboard. The program remains active for 10 seconds after the last key is pressed.
Syntax	**showkey [-sk --scancodes --keycodes]**
Important Flags and Options	• **-k/--keycodes**: Displays keycodes.
	• **-s/--scancodes**: Displays scancodes.

showmount

Description	Shows the current state of mounts from an NFS server. If a host is specified, then only mounts from the particular host are displayed.
Syntax	`showmount [-ade] [--all] [--directories] [--exports] [host]`
Important Flags and Options	• `-a/--all`: Displays both the client's host name and the mounted directory using `host:directory` format.
	• `-d/--directories`: Displays only directories.
	• `-e/--exports`: Displays the server's list of exported directories.

shutdown

Description	Shuts down the system, stopping logins and possibly delaying before shutting down and issuing an optional warning message. When a time is specified, the shutdown will occur at the specified time; otherwise it occurs immediately.
Syntax	`shutdown [-rkhc] time [warning]`
Important Flags and Options	• `-c`: Cancels a running shutdown.
	• `-h`: Halts after shutting down.
	• `-k`: Sends the warning message but doesn't actually shut down the system.
	• `-r`: Reboots after shutting down.
Notes	The time can be specified as an absolute time in the form *HH:MM* or as a number of minutes to wait before shutting down in the form `+minutes`.

sort

Description	Sorts the lines contained in one or more text files and displays the results. If no files are indicated, data is taken from the standard input and sorted. The resulting sorted data is displayed to the standard output.
Syntax	`sort [-cu] [-t separator] [-o file] [-T tempdir] [-bdfMnr]` ⮡`[+POS1 [-POS2]] [-k POS1[,POS2]] [file ...]`
Important Flags and Options	• `-b`: Ignores leading blanks in lines when trying to find sort keys.
	• `-c`: Checks whether the input data is sorted and prints an error message if it isn't. No sorting actually takes place.

- −d: Ignores all characters except letters, digits, and blanks in the sorting process.

- −f: Converts lowercase letters to uppercase letters during the sorting process.

- −k *POS1*[,*POS2*]: Specifies the field to use as the sorting key. The field will start at *POS1* and run up until *POS2* or the end of the line. Fields and character positions are specified starting at zero.

- −M: Sorts months. That is, any strings that starts with zero or more blanks followed by three letters are converted to uppercase and sorted as if they were abbreviated month names.

- −n: Compares strings numerically, which assumes that strings start with zero or more blanks followed by an optional sign and then a number.

- −o *file*: Outputs the results to the specified file instead of the standard output.

- +*POS1* [−*POS2*]: Specifies the field to use as the sorting key. The field will start at *POS1* and run up until *POS2* or the end of the line. Fields and character positions are specified starting at zero.

- −r: Reverses the sort order.

- −t *separator*: Indicates that the specified separator should serve as the field separator for finding sort keys on each line.

- −u: When two lines compare as equal, only outputs the first.

statserial

Description

Shows the status of a serial port by displaying the signals on the pins of the port and the status of the handshaking line. If no device is specified, the default will be the value of the MODEM environment variable, or /dev/cua1 if the variable isn't set. The program will loop continuously, providing an updated status every second until Ctrl+C is pressed.

Syntax

statserial [−n|−d|−x] [*device*]

Important Flags and Options

- −d: Displays the status of the port as a decimal number.

- −n: Disables looping and only displays a single status.

- −x: Displays the status of the port as a hexadecimal number.

su

Description

Runs a new shell under different user and group IDs. If no user is specified, the new shell will run as the root user.

Syntax	su [-flmp] [-c *command*] [-s *shell*] [--login] [--fast] [--preserve-↦environment] [--command=*command*] [--shell=*shell*] [-] [*user*]
Important Flags and Options	• -c command/--command=*command*: Passes the specified command as a single command line to the shell instead of running the shell in an interactive mode.
	• -f/--fast: Passes the -f option to the shell, which in the case of the C Shell and the Extended C Shell disables filename pattern expansion.
	• -/-l/--login: Forces the new shell to be a login shell. This means new environment variables will be set, the path will change, and the current directory will switch to the user's home directory.
	• -m/-p/--preserve-environment: Prevents the HOME, USER, LOGNAME, and SHELL environment variables from changing.
	• -s shell/--shell=*shell*: Runs the specified shell instead of the default shell included in the password file.

sync

Description	Saves the disk cache to the physical disks. This forces any changed information to be saved to the disk.
Syntax	sync
Important Flags and Options	None

tail

Description	Displays the last part of one or more files. By default, unless otherwise specified, the last 10 lines of each file are displayed. If no filenames are provided, then reads data from the standard input and displays the last section of the data following the same rules as for files.
Syntax	tail [-c *number*[bkm]] [-n *number*] [-q] [--bytes *number*[bkm]] ↦[--lines *number*] [--quiet] [--silent] [*file* ...]
Important Flags and Options	• -c/--bytes *number*: Displays the specified number of bytes from the end of each file. Optionally, the number can be followed by b for 512-byte blocks, k for kilobytes, or m for megabytes.
	• -n/--lines *number*: Displays the specified number of lines from the end of each file.
	• -q/--quiet/--silent: Prevents printing of filename headers when multiple files are being processed.

tar

Description   Creates an archive file of one or more files or directories.

Syntax   `tar [-crtuxz] [-f tarfile] [--file tarfile] [--create] [--delete]`
                                    `➥[--preserve] [--append] [--same-owner] [--list] [--update]`
                                    `➥[--extract] [--get] [--gzip] [--gunzip] [file|directory ...]`

Important Flags and Options
- `-c/--create`: Creates a new archive.
- `--delete`: Deletes files from an existing archive.
- `-f tarfile/--file tarfile`: Specifies the name of the archive file being created or read from.
- `--preserve`: Keeps permissions and order of files the same in the archive.
- `-r/--append`: Adds files to an existing archive.
- `--same-owner`: Signifies that extracted files keep their original owners.
- `-t/--list`: Displays a list of an archive's contents.
- `-u/--update`: Only adds files to an existing archive that are newer than the copy in the archive.
- `-x/--extract/--get`: Extracts files from an existing archive.
- `-z/--gzip/--ungzip`: Filters the archive through `gzip` when archiving and unarchiving.

timeconfig

Description   Configures time parameters. If a time zone is specified, then the system time zone is changed to the specified time zone. Otherwise, displays a list of available time zones.

Syntax   `timeconfig [--utc] [timezone]`

Important Flags and Options
- `--utc`: Assumes the system clock is running in Universal/Greenwich Mean Time.

timed

Description   Runs the time server daemon, which can synchronize the time with time on other machines on the local network.

Syntax   `timed [-M] [-i network] [-n network]`

Important Flags and Options
- −i *network*: Specifies which network the server belongs to, overriding any default choice made by timed.
- −M: Prepares to take on the job of the master time server if the master server crashes.
- −n *network*: Adds the specified network to the list of valid networks.

timedc

Description

Controls the timed daemon.

Syntax

`timedc [clockdiff host ...|msite [host ...]|election host]`

Important Flags and Options
- `clockdiff host ...`: Computes the difference between the system's clock and the time on the specified hosts.
- `election host`: Resets the election timer and ensures that a time master has been elected from among the slaves.
- `msite [host ...]`: Shows the master timeserver for the specified host or hosts. If no hosts are specified, shows the master for the current system.

top

Description

Displays a regularly updated report of processes running on the system.

Syntax

`top [d delay] [q] [c] [S] [s]`

Important Flags and Options
- c: Displays the complete command line of a process instead of just the command name.
- d *delay*: Specifies the delay between updates, in seconds.
- q: Causes updates to occur without any delays. If the root user runs **top** with this option, **top** will run with the highest possible priority.
- s: Runs in a secure mode that prevents the use of dangerous interactive commands.
- S: Statistics should be displayed in a cumulative manner. That is, CPU time should be reported for a process and its dead children as a total.

Notes

For a list of commands that can be used while **top** is running and for a description of the various fields in the reports, read the **top** man page.

touch

Description	Changes the timestamp of files without changing their contents. If a file doesn't exist, it will be created with a size of zero. By default, it uses the current time as the new timestamp.
Syntax	`touch [-acm] [-t MMDDhhmm[[CC]YY][.ss]] [--time=atime] [--time=access]` `➥[--time=use] [--time=mtime] [--time=modify] [--no-create] file ...`
Important Flags and Options	• `-a/--time=atime/--time=access/--time=use`: Changes only the access time.
	• `-c/--no-create`: Will not create files that don't exist.
	• `-m/--time=mtime/--time=modify`: Changes only the modification time.
	• `-t MMDDhhmm[[CC]YY][.ss]`: Sets the timestamp to the specified month, day, hour, and minutes plus, optionally, the specified century, year, or seconds. This overrides the default of using the current time.

traceroute

Description	Displays the route a packet travels to reach a remote host on the network.
Syntax	`traceroute [-ir] host`
Important Flags and Options	• `-i`: Specifies a network interface for outgoing packets. This is useful in systems with more than one network interface.
	• `-r`: Bypasses normal routing tables and attempts to send directly to an attached host.

true

Description	Does nothing and returns a successful exit status.
Syntax	`true`
Important Flags and Options	None

umount

Description	Unmounts a mounted file system. The file system is specified by either its device name, its directory name, or its network path.

Syntax	`umount -r device|directory|path ...`
Important Flags and Options	• `-r`: If unmounting fails, tries to remount the file system in read-only mode.

uname

Description	Displays selected system information. When no options are provided, the operating system name is displayed. When multiple pieces of information are requested, the display order is always: operating system, network host name, operating system release, operating system version, and machine type.
Syntax	`uname [-snrvma] [--sysname] [--nodename] [--release] [--machine] [--all]`
Important Flags and Options	• `-a/--all`: Displays all information. • `-m/--machine`: Displays the machine's type (that is, its hardware type). • `-n/--nodename`: Displays the machine's network host name. • `-r/--release`: Displays the operating system release. • `-s/--sysname`: Displays the operating system name. This is the default action when no options are specified. • `-v`: Displays the operating system's version.

uncompress

Description	Uncompresses files compressed with the **compress** program. If no files are specified, the standard input will be decompressed.
Syntax	`uncompress [-c] [file ...]`
Important Flags and Options	• `-c`: Sends the uncompressed data to the standard output instead of overwriting the old compressed file.

unzip

Description	Manipulates and extracts ZIP archives.
Syntax	`unzip [-cflptuz] [-d exdir] file[.zip]`
Important Flags and Options	• `-c`: Extracts files to the standard output, printing the name of each file as it is extracted.

- **-d** *exdir*: Uncompresses the archive to the specified directory instead of the current directory.

- **-f**: Extracts only those files that are newer than already-existing versions of the files.

- **-l**: Displays the contents of the archive without extracting.

- **-p**: Extracts files to the standard output without sending any other data such as filenames.

- **-t**: Tests the integrity of files in the archive.

- **-u**: Extracts files that are newer than already-existing versions of files as well as files that do not already exist in the extract directory.

- **-z**: Displays the archive comment.

Notes   This is a powerful program that supports many modifiers. See the **unzip** man page for details.

uptime

Description   Displays the length of time the system has been running.

Syntax   `uptime`

Important Flags and Options   None

useradd

Description   Adds a user to the system. Alternately, the default values for new users can be changed. If no options are provided, the program will display the current default values for new users.

Syntax   `useradd [-d home_dir] [-e expire_date] [-f inactive_time]`
➥`[-g initial_group] [-G group[,...]] [-s shell] [-u uid [-o]]`
➥`username`

`useradd -D [-g default_group] [-b default_home] [-f default_inactive]`
➥`[-e default_expiration] [-s default_shell]`

Important Flags and Options
- **-b** *default_home*: Sets the default home directory prefix to the specified path. Only to be used when **-D** is used.

- **-d** *home_dir*: Uses the specified home directory for the user instead of the default home directory.

- **-D**: Indicates that default values for new users should be changed rather than that a new user should be created.

- -e *expire_date*: Specifies the expiration date for the account. The data is provided in MM/DD/YY format. When -D is used, -e will be used to set the default expiration for all new passwords as a number of days instead of in a date format.

- -f *inactive_time*: Indicates that once a password expires, the specified amount of time should elapse before permanently disabling the password. When -D is used, -f will be used to set the default amount of time before passwords will be disabled after expiring.

- -g *initial_group*: Specifies the default login group for the user. When used with -D, -g will specify the default group for all new users.

- -G *group*[,...]: Specifies other groups the user should belong to.

- -s *shell*: Specifies the default shell for the user. If not provided, the default shell for new users will be used. When used with -D, -s will specify the default shell for all new users.

- -u *uid* [-o]: Specifies a user ID for the user rather than automatically assigning one. The value must be unique unless the -o flag is used.

userdel

Description	Deletes a user's account.
Syntax	userdel [-r] *user*
Important Flags and Options	• -r: Deletes the user's home directory when deleting the account.
Notes	If you choose to delete the user's home directory, keep in mind that any other files the user owns that are outside their home directory are not deleted when their account is deleted. These have to be deleted manually. Such files might include the user's mail inbox, for example.

usermod

Description	Modifies the settings for an existing user's account.
Syntax	usermod [-d *home_dir* [-m]] [-e *expire_date*] [-f *inactive_time*] ➡[-g *initial_group*] [-G *group*[,...]] [-l *login_name*] [-s *shell*] ➡[-u *uid* [-o]] *login*
Important Flags and Options	• -d *home_dir* [-m]: Changes the user's home directory as specified and, if the -m option is used, moves the current home directory to the new location.
	• -e *expire_date*: Sets a new expiration date for the account after which it will be disabled. The date should be in the form MM/DD/YY.

- **-f** *inactive_days*: Provides a new setting for the number of days after a password expires when it will be permanently disabled.

- **-g** *initial_group*: Defines a new login group for the user.

- **-G** *group*[,...]: Indicates which other groups a user should be a member of. If the user is currently a member of a group that is not on this list, they will be removed from the group.

- **-l** *login_name*: Changes the user's login name.

- **-s** *shell*: Changes the user's default shell as specified.

- **-u** *uid*: Changes the user's ID as specified.

users

Description	Displays the user names of current users on the system. This is normally found by looking at the contents of **/etc/utmp**. If a file is specified, the program will look in that file for the information.
Syntax	**users** [*file*]
Important Flags and Options	None

uudecode

Description	Decodes ASCII files created by **uudecode**, to recreate the original binary files. By default, the name of the decoded file will be the original name of the encoded file. If no files to decode are provided, then the standard input is decoded.
Syntax	**uudecode** [-o *outputfile*] [*file* ...]
Important Flags and Options	• **-o** *outputfile*: Specifies an alternate name for the resulting decoded file.

uuencode

Description	Encodes a binary file into a form that can be used where binary files cannot (such as with some mail software). If no file is provided, the standard input is encoded.
Syntax	**uuencode** [*file*]
Important Flags and Options	None

vipw

Description	Edits the system password file using the editor specified in the **EDITOR** environment variable.
Syntax	`vipw`
Important Flags and Options	None

vmstat

Description	Reports statistics about virtual memory.
Syntax	`vmstat [delay [count]]`
Important Flags and Options	• *count*: Indicates the number of times to repeat the report. If not specified, the report will repeat continuously until interrupted with Ctrl+C.
	• *delay*: Indicates how often to repeat the report, in seconds. If not specified, then only one report is provided.
Notes	For details of the report generated by **vmstat**, read the **vmstat** man page.

w

Description	Displays a list of current users and the tasks they are running. If a user is specified, then only that user's tasks are displayed.
Syntax	`w [user]`
Important Flags and Options	None

wc

Description	Prints the number of bytes (characters), words, and lines in one or more documents. When multiple filenames are provided, each file will be counted and displayed separately and then a cumulative total will be displayed. If no files are specified, then the standard input is counted.
Syntax	`wc [-clw] [--bytes] [--chars] [--lines] [--words] [file ...]`
Important Flags and Options	• `-c/--bytes/--chars`: Displays only the number of bytes.

- `-l`/`--lines`: Displays only the number of lines.

- `-w`/`--words`: Displays only the number of words.

Notes

The results are displayed in this order: characters, words, lines. The values are separated by spaces.

whereis

Description

Attempts to locate the binary, source code, and man page files for one or more commands.

Syntax

`whereis [-bms] [-BMS directory ... -f] file ...`

Important Flags and Options

- `-b`: Searches only for binary files.

- `-B directory ... -f`: Searches only the specified directories for binary files. The `-f` flag is necessary to delineate the end of the directory list and the start of the file argument list.

- `-m`: Searches only for man pages.

- `-M directory -f`: Searches only the specified directories for man pages. The `-f` flag is necessary to delineate the end of the directory list and the start of the file argument list.

- `-s`: Searches only for source code.

- `-S directory ... -f`: Searches only the specified directories for source code. The `-f` flag is necessary to delineate the end of the directory list and the start of the file argument list.

Notes

The **whereis** command will search, at a minimum, the following directories for the programs it is trying to locate:

`/bin`

`/usr/bin`

`/etc`

`/usr/etc`

`/sbin`

`/usr/sbin`

`/usr/games`

`/usr/games/bin`

`/usr/emacs/etc`

`/usr/lib/emacs/19.22/etc`

```
/usr/lib/emacs/19.23/etc
/usr/lib/emacs/19.24/etc
/usr/lib/emacs/19.25/etc
/usr/lib/emacs/19.26/etc
/usr/lib/emacs/19.27/etc
/usr/lib/emacs/19.28/etc
/usr/lib/emacs/19.29/etc
/usr/lib/emacs/19.30/etc
/usr/TeX/bin
/usr/tex/bin
/usr/interviews/bin/LINUX
/usr/bin/X11
/usr/X11/bin
/usr/X11R5/bin
/usr/X11R6/bin
/usr/X386/bin
/usr/local/bin
/usr/local/etc
/usr/local/sbin
/usr/local/games
/usr/local/games/bin
/usr/local/emacs/etc
/usr/local/TeX/bin
/usr/local/tex/bin
/usr/local/bin/X11
/usr/contrib
/usr/hosts
/usr/include
/usr/g++-include
```

which

Description   Displays the full pathname of one or more programs. Only programs that are on the
                                     path as specified by the **PATH** environment variable will be displayed.

Syntax   `which program ...`

Important Flags and Options   None

whoami

Description   Displays the current effective user ID.

Syntax   `whoami`

Important Flags and Options   None

ypdomainname

Description   Displays the system's NIS domain name.

Syntax   `ypdomainname`

Important Flags and Options   None

zcat

Description   Uncompresses one or more compressed files and displays the results to the standard
                                     output. If no files are specified, then the standard input is uncompressed and dis-
                                     played.

Syntax   `zcat [-f] [file ...]`

Important Flags and Options   • `-f/--force`: Forces uncompression even when a corresponding file already
                                       exists and will be overwritten by the uncompressed file.

zgrep

Description   Searches one or more compressed files for a specified pattern.

Syntax   `zgrep [options] pattern file ...`

Important Flags and Options	None
Notes	For a list of possible entries and a discussion of pattern syntax, refer to the `grep` command.

zip

Description	Creates a ZIP archive from one or more files and directories.
Syntax	`zip [-efFgmrSu@] [zipfile [file1 file2 ...]]`
Important Flags and Options	

- `-@`: Accepts the list of files to be archived from the standard input.

- `-e`: Encrypts the archive after prompting for a password. The password will be necessary to extract files from the archive.

- `-f`: Replaces entries in an existing archive only if the file is newer than the file currently in the archive.

- `-F`: Tries to fix a damaged archive.

- `-g`: Adds files to an existing archive.

- `-m`: Moves files into the archive, deleting them from their original location once they are in the archive.

- `-r`: Recursively works with directories, adding all files in subdirectories to the archive.

- `-S`: Includes system and hidden files in the archive.

- `-u`: Replaces entries in an existing archive if a file is newer than the file currently in the archive or if the file does not already exist in the archive.

Notes	The `zip` command offers many other options that have subtle, sometimes useful, impact on the behavior of the program. Consult the `zip` man page for more details.

zipgrep

Description	Searches for a pattern in one or more files in a ZIP archive using `egrep`. If no files in the archive are specified, then all files in the archive are searched.
Syntax	`zipgrep [egrepoptions] pattern zipfile file ...`
Important Flags and Options	None
Notes	«For a complete discussion of `egrep`'s and `zipgrep`'s pattern syntax, refer to the `egrep` command.

zipinfo

Description

Displays details about ZIP archives, including encryption status, compression type, operating system used to create the archive, and more. By default, information about each file in the archive is also listed on separate lines. If no ZIP files are specified, the standard input will be processed.

Syntax

`zipinfo [-121M] zipfile[.zip] [file ...]`

Important Flags and Options

- -1: Lists only filenames, each on a separate line.

- -2: Lists only filenames, including headers, trailers and comments.

- -1: Lists information in long format (similar to `ls -1`).

- -M: Displays information one page at a time in a fashion similar to **more**.

zmore

Description

Displays the contents of compressed text files, one screen at a time, allowing searching in much the same way as the **more** command. If no files are specified, the standard input will be used.

Syntax

`zmore [file ...]`

Important Flags and Options

None

Notes

See the **zmore** man page for a complete list of commands that can be used while viewing a file.

znew

Description

Converts files compressed with **compress** (.Z files) into the format used by **gzip** (.gz files). If no files are specified, then the standard input is processed.

Syntax

`znew [-ft9K] [file.Z ...]`

Important Flags and Options

- -9: Uses the best, but slowest, compression method.

- -f: Forces compression even when a .gz file already exists.

- -K: Keeps a .Z file if it will be smaller than the new .gz file.

- -t: Tests the new .gz file before deleting the original .Z file.

APPENDIX

D

GNU General Public License

Version 2, June 1991

Copyright (C) 1989, 1991 Free Software Foundation, Inc.

675 Mass Ave, Cambridge, MA 02139, USA

Preamble

The licenses for most software are designed to take away your freedom to share and change it. By contrast, the GNU General Public License is intended to guarantee your freedom to share and change free software—to make sure the software is free for all its users. This General Public License applies to most of the Free Software Foundation's software and to any other program whose authors commit to using it. (Some other Free Software Foundation software is covered by the GNU Library General Public License instead.) You can apply it to your programs, too.

When we speak of free software, we are referring to freedom, not price. Our General Public Licenses are designed to make sure that you have the freedom to distribute copies of free software (and charge for this service if you wish), that you receive source code or can get it if you want it, that you can change the software or use pieces of it in new free programs; and that you know you can do these things.

To protect your rights, we need to make restrictions that forbid anyone to deny you these rights or to ask you to surrender the rights. These restrictions translate to certain responsibilities for you if you distribute copies of the software, or if you modify it.

For example, if you distribute copies of such a program, whether gratis or for a fee, you must give the recipients all the rights that you have. You must make sure that they, too, receive or can get the source code. And you must show them these terms so they know their rights.

We protect your rights with two steps: (1) copyright the software, and (2) offer you this license which gives you legal permission to copy, distribute and/or modify the software.

Also, for each author's protection and ours, we want to make certain that everyone understands that there is no warranty for this free software. If the software is modified by someone else and passed on, we want its recipients to know that what they have is not the original, so that any problems introduced by others will not reflect on the original authors' reputations.

Finally, any free program is threatened constantly by software patents. We wish to avoid the danger that redistributors of a free program will individually obtain patent licenses, in effect making the program proprietary. To prevent this, we have made it clear that any patent must be licensed for everyone's free use or not licensed at all.

The precise terms and conditions for copying, distribution and modification follow.

Terms and Conditions for Copying, Distribution, and Modification

0. This License applies to any program or other work which contains a notice placed by the copyright holder saying it may be distributed under the terms of this General Public License. The "Program", below, refers to any such program or work, and a "work based on the Program" means either the Program or any derivative work under copyright law: that is to say, a work containing the Program or a portion of it, either verbatim or with modifications and/or translated into another language. (Hereinafter, translation is included without limitation in the term "modification".) Each licensee is addressed as "you".

   Activities other than copying, distribution and modification are not covered by this License; they are outside its scope. The act of running the Program is not restricted, and the output from the Program is covered only if its contents constitute a work based on the Program (independent of having been made by running the Program). Whether that is true depends on what the Program does.

1. You may copy and distribute verbatim copies of the Program's source code as you receive it, in any medium, provided that you conspicuously and appropriately publish on each copy an appropriate copyright notice and disclaimer of warranty; keep intact all the notices that refer to this License and to the absence of any warranty; and give any other recipients of the Program a copy of this License along with the Program.

   You may charge a fee for the physical act of transferring a copy, and you may at your option offer warranty protection in exchange for a fee.

2. You may modify your copy or copies of the Program or any portion of it, thus forming a work based on the Program, and copy and distribute such

modifications or work under the terms of Section 1 above, provided that you also meet all of these conditions:

a) You must cause the modified files to carry prominent notices stating that you changed the files and the date of any change.

b) You must cause any work that you distribute or publish, that in whole or in part contains or is derived from the Program or any part thereof, to be licensed as a whole at no charge to all third parties under the terms of this License.

c) If the modified program normally reads commands interactively when run, you must cause it, when started running for such interactive use in the most ordinary way, to print or display an announcement including an appropriate copyright notice and a notice that there is no warranty (or else, saying that you provide a warranty) and that users may redistribute the program under these conditions, and telling the user how to view a copy of this License. (Exception: if the Program itself is interactive but does not normally print such an announcement, your work based on the Program is not required to print an announcement.)

These requirements apply to the modified work as a whole. If identifiable sections of that work are not derived from the Program, and can be reasonably considered independent and separate works in themselves, then this License, and its terms, do not apply to those sections when you distribute them as separate works. But when you distribute the same sections as part of a whole which is a work based on the Program, the distribution of the whole must be on the terms of this License, whose permissions for other licensees extend to the entire whole, and thus to each and every part regardless of who wrote it.

Thus, it is not the intent of this section to claim rights or contest your rights to work written entirely by you; rather, the intent is to exercise the right to control the distribution of derivative or collective works based on the Program.

In addition, mere aggregation of another work not based on the Program with the Program (or with a work based on the Program) on a volume of a storage or distribution medium does not bring the other work under the scope of this License.

3. You may copy and distribute the Program (or a work based on it, under Section 2) in object code or executable form under the terms of Sections 1 and 2 above provided that you also do one of the following:

   a) Accompany it with the complete corresponding machine-readable source code, which must be distributed under the terms of Sections 1 and 2 above on a medium customarily used for software interchange; or,

   b) Accompany it with a written offer, valid for at least three years, to give any third party, for a charge no more than your cost of physically performing source distribution, a complete machine-readable copy of the corresponding source code, to be distributed under the terms of Sections 1 and 2 above on a medium customarily used for software interchange; or,

   c) Accompany it with the information you received as to the offer to distribute corresponding source code. (This alternative is allowed only for noncommercial distribution and only if you received the program in object code or executable form with such an offer, in accord with Subsection b above.)

   The source code for a work means the preferred form of the work for making modifications to it. For an executable work, complete source code means all the source code for all modules it contains, plus any associated interface definition files, plus the scripts used to control compilation and installation of the executable. However, as a special exception, the source code distributed need not include anything that is normally distributed (in either source or binary form) with the major components (compiler, kernel, and so on) of the operating system on which the executable runs, unless that component itself accompanies the executable.

   If distribution of executable or object code is made by offering access to copy from a designated place, then offering equivalent access to copy the source code from the same place counts as distribution of the source code, even though third parties are not compelled to copy the source along with the object code.

4. You may not copy, modify, sublicense, or distribute the Program except as expressly provided under this License. Any attempt otherwise to copy, modify, sublicense or distribute the Program is void, and will automatically terminate your rights under this License. However, parties who have

received copies, or rights, from you under this License will not have their licenses terminated so long as such parties remain in full compliance.

5. You are not required to accept this License, since you have not signed it. However, nothing else grants you permission to modify or distribute the Program or its derivative works. These actions are prohibited by law if you do not accept this License. Therefore, by modifying or distributing the Program (or any work based on the Program), you indicate your acceptance of this License to do so, and all its terms and conditions for copying, distributing or modifying the Program or works based on it.

6. Each time you redistribute the Program (or any work based on the Program), the recipient automatically receives a license from the original licensor to copy, distribute or modify the Program subject to these terms and conditions. You may not impose any further restrictions on the recipients' exercise of the rights granted herein. You are not responsible for enforcing compliance by third parties to this License.

7. If, as a consequence of a court judgment or allegation of patent infringement or for any other reason (not limited to patent issues), conditions are imposed on you (whether by court order, agreement or otherwise) that contradict the conditions of this License, they do not excuse you from the conditions of this License. If you cannot distribute so as to satisfy simultaneously your obligations under this License and any other pertinent obligations, then as a consequence you may not distribute the Program at all. For example, if a patent license would not permit royalty-free redistribution of the Program by all those who receive copies directly or indirectly through you, then the only way you could satisfy both it and this License would be to refrain entirely from distribution of the Program.

    If any portion of this section is held invalid or unenforceable under any particular circumstance, the balance of the section is intended to apply and the section as a whole is intended to apply in other circumstances.

    It is not the purpose of this section to induce you to infringe any patents or other property right claims or to contest validity of any such claims; this section has the sole purpose of protecting the integrity of the free software distribution system, which is implemented by public license practices. Many people have made generous contributions to the wide range of software distributed through that system in reliance on consistent application of that system; it is up to the author/donor to decide if he or she is willing to distribute software through any other system and a licensee cannot impose that choice.

This section is intended to make thoroughly clear what is believed to be a consequence of the rest of this License.

8. If the distribution and/or use of the Program is restricted in certain countries either by patents or by copyrighted interfaces, the original copyright holder who places the Program under this License may add an explicit geographical distribution limitation excluding those countries, so that distribution is permitted only in or among countries not thus excluded. In such case, this License incorporates the limitation as if written in the body of this License.

9. The Free Software Foundation may publish revised and/or new versions of the General Public License from time to time. Such new versions will be similar in spirit to the present version, but may differ in detail to address new problems or concerns.

   Each version is given a distinguishing version number. If the Program specifies a version number of this License which applies to it and "any later version", you have the option of following the terms and conditions either of that version or of any later version published by the Free Software Foundation. If the Program does not specify a version number of this License, you may choose any version ever published by the Free Software Foundation.

10. If you wish to incorporate parts of the Program into other free programs whose distribution conditions are different, write to the author to ask for permission. For software which is copyrighted by the Free Software Foundation, write to the Free Software Foundation; we sometimes make exceptions for this. Our decision will be guided by the two goals of preserving the free status of all derivatives of our free software and of promoting the sharing and reuse of software generally.

No Warranty

11. BECAUSE THE PROGRAM IS LICENSED FREE OF CHARGE, THERE IS NO WARRANTY FOR THE PROGRAM, TO THE EXTENT PERMITTED BY APPLICABLE LAW. EXCEPT WHEN OTHERWISE STATED IN WRITING THE COPYRIGHT HOLDERS AND/OR OTHER PARTIES PROVIDE

THE PROGRAM "AS IS" WITHOUT WARRANTY OF ANY KIND, EITHER EXPRESSED OR IMPLIED, INCLUDING, BUT NOT LIMITED TO, THE IMPLIED WARRANTIES OF MERCHANTABILITY AND FITNESS FOR A PARTICULAR PURPOSE. THE ENTIRE RISK AS TO THE QUALITY AND PERFORMANCE OF THE PROGRAM IS WITH YOU. SHOULD THE PROGRAM PROVE DEFECTIVE, YOU ASSUME THE COST OF ALL NECESSARY SERVICING, REPAIR OR CORRECTION.

12. IN NO EVENT UNLESS REQUIRED BY APPLICABLE LAW OR AGREED TO IN WRITING WILL ANY COPYRIGHT HOLDER, OR ANY OTHER PARTY WHO MAY MODIFY AND/OR REDISTRIBUTE THE PROGRAM AS PERMITTED ABOVE, BE LIABLE TO YOU FOR DAMAGES, INCLUDING ANY GENERAL, SPECIAL, INCIDENTAL OR CONSEQUENTIAL DAMAGES ARISING OUT OF THE USE OR INABILITY TO USE THE PROGRAM (INCLUDING BUT NOT LIMITED TO LOSS OF DATA OR DATA BEING RENDERED INACCURATE OR LOSSES SUSTAINED BY YOU OR THIRD PARTIES OR A FAILURE OF THE PROGRAM TO OPERATE WITH ANY OTHER PROGRAMS), EVEN IF SUCH HOLDER OR OTHER PARTY HAS BEEN ADVISED OF THE POSSIBILITY OF SUCH DAMAGES.

END OF TERMS AND CONDITIONS

Appendix: How to Apply These Terms to Your New Programs

If you develop a new program, and you want it to be of the greatest possible use to the public, the best way to achieve this is to make it free software which everyone can redistribute and change under these terms.

To do so, attach the following notices to the program. It is safest to attach them to the start of each source file to most effectively convey the exclusion of warranty; and each file should have at least the "copyright" line and a pointer to where the full notice is found.

```
<one line to give the program's name and a brief idea of what it does.>
Copyright (C) 19yy <name of author>
This program is free software; you can redistribute it and/or modify
```

```
it under the terms of the GNU General Public License as published by
the Free Software Foundation; either version 2 of the License, or
(at your option) any later version.
This program is distributed in the hope that it will be useful,
but WITHOUT ANY WARRANTY; without even the implied warranty of
MERCHANTABILITY or FITNESS FOR A PARTICULAR PURPOSE. See the
GNU General Public License for more details.
You should have received a copy of the GNU General Public License
along with this program; if not, write to the Free Software
Foundation, Inc., 675 Mass Ave, Cambridge, MA 02139, USA.
```

Also add information on how to contact you by electronic and paper mail.

If the program is interactive, make it output a short notice like this when it starts in an interactive mode:

```
Gnomovision version 69, Copyright (C) 19yy name of author
Gnomovision comes with ABSOLUTELY NO WARRANTY; for details type `show
w'.
This is free software, and you are welcome to redistribute it
under certain conditions; type `show c' for details.
```

The hypothetical commands "show w" and "show c" should show the appropriate parts of the General Public License. Of course, the commands you use may be called something other than "show w" and "show c"; they could even be mouseclicks or menu items—whatever suits your program.

You should also get your employer (if you work as a programmer) or your school, if any, to sign a "copyright disclaimer" for the program, if necessary. Here is a sample; alter the names:

```
Yoyodyne, Inc., hereby disclaims all copyright interest in the program
`Gnomovision' (which makes passes at compilers) written by James
Hacker.
<signature of Ty Coon>, 1 April 1989
Ty Coon, President of Vice
```

This General Public License does not permit incorporating your program into proprietary programs. If your program is a subroutine library, you may consider it more useful to permit linking proprietary applications with the library. If this is what you want to do, use the GNU Library General Public License instead of this License.

APPENDIX

E

Linux on Non-Intel Hardware

Linux is available for numerous hardware platforms other than the Intel *x*86 and Pentium microprocessors. This appendix serves as a quick overview of some of the major, interesting non-Intel versions of Linux that are available. For a comprehensive list of Linux ports that are available, consult Linux Online's list of hardware port projects at `http://www.linux.org/projects/ports.html`.

Linux for AP1000+

The AP1000+ is a multi-computer built by Fujitsu around the SPARC architecture. In the AP 1000+, multiple CPUs are connected by two networks. The system started with 16 CPUs and will be upgraded to 32 CPUs. The project for running Linux on this distributed multi-processing computer is being done at the Australian National University. Visit `http://cap.anu.edu.au/cap/projects/linux/` to learn more about the project.

Linux for the DEC Alpha Processor

DEC's Alpha CPU is widely hailed as an exemplary RISC CPU, offering one of the fastest processors on the market.

Linux for the Alpha CPU is perhaps among the most robust, stable, and highly tested versions of Linux for non-Intel hardware currently available. Everything from X Windows to networks to Web browsers works well, and emulation is even available to run many programs designed for the Intel *x*86 version of Linux. See `http://www.alphalinux.org/` for more information about Linux for the Alpha CPU.

Linux for Alpha runs on numerous DEC Alpha-based systems ranging from low-end Universal Desktop Boxes/Multias from Digital to high-end 500MHz systems.

Red Hat offers a version of Red Hat Linux for the Alpha processor along with its Intel *x*86 and SPARC versions.

Embedded Linux

The ELKS (Embedded Linux Kernel Subset) project is aiming to create a version of Linux for embedded systems such as older 8086 and 80286 PCs, handheld computers, and embedded controller systems. The current version of Linux available from the project runs on PCs and requires about 512K of RAM for a full system.

The current version is far from complete, offering only the ability to boot, use virtual consoles, access floppy disks, and run a collection of small programs. This is a development system, but it highlights the flexibility that enables Linux to run under a variety of hardware constraints.

The ELKS project is online at `http://www.uk.linux.org/ELKS-Home/index.html`.

Linux for Motorola 680x0 Processors

Linux/m68k is a port of Linux designed to run on Motorola 68020 through 68060 CPUs, such as those found in many Amiga, Atari, and Macintosh computers.

Robust, stable releases of Linux/m68k are currently available to run on Amiga, Atari, and Macintosh systems, including the following systems:

- Amiga A2500
- Amiga A3000
- Amiga A3000T
- Amiga A4000/040
- Amiga A4000T/040
- Amiga A4000T/060
- Atari Falcon
- Atari Falcon with AfterBurner 040
- Atari TT
- Atari Medusa

- Macintosh II (many models)
- Macintosh SE/30
- Macintosh Classic II
- Macintosh LC (many models)
- Macintosh Performa (many models)
- Macintosh Quadra (many models)
- Macintosh Centris (many models)
- In addition, development ports of Linux are under way to support other Motorola 680x0 systems, including:
  - HP 9000/300 workstations
  - NeXT workstations
  - Sun 3 workstations

More information is available at `http://www.linux-m68k.org/`.

Linux for MIPS Processors

Linux/MIPS is a port of Linux designed to run on most systems sporting MIPS processors, including the following:

- Acer PICA-61
- DECStation 5000/2x, 5000/100, and 3100
- MIPS Magnum 4000PC
- Olivetti M700-10

The current release is considered stable and includes networking and NFS support, with some shortcomings in support for on-board peripherals in some machines. While not yet available as a robust, complete distribution, it is possible to put together a complete distribution from the software on the project's Web site. Linux/MIPS is on the Web at `http://lena.fnet.fr/`.

Linux for the Power Macintosh

MkLinux is an attempt to run Linux on the Open Group Mach microkernel running natively on the Power Macintosh line of computers. Microkernel architecture is designed to ease porting of the OS, with the focus on porting the microkernel itself.

Apple Computer is fully supporting the MkLinux project, which has a Web site at `http://www.mklinux.apple.com/`. A complete distribution is currently available online or on CD-ROM.

Other projects aimed at porting Linux to the Power Macintosh include the PowerPC Linux distribution (which is discussed in the section on the PowerPC processor later in this appendix) and Powermac/Linux (`http://www.cs.wisc .edu/~tesch/linux_info/`). Both of these projects are versions of Linux that are native to the PowerPC processor (which is at the heart of Power Mac systems) instead of being layered on a microkernel. This design provides better performance but less portability to other hardware. The Powermac/Linux code, once a distinct project, has now been merged with the LinuxPPC source code developed by PowerPC Linux to produce one version of Linux for the PowerPC.

Linux for PowerPC Processors

Great strides have been made in supporting Linux on the PowerPC processor family. The LinuxPPC project (`http://www.linuxppc.org/`) is managed and developed by PowerPC Linux. It offers a stable and complete distribution that runs on a wide range of Power Macintosh computers, the BeBox from Be Computing, PowerPC-based RS/6000 systems from IBM, a wide range of systems from Power Computing, and workstations from Umax.

Supported applications and features include the following:

- PCI-bus systems
- SCSI and IDE hard disk drives
- Multimedia support
- Netscape Communicator

- X Windows and a wide range of window managers
- Java JDK 1.1.6

A project is also under way to develop an emulator of the Mac OS to run inside Linux on the PowerPC, just as Wine is an attempt to develop a Windows emulator for Linux for the Intel $x86$ CPU.

Linux for SGI Systems

SGI/Linux is a project of Silicon Graphics to port Linux to their hardware and then distribute it widely through Linux CD-ROM vendors. The project includes strong efforts to provide robust IRIX emulation in the distribution so that existing applications for SGI systems can be used under Linux, and consideration is being given to the ability to hot-swap between Linux and IRIX operating systems without completely rebooting the computer.

At the time of this writing, a pre-release distribution called Hard Hat 5.1 (a nearly-complete port of Red Hat Linux 5.1) is available. The major missing component is an X server, which is currently being developed.

SGI maintains a site for their Linux port at `http://www.linux.sgi.com/`.

Linux for SPARC Processors

UltraLinux (`http://www.ultralinux.org/`), formerly known as S/Linux, is a project to port Linux to Sun's SPARC and UltraSPARC processors. Currently, the port is quite stable, and Red Hat now has a SPARC version of their distribution available along with Intel and Alpha versions of their distribution.

INDEX

Note to the Reader: Throughout this index **boldfaced** page numbers indicate primary discussions of a topic. *Italicized* page numbers indicate illustrations.

(

E

F

H

I

K

O

P

Q

R

S

U

V

X

Y

Yggdrasil distribution, 19
ypdomainname command, 843

Z

Z Shell (zsh), 354
zcat command, 843
Zeus Web server, **679**
zgrep command, 843–844
zImage kernel, 454
zip command, **844**
ZIP files
    extracting, **836–837**
    in GNOME displays, 173
zipgrep command, 844
zipinfo command, **845**
zmore command, **845**
znew command, **845**
zooming, directive for, 256
zsh shell, 354

What's on the CD-ROM?

This book includes a CD-ROM. The disc contains the Publisher's Edition of the Red Hat Linux 6 operating system.

Due to space constraints, certain components present in the official Red Hat Linux are not available in the Red Hat Linux Publisher's Edition. Please check the file named README .publishers-edition on the CD-ROM for a list of missing files. The packages not present on this disc can be downloaded from the Red Hat Software Internet site (http://www.redhat.com).

System Requirements

- 486 MHz CPU or higher (In theory, you can run Linux on a 386 MHz system, but the performance will most likely be poor enough that it won't be worthwhile for most users.)

- 16MB of RAM or more (You will notice a significant performance gain with 32MB or more of memory.)

- At least 500MB of hard disk space (If you can afford 1GB or more, this will greatly enhance your freedom to experiment with Linux and Linux applications.)

- Bootable CD-ROM (preferably an ATAPI/IDE or SCSI drive)

- Red Hat Linux supports most modern Intel-compatible PC hardware. If you have any questions about your hardware's compatibility with Red Hat Linux 6, please check the hardware compatibility list at http://support.redhat.com.

- A backup of your current system in case you need to recover existing data or applications

- A video card and VGA or better monitor

- A keyboard and mouse

Software Support

Components of the supplemental Software and any offers associated with them may be supported by the specific Owner(s) of that material but they are not supported by SYBEX. Information regarding any available support may be obtained from the Owner(s) using the information provided in the appropriate README files or listed elsewhere on the media.

Should the manufacturer(s) or other Owner(s) cease to offer support or decline to honor any offer, SYBEX bears no responsibility. This notice concerning support for the Software is provided for your information only. SYBEX is not the agent or principal of the Owner(s), and SYBEX is in no way responsible for providing any support for the Software, nor is it liable or responsible for any support provided, or not provided, by the Owner(s).